NEO-SUMERIAN TEXTS FROM THE ROYAL ONTARIO MUSEUM

II

Administrative Texts Mainly from Umma

BY

MARCEL SIGRIST

CDL PRESS
BETHESDA MARYLAND

Library of Congress Cataloging-in-Publication

Sigrist, Marcel
Neo-Sumerian texts from the Royal Ontario Museum / by Marcel Sigrist
p. cm.
Includes index.
Contents: 2. Administrative Texts Mainly from Umma
ISBN 1883053-79x
1. Sumerian language—Texts. 2. Royal Ontario Museum. I. Title.
PJ4053.R66S55 1995
499'.95—dc20 95-12287
CIP

ISBN 1883053-79X

CONTENTS

CATALOGUE

Publication No.	*Collection No.*				
1	925.62.11	Š 47			Barley deliveries in Uruk for the king's beverage
2	967.287.19	ŠS [ ]	v		Beer deliveries for the governor
3	967.287.11	AS 4	i	26	Beer deliveries for the governor
4	967.287.6	ŠS 2	v	6	Beer deliveries for the governor
5	967.287.39	ŠS 1	v		Special rations of beer for the military governor
6	910x209.278	IS			Transfer of beer
7	925.62.485		i		Transfer of beer during the *bala*
8	925.62.488	AS 9			Summary tablet of barley deliveries
9	925.62.468	Š 38	ii		Fodder for donkeys
10	925.62.84	ŠS 5	ix		Fodder for donkeys
11	925.62.61	Š 46	diri		Fodder to fatten oxen
12	925.62.109	Š 46	iii		Barley to fatten oxen
13	925.62.419	Š 46	iii		Barley to fatten oxen
14	925.62.80	ŠS 7	iii		Recapitulative tablet of fodder deliveries
15	925.62.62	Š 48	xii		Barley for donkeys
16	925.62.500	ŠS 2	xii		Barley for donkeys
17	925.62.368	ŠS 3	vi		Barley for donkeys
18	967.287.41	Š 39	xi		Barley to fatten sheep
19	925.62.119	Š 39	xii		Barley to fatten sheep
20	925.62.545	Š 40			Barley to fatten oxen
21	925.62.388	Š 46	ii		Barley to fatten oxen
22	925.62.97	Š 36	xii		Barley to fatten donkeys
23	925.62.404	Š 38	x		Barley for donkeys
24	925.62.369	Š 39	viii		Barley for donkeys
25	925.62.441	Š 39	xii		Barley for donkeys
26	925.62.68	Š 40	xi		Fodder for donkeys
27	925.62.52	Š 40	xii		Fodder for donkeys
28	925.62.411	Š 41	ii		Fodder for donkeys
29	925.62.426	Š 41	viii		Fodder for donkeys
30	925.62.100	Š 42	vii		Fodder for donkeys
31	925.62.113	Š 42	ix		Fodder for donkeys
32	925.62.187	Š 42	ix		Fodder for donkeys
33	925.62.98	Š 42	iii		Fodder for donkeys
34	925.62.189	ŠS 4	xi		Fodder for donkeys
35	925.62.387	Š 37	xi		Barley for the regular deliveries of the donkeys
36	925.62.40	Š 39	vii		Fodder for donkeys
37	925.62.93	Š 40	xii		Fodder for donkeys
38	925.62.364	Š 41	v		Fodder for donkeys
39	925.62.394	Š 1	x		Fodder for donkeys

Publication No.	*Collection No.*			
40	925.62.510	Š 43	i	Fodder for donkeys
41	925.62.89	Š 44		Fodder for donkeys
42	910x209.606	Š 45	v	Fodder for donkeys
43	925.62.111	Š 46	x	Fodder for donkeys
44	925.62.478	Š 7	vii	Fodder for donkeys
45	925.62.79	Š 47	xi	Fodder for donkeys
46	925.62.530	Š 48	vii	Fodder for donkeys
47	925.62.435	ŠS 1	vi	Fodder for donkeys
48	925.62.412	ŠS 2	i	Fodder for donkeys
49	925.62.390a	Š 45	i	Fodder for donkeys
50	925.62.151	Š 47	x	Fodder for donkeys
51	925.62.96	Š 48	viii	Fodder for donkeys
52	925.62.198	Š 44	ix	Fodder for donkeys
53	925.62.202	Š 44	ix	Fodder for donkeys
54	925.62.45	Š 46	vii	Fodder for donkeys
55	925.62.110	Š 44	iv	Fodder for donkeys
56	925.62.83	[ ] [ ]		Fodder for donkeys
57	925.62.357	Š 41	x	Fodder for donkeys
58	925.62.374	Š 46	vii	Fodder for oxen
59	925.62.76	Š 46	x	Fodder for oxen
60	925.62.373	Š 44	vii	Fodder for donkeys
61	925.62.457	Š 40	i	Fodder for donkeys
62	925.62.442	Š 40	viii	Fodder for donkeys
63	925.62.102	Š 46	vii	Fodder for stags
64	925.62.94	Š 34	x	Fodder for donkeys
65	925.62.112	Š 35		Fodder for donkeys
66	925.62.487	Š 35	v	Fodder for donkeys
67	925.62.489	Š 35	vi	Fodder for donkeys
68	925.62.150	Š 39	vi	Fodder for donkeys
69	925.62.440	Š 39	vii	Fodder for donkeys
70	925.62.437	Š 39	I	Fodder for donkeys
71	925.62.92	Š 46	ix	Fodder for donkeys
72	925.62.409	Š 46	xii	Fodder for donkeys
73	925.62.438	Š 48	viii	Fodder for donkeys
74	925.62.405	[ ]	xii	Fodder for donkeys
75	967.287.36	Š 46	x	Fodder for donkeys
76	925.62.105	Š 48	xi	Fodder for donkeys
77	925.62.484	AS 2		Fodder for oxen
78	925.62.176	Š 44	diri	Fodder for oxen
79	925.62.179	Š 38		Fodder for donkeys
80	925.62.389	Š 38	x	Fodder for donkeys
81	925.62.118	Š 47	vii	Fodder for donkeys
82	925.62.379	ŠS 2	xi	Fodder for donkeys
83	910x209.259	Š 44		Fodder for oxen
84	925.62.447	Š 41	ix	Fodder for mules
85	925.62.428	Š 44	v	Fodder for mules
86	925.62.474	Š 37		Fodder for oxen
87	925.62.544			Fodder for donkeys and rations for guruš
88	925.62.69	Š 36		Barley

Publication No.	*Collection No.*			
89	925.62.192	Š 36		General account of barley
90	925.62.522	Š 46	ix	Barley for erin; envelop (Lagaš tablet)
91	925.62.44	ŠS 3	viii	Barley for ḫé-dab$_5$
92	910x209.586	[ ]	ii	Fodder for sheep (Lagash)
93	925.62.464			Regular deliveries for Šulgi; after Šulgi's reign;
94	925.62.496	ŠS 6	i–iv	Regular deliveries for Šulgi
95	925.62.41	Š 39	ii–i	Regular deliveries for Šulgi
96	925.62.415	AS 6	v	Regular deliveries for Šulgi
97	925.62.177	AS 8	vii	Regular deliveries for Amar-Sin
98	925.62.123	ŠS 7	xii	Regular deliveries for Amar-Sin
99	925.62.161	ŠS 1	iii	Regular deliveries for Amar-Sin
100	925.62.87	ŠS 7		Regular deliveries for Enki
101	925.62.385			Regular deliveries for Enki
102	910x209.123			Regular deliveries for Enki
103	967.287.8	ŠS 6	v	Regular deliveries for Enlil
104	963.159.2A	ŠS 3		Regular deliveries for Gula
105	925.62.51	Š 4	xi	Regular deliveries for Inanna in Uruk
106	925.62.103	AS 5		Regular deliveries for Inanna in Uruk
107	925.62.168	AS 7	ix	Regular deliveries for Inanna in Uruk
108	925.62.66	Š 45	vii	Regular deliveries for NindaLagaš
109	925.62.520	Š 35	vi	Regular deliveries for Ninee
110	925.62.393	Š 41	viii	Regular deliveries for Ninee
111	925.62.82	ŠS 5	ii	Regular deliveries for Ninsun
112	925.62.141	ŠS 1	vii	Regular deliveries for Ninurra
113	925.62.460	ŠS 2	vi	Regular deliveries for Nungal
114	925.62.359	Š 47	xii	Regular deliveries for Šara
115	925.62.433	Š 36	diri	Regular deliveries for Šara
116	925.62.29	AS 5	ii	Regular deliveries for Šara
117	925.62.72	AS 8	ix	Regular deliveries for Šara
118	967.287.12	AS 6		Regular deliveries for Šara
119	925.62.355	AS 9	iv	Regular deliveries for Šara
120	925.62.470	ŠS 7	ii	Regular deliveries for Šara
121	910x209.329	ŠS 1	ix	Regular deliveries for Šara
122	925.62.37	ŠS 4	iii	Regular deliveries for Šara
123	925.62.166	ŠS 3	xii	Regular deliveries for Šara
124	925.62.358	ŠS 3	xii	Barley and flour for Dumuzi
125	925.62.106	AS 9	xi	Regular deliveries for the gods
126	925.62.162	ŠS 6	xi	Regular deliveries for the temple emaš
127	925.62.146	Š 34	i	Regular deliveries for the temple enilagar
128	967.287.37	Š 34	vi	Regular deliveries for the temple enilagar
129	925.62.528	Š 34		Regular deliveries for the temple enilagar
130	925.62.116	ŠS 4	xii	Regular deliveries for the temple enilagar
131	925.62.78	Š 39	x	Regular deliveries for festival celebrations
132	925.62.446	Š 34	xi	Regular deliveries for the stair in the temple
133	925.62.138	ŠS 5		Regular deliveries for messengers
134	925.62.498	ŠS 6		Regular deliveries for messengers
135	925.62.57	Š 48	xii	Regular deliveries of beer for messengers
136	925.62.465	Š 44	ii	Regular deliveries
137	925.62.417	AS 8	ix–diri	Regular deliveries of dates

Publication No.	*Collection No.*		
138	925.62.495	ŠS 1 ii	Regular deliveries
139	989.259.9	Š 47	Earth to fill uncultivated land
140	925.62.122	ŠS 2	Building of a dam
141	910x209.56	IS 1	Cleaning a reservoir
142	925.62.453	ŠS 2	Women piling grain stack and compacting
143	925.62.25	ŠS 5	Guruš watching the level of the irrigation water
144	925.62.336	ŠS 5	Guruš watching the level of the irrigation water
145	925.62.101	ŠS 5	Guruš watching the level of the irrigation water
146	925.62.91	AS 6	Guruš watching the level of the irrigation water
147	967.287.54	Š 46	Irrigation activity
148	910x209.610	AS 3	Irrigation activity
149	925.62.370	AS 9 xii	Irrigation work
150	910x209.263	AS 5	Irrigation work
151	925.62.371a	ŠS 4 i	Irrigation work
152	925.62.65	ŠS 5	Irrigation work
153	967.287.21	ŠS 2	Irrigation work
154	925.62.381	ŠS 3	Irrigation work
155	925.62.30	AS 2	Irrigation work
156	967.287.59		Plowing
157	925.62.165	AS 5 viii	Field work
158	925.62.115	AS 9 xii	Wages for hired men
159	925.62.134		Wages
160	910x209.609	ŠS 3 ix	Wages for young ox-drivers
161	910x209.590		Rations for guruš
162	925.62.185	Š 44 vii	Rations for guruš
163	925.62.114	AS 6	Guruš work
164	925.62.154	AS 5	Guruš work
165	967.287.56	Š 44 xi	List of ḫé-dab$_5$ workers
166	925.62.173		Barley rations for reedmat-makers
167	925.62.88	ŠS 3	Instructions on the seeding of a field
168	967.287.27	ŠS 6	Pickax work
169	910x209.620	ŠS 6	Guruš weeding fields
170	967.287.43	ŠS 6	Guruš weeding fields
171	925.62.32a	ŠS 3	Guruš for seeding a field
172	967.287.10	ŠS 5	Guruš for harrowing fields
173	267.287.17	ŠS 5	Guruš for harrowing fields
174	925.62.117	ŠS 6	Guruš for harrowing fields
175	925.62.348	ŠS 9	Preparation of the furrows before seeding
176	925.62.241	ŠS 9	Preparation of the furrows before seeding
177	925.62.212	ŠS 9	Preparation of the furrows before seeding
178	925.62.377		Seeding of fields
179	925.62.90	AS 5	Threshing floor
180	967.287.51	AS 6 viii	Threshing floor
181	967.287.34	ŠS 5	Working days on the threshing floor
182	967.287.49	ŠS 5	Working days on the threshing floor
183	925.62.398	ŠS 8	Broken
184	910x209.611	ŠS 5	Wages for field workers
185	925.62.367	ŠS 5 ix–xi	Sick person
186	967.287.25	ŠS 7	Sick person

Publication No.	*Collection No.*				
187	925.62.542	Š 48			Un-íl workers
188	910x209.277	Š 41			Un-íl workers
189	925.62.28	AS 1	viii		Un-íl workers
190	910x209.577	AS 3	i		Un-íl workers
191	925.62.375	AS 6			Work contract
192	925.62.423	ŠS 7			Type of workers
193	967.287.29	ŠS 7			Work contract and transfer
194	925.62.47	ŠS 7	i		Work contract and transfer
195	925.62.256	AS 9	viii		Transfer of working force
196	925.62.480	Š 37			Female workers
197	925.62.12				Female workers
198	925.62.73	ŠS 3	vi		Female workers
199	925.62.536	AS 1	xii	15	Transfer of working force
200	910x209.255	ŠS 5			Work of a team
201	910x209.599	ŠS 2	vi		Balanced account of guruš work
202	925.62.430	Š 32			Items for a festival
203	910x209.210	IS 2	i	17	Sheep for a festival; Drehem
204	910x209.268	Š 46	viii	20	Animals for *nabrium*-festival; Drehem
205	910x209.524	AS 1	xii	12	Animals for dowry and encampment; Drehem
206	925.62.274	Š 32	vii		Receipt for goats
207	925.62.427	Š 48	v		Dead Sheep
208	925.62.99	AS 2			Return of a jackass
209	967.287.58	ŠS 2			Donkeys for Šara
210	925.62.160	IS 2	v	10	Receipt for sheep
211	925.62.194		x		Dead sheep
212	925.62.266	Š 47	v		Boars, doves, and ducks; Drehem
213	925.62.270	ŠS 1	iii		Dead gazelle
214	925.62.328				Sheep
215	910x209.589	ŠS 3	ix	15	Animals from various individuals
216	992.226.60	AS 3	i		Animals as *satukku* for the king; Drehem
217	925.62.511	Š 32	vi		Milk production
218	989.259.4	AS 5			Balanced account in silver
219	925.62.306	Š 45			Merchant dealings
220	925.62.434				Merchant dealings
221	925.62.431	IS 1			Merchant dealings
222	925.62.120	IS 3			About beverage
223	967.287.20	ŠS 5	xii		Flour delivery
224	925.62.493	Š 48		30	Flour delivery
225	967.287.2	ŠS 5	i		Flour delivery
226	967.287.5	AS 9	v	7	Flour delivery
227	967.287.13	ŠS 4	v		Regular deliveries for the governor
228	967.287.14	ŠS 4	ix	17	Regular deliveries for the governor
229	925.62.60	AS 5	iii		Yield in barley of fields
230	910x209.323				Barley deliveries
231	925.62.127				Barley
232	910.209.601				Barley deliveries
233	910x209.177				Statement about barley
234	925.62.443a	Š 31	x		Transfer of barley
235	925.62.42	ŠS 6			Expenditure of barley

Publication No.	*Collection No.*			
236	925.62.77	Š 30	ix	Expenditure of barley
237	975.35.11	IS 1	xii	Transfer of grain
238	925.62.16	Š 31	viii	Transfer of grain for the fattener
239	925.62.48	Š 40		Record of barley on tablets
240	925.62.55	Š 31	xii	Summary of barley accounts
241	925.62.195	Š 48	ix	Summary of barley records
242	910x209.279			Delivery of barley
243	910x209.58	Š 45		Barley adjustment in the accounts
244	925.62.543	AS 9	xii	Barley deliveries
245	925.62.513	AS 8	v	Transfer of barley and flour
246	925.62.54	Š 37		Barley for food of a household
247	989.259.2	Š 36	viii	Transfer of barley
248	910x209.194	Š 40	x	Transfer of barley
249	910x209.613	Š 32		Expenditure of barley
250	925.62.178	ŠS 7		Barley rations
251	925.62.472	ŠS 4		Barley rations for singers
252	910x209.283	ŠS 6		Administrative tablet
253	925.62.475	Š 32		Barley account
254	989.259.10	Š 42	vi	Transfer of barley, Drehem
255	925.62.43	ŠS 1	v	Barley deliveries
256	925.62.413	ŠS 1	ii	Removal of water from the barley
257	910x209.250a	Š 40	[ ]	Wages for hired men
258	925.62.126	AS 8		Barley for the plowmen
259	925.62.402	AS 8	i	Loan of barley
260	925.62.483	AS 5		Barley for a loan or for grinding
261	925.62.463	Š 46	v	Expenditure of barley for grinding
262	925.62.418	Š 39		Rations for specialized workers
263	925.62.23	Š 31	vii	Barley rations
264	925.62.452	Š 45	xii	Threshed barley
265	925.62.456	AS 9		Threshed barley
266	910x209.5	ŠS 9	iii	Barley account
267	925.62.108	ŠS 2	viii	Barley for guruš
268	925.62.71	ŠS 7	iii	Barley for guruš
269	925.62.67	Š 42		Barley for sowing
270	925.62.319	ŠS 4		Barley for sowing
271	925.62.537	ŠS 6		Barley on the threshing floor
272	925.62.17	AS 8	iii	Barley storage
273	925.62.524	AS 4	diri	Threshed barley
274	925.62.124	ŠS 3	vi	Barley for rations
275	925.62.414	ŠS 4	viii	Barley for rations
276	925.62.497	ŠS 3		Barley for rations
277	925.62.354			Barley for rations
278	925.62.121	Š 46	diri	Loan of barley
279	950.157.191	AS 5	xi	Loan of barley
280	925.62.216	Š 47	diri	Expenditure of barley
281	925.62.459	Š 47		Barley for flour
282	925.62.420	Š 31		Barley for flour
283	925.62.391	ŠS 1	xi	Barley for flour
284	910x209.604	Š 30	ix	Yield of several fields

Publication No.	*Collection No.*		
285	925.62.451	ŠS 2 iii	Barley for grinding
286	925.62.380	Š 46	Barley rations
287	925.62.285	Š 45 v	Barley rations
288	910x209.623		Barley rations
289	925.62.144	ŠS 2 ix	Barley rations
290	925.62.36	ŠS 4 xi	Barley rations
291	925.62.35	ŠS 1	Barley rations
292	925.62.50	ŠS 7 v	Barley rations
293	925.62.211	ŠS 8 viii	Barley rations
294	925.62.378	ŠS 6 iv	Barley rations
295	925.62.386	ŠS 7	Barley rations
296	925.62.432	ŠS 3 xii	Barley rations
297	925.62.445	ŠS 1 vi	Barley rations
298	925.62.534	ŠS 3 v	Barley rations
299	925.62.148	ŠS 3 v	Barley rations
300	925.62.477	ŠS 7 xi	Barley rations
301	925.62.167	Š 31	Barley rations for the *bala*
302	910x209.632	Š 34	Barley rations for women
303	925.62.27	ŠS 6 viii	Barley rations for weaver women
304	925.62.376	ŠS 3 vii	Barley for ḫé-dab$_5$ workers
305	925.62.397	ŠS 6 x	Barley rations
306	925.62.458	AS 9	New year rations
307	910x209.582	AS 8	Barley for seeding; envelope
308	910x209.582a	AS 8	Barley for seeding; tablet
309	925.62.10	ŠS 7	Account of barley
310	967.287.15	Š 48 diri	Barley for flour; envelope
311	925.62.356		Berley Rations
312	925.62.527	Š 27	Barley for the cult of Inanna
313	910x209.81	ŠS 1 v	Receipt for barley; Nippur
314	910x209.87	ŠS 8 iii	Receipt for barley
315	910x209.129	Š 44 vii 17	Loan of barley; Nippur
316	910x209.113	IS 2 xii diri	Loan of barley; Nippur
317	910x209.219	ŠS 7 xi	Loan of barley; Nippur
318	910x209.374	ŠS 9 xi	Loan of barley; Nippur
319	910x209.397	IS 1 iii	Barley receipt; Drehem
320	994.233.1	ŠS 3	Barley receipt
321	925.62.33	ŠS 4 x	Barley rations
322	925.62.34	Š 44 viii 10	Bread distributionš 43 xi to š 44 viii 10
323	967.287.63	AS 7	Bread distribution
324	910.209.602	ŠS 5	Bread distribution
325	925.62.74		Bread distribution
326	910x209.627	Š 32 ix	Bread distribution
327	925.62.392	ŠS 6 vi	Bread for messengers
328	925.62.491	Š 47 v	Flour
329	925.62.396		Flour
330	925.62.63	AS 8	Flour
331	925.62.473	Š 40 diri	Flour
332	910x209.249	IS 1 v	Barley flour for ḫedab-workers; Nippur
333	967.287.33	ŠS 2 xi	Flour for the governor

Publication No.	*Collection No.*		
334	967.287.47	ŠS 2 viii	Flour for the governor
335	910x209.282		Memorandum about flour
336	910x209.15	ŠS2–3	Flour for the dogs' house
337	910x209.588		Summary tablet about flour
338	925.62.59	Š 47 vii	Transfer of flour
339	925.62.399	Š 47 v	Transfer of flour
340	925.62.384	Š 47	Yield of palm trees
341	925.62.39	ŠS 6	Dates production
342	925.62.421	AS 9	Dates, beer, and flour
343	925.62.363	Š 33	Fish deliveries
344	925.62.400	AS 5	Fish deliveries
345	925.62.24	Š 37 xii	Fish deliveries
346	910x209.622	Š 48	Balanced account of oil expenses
347	910x209.286	ŠS 6 ii	Oil delivery in Nippur
348	993.201.1	Š 48	Lard collected as a tax
349	925.62.471	AS 6 v	Location of building
350	925.62.107	Š 42	Location of building
351	925.62.455a	Š 41	Location of building
352	967.287.30	ŠS 3	Watch function
353	925.62.499	AS 9 xii	Building
354	925.62.450	Š 48	Bitumen
355	925.62.466	ŠS 4	Bitumen
356	910x209.260		Reed
357	925.62.490	Š 46	Reed
358	925.62.410	Š 35	Bundles of reed
359	925.62.382	AS 4	Bundles of reed
360	925.62.19	Š 45	Bundles of reed
361	967.287.4	ŠS 5	Bundles of reed
362	967.287.40	ŠS 4	Bundles of reed
363	967.287.76	ŠS 7	Bundles of reed
364	925.62.136	ŠS 5	Bundles of reed
365	925.62.26	IS 2	Bundles of reed
366	910x209.290	IS 1	Bundles of reed
367	925.62.196	Š 48	Guruš to cut reed
368	925.62.140	ŠS 4	Door made out of reed
369	925.62.454	Š 48 xi	Guruš to carry reed
370	967.287.52	ŠS 5	Guruš to make reed bundles
371	925.62.38	Š 47	Reed mats
372	925.62.250	Š 39 i	Reed mats
373	910.209.71	ŠS 4 v	Reed mats
374	910x209.617	ŠS 7	Reed mats
375	910x209.600	ŠS 4	Reed mats
376	925.62.352	ŠS 4	Reed mats
377	925.62.49	ŠS 6	Reed mats
378	925.62.158	IS 1 x	Reed bundles
379	967.287.26	ŠS 6	Guruš to carry reeds
380	967.287.75	ŠS 5	Braided reed tips
381	925.62.145	ŠS 4 x	Transfer of baskets
382	910x209.640	ŠS 6	Baskets

Publication No.	*Collection No.*					
383	925.62.86	AS 6				Baskets covered with bitumen
384	925.62.242	AS 4				Guruš to carry baskets
385	925.62.207	AS 3				Large baskets to carry meat
386	925.62.383	ŠS 3	vii			Reed baskets
387	967.287.46	ŠS 3	v			Reed baskets for bread
388	925.62.429	ŠS 8				Sieves
389	910x209.247	Š 43				Bundles of reed
390	967.287.44	ŠS 4				Reed mats for boats
391	967.287.45	Š 46				Knifes
392	989.259.5	Š 44	iii			Baskets, Nippur
393	925.62.403	Š 32	vii			Copper and lead
394	925.62.209	Š 44	xi			Bronze
395	925.62.75	ŠS 1	viii			Guruš cleaning the field
396	925.62.46	AS 6				Wood
397	925.62.494	AS 6				Wood
398	925.62.276	Š 42				Wood
399	925.62.424	Š 3	vi		27	Wood
400	925.62.139	ŠS				Straw
401	925.62.22	ŠS 5				Leather
402	925.62.159	Š 38				Leather
403	967.287.9					Shoes
404	925.62.125	Š 45	vii			Hides
405	925.62.449	Š 35	iv			Hides
406	925.62.6	AS 5	i			Hides
407	910x209.281	AS 2				Sandals
408	910x209.272	ŠS 2	x			Loan of silver in Nippur
409	925.62.64	IS 3				Loan
410	925.62.257	Š 32	ix			Loan of silver
411	910x209.49	Š 44	iv		1	Loan of silver; Nippur
412	910x209.83	IS 3	vii			Loan of silver; Nippur
413	910x209.85	IS 3	vi			Delivery of silver; Nippur
414	910x209.104	IS 3	iv			Loan of silver; Nippur
415	910x209.106	AS 7	vi			Loan of silver; Nippur
416	910x209.117	IS 2	xi			Loan of silver; Nippur
417	910x209.218	IS 2	vi			Loan of silver; Nippur
418	910x209.220	ŠS 8	ix			Loan of silver; Nippur
419	910x209.239	ŠS 6	ix			Loan of silver; Nippur
420	910x209.254	AS 9	xii	diri		Loan of silver; Nippur
421	910x209.264	ŠS 6	iv			Loan of silver; Nippur
422	910x209.375	IS 2	vi			Loan of silver; Nippur
423	910x209.419	IS 1				Loan of silver; Nippur
424	925.62.439	Š 43				Tablet basket
425	967.287.3					Tablet basket
426	925.62.137					Tablet basket
427	925.62.448					Tablet basket
428	925.62.425	ŠS 6				Tablet basket
429	925.62.131	ŠS 9	vi			Inspection tablet
430	925.62.301	ŠS 2				Inspection tablet
431	925.62.132					Inspection tablet or exercise tablet

Publication No.	*Collection No.*				
432	925.62.529	ŠS 5			Inspection tablet
433	925.62.541	Š 32			Payment of taxes
434	925.62.372				Account correction
435	967.287.67	ŠS 9			Account of cattle
436	925.62.401				Memo of accounts
437	925.62.104	Š 44	ix		Excess to be returned
438	925.62.152	AS 7			Balanced account
439	925.62.56	AS 9	xi		Payment of taxes
440	925.62.467	Š 31			Account correction
441	925.62.479	Š 30			Account correction
442	925.62.512				Account correction
443	925.62.128	ŠS 9			Account correction
444	925.62.481	IS 3			Account correction
445	925.62.95	Š 30	diri		Account correction
446	925.62.360	Š 31	viii		Account correction
447	925.62.462	AS 7	vi		Loading of boats
448	925.62.153	AS 7	vi		Loading of boats
449	925.62.518a	AS 2			Loading of boats
450	925.62.85	AS 1			Canal navigation
451	910x209.146	AS 6	v–x		Work for navigation
452	925.62.208	ŠS 3			Navigation
453	925.62.492	ŠS 5			Navigation
454	910x209.641	ŠS 3			Navigation
455	925.62.157	ŠS 4	ix		Barley loaded onto boats
456	925.62.53	ŠS 5			Boat construction
457	989.259.8	Š 36	i		Work in the navigation office
458	975.35.8				Messenger tablet
459	967.287.50		viii		Messenger tablet
460	967.287.24	ŠS 4	ii		Messenger tablet
461	910x209.584	AS 8	iii		Messenger tablet; Lagaš
462	910x209.583		vii		Messenger tablet; Lagaš
463	967.287.22	ŠS 2	i	11	Messenger tablet
464	967.287.23	ŠS 4	xi		Messenger tablet
465	967.287.31	ŠS 3	xii	3	Messenger tablet
466	910x209.585		xii	22	Messenger tablet; Nippur
467	910x209.612				Messenger tablet
468	910x209.628				Special meals
469	989.259.1	ŠS 7	xi	4	Lamb for the euzga, Drehem
470	925.62.324	Š 46	ii		Fattening
471	989.259.3	AS 7	ix		Fattening
472	925.62.461		i		Food for harvesting
473	910x209.48	Š 40			Food for a festival
474	925.62.261	ŠS 4	xii		Food for a festival
475	910x209.621	AS8–9			Food for a lunar festival
476	925.62.422	Š or AS			Deliveries for the cult
477	925.62.469				Barley delivery; Old Akkadian
478	910x209.412				Wool rations
479	967.287.42	AS 5	ii		Wool for garments
480	925.62.81	Š 43	xii		Wool for the boat of the governor

Publication No.	*Collection No.*			
481	910x209.411	AS 9		Transfer of several items
482	910x209.607			Legal text
483	910x209.619			About garments
484	967.287.53	AS 9		About garments
485	925.62.259	AS 8	iii	About garments
486	967.287.65	ŠS 8	xii	Account of garments
487	925.62.538	ŠS 9	ix	About garments
488	925.62.8	IS 3		About garments
489	925.62.317	Š 33	vi	About garments, š 24, 31, 33 vi
490	925.62.486			About garments
491	925.62.307	Š 48		Transfer of wool
492	925.62.476			Letter order
493	925.62.234			Letter order
494	925.62.523			Letter order
495	267.287.16	Š		Letter order
496	910x209.438b			Exercise tablet
497	910x209.440			Exercise tablet
498	910x209.439			Exercise tablet
499	910x209.441			Exercise tablet
500	910x209.445			Exercise tablet
501	910x209.446			Exercise tablet
502	910x209.492			Exercise tablet
503	910x209.490			Exercise tablet
504	910x209.485			Exercise tablet
505	910x209.143			Exercise tablet
506	910x209.243			Exercise tablet(?)
507	967.287.55			
508	967.287.57			
509	967.287.35			
510	967.287.38			

UMMA

THE HISTORY OF THE CITY OF UMMA has not yet been written, although the site has yielded about ten thousand tablets published in various books and articles. The history of this site, built along the Iturungal canal (also called the Adab canal), starts long before Drehem was built, for the kings of Umma figure in the list of kings of ancient Sumer. During the Proto-Dynastic III period (ca. 2500–2300 BC), the urban areas multiplied in number and increased in size in the south of Mesopotamia. Thanks to irrigation, the cultivated land around the cities extended further and further, so that progressively the pasture land (the steppe, Sumerian "eden") claimed by one city would reach or encroach upon that of neighboring cities. This new proximity would lead to legal conflicts and wars over water rights and borders.

Eannatum, the great king of Lagash, conquered Elam, destroying its capital Susa and many other Iranian cities. His ambition extended over the land of Sumer and Akkad as well, where he assumed the title "King of Kish" after his victory over Akšak. But a great conflict was to erupt with Lagash's neighboring city, Umma. The geographic position of the two cities forced them to share the water of the Adab canal. For four generations the kings of these two cities had experienced successes and reversals. Finally the conflict was settled in favor of Umma, during a dynastic change in both cities. Lugalzagesi, the king of Umma, overpowered Uruinimgina, the reformer king of Lagash. Diverse accounts of the cities' rivalry, of the ensuing conflicts, and of the peace treaty are found in the literary text referred to as "The Holy Border of Shara."

With the rise of Sargon of Akkad (ca. 2300 BC), any conflict between Lagash and Umma was set aside so the two cities could unite against the menacing intruder. In fact, Umma participated in several anti-Sargon coalitions. Economic texts from this period survive and some are housed in the Royal Ontario Museum.

With the organization of the country under the Third Dynasty of Ur (ca. 2100 BC), southern Mesopotamia experienced a veritable renaissance, as the archives of Umma and Lagash attest. Yet abruptly the archive of Umma ceases in the fifth year of Ibbi-Sîn, similar to the archive of Drehem having been administratively shut down on the last day of the twelfth month of the second year of Ibbi-Sîn.

Umma's archive is, in certain respects, more intriguing than that of Lagash or Drehem because of its wide diversity of subject matter. I have classified the numerous tablets from Umma housed in the Royal Ontario Museum according to content, illustrating each archive by characteristic examples and annotations. Unfortunately, unlike Drehem, the Umma archives do not lend themselves to grand reconstructions of the accounting and administrative system. However, analysis of the tablets in the Royal Ontario Museum show that the economic structure of Umma was far more complex than what can be seen in Drehem. When the Umma tablets are eventually studied alongside the sealings from Umma, we will be able to construct a more accurate picture of the economic administration of that ancient city.

The administration has a regulatory function, overseeing various aspects in the production and distribution process of goods, including the management of resources need for production. All the related activities of the city were controlled through the administration, field work (irrigation, plowing, seeding, and harvesting), animal husbandry (herding, fattening, and wool shearing), and transformation activities (milling the grain, weaving the wool, working the leather). And for all these activities, the administration had to ensure a supply of manpower, making workers available and providing them with food. The royal palace, the office of the governor, and the temple complexes also were involved in this administrative apparatus.

Informations about all these activities can be found in the Umma tablets stored in the Royal Ontario Museum. It should be stressed that there is no perfect linear way to present the content of these tablets, as there is often an overlapping of responsibility between various sectors of the economy, such as between irrigation tasks and field work. For Umma, weaving activities could be considered to be at the end of the chain of pastoral activities. It could also be included among the transformation activities, such as grinding, melting, or tanning. Or, since its products are distributed among all the workers active in the economic sector of the city, we could place the accounting of garments as part of the wage-payment process, separating the fabrication process from its distribution system. Yet, to best understand the redistribution system it is beneficial to analyze together wages in barley, garments, oil, other food staples, as well as land attribution. The production sectors of the economy were interconnected and can, therefore, be approached and studied in several ways.

There is great diversity among the records of Umma, Drehem, Lagash, and Ur. The archives of the capital city Ur deal, to a large extent, with the palace and deliveries of food and precious items. There is also a private archive with many tablets about loans of barley or silver. The tablets of Lagash deal mainly with field work, barley yields, and loans. Drehem is almost completely devoted to the keeping of accounts of animals for Nippur and the palaces, as well as their fattening. Umma presents the widest scope of activities. Archives involving all these activities have been found, even if the documentation is not as extensive as it is for Lagash.

The tablets from the Royal Ontario Museum make a significant contribution to our understanding of this ancient economy. My sincerest thanks and appreciation to Dr. Dan Keal for permission to publish this second volume of the Ur III tablets housed in the Royal Ontario Museum.

Deliveries of Beer to High Officials (nos. 1 – 7)

Beer, with its many varieties, was the basic beverage throughout society, besides water, of course. It appears on the tables of the gods, kings, and governors, was among the provisions for messengers (rá-gaba or kaš$_4$), and constituted part of the normal rations of workers. This first text concerns requisitioning the barley used to make beer for the needs of the king.

no. 1 (Š 47) [copy]

Obverse	
5 še gur	5 gur of barley
ki Ur-^{d}Šara$_2$-ta	from Ur-Šara
nag-lugal-šè	for the royal beverages
gìr A-ba-ne-gim	responsible: Abanegim
Ur-mes šu-ba-ti	Urmes received
Reverse	
šà Unug^{ki}	in Uruk
mu-ús-sa Ki-maš^{ki} ba-ḫul	Š 47

5 gur of barley under the control of Ur-Šara was transferred to the control of Urmes, in order to provide the palace with the basics for the preparation of beer. Abanegim was the individual responsible for this transfer being carried out in Uruk.

Obviously the palace needed much more grain for beer than the 5 gur recorded on this tablet. Moreover, such deliveries were usually made to Ur, where the royal palace was located. Perhaps this tablet involves a special delivery for a ceremony taking place in Uruk, in the presence of the king. The gìr-official, in this case Abanegim, is the one who presents the request to the granary and forwards the barley to its destination, handing it over, in this case, to Urmes. The uncommon occurrence of a gìr-official for such a simple transfer reenforces the notion that this was for a special occasion.

The Umma administrative tablets provide no information about the actual preparation of beer, only the barley needed for its production and the redistribution of several types of beer.

The following tablets, bearing the seal of the governor of Umma, deal with almost daily deliveries of beer and flour for the household of the governor (ensi$_2$). Since the following documents lack any statement that these shipments were regular deliveries (sá-du$_{11}$), they may be additional deliveries to cover special or extra needs.

no. 2 (ŠS [ ] v) [copy]

Obverse	
17 sila$_3$ kaš sig$_5$	17 sila of top-quality beer
40 sila$_3$ kaš gin u$_4$-25-kam	40 sila of average-quality beer, on the 25th day
9 sila$_3$ kaš sig$_5$	9 sila of top-quality beer
30 sila$_3$ kaš gin	30 sila of average-quality beer

u$_4$-26-kam	on the 26th day
Reverse	
ki A-al-NI-ta	from AalNI
kišib ensi$_2$	(tablet has) the seal of the governor of Umma
iti ri	month 5
[mu]	[year Šu-Sîn]
Seal	
^{d}[Šu]-^{d}EN.ZU	to [Šu]-Sîn
lugal-kalag-ga	mighty king
lugal Uri$_5$^{ki}-ma	king of Ur
lugal an-ub-da limmu$_2$-ba	king of the four quarters of the universe
A-a-kal-la	Aakalla
ensi$_2$	the governor
Umma^{ki}	(of) Umma
ir$_{11}$-zu	(is) your servant

This document records the daily delivery for the 26th of the month of two types of beer—top quality and average quality—by AalNI, to the household of Aakalla, governor of Umma under King Šu-Sîn. The name A-al-NI could be read as either A-al-ni or A-al-lí.

The following two texts are similar in form and function to the previous example, except they cover three days of deliveries. Text no. 3 is for the household of Ur-Lisi, governor of Umma under King Amar-Sîn, and text no. 4 is for that of Aakalla, as above.

no. 3 (AS5 i 26) [copy]

Obverse	
12 sila$_3$ kaš sig$_5$	12 sila of top-quality beer
40 sila$_3$ kaš gin u$_4$-24-kam	40 sila of average-quality beer on the 24th day
14 sila$_3$ kaš sig$_5$	14 sila of top-quality beer
35 sila$_3$ kaš gin u$_4$-25-kam	35 sila of average-quality beer on the 25th day
10 sila$_3$ kaš sig$_5$	10 sila of top-quality beer
30 sila$_3$ kaš gin u$_4$-26-kam	40 sila of average-quality beer on the 26th day
Reverse	
kišib ensi$_2$	(tablet has) the seal of the governor
iti še-kin-ku$_5$	month 1
mu en-^{d}Nanna	AS 5
^{d}Amar-^{d}EN.ZU-ki-ág-an-na-kam	
Seal	
^{d}[Amar]-^{d}EN.ZU	Amar-Sîn
lugal-kalag-ga	mighty king
lugal Uri$_5$^{ki}-ma	king of Ur

lugal an-ub-da limmu$_2$-ba	king of the four quarters of the universe
Ur-^{d}Li$_9$-si$_4$	Ur-Lisi
ensi$_2$ Umma^{ki}-ka	the governor of Umma
ir$_{11}$-zu	(is) your servant

no. 4 (ŠS 2 v 6) [copy]

Obverse	
18 sila$_3$ [kaš sig$_5$]	18 sila of [top-quality beer]
50 sila$_3$ [kaš gin]	50 sila of [average-quality beer]
u$_4$-4-kam	on the 4th day
14 sila$_3$ kaš sig$_5$	14 sila of top-quality beer
30 sila$_3$ kaš gin	30 sila of average-quality beer
u$_4$-5-kam	on the 5th day
13 sila$_3$ kaš sig$_5$	13 sila of top-quality beer
25 sila$_3$ kaš gin	25 sila of average-quality beer
u$_4$-6-kam	on the 6th day
Reverse	
17 sila$_3$ kaš sig$_5$	17 sila of top-quality beer
0;1.2.5 sila$_3$ kaš gin	85 sila of average-quality beer
1 dug dida gin 15 sila$_3$	1 jug of average-quality beer ingredients of 15 sila
^{d}Šul-gi-ḫé-gál	Šulgi-ḫegal
ki Ur-mes-ta	from Urmes
kišib ensi$_2$-ka	(tablet has) the seal of the governor
iti ri	month 5
mu má ^{d}En-ki-ka ba-ab-du$_8$	ŠS 2
Seal	
^{d}Šu-^{d}EN.ZU	Šu-Sîn
lugal-kalag-ga	mighty king
lugal Uri$_5$^{ki}-ma	king of Ur
lugal an-ub-da limmu$_2$-ba	king of the four quarters of the universe
A-a-kal-la	Aakalla
ensi$_2$	the governor
Umma^{ki}	(of) Umma
ir$_{11}$-zu	(is) your servant

Text no. 5, again beer deliveries, is issued in Zabalam to the military governor (šaggina) of the province. The military governor's name may be Úr-ra-an or Úr-ra-ìl. Note that AalNI is once more the official in charge of the transfer.

no. 5 (ŠS I v) [copy]

Obverse	
10 sila$_3$ kaš sig$_5$	10 sila of top-quality beer
Úr-ra-AN šaggina	(for) UrraAN the military governor
ki A-al-NI-ta	from AalNI
kišib ensi$_2$	(tablet has) the seal of the governor
Reverse	
šà Zabalam^{ki}	in Zabalam
iti ri	month 5
mu ^{d}Šu-^{d}EN.ZU lugal	ŠS I
Seal	
^{d}Šu-^{d}EN.ZU	Šu-Sîn
lugal kalag-ga	mighty king
lugal Uri$_5$^{ki}-ma	king of Ur
lugal an-ub-da limmu$_2$-ba	king of the four quarters of the universe
A-a-kal-la	Aakalla
ensi$_2$	the governor
Umma^{ki}	of Umma
ir$_{11}$-zu	(is) your servant

The function and format of the following two transfers of beer are somewhat different. In these instances the individuals who takes charge of the beer (Urešdam and Egalesi) also impress their own seal on the tablet, thereby ratifying the transfer, and agreeing to the modalities as well as the quantity and quality of beer transferred. In text no. 6 the beer is transferred from the possession or account of Aḫanišu to that of Urešdam, in text no. 7 from the possession or account of Luinimgina to that of Egalesi.

no. 6 (IS)

Obverse	
45 sila$_3$ kaš sig$_5$	45 sila of top-quality beer
ki A-ḫa-ni-šu-ta	from Aḫanišu
kišib Ur-èš-dam	(tablet has) the seal of Urešdam
Reverse broken	
Seal	
^{d}I-bí-^{d}EN.ZU	Ibbi-Sîn
lugal kalag-ga	strong king
lugal Uri$_5$^{ki}-ma	king of Ur
lugal an-ub-da limmu$_2$-ba	king of the four quarters of the universe
Ur-èš-dam	Urešdam
dub-sar	the scribe
dumu [Lugal-úr-ra-ni]	son of [Lugalurrani]

[ir$_{11}$-zu]	[(is) your servant]

no. 7 (i) [copy]

Obverse	
o; 0.1.5 sila$_3$ kaš gin	15 sila of average-quality beer
ki Lú-inim-gi-na-ta	from Luinimgina
kišib É-gal-e-si	(tablet has) the seal of Egalesi
šà bala	part of the *bala*-obligation
Reverse	
iti še-kin-ku$_5$	month 1
Seal	
É-gal-e-si	Egalesi
dub-sar	the scribe
dumu Ur-[kù]	son of Ur[ku]

Over a one-year period, each city in the empire, participated in a rotation system called "bala," which required it to deliver all kind of items to the central administration to cover all the needs of the palace and temples for a certain portion of the year. The beer delivered in text no. 7 was part of this bala-obligation. By stating this explicitly on the tablet (šà bala), this document could be used for accounting purposes—to calculate how much of the bala-obligation has been delivered and how much was outstanding.

Egalesi is known to have used two seals, one during the years Š 48 to ŠS 2 and the second from ŠS 3 to ŠS 7. Both have identical inscriptions. Almost all the other tablets sealed by Egalesi concern reeds. Therefore, his role in text no. 7 seems to be an exception to his regular duties.

Deliveries of Fodder (nos. 8 – 92)

The Royal Ontario Museum collection contains a very extensive archive concerning the delivery of fodder for donkeys or mules. Only a few tablets deal with deliveries for barley-fed oxen or sheep. Normally, these animals receive a regular delivery (sá-du$_{11}$) of fodder. Since the following texts do not concern these regular deliveries, there must be a special occasion, which may be, to some extent, discerned in the mention of the donkeys of the chariot or of the festival or by the fact that the sealers of these tablets are often priests or servants of the god Šara. Therefore, perhaps these deliveries were made for special religious observances.

The major part of this archive spans Š 35 to Š 48. Only a few attestations come from the reign of Amar-Sîn. Some more date to the reign of Šu-Sîn.

The following is a chronological listing of this archive, with the name of the persons sealing these tablets.

Name on Seal	*Animal*	*Year*	*Text No.*
[Ur-dingir-ra kuš$_7$ ensi$_2$]	anše-kunga$_2$	[ ]	166
Ur-dingir-ra kuš$_7$ ensi$_2$	anše-kunga$_2$	Š 35	491
no seal	anše-kunga$_2$	Š 35	491
Lú-bàn-da ugula gu$_4$	anše	Š 36	151
Lú-dingir-ra	anše	Š 37	222
Ur-dingir-ra kuš$_7$ ensi$_2$	anše-kunga$_2$	Š 37	490
[ ]-kal-la	anše-kunga$_2$	Š 38	470
Lú-bàn-da ugula gu$_4$	anše-kunga$_2$	Š 38	410
Ur-^{ú}numun$_2$	anše	Š 38	172
Ur-^{ú}numun$_2$	anše	Š 38	218
Ur-^{ú}numun$_2$	anše	Š 38	400
Inim-^{d}Šara$_2$ kurušda	udu niga	Š 39	40
Inim-^{d}Šara$_2$ kurušda	udu niga	Š 39	173
Lú-[ ]	anše-kunga$_2$	Š 39	94
Lú-bàn-da ugula gu$_4$	anše-kunga$_2$	Š 39	377
Lú-bàn-da ugula gu$_4$	anše-kunga$_2$	Š 39	445
Lú-^{d}Nin-šubur ír	anše-kunga$_2$	Š 39	147
Ur-dingir-ra	anše-kunga$_2$	Š 39	198
Ur-dingir-ra	anše-kunga$_2$	Š 39	198
Ur-dingir-ra	anše-kunga$_2$	Š 39	444
Inim-^{d}Šara$_2$ kurušda	udu niga	Š 40	529
Lú-bàn-da ugula gu$_4$	anše-kunga$_2$	Š 40	106
Lú-bàn-da ugula gu$_4$	anše-kunga$_2$	Š 40	122
Ur-dingir-ra	anše-kunga$_2$	Š 40	446
Ur-dingir-ra	anše-kunga$_2$	Š 40	460
Lú-bàn-da ugula gu$_4$	anše-kunga$_2$	Š 41	416
Lú-bàn-da ugula gu$_4$	anše-kunga$_2$	Š 41	429
Puzur$_4$-ì-lí	anše	Š 41	366
[ ]	anše-kunga$_2$	Š 41?	450
Lú-bàn-da ugula gu$_4$	anše-kunga$_2$	Š 42	152
Lú-bàn-da ugula gu$_4$	anše-kunga$_2$	Š 42	154
Lú-bàn-da ugula gu$_4$	anše-kunga$_2$	Š 42	165
Lú-bàn-da ugula gu$_4$	anše-kunga$_2$	Š 42	221
Ur-dingir-ra	anše-kunga$_2$	Š 42	441
Lú-^{d}Nin-šubur ir$_{11}$	anše-kunga$_2$	Š 43	505
Lú-^{d}Nin-šubur ir$_{11}$	anše-kunga$_2$ zi-ku-um	Š 44	143
Lú-^{d}Nin-šubur ir$_{11}$	anše zi-ku-um	Š 44	658
Lugal-é-maḫ-e	anše-kunga$_2$	Š 44	230

Lugal-ḫé-gál	anše-kunga$_2$	Š 44	160
Ú-li	anše-kunga$_2$	Š 44	381
Ur-dingir-ra kuš$_7$ ensi$_2$	anše-kunga$_2$	Š 44	432
Ur-^{giš}gigir	gu$_4$ niga	Š 44	214
[ ]	gu$_4$ niga	Š 45	588
no seal	gu$_4$ niga	Š 45	488
En-ú-šim-e	gu$_4$-niga	Š 46	115
Ku-li	gu$_4$ niga	Š 46	396
Lú-[ ]	gu$_4$ niga	Š 46	398
Lú-^{d}Nin-šubur ir$_{11}$	anše zi-ku-um	Š 46	167
Lugal-é-maḫ-e	anše-kunga$_2$	Š 46	99
Lugal-é-maḫ-e	anše-kunga$_2$	Š 46	150
Lugal-é-maḫ-e	anše-kunga$_2$	Š 46	199
^{d}Nanše-kam	erin$_2$ bala tuš-a	Š 46	513
Šu-ú	gu$_4$ niga	Š 46	130
Šu-ú	gu$_4$ niga	Š 46	382
Gur$_4$-za-an	gu$_4$ niga	Š 46	164
Gur$_4$-za-an	gu$_4$ niga	Š 46	424
Ur-dingir-ra kuš$_7$ ensi$_2$	anše-kunga$_2$	Š 46	35
Ur-dingir-ra kuš$_7$ ensi$_2$	anše-kunga$_2$	Š 46	146
Ur-dingir-ra kuš$_7$ ensi$_2$	anše-kunga$_2$	Š 46	156
Ur-dingir-ra kuš$_7$ ensi$_2$	anše-kunga$_2$	Š 46	418
A-ḫu-a	udu-niga	Š 47	633
Lú-^{d}Nin-šubur ir$_{11}$	anše [ ]	Š 47	133
Lú-^{d}Nin-šubur ir$_{11}$	anše zi-ku-um	Š 47	517
Igi-^{d}Šara$_2$-šè	anše	Š 48	116
Ur-dingir-ra kuš$_7$ ensi$_2$	anše-kunga$_2$	Š 48	159
Ur-dingir-ra kuš$_7$ ensi$_2$	anše-kunga$_2$	Š 48	442
no seal	anše-kunga$_2$	AS 4	574
Lú-^{d}Nin-šubur kuš$_7$	anše	ŠS 1	440
Igi-^{d}Šara$_2$-šè	anše	ŠS 2	500
Lú-^{d}Nin-šubur kuš$_7$	anše	ŠS 2	420
Igi-^{d}Šara$_2$-šè	anše	ŠS 3	376
Lú-^{d}Nin-šubur kuš$_7$	anše-kunga$_2$	ŠS 3	373
Lú-^{d}Nám-an-ka	gan-tuš	ŠS 3	98
Lú-^{d}Nin-šubur kuš$_7$	anše-kunga$_2$	ŠS 3	402
Ad-da-kal-la	anše	ŠS 5	138
no seal	udu niga	ŠS 7	134
[ ]	anše	[ ]	137
no seal	anše-kunga$_2$	[ ]	412

The quantities delivered in these texts are small, from a few tens of sila to a few gur. Regular deliveries (sá-du$_{11}$) involve far larger quantities and should be divisible by 30 if for a month or by 12 if for a year. That such is not the case in this archive is further evidence that these deliveries were for exceptional needs.

The fodder was destined for animals of the governor, mules used by the dispatch service (zi-kum), for soldiers and workers, and religious occasions. The following indications are given in the texts:

šà-gal anše ensi$_2$ Ki-an^{ki}	fodder for the donkeys of the governor in Kian
šà-gal anše-kunga$_2$	fodder for the mules
šà-gal anše-kunga$_2$ ensi$_2$	fodder for the mules of the governor
šà-gal anše-kunga$_2$ Ki-an^{ki}	fodder for the mules of Kian
šà-gal anše-kunga$_2$ šà bala-a	fodder for the mules as part of the *bala*-obligation
šà-gal anše-kunga$_2$ zi-ku-um	fodder for the mules of the dispatch service
šà-gal anše-kunga$_2$ zi-ku-um ezem ^{d}Šul-gi	fodder for the mules of the dispatch service during the festival of Šulgi
šà-gal anše-kunga$_2$ siskur$_2$ ^{giš}gigir gu-la	fodder for the mules for the offering ceremony of the great chariot
šà-gal erin$_2$ bala tuš-a	fodder for the soldiers during their *bala*-obligation
šà-gal gu$_4$ niga	fodder for the barley-fed oxen
šà-gal ḫé-dab$_5$	fodder for the forced(?)-workers
šà-gal siskur$_2$-ra anše-kunga$_2$	fodder for the mules during the offering ceremony
šà-gal udu niga	fodder for the barley-fed sheep
lá-ni-ta su-ga … sá-du$_{11}$ anše	from the returned remainder delivered as regular delivery for the donkeys

These references indicate that the mules in the dispatch service of the governor in Kian were also used during religious occasions and, therefore, special fodder allotments were provided.

In this archive, the scribe always specifies the origin of the barley, whether from silos or mills. In most instances, the name of the field is given, that is, from a silo erected in that field. There was no central storage location for barley in the countryside. Such a facility would have to have been huge and difficult to manage. Every large area of cultivated land, therefore, had its own threshing floor and storage facilities, often in the vicinity of a canal for easy transportation of the grain. The following fields are mentioned:

a-šà ^{d}Šara$_2$
a-šà é-àr
a-šà é-àr gibil
a-šà ^{giš}ma-nu
a-šà saḫar-ú-ú

a-šà lá-maḫ

a-šà me-en-kár

Next to these fields are some buildings or storage places:

é-àr-àr

é-^{d}Nin-ur$_{4}$-ra

é-duru$_{5}$ Ur-gu (probably same as Ur-gu-la)

é-duru$_{5}$ Ur-gu-la

é-še-sumun

é-šu-tum

In a few instances granaries or threshing floors are named:

Granaries:

gur$_{7}$ íd-sal$_{4}$-la

gur$_{7}$ igi é-duru$_{5}$

Threshing floors:

ki-su$_{7}$ da-temen-na

ki-su$_{7}$ gu-la a-šà lá-maḫ

ki-su$_{7}$ a-šà lá-maḫ

(ki-su$_{7}$) šu-zu-gar-ra / šu-zu-gá-ra

The official most often mentioned in these tablets is Ir$_{11}$, who was the chief supervisor for all barley in the Umma region and was responsible for recording all disbursements. There were minor officials in charge of specific storages locations:

Ka-gur$_{7}$	(1) é-àr (gibil), (2) gur$_{7}$ íd-sal$_{4}$-la, (3) kar, (4) ki-su$_{7}$ da-temen-na, (5) ki-su$_{7}$ gu-la a-šà lá-maḫ
Lú-kiri$_{4}$-zal	šà bala-a
Lú-bala-sig$_{5}$	é-šutum
Lú-^{d}Šul-gi	é-àr gibil
Lugal-é-maḫ-e	a-šà ^{d}Šara$_{2}$

In these documents, the individual who sealed the tablet is also the person who actually took possession of the barley. Only in a few instances were two distinct individuals involved, one who receives and one who seals. The following is a list of all these individuals with the animals for which they provided:

[ ]	anše	[]	137
[ ]	gu$_{4}$ niga	Š 45	588
[ ]	anše-kunga$_{2}$	Š 41?	450
[ ]-kal-la	anše-kunga$_{2}$	Š 38	470
A-ḫu-a	udu-niga	Š 47	633

Ad-da-kal-la	anše	ŠS 5	138
En-ú-šim-e	gu_4-niga	Š 46	115
Gur_4-za-an	gu_4 niga	Š 46/AS 3	164
Gur_4-za-an	gu_4 niga	Š 46/AS 3	424
Igi-^{d}Šara$_2$-šè	anše	Š 48	116
Igi-^{d}Šara$_2$-šè	anše	ŠS 2	500
Igi-^{d}Šara$_2$-šè	anše	ŠS 3	376
Inim-^{d}Šara$_2$ kurušda	udu niga	Š 39	40
Inim-^{d}Šara$_2$ kurušda	udu niga	Š 39	173
Inim-^{d}Šara$_2$ kurušda	udu niga	Š 40	529
Ku-li	gu_4 niga	Š 46	396
Lú-[ ]	anše-kunga$_2$	Š 39	94
Lú-[ ]	gu_4 niga	Š 46	398
Lú-bàn-da ugula gu_4	anše-kunga$_2$	Š 38	410
Lú-bàn-da ugula gu_4	anše-kunga$_2$	Š 39	377
Lú-bàn-da ugula gu_4	anše-kunga$_2$	Š 39	445
Lú-bàn-da ugula gu_4	anše-kunga$_2$	Š 40	106
Lú-bàn-da ugula gu_4	anše-kunga$_2$	Š 40	122
Lú-bàn-da ugula gu_4	anše-kunga$_2$	Š 41	416
Lú-bàn-da ugula gu_4	anše-kunga$_2$	Š 41	429
Lú-bàn-da ugula gu_4	anše-kunga$_2$	Š 42	152
Lú-bàn-da ugula gu_4	anše-kunga$_2$	Š 42	154
Lú-bàn-da ugula gu_4	anše-kunga$_2$	Š 42	165
Lú-bàn-da ugula gu_4	anše-kunga$_2$	Š 42	221
Lú-bàn-da ugula gu_4	anše	Š 36	151
Lú-dingir-ra	anše	Š 37	222
Lú-^{d}Nám-an-ka	gan-tuš	ŠS 3	98
Lú-^{d}Nin-šubur ir$_{11}$	anše [ ]	Š 47	133
Lú-^{d}Nin-šubur ir$_{11}$	anše-kunga$_2$ zi-ku-um	Š 44	143
Lú-^{d}Nin-šubur ir$_{11}$	anše-kunga$_2$	Š 39	147
Lú-^{d}Nin-šubur ir$_{11}$	anše-kunga$_2$	Š 43	505
Lú-^{d}Nin-šubur ir$_{11}$	anše zi-ku-um	Š 44	658
Lú-^{d}Nin-šubur ir$_{11}$	anše zi-ku-um	Š 46	167
Lú-^{d}Nin-šubur ir$_{11}$	anše zi-ku-um	Š 47	517
Lú-^{d}Nin-šubur kuš$_7$	anše-kunga$_2$	ŠS 3	373
Lú-^{d}Nin-šubur kuš$_7$	anše-kunga$_2$	ŠS 3	402
Lú-^{d}Nin-šubur kuš$_7$	anše	ŠS 1	440
Lú-^{d}Nin-šubur kuš$_7$	anše	ŠS 2	420
Lugal-é-maḫ-e	anše-kunga$_2$	Š 44	230

Lugal-é-maḫ-e	anše-kunga$_2$	Š 46	99
Lugal-é-maḫ-e	anše-kunga$_2$	Š 46	150
Lugal-é-maḫ-e	anše-kunga$_2$	Š 46	199
Lugal-ḫé-gál	anše-kunga$_2$	Š 44	160
^{d}Nanše-kam	erin$_2$ bala tuš-a	Š 46	513
Puzur$_4$-ì-lí	anše	Š 41	366
Šu-ú	gu$_4$ niga	Š 46	130
Šu-ú	gu$_4$ niga	Š 46	382
Ú-li	anše-kunga$_2$	Š 44	381
Ur-dingir-ra	anše-kunga$_2$	Š 39	198
Ur-dingir-ra	anše-kunga$_2$	Š 39	198
Ur-dingir-ra	anše-kunga$_2$	Š 39	444
Ur-dingir-ra	anše-kunga$_2$	Š 40	446
Ur-dingir-ra	anše-kunga$_2$	Š 40	460
Ur-dingir-ra	anše-kunga$_2$	Š 42	441
Ur-dingir-ra kuš$_7$ ensi$_2$	anše-kunga$_2$	Š 35	491
Ur-dingir-ra kuš$_7$ ensi$_2$	anše-kunga$_2$	Š 37	490
Ur-dingir-ra kuš$_7$ ensi$_2$	anše-kunga$_2$	Š 44	432
Ur-dingir-ra kuš$_7$ ensi$_2$	anše-kunga$_2$	Š 46	35
Ur-dingir-ra kuš$_7$ ensi$_2$	anše-kunga$_2$	Š 46	146
Ur-dingir-ra kuš$_7$ ensi$_2$	anše-kunga$_2$	Š 46	156
Ur-dingir-ra kuš$_7$ ensi$_2$	anše-kunga$_2$	Š 46	418
Ur-dingir-ra kuš$_7$ ensi$_2$	anše-kunga$_2$	Š 48	159
Ur-dingir-ra kuš$_7$ ensi$_2$	anše-kunga$_2$	Š 48	442
[Ur-dingir-ra kuš$_7$ ensi$_2$]	anše-kunga$_2$	[ ]	166
Ur-^{giš}gigir	gu$_4$ niga	Š 44	214
Ur-^{ú}numun$_2$	anše	Š 38	172
Ur-^{ú}numun$_2$	anše	Š 38	218
Ur-^{ú}numun$_2$	anše	Š 38	400
no seal	anše-kunga$_2$	[ ]	412
no seal	anše-kunga$_2$	AS 4	574
no seal	anše-kunga$_2$	Š 35	491
no seal	gu$_4$ niga	Š 45	488
no seal	udu niga	ŠS 7	134

Rarely in this archive are the sealbearers scribes, dub-sar. Only for the fattening of sheep and oxen is dub-sar mentioned on the seal inscription. All the men sealing these tablets were active over the reigns of Šulgi, Amar-Sîn, and Šu-Sîn. Also, they all used more than one seal. The seal inscriptions usually indicate a connection with the divinity for whom the individual provided. The following are those who sealed the tablets:

A-ḫu-a	udu-niga	Š 47	633
[Ad-da]-kal-la	anše-kunga$_2$	Š 38	470
Ad-da-kal-la	anše	ŠS 5	138
Al-lu			
En-ú-šim-e	gu$_4$-niga	Š 46	115
Gur$_4$-za-an	gu$_4$ niga	Š 46	164, 424
Igi-^{d}Šara$_2$-šè	anše	Š 48-ŠS 3	116, 376, 500
Inim-^{d}Šara$_2$ kurušda	udu niga	Š 39-40	40, 173, 529
Ku-li	gu$_4$ niga	Š 46	396
Lú-bàn-da ugula gu$_4$	anše	Š 36-42	151, 410, 377, 445, 106, 122, 416, 165, 221, 429, 154, 152
Lú-dingir-ra	anše	Š 37	222
Lú-^{d}Nám-an-ka	ḫé-dab$_5$	ŠS 3	98
Lú-^{d}Nin-šubur ir$_{11}$	anše-kunga$_2$ zi-ku-um	Š 39-46	147, 505, 143, 658, 133, 517, 167
Lú-^{d}Nin-šubur kuš$_7$	anše	ŠS 1-3	440, 420, 402, 373
Lú-[ ]	anše-kunga$_2$	Š 39	94
Lú-[ ]	gu$_4$ niga	Š 46	398
Lugal-é-maḫ-e	anše-kunga$_2$	Š 44-46	99, 150, 160, 199, 230
Lugal-ḫé-gál		Š	
^{d}Nanše-kam	erin$_2$ bala tuš-a	Š 46	513
Puzur$_4$-ì-lí	anše	Š 41	366
Šu-ú	gu$_4$ niga	Š 46	130, 382
Ú-li	anše-kunga$_2$	Š 44	381
Ur-dingir-ra	anše-kunga$_2$	Š 39-42	198, 444, 460, 441, 446
Ur-dingir-ra kuš$_7$ ensi$_2$	anše-kunga$_2$	Š 35-48	490, 491, 431, 35, 418, 146, 156, 159, 442
[Ur-dingir-ra kuš$_7$ ensi$_2$]	anše-kunga$_2$	[ ]	166
Ur-^{giš}gigir	gu$_4$ niga	Š 44	214
Ur-^{ú}numun$_2$	anše	Š 38	172, 218, 400
[PN	gu$_4$ niga	Š 45	588

[PN]	anše-kunga$_2$	Š 41?	450
[PN]	anše	[ ]	137
no seal	anše-kunga$_2$	AS 4	574
no seal	anše-kunga$_2$	Š 35	491
no seal	anše-kunga$_2$	[ ]	412
no seal	gu$_4$ niga	Š 45	488
no seal	udu niga	ŠS 7	134

The following partially broken summary tablet does not contain the crucial administrative or accounting words that would highlight its function in the accounting system of the administration. Note that the fodder for fattening cattle comes from the same place as the regular deliveries for the divinities and those for grinding—a storage facility had to provide for multiple needs. This summary tablet is, itself, not sealed, because it is a simple internal administrative document, recapitulating the disbursement of barley for cattle (fattening of sheep and donkeys), for the regular deliveries to the gods Enki and Šulgi, and for the mill. All these disbursements are controlled by the same office.

no. 8 (AS 9)

Obverse	
10 gur šà-gal anše	10 gur fodder for donkeys
kišib A-ab-ba-ni	received by Aabbani
1; 1.0. gur šà-gal udu niga	1;1.0. gur fodder for barley-fed sheep
kišib A-du	received by Adu
0; 1.0. sá-du$_{11}$ ^{d}Šul-gi-ra	0;1.0. regular deliveries for the divine Šulgi
kišib Ur-ni$_9$-gar-ki-du$_{10}$	received by Urnigarkidu
0; 3.0. še-àr-ra kišib Lú-dingir-ra	0;3.0. barley for grinding; received by Ludingirra
1 gur sá-du$_{11}$ ^{d}En-ki	1 gur regular delivery for Enki
Reverse	
kišib Ni$_9$-gar-ki-du$_{10}$	received by Nigarkidu
1 gur še àr-ra kišib Du-ú-du$_{11}$	0;3.0. barley for grinding; received by Duudu
0; 3.0. še-àr-ra ^{d}Šara$_2$-kam	0;3.0. barley for grinding for Šarakam
0; 2.0. še-àr-ra Lú-dingir-ra	0;2.0. barley for grinding for Ludingirra
1 gur še-àr-ra Lú-gi-na	1 gur of barley for grinding for Lugina
1 gur še-àr-ra A-ab-ba	1 gur of. barley for grinding for Aabba
0; 1.0. še-àr-ra Al-lu	0;1.0. barley for grinding for Allu
[gìr] Inim-^{d}Nin-é-gal	[reponsible:] Inim-Ninegal
[ ]-ša	[ ]ša
[iti] mu-ús-	[month]
[-sa] en Eridu^{ki} ba-ḫun	AS 9

The tablets of the archive are grouped and ordered below according to the individual who sealed the document.

Sealer's name: [ ]-kal-la

no. 9 (Š 3 8 ii)

Obverse	
3 še gur-lugal	3 gur of barley according to the royal measurement
šà-gal anše-kunga$_2$	fodder for the mules
ki Ir$_{11}$-ta	from Ir
Lú-bàn-da	Lubanda
Reverse	
šu-ba-ti	received
iti sig$_4$-^{giš}ì-šub-ba-gá-ra	month 2
mu-ús-sa bàd ba-dù	Š 3
Seal	
[ ]-kal-la	[ ]kalla
dumu Lú-bàn-da	son of Lubanda

Sealer's name: Ad-da-kal-la

no. 10 (ŠS 5 ix) [copy]

Obverse	
1 še gur	1 gur of barley
šà-gal anše	fodder for donkeys
ki-su$_7$ da-temen-na-ta	from the threshing floor Datemena
ki ka-gur$_7$-ta	from the granary manager
kišib Ad-da-kal-la	(tablet has) the seal of Addakalla
Reverse	
iti ^{d}Li$_9$-si$_4$	month 9
mu-ús-sa ^{d}Šu-^{d}EN.ZU lugal-e	ŠS 5
bàd mar-tu mu-dù	
Seal	
Ad-da-kal-la	Addakalla
gir$_4$-díb	the official recorder
dumu Ur-^{d}Nin-[ur$_4$-ra]	son of Ur-Nin[urra]

Addakalla is known to have worked from ŠS 5 to ŠS 7. On his earlier seal he is titled gir$_4$-díb, the official recorder. On his later seal, the second line gir$_4$-díb is missing, probably erased. On almost all his tablets, Addakalla deals with barley fodder for donkeys delivered by the granary manager.

Sealer's name: En-ú-šim-e dumu Ir$_{11}$-dam

Only one seal of this man is known, dated to the time of Šulgi. The seal is quite exceptional, depicting a four-participant audience with goddess seated on a two-niched throne with festoons. The seal is known from Š 38 to at least Š 46. In two other tablets he is responsible for regular deliveries of barley. The present tablet deals only with barley for barley-fed oxen. The expected expression kišib En-ú-šim-e is not found, only his name in a line not completed with šu-ba-ti.

no. 11 (Š 46 diri) [copy]

Obverse	
1 še gur lugal	1 gur of barley according to the royal measurement
šà-gal gu$_4$ niga	fodder for barley-fed oxen
Ki-an^{ki}-ta	from the place Kian
ki Ir$_{11}$-ta	from Ir
En-ú-šim-e <šu-ba-ti>	Enušime <received>
Reverse	
iti diri	intercalary month
mu Ki-maš^{ki} ba-ḫul	Š 46
Seal	
En-ú-šim-e	Enušime
dumu Ir$_{11}$-dam	son of Irdam
sanga ^{d}Nin-e$_{11}$-e	chief temple official of Ninee

Sealer's name: Gur$_8$-za-an dumu Al-la

This seal owner had two seals. The first writes his name with the sign Gur$_8$ and presents a contest scene and deals with reed deliveries. The second seal uses the sign Gur$_4$ and depicts an introduction scene to a goddess. As noted in text 13, Gurzan held the title of throne-bearer. Many tablets sealed by Gurzan deal with reed deliveries, indicating that for the fodder of oxen and sheep reed was the more common fodder. Barley was used to produce fatter animals.

no. 12 (Š 46 iii)

Obverse	
0; 1.0. še lugal	60 sila of barley according to the royal measurement
šà-gal gu$_4$ niga	fodder for barley-fed oxen
é-àr-ta	from the mill
ki Ir$_{11}$-ta	from Ir

Reverse

Gur$_8$-za-an šu-ba-ti	Gurzan received
iti še-kar-ra-gál	month 3
mu-ús-sa Ur-bí-lum^{ki} ba-ḫul	Š 46

Seal

Gur$_8$-za-an	Gurzan
dumu Al-la	son of Alla

no. 13 (Š 46 iii)

Obverse

0; 1.0. še lugal	60 sila of barley according to the royal measurement
šà-gal gu$_4$ niga	fodder for barley-fed oxen
é-àr-ta	from the mill
ki Ir$_{11}$-ta	from Ir
Gur$_4$-za-an gu-za-lá	Gurzan the throne-bearer

Reverse

šu-ba-ti	received
iti še-kar-ra-gál-la	month 3
mu-ús-sa Ur-bí-ì-lum^{ki} ba-ḫul	Š 46

Seal

Gur$_4$-za-an	Gurzan
dumu Al-la	son of Alla

no. 14 (ŠS 7 iii) [copy]

Obverse

3; 0.4.5 sila$_3$ gur	3 gur and 45 sila
šà-gal udu niga	fodder for the barley-fed sheep
kišib Ur-^{d}Ma-mi	(tablet has) the seal of Ur-Mami
1; 1.2.5 <sila$_3$> šà-gal gu$_4$ niga <gur>	1 gur and 85 sila fodder for the barley-fed oxen
kišib Lú-^{d}Šara$_2$	(tablet has) the seal of Lu-Šara
0; 1.5. sá-du$_{11}$ kaš$_4$	110 sila regular deliveries for the messengers
kišib Gur$_4$-za-an	(tablet has) the seal of Gurzan
0; 0.4. še-ba Ur-^{d}Nin-tu	40 sila barley ration for Ur-Nintu

Reverse

šu-nigín [4;4.4.] gur	total : 4 gur and 280 sila
é še-sumun-ta	from the store of the old barley
iti še-kar-ra-gál-la	month 3
mu ma-da Za-ab-ša-li^{ki} ba-ḫul	ŠS 7

This recapitulative tablet mentions all those in this archive responsible for cattle fodder: Ur-Mami, Lu-Šara, and Gurzan. Note that Gurzan deals with messengers and not the fodder of donkeys or mules, a possible indication of the use of mules by messengers.

The practices of the administration are apparent on this tablet. All the individual tablets written during a given day are recapitulated on a general one, helping to keep the balance of what is still available at the storage location.

Sealer's name: Igi-^{d}Šara$_{2}$-šè

Two seals of this official are attested. On one is a presentation to an ascending god. On the other, which dates to the reign of Amar-Sîn, the relief is hardly visible and was used for sealing tablets dealing with donkey fodder.

Igi-Šarašè has a special relation to the god Šara, expressed through the word ir$_{11}$, servant of Šara. Even his name contains the mention of the god Šara.

no. 15 (Š 48 xii) [copy]

Obverse

1 še gur-lugal	1 gur of barley according to the royal measurement
šà-gal anše	fodder for donkeys
ki-su$_{7}$ gu-la a-šà lá-maḫ-ta	from the great threshing floor in the field Lamaḫ
ki Ir$_{11}$-ta	from Ir
Igi-^{d}Šara$_{2}$-šè	Igi-Šaraše

Reverse

šu-ba-ti	received
iti ^{d}Dumu-zi	month 12
mu Ar-ši^{ki} ù Ki-maš^{ki} ba-ḫul	Š 48

Seal

Igi-^{d}Šara$_{2}$-šè	Igi-Šaraše
ir$_{11}$-^{d}Šara$_{2}$	servant of Šara

no. 16 (ŠS 2 xii)

Obverse

3 še gur	3 gur of barley
šà-gal anše	fodder for donkeys
gur$_{7}$ íd-sal$_{4}$-la-ta	from the granary of the Salla-canal
ki ka-gur$_{7}$-ta	from the granary manager
kišib Igi-^{d}Šara$_{2}$-šè	received by Igi-Šaraše

Reverse

iti ^{d}Dumu-zi	month 12
mu má-^{d}En-ki ba-ab-du$_{8}$	ŠS 2

Seal

Igi-^{d}Šara$_2$-šè	Igi-Šaraše
ir$_{11}$ ^{d}Šara$_2$	servant of Šara

no. 17 (ŠS 3 vi)

Obverse

3 še gur-lugal	3 gur of barley according to the royal measurement
šà-gal anše	fodder for donkeys
ki-su$_7$ a-šà lá-maḫ-ta	from the threshing floor of the field Lamaḫ
ki ka-gur$_7$-ta	from the granary manager
kišib Igi-^{d}Šara$_2$-šè	received by Igi-Šaraše

Reverse

iti šu-numun	month 6
mu-ús-sa má-^{d}En-ki ba-ab-du$_8$	ŠS 3

Seal

Igi-^{d}Šara$_2$-šè	Igi-Šaraše
Ir$_{11}$ ^{d}Šara$_2$	servant of Šara

Sealer's name: Inim-^{d}Šara$_2$ dumu Ur-dingir-ra

Only one seal of this sheep fattener is known. His profession is noted on the seal and puts him in direct contact with the temple of Šara. Inim-Šara deals with barley for only the two years Š 39 and 40. In a later tablet, Š 46, he receives reeds for sheep.

no. 18 (Š 39 xi) [copy]

Obverse

0; 3.0. še lugal	180 sila of barley according to the royal measurement
šà-gal udu niga	fodder for barley-fed sheep
giš-KU-lagab-ta	from ?
ki Ir$_{11}$-ta	from Ir
Inim-^{d}Šara$_2$	Inim-Šara

Reverse

šu-ba-ti	received
iti pa$_4$-kùš-e	month 11
mu é Puzur$_4$-<iš-^{d}>Da-gan ba-dù	Š 39

Seal

Inim-^{d}Šara$_2$	Inim-Šara
dumu Ur-dingir-ra	son of Urdingirra
kurušda ^{d}Šara$_2$	fattener of Šara

Given the parallelism with other tablets giš-KU-lagab should be a toponym.

no. 19 (Š 39 xii)

Obverse	
2 še gur lugal	2 gur of barley according to the royal measurement
šà-gal udu niga	fodder for barley-fed sheep
é-^{d}Nin-ur$_4$-ra-ta	from the temple of Ninurra
ki Ir$_{11}$-ta	from Ir
Inim-^{d}Šara$_2$	Inim-Šara
Reverse	
šu-ba-ti	received
iti ^{d}Dumu-zi	month 12
mu é Puzur$_4$-<iš-^{d}>Da-gan ba-dù	Š 39
Seal	
Inim-^{d}Šara$_2$	Inim-Šara
dumu Ur-dingir-ra	son of Urdingirra
kurušda ^{d}Šara$_2$	fattener of Šara

no. 20 (Š 40)

Obverse	
2 še gur-lugal	2 gur of barley according to the royal measurement
šà-gal udu niga	fodder for barley-fed sheep
gú íd-da-ta	from (the storage place on) the bank of the canal
ki Ir$_{11}$-ta	from Ir
kišib! Inim-^{d}Šara$_2$	(tablet has) the seal of Inim-Šara
Reverse	
šu-ba-ti	he received
mu-ús-sa é Puzur$_4$-^{d}Da-gan ba-dù	Š 40
Seal	
Inim-^{d}Šara$_2$	Inim-Šara
dumu Ur-dingir-ra	son of Urdingirra
kurušda ^{d}Šara$_2$	fattener of Šara

Note the strange structure of the tablet. The scribe mixes two formulae: kišib PN and PN šu-ba-ti.

Sealer's name: Ku-li dumu Ur-ki-ág-mu

Most of Kuli's activity concerns deliveries of reeds and reed mats.

no. 21 (Š 46 ii)

Obverse	
0; 3.3. še lugal	210 sila of barley according to the royal measurement
šà-gal gu_4 niga	fodder for barley-fed oxen
é-àr-ta	from the mill
ki Ir_{11}-ta	from Ir;
mu Da-da-ga-šè	instead of Dadaga
Reverse	
A-du šu-ba-ti	Adu received
iti sig_4-^{giš}ì-šub-ba-gá-ra	month 2
mu-ús-sa Ur-bí-ì-lum^{ki} ba-ḫul	Š 46
Seal	
Ku-li	Kuli
dub-sar	scribe
dumu Ur-ki-ág-mu	son of Urkiagmu

The one who should have sealed the tablet is Adu (NBC 11764 is a similar tablet), not Kuli. Note that three persons were involved in this transaction. The scribe who seals, Kuli, is only an administrator supervising the transfer. Instead of Dadaga, Adu assumed control of the barley. The reason Adu substitutes for Dadaga is not stated.

Sealer's name: Lú-bàn-da dumu ^{giš}Gigir-re

Lubanda had at least four or five seals and was active from Š 32 to ŠS 4, almost thirty years. The activities of Lubanda during the reign of Amar-Sîn are not known.

Lubanda's profession, mu_6-šùb-^{d}$Šara_2$, "shepherd of Šara," is mentioned on all his seals. Each of his seals is new, same inscription but with a different scene. None are mere recuttings. The motifs of each are:

seal 1. Presentation scene to a divinity
seal 2. Divinity seated on single-niched throne
seal 3. A mace added as a filling motive
seal 4. Presentation to god, mace behind him
seal 5. Goddess seated on a single-niched throne, star-disk crescent above

no. 22 (Š 36 xii) [copy]

Obverse

8; 4.0. še gur-lugal	8 gur and 240 sila of barley according to the royal measurement
a-šà lá-maḫ-ta	from the field Lamaḫ
1; 1.0. gur é-àr-ta	1 gur and 60 sila of barley from the mill
šà-gal anše ki Ir_{11}-ta	fodder for donkeys, from Ir
Lú-bàn-da šu-ba-ti	Lubanda received
iti ^{d}Dumu-zi	month 12
Reverse	
mu ^{d}Nanna [kar-]	Š 36
zi-da a-rá 2-kam é-a-na ba-an-ku_4	
Seal	
Lú-bàn-da	Lubanda
mu_6-šùb-^{d}Šara_2	shepherd of Šara
dumu ^{giš}Gigir-re	son of Gigirre

Two storage places: the field Lamaḫ and the mill, are to provide for the fodder of the donkeys. The quantities are for once particularly important.

no. 23 (Š 38 x)

Obverse

2 gur še	2 gur of barley
šà-gal anše-$kunga_2$	fodder for the mules
šu-zu-gar-ra-ta	from (the threshing floor) Šuzugarra
ki Ir_{11}-ta	from Ir
Lú-bàn-da	Lubanda
Reverse	
šu-ba-ti	received
iti ezem-^{d}Šul-gi	month 10
mu-ús-sa bàd ba-dù	Š 38
Seal	
Lú-bàn-da	Lubanda
mu_6-šùb-^{d}Šara_2	shepherd of Šara
dumu ^{giš}Gigir-re	son of Gigirre

no. 24 (Š 39 viii)

Obverse

0; 2.0. še lugal	120 sila of barley according to the royal measurement
šà-gal anše-$kunga_2$	fodder for the mules

a-šà ^{giš}ma-nu-ta	from the field of willow
ki Ir$_{11}$-ta	from Ir
Lú-bàn-da	Lubanda
Reverse	
šu-ba-ti	received
iti é-iti-6	month 8
mu é Puzur$_4$-Da-gan ba-dù	Š 39
Seal	
Lú-bàn-da	Lubanda
mu$_6$-šùb-^{d}Šara$_2$	shepherd of Šara
dumu ^{giš}Gigir-re	son of Gigirre

no. 25 (Š 39 xii)

Obverse	
1 še gur-lugal	1 gur of barley according to the royal measurement
šà-gal anše-kunga$_2$	fodder for the mules
é-àr-ta	from the mill
ki Ir$_{11}$-ta	from Ir
Lú-bàn-da	Lubanda
šu-ba-ti	received
Reverse	
iti ^{d}Dumu-zi	month 12
mu é Puzur$_4$-^{d}Da-gan ba-dù	Š 39
Seal	
Lú-bàn-da	Lubanda
mu$_6$-šùb-^{d}Šara$_2$	shepherd of Šara
dumu ^{giš}gigir-re	son of Gigirre

no. 26 (Š 40 xi) [copy]

Obverse	
1 še gur-lugal	1 gur of barley according to the royal measurement
šà-gal anše-kunga$_2$	fodder for the mules
a-šà ^{giš}ma-nu-ta	from the field of willow
ki Ir$_{11}$-ta	from Ir
Lú-bàn-da	Lubanda
šu-ba-ti	received
Reverse	
iti pa$_4$-kùš-e	month 11
mu-ús-sa é Puzur$_4$-Da-gan ba-dù	Š 40

Seal

Lú-bàn-da	Lubanda
mu$_6$-šùb-^{d}Šara$_2$	shepherd of Šara
dumu ^{giš}Gigir-re	son of Gigirre

no. 27 (Š 40 xii) [copy]

Obverse

1; 3.0 še gur-lugal	1 gur and 180 sila of barley according to the royal measurement
šà-gal anše-kunga$_2$	fodder for the mules
ki Ir$_{11}$-ta	from Ir
Lú-bàn-da	Lubanda
šu-ba-ti	received

Reverse

iti ^{d}Dumu-zi	month 12
mu-ús-sa é Puzur$_4$-^{d}Da-gan ba-dù	Š 40

Seal

Lú-bàn-da	Lubanda
mu$_6$-šùb-^{d}Šara$_2$	shepherd of Šara
dumu ^{giš}Gigir-re	son of Gigirre

no. 28 (Š 41 ii)

Obverse

3 še gur-lugal	3 gur of barley according to the royal measurement
šà-gal anše-kunga$_2$	fodder for the mules
é-àr-ta	from the mill
ki Ir$_{11}$-ta	from Ir
Lú-bàn-da	Lubanda the shepherd
mu$_6$-šùb šu-ba-ti	received

Reverse

iti sig$_4$-^{giš}ì-šub-ba-gá-ra	month 2
mu-ús-sa é Puzur$_4$-<iš-^{d}>Da-gan ba-dù	Š 41
mu-ús-sa-a-bi	

Seal

Lú-bàn-da	Lubanda
mu$_6$-šùb-^{d}Šara$_2$	shepherd of Šara
dumu ^{giš}Gigir-re	son of Gigirre

Note that on this tablet Lubanda mentions his status of shepherd (mu$_6$-šùb) of Šara, usually noted only on his seal.

no. 29 (Š 41 viii)

Obverse	
2; 3.0. še gur-lugal	2 gur and 180 sila of barley in the royal measurement
šà-gal anše-kunga$_2$	fodder for mules
Ki-an^{ki}-ta	from Kian
lá-ni-ta su-ga	from the arrears that were returned
Lú-bala-sig$_5$	by Lubalasig
Lú-bàn-da	Lubanda
Reverse	
šu-ba-ti	received
iti é-iti-6	month 8
mu-ús-sa é Puzur$_4$-<Dagan>	Š 41
mu-ús-sa-a-bi	
Seal	
[Lú-bàn-da]	Lubanda
[mu$_6$-šùb-^{d}Šara$_2$]	shepherd of Šara
[dumu ^{giš}Gigir-re]	son of Gigirre

Also tablet no. 35 concerns barley that was returned after correction of the accounts. Lubalasig is mentioned in text no. 40. He managed the storehouse, the é-šu-tum or é-gi-na-ab-tum. To fulfill the needs here, the scribe balances the accounts of deliveries and returns, thereby not needing to request fodder from a storage location.

no. 30 (Š 42 vii) [copy]

Obverse	
4 še gur-lugal	4 gur of barley according to the royal measurement
šà-gal anše-kunga$_2$	fodder for mules
é-àr-ta	from the mill
ki Ir$_{11}$-ta	from Ir
Lú-bàn-da šu-ba-ti	Lubanda received
Reverse	
iti min-èš	month 7
mu Ša-aš-ru^{ki} ba-ḫul	Š 42
Seal	
Lú-bàn-da	Lubanda
mu$_6$-šùb-^{d}Šara$_2$	shepherd of Šara
dumu ^{giš}Gigir-re	son of Gigirre

no. 31 (Š 42 ix)

Obverse	
1 še gur-lugal	1 gur of barley, according to the royal measurement
é-àr-ta	from the mill
šà-gal anše-kunga$_2$	fodder for mules
ki Ir$_{11}$-ta	from Ir
Lú-bàn-da	Lubanda
šu-ba-ti	received
Reverse	
iti ^{d}Li$_9$-si$_4$	month 9
mu Ša-aš-ru-um^{ki} ba-ḫul	Š 42
Seal	
Lú-bàn-da	Lubanda
mu$_6$-šùb ^{d}Šara$_2$	shepherd of Šara
dumu ^{giš}Gigir-re	son of Gigirre

no. 32 (Š 42 ix)

Obverse	
1 še gur-lugal	1 gur of barley, according to the royal measurement
šà-gal anše-kunga$_2$	fodder for mules
é-àr-ta	from the mill
ki Ir$_{11}$-ta	from Ir
Lú-bàn-da	Lubanda
šu-ba-ti	received
Reverse	
iti ^{d}Li$_9$-si$_4$	month 9
mu Ša-aš-ru^{ki} ba-ḫul	Š 42
Seal	
Lú-bàn-da	Lubanda
mu$_6$-šùb ^{d}Šara$_2$	shepherd of Šara
dumu ^{giš}Gigir-re	son of Gigirre

no. 33 (Š 42 iii) [copy]

Obverse	
7 še gur-lugal	7 gur of barley, according to the royal measurement
šà-gal anše-kunga$_2$	fodder for the mules
^{giš}gigir gu-la	(who pull) the great chariot
ki Ir$_{11}$-ta	from Ir

Lú-bàn-da	Lubanda
Reverse	
šu-ba-ti	received
iti še-kar-ra-gar	month 3
mu Šà-aš-ru-um^{ki} ba-ḫul	Š 42
Seal	
Lú-bàn-da	Lubanda
mu_6-šùb-^{d}Šara$_2$	shepherd of Šara
dumu ^{giš}Gigir-re	son of Gigirre

This tablet gives a clue to the reason for this special delivery, which is not simply an addition to regular rations, which would have been noted as diri (extra, additional). These mules pulled a large chariot, presumably used in a cultic, or even a political, procession.

Sealer's name: Lú-dingir-ra dumu Da-da-a

no. 34 (ŠS 4 xi)

Obverse	
1; 1.0. še gur	360 sila barley
šà-gal anše	fodder for donkeys
kar-ta	from the quay
ki ka-gur$_7$-ta	from the granary manager
Ad-da-kal-la	Addakalla
Reverse	
šu-ba-ti	received
kišib Lú-dingir-ra	(tablet with) the seal of Ludingirra
iti pa$_4$-kùš-e	month 11
mu bàd mar-tu ba-dù	ŠS 4
Seal	
Lú-dingir-ra	Ludingirra
dub-sar	the scribe
dumu Da-da-a	son of Dadaa

Addakalla receives the barley, but Ludingirra, an otherwise unknown scribe, seals the tablet. Because Ludingirra is a scribe, he does not belong to those responsible for providing fodder for donkeys.

Sealer's name: Lú-^{d}Nin-šubur

Lu-Ninšubur never reveals his father's name—he is just the servant of the god Šara. Lu-Ninšubur has four or five seals, used from Š 34 to AS 6, some of which mention his being an equerry (kuš$_{7}$). Although his seals used after Š 44 include kuš$_{7}$, a tablet dated to AS 5 (YBC 445) is without kuš$_{7}$. The reasons for this pattern are unclear. The seal impressions, although plentifully attested, are in general of bad quality, and thus it is hard to discern the presentation scenes. The four seal inscriptions are:

seal 1 Lú-^{d}Nin-šubur
ir$_{11}$ ^{d}Šara$_{2}$
(Goddess seated on simple throne)

seal 2 Lú-^{d}Nin-
šubur kuš$_{7}$
ir$_{11}$ ^{d}Šara$_{2}$

seal 3 Lú-^{d}Nin-šubur
kuš$_{7}$
ir$_{11}$ ^{d}Šara$_{2}$

seal 4 Lú-^{d}Nin-šubur
[kuš$_{7}$]
ir$_{11}$ ^{d}Šara$_{2}$

In all the dealings recorded on the tablets he is connected to providing fodder to donkeys.

no. 35 (Š 37 xi)

Obverse	
0; 2.0. še lugal	120 sila of barley according to the royal measurement
lá-ni-ta su-ga	from the arrears that were returned
A-bí-a-núm	by Abianum,
sá-du$_{11}$ anše	regular delivery for the donkeys
A-kal-la	of Akalla
Reverse	
Lú-^{d}Nin-šubur	Lu-Ninšubur
šu-ba-ti	received
iti pa$_{4}$-kùš-e	month 11
mu-ús-sa ^{d}Nanna Ga-eš^{ki}	Š 37
é-a-na ba-ku$_{4}$	
Seal	
Lú-^{d}Nin-šubur	Lu-Ninšubur
ir$_{11}$ ^{d}Šara$_{2}$	servant of Šara

This tablet is a rectification of fodder accounts, similar to text no. 29.

Normally the scribe writes anše ensi$_2$, donkeys of the governor. In this instance he mentions Akalla, even though Ur-Lisi was then governor. Also note that the year name mentions Gaeš and not, as expected, the city Karzida.

no. 36 (Š 39 vii) [copy]

Obverse

0;1.0. še lugal	60 sila of barley according to the royal measurement
šà-gal anše-[kunga$_2$]	fodder for the mules
šu-zu-gá-ra-ta	from (the threshing floor) Šuzugarra
ki Ir$_{11}$-ta	from Ir
Lú-^{d}Nin-šubur	Lu-Ninšubur

Reverse

šu-ba-ti	received
iti min-éš mu [é]	month 7
Puzur$_4$-iš-[Dagan]	Š 39

Seal

Lú-Nin-šubur	Lu-Ninšubur
ir$_{11}$ ^{d}Šara$_2$	servant of Šara

no. 37 (Š 40 xii) [copy]

Obverse

0; 3.0. še lugal	180 sila of barley according to the royal measurement
šà-gal anše-kunga$_2$	fodder for the mules
šu-zu-gá-ra-ta	from (the threshing floor) Šuzugarra
ki Ir$_{11}$-ta	from Ir
Lú-^{d}Nin-šubur	Lu-Ninšubur
šu-ba-ti	received

Reverse

iti ^{d}Dumu-zi	month 12
mu é Puzur$_4$-Da-gan ba-dù	Š 40

Seal

Lú-^{d}Nin-šubur kuš$_7$	Lu-Ninšubur the equerry
ir$_{11}$-^{d}Šara$_2$	servant of Šara

no. 38 (Š 41 v)

Obverse

0; 0.3. še lugal	30 sila of barley according to the royal measurement
šà-gal anše-kunga$_2$	fodder for the mules

ki Lú-kiri$_3$-zal-ta	from Lukirizal
kišib Lú-^{d}Nin-šubur kuš$_7$	(tablet with) the seal of Lu-Ninšubur the equerry
Reverse	
šà bala-a iti ri	part of the bala-obligation; month 5
mu-ús-sa mu-	Š 41
ús-sa-a-bi	
Seal	
Lú-^{d}Nin-[šubur kuš$_7$?]	Lu-Nin[šubur the equerry?]
ir$_{11}$-^{d}Šara$_2$	servant of Šara

Rather than noting the location from which the fodder came, the tablet indicates that the fodder was part of the bala-obligation, i.e., from the amount the governor of the city had to deliver.

no. 39 (Š 41 x)

Obverse	
0; 1.0. še lugal	60 sila of barley according to the royal measurement
šà-gal anše-kunga$_2$	fodder for the mules
a-šà lá-maḫ-ta	from the field Lamaḫ
ki Ir$_{11}$-ta	from Ir
Lú-^{d}Nin-šubur	Lu-Ninšubur
šu-ba-ti	received
Reverse	
iti ezem-^{d}Šul-gi	month 8
mu-ús-sa mu-ús-sa-bi	Š 41
Seal	
Lú-^{d}Nin-[šubur kuš$_7$?]	Lu-Nin[šubur the equerry?]
ir$_{11}$-^{d}Šara$_2$	servant of Šara

no. 40 (Š 43 i)

Obverse	
0; 1.0. še lugal	60 sila of barley according to the royal measurement
šà-gal anše-kunga$_2$	fodder for the mules
é-šu-tum-ta	from (the storage facility) Ešutum
ki Lú-bala-sig$_5$-ta	from Lubalasig
Lú-^{d}Nin-šubur	Lu-Ninšubur
šu-ba-ti	received

Reverse	
iti še-kin-ku$_5$	month 1
mu-ús-sa Ša-aš-ru-um^{ki} ba-ḫul	Š 43
Seal	
Lú-^{d}Nin-šubur	Lu-Ninšubur
ir$_{11}$ ^{d}Šara$_2$	servant of Šara

no. 41 (Š 44) [copy]

Obverse	
1 še gur-lugal	1 gur of barley of the royal size
é-duru$_5$ Ur-gu-ta	from the encampment of Urgu(la)
šà-gal anše-kunga$_2$ zi-ku-um	fodder for the mules of the dispatch service
ki Ir$_{11}$-ta	from Ir
Lú-^{d}Nin-šubur	Lu-Ninšubur
Reverse	
šu-ba-ti	received
iti [ ]	month [ ]
mu Si-mu-ru-um^{ki}	Š 44
Lu-lu-bun a-rá 10 lá 1-kam ba-ḫul	
Seal	
Lú-^{d}Nin-šubur	Lu-Ninšubur
ir$_{11}$-^{d}Šara$_2$	servant of Šara

é-duru$_5$ denotes an encampment or small settlement outside the city gates. Urgu (or Urgula) would be the owner of this place, which contained storage facilities.

no. 42 (Š 45 v) [copy]

Obverse	
1; 1.3. še gur-lugal	1 gur and 90 sila of barley according to the royal measurement
šà-gal anše-zi-kum-ma	fodder for the donkeys of the dispatch service
ki Ir$_{11}$-ta	from Ir
Lú-^{d}Nin-šubur	Lu-Ninšubur
šu-ba-ti	received
Reverse	
iti ri	month 5
mu-ús-sa Si-mu-ru-um^{ki}	Š 45
Lu-lu-pu^{ki} a-rá 10 lá 1-kam ba-ḫul	
Seal	
Lú-^{d}Nin-šubur	Lu-Ninšubur
ir$_{11}$-^{d}Šara$_2$	servant of Šara

no. 43 (Š 46 x)

Obverse	
1; 2.3. še gur-lugal	1½ gur of barley according to the royal measurement
iti ^{d}Li$_{9}$-si$_{4}$-šè	for month 9
1; [ ] še gur	1 [ ] gur of barley
iti <ezem->^{d}Šul-gi	for month 10
šà-gal anše zi-ku-um-ma-ka	fodder for the donkeys of the dispatch service
Reverse	
ki Ir$_{11}$-ta	from Ir
Lú-^{d}Nin-šubur kuš$_{7}$ šu-ba-ti	Lu-Ninšubur the equerry received
a-šà me-en-kár-ta	from the field Menkar
mu Ki-maš^{ki} Ḫu-ur-ti^{ki} ba-ḫul	Š 46
Seal	
[Lú-^{d}Nin-šubur]	[Lu-Ninšubur
[ir$_{11}$-^{d}Šara$_{2}$]	servant of Šara]

no. 44 (Š 47 vii)

Obverse	
0; 2.0. še sumun lugal	120 sila of old barley according to the royal measurement
é-ús-sa é-im-sar-bi	(from) the house next to the tablet house
0; 1.3.5 sila$_{3}$ še lugal	95 sila of barley according to the royal measurement
igi-é-maḫ-šè-ta	from (the storage facility in the field) in front of the Emaḫ
šà-gal anše-kunga$_{2}$	fodder for the mules
ki Ir$_{11}$-ta	from Ir
Reverse	
Lú-^{d}Nin-šubur	Lu-Ninšubur
šu-ba-ti	received
iti min-èš mu-ús-	month 7
sa Ki-maš^{ki} ba-ḫul	Š 47
Seal	
Lú-^{d}Nin-šubur	Lu-Ninšubur
ir$_{11}$-^{d}Šara$_{2}$	servant of Šara

This document is as specific and detailed as such administrative tablets can be. We are informed that some of the fodder comes not from the current crop, but from the old, i.e., from the previous year's harvest. It was stored in the building next to the tablet house. This site was being emptied in the 7th month of its old barley, fed as fodder to the mules, presumably to be ready to store fresh barley to be harvested in the 12th month. The rest of the required fodder was obtained from a storage facility in a field in front of the Emaḫ.

no. 45 (Š 47 xi) [copy]

Obverse	
0; 3.4.5 sila$_3$ še [lugal]	225 sila of barley according to the [royal measurement]
šà-gal anše-[kunga$_2$]	fodder for the mu[les]
é-àr-ta	from the mill
ki Ir$_{11}$-ta	from Ir
Lú-^{d}Nin-[šubur]	Lu-Nin[šubur]
Reverse	
šu-ba-ti	received
iti pa$_4$-kùš-e	month 11
mu-ús-sa Ki-maš^{ki} ba-ḫul	Š 47
Seal	
Lú-^{d}Nin-šubur	Lu-Ninšubur
kuš$_7$	the equerry
ir$_{11}$ ^{d}Šara$_2$	servant of Šara

no. 46 (Š 48 vii)

Obverse	
1 še gur-lugal	1 gur of barley according to the royal measurement
šà-gal anše zi-ku-um-ma	fodder for the mules of the dispatch service
a-šà ^{giš}ma-nu-ta	from the field of willow
ki Ir$_{11}$-ta	from Ir
mu Igi-^{d}Šara$_2$-šè-šè	instead of (the seal of) Igi-Šaraše
kišib Lú-^{d}Nin-šubur	the seal of Lu-Ninšubur
Reverse	
ì-gál	it is.
iti min-èš	month 7
mu-ús-sa Ki-maš^{ki}	Š 46
ba-ḫul mu-ús-sa-a-bi	
Seal	
Lú-^{d}Nin-šubur	Lu-Ninšubur
ir$_{11}$-^{d}Šara$_2$	servant of Šara

The barley, despite the seal of Lu-Ninšubur, is for Igi-Šaraše.

no. 47 (ŠS 1 vi)

Obverse	
3 še gur	3 gur of barley
šà-gal anše	fodder for the donkeys
é-àr-gibil-ta	from the new mill
ki Lú-^{d}Šul-gi-ra-ta	from Lu-Šulgi
kišib Lú-^{d}Nin-šubur	(tablet has) the seal of Lu-Ninšubur
Reverse	
iti šu-numun	month 6
mu ^{d}Šu-^{d}EN.ZU lugal	ŠS 1
Seal	
Lú-^{d}Nin-šubur	Lu-Ninšubur
kuš 7	the equerry
ir$_{11}$ ^{d}Šara$_{2}$	servant of Šara

no. 48 (ŠS 2 i)

Obverse	
3 še gur-lugal	3 gur of barley according to the royal measurement
šà-gal anše	fodder for the donkeys
é-àr-gibil-ta	from the new mill
ki ka-gur$_{7}$-ta	from the granary manager
Reverse	
kišib Lú-^{d}Nin-šubur	seal of Lu-Ninšubur
iti še-kin-ku$_{5}$	month 1
mu-ús-sa ^{d}Šu-^{d}EN.ZU lugal	ŠS 2
Seal	
Lú-^{d}Nin-šubur	Lu-Ninšubur
kuš$_{7}$	the equerry
ir$_{11}$ ^{d}Šara$_{2}$	servant of Šara

The difference between texts nos. 47 and 48 is that text no. 48 indicates the granary manager (ka-gur$_{7}$), whereas text no. 47 uses the personal name Lu-Šulgi. Perhaps Lu-Šulgi is the unnamed granary manager in text no. 48.

Sealer's name: Lugal-á-zi-da dumu Lugal-kù-ga-ni

Lugalazida's seal is rarely attested. The scene is of a presentation to a god seated on a two-niched throne with a lion-standard behind him. From the text we know that Lugal-á-zi-da is a *gudu*-priest.

no. 49 (Š 45 i)

Obverse	
1 še gur lugal	1 gur of barley according to the royal measurement
šà-gal gu_4 niga	fodder for barley-fed oxen
ki Ir_{11}-ta	from Ir
Ki-an^{ki}-ta	from Kian
Lugal-á-zi-da $gudu_4$ šu-ba-ti	Lugalazida the purification-priest received
Reverse	
iti še-kin-ku_5	month 1
mu-ús-sa Si-mu-ru-um^{ki}	Š 45
Lu-lu-pu-um^{ki} a-rá 10 lá 1-kam ba-ḫul	
Seal	
Lugal-á-zi-da	Lugalazida
dumu Lugal-kù-ga-ni	son of Lugalkugani

Sealer's name: Lugal-é-maḫ-e dumu Lugal-kù-ga-ni

Lugal-é-maḫ-e owned two seals. One was used mainly from Š 31 to ŠS 6. The other is known from only a few impressions. Lugalemaḫe usually was involved with the assignment of workmen (guruš) for field duties. Therefore, sealing this tablet was outside the scope of his normal activities.

no. 50 (Š 48 x)

Obverse	
0; 3.0. še lugal	180 sila of barley according to the royal measurement
šà-gal anše-$kunga_2$	fodder for mules
ki-su_7 gu-la a-šà lá-maḫ-ta	from the large threshing floor of the field Lamaḫ
ki Ir_{11}-ta	from Ir
Reverse	
Lugal-é-maḫ-e	Lugalemaḫe
šu-ba-ti	received
iti ezem-^{d}Šul-gi	month 8
mu Ḫa-ar-$ši^{ki}$ Ḫu-ur_5-ti^{ki} ba-ḫul	Š 48

Seal

Lugal-é-maḫ-e	Lugalemaḫe
dub-sar	the scribe
dumu Lugal-kù-ga-ni	son of Lugalkugani

This seal owner, as well as Lugalazida in text no. 49, has a father named Lugalkugani. Perhaps they were brothers.

no. 51 (Š 47 viii) [copy]

Obverse

0; 3.0. še gur-lugal	180 sila of barley according to the royal measurement
šà-gal anše-kunga$_2$	fodder for mules
é-àr-ta	from the mill
ki Ir$_{11}$-ta	from Ir
Lugal-é-maḫ-e	Lugalemaḫe
šu-ba-ti	received

Reverse

iti é-iti-6	month 8
mu-ús-sa Ki-maš^{ki} ba-ḫul	Š 47
mu-ús-sa-a-bi	

Seal

Lugal-é-maḫ-e	Lugalemaḫe
dub-sar	the scribe
dumu Lugal-kù-ga-ni	son of Lugalkugani

Sealer's name: Lugal-é-maḫ-e dumu Lú-^{d}Nin-šubur kuš$_7$

Lugal-é-maḫ-e owned two seals, the second recording his new office of equerry (kuš$_7$). (Because it was added to an already carved seal, the sign kuš$_7$ was squeezed into the presentation scene.)

no. 52 (Š 44 ix)

Obverse

1 še gur-lugal	1 gur of barley according to the royal measurement
šà-gal anše-kunga$_2$	fodder for the mules
a-šà lá-maḫ-ta	from the field Lamaḫ
ki Ir$_{11}$-ta	from Ir
Lugal-é-maḫ-e	Lugalemaḫe
šu-ba-ti	received

Reverse	
iti ^{d}Li$_{9}$-si$_{4}$	month 9
mu Si-mu-ru-um^{ki} Lu-lu-pu^{ki}	Š 44
a-rá 10 lá 1-kam-aš ba-ḫul	
Seal	
Lugal-é-maḫ-e	Lugalemaḫe
dumu Lú-^{d}Nin-[šubur kuš$_{7}$]	son of Lu-Nin[šubur the equerry]

no. 53 (Š 44 ix)

Obverse	
1 še gur-lugal	1 gur of barley according to the royal measurement
šà-gal anše-kunga$_{2}$	fodder for the mules
a-šà lá-maḫ-ta	from the field Lamaḫ
ki Ir$_{11}$-ta	from Ir
Lugal-é-maḫ-e	Lugalemaḫe
šu-ba-ti	received
Reverse	
iti ^{d}Li$_{9}$-si$_{4}$	month 9
mu Si-mu-ru-um^{ki} Lu-lu-pu^{ki}	Š 44
a-rá 10 lá 1-kam-aš ba-ḫul	
Seal	
Lugal-é-maḫ-e	Lugalemaḫe
dumu Lú-^{d}Nin-šubur kuš$_{7}$	son of Lu-Ninšubur the equerry

no. 54 (Š 46 vii) [copy]

Obverse	
1 še gur-lugal	1 gur of barley according to the royal measurement
šà-gal anše-kunga$_{2}$	fodder for the mules
é-àr-ta	from the mill
ki Ir$_{11}$-ta	from Ir
Lugal-é-maḫ-e	Lugalemaḫe
Reverse	
šu-ba-ti	received
iti min-èš	month 7
mu ús-sa Ur-bí-lum^{ki} ba-ḫul	Š 46
Seal	
Lugal-é-maḫ-e	Lugalemaḫe
dumu Lú-^{d}Nin-šubur kuš$_{7}$	son of Lu-Ninšubur the equerry

Sealer's name: Lugal-ḫé-gál dumu Ur-ni$_9$-gar

Lugalḫegal owned two seals: (1) presentation to a goddess seated on single-niched throne, and (2) a simple presentation scene.

no. 55 (Š 44 iv)

Obverse	
8; 2.3. še gur-lugal	8½ gur of barley according to the royal measurement
šà-gal anše-kunga$_2$	fodder for the mules
Ki-an^{ki}-ta	from Kian
ki Ir$_{11}$-ta	from Ir
Lugal-ḫé-gál	Lugalḫegal
šu-ba-ti	received
Reverse	
iti nesag	month 4
mu Lu-lu-pu^{ki} Si-mu-ru-um^{ki}	Š 44
a-rá 10 lá 1-kam-aš ba-ḫul	
Seal	
Lugal-ḫé-gál	Lugalḫegal
mu$_6$-šùb-^{d}Šara$_2$	shepherd of Šara
dumu Ur-ni$_9$-gar	son of Urnigar

no. 56 [copy]

Obverse	
8; 1.3. še gur	8;1.3. gur of barley
šà-gal anše	fodder for the donkeys
é-àr-ta	from the mill
ki Ir$_{11}$-ta	from Ir
Lugal-ḫé-gál	Lugalḫegal
šu-ba-ti	received
Reverse	
[iti]	[month
[mu]	[year
Seal	
illegible	

Sealer's name: Puzur$_4$-ì-lí

Puzur-ili's seal is attested from Š 39 to Š 42, always regarding the same type of activity.

no. 57 (Š 41 x)

Obverse	
0; 3.0. še lugal	180 sila of barley according to the royal measurement
šà-gal anše	fodder for the donkeys
a-šà lá-maḫ-ta	from the field Lamaḫ
ki Ir$_{11}$-ta	from Ir
Puzur$_4$-ì-lí	Puzur-ili
Reverse	
šu-ba-ti	received
iti ezem-^{d}Šul-gi	month 8
mu-ús-sa é Puzur$_4$	Š 41
mu-ús-sa-a-bi	
Seal	
Ur-^{d}Li$_9$-si$_4$	Ur-Lisi
ensi$_2$ Umma^{ki}	governor of Umma
Puzur$_4$-ì-lí	Puzur-ili
gir$_4$-díb	the official recorder
ir$_{11}$-zu	(is) your servant

Sealer's name: Šu-ú dumu Ga-ni

no. 58 (Š 46 vii)

Obverse	
0; 4.0. še lugal	240 sila of barley according to the royal measurement
šà-gal gu$_4$ niga	fodder for barley-fed oxen
é-àr-ta	from the mill
ki Ir$_{11}$-ta	from Ir
Šu-ú<<ú>> šu-ba-ti	Šuu received
Reverse	
iti min-èš	month 7
mu-ús-sa Ur-bí-lum^{ki} ba-ḫul	Š 46
Seal	
Šu-ú	Šuu
dumu Ga-ni	son of Gani

There only other attestation of this seal is MVN 14 121, which also concerns the fattening of oxen.

no. 59 (Š 46 x) [copy]

Obverse

0; 3.0. še lugal	240 sila of barley according to the royal measurement
šà-gal gu$_4$-niga	fodder for barley-fed oxen
é-àr-ta	from the mill
ki Ir$_{11}$-ta	from Ir
Šu-ú šu-ba-ti	Šuu received

Reverse

iti ezem ^{d}Šul-gi	month 8
mu Ki-maš^{ki} ba-ḫul	Š 46

Seal illegible

Sealer's name: Ú-li

no. 60 (Š 44 vii)

Obverse

1 še gur-lugal	1 gur of barley according to the royal measurement
šà-gal anše-kunga$_2$	fodder for the mules
é-duru$_5$ Ur-gu-ta	from the encampment of Urgu(la)
ki Ir$_{11}$-ta	from Ir
Ú-li kir$_4$-díb	Uli the official recorder
šu-ba-ti	received

Reverse

iti min-èš	month 7
mu Lu-lu-bum^{ki} Si-mu-ru-um^{ki}	Š 44
a-rá 10 lá-1-kam-aš ba-ḫul	

Seal

Ú-li gir$_4$-díb	Uli the official recorder
ir$_{11}$ ^{d}Nin-líl-[lá]	servant of Ninlil

Sealer's name: Ur-dingir-ra dumu A-zi-da

Ur-dingir-ra was active from Š 37 to ŠS 8. Many of the tablets of the fodder tablets in the Royal Ontario Museum collection were sealed by him. He used four seals, two of which had the same inscription.

seal 1 Ur-dingir-ra kuš$_7$
dumu A-zi

seal 2 Ur-dingir-ra kuš$_7$
dumu A-zi-da

seal 3 Ur-dingir-ra
kuš$_7$ ensi$_2$-ka
dumu [A-zi-da]

seal 4 Ur-dingir-ra
kuš$_7$ ensi$_2$-ka
dumu A-zi-da

no. 61 (Š 40 i)

Obverse

1; 2.3. še gur-lugal	1½ gur of barley, gur according to the royal measurement
šà-gal anše-kunga$_2$	fodder for the mules
šu-zu-gá-ra-ta	from (the threshing floor) Šuzugara
ki Ir$_{11}$-ta	from Ir
Ur-dingir-ra	Urdingirra
šu-ba-ti	received

Reverse

iti še-kin-ku$_5$	month 1
mu-ús-sa Puzur$_4$-	Š 40
Da-gan ba-dù	

Seal

Ur-dingir-ra kuš$_7$	Urdingirra the equerry
dumu A-zi-da	son of Azida

no. 62 (Š 40 viii)

Obverse

0; 2.0. še lugal	120 sila of barley according to the royal measurement
šà-gal anše-kunga$_2$	fodder for the mules
a-šà lá-maḫ-ta	from the field Lamaḫ
ki Ir$_{11}$-ta	from Ir
Ur-dingir-ra kuš$_7$	Urdingirra the equerry
šu-ba-ti	received

Reverse

iti é-iti-6	month 8
mu-ús-sa Puzur$_4$-^{d}Da-gan ba-dù	Š 40

Seal

Ur-dingir-ra kuš$_7$	Urdingirra the equerry
dumu A-zi-da	son of Azida

no. 63 (Š 46 vii) [copy]

Obverse	
4; 2.3. še gur-lugal	4½ gur of barley according to the royal measurement
šà-gal anše-kunga$_2$ Ki-an^{ki}	fodder for the mules of Kian
iti še-kar-ra-gál-la-ta	from month 3
iti min-èš-šè	to month 7
é-àr-ta	from the mill
Reverse	
ki Ir$_{11}$-ta	from Ir
Ur-dingir-ra-ke$_4$	Urdingirra
šu-ba-ti	received
mu-ús-sa Ur-bí-lum^{ki} ba-ḫul	Š 46
Seal	
Ur-dingir-ra	Urdingirra
kuš$_7$ ensi$_2$-ka	the equerry of the governor
dumu A-zi-da	son of Azida

no. 64 (Š 34 x) [copy]

Obverse	
2 še gur-lugal	2 gur of barley according to the royal measurement
šà-gal anše-kunga$_2$	fodder for the mules
ki Ir$_{11}$-ta	from Ir$_{11}$
Ur-dingir-ra kuš$_7$	Urdingirra the equerry
šu-ba-ti	received
Reverse	
iti ezem-^{d}Šul-gi	month 8
mu An-ša-an^{ki} ba-ḫul	Š 34
Seal	
Ur-dingir-ra	Urdingirra
kuš$_7$ ensi$_2$-ka	the equerry of the governor
dumu A-zi-da	son of Azida

no. 65 (Š 35)

Obverse	
[ ] še gur-lugal	[ ] gur of barley according to the royal measurement
šà-gal anše ensi$_2$	fodder for the donkeys of the governor
0; 4.3. šà-gal anše-kunga$_2$	270 sila of fodder for the mules
é-àr-ta	from the mill
ki Ir$_{11}$-ta	from Ir$_{11}$
Reverse	
Ur-dingir-ra šu-ba-ti	Urdingirra received
mu-ús-sa [An-ša-an^{ki} ba-ḫul]	Š 35
Seal	
Ur-dingir-ra	Urdingirra
kuš$_7$ ensi$_2$-ka	the equerry of the governor
dumu A-zi-<da>	son of Azida

no. 66 (Š 35 v)

Obverse	
1; 2.3. še gur-lugal	1½ gur of barley according to the royal measurement
[šà-gal anše]	[fodder for the donkeys]
[é]-àr-[ta]	[from the m]ill
[ki] Ir$_{11}$-[ta]	[from] Ir
[Ur]-dingir-[ra]	[Ur]-dingir[ra]
Reverse	
šu-ba-ti	received
iti ri mu-ús-sa An-	month 5
ša-an^{ki} ba-ḫul	Š 35
Seal	
Ur-dingir-ra	Urdingirra
kuš$_7$ ensi$_2$-ka	the equerry of the governor
dumu A-zi	son of Azida

no. 67 (Š35 vi)

Obverse	
2 še gur-lugal	2 gur of barley according to the royal measurement
šà-gal anše-kunga$_2$	fodder for the mules
ki Ir$_{11}$-ta	from Ir
Ur-dingir-ra	Urdingirra
šu-ba-ti	received

iti šu-numun	month 6
Reverse	
mu-ús-sa An-ša-an^{ki} ba-ḫul	Š 35
Seal	
Ur-dingir-ra	Urdingirra
kuš$_7$ ensi$_2$-ka	equerry of the governor
dumu A-zi<-da>	son of Azida

no. 68 (Š 39 vi)

Obverse	
0; 2.0. še lugal	120 sila of barley according to the royal measurement
šà-gal anše-kunga$_2$	fodder for the mules
šu-zu-gá-ra-ta	from (the threshing floor) Šuzugarra
ki Ir$_{11}$-ta	from Ir
Ur-dingir-ra	Urdingirra
šu-ba-ti	received
Reverse	
iti šu-numun	month 6
mu Puzur$_4$-Da-gan ba-dù	Š 39
Seal	
Ur-dingir-ra kuš$_7$	Urdingirra the equerry
dumu A-zi-da	son of Azida

no. 69 (Š 39 vii)

Obverse	
0; 1.0. še lugal	60 sila of barley according to the royal measurement
šà-gal anše-kunga$_2$	fodder for the mules
šu-zu-gá-ra-ta	from (the threshing floor) Šuzugarra
ki Ir$_{11}$-ta	from Ir
Ur-dingir-ra	Urdingirra
Reverse	
šu-ba-ti	received
iti min-èš	month 7
mu é Puzur$_4$-Da-gan ba-dù	Š 39
Seal	
Ur-dingir-ra kuš$_7$	Urdingirra the equerry
dumu A-zi-da	son of Azida

no. 70 (Š 39 i)

Obverse	
1; 2.3. še gur-lugal	1½ gur of barley according to the royal measurement
šà-gal anše ensi$_2$	fodder for the donkeys of the governor
0; 4.3. še šà-gal anše Ki-an^{ki}	270 sila of barley, fodder for the donkeys of Kian
é-šu-tum-ta	from the (storage facility) Ešutum
Reverse	
ki Ir$_{11}$-ta	from Ir
Ur-dingir-ra šu-ba-ti	Urdingirra received
iti še-kin-ku$_5$	month 1
mu-ús-sa é-a	Š 39
mu-ús-sa-ba mu-ús-sa-bi	
Seal	
Ur-dingir-ra kuš$_7$	Urdingirra the equerry
dumu A-zi-da	son of Azida

no. 71 (Š 46 ix) [copy]

Obverse	
0; 4.3. še lugal	270 sila of barley according to the royal measurement
šà-gal anše-kunga$_2$	fodder for the mules
é-àr-ta	from the mill
ki Ir$_{11}$-ta	from Ir
Ur-dingir-ra	Urdingirra
šu-ba-ti	received
Reverse	
iti ^{d}Li$_9$-si$_4$	month 9
mu Ki-maš^{ki} ba-ḫul	Š 46
Seal	
Ur-dingir-ra	Urdingirra
kuš$_7$ ensi$_2$-ka	the equerry of the governor
dumu A-zi-da	son of Azida

no. 72 (Š 46 xii)

Obverse	
0; 4.3. še lugal	270 sila of barley according to the royal measurement
šà-gal anše-kunga$_2$	fodder for the mules
gur$_7$ igi-é-duru$_5$	from the silo in front of the encampment

a-šà lá-maḫ-ta	from the field Lamaḫ
ki Ir$_{11}$-ta	from Ir
Reverse	
Ur-dingir-ra kuš$_7$	Urdingirra the equerry
šu-ba-ti	received
iti ^{d}Dumu-zi	month 12
mu Ki-maš^{ki} ba-ḫul	Š 46
Seal	
Ur-dingir-ra	Urdingirra
kuš$_7$ ensi$_2$-ka	the equerry of the governor
dumu A-zi-da	son of Azida

no. 73 (Š 48 viii)

Obverse	
1 še gur lugal	1 gur of barley according to the royal measurement
šà-gal anše-kunga$_2$	fodder for the mules
é-àr-ta	from the mill
ki Ir$_{11}$-ta	from Ir
Ur-dingir-ra	Urdingirra
Reverse	
šu-ba-ti	received
iti é-iti-6	month 8
mu-ús-sa Ki-maš^{ki}	Š 48
mu-ús-sa-a-bi	
Seal	
Ur-dingir-ra	Urdingirra
kuš$_7$ ensi$_2$-ka	the equerry of the governor
dumu A-zi-da	son of Azida

no. 74 (xii)

Obverse	
2; 2.3. še gur	2½ gur of barley
šà-gal anše-kunga$_2$	fodder for the mules
ki Ir$_{11}$-ta	from Ir
Ur-dingir-ra kuš$_7$	Urdingirra the equerry
šu-ba-ti	has received
iti ^{d}Dumu-zi	month 12
Reverse	
[mu]	[year]

Seal

[Ur-dingir-ra	[Urdingirra
kuš$_7$ ensi$_2$-ka	the equerry of the governor
dumu A-zi-da]	son of Azida]

no. 75 (Š 46 x) [copy]

Obverse

0; 4.3. še lugal	270 sila of barley according to the royal measurement
šà-gal anše-kunga$_2$	fodder for the mules
é-àr-ta	from the mill
ki Ir$_{11}$-ta	from Ir
Ur-dingir-ra	Urdingirra

Reverse

šu-ba-ti	received
iti ezem-^{d}Šul-gi	month 10
mu Ki-maš^{ki} ba-ḫul	Š 46

Seal

Ur-dingir-ra	Urdingirra
kuš$_7$-ensi$_2$-ka	the equerry of the governor
dumu A-zi-da	son of Azida

no. 76 (Š 48 xi)

Obverse

1; 1.0. še gur lugal	360 sila of barley according to the royal measurement
šà-gal amar-amar-ra anše-kunga$_2$ ensi$_2$	fodder for the young(?) mules of the governor
ki-su$_7$ gu-la a-šà lá-maḫ-ta	from the great threshing floor of the field Lamaḫ
ki Ir$_{11}$-ta	from Ir

Reverse

Ur-dingir-ra kuš$_7$ šu-ba-ti	Urdingirra the equerry received
iti pa$_4$-kùš-e	month 11
mu Ḫa-ar-ši^{ki}	Š 48
Ki-maš^{ki} ba-ḫul	

Seal

Ur-dingir-ra	Urdingirra
kuš$_7$ ensi$_2$-ka	the equerry of the governor
dumu A-zi-da	son of Azida

It is unclear whether amar-amar-ra anše-kunga$_2$ indicates two distinct groups of animals, i.e., calves and mules, or whether the expression amar-amar-ra here denotes baby or young mules.

Sealer's name: Ur-^{d}En-líl-lá dumu Ḫa-la

Only one other tablet (YBC 12921) is known to be sealed by Ur-Enlilla. It dates to AS 3 and concerns regular deliveries (sá-du$_{11}$) of barley from Ir. Ur-Enlilla seems to have been active for only a short time in this capacity.

no. 77 (AS 2)

Obverse

2 še gur-lugal	2 gur of barley according to the royal measurement
šà-gal gu$_4$ niga	fodder for barley-fed oxen
é-àr-ta	from the mill
ki Ir$_{11}$-ta	from Ir
Ur-^{d}En-líl-lá	Ur-Enlilla

Reverse

šu-ba-ti	received
iti ^{d}Dumu-zi	month 12
mu Ur-bí-ì-lum^{ki} ba-ḫul	AS 2

Seal

Ur-^{d}En-líl-lá	Ur-Enlilla
dumu [Ḫa-la muḫaldim]	son of Ḫala the cook

Sealer's name: Ur-^{giš}gigir dumu Bar-ra-an

Only one seal belonging to Urgigir is known, although he was active from Š 33 to ŠS 4. He was a scribe (dub-sar) usually involved with the assignment of workmen (guruš). This tablet seems to represent an exception to his normal assignment.

no. 78 (Š 44 diri)

Obverse

2 še gur-lugal	2 gur of barley according to the royal measurement
šà-gal gu$_4$ niga	fodder for barley-fed oxen
é-àr-ta	from the mill
ki Ir$_{11}$-ta	from Ir
Ur-^{giš}gigir	Urgigir

Reverse

šu-ba-ti	received

iti diri	intercalary month
mu Si-mu-ru-um^{ki}	Š 44
Lu-lu-pu^{ki} a-rá	
10 lá 1-kam-aš ba-ḫul	
Seal	
Ur-^{giš}gigir	Urgigir
dub-sar	the scribe
dumu [Bar-ra-an]	son of [Barran]

Sealer's name: Ur-^{ú}numun$_2$

Urnumun owned three seals. One has a presentation scene to a seated divinity; the tablet impressions of the other two seals are not strong enough to discern. Urnumun, the servant of the goddess Ninurra (the spouse of Šara), deals with fodder for mules involved in cultic activities surrounding Šara.

no. 79 (Š 38)

Obverse	
1; 1.0. še gur lugal	1 1/5 gur of barley according to the royal measurement
šà-gal anše-kunga$_2$	fodder for mules
ki Lú-kiri$_3$-zal-ta	from Lukirizal
Ur-^{ú}numun$_2$	Urnumun
Reverse	
šu-ba-ti	received
šà bala	part of the bala-obligation
mu-ús-sa bàd ba-dù	Š 38
Seal	
Ur-^{ú}numun$_2$	Urnumun
ir$_{11}$ ^{d}Nin-ur$_4$-ra	servant of Ninurra

no. 80 (Š 38 x)

Obverse	
0; 1.2. še lugal	80 sila of barley according to the royal measurement
šà-gal anše	fodder for the donkeys
saḫar-ú-ú-ta	from (the field) Saḫaruu
ki Ir$_{11}$-ta	from Ir
Ur-^{ú}numun$_2$	Urnumun
<šu-ba-ti>	<received>

Reverse	
iti ezem-^{d}Šul-gi	month 8
mu-ús-sa bàd ba-dù	Š 38
Seal illegible	

no. 81 (Š 47 vii)

Obverse	
[0; 0].3. še lugal	[ ]+30 sila of barley according to the royal measurement
šà-gal anše-[kunga$_2$]	fodder for the mu[les]
é-àr-àr-ta	from the mill
ki Ir$_{11}$-ta	from Ir
Ur-^{ú}numun$_2$	Urnumun
Reverse	
<šu-ba-ti>	<received>
iti min-èš	month 7
mu-ús-sa Ki-maš^{ki} ba-ḫul	Š 47
Seal	
Ur-^{ú}numun$_2$	Urnumun
ir$_{11}$ ^{d}Nin-ur$_4$-ra	servant of Ninurra

no. 82 (ŠS 2 xi) [copy]

Obverse	
0; 3.4.5 sila$_3$ še	225 sila of barley
gìr Ur-^{ú}numun$_2$	responsible: Urnumun
1; 1.0. še gur	360 sila of barley
gìr Ur-^{d}Iškur	responsible: Ur-Iškur
šà-gal anše	fodder for the donkeys
kar-ta	from the quay
Reverse	
ki ka-gur$_7$-ta	from the granary manager
kišib Ur-^{ú}numun$_2$	(tablet has) the seal of Urnumun
iti pa$_4$-kùš-e	month 11
mu má ^{d}En-ki ba-ab-du$_8$	ŠS 2
Seal	
Ur-^{ú}numun$_2$	Urnumun
ir$_{11}$ ^{d}Nin-ur$_4$-ra	servant of Ninurra

This tablet mentions two *gir*-officials for the transfer. Barley was stocked on the quay and in two separate instances grain was taken from this pile, once under the responsibility of Urnumun and once under the responsibility of Ur-Iškur, both times for fodder for donkeys.

no. 83 (Š 44)

Obverse	
4 še gur-lugal	4 gur of barley according to the royal measurement
šà-gal gu_4 niga	fodder for barley-fed oxen
Ur-e_{11}-e	Uree
Reverse	
[šu-ba-ti]	[received]
mu Si-mu-ru-um^{ki}	Š 44
Lu-lu-pu-um a-rá 10 lá-1-kam-aš	
ba-ḫul	
Seal	
[^{d}Šul-gi]	[Šulgi]
nita kalag-ga	mighty man
lugal $Uri_5{}^{ki}$-ma	king of Ur
lugal an-ub-da $limmu_2$-ba	king of the four quarters of the universe
[ ]	[ ]
[ ]	[ ]
[ir_{11}-zu]	[(is) your servant.]

Although Uree would seem to be the sealer of text no. 83, no seal of this scribe dedicated to Šulgi has been found. Maybe the governor of Umma himself sealed the tablet.

no. 84 (Š 41 ix)

Obverse	
2 še gur lugal	2 gur of barley according to the royal measurement
šà-gal anše-$kunga_2$	fodder for the mules
ki-an^{ki}-ta	of Kian
ki Ir_{11}-ta	from Ir
Ur-dingir-ra $kuš_7$	Urdingirra the equerry
Reverse	
šu-ba-ti	received
iti $^{d}Li_9$-si_4	month 9
mu-ús-sa mu-ús-sa-a-bi	Š 41
Seal	
Ur-dingir-ra $kuš_7$	Urdingirra the equerry
dumu A-zi-da	son of Azida

no. 85 (Š 44 v)

Obverse

0;4.3. še lugal	270 sila of barley according to the royal measurement
šà-<gal> anše-kunga$_2$-šè	fodder for mules
ki Ir$_{11}$-ta	from Ir
kišib Ur-dingir-ra kuš$_7$	seal of Urdingirra the equerry

Reverse

šà ki-an^{ki}	in Kian
iti ri	month 5
mu lu-lu-bun^{ki}-na	Š 44
si-mu-ru-um^{ki} a-rá 9-kam ba-ḫul	

Seal

Ur-dingir-ra kuš$_7$	Urdingirra the equerry
dumu A-zi-da	son of Azida

no. 86 (Š 37)

Obverse

[ ] še gur lugal	[ ] gur of barley according to the royal measurement
[0;2.0] zíz	120 sila of emmer
še-numun mur-gu$_4$	barley for seeding and fodder for the oxen
[+]4;2.3. še gur	[ ] 4½ gur of barley
á-lú-ḫun-gá	wages for the hired men
šà-bi-ta	from it
38;.3.0.5 sila$_3$ ⅔ še gur	38 gur and 185⅔ sila of barley
0;2.0. zíz	120 sila of emmer
še-numun mur-gu$_4$	barley for seeding and fodder for the oxen

Reverse

1.20 še gur	80 gur of barley
á lú-ḫun-gá	wages for the hired men
šu-nigín 1.58;3.0.5⅔ sila$_3$	total 118 gur and 185⅔ sila of barley
zi-ga-àm	disbursement
diri 1;3.3.5⅔ sila$_3$ gur	difference 1 gur and 215⅔ sila
nì-ka$_9$-ak	account of
A-gu-gu	Agugu
a-dé-a	irrigation
mu bàd ba-dù	Š 37

no. 87 [copy]

This tablet, not being dated, could be just a memorandum to help the scribe compile a more comprehensive tablet at the end of the day or month.

Obverse

43 anše-kunga$_2$ 0; 1.3.-ta	43 mules, for each 90 sila (of barley)
2 anše-zi-zi 0; 2.3.	2 horses, for each ½ gur (of barley)
6 guruš 0; 1.0. zì-ta	6 workmen, for each 60 sila (of flour)
ugula Nir-ì-da-gál	overseer Niridagal
ki Ur-^{d}Šara$_2$-ta	from Ur-Šara
(*tablet uninscribed on the reverse*)	

no. 88 (Š 36) [copy]

Obverse

4 še gur-lugal	4 gur of barley according to the royal measurement
še kar-ra	from the barley of the quay
a-šà ^{d}Šara$_2$-ta	from the field of Šara;
mu-túm	delivery;
ki Lugal-é-maḫ-e-ta	from Lugalemaḫe
Ir$_{11}$ šu-ba-ti	Ir received

Reverse

mu ^{d}Nanna Kar-zi-da a-<rá> 2-kam	Š 36
é-a-na ba-an-ku$_4$	

This tablet has been included in this archive on the basis of the individuals involved. But the content is obviously of a different nature. Barley on the quay was left unutilized and, therefore, returned (mu-túm) to the account. Lugalemaḫe brings this remainder of barley to Ir—the official most often in charge of the disbursement of barley for fodder for cattle.

no. 89 (Š 36) [copy]

Obverse

30 še gur-lugal	30 gur of barley according to the royal measurement
še gub-ba a-šà sipad-e-ne	barley on hand in the field of the shepherds
sag-nì-ga-ra-kam	this is the capital
šà-bi-ta	from this (capital)
0; 3.1.5 <sila$_3$> še <<gur-lugal>>	195 sila of barley
še ì-šáḫ	barley (to buy) lard
kišib Lugal-ezem šabra	(tablet has) the seal of Lugalezem the steward
(*erased line*)	

7; 3.1.5 $sila_3$ še gur	7 gur and 195 sila of barley
še ši-ri-iq-tum-ma	barley (to buy) gifts
Reverse	
kišib Lugal-ezem	(tablet has) the seal of Lugalezem
12 <gur> A-kal-la Unug[ki]	12 gur for Akalla in Uruk
7; 2.3. sanga dub-sar	7½ gur for the head official over the temple scribes
2 gur šà-gal gu_4 niga	2 gur as fodder for barley-fed oxen
kišib Lugal-é-maḫ-e šeš Lugal-[giš]$kiri_6$	(tablet has) the seal of Lugalemaḫe brother of Lugalkiri
šu-nigín 30 lá 0;1. še gur	total 30 gur minus 60 sila of barley
še zi-ga-àm	disbursement of barley
ugula(?) Lugal-é-maḫ-e	overseer(?) Lugalemaḫe
mu [d]Nanna kar-zi-da a-rá 2-kam é-<a>-na ba-ku_4	Š 36

This tablet is a balanced account of barley produced in the field of the shepherds. The barley was used for multiple purposes: to purchase lard and gifts, for Akalla in Uruk, for the administrator of the scribes, and for fattening oxen. This balanced account is the final document, summarizing and recapitulating individual tablets written for each separate transaction, each under a separate seal.

There are a few tablets that concern barley rations or fodder (šà-gal) for persons, as well as equids, and for that reason have been included here.

no. 90 (Š 46 ix) envelope

The central administration was responsible for providing barley and wool to workgangs performing labor duty as part of the bala-obligation. This tablet is from Lagash.

Obverse	
9; 3.0. še gur-lugal	9; 3 gur of barley according to the royal measurement
šà-gal $erin_2$ bala tuš-a	rations for the workgangs as part of the *bala*
še mar-tu	barley for Amorites
ì-dub gir_4-u-ta	from the silo (in the field) Giru
kišib [d]Nanna-kam	(tablet has) the seal of Nannakam
Reverse	
iti mu-šu-du_7	month 9
nu-$banda_3$ Ur-[d]Ig-alim	lieutenant Ur-Igalim
é Nam-ḫa-ni	temple of Namḫani
mu Ki-maš[ki] ba-ḫul	Š 46

Seal

^{d}Nanna-kam	Nannakam
dumu Lú-du$_{10}$-ga	son of Luduga

no. 91 (ŠS 3 viii) [copy]

Obverse	
44 sila$_{3}$ dabin	44 sila of barley flour
šà-gal ḫé-dab$_{5}$-šè	rations for forced(?) workers
ki Lú-^{d}Nanna-šè	for Lu-Nanna
kišib Lú-^{d}Nám-an-ka	(tablet has) the seal of Lu-Namanka
Reverse	
iti é-iti-6	month 8
mu Si-ma-núm^{ki} ba-ḫul	ŠS 3
Seal	
Lú-^{d}Nám-an-ka	Lu-Namanka
dub-sar	the scribe
dumu Lú-^{d}Sara$_{2}$	son of Lu-Šara
sa$_{12}$-du$_{5}$-ka	the surveyor

During his last two years, the scribe Lu-Namanka controlled foodstuffs destined for workmen (guruš).

The ḫé-dab$_{5}$ form a category of workers probably lower than the most common classification of workmen, guruš. The term may derive from dab$_{5}$ "to be taken" and, thus, could indicate prisoners of war—the ^{giš}tukul-dab$_{5}$ are well attested. The same signs are sometimes read gan-tuš. If this reading is valid, the meaning might derive from tuš "to be settled," thus someone given an allotment to tend.

no. 92 (Š 48 ii) [copy]

Obverse	
1.52 še gur-lugal	112 gur of barley according to the royal measurement
šà-gal udu niga	fodder for barley-fed sheep
ì-dub a-šà da-ṣé	from the silo of the field Daṣe
uš é-duru$_{5}$ ^{d}Nanna	next to the encampment of Nanna
Reverse	
ki Ba-zi-ta	from Bazi
A-ḫu-a šu-ba-ti	Aḫua received
iti gu$_{4}$-rá-IZI-mú-<mú>	month 2
mu-ús-sa ki! ba-ḫul	Š 48

The area designated as the encampment of Nanna should be some small place outside the main cities of the Lagash/Girsu district.

Regular Deliveries (nos. 93 – 138)

Each institution of the Ur III empire had needs that required the establishment of a system to regularly provide certain goods. The term used for such deliveries was sá-du$_{11}$. These deliveries could be daily, weekly, monthly, or yearly deliveries of various products in fixed quantities.

Regular Deliveries for the King:

In the tablets of Drehem the reigning king was referred to as "lugal," while the dead kings of the dynasty were noted by their names. Such was not the practice in Umma. Therefore, to know whether the monarch mentioned in the text was alive or dead, there must be either a year date or information within the contents that indicates the purpose (such as the incantation-priests in text no. 90).

no. 93 (ii)

According to this document, two incantation-priests and Kirizal (also an incantation-priest?) received barley and emmer from the field of Šara to be delivered as a regular delivery for the cult of the deceased king, Šulgi. Perhaps this document is scribal memorandum to be later used for the redaction of his final tablet recording the expenditures of the day or the week.

Obverse

0; 4.0.5 sila$_3$ še	245 sila of barley
1 gur zíz	1 gur of emmer
Ur-^{giš}gigir išib	(for) Urgigir the incantation-priest
0; 4.0.5 sila$_3$ še	245 sila of barley
1 gur zíz	1 gur of emmer
Kirì-zal	(for) Kirizal
iti nesag-ta	from month 4
1; 1.3. še gur	3 gur and 90 sila of barley
Al-la išib	(for) Alla the incantation-priest

Reverse

iti sig$_4$-^{giš}ì-šub-ba-gá-ra	month 2
sá-du$_{11}$ ^{d}Šul-gi	regular delivery for the divine Šulgi
a-šà ^{d}Šara$_2$-ta	from the field of Šara

no. 94 (ŠS 6 i–iv)

Obverse

20+5?; 1.0. še gur	25 1/5 gur of barley

iti 2-kam	during 2 months
1; 3.4.7½ sila$_3$ gur	1 gur and 227½ sila
nì-[ ]-ba	[ ]
sá-du$_{11}$ ^{d}Šul-gi	regular deliveries for the divine Šulgi
0; 2.0.[ ] ^{d}Nin-líl-lá	120 sila for [ ] of the goddess Ninlil
iti še-kin-ku$_5$-ta iti nesag-šè	from month 1 to month 4
Reverse	
ki ka-gur$_7$-ta	from the granary manager
kišib-aš-a A-lu$_5$-lu$_5$	(consigned on) one sealed tablet of Alulu
mu-ús-sa ^{d}Šu-^{d}EN.ZU lugal-e	ŠS 6
bàd mar-tu mu-dù	
Seal	
A-lu$_5$-lu$_5$	Alulu
lú šim-^{d}Šara$_2$	the brewer of Šara
dumu Lugal-nì-lagar-e	son of Lugalnilagare

Since the tablet was sealed by a brewer, the consignment of barley was presumably for the production of beer. The partially preserved line 4 should record either the name of a person or circumstances surrounding this delivery for the cult of Šulgi.

The scribe writes kišib-aš-a, which should be understood as "(consigned) on one sealed tablet," thus the grain received by Alulu is recapitulated on one tablet, under one account. This document, then, is probably a summary of other documents, and it, in turn, was probably used to write larger summary ledgers.

no. 95 (Š 39 ii–i) [copy]

Like text no. 91, this tablet was sealed by a brewer, and thus the consignment of barley was presumably for the production of beer. Since the tablet is dated to the reign of Šulgi, it is obviously not for any cult of the deceased.

Obverse	
25; 3.0. še gur-lugal	25³⁄₅ gur of barley according to the royal measurement
sá-du$_{11}$ ^{d}Šul-gi	regular delivery for Šulgi
ki Ir$_{11}$-ta	from Ir
A-lu$_5$-lu$_5$	Alulu
šu-ba-ti	received
Reverse	
iti sig$_4$-^{giš}ù-šub-ba gál-la-ta	from month 2
iti še-kin-ku$_5$-šè	to month 1
mu é Puzur$_4$-^{d}Da-gan ba-dù	Š 39
Seal	
[A-lu$_5$-lu$_5$	[Alulu

lú šim-^{d}Šara$_{2}$	the brewer of Šara
dumu Lugal-nì-lagar-e]	son of Lugalnilagare]

no. 96 (AS 6 v)

Obverse	
1; 0.2. zíz gur	1 gur and 20 sila of emmer
sá-du$_{11}$ ^{d}Šul-gi	regular delivery for the divine Šulgi
é šu-tum-ta	from the (storage facility) Ešutum
ki Ir$_{11}$-ta	from Ir
Reverse	
kišib Ur-lugal	received by Urlugal
iti ri mu ^{d}Amar-^{d}EN.ZU lugal-e	month 5
Ša-aš-rum mu-ḫul	AS 6
Seal	
Šeš-[a-ni]	Šeš[ani]
gudu$_{4}$-[^{d}Šul-gi]	the purification-priest [of Šulgi]
dumu Inim-[kù]	son of Inim[ku]

This delivery of flour was for the cult of the dead Šulgi, because of the date of the tablet. The text of the tablet indicates the seal of Urlugal, while in fact Šeš[ani] the gudu$_{4}$-priest sealed it, clear indication that the delivery is for cultic purposes. An identical seal can be found on YBC 748, again grain as regular delivery for the divine Šulgi provided by Ir. YBC 748 also includes kišib Ur-lugal.

no. 97 (AS 8 vii)

Obverse	
1 še gur-lugal	1 gur of barley according to the royal measurement
sá-du$_{11}$ ^{d}Amar-^{d}EN.ZU	regular delivery for Amar-Sîn
é-àr-ta	from the mill
ki Lú-^{d}Šul-gi-ra-ta	from Lu-Šulgi
Reverse	
kišib Ur-ni$_{9}$-gar	(tablet with) the seal of Urnigar
iti min-èš	month 7
mu en Eridu^{ki} ba-ḫun	AS 8
	Seal
Ur-ni$_{9}$-gar	Urnigar
dumu Lugal-^{giš}gigir	son of Lugalgigir
en-dub-lá	archivist

Urnigar received the barley from Lu-Šulgi. The normal expression is šu-ba-ti ("he received"). Here, using the word kišib, we understand that this transfer was written on the tablet of Urnigar, i.e., put on his account. He is also the one who seals the tablet. MLC 2376 is the only other tablet with this same seal.

no. 98 (ŠS 7 xii) [copy]

This is a recapitulative tablet of deliveries of barley for bread and beer for the cult of the deceased king Amar-Sîn.

Obverse

13; 0.3. še ninda gur	13 gur and 30 sila of barley for bread
16; 1.0. še kaš gur	16 gur and 60 sila of barley for beer
sá-du$_{11}$ ^{d}Amar-^{d}EN.ZU	regular delivery for the divine Amar-Sîn
ki ka-gur$_{7}$-ta	from the granary manager
kišib-aš-a Al-la dumu Ur-ur	(recorded on) one sealed tablet of Alla son of Urur

Reverse

iti 10 lá 1-kam iti nesag-ta	over a period of 9 months, from month 4
iti ^{d}Dumu-zi-šè	to month 12
mu ^{d}Šu-^{d}EN.ZU lugal Uri$_{5}$^{ki}-ma-ke$_{4}$	ŠS 7
ma-da Za-ab-ša-li^{ki} mu-ḫul	

Seal

Lú-^{d}Šara$_{2}$	Lu-Šara
dumu Ur-[^{giš}gigir]	son of Ur[gigir]
išib ^{d}Šara$_{2}$	incantation-priest of Šara

no. 99 (ŠS 1 iii) [copy]

This summary tablet records on one document the deliveries of emmer for the cult of the two predecessors of Šu-Sîn, Šulgi and Amar-Sîn.

Obverse

1; 0.2. zíz gur	1 gur and 20 sila of emmer
sá-du$_{11}$ ^{d}Amar-^{d}EN.ZU	regular delivery for the divine Amar-Sîn
kišib A-kal-la	(tablet with) the seal of Akalla
1; 0.2. zíz gur	1 gur and 20 sila of emmer
sá-du$_{11}$ ^{d}Šul-gi	regular delivery for the divine Šulgi
kišib Ni$_{9}$-gar-ki-du$_{10}$	(tablet with) the seal of Nigarkidu
zíz gibil	fresh emmer
1; 4.0. gur šà-gal udu niga	1 gur and 240 sila fodder for barley-fed sheep

Reverse

kišib Ur-^{giš}gigir	(tablet with) the seal of Urgigir

0; 2.0. sá-du$_{11}$ ^{d}Amar-^{d}EN.ZU	120 sila regular delivery for the divine Amar-Sîn
kišib A-kal-la	(tablet with) the seal of Akalla
é-àr-ta	from the mill
iti še-kar-ra-gál-la	month 3
mu ^{d}Šu-^{d}EN.ZU lugal	ŠS 1

Regular Deliveries for the Gods:

no. 100 (ŠS7) [copy]

Obverse	
30; 0.4.5 sila$_{3}$ še gur	30 gur and 45 sila of barley
sá-du$_{11}$	regular delivery
1; 0.3. gur	1 gur and 30 sila
nì ezem-ma	provisions for the festival
sá-du$_{11}$ ^{d}En-ki	regular delivery for Enki
ki Ka-gur$_{7}$-ta	from the granary manager
Reverse	
kišib-aš-a Lú-Eridu^{ki}	(consigned on) one sealed tablet of Lu-Eridu
mu ^{d}Šu-^{d}EN.ZU lugal-e	ŠS 7
ma-da Za-ab-ša-li^{ki} mu-ḫul	
Seal	
Lú-Eridu^{ki}	Lu-Eridu
dumu Lugal-ga	son of Lugalga

no. 101 (ŠS4) [copy]

Obverse	
56; 3.0.4. ½ sila$_{3}$ še gur	56 gur and 184½ sila of barley
sá-du$_{11}$ ^{d}En-ki	regular delivery for Enki
iti 9-kam	for 9 months
ki ka-gur$_{7}$-ta	from the granary manager
Reverse	
kišib-aš-a Lú-Eridu^{ki}	(consigned on) one sealed tablet of Lu-Eridu
mu-ús-sa ^{d}Šu-^{d}EN.ZU lugal-e	ŠS 4
bàd mar-tu mu-dù	
Seal	
Lú-Eridu^{ki}	Lu-Eridu
dumu Lugal-ga	son of Lugalga

no. 102

The following poorly preserved tablet may be a balanced account or even an exercise tablet. It refers to provisions for the festivals of the gods Enki and Uškalimmu.

Obverse

[ ]	[ ]
[ ] gur [ ]	[ ] gur
[kišib] Ur-nì-[lagar-e]	[tablet with] the seal of Urni[lagare]
sá-du$_{11}$ ^{d}Uš-ka-limmu$_{2}$	regular deliveries for the god Uškalimmu
zi-ga-àm	disbursement
[ ] gur sá-du$_{11}$ Šu-[igi-du]	[ ] gur regular deliveries for Šu[igidu]
mu ^{d}Nanna Kar-zi-da	year Š 36
65 gur šà-bi-ta	from this 65 gur
35; 2.3. gur sá-du$_{11}$ ù nì ezem ^{d}En-ki	35½ gur for the regular delivery and for provisions for the festival of Enki
15; 2.0. gur sá-du$_{11}$ ù nì ezem-ma ^{d}Uš-ka-limmu$_{2}$	15 gur and 120 sila for the regular delivery and for provisions for the festival of Uškalimmu
zi-ga-àm	disbursement
[50;4.3.] gur sá-du$_{11}$ Šu-igi-du	[50;4.3.] gur regular deliveries for Šuigidu

Reverse

[mu bàd] ba-dù	year Š 37
[šà-]bi-ta	from this
35; 2.3. gur sá-du$_{11}$ ^{d}En-ki	35½ gur regular delivery for Enki
15; 2.0. gur ^{d}Uš-ka-limmu$_{2}$	$15^{2}/_{5}$ gur for Uškalimmu
zi-ga-àm	disbursement
ù sá-du$_{11}$ Šu-igi-du	and regular delivery for Šuigidu
mu-ús-sa bàd ba-dù	year Š 38
[ ] 16 gur [ ]	[ ] 16 gur [ ]
šà-bi-ta	from it
[ ]7; 1.0. gur	[ ]7;1.0. gur
[nì]-ka$_{9}$-ak	account
[ ]	[ ]

no. 103 (ŠS 6 v) [copy]

Obverse

0; 1.1. zíz-an	70 sila emmer flour
0; 1.0. še	60 sila of barley
0; 0.1. zú-lum	10 sila of dates
nì siskur$_{2}$-ra	provisions for the offering

0; 2.0. še gur-sal$_4$-la	120 sila of barley measured with the small gur
^{d}En-líl	for Enlil
Reverse	
ki Lú-bala-sig$_5$-ta	from Lubalasig
kišib ensi$_2$-ka	(tablet with) the seal of the governor
iti ri	month 5
mu ^{d}Šu-^{d}EN.ZU lugal Uri$_5$^{ki}-ma-ke$_4$	ŠS 6
na-rú-a maḫ ^{d}En-líl ^{d}Nin-líl-ra	
mu-ne-rú	
Seal	
^{d}Šu-^{d}EN.ZU	Šu-Sîn
lugal-kalag-ga	mighty king
lugal Uri$_5$^{ki}-ma	king of Ur
lugal an-ub-da limmu$_2$-ba	king of the four quarters of the universe
A-a-kal-la	Aakalla
ensi$_2$	governor
Umma^{ki}	of Umma
ir$_{11}$-zu	(is) your servant

no. 104 (AS 3) [copy]

Text no. 101 is a balanced account, enumerating individual transactions. This tablet could have been compiled only on the basis of the scribe having at his disposal records of the individual transactions. He notes this by writing kišib: tablet with the seal of PN, meaning (it is recorded on) the tablet of PN, or (this tablet was composed on the basis of the) tablets of PN.

Obverse	
12; 4.0. gig gur	12;4. gur of wheat
šà-bi-ta	from it
2; 1.3.4 sila$_3$ gig numun gur	2 gur and 94 sila of wheat seed
kišib Šeš-kal-la	(tablet with) the seal of Šeškalla
1 gig gur	1 gur of wheat
kišib ugula kikken é gibil	(tablet with) the seal of the overseer of the miller in the new building
20 sila$_3$ kišib ^{d}Šara$_2$-kam	20 sila (tablet with) the seal of Šarakam
30 sila$_3$ kišib Da-gu	30 sila (tablet with) the seal of Dagu
58 sila$_3$ kišib Lugal-nì-lagar-e	58 sila (tablet with) the seal of Lugalnilagare
0; 1.0. kišib Lugal-u$_4$-sùd-šè	60 sila (tablet with) the seal of Lugalusudše
30 sila$_3$ sá-du$_{11}$ ^{d}Gu-la	30 sila regular delivery for the goddess Gula
dam A-du-du	(for the) wife of Adudu

20 sila$_3$ nì-dab$_5$ ^{d}Li$_9$-si$_4$	20 sila provisions for the goddess Lisi
30 sila$_3$ nì-dab$_5$ šu-numun-na	30 sila provisions for the *šunumun*(-festival)
Reverse	
32 sila$_3$ ka-gur$_7$-šè	32 sila for the granary manager
8; 1.2. gur	8 gur 80 sila
ì-dub	for the silo
šu-nigín 12; 2.3.4 sila$_3$ gig gur	total 12;2.3.4 sila gur of wheat
zi-ga-àm	disbursement
mu Si-ma-núm^{ki} ba-ḫul	AS 3

no. 105 (Š 44 xi) [copy]

This text is a recapitulation of expenses, including regular deliveries, in the city of Zabalam.

Obverse	
7 še gur-lugal	7 gur of barley according to the royal measurement
sá-du$_{11}$ ^{d}<Inanna>-Zabalam^{ki}	regular delivery for Inanna of Zabalam
kišib Al-ba-ni-du$_{11}$	(tablet with) the seal of Albanidu
3 gur kišib Ba-a-ti	3 gur (consigned on the) tablet of Baati
3 gur kišib Ur-^{d}Nin-ildum-ma	3 gur (consigned on the) tablet of Ur-Ninilduma
kišib Sipa-da-rí	(total consigned on the) tablet of Sipadari
3 <gur> kišib Mùš-me	3 gur (consigned on the) tablet of Mušme
Reverse	
ki Šeš-kal-la	at the place of Šeškalla
šu-nigín 16 še gur	total 16 gur of barley
še zi-ga Zabalam^{ki}-ta	from the barley disbursement in Zabalam
gìr Lú-gi-na	responsible: Lugina
iti pa$_4$-kùš-e	month 11
mu Si-mu-ru-um^{ki}	Š 44
Lu-lu-pu^{ki} a-rá 10 lá-1-kam-aš ba-ḫul	

no. 106 (AS 5) [copy]

Obverse	
12 še gur	12 gur of barley
sá-du$_{11}$ ^{d}Inanna-Zabalam^{ki}	regular delivery for Inanna of Zabalam
ki ka-gur$_7$-ta	from the granary manager
kišib Ba-a-ti	(consigned under the) sealed tablet of Baati
Reverse	
mu en unu$_6$-gal ^{d}Inanna ba-ḫun	AS 5

Seal

Ba-a-ti	Baati
dumu Lugal-an-na-ab-tum	son of Lugalannatum
gudu$_{4}$ ^{d}Inanna-Zabalam^{ki}	purification-priest of Inanna of Zabalam

no. 107 (AS 7 ix)

Obverse

6 še gur-lugal	6 gur of barley according to the royal measurement
sá-du$_{11}$ ^{d}[Inanna-Zabalam^{ki}]	regular delivery [for Inanna of Zabalam]
ki Ba-a-[ti]-ta	from Baa[ti]
ki ka-gur$_{7}$-ta	from the granary manager
kišib Lugal-[an-na]-ba-a-túm	(consigned on the) sealed tablet of Lugal[anna]batum

Reverse

iti šu-numun-ta	from month 6
iti pa$_{4}$-kùš-e-šè	to month 11
mu Bi-tum-ra-bí-um^{ki} ba-ḫul	AS 7

Seal

Ba-a-ti	Baati
dumu Lugal-an-na-ab-tum	son of Lugalannabtum
gudu$_{4}$ ^{d}Inanna-Zabalam^{ki}	purification-priest of Inanna of Zabalam

*sattukku*s for NindaLagaš

no. 108 (Š 45 vii) [copy]

Obverse

[+]2; 1.0. še gur-lugal	[ ]+2;1. gur of barley according to the royal measurement
še kaš-gi$_{6}$	barley for black beer
9 še gur kaš-sig$_{5}$	9 gur of barley for top-quality beer
4; 0.2.4 sila$_{3}$ zì gur	4 gur and 24 sila of flour
1 ninda diri gur	1 additional gur of bread
sá-du$_{11}$ ^{d}[ ]	regular delivery for [the god]
é amar [ ]	house of the young [ ]

Reverse

1+[ ] še gur-lugal	1+[ ] gur of barley according to the royal measurement
sá-du$_{11}$ ^{d}Nin-da-Lagaš<^{ki}>	regular delivery for NindaLagaš
iti min-èš	month 7
mu-ús-sa Si-mu-ru-um	Š 45

Lu-lu-bun^{ki} a-rá 10 lá 1-kam ba-ḫul

Seal

Ur-àm-ma	Ur-àm-ma
išib ^{d}Nin-da-lagaš^{ki}	purification-priest of NindaLagaš
dumu [ ]	son of [ ]

Large deliveries of barley for bread and beer for two divinities, the second of which is NindaLagaš, "the Lady next to Lagaš." The seal occurs in HEU 86.

*sattukku*s for Ninee

no. 109 (Š 35 vi)

Text 106 records a single administrative operation, the transfer of barley for the *sattukku* of Ninee a divinity of Umma. This tablet would have been eventually used to form a recapitulation tablet.

Obverse

40 še gur-lugal	40 gur of barley according to the royal measurement
sá-du$_{11}$ ^{d}Nin-e$_{11}$-e	regular delivery of Ninee
ki Ir$_{11}$-ta	from Ir
Ir$_{11}$-dam	Irdam
šu-ba-ti	received

Reverse

iti šu-numun	month 6
mu-ús-sa An-ša-an^{ki} ba-ḫul	Š 35

no. 110 (Š 41 viii)

Obverse

3 še gur-lugal	3 gur of barley according to the royal measurement
sá-du$_{11}$ ^{d}Nin-e$_{11}$-e	regular delivery for Ninee
a-šà lá-maḫ-ta	from the field Lamaḫ
ki Ir$_{11}$-ta	from Ir
En-mí-ús-sa	Enmussa

Reverse

šu-ba-ti	received
iti é-iti-6	month 8
mu-ús-sa é Puzur$_{4}$ mu-ús-sa-a-bi	Š 41

Seal

En-mí-ús-sa	Enmussa
dumu Lu$_{5}$-ú-lu$_{5}$	son of Luulu

gudu$_4$-e$_{11}$-e-[x]	purification-priest of <Nin>ee

*sattukku*s for Ninsun

no. 111 (ŠS 5 ii) [copy]

Obverse	
2 še gur	2 gur of barley
sá-du$_{11}$ ^{d}Nin-sún$^{?}$	regular delivery for Ninsun
šu-igi-du	first delivery
é-àr-gibil-ta	from the new mill
ki ka-gur$_7$-ta	from the granary manager
Reverse	
mu Ur-ma-am$_6$-šè	instead of the seal of Urmam
kišib Lú-du$_{10}$-ga	the seal of Luduga (was used)
iti sig$_4$-giš-gá-ra	month 2
mu-ús-sa bàd mar-tu ba-dù	ŠS 5
Seal	
Lú-du$_{10}$-ga	Luduga
dub-sar	scribe
dumu Ur-^{d}Nin-[tu]	son of Ur-Nin[tu]
gudu$_4$-E$_{11}$-e-[ka]	purification-priest of Ee

The third line is difficult to understand, for it might be a descriptive phrase referring to the goddess Ninsun, thus "Ninsun, the Leader." However, I have interpreted it here as qualifying the regular offering, indicating the first delivery of the total amount.

Various seals of Lú-du$_{10}$-ga son of Ur-Nintu are attested. This one seems identical to the one depicted in MVN 16 1303.

*sattukku*s for Ninurra

no. 112 (ŠS 1 vii) [copy]

This text is a memorandum concerning two expenses, written in the storeroom of Ninurra, the wife of Šara, the main deity of Umma.

Obverse	
36 še gur	36 gur of barley
sá-du$_{11}$ ^{d}Nin-ur$_4$-ra	regular delivery for Ninurra
kišib Šà-kù-ge	seal of Šakuge
3 gur mu-ša	3 gur of ... (barley)
kišib Ur-^{d}Šul-pa-è	seal of Ur-Šulpae
Reverse	
é-šu-tum ^{d}Nin-ur$_4$-ra-ta	from the storeroom of (the temple) of Ninurra

iti min-èš	month 7
mu ^{d}Šu-^{d}EN.ZU lugal	ŠS 1

*sattukku*s for Nungal

no. 113 (ŠS 2 vi)

Obverse

8 zíz gibil gur	8 gur of fresh emmer
4; 1.0. zíz sumun gur	4;1.0. gur of old emmer
mu-ša	… (emmer)
kišib Ur-^{d}EN.ZU	seal of Ur-Sîn
8 zíz gibil gur	8 gur of fresh emmer
4; 2.0. zíz sumun gur	4;2.0. gur of old emmer
kišib Lugal-é-maḫ-e	seal of Lugalemaḫe
8 zíz-gibil gur	8 gur of fresh emmer
4; 1.0. zíz-gibil gur	4;1.0. gur of old! emmer

Reverse

kišib ^{d}Šara$_{2}$-za-me	seal of Šara-zame
mu-ša	… (emmer)
6 še gur	6 gur of barley
sá-du$_{11}$ ^{d}Nun-[gal]	regular delivery for Nungal
kišib dam$^{?}$ Ur-ša$_{6}$-ša$_{6}$	seal of the wife(?) of Uršaša
é-àr-gibil-ta	from the new mill
iti šu-numun-na	month 6
mu má ^{d}En-ki	ŠS 2
ba-ab-du$_{8}$	

This recapitulation tablet was not sealed because it was for internal administrative use only. Based on the previous line, zíz-gibil in the last line on the obverse is probably an error for zíz-sumun, "old emmer."

*sattukku*s for Šara

no. 114 (Š 47 xii) [copy]

This text concerns barley to be processed into beer for Šara.

Obverse

0; 1.3. še lugal	90 sila barley according to the royal measurement
še kaš-kam	barley for beer
sá-du$_{11}$ ^{d}Šara$_{2}$	regular delivery for Šara
saḫar-ú-ú-ta	from the field Saḫaruu

Reverse

ki Ù-ma-ni-ta	from Umani
Lú-dingir-ra	Ludingirra
šu-ba-ti	received
iti ^{d}Dumu-zi mu-ús-sa	month 12; year following the year
Ki-maš^{ki} ba-ḫul	Š 47

Seal

Lú-dingir-ra	Ludingirra
dumu Ù-ma-ni	son of Umani

no. 115 (Š 36 diri) [copy]

Obverse

2; 3.0. še gur-lugal	2;3.0. gur of barley according to the royal measurement
sá-du$_{11}$ ^{d}Šara$_{2}$ é nì-lagar-ka	regular delivery for the god Šara in the Enilagar-temple
ki-su$_{7}$ íd-sal$_{4}$-la-ta	from the threshing floor of <the field> Idsalla
ki Ir$_{11}$-ta	from Ir

Reverse

Šeš-kal-la	Šeškalla
šu-ba-ti	received
iti diri	intercalary month
mu ^{d}Nanna Kar-zi-da a-rá 2-kam	Š 36
é-a-na ba-an-ku$_{4}$	

no. 116 (AS 5 ii) [copy]

Obverse

1; 2.3. zíz gur lugal	1½ gur of emmer according to the royal measurement
sá-du$_{11}$ ^{d}Šara$_{2}$-šè	regular delivery for Šara
ki-su$_{7}$ a-šà lá-tur-ta	from the threshing-floor of the field Latur
ki Ir$_{11}$-ta	from Ir
Ur-^{d}EN.ZU-ke$_{4}$	Ur-Sîn
šu-ba-ti	received

Reverse

mu Ur-^{d}EN.ZU-šè	instead of the seal of Ur-Sîn
kišib Ur-^{d}Ma-mi ì-gál	the seal of Ur-Mami (was used)
iti sig$_{4}$-giš-ì-ba!-šub!-gar	month 2
mu-ús-sa en-maḫ-gal-an-na ba-ḫun	AS 5

Seal

Ur-^{d}EN.ZU	Ur-Sîn

dumu Lú-^{d}Šara$_2$	son of Lu-Šara
nu-banda$_3$	lieutenant

no. 117 (AS 8 ix) [copy]

Obverse

6; 1.0. zì gur	$6\frac{1}{5}$ gur of flour
sá-du$_{11}$ ^{d}Šara$_2$	regular delivery for Šara
ki-su$_7$ é-duru$_5$ gu-la-ta	from the threshing floor of the encampment of [Ur]gula
ki Lú-^{d}Šul-gi-ra-ta	from Lu-Šulgira
mu Ur-^{d}EN.ZU-šè	instead of (the seal of) Ur-Sîn

Reverse

kišib Ur-^{d}Ma-mi	the seal of Ur-Mami (was used)
iti 4-šè iti šu-numun-ta iti ^{d}Li$_9$-si$_4$-šè	for 4 months, from month 6 to month 9
mu en Eridu^{ki} ba-ḫun	AS 8

Seal

Ur-^{d}EN.ZU	Ur-Sîn
dumu Lú-^{d}Šara$_2$	son of Lu-Šara
nu-banda$_3$	lieutenant

no. 118 (AS 6) [copy]

This tablet concerns cattle deliveries for observances connected with the cycle of the moon.

Obverse

1 udu niga 2 udu ú	1 barley-fed sheep 2 grass-fed sheep
u$_4$-sakar$_x$-gu-la	for the ceremony of the new moon;
1 udu niga 3 udu ú	1 barley-fed sheep 3 grass-fed sheep
1 máš ^{giš}gigir u$_4$-6	1 goat for the chariot on the 6th day
1 udu niga 4 udu ú 1 sila$_4$	1 barley-fed sheep 4 grass-fed sheep 1 lamb
^{giš}gigir u$_4$-7	for the chariot on the 7th day;
1 udu niga 2 udu ú	1 barley-fed sheep 2 grass-fed sheep
á u$_4$-da	daily;

Reverse

1 udu ú nì-dab$_5$ sig$_4$-giš-ì-šub-ba gá-ra [erasure]	1 grass-fed sheep, provision for the ceremony of the laying of the brickmold
1 udu niga 1 udu ú	1 barley-fed sheep 1 grass-fed sheep
é-maḫ	for the Emaḫ;
sá-du$_{11}$ ^{d}Šara$_2$	regular delivery for Šara
ki A-lu$_5$-lu$_5$-ta	from Alulu
zi-ga-àm	disbursement

iti sig_4-giš-ì-šub-ba-gar	month 2
mu-ús-sa en unu_6-gal ^{d}Inanna ba-ḫun	AS 6

The expression u_4-$sakar_x$ denotes the new crescent of the moon, followed by the half moon ^{giš}gigir u_4-7. The expression á-u_4-da indicates the wages for a working day, apparently three sheep for the participants of these liturgies.

no. 119 (AS 9 iv) [copy]

Obverse

24; 4.0. še gur-lugal	24⁴/₅ gur of barley according to the royal measurement
mu-túm $^{d}Šara_2$	delivery for Šara
ki Lú-$^{d}Šara_2$ šabra gu_4-ta	from Lu-Šara the steward of the oxen
iti nesag	month 4

Reverse

mu-ús-sa en $Eridu^{ki}$ ba-ḫun-gá	AS 9

Note the expression mu-túm, instead of sá-du_{11}. Although in both cases the terms deal with deliveries, their administrative status is different.

no. 120 (ŠS 7 ii) [copy]

Obverse

0; 2.2. še [lugal]	140 sila of barley according to the royal measurement
sá-du_{11} $^{d}Šara_2$	regular delivery for Šara
é-àr-sumun-ta	from the old mill
ki ka-gur_7-ta	from the granary manager

Reverse

iti sig_4-giš-ì-šub-ba-gar	month 2
mu ^{d}Šu-^{d}EN.ZU lugal-e	ŠS 7
ma-da Za-ab-ša-li^{ki} mu-ḫul	

no. 121 (ŠS 1 ix)

Obverse

7; 1.0. še gur	7¹/₅ gur of barley
sá-du_{11}-$^{d}Šara_2$	regular delivery for Šara
kišib Ḫa-la	seal of Ḫala
2; 2.0. gur	2²/₅ gur of barley
kišib Ur-ab-ba-sig_5	seal of Urabbasig
sá-du_{11}-$^{d}Šara_2$	regular delivery for Šara

Reverse	
é-àr sumun-ta	from the old mill
iti ^{d}Li$_{9}$-si$_{4}$	month 9
mu ^{d}Šu-^{d}EN.ZU lugal	ŠS 1

no. 122 (ŠS 4 iii) [copy]

Obverse	
3; 4.0. zíz gur	$3\,^{4}/_{5}$ gur of emmer
sá-du$_{11}$-^{d}Šara$_{2}$	regular delivery for Šara
ki-su$_{7}$ gana$_{2}$ Ur-gu-ta	from the threshing floor of Urgu
ki ka-gur$_{7}$-ta	from the granary manager
Reverse	
kišib Al-lu	seal of Allu
iti 2-kam	during 2 months
iti sig$_{4}$-giš-ì-šub-ba-gar-ta	from month 2
iti še-kar-ra-gál-la-aš	to month 3
mu-ús-sa Si-ma-núm^{ki} ba-ḫul	ŠS 4
Seal	
Al-lu	Allu
[ ] nin-[ ]	[ ] nin-[ ]
nu-banda$_{3}$ é-nin-[ ]	lieutenant of the temple of Nin-[ ]

no. 123 (ŠS 3 xii) [copy]

Obverse	
3; 0.3. zíz gur	3 gur and 30 sila of emmer
sá-du$_{11}$-^{d}Šara$_{2}$	regular delivery for Šara
0; 1.1.1 sila$_{3}$ zíz	71 sila of emmer
nì-mí-ús-sa-	bridal gift for Dumuzi
^{d}Dumu-zi-da	
Reverse	
iti ^{d}Dumu-zi	month 12
mu Si-ma-núm^{ki} ba-ḫul	ŠS 3
Seal	
Da-da	Dada
nu-banda$_{3}$ gu$_{4}$	lieutenant of the oxen

no. 124 (ŠS 3 xii)

Obverse	
0;1.0. zì	$^{1}/_{5}$ gur of flour
0;1.0. še	$^{1}/_{5}$ gur of barley

gur ^{d}Dumu-zi-da Ki-an^{ki}	for the … of Dumuzi of Kian
é [àr]-ta	from the mill
Reverse	
iti ^{d}Dumu-zi	month 12
mu Si-ma-núm^{ki} ba-ḫul	ŠS 3

The first sign on line 3 is problematic. A reading é ("the temple of Dumuzi") makes sense in context, but the sign appears to be gur. For ritual provisions for the ^{kuš}gur-dumu-zi-da at Umma, a leather object, see TCL 5 pl. vi AO 5672 iii.

sattukkus for unnamed deities

no. 125 (AS 9 xi) [copy]

Obverse	
1; 3.1.5 sila$_3$ <še> gur-lugal	1 gur and 195 sila of barley according to the royal measurement
sá-du$_{11}$ dingir-re-ne	regular deliveries for the gods
kišib Ur-^{d}Ma-mi	seal of Ur-Mami
0; 2.0. zì mu-ša	120 sila of … flour
kišib A-gu	seal of Agu
30 sila$_3$ zì kišib dam Šeš-a-ni	30 sila of flour, seal of the wife of Šešani
Reverse	
iti pa$_4$-kùš-e	month 11
mu en Ga-eš^{ki} ba-ḫun	AS 9

Regular Deliveries for Temples:

sattukkus for the é-maš

The Emaš temple at Umma includes a chapel for Enki.

no. 126 (ŠS 6 xi) [copy]

Obverse	
0; 1.2. zíz	80 sila of emmer
sá-du$_{11}$ é-maš	regular delivery for the Emaš
é-àr sumun-ta	from the old mill
ki ka-gur$_7$-ta	from the granary manager
kišib Nam-ḫa-ni	seal of Namḫani
Reverse	
iti pa$_4$-kùš-e	month 11
mu na-rú-a maḫ ba-rú	ŠS 6
Seal	
[Nam-ḫa-ni]	[Namḫani]
[dumu Ur-ni$_9$-gar]	[son of Urnigar]

This tablet deals with the delivery of emmer wheat, probably monthly, since specific day is indicated. However, 80 sila is not easily divisible by 30. Therefore, most likely other storage facilities were contributing their share for the *sattukku*s during this period.

The administrative structure of this tablet is identical with those analyzed previously concerning donkey fodder—utilization and origin of the items, name of those responsible for the expense, and the recipient of the transfer have to be indicated.

*sattukku*s for the é-nì-lagar

At Umma, the é-nì-lagar temple stood beside the temples of Šara and Ninurra. It contained a statue of Šara.

The following tablets record regular deliveries of barley. Most of these tablets are not sealed. (See Text 112 for sá-du$_{11}$ ^{d}Šara$_{2}$ é-nì-lagar-ka, "regular delivery for Šara in the Enilagar.")

no. 127 (Š 34 i) [copy]

Obverse

10; 2.0. še gur-lugal	10⅖ gur of barley according to the royal measurement
5; 2.0. zìz gur	5⅖ gur of emmer
sá-du$_{11}$ é-nì-lagar-ka	regular delivery for the Enilagar-temple
ki Ir$_{11}$-ta	from Ir
Lugal-^{giš}gigir-re dumu Gìr-ni	Lugalgigir son of Girni

Reverse

šu-ba-ti	received
iti še-kin-ku$_{5}$	month 1
mu é An-ša-an^{ki} ba-ḫul	Š 34

no. 128 (Š 34 vi) [copy]

Obverse

5; 1.0. še gur-lugal	5⅕ gur of barley according to the royal measurement
2; 2.0. zíz gur	2⅖ gur of emmer
sá-du$_{11}$ é-nì-lagar	regular delivery for the Enilagar-temple
a-šà ka-gu$_{4}$-gu-sag-gá-ta	from the field Kagugusag

Reverse

ki Ir$_{11}$-ta	from Ir
Gìr-ni šu-ba-ti	Girni received
iti šu-numun	month 6
mu-ús-sa a-rá 3-kam	Š 34
Si-mu-ru-um^{ki} ba-ḫul	

In line 4, the scribe has written ka-gu$_{4}$-gu-sag-gá instead of the expected ka-gu$_{4}$-ku$_{6}$-sag-gá.

no. 129 (Š 34) [copy]

Obverse

20; 4.0. še gur-lugal	$20\frac{4}{5}$ gur of barley according to the royal measurement
10 gur lá 0; 2.0. zì	10 gur minus 120 sila of flour
sá-du$_{11}$ é-nì-lagar	regular delivery for the Enilagar-temple
ki Ir$_{11}$-ta	from Ir
Ur-^{d}EN.ZU	Ur-Sîn
šu-ba-ti	received

Reverse

mu An-ša-an^{ki} ba-ḫul	Š 34

Seal

Ur-^{d}EN.ZU (*written upside down*)	Ur-Sîn
dumu ^{d}Šara$_2$-ka	son of Šaraka

no. 130 (ŠS 4 xii) [copy]

It can be presumed that this tablet concerns deliveries for brewing beer since the tablet is sealed by a brewer.

Obverse

1.02; 2.0. še gur	$62\frac{2}{5}$ gur of barley
28; 4.0. zíz gur	$28\frac{4}{5}$ gur of emmer
sá-du$_{11}$ É-nì-lagar	regular delivery for the Enilagar-temple
iti 12-kam	over a period of 12 months
ki ka-gur$_7$-ta	from the granary manager

Reverse

kišib Lugal-zag-ge-si	seal of Lugalzagesi
mu Si-ma-núm^{ki} ba-ḫul	ŠS 4

Seal

Lugal-zag-ge-si	Lugalzaggesi
lú-šim-^{d}Šara$_2$	brewer of Šara
dumu [Lugal]-lú-ni	son of [Lugal]luni

no. 131 (Š 39 x) [copy]

Obverse

1; 1.0. zì gur-lugal	$1\frac{1}{5}$ gur of flour according to the royal measurement
sá-du$_{11}$ <é->nì-lagar-e	regular delivery for the Enilagar-temple
é-šu-tum-ma	in the storehouse
ki Ir$_{11}$-ta	from Ir
A-bu-da	Abuda

Reverse	
šu-ba-ti	received
iti ezem-^{d}Šul-gi	month 8
mu é Puzur$_4$-Da-gan ba-dù	Š 39
Seal	
A-bù-da	Abuda
dumu Gìr-ni-ì-ša$_6$	son of Girniiša

*sattukku*s for the ib-gal

The Ibgal is the great stairway of the ziggurat at Umma. (See also Text 135 below.)

no. 132 (Š 34 xi)

Obverse	
1 še gur-lugal	1 gur of barley according to the royal measurement
sá-du$_{11}$ ib-gal	regular delivery for the Ibgal
ki Ir$_{11}$-ta	from Ir
Ur-gi$_6$-par$_4$ šu-ba-ti	Urgipar received
iti pa$_5$-kùš-e mu	month 11
An-ša-an^{ki} ba-ḫul	Š 34
Seal	
Ur-gi$_6$-par$_4$	Urgipar
dumu Ur-^{d}Ištaran	son of Ur-Ištaran

Regular Deliveries for Messengers and Scribes:

no. 133 (ŠS 5) [copy]

This tablet does not record the transfer of barley, but the handing over of the tablets on which the transfers are recorded. The verb is not šu-ba-ti "he received," but díb "he took." The three tablets recording the regular allocations for the three messengers who have returned from a mission in the fields are given to Ur-Nungal, who administers their accounts.

These three messengers were sent to the fields to check the status of several work projects: irrigation, plowing, and seeding or harvesting. They were supposed to provide the palace administration with reports on the actual situation in the field.

Obverse

1 še gur	1 gur of barley
kišib Lú-du$_{10}$-ga	on the tablet of Luduga
0; 3.0. kišib ^{d}Šara$_{2}$-za-me	180 sila on the tablet of Šara-zame
0; 2.0. kišib Ur-ni$_{9}$-gar	120 sila on the tablet of Urnigar
sá-du$_{11}$ kaš$_{4}$	regular delivery for the messengers
Reverse	
gana$_{2}$-ta DU-a	coming from the field
Ur-^{d}Nun-gal ba-an-díb	Ur-Nungal took (the tablets)
mu-ús-sa ^{d}Šu-^{d}EN.ZU lugal	ŠS 5
bàd mar-tu mu-dù	

no. 134 (ŠS 6)

Messenger accounts were always complicated. Because of the wide area the messengers traversed, they obtained rations at different locations. At the conclusion of each mission all pertinent records would be assembled at the central office for verification. Such administrative and accounting procedures often necessitated several copies of the original. This tablet is such a copy.

Obverse

4; 1.0. še gur	$4^{1}/_{5}$ gur of barley
sá-du$_{11}$ kaš$_{4}$	regular delivery for messengers
kišib ^{d}Šara$_{2}$-za-me	tablet of Šara-zame
ki Lugal-nì-lagar-e-ta	from Lugalnilagare
gaba-ri kišib ^{d}Šara$_{2}$-ì-zu	a copy of the tablet of Šara-izu
Reverse	
mu na-rú-a maḫ ba-rú	ŠS 6

no. 135 (Š 48 xii) [copy]

This text records an expenditure of beer, probably for messengers. The tablet adds the statement that the entire delivery was made in one installment.

Obverse

20 sila$_{3}$ kaš [sig$_{5}$]	20 sila of [top-quality] beer
20 sila$_{3}$ kaš gin	20 sila of average-quality beer
sá-du$_{11}$ ku$_{5}$-rá	complete regular delivery
u$_{4}$ 1-ta	for one day
[šu-a]-gi-na-àm	fixed and complete allocation
Reverse	
ki Al-la-di muḫaldim-ta	from Alladi the cook
kišib Lú-gi-na	seal of Lugina
iti še-kin-ku$_{5}$	month 12

mu Ḫa-ar-ši^{ki} ba-ḫul	Š 48
Seal	
Lú-gi-na	Lugina
dub-sar	scribe
dumu Da-da	son of Dada

Other Regular Deliveries:

no. 136 (Š 44 ii)

Obverse	
3 še gur-lugal	3 gur of barley according to the royal measurement
sá-du$_{11}$-šè	for the regular delivery
ki Ir$_{11}$-ta	from Ir
Nam-lugal-a-ni-du$_{10}$	Namlugalanidu
šu-ba-ti	received
Reverse	
iti sig$_4$-giš-ì-šub-ba-gá-gar	month 2
mu-ús-sa a-rá 10 lá 1-kam	Š 44
[Si-mu-ru]-um^{ki} ba-ḫul	
Seal	
Nam-lugal-ni-du$_{10}$	Namlugal(a)nidu
ir$_{11}$ ^{d}Šara$_2$	servant of Šara

These *sattukku*s are probably for the temple of Šara, because of the person sealing the tablet; he is servant of Šara.

Only one other tablet of the exact same type is known for Namlugalidu, and is dated eleven years earlier. This personal name should be written Nam-lugal-a-ni-ì-du$_{10}$ meaning "his kingship is good." But it can be abbreviated as Nam-lugal-a-ni-du$_{10}$, Nam-lugal-ni-du$_{10}$, or Nam-lugal-ì-du$_{10}$. This seal occurs on YBC 10978.

no. 137 (AS 8 ix–diri)

Obverse	
35 sila$_3$ zú-lum	35 sila of dates
sá-du$_{11}$ iti 5-kam	regular deliveries over 5 months
iti ^{d}Li$_9$-si$_4$-ta	from month 9
iti diri-šè	to the intercalary month
mu en Eridu^{ki} ba-ḫun-gá	year AS 7
0; 1.3.4 sila$_3$ zú-lum	94 sila of dates
Reverse	
sá-du$_{11}$ iti 12-kam	over a period of 12 months

iti še-sag-ku$_5$-ta	from month 1
iti ^{d}Li$_9$-si$_4$-šè	to month 9
mu-ús-sa en Eridu^{ki} ba-ḫun-gá	AS 8
^{d}Gu-la Zabalam^{ki}	(regular delivery) for Gula of Zabalam

The amounts of these regular deliveries are quite small, just 7 sila of dates per month. It is obvious that such small portions did not constitute a major source of sustenance for the personnel of this divinity.

no. 138 (ŠS 1 ii)

This is a summary tablet of multiple deliveries. The first delivery is for the Great Stairway, the ib-gal. (See also Text 129 above.) The second delivery is for the emblem of Ninurra. The archive of Umma offers many texts dealing with deliveries for the emblems. The food would have been for the emblem-bearer. Sometimes the regular deliveries are for the maintenance or refitting of the emblem, in silver, gold, or other precious items. Other emblems are those of the Gudenna in Apisal and in Umma or the emblems of Ninurra in Apisal and Kian.

Obverse	
3 še gur-lugal	3 gur of barley according to the royal measurement
sá-du$_{11}$ ib-gal	regular delivery for the Ibgal
kišib Lú-sig$_5$	seal of Lusig
é-šu-tum-[ta]	[from] the storehouse
30 še gur	30 gur of barley
sá-du$_{11}$ šu-nir-ra-^{d}Nin-ur$_4$-ra	regular delivery for the emblem of Ninurra
Reverse	
kišib Šà-kù-ge	seal of Šakuge
é-šu-tum ^{d}Nin-ur$_4$-ra-<ta>	<from> the storehouse of Ninurra
5 gur mu-ša	5 gur of ... (barley)
kišib Ur-^{d}EN.ZU	seal of Ur-Sîn
é gú-íd-da-ta	from the (store)house by the edge of the canal
4 gur šà-gal udu niga	4 gur as fodder for the barley-fed sheep
kišib Ur-^{giš}gigir	seal of Urgigir
é ús-sa-šabra	from the (store)house next to that of the steward
šà é-àr gibil	from the new mill
Edge	
iti sig$_4$-giš-ì-šub-ba-gar	month 2
mu-ús-sa en Ga-eš^{ki} ba-ḫun	ŠS 1

IRRIGATION PRACTICE (nos. 139 – 155)

Workers exploited the small canals resulting from the spring flooding. From them were cut smaller channels that, through an intricate system, would bring the water to the fields. Since the water did not have to flow continually onto the fields, but only for specific periods of time, the sides of the irrigation ditches were broken at certain points to enable the water to flood the adjoining land, which sometimes was prepared with smaller irrigation ditches dividing the field into small strips. The furrows ran down the slope from the irrigation ditch and water poured onto the furrows by breaching the ditch wall, or some form of lifting device was used. Sometimes the land was divided into rectangular basins by building low earth levees on flat land, which were filled to the required depth with water which was allowed to percolate in the soil.

Workers were always busy in the fields. Control of the irrigation system was a major task. The flow of water, which was needed for growing crops, could be dangerous, by destroying riverbanks or canals through overflowing, thereby causing crops to rot. Another problem was the possibility of inducing salinization of the field through allowing standing water to stagnate.

There is an extensive terminology to speak about the irrigation techniques:

a bal : to draw water

a-da-gub-ba : in charge of the control of the water level

a dé : to flood

a du_{11} : to irrigate

a saḫar si-ga : to fill with soil

a zig : to elevate the level of the water

bar-lá : water divider

e: barrage, but also ditch

e-sa-KU/dúr-ra : connection-canal, derivation-canal

e-sag-du : main ditch / barrage

e-zi-DU : erected barrage

nag-ku_5 : reservoir for the flooding

pa_4 / pa_4 : water canal

pa_4-a-da-ga : irrigation ditch, irrigation canal

kun-zi-da : reservoir at the outlet

Whereas the scribes who sealed the tablets concerning donkey fodder seem to have been active for short periods, those in charge of the management of irrigation had very long tenures in the administration. They must be considered as high officials controlling the whole irrigation operation of the city.

no. 139 (Š 47) [copy]

This tablet records an activity involving moving earth, but not necessarily connected with irrigation. Workmen are moving about 100 cubic meters, filling either a threshing floor or the fallow land of Kar-Baba. They are either compacting the ground for threshing or adding to a strip of uncultivated land whose water level has to be heightened by accumulating more soil.

5 sar saḫar	5 sar of earth
guruš-e 10 gín-ta	each workman's task: 10 shekels of earth
guruš-bi 30 u$_4$-1-šè	30 such workmen for 1 day
su$_7$ kar-ba$_6$-ba$_6$ saḫar si-ga	to fill with earth the … of Kar-baba
Reverse	
ugula Lú-gi-na	overseer Lugina
kišib nam-šà-tam Lugal-é-maḫ-e	seal of the office of the high administrator, Lugalemaḫe
mu-ús-sa Ki-maš^{ki} ba-ḫul	Š 47
Seal	
Lugal-é-maḫ-e	Lugalemaḫe
dub-sar	scribe
dumu Lugal-kù-ga-ni	son of Lugalkugani

One sar is equivalent to 60 gín. 5 sar is 300 gín, exactly the task of the 30 moving 10 gín, i.e. 300 gín.

Many of the tablets sealed by Lugalemaḫe date from Š 31 to ŠS 6 and deal with irrigation and field work.

no. 140 (ŠS 2) [copy]

Obverse	
34 geme$_2$ u$_4$-1-[šè]	34 workwomen for 1 day
a-e-bu$_6$-a kun íd-da-ka saḫar si-ga	to fill with earth the channel of the tail of the canal
ugula ^{d}Šara$_2$-za-me	overseer Šara-zame
Reverse	
kišib Da-da-ga	seal of Dadaga
mu má-^{d}En-ki ba-ab-du$_8$	ŠS 2
Seal	
Da-da-ga	Dadaga
dub-sar	scribe
dumu Ur-ni$_9$-gar kuš$_7$	son of Urnigar the equerry

The expression a-e-bu$_6$-a is rare. It probably designates a small water canal. The34 women are trying to stop the water flow by building a dam through piling up earth.

The activity of Dadaga, which spans AS 9 to ŠS 6, mainly concerns the assignment of men and women on irrigation projects, and the carrying of reeds to construct dams and ditches.

no. 141 (IS 1) [copy]

This text refers to the completion of cleaning out a reservoir by removing the accumulated silt.

Obverse	
15 sar saḫar zi-ga	15 sar of earth removed
Me-^{d}Nisaba lukur lugal	(in the domain of) Me-Nisaba the royal votary
kin-til-la-àm	the work is done
šà íd ma-ma-šar-ra	in the canal Mamašar
Reverse	
gìr Ku-lu-a-ti lú kin-gi$_4$-a lugal	responsible: Kuluati the messenger of the king
ù I-la-ak-šu-qir dub-sar	and Ilak-šuqir the scribe
mu ^{d}I-bí-^{d}EN.ZU lugal	IS 1
Seal	
I-la-ak-šu-qir	Ilak-šuqir
dumu Ur-^{giš}kiri$_6$	son of Ur-kiri
dub-sar	scribe

The relationship between lines 1 and 2 is not clear. The cleaning was ordered by the palace and most likely concerns a canal on the property of the royal votary Me-Nisaba. Because of the votary's status, no less than two parties, one a royal messenger and the other a scribe, are responsible for supervising the work and attesting to its completion.

no. 142 (ŠS 2)

Female workers were not restricted to the mill or the weaving house. They labored in the fields and performed canal work, quite often piling up grain stacks and compacting earth.

Obverse	
4.30 geme$_2$ u$_4$-1-šè	270 workwomen for 1 day
zar-tab-ba šu-ùr-[ra]	to pile and compact grain stacks
a-šà ^{d}Nin-ur$_4$-ra	in the field of Ninurra
ugula Lugal-é-[maḫ-e]	overseer Lugalemaḫe
kišib Ukken-né	seal of Ukkenne
Reverse	
mu má ^{d}En-ki ba-ab-du$_8$	ŠS 2
Seal	
Ukken-né	Ukkenne
dub-sar	scribe
dumu Ur-^{giš}gigir	son of Urgigir

d - a-da gub-ba = watch of the irrigation

no. 143 (ŠS 5) [copy]

It was very important to monitor constantly the flow of water and the ability of dams and canals to resist flood. In this tablet workmen watch over the water supply of a field.

Obverse	
59½ guruš u$_4$-1-šè	59½ workmen for 1 day
a-da gub-ba	watching (the level of) the irrigation water
du$_6$ giš-ì-ka	on the hill of the field Giši
ugula A-du-mu	overseer Adumu
Reverse	
kišib Gu-ú-g[u-a]	seal of Guugua
mu-ús-sa bàd ba-dù	ŠS 5
Seal	
Gu-ú-gu-a	Guugua
dub-sar	scribe
dumu Ma-an-sum	son of Mansum

Gugua was active from AS 8 to ŠS 7. His texts concern workmen employed in agricultural or irrigation work.

no. 144 (ŠS 5)

Obverse	
3.45 guruš u$_4$-1-šè	225 workmen for 1 day
a-da gub-ba a-šà	watching (the level of) the irrigation water in the field
gaba apin-ba-zi	opposite (the field) Apin-Bazi
ù sig$_7$-tur-tur-bi	and (the field) Sigturturbi
Reverse	
ugula [Ur]-^{d}Šara$_2$	overseer Ur-Šara
kišib Lugal-ḫé-gál	seal Lugalḫegal
mu-ús-sa bàd mar-tu ba-dù	ŠS 5
Seal	
Lugal-ḫé-gál	Lugalḫegal
dub-sar	scribe
dumu [Ur-ni$_9$-gar]	son of [Ur-nigar]

During the reign of Šulgi, Lugalḫegal was mu$_6$-šùb Šara$_2$ "shepherd of the god Šara" and was in charge of providing barley for the donkeys. Beginning with the reign of Amar-Sîn, two of his seals are attested. He remained active until ŠS 6, dealing with workers on irrigation projects.

no. 145 (ŠS 5) [copy]

This text involves the flooding of three fields, cutting the mouth of the water outlet, and compacting it after closure.

Obverse	
8 guruš u$_{4}$ 40-šè	8 workmen for 40 days
á-bi u$_{4}$ 5.20-[kam]	320 workdays
a-da gub-ba	watching (the level of) the irrigation water
a-šà amar-^{giš}kišig$_{5}$	in the field Amar-kišig
a-šà muru$_{13}$	in the field Muru
a-šà íd-lugal-ka	in the field at the canal of the king
a-dé-a	to control the waterflow
ka íd-è-ka ku$_{5}$-rá	to open the mouth of the canal Ide
Reverse	
ka íd-è-ta	from the mouth of the canal Ide
a-šà amar-^{ú}kišig$_{2}$-da šu-ùr-ra	to the field Amarkišig to compact soil
ugula [ ]	overseer [ ]
gìr [ ]	responsible: [ ]
kišib É-gal-e-si	seal of Egalesi
mu-ús-sa ^{d}Šu-^{d}EN.ZU	ŠS 5
lugal-e bàd mar-tu	
mu-dù	
Seal	
É-gal-e-si	Egalesi
dub-sar	scribe
dumu Lú-^{d}Šara$_{2}$	son of Lu-Šara
sa$_{12}$-du$_{5}$-ka	field surveyor

During his long career, from Šulgi to Šu-Sîn, Egalesi was active exclusively in irrigation projects.

no. 146 (AS 6) [copy]

Obverse	
26 guruš u$_{4}$-1-šè	26 workmen for 1 day
a-da gub-ba	watching (the level of) the irrigation water
a-šà buru$_{x}$(GANA$_{2}$)-maḫ	in the field Burumaḫ
nu-banda$_{3}$-gu$_{4}$ Da-a-ga	Daaga, lieutenant of the oxen
Reverse	
kišib Lugal-kù-ga-ni	seal of Lugalkugani
mu a-rá 2-kam ša-aš-ru-um^{ki} <ba>-ḫul	AS 6

Seal

Lugal-kù-ga-ni	Lugalkugani
dumu Ur-mes	son of Urmes

Lugalkugani was not a scribe, but, like the previous seal owners, he was in charge of agricultural and irrigation work. He was active mainly during the reigns of Amar-Sîn and the beginning of Šu-Sîn.

no. 147 (Š 46) [copy]

The irrigation activity a-du$_{11}$-ga occurs during months 10 and 12. The workmen watched the water flowing down from a basin situated at a higher level to the field, totally submerging the field.

Obverse

12 guruš u$_4$-6-šè	12 workmen for 6 days
a-šà-ge a-du$_{11}$-<ga>	to inundate the field
a-šà íd-lugal	the field Idlugal
ugula Lugal-gu$_4$-e	overseer Lugalgue

Reverse

kišib Lugal-iti-da	seal Lugalitida
mu Ki-maš^{ki} ba-ḫul	Š 46

Seal illegible

no. 148 (AS 3)

This summary tablet involves several irrigation activities undertaken by workmen: inundating the field with the waters of the first flood; carrying earth and grass; and digging.

Obverse

19 guruš u$_4$-1-šè	19 workmen for 1 day
a-šà-ge a-du$_{11}$-ga	to inundate the field
$30^{5}/_{6}$ sar 7 gín kin ú saḫar-ba	$30^{5}/_{6}$ sar and 7 gin of work on grass and earth
7 guruš u$_4$-1-šè ú íl-la	7 workmen for 1 day to carry grass
kun-zi-da íd	at the dam of the canal
Ur-sig$_5$ nag-ku$_5$	Ursig, the canal
a-šà ka-ma-rí	of the field Kamari;
13 sar 10 gín	13 sar and 10 gin (of soil)
pa$_5$ a-da-ga ba-al-la	to dig the canal
1.44 guruš u$_4$-1-šè	104 workmen for 1 day

Reverse

kun-zi-da íd Ur-sig$_5$	the reservoir Ursig
kišib Lugal-nì-lagar-e	seal Lugalnilagare
dumu Da-da	son of Dada
mu gu-za ^{d}En-líl-lá ba-dím	AS 3

Seal

Lugal-nì-lagar-e	Lugalnilagare
dub-sar	scribe
dumu Da-da	son of Dada

No overseer is mentioned, since this is a summary tablet. Lugalnilagare son of Dada has only one known sealed tablet sealed from the reigns of AS and ŠS involving guruš work in connection with irrigation.

no. 149 (AS 9 xii) [copy]

This text is a record of workmen assigned irrigation work: controlling the flow of water of the small inlets in the field and pulling grass on the threshing floor.

Obverse

17 guruš u_4-6-šè	17 workmen for 6 days
e-sa-dúr-a a-šà ^{giš}ma-nu	at the outlet of the field of willow
a-da [gub]-ba a-è-da gub-ba	watching the water level and its flow
9 guruš u_4-3-šè	9 workmen for 3 days
su_7 má-bíl-la-ka	pulling grass
$^{ú}numun_2$ bù-ra	at the threshing floor Mabilla

Reverse

ugula Lú-bala-sig_5	overseer Lubalasig
kišib Da-da-ga	seal of Dadaga
gìr Lú-du_{10}-ga dumu Lugal-nesag-e	responsible: Luduga son of Lugalnesage
iti ^{d}Dumu-zi	month 12
mu en Ga-èš^{ki} ba-ḫun	AS 9

Seal

Da-da-ga	Dadaga
dub-sar	scribe
dumu Ur-ni_9-gar $kuš_7$	son of Urnigar the equerry

Dadaga was active from the last year of AS through the entire reign of ŠS. He was mainly concerned with the assignment of workmen for irrigation work.

no. 150 (AS 5)

Obverse

3 guruš u_4-1-šè	3 workmen for 1 day
kun-zi-da ki-	(to be) stationed at the Kigamma-reservoir
gam-ma-ka gub-ba	
ugula Da-du-mu	overseer Dadumu

Reverse	
kišib Lugal-é-maḫ-e	seal of Lugalemaḫe
mu en unu$_6$-gal ^{d}Inanna ba-ḫun	AS 5
Seal	
Lugal-é-maḫ-e	Lugalemaḫe
dub-sar	scribe
dumu Lugal-kù-ga-ni	son of Lugalkugani

no. 151 (ŠS 4 i)

Obverse	
31 geme$_2$ 30 sila$_3$	31 workwomen receiving a ration of 30 sila
u$_4$-1-šè	for one day
kun-zi-da	on hand at the reservoir
amuš ^{giš}kiri$_6$ Lugal-ša$_6$	of the Amuš-canal of the garden of Lugalša
dub-lá-^{d}Utu gub-ba	at the dubla-Utu
ugula Ur-^{d}Nin-tu	overseer Ur-Nintu
Reverse	
kišib Gu-ú-gu-a	seal of Guugua
iti še-kin-ku$_5$	month 1
mu-ús-sa Si-ma-núm^{ki} ba-ḫul	ŠS 4
Seal	
Gu-ú-gu-a	Guugua
dub-sar	scribe
dumu Ma-an-sum	son of Mansum

no. 152 (ŠS 5) [copy]

Obverse	
31 geme$_2$ u$_4$-4-šè	31 workwomen for 4 days
kun-zi-da	(to be stationed at) the reservoir
ki Ur-^{d}Nin-šubur-ta	from Ur-Ninšubur
Reverse	
kišib Ukken-né	seal of Ukkenne
mu-ús-sa bàd mar-tu ba-dù	ŠS 5
Seal	
Ukken-né	Ukkenne
dub-sar	scribe
dumu Ur-^{giš}gigir	son of Urgigir

no. 153 (ŠS 2) [copy]

Obverse	
15 geme$_2$ u$_4$-1-šè	15 workwomen for one day
kun-zi-da dub-lá ^{d}Utu gub-ba	to be stationed at the reservoir of the dubla-Utu
ugula Lugal-é-maḫ-<e>	overseer Lugalemaḫe
kišib A-du-mu	seal of Adumu
Reverse	
mu má ^{d}En-ki ba-ab-du$_8$	ŠS 2
Seal	
Ur-^{d}EN.ZU	Ur-Sîn
dub-sar	scribe
dumu Ur-^{giš}gigir	son of Urgigir
šà-tam	high administrator

Ur-^{d}EN.ZU is another scribe whose activity was almost exclusively relegated to irrigation.

no. 154 (ŠS 3) [copy]

This is a record of ox-drivers utilized for irrigation duties. Their assignment was to widen the dam, if necessary, to let the irrigation water flow into the fields and to be ready to intervene in case of disaster. A large labor force was needed for this task.

Obverse	
24 guruš šà-gu$_4$ u$_4$-2-šè	24 workmen (to serve as) ox-drivers for 2 days
kun-zi-da ku$_5$-rá-a gub-ba	standing at the opened dam
ugula Ur-lugal	overseer Urlugal
Reverse	
kišib Lú-^{d}Ḫa-ià	seal of Lu-Ḫaia
mu Si-ma-núm^{ki} ba-ḫul	ŠS 3
Seal	
Lú-^{d}Ḫa-ià	Lu-Ḫaia
dub-sar	scribe
dumu Ur-e$_{11}$-e kuš$_7$	son of Uree the equerry

The scribe Lu-Ḫaia, the brother of the Lukalla who was active in the offices dealing with cattle, was active during the second half of the reign of AS, throughout the reign of ŠS, and to the second year of Ibbi-Sîn. Although he was often involved with the assignment of workmen, Lu-Ḫaia's activity was not limited to irrigation.

no. 155 (AS 2) [copy]

The nag-ku$_5$ was a water reservoir for the flooding the fields. Workmen were assigned to the site to maintain the water flow by cutting the earth at the dam deep enough to secure a regular flow.

Obverse	
10 guruš u$_4$-1-šè	10 workmen for 1 day
nag-ku$_5$ en-GABA-rá gub-ba	stationed at the reservoir of the field EnGABAra
ugula Lú-^{d}Nin-ur$_4$-ra	overseer Lu-Ninurra
kišib nam-šà-<tam> A-du-mu	seal of the office of the high administrator, Adumu
Reverse	
mu ^{d}Amar-^{d}EN.ZU lugal-e	AS 2
Ur-bí-lum^{ki} mu-ḫul	
Seal	
Ur-^{d}[EN].ZU	Ur-Sîn
dub-sar	scribe
dumu Ur-^{giš}gigir šà-tam	son of Urgigir the high administrator

AGRICULTURAL WORK (nos. 156–217)

The working force:

1. The draught animals are the gu$_4$-apin, i.e., plowoxen, used for plowing and to tract the harrow, the seeder-plow, and carts.
2. Various categories of laborers participated in these activities: lú-ḫun-gá, guruš, šà-gu$_4$, erin$_2$, engar, nu-banda$_3$-gu$_4$, un-íl.

Field operations:

To prepare the field for seeding it was necessary to open the ground by plowing. based on the condition of the ground, there are different ways of plowing the fields:

1. Plowing the land with a túg-ŠE.KIN plow and then harrowing it with a team of two or three persons;
2. Plowing the land with a túg-gur$_8$ plow and then harrowing it with a team of three persons;
3. Plowing the land with a túg-ŠE.KIN plow and then harrowing it with a team of a number of persons;
4. or harrowing the land with a team of a number of persons without plowing. It is possible that this type of land was unsuited for plowing because of weeds and reeds growing there. Therefore, it would be necessary to break the clods of soil with a hammer-like instrument and to cut or extract the weeds from the fields.

After this preliminary operation, furrowing and planting the land would take place. There were three types of land:

1. gán-gu$_4$ uru$_4$-a
2. gán-gu$_4$ a-šà bal-a
3. šukur engar uru$_4$-a (allotment of land for the cultivators)

The workers were set ten furrows per square *nindan*. In some cases they would use a wooden pole for manual seeding. With this pole on the breast (^{giš}gaba-tab), a team of ten or twelve laborers would advance in one row, dropping cereal seeds onto each furrow.

A preliminary flooding of the fields was common practice before plowing. Oxen with covered hooves were brought onto these fields to puddle and make the bottom ground smooth. These fields of rather poor soil were also sown with the ^{giš}gaba-tab pole.

Many tablets deal with the grain needed to perform plowing, furrowing, harrowing, and digging with the spade and other tasks.

156 [copy]

This tablet records a plowing commitment, with an oath in the name of the king.

Obverse

1 bur'u gana$_2$ uru$_4$-a	1 *buru* of land to plow
a-rá 1-kam	once
4 bur'u gana$_2$ uru$_4$-a	4 *buru* of land to plow
a-rá 2-kam	twice
5 gana$_2$ uru$_4$-a	5 *buru* of land to plow

Reverse

A-pi-lí nu-banda$_3$	Apili the lieutenant
Ša-ga-pu egir-ra-ni	(and) Šagapu his follower
mu lugal-bi in-pàd	swore in the name of the king (to do it)
igi Pu-úḫ-lim-šè	witness Puḫlim
igi Na-ra-am-É-a-šè	witness Naram-Ea
šà Lu-lu-pu-um^{ki}	in Lulubum
gìr A-da-làl aga$_3$-uš	responsible: Adalal the soldier

157 (AS 5 viii) [copy]

When plowing could not be performed in a field, it was necessary to weed out the thorny plants that were growing in the field, digging with a spade or cutting them. These operations were, obviously, manpower intensive.

Obverse

50 guruš u$_4$-1-šè al 5 sar-ta	50 workmen for 1 day to dig with the spade 5 *sar* per day
20½ guruš u$_4$-1-šè	20½ workmen for 1 day
^{ú}kiší ku$_5$-a 10 sar-ta	to cut thorny weeds at the rate of 10 *sar* per day
á lú ḫun-gá še 6 sila$_3$-ta	wages for the hired men per day 6 *sila* of barley

Reverse

[ ] giš ab-zu	[ ]...
a-šà šu-nu-kúš	in the field Šunukuš

kišib Lugal-kù-zu	seal of Lugalkuzu
iti é-iti-6	month 8
mu en unu$_6$-gal ^{d}Inanna ba-ḫun	AS 5
Seal	
Lugal-kù-zu	Lugalkuzu
dub-sar	scribe
dumu Ur-ni$_9$-gar kuš$_7$	son of Urnigar the equerry

no. 158 (AS 9 xii) [copy]

Manpower had to be paid or at least fed. The administrative expression is á lú-ḫun-gá, salary/wages for the hired men or all other type of workers. This tablet summarizes all the barley expenses made by Lu-Šulgi from various places. This is a clear indication that one individual could be responsible for more than one storage place.

Obverse	
9 še gur	9 gur of barley
á lú-ḫun-gá	wages for hired men
kišib Lú-ḫé-gál dumu Ur-^{d}Šara$_2$	tablet of Luḫegal son of Ur-Šara
še gibil ús-sa é-šu-tum šabra-ta	fresh barley from <the building> next to the (storage facility) Ešutum of the steward
0; 2.3. še-ba e-daḫ-ḫa ḫé-dab$_5$	½ gur barley rations additional for the forced(?) workers
kišib ensi$_2$-ka	tablet of the governor
Reverse	
1; 1.0. še àr-ra zì-da gur	1⅕ gur of barley ground into flour
kišib Lugal-e-ba-an-ša$_6$	tablet of Lugalebanša
2; 4.0. še gibil gur	2⅘ gur of fresh barley
bar-ta-gál-la	outstanding
é-àr-gibil-ta	from the new mill
ki Lú-^{d}Šul-gi-ta	from Lu-Šulgi
iti ^{d}Dumu-zi	month 12
mu en Ga-eš^{ki} ba-ḫun	AS 9

no. 159 [copy]

Recapitulative tablet of wages paid to 6 individuals, usually in barley. The reason for the payment is not given.

Obverse	
0;1.0. še lugal	60 sila of barley according to the royal measurement
gur ⌜Ab(?)⌝-ba-sig$_5$	<gur> for Abbasig
0; 2.0. Ur-e$_{11}$-e	120 sila for Uree

0; 2.3. Ur-^{d}Neraḫ	½ gur for Ur-Neraḫ
0;1.0. Ur-gú-la	60 sila for Ur-gula
0;1.0. Ur-li	60 sila for Urli
0;1.0. Ur-^{d}Ištaran	60 sila for Ur-Ištaran

The significance of gur at the beginning of the second line is unclear.

no. 160 (ŠS 3 ix)

Long list of wages for young (banda$_3$) ox-drivers.

Obverse	
20 sila$_3$ banda$_3$ Lú-gu-la	20 sila for the young Lugula
40 sila$_3$ banda$_3$ A-ḫu-šu-ni	40 sila for the young Aḫušuni
20 sila$_3$ banda$_3$ Lugal-má-gur$_8$-re	20 sila for the young Lugalmagurre
30 sila$_3$ banda$_3$ Lugal-zi-mu	30 sila for the young Lugalzimu
20 sila$_3$ banda$_3$ Ur-^{d}A-šár	20 sila for the young Ur-Asar
20 sila$_3$ banda$_3$ Lú-^{d}Šara$_2$	02 sila for the young Lu-Šara
40 sila$_3$ banda$_3$ Lugal-dub-lá	40 sila for the young Lugaldubla
20 sila$_3$ banda$_3$ Ilum-qàr-ad	20 sila for the young Ilum-qarrad
20 sila$_3$ banda$_3$ Uru-bar-re	20 sila for the young Urubarre
35 sila$_3$ banda$_3$ Lú-me-lám	35 sila for the young Lumelam
15 sila$_3$ banda$_3$ Na-ga-LUG	15 sila for the young NagaLUG
35 sila$_3$ banda$_3$ Ur$_4$-šà-ki-du$_{10}$	35 sila for the young Uršakidu
60 sila$_3$ banda$_3$ Ur-lugal	06 sila for the young Urlugal
20 sila$_3$ banda$_3$ Lú-^{d}Utu	20 sila for the young Lu-Utu
20 sila$_3$ banda$_3$ Ur-^{d}Iškur	20 sila for the young Ur-Iškur
20 sila$_3$ banda$_3$ Lugal-iti-da	20 sila for the young Lugalitida
Reverse	
35 sila$_3$ banda$_3$ Lú-ib-gal	35 sila for the young Lu-ibgal
20 sila$_3$ banda$_3$ Ur-e$_{11}$-e	20 sila for the young Uree
70 sila$_3$ banda$_3$ Ur-é-an-na	70 sila for the young Ur-Eanna
20 sila$_3$ banda$_3$ Ur-^{d}[Gu-nu-ra]	20 sila for the young Ur-[Gunura]
35 sila$_3$ banda$_3$ Šeš-[ ]	35 sila for the young Šeš-[ ]
35 sila$_3$ banda$_3$ A-za-lú	35 sila for the young Azalu
20 sila$_3$ banda$_3$ Ur-^{d}Nun-[gal]	120 sila for the young Ur-Nun[gal]
35 sila$_3$ banda$_3$ Lú-me-lám	35 sila for the young Lu-melam
šu-nigín 2;3.2.5 sila$_3$ gur banda$_3$ šà-gu$_4$-me	total 2 gur 35 sila for the young ox-drivers
iti ^{d}Li$_9$-si$_4$	month 9
mu Si-ma-núm^{ki}	ŠS 3

It is possible to translate in the first line dumu Lú-gu-la "son of Lugula" or banda$_3$ Lú-gu-la "the young Lugula" as proposed. In this latter instance Lú-gu-la would be the name of the young ox-driver and not that of his father.

no. 161

The guruš make up the largest part of the working force and, therefore, are present in every sector of 'industrial' activity, irrigation, agricultural work, navigation, including pulling boats upstream and building reed rafts. The un-íl are another category of personnel, probably of a lower rank than the guruš but performing the same duties.

Obverse

<table>
<tr><td>ug$_7$ Ur-^{d}Šul-pa-è</td><td>dead Ur-Šulpae</td></tr>
<tr><td>½ Lugal-zu-[ab]</td><td>½ Lugalabzu</td></tr>
<tr><td>½ Lugal-dub-lá</td><td>½ Lugaldubla</td></tr>
<tr><td>½ Lugal-á-zi-da</td><td>½ Lugalazida</td></tr>
<tr><td>½ Ur-^{d}Šul-pa-è</td><td>½ Ur-Šulpae</td></tr>
<tr><td>½ Da-gi$_4$</td><td>½ Dagi</td></tr>
<tr><td>½ dumu Á-na-na</td><td>½ son of Anana</td></tr>
<tr><td>½ Ur-^{d}Šara$_2$</td><td>½ Ur-Šara</td></tr>
<tr><td>| Ur-^{giš}gigir</td><td>1 Urgigir</td></tr>
<tr><td>| Ur-^{giš}gigir min-kam</td><td>1 Urgigir, second one</td></tr>
<tr><td>| Šeš-a-ni</td><td>1 Šešani</td></tr>
<tr><td>| Lú-^{d}Šara$_2$</td><td>1 Lu-Šara</td></tr>
<tr><td>| Lú-^{d}Nin-ur$_4$-ra</td><td>1 Lu-Ninurra</td></tr>
<tr><td>½ Šeš-kal-la</td><td>½ Šeškalla</td></tr>
</table>

Reverse

<table>
<tr><td>šu-nigín 8 guruš ½ ||||| guruš</td><td>total: 8 workmen ½ (and) 5 workmen</td></tr>
<tr><td>ugula A-a-kal-la</td><td>overseer Aakalla</td></tr>
</table>

The sign preceding the workers' names is an indication of status, reflecting the rations attributed. Sometimes a second sign indicating the amount of wool is added next to the barley amount. In the present tablet the sign | indicates a full ration, often 60 sila of barley per month and 4 mana of wool, while the sign ½ indicates a half-ration of wool and barley

no. 162 (Š 44 vii)

This tablet concerns workers driving cattle from Umma to Ibtur.

Obverse

<table>
<tr><td>2 guruš u$_4$ 7-šè</td><td>2 workmen for 7 days</td></tr>
<tr><td>Ib-tùr^{ki}-šè</td><td>to Ibtur</td></tr>
<tr><td>gu$_4$-niga laḫ$_4$-a</td><td>to bring barley-fed oxen</td></tr>
<tr><td>gìr ensi$_2$-ka</td><td>the governor is responsible</td></tr>
</table>

ugula Ba-ša$_6$	overseer Baša
iti min-èš	month 7
Reverse	
mu-ús-sa a-rá 10 lá 1-kam	Š 44
Si-mu-ru-um^{ki} Lu-lu-pu^{ki} ba-ḫul	
Seal	
Ur-^{d}Li$_9$-si$_4$	Ur-Lisi
ensi$_2$ Umma^{ki}	governor of Umma
[Ba-ša$_6$]	[Baša]
sagi ir$_{11}$-zu	the cupbearer is your servant

no. 163 (AS 6) [copy]

Obverse	
20 guruš u$_4$-2-šè	20 workmen for 2 days
a-šà lá-maḫ-ta	from the field Lamaḫ
a-šà muš-bi-an-<na>-šè	to the field Mušbianna
gu$_4$ bù-ra	to drive oxen
20 guruš u$_4$-2-šè	20 workmen for 2 days
a-šà muš-bi-an-na [Umma]^{ki}-šè	from the field Mušbianna to [Umma]
Reverse	
gu$_4$ bù-ra	to drive oxen
ugula Lú-dingir-ra	overseer Ludingirra
kišib nam-šà-tam	seal of the high administrator's office
A-du-mu	Adumu
mu Ša!-šà-ru-um^{ki}	AS 6
a-rá 2-kam ba-ḫun	
Seal	
Ur-^{d}EN.ZU	Ur-Sîn
dub-sar	scribe
dumu Ur-^{giš}gigir	son of Urgigir

no. 164 (AS 5) [copy]

Obverse	
1 guruš u$_4$-12-šè	1 workman for 12 days
lú a-da [šè?] tuk-a gub-ba	stationed [ ]
ugula Da-a-ga	overseer Daaga
Reverse	
kišib Lugal-kù-ga-ni	seal of Lugalkugani
mu en unu$_6$-gal ^{d}Inanna ba-ḫun	AS 5

Seal

<table>
<tr><td>Lugal-kù-ga-ni</td><td>Lugalkugani</td></tr>
<tr><td>dumu Ur-mes</td><td>son of Urmes</td></tr>
</table>

no. 165 (Š 44 xi) [copy]

Obverse

<table>
<tr><td>| Ìl-su-ba-[ni]</td><td>Ilsu-bani</td></tr>
<tr><td>| Ur-^{d}Dam-gal-nun-ka</td><td>Ur-Damgalnunka</td></tr>
<tr><td>| Šeš-kal-la</td><td>Šeš-kalla</td></tr>
<tr><td>| Lú-^{d}Šara$_{2}$</td><td>Lu-Šara</td></tr>
<tr><td>| Ì-lí-iš-^{d}Da-gan</td><td>Iliš-Dagan</td></tr>
<tr><td>| ^{d}Nanna-ki-ág</td><td>Nanna-kiag</td></tr>
<tr><td>| Engar-zi</td><td>Engarzi</td></tr>
<tr><td>| É-gal-e-si</td><td>Egalesi</td></tr>
<tr><td>| Lú-^{d}Utu</td><td>Lu-Utu</td></tr>
</table>

Reverse

<table>
<tr><td>| Igi-^{d}Šara$_{2}$-šè</td><td>Igi-Šaraše</td></tr>
<tr><td>ḫé-dab$_{5}$ libir</td><td>forced(?) workers from the old (team)</td></tr>
<tr><td>iti pa$_{4}$-kùš-e</td><td>month 11</td></tr>
<tr><td>mu Si-mu-ru-um^{ki} ba-ḫul</td><td>Š 44</td></tr>
</table>

no. 166 [copy]

Rations for reedmat-makers that were not received.

Obverse

<table>
<tr><td>0; 1.0. Ur-^{d}Nin-[ti]</td><td>60 sila Ur-Nin[ti]</td></tr>
<tr><td>0; 1.1.5 <sila$_{3}$> Lú-^{d}Nin-ur$_{4}$-ra dumu-ni</td><td>75 sila Lu-Ninura, his son</td></tr>
<tr><td>ad-kub$_{4}$-me</td><td>reedmat-makers</td></tr>
<tr><td>šu nu-ti-a</td><td>it (this barley) was not received</td></tr>
<tr><td>ki A-gu</td><td>from Agu</td></tr>
<tr><td>[ ]</td><td>…</td></tr>
</table>

no. 167 (ŠS 3) [copy]

Obverse

<table>
<tr><td>1 ešè 1 iku gana$_{2}$ a-šà bala-a</td><td>1 eše 1 iku of land …</td></tr>
<tr><td>ab-sín 10-ta</td><td>prepared with 10 furrows</td></tr>
<tr><td>a-šà lá-tur</td><td>in the field Latur</td></tr>
</table>

Reverse

<table>
<tr><td>ugula Lugal-kù-zu</td><td>overseer Lugalkuzu</td></tr>
<tr><td>kišib Ur-^{d}Ùr-bar-tab</td><td>seal Ur-Urbartab</td></tr>
<tr><td>mu Si-ma-núm^{ki} ba-ḫul</td><td>ŠS 3</td></tr>
</table>

Seal

Ur-^{d}Ùr-bar-tab	Ur-Urbartab
dumu Lugal-á-zi-da	son of Lugalazida
gudu$_4$ é-maḫ	purification-priest of the Emaḫ

The setting up of 10 furrows per square *nindan* (36 sq. meters) was the most common practice in the Ur III period (see *BSA* 5 125). Knowing this practice, the scribe, although sitting in his office, could nevertheless compute the yield to be expected from every field and keep a clear view of the use and category of exploitation of the land and, therefore, determine the type of manpower needed at the time of irrigation and seeding and the quantity of grain for seeding, the labor force, and the oxen.

This tablet mentions a special category of field: gana$_2$ a-šà bala-a. Its nature is not yet clearly understood.

Ur-Urbartab was active from ŠS 2 to ŠS 6 in agriculture and irrigation.

no. 168 (ŠS 6) [copy]

Obverse

12.45 sar	765 sar
al 5 sar-ta	(each worker) dug 5 sar
á-bi u$_4$ 2.33 kam	153 workdays
2.30 sar al 3 sar-ta	150 sar (each worker) dug 3 sar
á u$_4$ 50-kam	50 workdays

Reverse

a-šà ^{giš}ma-nu	field of willow
a-šà igi-dag?-ga-ka	field Igidagga
á lú ḫun-gá 6 sila$_3$-ta	the wage of each hired man is 6 sila (of barley)
ugula Lú-kù-ga-ni	overseer Lu-kugani
kišib Ur-^{giš}gigir	seal Urgigir
mu na-rú-a maḫ ba-rú	ŠS 6

Seal

Ur-^{giš}gigir	Urgigir
dub-sar + picture	scribe
dumu Lugal-é-maḫ-e	son of Lugalemaḫe

Some fields were not plowed either because of the hardness of the soil or because of too many weeds and thorny bushes. Before sowing the ground would have to be hoed with a spade. According to the hardness of the soil and nature of the field, a guruš could hoe 3 or 5 *sar* per day. One *sar* equals 36 sq. meters; 5 *sar* equal 180 sq. meters, i.e., between 13 and 14 sq. meters. Each worker was paid around 6 *sila* barley per working day. In the present text, as no guruš were available, hired men would have to do the work.

Only a few tablets sealed by Urgigir, who was active during the reign of Šu-Sîn, are known. In this seal there is an unusual placement of the picture in the cartouche.

no. 169 (ŠS 6) [copy]

Obverse	
11.35 sar <al> 5 sar-ta	695 sar dug at the rate of 5 sar par work-day
á-bi u$_4$ 2.19	139 workdays
2.16 sar al 4-sar	136 sar dug at the rate of 4 sar par work-day
á-bi u$_4$ 34	34 workdays
2.40 sar $^{<ú>}$ḫar!-an bù 20 sar-ta	160 sar cleaned of *ḫaran*-weed at the rate of 20 sar par work-day
á-bi u$_4$ 8	8 workdays
á lú ḫun-gá 7 sila$_3$-ta	the wages of a hired man is 7 sila per day
a-šà sag-dù	in the field Sagdu
gìr Lú-^{d}Šara$_2$	responsible: Lu-Šara
36.0 sar ^{ú}kiši 20 sar-ta	21600 sar cleaned if *kiši*-weed at the rate of 20 sar
á-bi u$_4$ 1.40+[8]	108 workdays
Reverse	
2.52 sar 4 sar-ta	172 sar at the rate of 4 sar
á-bi u$_4$ 43	43 workdays
2.55 sar al 5 sar-ta	175 sar dug at the rate of 5 sar
á-bi u$_4$ 35	35 workdays
á lú-ḫun-gá 7 sila$_3$-ta	the wages of the hired men is 7 sila per person
a-šà šu-nu-kúš	field Šunukuš
gìr a-du-[mu]	responsible: Adumu
ugula Íd-pa-è	overseer Idpae
kišib Lú-dingir-ra	seal Ludingirra
mu ^{d}Šu-^{d}EN.ZU lugal Uri$_5^{ki}$-ma-ke$_4$	ŠS 6
na-rú-a-maḫ ^{d}En-líl ^{d}Nin-líl-ra mu-ne-rú	
Seal	
Lú-dingir-ra	Ludingirra
dub-sar	scribe
dumu Ḫa-ba-lug-gé	son of Ḫabalugge

The few sealed tablets of this scribe all date to Šu-Sîn and deal with irrigation or rations.

no. 170 (ŠS 6) [copy]

Obverse	
12 guruš ḫun-gá	12 hired workmen
^{giš}dìḫ ku$_5$-a ù ^{ú}numun$_2$ bù-ra 20 sar-ta	thorny weed and weed to be cut
a-šà ^{d}Nin-ur$_4$-ra	in the field of Ninurra
gana$_2$ Lugal-kù-zu	land of Lugalkuzu
Reverse	
gìr Ur-^{d}Ma-mi	responsible: Ur-Mami
kišib Ur-^{giš}gigir	seal of Urgigir
mu ^{d}Šu-^{d}EN.ZU lugal-e	ŠS 6
na-rú-a maḫ mu-rú	
Seal	
Ur-^{giš}gigir	Urgigir
dub-sar	scribe
dumu Ba-ša$_6$ (lion representation)	son of Baša

no. 171 (ŠS 3) [copy]

Obverse	
10.56½ guruš šà-gu$_4$ u$_4$-1-šè	656½ workmen (to serve as) ox-drivers for 1 day
^{giš}gaba-tab gíd-da	to hold the chest-pole
á-bi 30 sila$_3$ še-ta	the wages are 30 sila
guruš-bi 15-ta	of these, 15 workmen are to work
a-šà ^{d}Šul-pa-è	in the field of Šulpae
ugula Lugal-^{d}Ištaran	overseer Lugal-Ištaran
Reverse	
kišib Inim-^{d}Šara$_2$	seal Inim-Šara
mu ^{d}Šu-^{d}EN.ZU lugal-e	ŠS 3
<Si->ma-núm^{ki} mu-ḫul	
Seal	
Inim-^{d}Šara$_2$	Inim-Šara
dub-sar	scribe
dumu Ur-ni$_9$-gar kuš$_7$	son of Urnigar the equerry

^{giš}gaba-tab is the wooden pole of one *nindan* length (6 m.), held against the chest. All the members in a team of 10 or 12 laborers advance in a single line, dropping seeds by hand into each furrow. This was done for the fields where the regular plowing and seeding with the plow was impossible. One must wonder at the low wages of the guruš, only 2 sila of barley per day. The 15 guruš needed around 44 days to perform this task.

Urnigar had several children, all scribes active in the Umma administration (though there could have been than one Urnigar). His son, Inim-Šara, active during the reign of Amar-

Sîn, had many seals (12 or 13). In two of them Urnigar is qualified as kuš$_7$, equerry. He even has a small tablet dated to the middle of his active life where he is not given the title of dub-sar. According to his tablets, he appears to have been restricted to the agricultural sector.

no. 172 (ŠS 5) [copy]

Obverse	
1 bùr 1 ešè gana$_2$ ^{giš}[ùr]	1 bur and 1 ese of field to harrow
a-[rá 3 4½ iku gana$_2$-ta]	team of 3, at the rate of 4½ iku
á erin$_2$-na u$_4$ 11-[kam]	work (performed) by workgangs in 11 days
a-šà du$_6$-giš-ì-ka	for the field Dugiši
ugula Ab-ba-sig$_5$	overseer Abbasig
kišib Lú-^{d}Šara$_2$	seal of Lu-Šara
Reverse	
mu-ús-sa ^{d}Šu-^{d}EN.ZU lugal Uri$_5$^{ki}-ma-ke$_4$	ŠS 5
bàd mar-tu mu-dù	
Seal	
Lú-^{d}Šara$_2$	Lu-Šara
dub-sar	scribe
dumu Ur-^{giš}gigir	son of Urgigir

After plowing it was necessary to smooth out the surface of the field by breaking the large clods of hard, dried soil with the harrow. The work was done by team of three and an ox. An ugula and kišib is always active in this instance. It could also be accomplished by hand, expressed in by the words la-ag ab-sin-ta ri-ri-ga "clods cleared from the furrow."

no. 173 (ŠS 5) [copy]

Obverse	
1 ešè 3 iku gana$_2$ tuk-še-sig$_{18}$	1 eše 1 iku to plow per deep-going plow
túg-gur$_8$ 1 ubu 1 sar gana$_2$-ta ^{giš}ùr-ra a-rá 3	1 ubu 1 sar per plow;
4½ iku gana$_2$-ta	4½ iku by a team of 3 (men)
á erin$_2$-na-bi u$_4$ 1.30	90 workgang days
1 bùr gana$_2$ túg-ŠE.KIN	1 bur to plow
1 ubu 1 sar gana$_2$-ta giš a-rá 3	1 ubu 1 sar per plow, harrowed
4½ iku gana$_2$-ta	4½ iku by a team of 3 (men)
á erin$_2$-na-bi u$_4$ 1.46	106 workgang days
Reverse	
1 bùr 1 ešè 3 iku gana$_2$ giš-ùr-ra a-rá 2	1 bur 1 eše 3 iku land harrowed a second time
4½ iku gana$_2$-ta	4½ iku by a team of 2 (men)
á erin$_2$-na-bi u$_4$ 54	54 workgang days
a-šà muru$_{13}$	field Muru
ugula Lugal-iti-da	overseer Lugalitida

kišib Mes-é	seal of Mese
mu-ús-sa bàd mar-tu ba-dù	ŠS 5
Seal	
Mes-é	Mese
dub-sar	scribe
dumu Da-da	son of Dada

Given the area and the plowing and harrowing to be performed per workmen, the scribe could determine the workdays needed. All this work is done in 3 parcels of the field Muru.

This seal engraving depicts three participants in a royal audience with a star disk-crescent above; the *anzu*-bird is under the inscription (ENES 645, Nikolsky pl. 3).

no. 174 (ŠS 6) [copy]

Obverse	
2 bùr gana$_2$ giš-ùr-ra	2 bur of land to harrow
a-rá 3 4½ iku gana$_2$-ta	team of 3 at the rate of 4½ iku
á erin$_2$-na-bi u$_4$ [1.12]	[72] workgang days
[ ] giš-ùr-ra	[ ] land to harrow
[a-rá 3] 4½ iku gana$_2$-ta	team of 3 at the rate of 4½ iku
[á erin$_2$-na]-bi u$_4$ [$21^{5}/_{6}$]	[$21^{5}/_{6}$] workgang days
Reverse	
a-šà me-en-kár	field Menkar
ugula Gú-tar	overseer Gutar
kišib Šeš-kal-la	seal of Šeškalla
mu na-rú-a maḫ ba-rú	ŠS 6
Seal	
Šeš-kal-la	Šeškalla
dub-sar	scribe
dumu Na-[di]	son of Na[di]

Harrowing was performed by a team of 3 persons, a guruš-workman, and a ox, which explains the regular form a-rá 3-kam and not that the work was done three times by one person.

The scribe Šeš-kal-la owns five seals, the first one dedicated to Ur-Lisi the governor of Umma. He was like in this tablet mostly busy with labor work in the fields during the reigns of Šulgi, Amar-Sîn and Šu-Sîn.

no. 175 (ŠS 9) [copy]

Obverse	
1 ešè 2 iku gana$_2$ a-šà bala-a 9-ta	1 eše 2 iku of land, a field provided with 9 furrows,
a-šà a-ba-gal-^{giš}ì-šub-ba	the field Abagal-išub
gana$_2$ engar-zi	the field Engarzi
Reverse	
nu-banda$_3$ gu$_4$ Šeš-kal-la	lieutenant of the oxen Šeškalla
kišib Ur-àm-ma	seal Uramma
mu é ^{d}Šara$_2$ ba-dù	ŠS 9
Seal	
Ur-àm-ma	Uramma
dumu Lugal-ezem	son of Lugalezem
sukkal lugal	vizier of the king

The meaning of the first line is unclear. Since no activity was performed nine times, most likely 9-ta refers to nine furrows, although ten is a more common figure. The type of field may be bala-a, a category not clearly defined. Apparently in this type of field the number of furrows was slightly less than in the fields with good soil.

This seal is known from only one other tablet from the reign of Šulgi. Sparse attestation of the use of a seal, which can extend over two or three reigns, is an indicator of the many tablets still missing. If all these men were in charge of agriculture, it is likely they would have sealed hundred of tablets, of which only a few have been found.

no. 176 (ŠS 9) [copy]

Obverse	
2 bùr 4 iku gana$_2$ a-šà bala-a 10 lá-1-ta	2 bur 4 iku land prepared for 9 furrows
a-šà a-ba-gal-gu-la	field Abagalgula
3 iku gana$_2$ a-šà bala-a [9]-ta	3 iku land returned prepared for [9 furrows]
Reverse	
a-šà igi-é-maḫ-šè	field in front of the Emaḫ
Lú-dingir-ra-ke$_4$	Ludingirra
šu sum-mu-dam	will hand over
mu é ^{d}Šara$_2$ ba-dù	ŠS 9
Seal	
Lú-dingir-ra	Ludingirra
dub-sar	scribe
dumu Ḫé-ma-túm	son of Ḫematum

Ludingirra is to prepare the land for seeding, with nine furrows since it is a bala-a field, slightly inferior to a regular field.

Three seals of this scribe are attested. Ḫematum is involved with labor for agricultural duties.

no. 177 (ŠS 9)

Obverse

[x ešè é-duru$_5$ 3 sa] 9-ta	… eše of the enclosure … with 9 furrows
a-šà ukù-nu-ti	field Ukunuti
2 ešè é-duru$_5$ 3 sa 9-ta	… eše of the enclosure … with 9 furrows
1 ešè 4 iku é-duru$_5$ 3 sa 9-ta Ur-^{d}[ ]	1 eše 4 iku of the enclosure with 9 furrows Ur[…]

Reverse

a-šà bala-a	field …
Ur-^{d}Šul-pa-è-ke$_4$	Ur-Šulpae
šu sum-mu-dam	will hand over
mu é ^{d}Šara$_2$ ba-dù	ŠS 9

Seal

Ur-^{d}Šul-pa-è	Ur-Šulpae
dub-sar	scribe
dumu Lugal-kù-ga-ni	son of Lugalkugani

Ur-Šulpae is rarely involved with field work. A clear understanding of this document is difficult. The significance of the compound verb šu sum-mu-dam and of the expression é-duru$_5$ 3 sa is unclear.

no. 178

Obverse

1 su$_7$ 12 gur	1 measure of fallow land needing 12 gur (of seeding grain)
šà aga$_3$-uš A-kal-la-ke$_4$-ne 6-kam	for the 6 soldiers of Akalla
Ab-ba-gi-na in-uru$_4$	Abbagina plowed
2 su$_7$ 10 gur É-gi$_4$-a ù Ur-èš-dam íb-uru$_4$	2 measures of fallow land needing 10 gur Egia and Ur-ešdam plowed
1 su$_7$ 8 gur Lugal-é-maḫ-e in-uru$_4$	1 measure of fallow land needing 8 gur Lugalemaḫe plowed
šà saḫar-ra ugula Lugal-mu-ma-ág	for the men busy with the field work, overseer Lugalmumag
1 su$_7$ 2 gur šukur ^{giš}dúr-gar-ni [ ]	1 measure of fallow land needing 2 gur, *šukur*-ration of Durgarni (…)
A-kal-la muḫaldim in-uru$_4$	Akalla the cook plowed

1 su_7 3 gur šukur šà saḫar-ra	1 measure of fallow land needing 3 gur ration for the men busy with the field work,
Ur-lugal dumu Da-a-gi_4 in-uru_4	Ur-lugal son of Dagi plowed
1 su_7 6 gur šukur šà saḫar-ra	1 measure of fallow land needing 6 gur ration for the men busy with the field work,
Lugal-ukken-né-me! in-uru_4	(the men of) Lugalukkene plowed
Reverse	
ugula Lugal-mu-ma-ág	overseer Lugalmumag
1 su_7 1; 2.0. gur	1 measure of fallow land needing 1;2. gur
Lugal-nesag-e	Lugalnesage
1 su_7 4 gur šà A-tu [dumu] Lugal-á-zi-da [in-uru_4]	1 measure of fallow land needing 4 gur from Atu [son of] Lugalazida [plowed]
Lugal-nesag-e nu-$banda_3$ gu_4 [ ]	Lugalnesage the lieutenant of the oxen [...]
1 su_7 30 gur Lugal-nesag-e nu-$banda_3$ nu-$banda_3$-gu_4	1 measure of fallow land needing 30 gur Lugalnesage, a lieutenant, lieutenant of the oxen
1 su_7 3 gur Lú-sig_5 dumu Ur-ág-mu	1 measure of fallow land needing 3 gur Lusig son of Uragmu
su_7 šu-sum-ma ki-su_7 a-šà $muru_{13}$	1 measure of fallow land handed over for a threshing floor in the field Muru
mu [ ] kišib Lugal-kù-ga-ni	instead of [ ] seal of Lugalkugani
[ ] mu en šè	
Seal	
Lugal-kù-ga-ni	Lugalkugani
dumu Lú-^{d}Nin-[ur_4-ra]	son of Lu-Nin[urra]

No other tablet of this type is known. The word su_7 could be the threshing floor (*maškattu*) or the *nidītu* (fallow land) put again in use. For each plot of fallow land the barley needed by the plowman for seeding (šukur šà saḫar-ra) is listed. This summary tablet is for the use of the land registrars, who kept track of every piece of land as well as the laborer required for it.

no. 179 (AS 5) [copy]

Obverse	
12 guruš u_4 33-šè	12 workmen for 33 days
ki-su_7 a-šà ^{d}Nin-ur_4-ra-ka gub-ba	stationed at the threshing flour of the field of Ninurra
ugula Lugal-kù-zu	overseer Lugalkuzu
Reverse	
kišib nam-šà-tam	seal of the high administrator's office
Ì-kal-[la]	Ikalla
mu en unu_6-gal ^{d}Inanna ba-ḫun	AS 5

Seal

Ì-kal-la	Ikalla
dub-sar	the scribe
dumu Lú-ša$_6$-ga	son of Lu-šaga

Immediately after the harvest, the stack of barley was brought to the threshing floor, where it was trampled by oxen or beaten with a flail. Tossed into the air, the wind would blow away the chaff while the heavier grain would fall down.

Ikalla has three known seals. Active during the reigns from Šulgi to Ibbi-Sîn, he rarely was involved with the labor force, more often with clothes, reeds, and reed mats.

no. 180 (AS 6 viii) [copy]

Obverse

1.02; 2.0. še [numun gur-lugal]	62 2/5 gur of old barley according to the royal measurement
bar-ta-gál-la	outside of the account
gìr Lú-gi-na	responsible: Lugina
9 gur á lú ḫun-gá	9 gur, wages of the hired men
kišib Ur-dun	seal of Urdun
1 še <gur> šukur guruš kišib Íd-pa-è	1 gur of barley, ration for workmen, seal of Idpae
0; 3.0. še-numun kišib Ur-^{giš}gigir	180 sila of old barley seal of Urgigir
dumu Ur-kal-la	seal of Urkalla

Reverse

0; 2.0. á lú ḫun-gá	2/5 gur wages for the hired men
kišib Da-du	seal of Dadu
0; 2.0. še šukur kišib A-kal-la dumu ^{d}Utu-mu	2/5 gur rations seal of Akalla son of Utumu
kišib A-kal-la nu-banda$_3$	seal of Akalla the lieutenant
šu-nigín 63 gur	total 63 gur
gur še-numun-ta	gur of the old barley
šu-nigín 10; 4.0. gur sá-du$_{11}$	total 10 4/5 gur according to the *satukku* measurement
ki-su$_7$ a-šà ^{d}Nin-[ur$_4$-ra]	threshing floor of the field of Nin[urra]
gìr A-kal-la nu-banda$_3$	responsible: Akalla the lieutenant
iti é-iti-6	month 8

Edge

mu a-rá 2-kam Ša-aš-ru-um ba-ḫul	AS 6

This tablet reviews the grain stored on the threshing floor at the close of the season's activities, in preparation for the next harvest. A gìr certifies the correctness of this summary tablet.

no. 181 (ŠS 5) [copy]

Obverse	
1.10 lá-1 guruš u_4-1-šè	69 workmen for 1 day
ki-su_7 a-šà ^{d}Nin-ur_4-ra gub-ba	stationed at the threshing floor of the field of Ninurra
ugula Lugal-kù-zu	overseer Lugalkuzu
Reverse	
kišib Ur-^{d}Šul-pa-è	seal of Ur-Šulpae
mu-ús-sa bàd mar-tu ba-dù	ŠS 5
Seal	
[Ur-^{d}Šul-pa-è	[Ur-Šulpae
dub sar	scribe
dumu Lugal-kù-ga-ni]	son of Lugalkugani]

no. 182 (ŠS 5) [copy]

Obverse	
40 lá-1 guruš u_4-1-šè	39 workmen for 1 day
ki-su_7 a-šà ^{giš}ma-nu gub-ba	stationed on the threshing floor of the field of willow
ugula Ur-mes	overseer Urmes
kišib ^{d}$Šara_2$-ba-an-zi-ge	seal of Šara-banzige
Reverse	
mu-ús-sa ^{d}Šu-^{d}EN.ZU lugal-e	ŠS 5
bàd mar-tu mu-dù	
Seal	
Ur-^{d}Li_9-si_4	Ur-Lisi
$ensi_2$ $Umma^{ki}$	governor of Umma
dumu ^{d}$Šara_2$-ba-zi-ge	son of Šara-bazige
dub-sar ir_{11}-zu	the scribe is your servant

no. 183 (ŠS 8)

Obverse	
20 [ ]	20 [ ]
saḫar-[ ]-me-bi	… [ ]
en-gaba-rá-ta	from the field Engabara
En-za-gu	Enzagu

Reverse

mu má-gur$_8$ maḫ	ŠS 5

Seal illegible

no. 184 (ŠS 5) [copy]

Obverse

[0]; 4.5.8 sila$_3$ ninda sig$_5$ gur	[ ] 298 sila of top-quality bread
2.42; 0.3.1 sila$_3$ ninda gin gur	162 gur 31 sila of average-quality bread
4; 1.1.7 sila$_3$ ninda zì-gu gur	4 gur 77 sila of bread with pea-flour
šaggina ensi$_2$	for the military governor (of) the governor
3; 3.2. ninda gin gur	3⅖ gur of average-quality bread

Reverse

nu-banda$_3$ u$_4$ 2-kam	for the lieutenant for 2 days
ki á-u$_4$-da	for the daily wages
gìr Ir$_{11}$-^{d}Šara$_2$	responsible: Ir-Šara
kišib Ḫu-wa-wa	tablet of Ḫuwawa
mu-ús-sa ^{d}Šu-^{d}EN.ZU lugal Uri$_5$^{ki}-ma-ke$_4$	ŠS 5
bàd mar-tu mu-dù	

Seal

Lú-ib-gal	Lu-ibgal
dub-sar	scribe
dumu Ur-gi$_6$-par$_4$	son of Urgipar
gudu$_4$ ^{d}Inanna	purification-priest of Inanna

The expression ki á-u$_4$-da is unique. á-u$_4$-da is well known as wages for a day's work. One could interpret it as "at the place where the wages are distributed" or "as (=ki) daily wages." A gìr is supervising this distribution as high officials are involved.

Lu-ibgal has at least three seals from Šulgi to Šu-Sîn. His last seal, from the reign of Šu-Sîn, adds a fourth line in the inscription: gudu$_4$ ^{d}Inanna. Remarkable is the fact that on all the tablets sealed by Lu-ibgal, we find kišib Ḫuwawa. It is difficult to understand the working relationship between these two functionaries.

The following texts deal with the sick persons (tu-ra). In order to keep straight the ledgers, it was necessary to keep records of the sick persons, who had to be fed and replaced at work.

no. 185 (ŠS 5 ix–xi)

Obverse

tu-ra Lú-^{d}Ìr-ra	sick man Lu-Irra
iti ^{d}Li$_9$-si$_4$-ta	from month 9
iti pa$_4$-kùš-e-šè	to month 11

Reverse	
ugula Lú-du$_{10}$-ga	overseer Lu-duga
kišib Kaš$_4$	seal of Kaš
mu-ús-sa ^{d}Šu-^{d}EN.ZU lugal-e	ŠS 5
bàd mar-tu ba-dù	
Seal	
En-kaš$_4$	Enkaš
dub-sar	scribe
dumu Ur-^{d}Ištaran	son of Ur-Ištaran

Enkaš was busy from Šulgi through Ibbi-Sîn. One of his seals is dedicated to Ur-Lisi, the governor of Umma, and the latest is dedicated to Ibbi-Sîn. His activity mainly concerns the work of guruš workmen. Note that on the tablets the name inscribed on the seal is En-kaš$_4$ yet the name on the actual tablet is simply Kaš$_4$. Our reading kaš$_4$ may not be correct; some propose girim$_2$.

no. 186 (ŠS 7) [copy]

Obverse	
tu-ra Lú-bala-sig$_5$	sick man Lu-balasig
iti ri-ta	from month 5
iti ^{d}Li$_9$-si$_4$-šè	to month 9
Reverse	
ugula Lú-dingir-ra	overseer Ludingirra
kišib Lú-^{d}Šul-gi-ra	seal Lu-Šulgira
mu ma-da Za-ab-ša-li^{ki} ba-ḫul	ŠS 7
Seal	
Lú-^{d}Šul-gi-ra	Lu-Šulgira
dub-sar	scribe
dumu Da-da-ga	son of Dadaga

Another category of workers were the un-íl workers, which are the subject of the following texts. un-íl can work alongside guruš, but there status seems to be lower.

no. 187 (Š48)

Obverse	
1 un-<íl> Lú-dingir-ra	1 un-il Ludingirra
iti pa$_4$-kùš-e-ta	from month 11
1 un-<íl> Ba-zi-ge	1 un-il Bazige
iti ^{d}Dumu-zi-ta	from month 12

Reverse

mu-ús-sa Ki-maš^{ki} ba-ḫul-ta	from the year following the year Kimaš was destroyed
ugula Ù-dag-ga	overseer Udagga
kišib Ir$_{11}$ ugula	seal of Ir the overseer
mu Ḫa-ar-ši^{ki} ba-ḫul-šè	Š 48

Seal

Ù-dag-ga	Udagga
dumu Ú-[da-li]	son of U[dali]
ir$_{11}$ ^{d}[Šara$_{2}$]	servant of [Šara]

no. 188 (Š 41)

Obverse

4.30 un-íl u$_{4}$-1-šè	270 un-il for 1 workday
ú sig$_{7}$-a la-ag ab-sín-ta	cutting grass and collecting clods from the
ri-ri-ga a-šà lá-maḫ	furrows in the field Lamaḫ
a-šà gana$_{2}$ Ur-gu	in the field Urgu

Reverse

ù a-šà lá-tur	and the field Latur
ugula Šeš-kal-la	overseer Šeškalla
kišib Lú-gi-na	seal of Lugina
mu-ús-sa é Puzur$_{4}$-Da-gan	Š 41
ba-dù mu-ús-sa-bi	

Seal

Lú-gi-na	Lugina
dumu É-gal-e-si	son of Egal-esi

All agricultural or irrigation work necessitated at least two tablets, one to indicate the nature of work to be performed, the other the manpower required. This information could have been combined onto a single tablet, but distinct offices needed separate information—one for the labor needed, the other a highly sophisticated definition of the task to be performed, fixed by the administration of the land.

no. 189 (AS 1 viii) [copy]

Obverse

21 un-íl 40 sìla	21 un-il receiving 40 sila (of barley per month)
u$_{4}$-1-šè	for a day work
kun-zi-da íd ^{d}Nin-ḫur-sag gub-ba	stationed at the dam of the Ninḫursag canal

Reverse

iti é-iti-6	month 8
mu ^{d}Amar-^{d}EN.ZU lugal	AS 1

Seal

Ur-[e_{11}-e]	Uree
dub-sar	scribe
dumu Ur-[ni_9-gar]	son of Ur-nigar

Compare the 40 sila barley per month with the 180 sila given to some laborers, guruš. These small rations would have been very inadequate for heavy field work if not supplemented with other food, not recorded on these tablets.

no. 190 (AS 3 i)

Obverse

Ab-ba-mu šeš Nir-ì-da-gál	Abbamu brother of Niridagal
Ma-an-sum	Mansum
Ì-la-a dumu Ki-gi-na	Ilaa son of Kigina
Lú-^{d}EN.ZU dumu dab_5-ba-me	Lu-Sîn, all young captured people
Ba-an-zi-ge	Banzige
Ur-numun-du_{10}-ga	Urnumunduga
Ur-mes	Urmes
$geme_2$ Ur-sag-pa-è dumu Ba-an-zi-ge-me	the daughter of Ursagpae, the children of Banzige
Nì-^{d}Ba-ba_6	Ni-Baba
un-íl-me	they are un-il
5 guruš ⅔ $geme_2$	5 workmen ⅔ of workwomen time
iti maš-dù-kú-ta	from month 2
iti še-kin-ku_5-šè	to month 1
á-bi 15.10 guruš dumu ḫun u_4-1-šè	their work 910 workdays for young hired men
á-bi 18.25 guruš un-íl u_4-1-šè	their work 1105 workdays un-il working time
á-bi 4.20 $geme_2$ u_4-1-šè	their work 260 workwomen days
iti 13-kam	13 months
šà-ba iti diri 1-àm ì-gál	the year having an intercalary month
Dan-ì-lí	Dan-ili

Reverse

A-ma-an-bí-in	Amanbin
Gu-la	Gula
$Puzur_4$-É-a	Puzur-Ea
Mu-mu	Mumu
dumu-dab_5-ba-me	their are captured young men
2 guruš	2 workmen
iti maš-dù-kú-ta	from month 2
iti á-ki-ti-šè	to month 7

á-bi 6 guruš dumu ḫun u_4-1-šè	their work 6 workmen days for young hired men
iti 6-kam	for 6 months
Ma-ka-ùb-ba	Maka-ubba
Ir_{11}-dam	Irdam
⅔ guruš	⅔ guruš time
iti ezem-[d]Šul-gi-ta	from month 8
iti še-kin-ku_5-šè	to month 1
á-bi 2.20 guruš dumu ḫun u_4-1-šè	their work 140 workmen days for young hired men
iti 7-kam	7 months
šà-ba iti diri 1-àm ì-gál	the year having an intercalary month
šu-nigín 23.30 á guruš dumu ḫun u_4-1-šè	total 1410 workmen days for young hired men
šu-nigín 18.25 á guruš un-íl u_4-1-šè	total 1105 workmen days of un-il
šu-nigín 4.20 á $geme_2$ u_4-1-šè	total 260 workwomen days
Bù-lu_5-lu_5 ì-dab_5	Bululu has taken into possession
mu gu-za [d]En-líl-lá ba-dím	AS 3

no. 191 (AS 6) [copy]

This tablet records a work contract.

Obverse	
| Lú-[d]$Šara_2$ dumu La-al-ú-a	Lu-Šara son of Lalua
iti šu-numun-ta	from month 6
ki Lugal-nesag-e-ta	from Lugalnesage
Ur-mes ì-dab_5	Urmes has taken into possession
Reverse	
kišib Lugal-é-maḫ-e	seal of Lugalemaḫe
mu Ša-aš-ru[ki] ba-ḫul	AS 6
Seal	
Lugal-é-maḫ-e	Lugalemaḫe
dub-sar	scribe
dumu Lugal-kù-ga-ni	son of Lugalkugani

Lu-Šara is transferred from the authority of Lugalnesage to Urmes, probably from one team to another or even from one household to another. Lugalemaḫe, whose activity involves guruš workmen, supervises the transfer.

no. 192 (ŠS 7) [copy]

Obverse	
2.0.20+[še gur lugal]	7220+[ ] gur [barley according to the royal measurement]
lú-šukur-e-[ne]	for the rationaries
šà saḫar-ra ù lú šukur dab$_5$-ba	working in the soil and the rationaries who were captured
ensi$_2$ Umma$^{\langle ki\rangle}$-ka	of the governor of Umma
Reverse	
mu ^{d}Šu-^{d}EN.ZU lugal Uri$_5$^{ki}-ma-<ke$_4$>	ŠS 7
ma-da Za-ab-ša-li^{ki} mu-ḫul-<<ke>>	

The lú-šukur are rationaries, whose status is difficult to differentiate from guruš or un-íl as these groups too received rations, še-ba or šà-gal.

šà saḫar designates all the guruš and other workers busy with moving soil for the irrigation or preparing fields for seeding.

no. 193 (ŠS 7) [copy]

This work contract is similar to no. 191. Here the description of the job is given, to watch the sheepfold.

Obverse	
1 guruš	1 workman
iti sig$_4$-giš-ì-šub-ba-gar-ta	from month 2
iti nesag-šè	to month 4
é-udu-ka gub-ba	stationed in the sheepfold
ugula Ur-àm-ma	overseer Uramma
Reverse	
kišib I-šar-ru-um	seal Išarrum
mu ma-da Za-ab-ša-li^{ki} ba-ḫul	ŠS 7
Seal	
I-šar-ru-um	Išarrum
dub-sar	scribe
dumu Ur-^{d}En-líl-lá	son of Ur-Enlilla

Išarrum is attested for only four years during the reign of Šu-Sîn.

no. 194 (ŠS 6 x – ŠS 7 i) [copy]

Obverse	
2 guruš	2 workmen
iti ezem-^{d}Šul-gi	from month 8
mu ^{d}Šu-^{d}EN.ZU lugal-e	of the year ŠS 6

^{d}En-líl ^{d}Nin-líl-ra	
na-rú-a maḫ mu-ne-rú-ta	
Reverse	
iti še-kin-ku$_{5}$ mu ^{d}Šu-^{d}EN.ZU lugal-e	to month 1 of the year ŠS 7
ma-da Za-ab-ša-li^{ki} mu-ḫul-šè	
é-udu-ka gub-ba	stationed in the sheepfold
ugula Ur-mes	overseer Urmes
kišib I-šar-ru-um	seal of Išarrum
Seal	
I-šar-ru-um	Išarrum
dub-sar	scribe
dumu Ur-^{d}En-líl-lá	son of Ur-Enlilla

no. 195 (AS 9 viii)

Obverse	
6 guruš	6 workmen
u$_{4}$ 5-àm	5 days
ki A-tu-ta	from Atu
Kù-ga-ni ì-dab$_{5}$	Kugani has taken into possession
iti é-iti-6	month 8
Reverse	
mu-ús-sa	AS 9
en Eridu^{ki} ba-ḫun-gá	

no. 196 (Š37) [copy]

Obverse	
1.11 á geme$_{2}$	71 workwomen
u$_{4}$-1-šè	for 1 day
4 túg gú-anše	4 garments …
ki A-kal-la-ta	from Akalla
ugú Kù-ga-ni ba-a-gar	on the account of Kugani
Reverse	
kišib Lugal-ezem	seal of Lugalezem
á zì-àr-a	wages for grinding flour
mu bàd ba-[dù]	Š 37
Seal 1	
Lugal-ezem dub-sar	Lugalezem scribe
dumu Lugal-é-maḫ-e	son of Lugalemaḫe
šabra	steward

Seal 2	
A-kal-la	Akalla
dub-sar	scribe
dumu Lugal-nì-lagar-e	son of Lugalnilagare
aga$_3$-uš lugal	soldier of the king

no. 197 (Š 46) [copy]

Obverse	
1.0 še gur-lugal	60 gur of barley according to the royal measurement
ì-dub ^{giš}asál-ta	from the silo of the poplar
ki Ba-zi-ta	from Bazi
á geme$_2$ àr-šè	for the wages of the grinder women
mu Lugal-^{d}Igi-ma-šè	instead of the seal of Lugal-Igimaše
kišib Lugal-Anzu^{mušen}	seal of Lugal-Anzu (was used)
kišib Ur-^{d}Nin-giš-zi-da	seal of Ur-Ningišzida
Reverse	
ù kišib Ur-^{d}Nanše	and the seal of Ur-Nanše
iti munu$_4$-kú	month 5
mu-ús-sa Ur-bí-lum^{ki} ba-ḫul	Š 46
Seal 1	
Ur-^{d}Nin-giš-zi-da	Ur-Ningišzida
gu-za-lá	throne-bearer
dumu Igi-[ ]	son of [ ]
Seal 2	
Lugal-Anzu^{mušen}	Lugal-Anzu
dub-sar	scribe
dumu Ba-[ ]	son of Ba-[ ]
Seal 3	
Ur-^{d}Nanše	Ur-Nanše
dub-sar	scribe
dumu A-	son of [ ]
[ ]	[ ]

no. 198 (ŠS 3 vi) [copy]

Obverse	
5 še gur	5 gur of barley
á geme$_2$ ḫun-gá	wages for the work of hired women
kišib Ur-^{d}Nu-muš-da	seal of Ur-Numušda

Reverse

še gibil é-àr ús-sa é im-sar-ta	fresh barley of the mill next to the tablet building
iti šu-numun	month 6
mu-ús-sa má ^{d}En-ki ba-ab-du$_{8}$	ŠS 3

Seal

[Ur-^{d}Nu-muš-da	[Ur-Numušda
dub-sar	scribe
dumu Lugal-gu$_{4}$-e]	son of Lugalgue]

no. 199 (AS 1 xii15) [copy]

Obverse

| Lugal-íb-gu-ul	Lugalibgul
| ^{d}Šara$_{2}$-ì-ša$_{6}$ é kuš$_{7}$-ta	Šara-iša from the house of the equerry
| Lugal-mu-ma-ág	Lugalmumag
A-ši-dingir ì-dab$_{5}$	Ašidingir has taken into possession (under his orders)

Reverse

iti ^{d}Dumu-zi-ta	month 12
u$_{4}$ 15 ba-ra-zal	the 15th day has elapsed
mu Amar-^{d}EN.ZU lugal	AS 1

Seal

A-ši-dingir	Ašidingir
ir$_{11}$-^{d}Šara$_{2}$	servant of Šara
dumu Lugal-ša$_{6}$-ga	son of Lugalšaga

Ašidingir has five attested seals. He worked in the administration from the reign of Šulgi to that of Šu-Sîn. He was concerned with agricultural tasks and irrigation. Like those responsible for donkey fodder, he was a servant of Šara, probably in charge of the administration of one of his temples.

no. 200 (ŠS 5 i 23)

The scribes would write daily inspection tablets such as this one, to keep track of all the persons on the team.

Obverse

3 guruš uru$_{4}$-lá	3 workmen for plowing
24 guruš šà-gu$_{4}$	24 workmen (as) ox-drivers
14 geme$_{2}$	14 women
šu-nigín 27 guruš 14 geme$_{2}$	total 27 workmen and 14 workwomen

Reverse

50 giš šeg$_{6}$ íb-šà	50 pieces of dried wood gathered(?)

gurum$_2$-ak a-šà [ ] gu$_4$	inspection (of the workers) in the field [ ]
iti še-kin-ku$_5$ u$_4$ 23 ba-zal	month 1 day 23
mu-ús-sa bàd mar-tu ba-dù	ŠS 5

It is difficult to determine what exactly occurred in the field. It appears that approximately one person was needed to carry a tree. šà as a verb is unique.

no. 201 (ŠS 2 vi) [copy]

Obverse

34 šà-bi-ta	34 (men); from them
5 im íl bahar$_3$	5 clay carriers (for) the potter
2 nì-dab$_5$ ^{giš}kin-ti	2 (working with) material for the artisan
šà Uri$_5$^{ki}-ma	in Ur
6 má-lá-a giš	6 (men for) the raft with wood
15 gá-nun	15 (men) in the atelier storehouse
šà é-temen-na	in the Etemena
2 má hun-gá ka sahar [ ] šè gur	2 (men for the) hired boats with earth [ ] gur of barley
1 [ ]	1 [ ]
1 [ ]	1 [ ]

Reverse

šu-nigín 32 guruš	total 32 workmen
zi-ga-àm	disbursement
lá-ni | ^{d}Šara$_2$-kam	difference 1 Šarakam
| Lú-kal-la	1 Lukalla
lá-ni-àm	is the difference
nì-ka$_9$-ak Ur-é-maš	account of Uremaš
bala 5-àm im-da-gál	it is the 5th turn
iti šu-numun	month 6
mu má ^{d}En-ki	ŠS 2

no. 202 (Š 32)

Additional flour(?) for a festival. sig$_7$-a is a category of workers.

Obverse

3; 2.2.5? sila$_3$ zì?	3 gur and 145(?) sila of flour(?)
nì diri u$_4$-sakar-ra sig$_7$-a-ka	supplementary provisions for the new moon festival for the sig$_7$-a
mu-ús-sa a-rá 3-kam	Š 32
Si-mu-ru-um^{ki} ba-hul	

Reverse	
iti [ ]	month [ ]
im-e daḫ-ḫe-[dam]	to be added on the tablet
Seal	
Ur-^{d}Šara$_2$	Ur-Šara
dub-sar	scribe
dumu Lugal-nanga	son of Lugalnanga
nu-banda$_3$-gu$_4$-^{d}Šara$_2$	lieutenant of the oxen of Šara

This tablet, sealed by Ur-Šara, is one of the earliest of the Umma archive. The tablet records an additional transfer of flour on the occasion of the new moon for the sig$_7$-a, perhaps some type of crippled persons. The expression im-e daḫ-ḫe-dam is rarely found—it is a note for the scribe.

no. 203 (IS 2 i 17)

Obverse	
2 udu niga gu$_4$-e-ús-sa ^{d}Šul-gi	2 barley-fed sheep of last category for Šulgi
4 udu niga a-rá 1-kam	4 barley-fed sheep, the first portion,
4 udu niga a-rá 2-kam ^{d}[ ]	4 barley-fed sheep, the second portion, for the goddess [ ]
1 udu niga gu$_4$-e-ús-sa ^{d}Gu-la	1 barley-fed sheep of last category for Gula
2 udu niga gu$_4$-e-ús-sa ka gi$_6$-par$_4$	2 barley-fed sheep of last category for the entrance(?) of the *gipar*-building.
2 udu niga gu$_4$-e-ús-sa ^{d}Na-na-a	2 barley-fed sheep of last category for Nanaya
1 udu niga gu$_4$-e-ús-sa	1 barley-fed sheep of last category
Reverse	
^{d}Nin-sún	for Ninsun
1 udu niga gu$_4$-e-ús-sa ^{d}[ ]	1 barley-fed sheep of last category for the goddess [ ]
1 udu niga gu$_4$-e-ús-sa ^{d}[ ]	1 barley-fed sheep of last category for the goddess [ ]
ezem [ ]	(for) the festival [of]
gìr [ ]	responsible: [ ]
½ [ ]	½ [ ]
iti še-kin-ku$_5$	month 1
mu en ^{d}Inanna ba-ḫun	IS 2
Edge	
18	18

no. 204 (Š 46 viii 20)

Obverse	
1 gu_4 ú	1 grass-fed ox
2 udu niga sá-du_{11}	2 barley-fed sheep for regular delivery
1 udu ú	1 grass-fed sheep
1 máš-gal	1 full-grown goat
ezem na-ab-rí-um an-nu-ni-tum	for the *nabrium*-festival of the Annunitum
Reverse	
šà Uri_5^{ki}-ma	in Ur
gìr Ur-^{d}Dumu-zi-da	responsible: Ur-Dumuzida
iti-ta u_4 20 ba-ra-zal	the 20th day having elapsed
iti šu-eš-ša	month 8
mu Ki-maš^{ki} ba-ḫul	Š 46

no. 205 (AS 1 xii 12)

Obverse	
2 gu_4 niga sag-gu_4	2 barley-fed lead oxen
5 udu niga	5 barley-fed sheep
Apin-du_{10} u_4 é-ùr-ra-na-šè nì-mussa in-ak-a	for Apindu, the day he brought the dowry into his house
1 udu niga	1 barley-fed sheep
Ki-wi lú Du_8-du_8-lí-um^{ki}	for Kiwi the man of Duduli
1 máš-gal niga	1 barley-fed full-grown goat
Ra-ši lú Zi-da-núm^{ki}	for Raši the man of Zidanum
1 udu niga	1 barley-fed sheep
Reverse	
Ama-kiš-ir	for Amakišir
é-$duru_5$-ne-ne-šè	in their encampments
gìr PU-ù sukkal	responsible: PUu the vizier
Ir_{11}-mu maškim	Irmu is the conveyer;
šà Nibru^{ki}	in Nippur
iti u_4 12-ba-zal	day 12
ki Lú-dingir-ra-ta	disbursed
ba-zi	by Ludingirra
iti še-kin-ku_5	month 12
mu ^{d}Amar-^{d}EN.ZU lugal	AS 1

no. 206 (Š 32 vii) [copy]

The *šabra* entrusts Abbamu with ovines probably for shepherding.

Obverse

12 ^{munus}ašgar	12 female kids
[ ] máš nitá	[ ] male goats
[ki] šabra-ta	from the steward
Ab-ba-mu sipa	Abbamu the shepherd

Reverse

ì-dab$_5$	has taken into possession
iti min-èš	month 6
mu Si-mu-ru-um^{ki} a-rá 3-kam ba-ḫul	Š 32

no. 207 (Š 48 v)

Obverse

2 udu kur-ra ba-ug$_7$	2 dead mountain sheep
ki Ur-ru-ta	from Urru
kišib Da-da-ga	received by Dadaga

Reverse

iti ri	month 5
mu-ús-sa Ki-maš^{ki}	Š 38
ba-ḫul mu-ús-sa-a-bi	

Seal

Lú-du$_{10}$-ga	Lu-duga
dub-sar	scribe
dumu Ur-ni$_9$-gar	son of Urnigar

Lu-duga on his later seal mentions his father as kuš$_7$. In a number of tablets he is in charge of receiving dead cattle from Urru.

no. 208 (AS 2) [copy]

Internal transfer of one donkey. The kind of transaction recorded in this tablet is unusual.

Obverse

1 dùr giš	1 jackass for the yoke
su-su Lú-du$_{10}$-ga ù-kul	returned by Lu-duga …
Ur-^{d}EN.ZU engar	Ur-Sîn the farmer
kišib Lú-du$_{10}$-ga	seal of Lu-duga

Reverse

mu ^{d}Amar-^{d}EN.ZU lugal-e	AS 2
Ur-bí-lum^{ki} mu-ḫul	

Seal	
Lú-du_{10}-ga	Lu-duga
dub-sar	scribe
dumu Ḫé-ma-túm	son of Ḫematum

This donkey was in the care of Luduga. After having been returned to the central administration, Ur-Sîn the farmer takes him into account. The profession ù-kul is not yet understood. The ù-kul is often mentioned in messenger tablets along with the lú-^{giš}tukul, probably a kind of armed man accompanying messengers or the dispatch service.

Lu-duga son of Ḫematum is usually in charge of guruš during the reigns of Amar-Sîn.

no. 209 (ŠS 2) [copy]

A scribe and a ḫa-za-núm (city mayor) make deliveries for Šara in Apisal.

Obverse	
[anše] nitá mu 3	1 male 3-year-old donkey
[ ]-ni dub-sar	[from ...]ni the scribe
1 anše-$kunga_2$ nitá mu 3	1 male 3-year-old donkey
Ur-^{d}Nu-muš-da ḫa-za-núm	from Ur-Numušda the mayor
mu-túm ^{d}$Šara_2$-A-pi_4-sal^{ki}	delivery for Šara of Apisal
Reverse	
ki Šà-kù-gi	from Šakuge
Ur-^{d}Dumu-zi-da ugula gu_4 ì-dab_5	Ur-Dumuzida the overseer of the oxen has taken into possession
mu má ^{d}En-ki ba-ab-du_8	ŠS 2
Seal	
Ur-^{d}Dumu-zi-da	Ur-Dumuzida
dumu La-a-a	son of Laaa

no. 210 (IS 2 v 10) [copy]

Obverse	
1 udu	1 sheep
ki A-bu-ù-ta	from Abuu
Lú-bala-$ša_6$-ga-ke_4	Lubalašaga
Reverse	
ì-dab_5	has taken into possession
iti ne-IZI-gar	month 5
u_4 10 ba-zal	the 10th day having elapsed
sum-mu-da	he will give (it back)
mu en ^{d}Inanna Unug^{ki} máš-e ì-pàd	IS 2
Seal	
Lugal-á-zi-da	Lugalazida

dub-sar	scribe
dumu Ur-du$_6$-kù-ga?	son of Urdukuga?

no. 211 (x) [copy]

Obverse	
1 udu ba-ug$_7$	1 dead sheep
bar-gál	with its fleece
ki Ur-ru-ta	from Urru
Šeš-kal-la	Seškalla
šu-ba-ti	received
Reverse	
iti ezem-^{d}Šul-gi	month 8
Seal	
Šeš-kal-la	Šeškalla
dub-sar	scribe
dumu Ur-ni$_9$-gar kuš$_7$	son of Urnigar the equerry

no. 212 (Š 47 vi)

Obverse	
1 šáh-izi-tur nitá ^{giš}gi	1 male boar (to be roasted)
2 tu-gur$_5^{mušen}$	2 turtle-doves
nì-kú nin-gá-šè	food for My Lady
Reverse	
1 uz-tur	1 duck
ba-ug$_7$ é-gal-la ba-an-ku$_4$	dead, brought to the palace
iti-ta u$_4$ 14 ba-ra-zal	the 14th of the month having elapsed
zi-ga ^{d}Šul-gi-ì-lí	disbursement of Šulgi-ili
iti ezem-^{d}Nin-a-zu	month 6
Edge	
mu-ús-sa Ki-maš^{ki} ba-hul	Š 47

no. 213 (ŠS 1 iii)

Obverse	
1 amar-mašda nitá	1 young male gazelle
ba-ug$_7$	dead
é-kišib-ba-šè	for the storehouse
u$_4$ 1-kam	on the first day
ki Du$_{11}$-ga-ta	disbursed
Reverse	
ba-zi	by Duga

gìr Nu-úr-^{d}Adad dub-sar	reponsible: Nur-Adad the scribe
iti u$_{5}$-bí-kú	month 4
mu ^{d}Šu-^{d}EN.ZU lugal	ŠS 1
Edge	
1 udu	1 sheep

no. 214

Obverse	
1 u$_{8}$ kun-gíd 1 sila$_{4}$-ga	1 fat-tailed ewe, 1 milk lamb
[ ] udu nitá niga ù síg-ta sa$_{10}$	[ ] barley-fed ram bought for the price of (its) wool
Lú-me-lám	Lu-melam
1 u$_{8}$ 1 sila$_{4}$ kir$_{11}$ ^{giš}ḫum	1 ewe 1 ewe-lamb …
1 udu nitá ^{giš}si nam ùr-ta	1 ram [ ]
1 u$_{8}$ Lú-^{d}Nanna a-zu	1 ewe Lu-Nanna the physician
1 udu nitá Lú-dingir-ra dumu Ir$_{11}$-ḫu-la	1 ram Ludingira son of Irḫula
é-ta	from the house
1 u$_{8}$ Za-ga-mu	1 ewe Zagamu
Reverse	
[ ] kir$_{11}$ ki [ ] sila$_{4}$ kir$_{11}$ ^{giš}ḫum	[ ] ewe-lamb [ ] ewe-lamb …
[ ] ba-gar	
1 kir$_{11}$ [ ] Ur-ni$_{9}$-gar dam-gàr	1 ewe-lamb Urnigar the merchant
1 kir$_{11}$ Lugal-[ ]	1 ewe-lamb Lugal-[ ]
1 [ ] Ḫa-ni-mu	1 [ ] Ḫanimu
1 [A]-pi$_{4}$-sal$_{4}^{ki}$	1 [A]pisal
1 u$_{8}$ [ ]-zu nar	1 ewe [ ]zu the singer

no. 215 (ŠS 3 ix 15) [copy]

Obverse	
2 sila$_{4}$ En-[ ]	2 lambs from En[ ]
1 máš Al-la-[mu]	1 goat from Allamu
1 sila$_{4}$ A-[ ]	1 lamb from A[ ]
1 sila$_{4}$ Šà-gú-bi	1 lamb from Šagubi
1 lulim Ir$_{11}$-[ ]	1 gazelle from Ir[mu]
15 udu Lú-[ ]	15 sheep from Lu[ ]
6 máš [ ]	6 goats from [ ]
6 udu Lú-[ ]	6 sheep from Lu[ ]
4 máš-gal Lú-[ ]	4 full-grown goats from Lu[ ]
1 [ ]	1 [ ]
Ṣe-lu-uš-^{d}Da-gan	from Ṣelluš-Dagan

Reverse

1 gu$_4$ niga	1 barley-fed ox
7 udu ú	7 grass-fed sheep
2 máš-gal ú	2 grass-fed full-grown goats
1 sila$_4$	1 lamb
Be-lí-ba-ni gudu$_4$	from Beli-bani the purification-priest
u$_4$-15-kam	on the 15th day
mu-túm	delivery
In-ta-è-a ì-[dab$_5$]	Intaea has taken into possession
gìr Nu-úr-^{d}EN.ZU dub-sar	responsible: Nur-Sîn the scribe
iti ezem-maḫ	month 9
mu ^{d}Šu-^{d}EN.ZU lugal-[e]	ŠS 3
Si-ma-[núm^{ki} ba-ḫul]	

Edge

1 gu$_4$ 1 lulim 46! udu (for 47)	1 ox, 1 gazelle, 47 sheep

no. 216 (AS 3 i)

Obverse

15 sila$_4$ niga šu-a-gi-na	15 barley-fed lambs, constituting the complete delivery
2 sila$_4$ niga uzu-NIM	2 barley-fed lambs of superior meat quality
1 sila$_4$ niga a-suḫuš-še	1 barley-fed lamb …
6 sila$_4$ ga ka-šeg$_6$-šè	6 milk-fed lambs for roasting
A-a-kal-la ì-dab$_5$	Aakalla has taken into possession
14 sila$_4$ niga šu-a-gi-na	14 barley-fed lambs, constituting the complete delivery
4 sila$_4$ ga ka-NE-šè	4 milk-fed lambs for roasting
Ur-^{d}Ba-ba$_6$ ì-dab$_5$	Ur-Baba has taken into possession

Reverse

sá-du$_{11}$ lugal	regular deliveries for the king
ki Na-lu$_5$-ta	disbursed
ba-zi	by Nalu
iti maš-dù-kú	month 1
mu ^{d}gu-za ^{d}En-líl-lá ba-dím	AS 3

no. 217 (Š 32 vi)

Obverse

0; 3.4.7 sila$_3$ ga muru$_{13}$ sumun lugal	227 sila of old …-milk according to the royal measurement
ki ^{giš}Dúr-gar-ni-ta	from Durgarni

Lugal-má-gur$_{8}$-re	Lugalmagurre
šu-ba-ti	received
Reverse	
iti šu-numun	month 6
mu Si-mu-ru-um	Š 32
ki a-rá 3-kam ba-ḫul	

Merchant Activities (nos. 218–221)

Weights of silver were the conventional means to express the price of items traded. In merchant's balanced accounts the price of every item is expressed in silver. Loans were often expressed directly in weights of barley or in its corresponding value in silver. In the first instance the interest rate is 33%, in the second 20%.

no. 218 (AS 5)

10 gín kù-babbar mu Ḫa-da kaš$_{4}$ ^{d}EN.ZU-šè	10 gin of silver loan Ḫada the runner of Sîn
ki Ur-^{d}EN.ZU šu-ḫa-ta	from Ur-Sîn the fisherman
5 gín ki A-kal-la muḫaldim-ta	5 gin from Akalla the cook
5 gín ki Ur-gi$_{6}$-par$_{4}$ lunga-ta	5 gin from Urgipar the brewer
5 gín ki Ur-ni$_{9}$-gar gudu$_{4}$-ta	5 gin from Urnigar the purification-priest
5 gín ki Lú-bala-sig$_{5}$-ta	5 gin from Lubalasig
maš-da-rá-a ki ensi$_{2}$-ta	*mašdaria*-offering from the governor
1.40; 1.0. še gur	100;1. gur of barley
kù-bi 1⅓ ma-na 3½ gín	its silver value 1⅓ mana 3½ gin
gìr Ir$_{11}$-da	responsible: Irda
2.12 še gur	132 gur of barley
kù-bi 1$\frac{5}{6}$ ma-na 0 gín	its silver value 1$\frac{5}{6}$ mana 0 gin
gìr Lú-kal-la	responsible: Lukalla
Reverse	
ki Ir$_{11}$-ta	from Ir
šu-nigín 3⅔ ma-na 3½ gín kù-babbar	total 3⅔ ma-na 3½ gín of silver
šà-bi-ta	from it
7⅔ gín 15 še kù-gi	7⅔ gin 15 grains of gold
10⅓ gín 7½ še 8-ta	10⅓ gin 7½ grains of gold for 8 times
3 gín kù-sig$_{17}$ 7-ta	3 gin of gold for 7 times
kù-bi 3 ma-na 1½ gín	its silver value is 3 mana and 1½ gin
½ ma-na 5 gín kù	½ mana 5 gin of silver
ugu Šu-^{d}Lama-^{d}Amar-^{d}EN.ZU-ka ba-a-gar	on Šu-Lama-Amar-Sîn

2 gín 4/ZA-NIM igi Šu-^{d}Lama	2 gin for precious stones(?)
<-^{d}Amar>-^{d}EN.ZU-ka dù-a	to fix in front of Šu-Lama-Amar-Sîn
šu-nigín 3½ ma-na 8½ gín kù	total 3½ mana 8½ gin of silver
zi-ga-àm	disbursement
lá-ni 5 gín mu en unu$_6$-gal ^{d}Inanna ba-ḫun	deficit of 5 gin; AS 5

Merchants played an important role in the economic life in the Ur III kingdom. Through their business ventures they provided Sumer with the products otherwise not available in the country, such as timber and precious stones. Their accounts list the value of an object converted to its silver value.

no. 219 (Š 45) [copy]

Obverse

sag-nì-ga-ra	capital sum
šà-bi su-ga	its capital has been returned
kù dam-gàr	silver of the merchant Dadaga
Da-da-ga	
mu Ur-bí-lum^{ki} ba-ḫul	Š 45

Seal

Lú-du$_{10}$-ga	Luduga
dub-sar	scribe
dumu Ur-ni$_9$-gar	son of Urnigar

no. 220

This text records the transfer of barley brought in by several important persons. The barley entrusted to the merchant may have been intended to pay for a product that he was to procure for them. If this interpretation is correct, it would mean that not only the palace, but also individuals of the upper class, could pass orders to the merchants for their private needs.

Obverse

6 še gur lugal	6 gur of barley according to the royal measurement
ki Ir$_{11}$-ta	from Ir
2; 4.0. še ki Šà-da túg-du$_8$-ta	$2\frac{4}{5}$ gur of barley from Šada the garment-maker
3 gur ki Ur-^{d}Li$_9$-si$_4$-ta	3 gur from Ur-Lisi
1 gur ki gala-ne-ta	1 gur from the lamentation-priests

Reverse

Ur-^{giš}gigir dam-gàr	Urgigir the merchant
šu-ba-ti	received

no. 221 (IS 1)

A granary manager gives grain to a merchant to serve as exchange for buying other things.

Obverse	
[ ] še gur	[ ] gur of barley
nì/ninda sa$_{10}$-àm zi-ga Uri$_{5}^{ki}$-ma	for buying stuff/bread, disbursement in Ur
ki ka-gur$_{7}$-ta	from the granary manager
Reverse	
ugú dam-gàr gá-gá-dam	to be put on the account of the merchants
mu ^{d}I-bí-^{d}EN.ZU lugal-e	IS 1

Commodities: Barley (nos. 222–321)

no. 222 (IS 3) [copy]

Obverse	
[ ]	[ ]
[ ] 2 dug 40 sila$_{3}$-ta	[ ] 2 vessels of 40 sila each
[ ] 5 zì še-bi 0; 3.2.	[ ] 5 of flour, the needed barley ⅔ gur
[ ] dida-šè	[ ] for *billatu*-beverage
gìr Da-di-a	responsible: Dadia
Reverse	
ki Sag-rig$_{7}^{ki}$-šè ba-a-gar	to be brought to Sagrig
gìr Lú-^{d}Šara$_{2}$	responsible: Lu-Šara
ki Ur-gú-dè-na-ta	from Urgudena
kišib Gìr-^{d}Šara$_{2}$-ì-dab$_{5}$	seal of Gir-Šara-idab
šà bala-a mu en-^{d}Inanna	during the *bala*
Unug^{ki} máš-e ì-pàd	IS 3
Seal illegible	

This tablet mentions two individuals responsible for a transfer. We expect the city to be written as Uru-sag-rig$_{7}$. Here the expression is only sag-rig$_{7}$, but with the final ki-sign for the place name. This first line of the reverse remains ambiguous.

dida *billatu* was a nonfermented beverage, made out of titab (bappir+munu$_{4}$) and a substance rich in sugar.

no. 223 (ŠS 5 xii) [copy]

Daily deliveries of flour and dates. Unground barley flour often is found in ration allowances.

Obverse	
6 sila$_{3}$ dabin	6 sila of barley flour

2 sila$_3$ zì-sig$_{15}$	2 sila of coarse flour
1 sila$_3$ zú-lum	1 sila of dates
u$_4$-1-kam	day 1
6 sila$_3$ dabin	6 sila of barley flour
3 sila$_3$ zì-sig$_{15}$	3 sila of coarse flour
1 sila$_3$ zú-lum	1 sila of dates
u$_4$-2-kam	day 2
Reverse	
6 sila$_3$ dabin	6 sila of barley flour
3 sila$_3$ zì-sig$_{15}$	3 sila of coarse flour
1 sila$_3$ zú-lum	1 sila of dates
u$_4$-3-kam	day 3
6 sila$_3$ dabin	6 sila of barley flour
1 sila$_3$ zì-sig$_{15}$	1 sila of coarse flour
1 sila$_3$ zú-lum	1 sila of dates
u$_4$-4-kam	day 4
nì sì-ga	items given
iti ^{d}Dumu-zi	month 12
mu-ús-sa bàd mar-tu	ŠS 5
Seal	
^{d}Šu-^{d}EN.ZU	Šu-Sîn
lugal-kalag-ga	strong king
lugal Uri$_5$^{ki}-ma	king of Ur
lugal an-ub-da limmu$_2$-ba	king of the four corners of the universe
A-a-kal-la	Aakalla
ensi$_2$	the governor
Umma^{ki}	of Umma
ir$_{11}$-zu	is your servant

The expression nì-sì-ga is unattested in other texts. dabin is barley flour; zì is a non-specific term for flour.

no. 224 (Š 48 [ ] 30) [copy]

Transfer of flour to the singers of Hašanmegar. This ration was among the items to be delivered during the *bala*/rotation deliveries.

Obverse	
10 sila$_3$ dabin	10 sila of barley floor
šu-a-gi-na	complete delivery as imposed
nar-munus Ḫa-ša-an-me-gár^{ki}-me	for the female singer of Ḫašanmegar

ki Lú-dingir-ra-ta	from Ludingirra
Reverse	
kišib Lú-gi-na	seal of Lugina
šà bala-a	during the *bala*
mu Ḫa-ar-ši^{ki} ba-ḫul	Š 48
u_4-30-šè	for 30 days
Seal	
Lú-gi-na	Lugina
dub-sar	scribe
dumu Da-da	son of Dada

no. 225 (ŠS 5 i) [copy]

Obverse	
5 $sila_3$ dabin sa-a	5 sila of roasted barley flour
ki Da-gu-ta	from Dagu
kišib $ensi_2$-ka	sealed by the governor
Reverse	
iti še-kin-ku_5	month 1
mu-ús-sa bàd mar-tu ba-dù	ŠS 5
Seal	
^{d}Šu-^{d}EN.ZU	Šu-Sîn
lugal-kalag-ga	strong king
lugal Uri_5^{ki}-ma	king of Ur
lugal an-ub-da $limmu_2$-ba	king of the four quarters of the universe
A-a-kal-la	Aakalla
$ensi_2$	governor of
Umma^{ki}	Umma
ir_{11}-zu	is your servant

no. 226 (AS 9 v 7) [copy]

Obverse	
40 $sila_3$ dabin	40 sila of barley flour
u_4 5-kam	fifth day
40 $sila_3$ dabin	40 sila of barley flour
u_4 6-kam	sixth day
31 $sila_3$ dabin	31 sila of barley flour
Reverse	
u_4 7-kam	seventh day
ki Lú-dingir-ra-ta	from Ludingirra
kišib $ensi_2$-ka	seal of the governor

iti ri	month 5
mu-ús-sa en Ga-eš^{ki} ba-ḫun	AS 9
Seal	
^{d}Šu-^{d}EN.ZU	Šu-Sîn
lugal-kalag-ga	strong king
lugal Uri$_5$^{ki}-ma	king of Ur
lugal an-ub-da limmu$_2$-ba	king of the four quarters of the universe
A-a-kal-la	Aakalla
ensi$_2$	governor of
Umma^{ki}	Umma
ir$_{11}$-zu	is your servant

no. 227 (ŠS 4 v) [copy]

Obverse	
52 sila$_3$ dabin	52 sila of barley flour
u$_4$ 22-kam	on the 22nd day
37 sila$_3$ dabin	37 sila of barley flour
u$_4$ 23-kam	on the 23rd day
31 sila$_3$ dabin	31 sila of barley flour
Reverse	
u$_4$ 24-kam	on the 24th day
ki ^{d}Šara$_2$-kam-ta	from Šarakam
kišib ensi$_2$-ka	seal of the governor
iti ri	month 5
mu-ús-sa Si-ma-núm^{ki} ba-ḫul	ŠS 4
Seal	
^{d}Šu-^{d}EN.ZU	Šu-Sîn
lugal-kalag-ga	strong king
lugal Uri$_5$^{ki}-ma	king of Ur
lugal an-ub-da limmu$_2$-ba	king of the four quarters of the universe
A-a-kal-la	Aakalla
ensi$_2$	governor of
Umma^{ki}	Umma
ir$_{11}$-zu	is your servant

no. 228 (ŠS 4 ix 17) [copy]

Obverse	
24 sila$_3$ dabin	24 sila of barley flour
u$_4$ 11-kam	on the 11th day
12 sila$_3$ zì u$_4$-12-kam	12 sila of flour on the 12th day

32 sila$_3$ zì u$_4$-13-kam	32 sila of flour on the 13th day
22 sila$_3$ zì	22 sila of flour
u$_4$ 14-kam	on the 14th day
Reverse	
33 sila$_3$ u$_4$-15-kam	33 sila of flour on the 15th day
31 sila$_3$ u$_4$-16-kam	31 sila of flour on the 16th day
15 sila$_3$ u$_4$-17-kam	15 sila of flour on the 17th day
ki ^{d}Šara$_2$-kam-ta	from Šarakam
iti ^{d}Li$_9$-si$_4$	month 9
mu bàd mar-tu ba-dù	ŠS 4
Seal	
^{d}Šu-^{d}EN.ZU	Šu-Sîn
lugal-kalag-ga	strong king
lugal Uri$_5$^{ki}-ma	king of Ur
lugal an-ub-da limmu$_2$-ba	king of the four quarters of the universe
A-a-kal-la	Aakalla
ensi$_2$	governor of
Umma^{ki}	Umma
ir$_{11}$-zu	is your servant

no. 229 (AS 5 iii) [copy]

A threshing floor yields 802 gur of barley and 41 gur of emmer wheat.

Obverse	
13.7 še gur	787 gur of barley
41 zíz gur	41 gur of emmer
še gán-gu$_4$	barley from state-owned land
nu-banda$_3$ gu$_4$ Da-du-mu	lieutenant of the oxen Dadumu
15; 2.0. še gur	15$^2/_5$ gur of barley
še šukur-ra šà-gu$_4$-ka	barley for the ox-driver sustenance
Reverse	
šu-nigín 13.22; 2.0. še gur	total 802$^2/_5$ gur of barley
šu-nigín 41 zíz gur	total 41 gur of emmer
še giš-è-a	threshed barley
ki-su$_7$ šár-a-bar-ra	on the threshing floor Šarabarra
gìr Ur-èš ù Ur-dingir-ra dub-sar	responsible: Ureš and Urdingirra the scribe
iti še-kar-ra-gál-la	month 3
mu en unu$_6$-gal ^{d}Inanna ba-ḫun	AS 5

no. 230

Obverse

1 še gur-[lugal]	1 gur of barley according to the royal measurement
Lú-dingir-ra <dumu> Da-da-ti	Ludingirra son of Dadati
4; 2.0. gur A-tu šeš Lú-usar	4 2/5 gur Atu brother of Lu-usar
2; 1.0. gur Ur-^{d}Li$_{9}$-si$_{4}$	2 1/5 gur Ur-Lisi
1 gur Lú-dingir-ra	1 gur Ludingirra
2 gur a-rá 1-a-kam	2 gur first time
0; 3.0. a-rá 2-<kam>	180 sila the second time
2; 3.0. a-rá 3-<kam>	2 3/5 third time
dumu A-za-ru-um-a-pil	son of Azarum-Apil
2 gur a-rá 1-a-kam	2 gur first time
2; 2.0. a-rá 2-kam	2 2/5 gur the second time

Reverse

2; 1.0. a-rá 3-kam	2 1/5 third time
dumu É-a-^{d}Nin-gal	son of Ea-Ningal
4; 3.0. Šu-Ma-ma	4 3/5 gur Šu-Mama
2; 1.0. I-ti-^{d}EN.ZU	2 1/5 Iti-Sîn
2 gur gìr Lú-nin-gá	2 gur, responsible: Luninga
1; 3.0. gìr Lú-kal-la	1 3/5 gur responsible: Lukalla
lú-^{d}En-líl-lá	servant of Enlilla
3; 0.3. a-rá 1-a-kam	3 gur 30 sila first time
3 a-rá 2-kam	3 gur second time
Šu-Ma-ma	Šu-Mama
[ ]Nimgir-ša$_{6}$-ga	[ ] Nimgiršaga

no. 231

Obverse

53 še gur	53 gur of barley
10 zíz gur kišib Lugal-é-maḫ-e	10 gur of emmer seal of Lugalemaḫe
53 še gur 10 zíz gur kišib Ur-^{d}EN.ZU	53 gur of barley 10 gur of emmer seal of Ur-Sîn
53 še gur 10 zíz gur kišib ^{d}Šara$_{2}$-za-me	53 gur of barley 10 gur of emmer seal of Šara-zame

Reverse

48 gur 9; 3.0. zíz gur kišib Lú-bala-[sig$_{5}$]	48 gur <of barley> 10 gur of emmer seal of Lu-balasig
šu-nigín	total
3.27 gur 39; 3.0. zíz gur	207 gur 39 3/5 gur of emmer

(last line illegible)

Left Edge

3.24?	204

no. 232

Barley deliveries brought to or taken from storage facilities by various individuals.

Obverse	
[ ] še gur	[ ] gur of barley
[ ]-nir	[ ]nir
[ ] gur Ur-^{d}Nun-gal	[ ] gur Ur-Nungal
[ ]+30 gur Ab-ba-gi-na	[ ] + 30 gur Abbagina
[ ] gur Úr-ra-ni	[ ] gur Urrani
[ ]+2.30 gur ^{d}Šara$_2$-ì-zu	[ ] 150 gur Šara-izu
14.40 gur Gu-du-du	[ ] 880 gur Gududu
11.30 gur Šà-nin-gá	[ ] 690 gur Šaninga
[ ]+4.0 gur Uš-mu	[ ]+240 gur Ušmu
[ ]+4.0 gur Šeš-kal-la	[ ]+240 gur Šeškalla
12.0 gur Kaš$_4$	720 gur Kaš$_4$
12.0 gur Lugal-^{d}Utu	720 gur Lugal-Utu
Reverse	
[ ] gur gu$_4$ diri	[ ] gur additional oxen
šu-nigín 2 gur$_7$ 25.0 še gur	total 2 gur$_7$ 1500 gur of barley

no. 233 [copy]

Obverse	
5; 2.0. še gur	$5^{2}/_{5}$ gur barley
ki U-bar-um-ta	from Ubarum
Ú-da-li	are with Udali
in-da-gál	
Seal	
Ú-da-li	Udali
dub-sar	scribe
nu-banda$_3$-ne-ne	of the lieutenants
ir$_{11}$ ^{d}Šu-^{d}EN.ZU	servant of Šu-Sîn

Note the presence of an unusual form in-da-gál "it is with him." Normally the scribe writes šu-ba-ti "received." Here it is a statement that the $5^{2}/_{5}$ gur of barley are with Udali.

no. 234 (Š 31 x)

6; 2.0. še gur-lugal	6$^{2}/_{5}$ gur of barley according to the royal measurement
ki Ur-^{d}Li$_{9}$-si$_{4}$-ta	from Ur-Lisi
Ukken-né	Ukkene
šu-ba-ti	received
Reverse	
iti ezem-^{d}Šul-gi	month 8
mu a-rá-2-kam	Š 31
Kara$_{2}$-ḫar^{ki} ba-ḫul	

no. 235 (ŠS 6) [copy]

Obverse	
3; 3.0. še gur	3 gur 180 sila of barley
a-šà kar$^{!}$(TE)-^{d}Inanna	in the field Kar-Inanna
ki Ka-gur$_{7}$-ta	from Kagur
kišib-aš-a Ur-Da-da	(consigned) on one tablet belonging to Ur-Dada
Reverse	
mu ^{d}Šu-^{d}EN.ZU lugal-e na-rú-a maḫ ^{d}En-líl ^{d}Nin-líl-ra mu-ne-rú	ŠS 6
Seal	
Ur-Da-da	Ur-Dada
išib ^{d}Šara$_{2}$-bàn-da	purification-priest of Šarabanda

The god Šara-bàn-da is elsewhere unattested.

no. 236 (Š 30 ix) [copy]

Obverse	
23.18; 0.3. še gur-lugal	1398 gur and 30 sila of barley according to the royal measurement
6 gur gig	6 gur of wheat
2 <gur> á guruš ḫun-gá	2 gur as wages for the hired workmen
ki Lugal-inim-gi-na-ta	from Lugalinimgina
Ir$_{11}$-mu	Irmu
šu-ba-ti	received
Reverse	
zi-ga Uri$_{5}$^{ki}-ma	disbursement in Ur
iti ^{d}Li$_{9}$-si$_{4}$	month 9
mu dumu-munus lugal ensi$_{2}$ An-ša-na-ke$_{4}$ ba-tuk-a	Š 30

no. 237 (IS 1 xii) [copy]

Obverse	
0;1. še	60 sila of barley
ki Ab-ba-gi-na-ta	from Abbagina
kišib Al-lu	seal of Allu
Reverse	
iti ^{d}Dumu-zi	month 12
mu ^{d}I-bi-^{d}EN.ZU lugal	IS 1
Seal	
Al-lu	Allu
dub-sar	scribe
dumu [ ]	son of [ ]

Note that the name I-bi-^{d}EN.ZU is unexpectedly written with -bi- instead of -bí-.

no. 238 (Š 31 viii) [copy]

Transfer of barley to the fattener.

Obverse	
0; 2.3. še lugal	½ gur of barley according to the royal measurement
ki Ir_{11}-ta	from Ir
0;1.0 Šeš-kal-la	(and) 60 $sila_3$ (brought by) Šeškalla
ki Ur-$^{d}Li_9$-si_4-ta	from Ur-Lisi
$^{d}Šara_2$-ki-ág kurušda	Šara-kiag the fattener
Reverse	
šu-ba-ti	received
iti é-iti-6	month 8
mu a-rá 2-kam $Kara_2$-ḫar^{ki} ba-ḫul	Š 31

no. 239 (Š 40) [copy]

Summary tablet of the accounts written for the central administration.

Obverse	
9; 3.1. še gur	9 gur 190 sila of barley
kišib A-kal-la Unug^{ki}	tablet of Akalla in Uruk
11; 2.5. še gur	11 gur and 170 sila of barley
kišib A-kal-la dumu Ba-ne	tablet of Akalla son of Bane
19; 2.1. še gur	19 gur 130 sila of barley
kišib Sag-ku_5 dam-gàr	tablet of Sagku the merchant
Reverse	
kišib Lú-[ ] ù-túm	if the tablet of Lu-[ ] is brought

kišib La-ni muḫaldim zi-re-dam	the tablet of Lani the cook shall be destroyed
mu-ús-sa Puzur$_4$-<^{d}Da->gan ba-dù	Š 40
Seal	
La-ni muḫaldim	Lani the cook
dub-sar	scribe
dumu Ur-ni$_9$-gar	son of Urnigar

In this context it is obvious that kišib cannot be translated "seal" but as "tablet" or in a broader way, "account." It is said that, if the tablet of Šagku shows up or is presented in the office, the one of Lú-[ ] shall be destroyed. In other words, the valid tablet is that of Sag-ku$_5$. But as long as it is not available, the tablet of Lú-[ ] is to be considered as sufficient proof.

La-ni had three seals, two with the name La-ni and the third La-ni muḫaldim "Lani the cook." On some tablets sealed La-ni, the name written on the tablet adds muḫaldim. Therefore it is obvious that the name cannot be read Lanimu.

no. 240 (Š 31 xii) [copy]

Summary of accounts of barley and flour transferred to Lu-ḫegal.

Obverse	
8 zì gur-lugal	8 gur of flour according to the royal measurement
ki Ur-^{d}Li$_9$-si$_4$-ta	from Ur-Lisi
7 še gur	7 gur of barley
še àr-ra zì-da	barley to be ground into flour
ki Lú-ḫé-gál-ta	from Lu-ḫegal
2.9; 3.4. še gur	129 gur and 220 sila of barley
gur-zabar-ta	according to the bronze gur
ki Ur-^{d}Li$_9$-si$_4$-ta	from Ur-Lisi
Lú-ḫé-gál	Lu-ḫegal
Reverse	
šu-ba-ti	received
gaba-ri šà-dub-ba	[copy] of the tablet of the archivist
šu-nigín 2.24; 3.4 še gur	total 144 gur 220 sila
iti ^{d}Dumu-zi	month 12
mu a-rá 2-kam Kara$_2$-ḫar^{ki} ba-ḫul	Š 31

The scribes would write copies (gaba-ri) of the same tablet for the needs of different offices, one keeping the accounts of storage places, the others following the accounts of persons making deliveries.

no. 241 (Š 48 ix) [copy]

Summary of barley records combining the wages of sowers and barley outstanding (bar-ta-gál-la).

Obverse

20 še gur-lugal	20 gur of barley according to the royal measurement
á lú ḫun-gá ^{giš}gaba-<gíd-da> a-šà ì-sum	wages for the hired men for seeding the field Isum with the breast-pole
mu Šu-Eš$_4$-tár-šè	for Šu-Eštar
kišib Lú-kal-la	seal of Lukalla
5 gur bar-ta-gál-la	5 gur not yet available (outstanding)

Reverse

šu-nigín 25 še gur	total 25 gur of barley
ki-su$_7$ é-duru$_5$ gu-la-ta	from the threshing floor of the great encampment
gìr Ur-^{d}EN.ZU	responsible: Ur-Sîn
iti ^{d}Li$_9$-si$_4$	month 9
mu Ḫa-ar-ši^{ki} ù Ki-maš^{ki} ba-ḫul	Š 48

The gaba-gíd-da pole was fixed on the breast of the sowers, who were forced, in this way, to move together.

no. 242

Deliveries or expenditures of barley. This tablet could be Old Babylonian.

Obverse

1 še gur	1 gur of barley
Ḫi-gi	Ḫigi
0; 2.0. Ilum-ra-bé	2/5 gur Ilum-rabe
1 gur I-ti-ilum	1 gur Iti-ilum
0; 3.0. Na-ki-ki	180 sila Nakiki

Reverse

0; 2.0. Nu-ḫi-ilum	120 sila Nuḫilum
0; 2.0. Ti-ti	120 sila Titi
šu-nigín 3; 4.0. gur	total 3 4/5 gur
Šu-nir-ru-ku maškim	Šunirruku is the conveyer

no. 243 (Š 45)

Obverse

3; 2.0. še gur-lugal	3 2/5 gur of barley according to the royal measurement

še nam-lá é-duru$_5$ si-ga	barley from leftover filled in the encampment
[ki -ta]	from [ ]
Reverse	
[ ]-ni	[Aal]-ni
šu]-ba-an-ti	received
iti ki-ir-ki-ma	month kirkima
mu-ús-sa a-rá	Š 45
9 Si-mu-ru-um^{ki}	
Lu-lu-pu-um^{ki} ba-ḫul	

ki-ir-ki-ma is a month name of Elam. The tablet has the unusual expression nam-lá. I understand it as leftover, from nam-lá-<ni>. Of course, nam would be superfluous.

no. 244 (AS 9)

Obverse	
2; 2.0. še gur	140 sila of barley
^{d}Šara$_2$-za-me	Šara-zame
3; 2.0. gur	$3\,{}^{2}/_{5}$ gur
Ur-^{d}En-líl	Ur-Enlil
1; 1.0. gur	$1\,{}^{1}/_{5}$ gur
Lugal-é-maḫ-e	Lugalemaḫe
1; 1.0. gur	1 [1] gur
Reverse	
Lú-bala-sig$_5$	Lu-balasig
mu-ša	... (barley)
iti ^{d}Šul-gi	month [the festival of] Šulgi
mu en Ga-eš^{ki} ba-ḫun	AS 9

The expression mu-ša is known as characterizing barley, but its exact meaning eludes us. Its position in the text is unusual. It should appear in the first line.

no. 245 (AS 8 v) [copy]

Obverse	
30;4.1. še gur	30 gur and 250 sila of barley
0; 1.0. dabin	${}^{1}/_{5}$ gur of barley flour
ki Lugal-usar$_x$(LÁL.TÚG)-ta	from Lugalusar
gaba-ri kišib Lú-gi-na	copy; the tablet of Lugina
kišib-aš-a	one tablet
Reverse	
iti ri	month 5
mu en Eridu^{ki} ba-ḫun	AS 8

no. 246 (Š 37)

Record of barley made available for a household or personnel in Zabalam.

Obverse

7; 3.2.5 sila$_3$ še gur-lugal	7 gur 205 sila of barley according to the royal measurement
mu nì-gál-la	as disponibilities to be eaten by the
gìr-sì-ga Zabalam^{ki}	household in Zabalam
Reverse	
ke$_4$ íb-kú-šè	
ki Ur-^{d}Nun-gal-ta	from Ur-Nungal
Ir$_{11}$ šu-ba-ti	Ir received
mu bàd ba-dù	Š 37
Seal	
Ir$_{11}$-mu	Irmu
dub-sar	scribe
dumu Ur-ni$_9$-gar kuš$_7$	son of Urnigar the equerry

no. 247 (Š 36 viii) [copy]

A transfer of barley between two governors. A *gir*-official supervises the operation. One can only speculate on the reason of the transfer. Normally every delivery moves items towards the center, i.e., to the king in Ur. Perhaps the governor of Umma is helping out the governor of Marad with a shortage of grain, three or four months before harvest. Curiously despite the importance of this transfer and the importance of the persons involved, this tablet is not sealed.

Obverse

12.12 še gur lugal	732 gur of barley according to the royal measurement
ki ensi$_2$ Umma^{ki}-ta	from the governor of Umma
É-a-ba-ni	Ea-bani
lú ensi$_2$ Ma-ra-ad^{ki}-ka	the man of the governor of Marad
Reverse	
šu-ba-ti	received
šà Uri$_5$^{ki}-ma	in Ur
gìr Lugal-é-maḫ-e	responsible: Lugalemaḫe
iti é-iti-6	month 8
mu ^{d}Nanna kar-zi-da a-rá-2-kam	Š 36
é-a-na in-ku$_4$	

no. 248 (Š 40 x)

Obverse	
5 še gur-lugal	5 gur of barley according to the royal measurement for / from
Ìr-ra-dan	Irradan
| Puzur$_4$-lum	Puzurlum
| Iš-gu	Išgu
Reverse	
ki-še 23 še gur	in the place of barley; 23 gur of barley
gá-nun-ta	from the storehouse
iti ezem-^{d}Šul-gi	month 10
mu-ús-sa é Puzur$_4$-iš-^{d}Da-gan ba-dù	Š 40

It is difficult to understand this tablet, in particular the quantities delivered. Note also the expression ki-še: the place of barley, so far unattested.

no. 249 (Š 32) [copy]

Expenditures of barley consigned on the tablet of 4 persons. The grain comes from the gardens, probably to be understood, the storehouses of the gardens.

Obverse	
1.40; 3.0.6 sila$_3$ še gur-lugal	100 gur 186 sila of barley according to the royal measurement
kišib Ur-^{d}Li$_9$-si$_4$	tablet of Ur-Lisi
25 gur	25 gur
kišib Lugal-inim-gi-na	tablet of Lugalinimgina
55 gur	55 gur
lú Šu-^{d}Utu	the man of Šu-Utu
10+[ ] gur	10+[ ] gur
Kù-[ ]	Ku[ ]
Reverse	
zi-ga ki ^{giš}kiri$_6$ ^{giš}kiri$_6$-ta	disbursement from the gardens
mu Si-mu-ru-um^{ki}	Š 32
a-rá 3-kam ba-ḫul	

no. 250 (ŠS 7) [copy]

Barley rations delivered by the granary manager. All the expenses are consigned on the one tablet of Adumu.

Obverse	
2 še gur	2 gur of barley
Á-nin-gá-ta	Aningata

2; 2.0. gur	$2^{2}/_{5}$ gur
Šeš-a-ni dumu-ni	Šešani his son
4 gur	4 gur
[Ḫa]-ba-lug-<gé>	Ḫabalugge
4 gur	4 gur
É-ki	Eki
Reverse	
2; 2.0. gur	$2^{2}/_{5}$ gur
Lú-du$_{10}$-ga dumu ^{d}Šara$_{2}$-a-zi	Luduga son of Šara-azi
šu-nigín 14; 4.0. še-ba gur	total $14^{4}/_{5}$ gur for rations
ki Ka-gur$_{7}$-ta	from the granary manager
kišib-aš-a A-du-mu	on one tablet of Adumu
mu ^{d}Šu-^{d}EN.ZU lugal-e ma-da	ŠS 7
Za-ab-ša-li^{ki} ba-ḫul	
Seal	
Ur-^{d}EN.ZU	Ur-Sîn
dub-sar	scribe
dumu Ur-^{giš}gigir	son of Urgigir
šà-tam	high administrator

The connection between Ur-Sîn and the mention of Adumu on all the tablets sealed by Ur-Sîn is striking and deserving of special study.

no. 251 (ŠS 4)

Barley rations for singers received in leather containers. Although the text is not absolutely clear, it seems that these rations are given for the turn of service of these singers: <šà> bala-a.

Obverse	
0; 1.0. še ^{kuš}a-gá-lá kéš-rá	$^{1}/_{5}$ gur to put in the leather bag
Ur-^{d}En-líl-lá	for Ur-Enlilla
0; 1.0. Ur-àm-ma	$^{1}/_{5}$ gur for Uramma
0; 1.0. ^{d}Šara$_{2}$-mu-túm	$^{1}/_{5}$ gur for Šara-mutum
0; 1.0. Di-né	$^{1}/_{5}$ gur for Dine
0; 1.0. Ur-ab-ba	$^{1}/_{5}$ gur for Urabba
Reverse	
0; 1.0. Ur-ni$_{9}$-gar	$^{1}/_{5}$ gur for Urnigar
0; 1.0. Lú-ib-gal	$^{1}/_{5}$ gur for Lu-ibgal
0; 1.0. Lú-dingir-ra	$^{1}/_{5}$ gur for Ludingirra
mu nar-šè	for the singers
šu-nigín 1; 3.0. še gur-lugal	total $1^{3}/_{5}$ gur of barley according to the royal measurement

še ^{kuš}a-gá-lá kéš bala-a	barley in leather bags for the *bala*
ki ka-gur$_{7}$-ta	from the granary manager
kišib Inim-ma-ni-zi	seal of Inimmanizi
mu-ús-sa Si-ma-núm^{ki} ba-ḫul	ŠS 4
Seal	
Inim-ma-ni-zi	Inimmanizi
dumu Ba-a-mu	son of Baamu
lú bappir nì-lagar	the brewer of Nilagar

no. 252 (ŠS 6)

This is a most interesting tablet as it is not apparently an official tablet, i.e., a tablet from the administration. Kaamu brother of Adumu gives barley to Ur-Nammaḫka, according to the seal, his natural father.

Obverse	
1 še gur	1 gur of barley
mu Ur-^{d}Nám-maḫ-ka-šè	for Ur-Nammaḫka
Ka5-<a>-mu	Kaamu
šeš A-du-mu	the brother of Adumu
Reverse	
ì-na-sum	gave
mu na-rú-a maḫ ba-rú	ŠS 6
Seal	
nu-banda$_{3}$ Ur-[^{d}Nám-maḫ-ka]	of the lieutenant Ur-Nammaḫka
Ka5-<a>-mu	Kaamu
dumu-ni	is his son

no. 253 (Š 32)

Obverse	
15 še gur-lugal	15 gur of barley according to the royal measurement
kišib Ur-^{d}En-ki	seal of Ur-Enki
15 gur kišib ugú ki baḫar-me	15 gur on the account of the brewer
gur zabar-ta	according to the bronze gur
Reverse	
ugú ba-a-gar	it is imposed
Ur-^{d}Li$_{9}$-si$_{4}$-ra	from (the account of) Ur-Lisi
zi-zi-dam	it will be subtracted
mu Si-mu-ru-um^{ki}	Š 32
a-rá 3-kam ba-ḫul	

no. 254 (Š 42 vi) [copy]

Simple transfer of barley. But, as the brother of the *sukkalmaḫ* is involved, a *gir*-official oversees the transfer.

Obverse	
2.0 še gur-lugal	120 gur of barley according to the royal measurement
ki Bu-zu-a-ta	from Buzua
Ur-^{d}Nanna šeš sukkal-maḫ-ke$_4$	Ur-Nanna the brother of the grand vizier
šu-ba-ti	received
gìr Lugal-uru-da	responsible: Lugaluruda
Reverse	
šà Ti-im-tum^{ki}	in Timtum
Ur-ša$_6$-ga	Uršaga
iti á-ki-ti	month 7
mu Ša-aš-ru^{ki} ba-ḫul	Š 42

no. 255 (ŠS 1 v) [copy]

Obverse	
0; 4.4. še gub-ba	280 sila of available barley
Ur-e$_{11}$-e	Uree
40 sila$_4$ A-gu-du	40 sila Agudu
40 sila$_3$ Ur-^{giš}gigir	40 sila Urgigir
a-šà ^{d}Inanna	in the field of Inanna
gìr Lugal-á-zi-da	responsible: Lugalazida
Reverse	
1; 1.0. gur Lú-^{d}Ùr-bar-tab	1 1/5 gur Lu-Urbartab
a-šà sipad-da	in the field Sipad
gìr Ur-zi-ku-um-ma	responsible: Urzikumma
še [giš è?] mu-túm	delivery of [threshed] barley
iti ri	month 5
mu ^{d}Šu-^{d}EN.ZU lugal	ŠS 1

Apparently barley is being brought (mu-túm) to a central storage place, but the quantities are so small that one wonders on what terms this delivery took place.

no. 256 (ŠS 1 ii) [copy]

Obverse	
1.1 guruš u$_4$-1-šè	61 workmen for one day
a-šà igi é-maḫ-ta	from the field in front of the Emaḫ
še a-ta du$_8$-a	to remove the water from the barley

ù a-šà ^{d}Nin-ur$_{4}$-ra-ka-an^{ki}	and in the field Ninurra-ka-an
Reverse	
u$_{4}$-4-kam	for the 4 days
zar-tab-ba šu-ùr-ra	for placing piled grain stacks and leveling
ugula É-gal-e-si	overseer Egalesi
kišib Ur-e$_{11}$-e	seal of Uree
iti sig$_{4}$-giš ì-šub-ba-gar	month 2
mu-ús-sa en Ga-eš^{ki} ba-ḫun	ŠS 1
Seal	
Ur-e$_{11}$-e	Uree
dub-sar	scribe
dumu Ur-ni$_{9}$-gar	son of Urnigar

After the first irrigation period, to permit the growth of the barley, the water must be removed from the roots. To stop the irrigation flow the workers must close the breach made in the bank of the canal by bringing soil and mixing it with grain stacks. To reinforce the place the soil would be compacted.

no. 257 (Š 40)

Summary tablet of expenses of barley, flour, thread, and fish, for hired men working on the irrigation system and on other small tasks.

Obverse	
0; 1.0. še lugal	60 sila of barley according to the royal measurement
še á lú ḫun-gá	barley for the wages of the hired men
10 sila$_{3}$ Ur-lul-UD	10 sila for UrlulUD
0;1.0 kaš-ú-sa (dida)	60 sila of beer bread
še nì-sa$_{10}$ 25 sila$_{3}$	the barley for buying it is 25 sila
5 sila$_{3}$ gu	5 sila of thread
kun-zi-da a-za-ru	at the reservoir azaru
uru-^{d}Šul-gi	in uru-Šulgi
Ur-^{d}Lama nu-banda$_{3}$ gu$_{4}$	Ur-Lama lieutenant of the oxen
Reverse	
0;1.0. še á lú ḫun-gá	60 sila of barley according to the royal measurement
a-šà tur-an-na	in the field Turanna
Ad-da-ga-da	(of) Addagada
10 sila$_{3}$ dabin A-kal-la	10 sila of barley flour for Akalla
ù Nimgir-šà-kúš	and Nimgiršakuš
10 sila$_{3}$ dabin Nam-ḫa-ni	10 sila barley flour Namḫani

10 sila$_3$ ku$_6$-gibil ḫa-ar-[ ]	10 sila of fresh fish Ḫar-[ ]
iti ezem-^{d}[ ]	month [ ]
mu-ús-sa é Puzur$_4$-Da-gan ba-dù	Š 40

The personal name Ur-lul-UD is unknown to me. The first and second lines: 60 sila$_3$ dabin / še nì sa$_{10}$ 25 sila$_3$ is difficult to interpret. One would expect "60 sila of barley to buy 25 sila of barley flour."

The use of the term gu is difficult to understand. Does it mean linen fiber for the reservoir? As such, this tablet is odd by mixing several categories, unless one should understand zì-gu "pea-flour."

no. 258 (AS 8) [copy]

Obverse	
4.10; 4.3.[ ] sila$_3$ še gur	250 gur and 270+[ ] sila of barley
še uru$_4$-lá da-ba-a	barley requisitioned for (those) plowing
mu-túm	delivery
ì-dub a-šà A-ka$_4$-sal$_4$^{ki}	silo of the field of Apisal
Reverse	
kišib Gu-du-du	seal of Gududu
mu en Eridu^{ki} ba-ḫun	AS 8
Seal	
Inim-^{d}Šara$_2$	Inim-Šara
dub-sar	scribe
dumu Ur-ni$_9$-gar kuš$_7$	son of Urnigar the equerry

da-ba-a is a syllabic writing, not uncommon in Umma, for writing dab$_5$-ba-a "taken" or even better "requisitioned." In the present case the barley is earmarked for the requisitioned plowmen, for the guruš, and the oxen working in the field. The same writing is found in the expression ^{giš}tukul da-ba-a / dab$_5$-ba.

This scribe had many different seals. In two instances his father is given as kuš$_7$ "equerry." On the tablets sealed with this specific seal, one finds written kišib Gududu, while in all the other cases we find kišib Inim-^{d}Šara$_2$.

no. 259 (AS 8 I)

Obverse	
4 še ur$_5$ gur	4 gur of barley for loan
mu Lú-gi-na lú Sì-pú$^{[ki]}$-šè	for Lugina servant of (the man of) Sipu
1 še ur$_5$ gur	1 gur of barley for loan
mu Da-da dub-sar-šè	for Dada the scribe
ki Lú-^{d}Šul-gi-ra-ta	from Lu-Šulgi

Reverse

gaba-ri kišib Lú-gi-na	copy of the tablet of Lugina
iti še-kin-ku$_5$	month 1
mu en-nun-né en Eridu^{ki} ba-ḫun	AS 8

Some of the tablets of barley for loan could also be read as barley for grinding, since the sign ḪAR can be read ur$_5$ or àr. In the present case it is more likely that barley was loaned to two persons.

no. 260 (AS 5)

Obverse

3; 4.4.8 sila$_3$ gur <še>	3 gur 288 sila <of barley>
A-a-gi-na	for Aagina
0; 2.3. Ur-^{d}Ùr-bar-<tab>	½ gur for Ur-Urbartab
dumu Dingir-ra	son of Dingirra
diri kišib še àr-ra-ka	additional to the tablet of barley for grinding
gìr Lú-^{d}Nin-šubur	responsible: Lu-Ninšubur

Reverse

mu en unu$_6$-gal ^{d}Inanna ba-ḫun	AS 5

no. 261 (Š 46 v)

Obverse

2; 3.5. še gur-lugal	2 gur 230 sila of barley according to the royal measurement
á má ḫun-gá	wages for the hired boats
kišib Lugal-e-ba-an-ša$_6$	tablet of Lugalebanša
6; 2.3.5 sila$_3$ gur	6 gur 155 sila
šà-gal udu niga	fodder for barley-fed sheep
kišib kurušda-e-ne	tablet of the fatteners
0; 1.0. šà-gal anše-kunga$_2$	60 sila fodder for the mules
kišib Lú-banda$_3$	tablet of Lubanda

Reverse

0; 2.5. še gìr Lugal-nì-lagar-e	170 sila responsible: Lugalnilagare
0; 1.0. še é-àr ku$_4$-ra	60 sila barley for the mill
šu-nigín 10; 1.1.5 sila$_3$ še gur	total 10 gur 75 sila of barley
še àr-ra zi-ga	disbursement of barley for grinding
é-àr-ta	from the mill
iti ri mu-ús-sa	Š 46
Ur-bí-lum^{ki} ba-ḫul	

At first reading this tablet recapitulates different expenses of barley, which was stocked in the mill (é-àr-ta). Therefore, the previous line (line 12) še àr-ra zi-ga must mean "expenditure of barley that was (kept) for milling." The mill stocked barley for grinding. In this instance, because of need or because of a surplus, it was possible to draw on this reserve to satisfy other needs.

no. 262 (Š 39)

Obverse	
2 še gur-lugal	2 gur of barley according to the royal measurement
A-pi$_4$-sal$_4^{ki}$-ta	from Apisal
ki Ir$_{11}$-ta	from Ir
mu gašam-šè	for the craftsmen
Al-ba-ni-du$_{11}$	Albanidu
šu-ba-ti	received/took in account
Reverse	
kišib ^{d}Šara$_2$-mu-túm	seal of Šara-mutum
iti ^{d}Dumu-zi	month 12
mu é Puzur$_4$-Da-gan ba-dù	Š 39
Seal	
^{d}Šara$_2$-mu-túm	Šara-mutum
lú-šim	the brewer
dumu Ur-[ ]	son of Ur-[ ]

The sign gašam (nun-me-tag) is written more like mùš-me than nun-me.

no. 263 (Š 31 vii) [copy]

Barley rations drawn from the threshed barley. As such the indication še giš è-a must help the scribe know from which pile the barley was taken.

Obverse	
1.0 še [gur-lugal]	60 gur of barley according to the royal measurement
Lú-ḫé-[gál]	for Luḫegal
25 še gur	25 gur of barley
Šeš-a-ni	for Šešani
22; 4.0. še gur	$22\frac{4}{5}$ gur of barley
še-ba išib-e-ne	barley rations of the incantation-priests
10 še gur	10 gur of barley
Reverse	
Lú-ga-ti-e	for Lugatie
3; 2.0. še-ba zag-mu	$3\frac{2}{5}$ barley ration for the beginning of the year

0; 4.0. Al-la	4/5 gur for Alla
10 še gur	10 gur of barley
kišib Ḫa-lu$_5$-lu$_5$	seal of Ḫalulu
1 gur Ur-^{d}Šul-[gi]	1 gur for Ur-Šulgi
šu-nigín 2.13 še gur-lugal	total 133 gur of barley according to the royal measurement
šà še giš è-a	from the threshed barley
gìr Ur-^{d}[ ]	responsible: Ur-[ ]
Edge	
iti min-èš	month 7
mu a-rá 2-kam Kara$_2$-ḫar^{ki} ba-ḫul	Š 31

no. 264 (Š 45 xii)

During threshing, immediately after the harvest, the scribe had to record from which pile of grain barley was taken. Probably the grain had already been brought to the granary, but not yet stacked.

Obverse	
[še] gur	[ ] gur of barley
[ ]-da	[ ]-da
[ ]-zu	[ ]-zu
[šà]-gal gu$_4$ niga	[ ] fodder to fatten donkeys
[ ] ì-šáḫ-ka	[ ] lard
kišib Lugal-é-maḫ-e	tablet of Lugalemaḫe
Reverse	
šu-nigín 43 še gur	total 43 gur of barley
gur$_7$ a-šà lá-maḫ gàr-banda$_3$ igi é-duru$_5$	granary in the field Lamaḫ gar-banda in front of the encampment
še giš è-a Na-bí-^{d}EN.ZU	threshed barley of Nabi-Sîn
iti ^{d}Dumu-zi	month 12
mu Ur-bí-ì-lum^{ki} ba-ḫul	Š 45

no. 265 (Š 36)

Summary of threshed barley from state-owned land, as opposed to the gana$_2$ šukur-ra and gana$_2$ apin-lá. Each steward brings the yield of the state land over which he was in charge.

Obverse	
1; 1.0. še gur-lugal	1 1/5 gur of barley according to the royal measurement
[Ur]-ab-ba šabra	[Ur]abba is the steward
[x+]8; 2.0. še gur	[ ]+8 2/5 gur of barley
Lú-gi-na šabra	Lugina is the steward
[ ]+1; 3.0. še gur	[ ]+1 23/5 gur of barley

Lugal-kù-ga-ni šabra	Lugalkugani is the steward
2.0 gur lá 0;2.0. sila$_3$ še gur	120 minus $^2/_5$ gur of barley
Nì-lagar-e šabra	Nilagare is the steward
4.28 še gur	268 gur of barley
[ ] ù	[ ] and
[ ] ab / kurušda	[ ] …
Reverse	
36? še gur	[ ]+8$^2/_5$ gur of barley
[ ]-ga nu-banda$_3$-gu$_4$	[ ] the lieutenant of the oxen
[ ] še gur	[ ]+8$^2/_5$ gur of barley
[ ] Ur-líl [ ]-na	[ ] Urlil [ ]na
šu-nigín 17.30+[ ] še gur lugal	total : 1050+[ ] gur of barley according to the royal measurement
še giš-è-a gán-gu$_4$	threshed barley from state-owned land
a-šà A-pi$_4$-sal$_4$^{ki}	in the field of Apisal
mu ^{d}Nanna Ga-eš^{ki} é-a-na ba-an-ku$_4$	Š 36

no. 266 (ŠS 9 iii)

This tablet is elliptically shaped; perhaps an office memorandum about fresh barley.

Obverse	
1;2[še-giš] è-a gur	[ ] threshed barley
^{d}Šara$_2$-mu-túm	from Šara-mutum
^{giš}kiri$_6$ Ki-maš^{ki}	from the orchard of Kimaš
Reverse	
kab-du$_{11}$-ga	tax
iti še-kar-ra-gál-la	month 3
mu é ^{d}Šara$_2$ Umma^{ki} mu-dù	ŠS 9

no. 267 (ŠS 2 viii) [copy]

Leftover barley in the granary handed over for the bala requirements.

Obverse	
0; 1.4. še Igi-^{d}Šara$_2$-šè kuš$_7$	⅓ gur of barley for Igi-Šara-še the equerry
0; 1.3. Ú-li	90 sila for Uli
0; 1.4. Lú-^{d}Nin-šubur	⅓ gur for Lu-Ninšubur
mu A-kal-la dumu Ir$_{11}$-da-ni-šè	for Akalla the son of Irdani
gur$_7$-a tag$_4$-a	left over in the granary
ugula Igi-^{d}Šara$_2$-šè	overseer Igi-Šara-še
ki Lú-du$_{10}$-ga ugula	from Lu-duga the overseer

0; 1.0. ^{d}Šara$_{2}$-mu-túm dub-<sar> nar	⅕ gur for Šara-mutum, the scribe of the singer
Reverse	
mu Ur-^{d}Nun-gal-<šè>	for Ur-Nungal
mu-túm mu nì-bala-a-ka-šè	delivery for the stuff of the *bala*
ki Ur-^{d}Geštin-an-ka-ta	from Ur-Geštinanka
iti é-iti-6	month 8
mu má-^{d}En-ki ba-ab-du$_{8}$	ŠS 2

no. 268 (ŠS 7 iii) [copy]

Obverse	
1; 0.2. še guruš? da-ba gur	1 gur 20 sila for seized workmen
A-du-du IM	Adudu …
5; 2.3. Ur-^{d}Nun-gal gá-ra	5½ gur put on the account of Ur-Nungal
Reverse	
še uru$_{4}$-lá gub-ba	barley destined to the plowmen
ki-su$_{7}$ gana$_{2}$ Ur-gu	the threshing floor of the field Urgu
iti še-kar-<ra>-gál-la	month 3
mu ma-da Za-ab-ša-li^{ki} mu!-ḫul	ŠS 7

no. 269 (Š 42) [copy]

Obverse	
0; 2.3. še	½ gur of barley
20 sila$_{3}$ gig	20 sila of wheat
še numun mur-gu$_{4}$	barley for seed and fodder for the oxen
a-šà ^{giš}kiri$_{6}$-gu-la	for the field called the great garden
ki Ka-gur$_{7}$-ta	from the granary manager
Reverse	
kišib Šeš-kal-la	seal of Šeškalla
dumu A-ka-DUL	son of Akadul
mu Ša-aš-ru-um^{ki} ba-ḫul	Š 42
Seal illegible, but most likely	
[Šeš-kal-la]	[Šeškalla
[dub-sar]	scribe
[dumu A-ka-DUL]	son of Akadul]

no. 270 (ŠS 4)

Obverse	
1 ešè [še]-bi 0; 4.0. gur	1 eše [of land …] 4 gur
apin-ta	from plowing

A-a-kal-la rá-gaba	for Aakalla the messenger
1 ešè gana$_2$ 1; 1.0. gur	1 eše of land 360 sila
Šeš-a-ni munu$_4$-mú	for Šešani who makes the malt germinate
1 bùr gana$_2$ 10 še gur	1 bur land 10 gur of barley
Reverse	
^{d}Šul-gi-ì-lí sagi	for Šulgi-ili the cupbearer
ki Gu-ú-gu-a-ta	from Guugua
mu ^{d}Šu-^{d}EN.ZU lugal-e	ŠS 4
bàd mar-tu mu-dù	

no. 271 (ŠS 6) [copy]

Account of the old barley in the threshing floor.

Obverse	
29; 4.1. še gur	29 gur and 250 sila of barley
1.6; 1.0. še gur	66⅕ gur of barley
še ur$_5$-ra gibil sila-a gál-la	loan of barley, new in the account
1.40 še zì gú-na gur	100 gur barley for flour from the tax
3.56 še <gur> kaš bala-a	236 gur of barley for beer for the *bala*
5.40 še gur	290 gur of barley
ì-dub	in the silo
Reverse	
ki-su$_7$ kam-sal$_4$-la	in the threshing floor Kamsalla
šu-nigín 12.52; 0.1. gur	total 772 gur and 10 sila
še sumun	of old barley
mu ^{d}Šu-^{d}EN.ZU lugal Uri$_5^{ki}$-ma-ke$_4$	ŠS 6
na-rú-a maḫ ^{d}En-líl ^{d}Nin-líl-ra mu-ne-rú	

This account shows the variety and complexity of the accounts kept in the threshing floor. This inventory of barley was written probably before the new barley was about to enter. The inventory indicates:

- l. 1: barley physically present in the storage place;
- l. 2: barley loaned and due to be returned (sila-a gál-la), present in the accounts;
- l. 4: barley for flour, coming from the tax;
- l. 5: barley earmarked for beer;
- l. 6: barley in the silo, the storage place.

no. 272 (AS 8 iii) [copy]

Storage of barley in the temple of Ninurra, in the é-nesag "house of first offerings." The delivery is made by a šabra under the supervision of a nu-banda$_3$.

Obverse

2.48 še gur lugal	168 gur of barley according to the royal measurement
še gana$_2$ a-šà en-gaba-rá-ta	barley from the field Engabara
ki Ìr-ḫu-la šabra-ta	from Irḫula the steward
gìr Ur-^{giš}gigir nu-banda$_3$	responsible: Urgigir the lieutenant

Reverse

[šà] é-nesag-ka si-ga	filled in the Enesag
é ^{d}Nin-ur$_4$-ra	temple of Ninurra
iti še-kar-gál-la	month 3
mu-ús-sa en Eridu^{ki} ba-ḫun	AS 8

no. 273 (AS 4 diri)

Obverse

[ ] gur-lugal	[ ] gur according to the royal measurement
[ ] LÚ×GÁ im-du$_8$	[ ] ... clay backer
38 še ŠE.KIN gur	30 gur of harvested barley
kišib Íd-pa-è	seal of Idpae
[ ] še-ba gur	[ ] gur for rations
[ ] bala ki-sur-ra	[ ] the *bala* in Kisurra
(space)	
[ ] še gur	[ ] gur of barley

Reverse

gur sá-du$_{11}$-ta	from the gur for the regular deliveries
ki-su$_7$ a-šà ì-sum-ta	from the threshing floor of the field Isum
gìr Lú-gi-na	responsible: Lu-gina
ù ^{d}Šara$_2$-ba-zi-ge	and Šara-bazige
iti diri	intercalary month
mu en-maḫ-gal-an-na ba-ḫun	AS 4

no. 274 (ŠS 3 vi) [copy]

Obverse

0; 2.3. še šukur-e tag$_4$-a	½ gur of barley for rationaries, left over
A-gu	Agu
0; 1.0. Lú-^{d}EN.ZU	⅕ gur Lu-Sîn
é-àr-gibil-ta	from the new mill
ki ka-gur$_7$-ta	from the granary manager

Reverse	
kišib A-gu	seal of Agu
iti šu-numun	month 6
mu-ús-sa má ^{d}En-ki ba-ab-du_8	ŠS 3
Seal	
A-gu	Agu
dub-sar	scribe
dumu Ur-é-maḫ-e	son of Uremaḫe

This tablet allows to grasp the intricacy of the administration. Agu and Lu-Sîn receive barley from the new mill. The one who authorizes it or under whose jurisdiction the operation is carried out is the granary manager. The one checking the whole operation is Agu.

Agu has several seals. In general his activities are connected with objects or reeds. This tablet is odd unless this barley is meant for some of the workers he was controlling.

no. 275 (ŠS 4 viii) [copy]

Obverse	
0; 2.0. še šukur-ra	2/5 gur of rations
Ḫu-wa-wa dub-sar	for Ḫuwawa the scribe
0; 2.0. še šukur-ra	2/5 gur barley for rations
á gál nu-tuk	the collector did not take
é-àr sumun-ta	from the old mill
Reverse	
ki ka-gur_7-ta	from the granary manager
kišib nu-ra-a	the tablet was not sealed
iti é-iti-6	month 8
mu bàd mar-tu ba-dù	ŠS 4

no. 276 (ŠS 3)

Obverse	
0; 1.0. še šukur-ra	1/5 gur of barley as rations
Lú-dingir-ra	for Ludingirra
ki ka-gur_7-ta	from the granary manager
kišib Lugal-ḫé-gál	seal of Lugalḫegal
Reverse	
mu Si-ma-núm^{ki} ba-ḫul	ŠS 3
Seal	
Lugal-ḫé-gál	Lugalḫegal
dub-sar	scribe
dumu Ur-^{d}Utu	son of Ur-Utu

no. 277 [copy]

Obverse

2.0. šukur? ba-lá 9$\frac{2}{3}$ ma-na	*(no translation proposed)*
šukur 1 ma-na 12 gín	
Ur-e$_{11}$-e	

no. 278 (Š 46 diri) [copy]

Obverse

2 še ur$_{5}$-ra gur-lugal	2 gur of barley on loan according to the royal measurement
kišib Lugal-e-ba-an-ša$_{6}$	tablet of Lugalebanša
1 še ur$_{5}$-ra gur	1 gur of barley on loan
kišib Lugal-mu-ma-ág	tablet of Lugalmumag
1; 3.0. gur šà-gal gu$_{4}$ niga	1$\frac{3}{5}$ gur fodder for the barley-fed oxen
kišib Lugal-é-maḫ-e šeš A-ab-ba-ka	tablet of Lugalemaḫe brother of Aabba
4; 1.2. še-ba má-laḫ$_{4}$-e-ne	4 gur 80 sila barley rations for the sailors
kišib Ir$_{11}$ ka-gur$_{7}$-ka	tablet of Ir the granary manager

Reverse

šu-nigín 8; 4.2. še gur-lugal	total 8;4.2. gur of barley according to the royal measurement
gur$_{7}$ a-šà ^{giš}ma-nu-ta	from the granary of the field of willow
a-rá 6-kam	for the 6th time
gìr Lú-gi-na ù Kù-ga-ni	responsible: Lugina and Kugani
iti diri mu Ki-maš^{ki} ba-ḫul	intercalary month, Š 46

no. 279 (AS 5 xi) [copy]

This tablet inside an envelop is a loan of barley. In a rarely attested statement it specifies that the barley should be returned to the place from which it was taken, the granary in the field of Ninurra. The loan is made to an official, the throne-bearer. Therefore the transaction needs the supervision of the governor.

Obverse

10 še ur$_{5}$-<ra> gur lugal	10 gur of barley according to the royal measurement, for loan
še še ki-ba si-gi$_{4}$	barley to be returned at its right place
gur$_{7}$ a-šà ^{d}Nin-ur$_{4}$-ra	granary in the field of Ninurra
ki Ur-^{d}Li$_{9}$-si$_{4}$	from Ur-Lisi
ensi$_{2}$ Umma^{ki}-ta	governor of Umma

Reverse

Lugal-ḫé-gál gu-za-lá	Lugalḫegal the throne-bearer
šu-ba-ti	received

kišib Ur-é-gu-la dumu-na	seal of Ur-egula his son
iti pa$_4$-kùš-e mu	month 11
en unu$_5$-gal-<an-na> ^{d}Inanna ba-ḫun	AS 5
Seal	
Ur-é-gu-la	Ur-egula
ir$_{11}$-^{d}[ ]	servant of [ ]
aga$_3$-uš A-a-kal-la	soldier of Aakalla

no. 280 (Š 47 diri) bulla

2.2; 0.4.8 sila$_3$ še gur	122 gur 48 sila of barley
še-ba zi-ga	disbursement of rations
ki A-lu$_5$-lu$_5$	from Alulu
iti diri še-kin-ku$_5$	from the intercalary month
mu-ús-sa Ki-maš^{ki} ba-ḫul-ta	year Š 47
iti ezem-an-na mu Ḫa-ar-ši^{ki} ù	to month 11 year Š 48
iti 11-kam	it is [11] months
šà-ba iti diri 1-àm ì-gál	among these months is an intercalary month
kit-tum	this tablet is verified
Seal	
^{d}Šul-gi	Šulgi
nita kalaga-ga	the strong man
lugal Urí^{ki}-ma	king of Ur
Col. ii	
Lú-^{d}[ ]	Lu-[ ]
dub-sar	scribe
ir$_{11}$-zu	is your servant

no. 281 (Š 47)

Obverse	
54; 1.0. še zì-gu gur-lugal	54$\frac{1}{5}$ gur of barley for pea-flour according to the royal measurement
ki [Ir$_{11}$]-ta	from Ir
Lú-^{d}Nin-šubur-ke$_4$	Lu-Ninšubur
šu-ba-ti	received
Reverse	
mu-ús-sa Ki-maš^{ki} ba-ḫul	Š 47
Seal	
Lú-dingir-ra	Ludingirra
dub-sar	scribe
dumu Á-an-du-ru	son of Aanduru

The tablets sealed by this scribe deal mostly with guruš workers.

no. 282 (Š 31) [copy]

Dry flour for the boat of the king.

Obverse

o; 3.o. še zì ḫád	180 sila barley for dry flour
ki Ku-li ensi$_2$-ta	from Kuli the governor
A-na-a? sukkal?	Anaa(?) the vizier(?)
mu má lugal-šè	for the boat of the king

Reverse

šu-ba-ti	received
mu a-<rá>-2-kam	Š 31
Kara$_2$-ur^{ki} ba-ḫul(ŠI)	
šà Iš-zu$^{\langle ki\rangle}$-šè	in Iššu

This tablet is not clear. Anaa the vizier should directly precede šu-ba-ti. The reading mu a-<rá>-2-kam Kara$_2$-ur^{ki} ba-ḫul(ŠI) is not at all sure.

no. 283 (ŠS 1 xi) [copy]

Obverse

o; 2.o. še zì-gu	⅖ gur of pea-flour
kišib ^{d}Šara$_2$-za-me	tablet of Šara-zame
o; 2.o. kišib Ur-^{d}EN.ZU	⅖ gur tablet of Ur-Sîn
o; 2.o. kišib Lugal-é-maḫ-e	⅖ gur tablet of Lugalemaḫe
o; 2.o. kišib Lú-bala-sig$_5$	⅖ gur tablet of Lu-balasig
2 gur kišib Ur-^{d}Šul-pa-è	2 gur tablet of Ur-Šulpae

Reverse

še gibil$_4$ mu-ša	fresh barley
igi é-maḫ-šè-ta	from the igiemaḫše
iti pa$_4$-kùš-e	month 11
mu ^{d}Šu-^{d}EN.ZU lugal	ŠS 1

no. 284 (Š 30 ix)

Yield of wheat, barley, and emmer from several fields. The highest yield is always barley. Emmer-wheat is second, but far behind barley; the smallest is wheat. These proportions are well known and caused by the salinization of the soil.

Obverse

6.11;3.4.5 sila$_3$ še gur	370 gur of barley
14; 3.4. zíz gur	14 gur 220 sila of flour

a-šà dingir-ra-ta	from the field Dingirra
14.18; 1.0. še gur	$858\frac{1}{5}$ gur of barley
10; 1.0. zíz gur	$10\frac{1}{5}$ gur of flour
5; 2.0. gig gur	$5\frac{2}{5}$ gur of wheat
a-šà a-ú-da-ta	in the field Auda
4.0 lá 2 gur	238 gur <of barley>
[2;02.1 sila$_3$] zíz gur	[ ] gur of flour
Reverse	
a-šà muš-bi-an-na	in the field Mušbianna
4.46; 1.0. še gur	$286\frac{1}{5}$ gur of barley
2; 1.0. zíz <gur>	$2\frac{1}{5}$ gur of flour
1 gur gig	1 gur of wheat
a-šà sag-dù-ta	from the field Sagdu
šu-nigín 29.14; 0.4.5 sila$_3$ še gur-lugal	total 1754 gur and 45 sila of barley according to the royal measurement
šu-nigín 29; 1.0. zíz gur	total $29\frac{1}{5}$ gur of flour
šu-nigín 5; 2.0. gig gur	total $5\frac{2}{5}$ gur of wheat
Lugal-kù-zu [ì-dab$_5$]	Lugalkuzu [has taken into possession]
iti ^{d}Li$_9$-si$_4$-ta	from month 9
[iti sig$_4$-giš-ì-šub-]ba-[gar-šè]	to month 2
Edge	
mu dumu-lugal	Š 30

no. 285 (ŠS 2 iii)

Obverse	
0; 3.3.6 sila$_3$ še-àr-ra mu-túm	delivery of 216 sila of barley for grinding
kaš$_4$ má-laḫ$_4$ Ur-gar	for the messengers and the boatmen of Urgar
0; 1.0. Lú-^{d}Nagar-pa-è lú-lunga	$\frac{1}{5}$ gur of barley for Lu-Nagarpae the brewer
0; 1.2.6 sila$_3$ ^{giš}Dúr-gar-ni ašgab	86 sila for Durgarni the leatherworker
Reverse	
šu-nigín 1; 1.0.2 sila$_3$ gur	total 1 gur 62 sila
še-àr-ra mu-túm	delivery of barley for grinding
[kišib] ^{d}Šara$_2$-kam	seal of Šarakam
iti še]-kar-ra-gál-la	month 3
[mu má] ^{d}En-ki ba-ab-du$_8$	ŠS 2

no. 286 (Š 46)

Obverse	
22 še gur	22 gur of barley
še-ba [ ]	wages of [ ]

šà Umma^{ki}	in Umma
kišib Gur$_4$-za-an	seal of Gurzan
mu Ki-maš^{ki} ba-ḫul	Š 46

Seal

Gur$_4$-za-an	Gurzan
dumu Du-la-a-bi	son of Dulabi
muḫaldim ensi$_2$	cook of the governor

no. 287 (Š 45 v)

Obverse

0; 0.1. še-ba lugal	60 sila barley rations according to the royal measurement
Ur-^{d}Šara$_2$	for Ur-Šara
A-ba-ša$_6$	for Abaša
kišib Lugal-ukken-né	seal of Lugalukkenne
še sumun é-gal íd-lugal-ta	old barley from the palace of the royal canal

Reverse

iti ri mu-ús-sa	month 5
Si-mu-ru-um^{ki} Lu-lu-pu-um	Š 45
a-rá 10 lá 1-kam ba-ḫul	

Seal

Lugal-ukken-né	Lugalukkenne
dumu Lugal-nì-lagar-e	son of Lugalnilagare
nu-banda$_3$ gu$_4$	lieutenant of the oxen

no. 288 [copy]

Obverse

20 sila$_3$ še-ba Lú-uš-gi-na dumu Ur-^{d}EN.ZU šà-gu$_4$	20 sila barley rations for Lu-ušgina son of Ur-Sîn the ox-driver
30 sila$_3$ Ur-^{d}A-šár dumu Lú-bàn-da šà-gu$_4$	30 sila Ur-Ašar son of Lubanda the ox-driver
20 sila$_3$ ^{d}Amar-^{d}EN.ZU-me-an-ta dumu Dingir-ama geme$_2$ kikken-e-na	20 sila Amar-Sîn-meanta son of Dingirama the mill woman
20 sila$_3$ Lú-^{d}Utu dumu Lugal-é dumu Gu-du-ni	20 sila Lu-Utu son of Lugale son of Guduni
zàḫ Gemé-e$_{11}$-e ^{giš}ì-sur	the fugitive Geme-ee employed at the oilpress

Reverse

[ ]-ta	from [ ]
[ ]-nir-zi-mu	[ ]-nirzimu
[ ]	[ ]
[ ]-5-ta	[ ] five [ ]
[mu um]^{ki} ba-ḫul	[year]

no. 289 (ŠS 2 ix) [copy]

Obverse	
0; 1.4. še-ba	⅓ gur barley for rations
Ur-^{giš}gigir dumu E-a	Urgigir son of Ea
0; 1.4. Lú-^{d}Šara$_2$	⅓ gur barley for Lu-Šara
0; 1.3. Ur-^{giš}gigir banda$_3$	90 sila barley for young Urgigir
0; 1.3. Šeš-a-ni	90 sila barley for Šešani
Reverse	
šu-nigín 1; 1.2. še-ba gur	total 380 sila of rations
gur$_7$ ì-sum-ta	from the granary of the field Isum
ki ka-gur$_7$-ta	from the granary manager
kišib Šeš-a-ni	seal of Šešani
iti ^{d}Li$_9$-si$_4$	month 9
mu ma-da Za-ab-ša-li^{ki} ba-ḫul	ŠS 2
Seal	
Šeš-a-ni	Šešani
dub-sar	scribe
dumu Lugal-nì-lagar-e	son of Lugalnilagare

no. 290 (ŠS 4 xi) [copy]

Obverse	
0;1.0. še-ba	60 sila barley rations
Lú-bala-sig$_5$	Lu-balasig
kar-ta	from the quay
ki Ka-gur$_7$-ta	from the granary keeper
Reverse	
kišib ^{d}Šara$_2$-a-mu	seal of Šara-amu
iti pa$_4$-kùš-e	month 11
mu bàd mar-tu ba-dù	ŠS 4
Seal	
^{d}Šara$_2$-a-mu	Šara-amu
dumu ^{d}Šara$_2$-uru$_x$(ŠEŠ)	son of Šara-šeš

no. 291 (ŠS 1 [v]) [copy]

Obverse	
40 sila$_3$ še-ba banda$_3$ Ur-é-an-na	40 sila of barley rations for the young Ur-Eanna
35 <sila$_3$> banda$_3$ Lú-me-lám	35 sila for the young Lumelam
30 sila$_3$ banda$_3$ Lugal-zi-mu	30 sila for the young Lugalzimu
20 sila$_3$ banda$_3$ Ur-^{d}Gu-nu-ra	20 sila for the young Ur-Gunura

20 sila$_3$ banda$_3$ A-ba-^{d}Šara$_2$-gim	20 sila for the young Aba-Šara-gim
Reverse	
banda$_3$ šà-gu$_4$	young ox-drivers
iti [ri]	month 5
mu ^{d}Šu-^{d}EN.ZU lugal	ŠS 1

no. 292 (ŠS 7 v) [copy]

Obverse	
0; 1.4. še-ba	⅓ gur of barley rations
Ur-^{giš}gigir	Urgigir
0; 1.4. Lú-^{d}Šara$_2$	100 sila Lu-Šara
dumu A-tá-na-aḫ	son of Atanaḫ
0; 1.3. Ur-^{giš}gigir 2-kam	90 for Urgigir, the second
Reverse	
0; 1.3. Šeš-a-ni	90 sila for Šešani
lú-azlág-me	garment-makers
ugula Ì-kal-la	overseer Ikalla
šu-nigín 1; 1.2. še-ba gur	total 1 gur 80 sila of barley rations
a-šà ^{giš}ma-nu-ta	from the field of willow
ki Ka-gur$_7$-ta	from the granary manager
kišib Ur-^{giš}gigir dumu E-a	seal of Urgigir son of Ea
iti ri mu ma-da Za-ab-ša-li^{ki} ba-ḫul	month 5 ŠS 7
Seal	
Ur-^{giš}gigir	Urgigir
dub-sar	scribe
dumu [Ba-ša$_6$]	son of Baša

no. 293 (ŠS 8 viii) [copy]

Obverse	
0; 1.1.5 sila$_3$ še-ba	75 sila of barley rations
^{d}Šara$_2$-ù-túm	Šara-utum
0; 1.4. Ur-^{d}Ištaran?	⅓ gur Ur-Ištaran
0; 0.4. dumu Dingir-gá	40 sila son of Dingirga
0; 0.3.5 sila$_3$ dumu Ur-gi$_6$-par$_4$	35 sila son of Urgipar
Reverse	
0; 1.1.5 sila$_3$ Ur-dun	75 sila Urdun
0; 1.1.5 sila$_3$ Lugal-gar-ni	75 sila Lugalgarni
0; 1.0. Ur-ni$_9$-gar	⅕ gur Urnigar
šu-nigín 1; 2.4. še-ba gur	total 1 gur 160 sila barley rations
gur$_7$ gu-<la>-ta	from the great granary

ki ka-gur$_7$-ta	from the granary manager
kišib Lú-kiri$_3$-zal	seal of Lukirizal
iti é-iti-6	month 8
mu-ús-sa Za-ab-ša-li^{ki} ba-ḫul	ŠS 8
Seal	
[Ur-gú-dè]-na	Urgudena
dub-sar	the scribe
dumu Lú-[kiri$_3$-zal]	son of Lukirizal

no. 294 (ŠS 6 iv)

Obverse	
0; 1.2.5 sila$_3$ še-ba	85 sila of rations
Al-lu	for Allu
0; ?.1.5 sila$_3$ Lú-^{d}Nin-šubur	x+15 sila for Lu-Ninšubur
[ ] Šeš-kal-la	[ ] sila for Šeškalla
[ ] Ir$_{11}$-^{d}Šara$_2$	x for Ir-Šara
ugula Lugal-nesag-e	overseer Lugalnesage
0; 1.2.5 sila$_3$ Lugal-nam-maḫ-zu	85 sila of rations for Lugalnammaḫzu
Reverse	
àr-àr sá-du$_{11}$-me	millers for the regular deliveries
0; 1.1. Ur-tar-luḫ ir$_{11}$ Lugal-ezem	75 sila of rations for Urtarluḫ servant of Lugalezem
gìr-sì-ga ensi$_2$-ka	members of the household of the governor
iti nesag	month 4
mu ^{d}Šu-^{d}EN.ZU lugal-e	ŠS 6
na-rú-a maḫ mu-dù	

no. 295 (ŠS 7)

Obverse	
0; 1.1.5 sila$_3$ še-[ba] Nam-zi-tar-ra	75 sila rations for Namzitarra
0; 1.4.5 sila$_3$ Ḫa-ni-[eš]	105 sila for Ḫanieš
0; 1.1.5 sila$_3$ Lugal-a-[ma-ru]	75 sila for Lugalamaru
0; 1.1.5 sila$_3$ Ur-^{d}Šara$_2$	75 sila for Ur-Šara
0; 1.1.5 sila$_3$ La-qí-ip	75 sila for Laqip
0; 0.4.5 sila$_3$ Na-an-na	45 sila for Nanna
0; 0.3. Inim-^{d}Šara$_2$	30 sila for Inim-Šara
Reverse	
šu-nigín 1; 3.0. še-ba gur [ ]-ne	total 1 3/5 gur rations for the [ ]
ki Ka-gur$_7$-ta	from the granary manager
[kišib] Lú-ša$_6$-ša$_6$	seal of Lušaša

ki-su$_7$ a-šà Lugal-AB	threshing floor of the field LugalAB
mu ^{d}Šu-^{d}EN.ZU lugal Uri$_5$^{ki}-ma-ke$_4$	ŠS 7
ma-da Za-ab-ša-li^{ki} mu-ḫul	
Seal	
Lú-ša$_6$-ša$_6$	Lu-šaša
dub-sar	scribe
dumu Bí-du$_{11}$-ga	son of Biduga

no. 296 (ŠS 3 xii) [copy]

Obverse	
0; 1.1.5 sila$_3$ še-ba	75 sila of rations
Lú-kiri$_3$-zal	for Lukirizal
0; 1.0. Lú-du$_{10}$-ga	⅕ gur for Luduga
ki-su$_7$ saḫar-ú-ú-ta	from the threshing floor Saḫaruu
ki ka-gur$_7$-ta	from the granary manager
Reverse	
kišib Ur-^{giš}gigir	seal of Urgigir
iti ^{d}Dumu-zi	month 12
mu Si-ma-núm^{ki} ba-ḫul	ŠS 3
Seal	
Ur-^{giš}gigir	Urgigir
dub-sar	scribe
dumu Ba-ša$_6$	son of Baša

no. 297 (ŠS 1 vi) [copy]

Obverse	
0; 2.1. še-ba	130 sila of barley rations
mu še-àr-ra-ka-šè	destined for flour
gur$_7$-a tag$_4$-a	(but) left over in the granary
ki Ur-dingir-ra-ta	from Urdingirra
Reverse	
[kišib] Lú-^{d}Šul-gi-ra	seal of Lu-Šulgi
gìr Ur-^{d}Šara$_2$	responsible: Ur-Šara
iti šu-numun	month 6
mu ^{d}Šu-^{d}EN.ZU lugal	ŠS 1
Seal	
Lú-é-maḫ-e	Lu-emaḫe
dub-sar	scribe
dumu Ur-^{d}Li$_9$-si$_4$-na	son of Ur-Lisi
ensi$_2$ Umma^{ki}-ka	governor of Umma

Grain to be handed out as rations to be ground is left over in the granary. Either this grain is given to Lu-Šulgi under the supervision of a *gir*-official or Lu-Šulgi guaranties the exactness of the statement.

no. 298 (ŠS 3 v)

Obverse	
0; 1.3. še-ba ^{d}Šara$_2$-a-mu	90 sila ration for Šara-amu
0; 0.5.5 sila$_3$ šim-ta	55 sila from the brewer
0; 1.0. Lugal-nì-lagar-e	$^{1}/_{5}$ for Lugalnilagare
0; 0.3. Ur-^{d}Hal-mu-túm	30 sila for Ur-Ḫalmutum
0; 1.2.5 <sila$_3$> ^{giš}Apin-ki-du$_{10}$	85 sila for Apinkidu
0; 1.3. Lú-dingir-ra	90 sila for Ludingirra
0; 1.2.5 sila$_3$ ^{d}Šara$_2$-ì-zu	85 sila for Šara-izu
0; 1.0. Kù-^{d}Šara$_2$	$^{1}/_{5}$ gur for Ku-Šara
Reverse	
šu-nigín 1; 4.2.5 sila$_3$ še gur	total 1 gur 265 sila barley
ki-su$_7$ a-šà lá-maḫ-ta	from the threshing floor of the field Lamaḫ
ki ka-gur$_7$-ta	from the granary manager
ugula ^{d}Šara$_2$-a-mu	overseer Šara-amu
kišib Ur-^{d}Šara$_2$	seal of Ur-Šara
iti ri	month 5
mu-ús-sa má ^{d}En-ki ba-ab-du$_8$	ŠS 3
Seal	
^{d}Šara$_2$-a-mu	Šara-amu
dumu ^{d}Šara$_2$-uru$_x$(ŠEŠ)	son of Šara-uru

Line 2 presents a difficulty, since we expect a destination, not a source.

no. 299 (ŠS 3 v) [copy]

Obverse	
0; 1.5. še-ba lugal	110 sila rations according to the royal measurement
^{d}Ìr-ra-ba-ni	Irra-bani
0; 1.3. Igi-ḫuš	90 sila Igiḫuš
0; 1.0. Lú-^{d}Nanna	$^{1}/_{5}$ gur Lu-Nanna
0; 1.0. ^{d}Nin-ur$_4$-ra-kam	$^{1}/_{5}$ gur Ninurrakam
Reverse	
šu-nigín 1; 0.2. še-ba gur	total: 1 gur 20 sila rations
ki ka-gur$_7$-ta	from granary manager
kišib Lil-la	seal of Lilla

a-šà lá-maḫ-ta	from the field Lamaḫ
iti ri mu-ús-sa	month 5
má ^{d}En-ki ba-ab-du$_{8}$	ŠS 3
Seal	
Ur-^{d}Li$_{9}$-si$_{4}$	Ur-Lisi
ensi$_{2}$ Umma^{ki}	governor of Umma
Lil-la	Lilla
dumu [ ]	son of [ ]
ir$_{11}$-zu	his servant

no. 300 (ŠS 7 xi) [copy]

Obverse	
0; 1.1.5 sila$_{3}$ še-ba	75 sila of barley rations
Kù-^{d}Šara$_{2}$	for Ku-Šara
ki Ka-gur$_{7}$-ta	from the granary manager
kišib ^{d}Šara$_{2}$-a-mu	seal of Šara-amu
Reverse	
iti pa$_{4}$-kùš-e	month 11
mu ma-da Za-ab-ša-li^{ki}	ŠS 7
ba-ḫul	
Seal	
^{d}Šara$_{2}$-a-mu	Šara-amu
dumu ^{d}Šara$_{2}$-uru$_{x}$(ŠEŠ)	son of Šara-šeš

no. 301 (Š 31) [copy]

Obverse	
0; 1.1. še lugal	70 sila of barley according to the royal measurement
0; 0.3. dabin	30 sila of barley flour
5 sila$_{3}$ zì-[dub-dub]	5 sila flour [for offering]
1 sila$_{3}$ gig	1 sila of wheat
ki Lugal-mu-ma-ág-ta	from Lugalmumag
Reverse	
^{giš}Dúr-gar-ni	Durgarni
šu-ba-ti	received
šà bala	during the *bala*
mu a-rá 2-kam Kara$_{2}$-ḫar^{ki} ba-ḫul	Š 31
Seal	
^{giš}Dúr-gar-ni	Durgarni
dub-sar	scribe

dumu Lugal-gaba	son of Lugalgaba
šabra	steward

no. 302 (Š 34)

Summary of the temples of deities in which young women were active.

Obverse	
5; 4.0. gur še-ba geme$_2$ banda$_3$ iti 12-kam	$5^{4}/_{5}$ gur rations for young women over 12 months
^{d}Nin-sún	for Ninsun
15; 2.0.6 sila$_3$ gur sá-du$_{11}$	15 gur 126 sila as regular deliveries
8; 2.3. gur še-ba geme$_2$ banda$_3$ iti 12-kam	8½ gur rations for young women over 12 months
^{d}Nin-ib-gal	for Nin-ibgal
10; 1.1.7 sila$_3$ sá-du$_{11}$ iti 12-kam	10 gur 77 sila regular deliveries over 12 months
^{d}Nanše Umma^{ki}	for Nanše of Umma
10 gur sá-du$_{11}$ iti 12-kam	10 gur regular deliveries over 12 months
10; 3.0. še-ba geme$_2$-banda$_3$ iti 12-kam	$10^{3}/_{5}$ gur rations for young women
^{d}Nin-e$_{11}$-e	for Ninee
9; 0.5.1½ sila$_3$ gur sá-du$_{11}$	9 gur 51½ sila regular deliveries
7; 2.0. gur sá-du$_{11}$ geme$_2$ banda$_3$ iti 12-kam	$7^{2}/_{5}$ gur rations for young women over 12 months
^{d}En-ki ù ^{d}Uš-ka-limmu$_2$	for Enki and for Uskalimmu
21; 4.[1.6½ sila$_3$]. gur sá-du$_{11}$	21 gur 256½ sila regular deliveries
1; 1.0. gur še-ba geme$_2$ banda$_3$ iti 12-kam	$1^{1}/_{5}$ gur rations for young women over 12 months
^{d}Nun-gal	for Nungal
32; 0.0.7 sila$_3$ gur [sá-du$_{11}$]	32 gur 7 sila regular deliveries
3; 3.0. gur še-ba geme$_2$ banda$_3$ iti 12-kam	$3^{3}/_{5}$ gur rations for young women over 12 months
^{d}Nin-da-Lagaš^{ki}	for NindaLagaš
7; 1.0. gur ninda nì-gál-la Gir$_{13}$-giš^{ki}	$7^{1}/_{5}$ gur of barley for bread available in Girgiš
ugú Ur-zu-ka ba-a-gar	to be put on the account of Urzu
Reverse	
šu-nigín 143; 0.0. 8 sila$_3$ še-ba	total 143 gur and 8 sila
še-ba še ninda nì-gál-la	barley rations and barley for bread
ki Ur-^{d}Šara$_2$ ša$_{13}$-dub-ba-ta	from Ur-Šara the archivist
Ir$_{11}$ ka-gur$_7$-ke$_4$ šu-ba-ti	Ir the granary manager received
mu An-ša-an^{ki} ba-ḫul	Š 34

no. 303 (ŠS 6 viii) [copy]

This tablet deals with weaver women employed at irrigation work.

Obverse	
12 geme$_2$ uš-bar u$_4$-3-šè	3 workdays for 12 female weavers
a-è-a nin-ḫé-gál-ka-ta	on the water outlet of <the field> of Ninḫegal
ugula Šeš-sig$_5$	overseer Šeššig
Reverse	
kišib nam-šà-tam Lugal-kù-zu	seal of the office of the high administrator, Lugalkuzu
iti é-iti-6	month 8
mu ^{d}Šu-^{d}EN.ZU lugal-e	ŠS 6
na-rú-a maḫ mu-rú	
Seal	
Lugal-kù-zu	Lugalkuzu
dub-sar	scribe
dumu Ur-ni$_9$-gar kuš$_7$	son of Urnigar the equerry

At least two seals of this scribe are known. He is usually concerned with guruš work, fields, irrigation, and navigation.

no. 304 (ŠS 3 vii)

Obverse	
0; 2.0. še-ba ḫé-dab$_5$	$\frac{2}{5}$ gur rations for the forced(?) workers
gur$_7$-a tag$_4$-a	leftover in the granary
šà é-àr sumun	in the old mill
kišib Lú-^{d}Nám-an-ka	seal of Lu-Namanka
gìr Dingir-ra	responsible: Dingirra
Reverse	
iti min-èš	month 7
mu Si-ma-núm^{ki}	ŠS 3
Seal	
Lú-^{d}Nám-an-ka	Lu-Namanka
dub-sar	scribe
dumu Lú-^{d}[Sara$_2$]	son of Lu-[Šara]
sa$_{12}$-du$_5$-ka	field surveyor

no. 305 (ŠS 6 x)

Obverse	
0; 1.0. še-ba lugal	⅕ gur of rations according to the royal measurement
Lú-uš-gi-na	for Lušgina
0; 1.2.5 $sila_3$ ^{d}$Šara_2$-ba-zi-ge	85 sila for Šara-bazige
0; 1.1. Lú-ib?-gal	70 sila for Lu-ibgal
0; 1.4. Gur_4-za-an	⅓ gur for Gurzan
Reverse	
šu-nigín 1; 0.1.5 $sila_3$ še-ba	total 1 gur 15 sila of rations
ki Ka-gur_7-ta	from the granary manager
kišib A-kal-la	seal of Akalla
iti ezem-^{d}Šul-gi	month 8
mu na-rú-a maḫ	ŠS 6
^{d}Šu-^{d}EN.ZU lugal-e	Šu-Sîn the king
^{d}En-líl ^{d}Nin-líl-ra mu-rú	for Enlil and Ninlil erected
Seal	
A-kal-la	Akalla
dub-sar	scribe
dumu Lú-[$ša_6$-ga]	son of Lu[šaga]

no. 306 (AS 9)

Obverse	
5 še gur-lugal	5 gur of barley according to the royal measurement
I-ti-a	for Itia
5 gur I-din-^{d}Adad	5 gur for Idin-Adad
5 gur A-ti-núm	5 gur for Atinum
5 gur Ḫi-li-ib	5 gur for Ḫilib
5 gur Du-šu-um	5 gur for Dušuum
5 gur E-la-ak-šu-qir	5 gur for Elakšuqir
Reverse	
ka-kéš-me	making belts
5 gur Da-da	5 gur for Dada
5 gur Lú-dingir-ra	5 gur for Ludingirra
ì-rá-rá-me	perfumers
30 gur ^{d}En-líl-da	30 gur for Enlilda
lú kur-mu-gam-ma	who submits *the land*(?)
šu-nigín 70 še gur-lugal	total 70 gur of barley according to the royal measurement

še-ba zag-mu	barley rations for the beginning of the year
ki Ur-^{giš}gigir ensi$_2$ Umma^{ki}-ta	from Urgigir governor of Umma
Edge	
ki Ab-ba-ti	at the place of Abbati
mu-ús-sa en Eridu^{ki} ba-ḫun	AS 9

no. 307 (AS 8) envelop [copy]

Obverse	
5; 2.0. še gur-lugal	5 gur ⅖ gur of barley according to the royal measurement
še-numun-šè	for the seeding-barley
ì-dub a-šà du$_6$-tir	silo on the field Dutir
ki Lugal-Nina^{ki}-šè-ta	from Lugal-Ninaše
Reverse	
kišib Ur-^{d}Lama dumu Nam-maḫ	seal of Ur-Lama son of Nammaḫ
mu en-nun-e! Eridu^{ki} ba-ḫun	AS 8
Seal	
Ur-^{d}Lama	Ur-Lama
[dub-sar]	[scribe]
[dumu]	[son of]

no. 308 (AS 8) tablet

5; 2.0. še gur-lugal	5⅖ gur of barley according to the royal measurement
še-numun-šè	for seeding barley
ì-dub a-šà du$_6$-tir	silo on the field Dutir
ki Lugal-Nina^{ki}-šè-ta	from Lugal-Ninaše
(The rest of the tablet is illegible.)	

no. 309 (ŠS 7) [copy]

Copy of an account tablet in which the scribe recapitulates the special status of some deliveries. One is a loan, two others are of excess barley available and returned, and the last a delivery for buying silver. A *gir*-official is present to authenticate this account and guaranty its accounting accuracy.

Obverse	
40 še-ur$_5$-ra gur	40 gur of barley for loan
Lú-^{d}Nin-šubur dumu Inim-^{d}Šara$_2$	for Lu-Ninšubur son of Inim-Šara
11 še gur lá-ni su-ga	11 gur of barley, from the arrears that were returned
Lugal-é-maḫ-e	for Lugalemaḫe

9 še gur lá-ni su-ga	9 gur of barley, from the arrears that were returned
Lugal-^{d}Ištaran	for Lugal-Ištaran
7 še gur šám kù-babbar	7 gur of barley to buy silver
Reverse	
Lú-^{d}Šul-gi-ra	for Lu-Šulgi
ki Ur-^{d}Nun-gal-ta	from Ur-Nungal
gaba-ri kišib ^{d}Šara$_{2}$-kam)	[copy] of the tablet of Šarakam
gìr Gu-du-du	responsible: Gududu
mu ^{d}Šu-^{d}EN.ZU lugal-e	ŠS 7
ma-da Za-ab-ša-li^{ki} mu-ḫul	

no. 310 (Š 48 diri) envelope [copy]

Obverse	
15; 2.0. še gur lugal	15$^{2}/_{5}$ gur of barley according to the royal measurement
še-zì-ka nu-banda$_{3}$-gu$_{4}$-ne	barley for flour for the lieutenants of the oxen
ki Ur-^{d}Ba-ba$_{6}$-ta	from Ur-Baba
ì-dub ḫi-gál-ta	from the silo (on the field) Ḫigal
kišib Ur-^{d}Ba-ba$_{6}$ dumu Lugal-sig$_{5}$	seal of Ur-Baba son of Lugalsig
ugula sanga ^{d}Nin-gír-su	overseer the chief temple official of Ningirsu
Reverse	
iti diri še-kin-ku$_{5}$	intercalary month
mu Ḫa-ar-ši^{ki}	Š 48
Ḫu-ur$_{5}$-ti^{ki} ba-ḫul	
Seal	
[Ur-^{d}Ba-ba$_{6}$	Ur-Baba
dub-sar	scribe
dumu Lugal-sig$_{5}$]	son of Lugalsig

This seal has been reconstructed from the tablet and is not otherwise attested.

no. 311

Obverse	
[ ] še-ba	[ ] barley ration
[ ] Ku-li	[ ] for Kuli
0;1.0. Ur-^{d}Pirig	$^{1}/_{5}$ gur for Ur-Pirig
0;3.3.5 sila$_{3}$ iti ri-ta iti min-èš-šè	215 sila from month 5 to month 7
Reverse	
ur-^{giš}gigir-re mušen-dù	for Urgigire, the fowler
0;4.0. še-ba a-bal Ka-ma-rí^{ki}	240 sila for the water-carrier in Kamari

ki Ur-mes	at the place of Urmes

no. 312 (Š 27)

Obverse

20 lá 2 še gur lugal	18 gur of barley according to the royal measurement
a-šà-ga <Ka>-ma-rí^{ki}-ta	from the fields of Kamari
6;1.0. é-àr-ta	6 1/5 gur from the mill
ki Ir$_{11}$-ta	from Ir
iti ezem-^{d}Šul-gi	month 10

Reverse

sá-du$_{11}$ ^{d}Inanna [unu$_{6}$-gal-ka-šè]	regular delivery for Inanna [in the great kitchen]
Ur-é-gi$_{6}$-par$_{4}$	Ur-egipar
šu-ba-ti	received
mu-ús-sa a-rá 2-kam	Š 27
si-mu-ru-um^{ki} ba-ḫul	

no. 313 (ŠS 1 v) [copy]

Obverse

4;3.4. še gur	4 gur and 220 sila of barley
ki ^{d}Nanna-ma-ba-ta	from Nanna-maba
mu [-šè]	for [ ]

Reverse

iti ne-IZI-gar	month 5
mu ^{d}Šu-^{d}EN.ZU lugal-àm	ŠS 1

no. 314 (ŠS 8 iii) [copy]

Obverse

12 še gur	12 gur of barley
še Ilum-ki-in	barley of Ilum-kin
10 gur	10 gur
ki U-bar-um-ta	from Ubarum
^{d}Šul-gi-^{d}Lama-mu	Šulgi-Lamamu

Reverse

šu-ba-an-ti	received
iti zaḫ$_{x}$-da-gu$_{7}$	month 3
mu ^{d}Šu-^{d}EN.ZU lugal Uri$_{5}$^{ki}-ma-ke$_{4}$	ŠS 8
má-gur$_{8}$ maḫ ^{d}En-líl ^{d}Nin-líl-ra mu-ne-dím	

Seal

[ ]	[ ]

dub-sar ir$_{11}$ lugal	scribe servant of the king

no. 315 (Š 44 vii 17)

Obverse	
15 še gur ur$_{5}$-ra	15 gur of barley for loan shekel of silver
máš-bi 1 gur 100 sila$_{3}$-ta	interest 100 sila for 1 gur
ki Ur-^{d}EN.ZU-ta	from Ur-Sîn
Gemé-é-zi-da-ke$_{4}$	Geme-ezida
Reverse	
šu-ba-ti	received
iti du$_{6}$-kù-ga u$_{4}$ 17 ba-zal	month 7 day 17
mu Si-mu-ru-um^{ki} ba-ḫul	Š 44
Seal	
Ba-ša$_{6}$ [ ]	
[ ]	

no. 316 (IS 2 diri)

Obverse	
7 še gur lugal máš DIŠ-ta	7 gur of barley according to the royal measurement interest as usual(?)
4 gín máš 5 gín 1 gín-àm	4 shekels interest 1 shekel for 5 shekels
ki Ur-^{d}EN.ZU-ta	from Ur-Sîn
Ur-^{d}EN.ZU dumu šeš aga$_{3}$-uš-ke$_{4}$	Ur-Sîn the son of the assistant soldier
Reverse	
šu-ba-ti	received
iti diri	intercalary month
mu en ^{d}Inanna Unug^{ki}	IS 2
máš-e ì-pàd	

no. 317 (ŠS 7 xi)

Obverse	
0;2.0 še ur$_{5}$-šè	120 sila of barley for loan
máš-bi 0;0.4.	interest 40 sila
ki Ur-^{d}EN.ZU-ta	from Ur-Sîn
Aš-ka-e?	Aškae
šu-ba-ti	received
Reverse	
Lugal-ḫé-gál	Lugalḫegal
Á-da-da	Adada
Ur-dingir-si$_{4}$-an-na	Urdingirsianna

lú inim-ma-bi-me	the witnesses
iti úd-duru$_5$ [ ] u$_4$ 17 ba-zal	month 11 [ ] day 17
mu ma-da [ ]	ŠS 7
Seal	
Ba-ša$_6$ [ ]	Baša
[ ]	
Seal illegible	

no. 318 (ŠS 9 xi)

Obverse	
2 še gur	2 gur of barley
máš gur-ra 100 sila$_3$-ta	interest of 100 sila per gur
ki U-bar-ta	from Ubar
Iš-me-^{d}En-líl	Išme-Enlil
šu-ba-ti	received
Reverse	
iti úd-duru$_5$	month 11
mu ^{d}Šu-^{d}EN.ZU lugal-e	ŠS 9
é ^{d}Šara$_2$ Umma^{ki}-ka mu-dù	
Seal	
Da-ḫi-ša-tal	(O) Daḫištal
máš-šu-gíd-gíd	the augur
Šu-^{d}En-líl	Šu-Enlil
[engar] ir$_{11}$-zu	[the farmer] is your servant

no. 319 (IS 1 iii)

Obverse	
30 sila$_3$ še	30 sila of barley
ki Du$_{11}$-ga-ta	from Dugga
Ur-^{d}Ba-ba$_6$	Ur-Baba
šu-ba-ti	received
Reverse	
iti zaḫ$_x$-da-gu$_7$	month 3
mu ^{d}I-bí-^{d}EN.ZU lugal	IS 1
Seal	
Ur-^{d}Ba-ba$_6$	Ur-Baba
dumu Ab-ba-dul	son of Abbadul

no. 320 (ŠS 3)

Obverse	
15 $sila_3$ še	15 sila of barley
ki Šeš-kal-la-ta	from Šeš-kal-la
kišib $ensi_2$	seal of the governor
Reverse	
mu Si-ma-$núm^{ki}$ ba-ḫul	ŠS 3
Seal	
^{d}Šu-^{d}EN.ZU	Šu-Sîn
lugal kalag-ga	the mighty king
lugal $Uri_5{}^{ki}$-ma	king of Ur
lugal an-ub-da limmu-ba	king of the four quarters of the universe
A-a-kal-la	Aakalla
$ensi_2$ $Umma^{ki}$	the governor of Umma
ir_{11}-zu	is your servant

no. 321 (ŠS 4 x) [copy]

Obverse	
2 $sila_3$ še Igi-$^{d}Šara_2$-šè	2 sila of barley for Igi-Šaraše
12 $sila_3$ Ur-dun	12 sila for Urdun
6 $sila_3$ Bí-da	6 sila for Bida
6 $sila_3$ Ur-ab-ba	6 sila for Urabba
6 $sila_3$ $^{d}Šara_2$-ù-túm	6 sila for Šara-utum
Reverse	
mu ninda-še gur_7-[a] tag_4-a	for bread, from the barley leftover in the granary
ki In-$ša_6$-$ša_6$-ta	from Inšaša
kišib Lú-$^{d}Šara_2$	seal of Lu-Šara
šà kar-ra-ka	on the quay
ugula Lú-$kiri_3$-zal	overseer Lukirizal
iti ezem-^{d}Šul-gi	month 8
mu bàd mar-tu ba-dù	ŠS 4
Seal	
Lú-$^{d}Šara_2$	Lu-Šara
dub-sar	scribe
dumu [ ]	son of [ ]

COMMODITIES: BREAD AND FLOUR (nos. 322–339)

no. 322 (Š 43 xi – Š 44 viii 10)

Three workers give back to the temple bread and flour, owned by this institution.

Obverse	
2; 2.1.3 sila$_3$ ninda zì-sig$_{15}$ gur-lugal	2 gur 133 sila of bread made from coarse flour
1; 2.0.2 sila$_3$ ninda dabin gur	1 gur 122 sila of bread made of barley flour
sag nì-<<pa>>-ga é-nì-lagar-ka	total amount in the Enilagar-temple
Reverse	
Ba-a-mu	Baamu
Gìr-ni	Girni
Ḫa-la-mu	Ḫalamu
ù Lú-iti-da	and Luitida
íb-su-su-ne	returned
iti 8 u$_4$ 10-kam	on the 10th day
iti pa$_4$-kùš-e mu en ^{d}Nanna ša iti min-èš-ta	month 11 year Š 43
u$_4$ 10 zal-la mu Si-mu-ru-um^{ki} a-rá-a	to the 10th day Š 44
10 lá 1-šè	

no. 323 (AS 7) [copy]

Obverse	
10 nagar ninda-dag 30-ta	10 carpenters receiving 30 bread each
16 ad-kub$_4$ 30-ta	10 reedmat-makers receiving 30 bread each
12 ašgab 30-ta	10 leather-workers receiving 30 bread each
ki Da-da-ga	from Dadaga
8 šitim 30-ta	8 builders receiving 30 bread each
30 ḫé-dab$_5$ 30-ta	8 forced(?) workers receiving 30 bread each
5 má-gín 30-ta	5 sailors receiving 30 bread each
15 ad-kub$_4$ 30-ta	15 reedmat-makers receiving 30 bread each
šà é-maš	in the Emaš
ninda-bi 48.0-àm	the bread is 2880
0; 2.3. ninda dabin	½ gur bread with barley flour
27 sila$_3$ ninda al-zi-ra	27 sila of broken bread
3.40.0 ninda dag	13200 pieces of …-bread
geme$_2$-bàn-da íb-kú	eaten by the young women
10.0 ninda a-rá 1-kam	600 bread the first time
3.0 ninda a-rá 2-kam	180 bread the second time
Reverse	
gìr Ba-sig$_5$	responsible: Basig

3.0 ninda gìr A-kal-la gu-za-lá	180 breads, responsible: Akalla the throne-bearer
2.0 ninda gìr Nam-ḫa-ni	120 breads, responsible: Namḫani
1.0.0 ninda gìr Ur-gú-dè-na	3600 breads, responsible: Urgudena
1.0.0 ninda gìr ^{d}Ḫa-ià-ù-túm ù Lugal-nì-lagar-è	600 breads, responsible: Ḫaia-utum and Lugalnilagare
1.40 ninda gìr En-gi_7	100 breads, responsible: Engi
4.0 ninda gìr Lú-^{d}Utu	24 breads, responsible: Lu-Utu
8.50 ninda Lú-du_{10}-ga	370 breads, <responsible:> Luduga
gìr A-kal-la $gudu_4$	responsible: Akalla the purification-priest
šu-nigín 7.0.30 ninda dag	total 25230 pieces of ...-bread
zi-ga ki Ad-da-ta	disbursement from Adda
mu Ḫu-úḫ-nu-ri^{ki} ba-ḫul	AS 7

no. 324 (ŠS 5)

Obverse

33; 2.0. ninda gin gur ki Lugal-kù-zu	$33^2/_5$ gur of average-quality bread from Lugalkuzu
18; 0.2.7 $sila_3$ gur ninda gin ì-du_8 rá-gaba	18 gur 27 sila of average-quality bread for the doorkeeper and the messenger,
gìr Lú-tur-tur	responsible: Luturtur
6; 0.3. gur ninda zì-gu sig_5	6 gur and 30 sila bread from top-quality pea-flour
6; 2.0. gur ninda zì-gu gin	$6^2/_5$ gur bread from average-quality pea-flour
1.5; 3.3. gur ninda gin	65 gur 210 sila of average-quality bread
11; 4.0. gur ninda šu	$11^4/_5$ gur of bread šu
13; 4.3. gur ninda zì-gu sig_5	13 gur 270 sila bread from top-quality pea-flour
1; 2.0. gur <ninda> zì-gu gin	$1^2/_5$ gur bread from average-quality pea-flour
3.20; 0.1. gur dabin	200 gur 10 sila of barley flour
0; 3.3.5 $sila_3$ nì-àr-sig_5	215 sila of top-quality groats
šu-a-gi-na iti-da	complete delivery for the month
1; 2.3. gur zì-sig_{15}	1½ gur of coarse flour
1 gur ninda gin	1 gur of average-quality bread
0; 0.3. [ ]	30 sila [ ]

Reverse

0;1.0. [ ]	60 sila [ ]
0;2.0 ninda ù-du_8-[ ]	120 sila bread [ ]
0;1.0 $sila_3$ ninda šu-ùr-ra	60 sila ...-bread
20 $sila_3$ še sa zíz-an	20 sila roasted barley and emmer flour

30 sila$_3$ še sa še	30 sila roasted barley and barley
nin giš LU-LU è-a	...
šà á-u$_4$-da-ka	in the workdays
gìr Lugal-usar	responsible: Lugalusar
kišib Ḫu-wa-wa	seal of Ḫuwawa
mu-ús-sa ^{d}Šu-^{d}EN.ZU lugal Uri$_5$^{ki}-ma-ke$_4$	ŠS 5
bàd mar-tu ba-ab-dù	
Seal	
Lú-ib-gal	Lu-ibgal
dub-sar	scribe
dumu Ur-gi$_6$-par$_4$	son of Urgipar

no. 325 [copy]

Obverse	
10 sila$_3$ ninda PU	10 sila ...-bread
10 sila$_3$ ninda u$_4$-ú-x	10 sila ...-bread
2 má-gur$_8$	2 boats
a-rá 1-kam	the first time
10 sila$_3$ ninda PU	10 sila ...-bread
4 x-èš	4 [ ]
4 má gur$_8$	4 boats
Reverse	
a-rá 2-kam	for the second time
Šeš-zi-mu	Šešzimu
šu-ba-an-ti	received
gi$_4$-gi$_4$-dam	to be returned
kišib E-lu-lu	seal of Elulu
Seal	
E-lu-lu	Elulu
dub-sar	scribe
dumu Dingir-a-zu	son of Dingirazu

no. 326 (Š 32 ix)

Large bread deliveries for several high officials and messengers.

Obverse	
2; 4.3.8 sila$_3$ ninda giš-AŠ gur lugal	2 gur 278 sila of ...-bread according to the royal measurement
šukur gal-gal ^{giš}banšur šaggina	great ration for the table of the military governor
1 ninda-sig$_5$ gur nar um-mi-a ù	1 gur of top-quality bread for the master

dumu um-mi-a	singer and the students
0; 0.5.6 sila$_3$ ninda sig$_5$ gala	56 sila of top-quality bread for the lamentation-priest
0; 1.5.2 sila$_3$ ninda sig$_5$ di$_5$-di$_5$-la	112 sila of top-quality bread for the young lamentation-priest
0; 0.2.6 sila$_3$ ninda sig$_5$ mar-tu	26 sila of top-quality bread for the Amorites
ki Kur-gìr-ni-ì-šè	from Kurgirniše
0; 0.2. la 2 sila$_3$ ninda-šu nar-munus	18 sila of bread for the female singer
ki I-ti-^{d}Adad	from Iti-Adad
0; 1.2. ninda ^{giš}AŠ máš-šu-gíd-gíd	80 sila of ...-bread or the augurs
zi-ga na-ap-tá-núm	disbursement for the banquet
0; 0.5. ninda sig$_5$ nar ^{d}Nin-líl-lá	50 sila of top-quality bread for the singer of Ninlil
0; 0.2.2 sila$_3$ ninda sig$_5$ Lú-giš-šà-lá	22 sila of top-quality bread for Lugiššala
9; 0.1.6 sila$_3$ ninda sig$_5$ gur Nar-ša$_6$-a-ga	9 gur 16 sila of top-quality bread for Naršaga
Reverse	
0; 0.2. ninda sig$_5$ mar-tu	20 sila of top-quality bread for the Amorite
Nin-ù-numun-ki-ág maškim	Ninunumnkiag is the conveyer;
0; 0.1. ninda sig$_5$ lú-kin-gi$_4$-a	10 sila of top-quality bread for the messenger
u$_4$ 4-a	for 4 days
6 ninda sig$_5$ lú kin-gi$_4$-a	6 sila of top-quality bread for the messenger
Ur-ki-um šaggina	Urkium the military governor
2 ninda ^{giš}AŠ numun gur Nin$_9$-kal-la	2 gur of ...-bread ... for Ninkalla
1 ninda ^{giš}AŠ gur	1 gur of ...-bread
1; 2.0. ninda sig$_5$ gur	$1\frac{2}{5}$ gur of top-quality bread
kaš$_4$-me	for the messengers
0; 1.0. dabin Ba-ša$_6$	60 sila of barley flour for Baša
šu-nigín 6 ninda ^{giš}AŠ gur-lugal	total 6 gur of ...-bread, according to the royal measurement
šu-nigín 3; 1.2. lá 1 sila$_3$ ninda sig$_5$ gur	total 3 gur 79 sila of top-quality bread
šu-nigín 0; 0.2. lá 2 sila$_3$ ninda šu gur	total 18 sila of ...-bread
šu-nigín 0; 1.0. dabin	total 60 sila of barley flour
iti ^{d}Li$_9$-si$_4$	month 9
mu a-rá 3-kam Si-mu-ru-um^{ki} ba-ḫul	Š 32
Edge	
u$_4$ 30 lá 2-kam	the 28th day

no. 327 (ŠS 6 vi) [copy]

Obverse	
1.6; 2.3.6 sila$_3$ ninda gin gur	66 gur and 156 sila of average-quality bread
šà á u$_4$-da-ka	from the wages of the daily work
rá-gaba šà é-gal	for the messengers in the palace
gìr Lugal-á-zi-da	responsible: Lugalazida
Reverse	
šà bala-a	during the *bala*
iti šu-numun-na	month 6
mu ^{d}Šu-^{d}EN.ZU lugal-e	ŠS 6
na-rú-a maḫ ^{d}En-líl	
^{d}Nin-líl-ra mu-ne-rú	

no. 328 (Š 47 v)

Obverse	
4.0; 2.3. lá 1 sila$_3$ dabin gur	4.0; 2.3. - 1 sila gur of barley flour
22; 2.2.2⅓ sila$_3$ zì-sig$_{15}$ gur	22; 2.2.2⅓ sila gur of coarse flour
šu-nigín 4.0; 2.3. lá 1 sila$_3$ dabin gur	total 4.0; 2.3. - 1 sila gur of barley flour
šu-nigín 22; 2.2.2⅓ sila$_3$ zì-sig$_{15}$ gur	total 22; 2.2.2⅓ sila gur of coarse flour
šà-bi-ta	from it
4.1; 2.0.7 ⅔ sila$_3$ dabin gur	4.1; 2.0.7 ⅔ sila gur of barley flour
24; 0.3.5 sila$_3$ zì-sig$_{15}$ gur	24; 0.3.5 sila gur of coarse flour
zi-ga-àm	disbursement
diri 0; 4.3.8 ⅔ sila$_3$ dabin gur	difference 0; 4.3.8 ⅔ sila gur of barley flour
Reverse	
diri 1; 3.1.2. ⅔ sila$_3$ zì-sig$_{15}$ gur	difference 1; 3.1.2. ⅔ sila gur of coarse flour
nì-ka$_9$-ak Ur-zu	account of Urzu
iti ri mu-ús-sa Ki-ma-aš^{ki} ba-ḫul	month 5 Š 47

This is a simple account of two types of flour. lá-ni here indicates a positive balance, left overs that have to be returned (su-su-dam). On the other hand, diri indicates an excess in spending, therefore an overdraft, a debt, which can be compensated only by less spending next time.

no. 329

Obverse	
15 dabin gur	15 gur of barley flour
0; 2.0. zì-sig$_{15}$	120 sila of coarse flour
kišib ^{d}Ìr-ra-dingir-šè	seal of Irra-dingirše
[ ]-gú-[ ]	[ ]

Reverse	
zì àr-ra	milled flour
gìr ^{giš}Gigir-[re]	responsible: Gigirre

no. 330 (AS 8) [copy]

Obverse	
19 dabin gur	19 gur of barley flour
zì gú-na èš-didli	flour from the tax for various sanctuaries
ki Lugal-nì-lagar-e-ta	from Lugalnilagare
ugú Lú-kal-la ba-a-gar	put on the account of Lukalla
Reverse	
kišib Lú-^{d}Šul-gi	seal of Lu-Šulgi
mu en Eridu^{ki} ba-ḫun	AS 8
Seal	
Lú-é-maḫ-e	Lu-emaḫe
dub-sar	scribe
dumu Ur-^{d}Li$_{9}$-si$_{4}$	son of Ur-Lisi
ensi$_{2}$ Umma^{ki}-ka	governor of Umma

The barley flour is a tax (gú-na) for various sanctuaries. The barley is delivered by Lugalnilagare, but nevertheless is put on the account of Lukalla. The expression ugú gar *eli išû* indicates that things should be put on the right accounts. Another interpretation is possible. As the sanctuaries were landowners, perhaps they were paying a tax (gú-na) rather than receiving the flour

no. 331 (Š 40 diri)

Obverse	
2 še gur lugal	2 gur of barley according to the royal measurement
še zì-da àr-ra	barley to be ground into flour
Ki-an^{ki}-ta	from Kian
ki Ir$_{11}$-ta	from Ir
Ḫu-ma-ti	Ḫumati
mí-ús-sa lú-maḫ-e	the daughter-in-law of the *lumaḫ*-priest
Reverse	
šu-ba-ti	received
iti diri mu-ús-sa é	intercalary month
Puzur$_{4}$-^{d}Da-gan ba-dù	Š 40
Seal	
Lugal-zag-ge-[si]	Lugalzagesi
dumu Ur-^{d}Dumu-zi-da	son of Ur-Dumuzida
dub-sar	the scribe

no. 332 (IS 1 v)

Obverse

0;2.0. dabin Ka-ba-ab-du$_7$	120 sila of barley flour for Kababdu
0;2.0. Lú-^{d}Lama	120 sila Lu-Lama
[ ] Lú-^{d}Nin-šubur	[120 sila] Lu-Ninšubur
[ ]-ka-ì-ša$_6$	[120 sila]kaiša
[ugula ur-]^{d}Ig-alim	[overseer Ur]-Igalim

Reverse

ḫé-<dab$_5$>-me	*ḫedab*-workers
0;2.0. Lú-^{d}Nin-gír-su	120 sila Lu-Ningirsu
0;1.0. Lú-^{d}Nin-šubur šà-tam	60 sila$_3$ Lu-Ninšubur high administrator
2;1.0. dabin gur	2$^{1}/_{5}$ gur of barley flour
má Ur-^{giš}gigir dù	for fixing the boat of Urgigir
iti munu$_4$-kú	month 5
mu ^{d}I-bí-^{d}EN.ZU lugal	IS 1

no. 333 (ŠS 2 xi) [copy]

Obverse

0; 1.1.5½ sila$_3$ dabin	75½ sila of barley flour
u$_4$ 18-kam	the 18th day
0; 0.5.8 sila$_3$ dabin	58 sila of barley flour
u$_4$ 20 lá 1-kam	the 19th day
ki ^{d}Šara$_2$-kam-ta	from Šarakam

Reverse

kišib ensi$_2$-ka	seal of the governor
iti pa$_4$-kùš-e	month 11
mu má ^{d}En-ki ba-ab-du$_8$	ŠS 2

Seal

d[Šu]-^{d}EN.ZU	Šu-Sîn
lugal-kalag-ga	mighty king
lugal Uri$_5$^{ki}-ma	king of Ur
lugal an-ub-da limmu$_2$-ba	king of the four quarters of the universe
A-a-kal-la	Aakalla
ensi$_2$	governor of Umma
Umma^{ki}	
ir$_{11}$-zu	(is) your servant

no. 334 (ŠS 2 viii) [copy]

Obverse

0; 1.0.6 sila$_3$ dabin u$_4$-16-kam	66 sila of barley flour the 16th day
0; 1.0.5 sila$_3$	65 sila <of barley flour>
u$_4$-17-kam	the 17th day
0; 1.0.2 sila$_3$	62 sila <of barley flour>
u$_4$-18-kam	the 18th day
0; 0.4.6 sila$_3$	46 sila <of barley flour>
u$_4$-19-kam	the 19th day
0; 1.0.6 sila$_3$	66 sila <of barley flour>
u$_4$-20-kam	the 20th day
0; 0.3.6 sila$_3$	36 sila <of barley flour>
u$_4$-21-kam	the 21st day

Reverse

0; 0.5.4 sila$_3$	54 sila <of barley flour>
u$_4$-22-kam	the 22nd day
0; 0.5	50 sila <of barley flour>
u$_4$-23-kam	the 23rd day
0; 0.5 kaš 1 sila$_4$ <a>-ra-zu	50 sila of beer 1 lamb for the prayer-offering
kišib ensi$_2$-ka	seal of the governor
iti é-iti-6	month 8
mu má ^{d}En-ki ba-ab-du$_8$	ŠS 2

Seal

^{d}[Šu]-^{d}EN.ZU	Šu-Sîn
lugal-kalag-ga	mighty king
lugal Uri$_5$^{ki}-ma	king of Ur
lugal an-ub-da limmu$_2$-ba	king of the four quarters of the universe
A-a-kal-la	Aakalla
ensi$_2$	governor of Umma
Umma^{ki}	
ir$_{11}$-zu	(is) your servant

no. 335

Obverse

0; 2.0. dabin	120 sila of barley flour
kišib Lú-^{d}Nin-šubur	seal of Lu-Ninšubur
dumu Ur-^{d}Šul-pa-è	son of Ur-Šulpae

no. 336 (ŠS 2) [copy]

Transfer of barley to be ground into *isimmanu*-flour for the food of the dogs.

Obverse

1; 2.3 še gur	1½ gur of barley
mu zì-munu$_4$ zì-ur-šè	for flour for the dogs
ki Inim-^{d}Šara$_2$-ta	from Inim-Šara
kišib A-tu	seal of Atu

Reverse

šà bala-a	during the *bala*
mu má ^{d}En-ki ba-ab-du$_8$	ŠS 2

Seal

A-tu dub-sar	Atu the scribe
dumu Šeš-kal-la	son of Šeškalla

no. 337 (ŠS 2–3)

Obverse

[ ] sila$_3$ zì-sig$_{15}$	[ ] sila of coarse flour
[kišib] Ur-^{d}Šara$_2$-kam	seal of Ur-Šarakam
1 še gur 0; 2.0. zì-sig$_{15}$	1 gur of barley ⅖ gur of coarse flour
kišib Kù-^{d}Nin-ur$_4$-ra	seal of Ku-Ninurra
mu má ^{d}En-ki ba-ab-du$_8$	ŠS 2
0; 0.4.5 sila$_3$ zì-sig$_{15}$ mu Si-ma-núm^{ki}	45 sila of coarse flour ŠS 3
kišib Kù-^{d}Nin-ur$_4$-ra	seal of Ku-Ninurra
ki Lú-^{d}EN.ZU-ta	from Lu-Sîn
2 še gur šukur-ra	2 gur of barley for the ration
Ur-^{d}Kal-kal	for Ur-Kalkal
mu na-rú-a maḫ ba-rú	ŠS 6
kišib ^{d}Šara$_2$-ì-zu	seal of Šara-izu

Reverse

1; 0.2.1½ sila$_3$ ninda giš-AŠ gur	1 gur and 21½ sila of ...-bread
kišib ^{d}Šara$_2$-kam	seal of Šarakam
mu Si-ma-núm^{ki} ba-ḫul	ŠS 3
ki Šà-kù-gi-ta	from Šakuge
ki Na-ba-sá-ta	from Nabasa
gaba-ri kišib Lú-kal-la	copy of the tablet of Lukalla

no. 338 (Š 47 vii) [copy]

Obverse	
1; 3.1. zíz gur	490 sila of emmer wheat
ki Lú-^{d}Šara$_2$-ta	from Lu-Šara
kišib Ir$_{11}$	seal of Ir
iti min-èš	month 7
Reverse	
mu-ús-sa Ki-maš^{ki} ba-ḫul	Š 47
Seal	
Ir$_{11}$-mu	Irmu
dub-sar	scribe
dumu Ur-ni$_9$-gar kuš$_7$	son of Urnigar the equerry

no. 339 (Š 47 v)

Obverse	
[ ] zíz-an gur	[ ] gur of emmer flour
[ ] gi-gur-dub	[ ] reed basket
kišib Lú-^{d}Šara$_2$	seal of Lu-Šara
ki Ir$_{11}$-ta	from Ir
Da-da-ga	Dadaga
šu-ba-ti	received
Reverse	
iti ri	month 5
mu-ús-sa Ki-maš^{ki} ba-ḫul	Š 47

COMMODITIES: DATES (nos. 340–342)

no. 340 (Š 47)

Obverse	
22 giš 5 sila$_3$	22 trees (taxed at) 5 sila of dates
16 giš šà-sù	16 trees of bad fruits
15 giš 20 sila$_3$	15 trees (taxed at) 20 sila of dates
13 giš 10 sila$_3$	13 trees (taxed at) 10 sila of dates
25 giš 30 sila$_3$	25 trees (taxed at) 30 sila of dates
1 giš 40 sila$_3$	1 trees (taxed at) 40 sila of dates
2 giš 60 sila$_3$	2 trees (taxed at) 60 sila of dates
zú-lum-bi 4; 4.1. gur	its dates amount 4 gur 2500 sila
šu-nigín 1.34 ^{giš}hi-a	total: 94 trees
^{giš}kiri$_6$ ḫun?-na	from the palm grove Ḫunna(?)

Reverse

šà a-šà ^{d}Inanna-inim-gál-la	in the field Inanna-inimgal
mu-ús-sa Ki-maš^{ki} ba-ḫul	Š 47

It is unclear whether the scribe is stipulating the tax in dates to be paid according to the types of trees or according to the actual yield of the palm trees. The expression šà-sùd *šiṣūtum* indicates trees not bearing fruit or having bad fruit.

no. 341 (ŠS6) [copy]

Dates subtracted from the delivery in order to pay the daily work performed in the palm grove.

Obverse	
3 zú-lum gur	3 gur of dates
gìr-lam gur	according to the basket-gur
gìr Lú-^{d}Nin-šubur	responsible: Lu-Ninšubur
šà á-u$_4$-da	from the wages of the daily work
Reverse	
santana-ke$_4$-ne	of the palm tree growers
ba-an-na-zi	were expended
kišib Ḫu-wa-wa	seal of Ḫuwawa
mu ^{d}Šu-^{d}EN.ZU lugal-e	ŠS 6
na-rú-a maḫ ^{d}En-líl-^{d}Nin-líl-ra	
mu-ne-rú	
Seal	
Lú-ib-gal	Lu-ibgal
dub-sar	the scribe
dumu Ur-gi$_6$-par$_4$	son of Urgipar

no. 342 (AS 9)

Obverse	
0; 2.1. kaš sig$_5$ lugal	130 sila of top-quality beer
3; 1.4. kaš gin gur	3 gur 100 sila of average-quality beer
1; 2.0. dabin gur	420 sila of barley flour
0; 4.0. lá 10 sila$_3$ zì-sig$_{15}$	230 sila of coarse flour
0; 0.3. zú-lum	30 sila of dates
0; 0.2.5 sila$_3$ eša	25 sila of eša-flour
0; 0.2. lá ½ sila$_3$ nì-àr-ra-sig$_5$	19½ sila of top-quality groats
Reverse	
5 ma-na ^{ú}ḫáb	5 mana of tanning stuff
kišib Lú-ì-zu	seal of Luizu
mu-ús-sa en Eridu^{ki} ba-ḫun-gá	AS 9

COMMODITIES: FISH (nos. 343–345)

no. 343 (Š 33) [copy]

Obverse	
11.0 gín-suḫur ku$_6$-gal	660 large fish
2.30 ku$_6$ ti-la	150 live fish
ku$_6$-kun-zi-bi 10-ta	its *kunzi*-fish 10 for each
4.10 ku$_6$-kun-zi	250 *kunzi*-fish
4.10 ku$_6$ sag-kešda$_2$	250 *sagkešda*-fish
ku$_6$ sag-kešda$_2$-ba ùr-šè ku$_6$ kun-zi 1.40-ta	*sagkešda*- fish for the *kunzi*-fish 100 for each
3.0 ku$_6$ sag-kešda$_2$	180 *sagkešda*-fish
ku$_6$ sag-kešda$_2$-ba ùr-šè 0;1.1.5-sila$_3$-ta	*sagkešda*-fish for ... 75 sila each
Reverse	
[ ]	
[ ]	
[ ]	
mu-ús-sa a-rá 3-kam	Š 33
Si-mu-ru-um^{ki} ba-ḫul	

no. 344 (AS 5)

Obverse	
6; 3.0. ku$_6$ šeg$_6$ gur	6$^{3}/_{5}$ gur of dried fish
ki Ur-^{d}En.[ ]-ta	from Ur-En[ ]
ugú Lú-kal-la ba-a-gar	put on the account of Lukalla
kišib Ur-^{d}Šara$_2$	seal of Ur-Šara
Reverse	
mu-ús-sa en maḫ gal-an-na ba-ḫun	AS 5
Seal	
Ur-gi$_6$-par$_4$	Urgipar
dub-sar	scribe
dumu A-a-kal-la	son of Aakalla

no. 345 (Š 37 xii) [copy]

Obverse	
9 gín kù-babbar	9 shekels of silver
kù ku$_6$-mun	silver for fish and salt
ki Na-ú-a-ta	from Naua
A-kal-la šu-ba-ti	Akalla received
Reverse	
iti ^{d}Dumu-zi	month 12

mu bàd ba-dù	Š 37
9 gín	9 shekels
Seal	
A-kal-la	Akalla
dub-sar	scribe
dumu Ur-ni$_9$-gar kuš$_7$	son of Urnigar the equerry

Commodities: Oil and Fat (nos. 346–348)

no. 346 (Š 48) [copy]

Obverse	
0; 1.4.8. sila$_3$ 1 gín ì	108 sila and 1 gin of oil
mu Ur-bí-lum^{ki}	year Š 45
0; 0.5.3 sila$_3$ 1 gín ì	53 sila and 1 gin of oil
mu Ki-maš^{ki}	year Š 46
0; 1.1.6⅓ sila$_3$ ì	76 sila and ⅓ gin of oil
mu-ús-sa Ki-maš^{ki} ba-ḫul	year Š 47
šu-nigín 0;3.5.7⅓ sila$_3$ 2⅓ gín	total 237⅓ sila 2⅓ gin
šà-bi-ta	from it
0; 0.2.9 sila$_3$ 12 gín ì šu-gír sá-du$_{11}$ ^{d}Šara$_2$	29 sila and 12 gin of …-oil regular delivery for Šara
mu Ur-bí-lum^{ki} ba-ḫul	year Š 45
29 sila$_3$ 12 gín ì	29 sila and 12 gin of oil
mu Ki-maš^{ki}	year Š 46
29 sila$_3$ 12 gín ì	29 sila and 12 gin of oil
mu-ús-sa Ki-maš^{ki}	year Š 47
zi-ga-àm	disbursement
Reverse	
šu-nigín 0; 1.2.7½ sila$_3$ 6 gín	total 87½ sila 6 gin
zi-ga-àm	disbursement
0;2.2.9 ⅔ sila$_3$ 7½ gín	14⅔ sila 7½ gin
ki A-tu-ta	from Atu
a-rá-2-kam	for the second time

no. 347 (ŠS 6 ii)

Obverse	
1 ì-giš gur	1 gur of sesame seed oil
ki [ka$_5$]-a-ta	from [Ka]a
nu-banda$_3$ Lugal-zi-mu	the lieutenant is Lugalzimu

ugula Al-ùr-dingir	overseer Alurdingir
mu-túm	delivery
Reverse	
iti gu$_4$-si-su	month 2
mu-ús-sa bàd mar-tu	ŠS 6
ba-dù-a mu-ús-sa-a-bi	
Seal	
Lú-ezem	Lu-ezem
dub-sar	scribe
dumu Al-ùr-dingir	son of Alurdingir

no. 348 (Š 48)

Obverse	
30 sila$_3$ ì-šáh̬	30 sila of lard
Ur-^{d}Šakan engar	from Ur-Šakan the field worker
30 sila$_3$ Gu-gu-a engar	30 sila from Gugua the field worker
30 sila$_3$ A-kal-la engar	30 sila from the field worker
30 sila$_3$ Šu-ma-àm engar	30 sila from Šumam the field worker
ì gú-na mu-túm	delivery of lard as tax
ki Lugal-^{giš}gigir-re nu-banda$_3$-ta	from Lugalgigire the lieutenant
Reverse	
Ì-kal-la	Ikalla
šu-ba-ti	received
mu H̬a-ar-ši^{ki} ba-h̬ul	Š 48
Seal	
Ì-kal-la	Ikalla
dub-sar	the scribe
dumu Lú-[ ]	son of Lu[ ]

Commodities for Buildings (nos. 349–353)

no. 349 (AS 6 v) [copy]

Obverse	
0; 3.0. Íd-pa-è	3/5 gur from Idpae
dumu Šeš-kal-la	son of Šeškalla
0; 2.0. ^{d}Šara$_2$-kam	2/5 gur from Šarakam
šu-nigín 1 gur	total 1 gur
Reverse	
še àr-ra mu-túm	delivery of barley for grinding

gìr Lú-dingir-ra gu-za-lá	responsible: Ludingirra the throne-bearer
é-šu-tum šabra ús-sa si-ga	filled in the building next to the (storage facility) Ešutum of the steward
iti ri mu ^{d}Amar-^{d}EN.ZU	month 5
Ša-aš-šú! mu-ḫul	AS 6

no. 350 (Š 42) [copy]

Obverse

0; 2.0. ^{d}Šara$_2$-kam	120 sila from Šarakam
0; 4.0. Ma-an-ba	240 sila from Manba
0; 1.0. Lugal-kù-zu	60 sila from Lugalkuzu
0; 1.0. Kù-sig$_5$	60 sila from Kusig
0; 0.2. Íd-pa-è	20 sila from Idpae

Reverse

0; 4.0. Lú-^{d}Nin-šubur	240 sila from Lu-Ninšubur
šu-nigín 2; 2.2. gur	total 2 gur 140 sila
é-àr mu-túm	delivery of barley for grinding
é-šu-tum šabra ús-sa si-ga	filled in the building next to the (storage facility) Ešutum of the steward
gìr Lú-dingir-ra	responsible: Ludingirra
mu Ša-aš-šú-ru mu!-ḫul	Š 42

no. 351 (Š 41)

Obverse

| Ur-^{d}Šara$_2$	Ur-Šara
| Šul-la	Šulla
| Bù-ú-me	Buume
| Ur-^{d}Gu-nu-ra	Ur-Gunura
| Ḫé-lí-a	Ḫelia
iti šu-numun-ta	from month 6
| Lú-^{d}Nin-ur$_4$-ra	Lu-Ninurra
iti šu-numun-ta iti é-iti-6-šè	from month 6 to month 8
šà-gu$_4$-šè	for ox-drivers

Reverse

(*erasure*)	(were hired)
iti ezem-^{d}Šul-gi-šè	from month 8
gá-nun-gi-da tuš-a	they are settled in the reed storehouse
ki Bí-du$_{11}$-ga-ta	from Biduga
kišib nam-šà-tam Ur-^{giš}gigir šabra	seal of the office of the high administrator, Urgigir the steward

mu-ús-sa é Puzur$_4$-Da-gan ba-dù	Š 41
mu-ús-sa-bi	
Seal	
Ur-^{giš}gigir	Urgigir
dub-sar	scribe
dumu Bar-ra-an	son of Barran

no. 352 (ŠS 3) [copy]

Obverse	
1 guruš u$_4$-50-šè	1 workman for 50 workdays
é-da tuš	stationed in the house
šà Zabalam^{ki}	in Zabalam
ugula Lugal-igi-ḫuš	overseer Lugaligiḫuš
Reverse	
kišib ^{d}Šara$_2$-kam	seal of Šarakam
mu-ús-sa Si-ma-núm^{ki}	ŠS 3
Seal	
^{d}Šara$_2$-kam	Šarakam
dub-sar	scribe
dumu Lugal-^{giš}kiri$_6$	son of Lugalkiri

no. 353 (AS 9 xii)

Obverse	
2.32; 2.0. še gur	152 2/5 gur of barley
má A-gu	on the boat of Agu
1.3 gur [ ]	63 gur [ ]
má Ur-^{d}Ištaran ù Da-du-mu	on the boat of Ur-Ištaran and Dadumu
2.4; 3.0. gur	124 3/5 gur
má Lú-dingir-ra ù Ur-ZU.AB	on the boat of Ludingirra and Urabzu
3.4; 0.5. gur	184 gur and 50 sila
má Lugal-nì-lagar-e ù É-an-né	on the boat of Lugalnilagare and Eanne
Reverse	
56 še gur še è-a	56 gur of threshed barley
4; 3.0. gur sá-du$_{11}$-ta	4 3/5 gur from the regular deliveries
^{d}Šara$_2$-za-me	Šara-zame
56; 1.2.5 sila$_3$ gur	56 gur 85 sila
má Lugal-bala-sig$_5$	on the boat of Lugalbalasig
1.1 gur má Ur-^{d}En-[ ]	61 gur of the boat of Ur-En[ ]
1.0; 2.3. gur má Lugal-é-maḫ-e	60½ gur of the boat of Lugalemaḫe
še mu-túm é-àr-gibil	delivery of barley (for) the new mill

ús-sa é-šu-tum šabra ku$_4$-ra	next to the (storage facility) Ešutum of the steward
ki-su$_7$ gu-la a-šà lá-maḫ-ta	great threshing floor of the field Lamaḫ
Edge	
iti ^{d}Dumu-zi mu en Ga-eš^{ki} ba-ḫun	month 12, AS 9
11.42; 2.4.5 <sila$_3$ gur>	702 gur 165 sila

Commodities: Bitumen (nos. 354–355)

Bitumen is easily available in Mesopotamia, as oil wells spouting at ground level or coagulating bitumen on the river waters. Bitumen was used for caulking boats, reed mats, and vessels. Nothing is known about the way bitumen was liquefied and applied on the boats or vessels. Intense fires were needed. It was used in tombs to seal the opening. In the building of ziggurats bitumen was used as mortar between the bricks.

no. 354 (Š48) [copy]

Obverse	
28 ma-na igi-esír	28 mana of bitumen
52 ma-na esír ḫád	52 mana of dried bitumen
ki Nì-lagar-e-ta	from Nilagare
La-ni-mu	Lanimu
šu-ba-ti	received
Reverse	
mu Ḫa-ar-ši^{ki}	Š 48
Ki-maš^{ki} ba-ḫul	

no. 355 (ŠS 4) [copy]

Obverse	
17; 4.0. esír ḫád gur	17$\frac{4}{5}$ gur of dried bitumen
0; 2.5.6 sila$_3$ esír é-a	176 sila of bitumen
šà-á-u$_4$-da	(constituting) the daily amount of work
gìr Lugal-usar	responsible: Lugalusar
kišib Ḫu-wa-wa	seal of Ḫuwawa
Reverse	
mu bàd mar-tu ba-dù	ŠS 4
Seal	
Lú-ib-gal	Lu-ibgal
dub-sar	scribe
dumu Ur-gi$_6$-par$_4$	son of Urgipar
gudu$_4$ ^{d}Inanna	purification-priest of Inanna

COMMODITIES: REEDS (nos. 356–390)

Reed is another natural product abundant in southern Mesopotamia and was used as fuel for fires, fodder for all the ruminants—especially when barley was not available—material for building rafts, boats, for mats, as a stabilizer of soil on the shores of rivers and canals.

no. 356 [copy]

Obverse	
1.0 sa gi-zi	60 bundles of fresh reed
šabra nin Da-da	for Dada the steward of the queen
1.0 sa ugula Ir$_{11}$-mu	60 bundles for the overseer Irmu
20 sa Lugal-sig$_5$	20 bundles for Lugalsig
30 sa Á-ti-mu	30 bundles for Atimu
maškim A-bí-a	Abia is the conveyer;
Reverse	
1.40 sa	100 bundles
é-da-na	for Edana
zi-ga	disbursement
gìr Bí-<du$_{11}$>-ga	responsible: Biduga
ugula Lú-làl	overseer Lulal

no. 357 (Š46) [copy]

Obverse	
20.0 sa gi	1200 bundles of reed
gu kilib-ba 12-ta	in each bale there are 12 bundles
Ur-^{giš}gigir dumu Ur-ur	for Urgigir son of Urur
50.0 sa gi	3000 bundles of reed
gu kilib-ba 13-ta	in each bale there are 13 bundles
aga$_3$-uš ensi$_2$	for the soldier of the governor
10.0 sa gi	600 bundles of reed
Reverse	
gu kilib-ba 13 sa-ta	in each bale there are 13 bundles
Bù-bù	for Bubu
ki Lú-^{d}Utu-ta	from Lu-Utu
gi zi-ga didli	various disbursements of reeds
inim-ensi$_2$-ta	by order of the governor
gi zi-ga šà a-šà-ga-ta	reed taken from the field
kišib A-tu	seal of Atu
mu Ki-maš^{ki} ba-ḫul	Š 46

Seal

A-tu dub-sar	Atu the scribe
dumu Lugal-ša$_6$-ga	son of Lugalšaga

no. 358 (Š 35)

Obverse

10.0 sa gi šeg$_6$	600 bundles of dry reed
á guruš 12 sa-ta	each workman to make 12 bundles
^{d}Nin-ki-du-ka	for the god Ninkiduka
ab-ba sig$_7$-a	...
Ur-^{giš}gigir-ke$_4$	Urgigir
šu-ba-ti	received

Reverse

mu-ús-sa An-ša-an^{ki} ba-ḫul	Š 35

Seal

Ur-^{giš}gigir	Urgigir
dumu Lugal-má-gur$_8$-re	son of Lugalmagurre

no. 359 (AS 4)

This is a transfer of tablets dealing with reeds. It is rare that reed is weighed rather than counted in bundles (gu kilib-ta è). The tablet of Ur-Nanše is handed over to Ur-Šulpae, who also seals the tablet.

Obverse

4.34 gú gi	274 talents of reed
ki Lú-igi-ša$_6$-ša$_6$	at the place of Luigišaša
20 gú ki Ab-ba-gi-na	20 talents at the place of Abbagina
5.11 gú	311 talents

Reverse

ki Lú-du$_{10}$-ga	at the place of Luduga
gu kilib-ta è	(this reed) coming from bundles
gi Dub-ru-um^{ki}	(this reed is) from Dubrum
kišib Ur-^{d}Nanše-ka	the tablet of Ur-Nanše
Ur-^{d}Šul-pa-è-ke$_4$ ba-dáb	Ur-Šulpae took into his account
mu En-<maḫ>-gal-an-na	AS 4
en ^{d}Nanna ba-ḫun	

Seal

Ur-^{d}Šul-pa-è	Ur-Šulpae
dub-sar	scribe
dumu Lugal-kù-ga-ni	son of Lugalkugani

no. 360 (Š 45) [copy]

Obverse

20.0+[ ] sa gi-zi	12300+[ ] bundles of fresh reed
ki-su$_7$ [A]-pil-lí	from the threshing floor of [A]pilli
má-a si-ga Nibru^{ki}-šè	loaded onto a boat to Nippur
gìr Nam-ḫa-ni	responsible: Namḫani
Reverse	
dumu Ur-ZU.AB	son of Urabzu
mu Ur-bí-ì-lum^{ki} ba-ḫul	Š 45

no. 361 (ŠS 5) [copy]

Obverse

5 or 5.0 sa gi	300 bundles of reed
má ì é-gal-šè du-a ba-a-dù	brought to the palace to build a boat to carry oil
gi sig$_7$-a	reed being plucked
Reverse	
ki A-kal-la-ta	from Akalla
kišib ^{d}Šara$_2$-kam	seal of Šarakam
mu-ús-sa bàd mar-tu ba-dù	ŠS 5
Seal	
^{d}Šara$_2$-kam	Šarakam
dub-sar	scribe
dumu Lugal-^{giš}kiri$_6$	son of Lugalkiri

no. 362 (ŠS 4) [copy]

Obverse

11.0 sa gi gu kilib-ba 10 sa-ta	660 bundles of reed, in each bale are 10 bundles
ka íd.^{d}Amar-^{d}EN.ZU-ke$_4$ gar	on the opening of the canal Amar-Sîn
gú-bi kéš-rá	to consolidate its bank
Reverse	
ugula A-gu	overseer Agu
kišib Da-da-ga	seal of Dadaga
mu bàd mar-tu ba-dù	ŠS 4
Seal	
Da-da-ga	Dadaga
dub-sar	scribe
dumu Ur-ni$_9$-gar kuš$_7$	son of Urnigar the equerry

no. 363 (ŠS 7) [copy]

Obverse	
25.30 sa gi gu kilib-ba 9-ta	1530 bundles of reed; in each bale 9 bundles
gá-nun en-gaba-rá-ta	from the storeroom of the field Engabara
ki Ur-é-maḫ-ta	from Uremaḫ
Reverse	
kišib Lugal-nir	seal of Lugalnir
mu ma-da Za-ab-ša-li$^{\langle ki \rangle}$ ba-ḫul	ŠS 7
Seal	
Lugal-nir	Lugalnir
dub-sar	scribe
dumu Ur-^{d}Šara$_{2}$	son of Ur-Šara
ša$_{13}$-dub-ba-ka	field surveyor

no. 364 (ŠS 5) [copy]

Obverse	
16.0 sa gi gu kilib-ba 12 sa-ta	960 bundles of reed, in each bale 12 bundles
é-maš-a ku$_{4}$-ra	to be brought in the Emaš
ki A-kal-la-ta	from Akalla
Reverse	
kišib [^{d}Šara$_{2}$-kam]	seal of [Šarakam]
mu-ús-sa bàd mar-tu ba-dù	ŠS 5
Seal	
^{d}Šara$_{2}$-kam	Šarakam
dub-sar	scribe
dumu Lugal-^{giš}kiri$_{6}$	son of Lugalkiri

no. 365 (IS 2) [copy]

Obverse	
13.0 sa gi	780 bundles of reed
gu kilib-ba 10 sa-ta	in each there are 10 bundles
3.40 sa gi še-ta sa$_{10}$	220 bundles of reed bought with barley
ki Inim-^{d}Šara$_{2}$	from/ in the place of Inim-Šara
kišib Lú-gišgal	seal of Lugišgal
Reverse	
šà bala-a	in each *bale*
mu en-^{d}Inanna	IS 2
máš-e ì-pàd	
Seal	
Lú-gišgal	Lugišgal
dumu Bí-du$_{11}$-mu	son of Bidumu

no. 366 (IS 1)

Obverse	
3.21 sa gi-zi	201 bundles of fresh reed
gu kilib-ba 5-ta	in each bale are 5 bundles
ki Ur-é-maḫ-ta	from Ur-emaḫ
Reverse	
kišib A-lu$_5$-lu$_5$	seal of Alulu
gìr Lú-ḫé-gál	responsible: Luḫegal
mu ^{d}I-bí-^{d}EN.ZU lugal	IS 1
Seal	
A-lu$_5$-lu$_5$	Alulu
dumu Inim-^{d}Šara$_2$	son of Inim-Šara
kurušda ^{d}Šara$_2$-ka	fattener of Šara

no. 367 (Š 48) [copy]

Obverse	
7 guruš ḫun-gá	7 hired workmen
gi ku$_5$-a 30 sar-ta	each cutting 30 sar of reed
á 5 sila$_3$-ta	at the wage of 5 sila per day
gurum-ak u$_4$ 16-kam	inspection done on the 16th day
é Ur-^{d}EN.ZU	in the domain of Ur-Sîn
ugula A-da-ga	overseer Adaga
Reverse	
a-šà lá-maḫ	in the field Lamaḫ
kišib Lugal-kù-zu	seal of Lugalkuzu
mu Ḫa-ar-ši^{ki} Ḫu-ur$_5$-ti$^{\langle ki\rangle}$	Š 48
ù Ki-maš^{ki} ba-ḫul	
Seal	
Lugal-kù-zu	Lugalkuzu
dub-sar	scribe
dumu Lugal-é-maḫ-e	son of Lugalemaḫe

no. 368 (ŠS 4) [copy]

Obverse	
1 gi ig é-nin	1 reed door for the palace of the queen
ki A-gu-ta	from Agu
kišib Ur-^{giš}gigir	seal of Urgigir
Reverse	
mu-ús-sa Si-ma-núm^{ki} ba-ḫul	ŠS 4
Seal	
Ur-^{giš}gigir	Urgigir

dub-sar	scribe
dumu Lugal-é-maḫ-e	son of Lugalemaḫe

In line 1, I prefer to read of é-nin rather than é-sal$_4$-la, although the sign read nin is not accurately written.

no. 369 (Š 48 xi) [copy]

Obverse	
26 guruš u$_4$-1-šè	26 workmen for 1 day
en-gaba-rá-ta	from the field Engabara
gi íl	to carry reed
gá-nun-šè	to the storehouse
ugula Lugal-nesag-e	overseer Lugalnesage
Reverse	
kišib nam-šà-tam A-tu	seal of the office of the high administrator, Atu
iti pa$_4$-kùš-e	month 11
mu Ḫa-ar-<ši>^{ki} Ki-maš^{ki} ba-ḫul	Š 48
Seal	
A-tu	Atu
dub-sar	scribe
dumu Lugal-ša$_6$-ga	son of Lugalšaga

no. 370 (ŠS 5) [copy]

Obverse	
1.13 guruš u$_4$-1-šè	73 workmen for 1 day
gi kéš-rá a-šà <lá>-maḫ	to tie reeds in the field Lamaḫ
gìr Ur-àm-ma	responsible: Uramma
17 guruš u$_4$-1-šè	17 workmen for 1 day
gi kéš-rá a-šà ki-šul	to tie reeds in the field Kišul
Reverse	
gìr Da-da	responsible: Dada
á lú ḫun-gá 6 sila$_3$-ta	the wages of the hired men is 6 sila per day
ugula Ab-ba-sig$_5$	overseer Abbasig
kišib Gu-ú-gu-a	seal of Guugua
mu-ús-sa ^{d}Šu-^{d}EN.ZU lugal-e	ŠS 5
bàd mar-tu mu-dù	
Seal	
Gu-ú-gu-a	Guugua
dub-sar	scribe
dumu Ma-an-sum	son of Mansum

no. 371 (Š 47) [copy]

Obverse	
4 gi kid ùr-ra	4 reed mats for the roof
ki-lá-bi 1½ sar	its weight 1½ sar
má-[zì]-ka ba-a-dul$_9$	to cover a boat loaded with flour
ki Lú-igi-ša$_6$-ša$_6$-ta	from Luigišaša
kišib Ukken-né	seal Ukkenne
Reverse	
mu-ús-sa Ki-maš^{ki} ba-ḫul	Š 47
Seal	
Ukken-né	Ukkenne
dub-sar	scribe
dumu Ur-^{giš}gigir	son of Urgigir

no. 372 (Š 39 i) [copy]

Obverse	
5 gi kid	5 reed mats
ki-lá-bi 2½ sar	its weight 2½ sar
19 gi-ḫa-an	19 baskets
ki gá kaš túg še lugal…	
Reverse	
ki Ur-e$_{11}$-e	from Uree
kišib Šeš-kal-la	seal of Šeškalla
iti še-sag-ku$_5$	month 1
mu é Puzur$_4$-Da-<gan> ba-dù	Š 39
Seal	
Ur-^{d}Li$_9$-si$_4$	Ur-Lisi
ensi$_2$	governor
Umma^{ki}	of Umma
Col. ii	
Šeš-kal-la	Šeškalla
dub-sar	scribe
dumu Na-di	son of Nadi
ir$_{11}$-zu	your servant

no. 373 (ŠS 4 v)

Obverse	
3 kid šer$_7$-ru-um	3 *šerrum*-reed mats
ki-lá-bi 1 sar	its weight 1 sar
Nibru^{ki}-šè má-zì-da-ka ba-a-gar	put on a boat carrying flour (going) to Nippur

ki Lú-ib-gal-ta	from Lu-ibgal
kišib Lú-^{d}Šara$_{2}$	seal of Lu-Šara
Reverse	
iti ri	month 5
mu-ús-sa Si-ma-núm^{ki} ba-ḫul	ŠS 4
Seal	
Lú-^{d}Šara$_{2}$	Lu-Šara
dub-sar	scribe
dumu Lugal-inim-gi-na	son of Lugalinimgina

no. 374 (ŠS 7) [copy]

Obverse	
15 gi kid mu[nu$_{4}$] sig$_{5}$ esír su-ba	15 reed mats covered with bitumen for top-quality malt
1 gi kid zì-munu$_{4}$	1 reed mat for flour
ki-lá-bi 12 gín	its weight 12 gin
1 gi su$_{7}$-su$_{7}$	1 basket
1 ma-an-sim dabin	1 basket for barley flour
1 ma-an-sim nì-àr-ra	1 basket for groats
1 ma-an-sim duḫ-ḫu!(ri)	1 basket for bran
1 gi-kaskal ba-ba-kesda$_{2}$	1 fastened basket
4 gi-kaskal nì-àr-ra esír su-ba	4 reed baskets covered with bitumen for groats
Reverse	
[gi]-ḫal gíd-da mušen	long baskets for poultry
[ ] gi-gur-dub 60 sila$_{3}$	[ ] baskets of 60 sila capacity
6 gi-gur dub 0; 2.3.-ta	6 baskets of ½ gur
zì-munu$_{4}$ ba-an-si	filled with flour
12 gi-ḫal gur-dub 120 sila$_{3}$-ta	12 baskets containing 120 sila
sum-sikil sum-gaz ba-an-si	filled with 'pure'-onions and 'crush'-onions
zi-ga nì-ebur-ke$_{4}$ DU-a	disbursement brought for harvest
kišib ^{d}Šara$_{2}$-kam	seal of Šarakam
mu-ús-sa ^{d}Šu-^{d}EN.ZU lugal-e	ŠS 7
na-rú-a maḫ mu-rú	
Seal	
^{d}Šara$_{2}$-kam	Šarakam
dub-sar	scribe
dumu Lugal-^{giš}kiri$_{6}$	son of Lugalkiri

no. 375 (ŠS 4) [copy]

Obverse	
2 gi kid zu!-zu!-ra	2 reed mats for the threshing floor(?)
ki-lá-bi ⅓ sar	its weight ⅓ sar
20 gi <ma>-an-sim sig$_5$	20 top-quality baskets
7 ma-an-sim nì-àr-ra	7 baskets for groats
20 gi su$_7$-su$_7$	20 sieves
30 gi-gur-kam	30 baskets
5 gi-gur zì-íl	5 baskets to carry flour
1 [ ] esír su-ba	1 [basket] covered with bitumen
Reverse	
[ ] gi-gur-kam en	[ ] basket of excellent quality
[ ] gi kid má-a ba-si	[ ] basket to load on the boat
ki-lá-bi ⅔ sar	its weight ⅔ of sar
ki A-gu-ta	from Agu
kišib Lugal-é-maḫ-e	seal of Lugalemaḫe
mu-ús-sa Si-ma-núm^{ki} ba-ḫul	ŠS 4
Seal	
Lugal-é-maḫ-e	Lugalemaḫe
dumu Ur-^{d}Dumu-zi	son of Ur-Dumuzi

In line 1, the suggested reading zu!-zu!-ra is only tentative. I expect šer$_7$-ru-um, but this cannot be reconciled with the contents of the tablet.

no. 376 (ŠS 4) [copy]

Obverse	
1 gi kid šer$_7$-ru-um	1 *šerrum*-reed mat
ki-lá-bi ⅓ sar	its weight ⅓ sar
má zì-da-šè	for the boat of flour
ki A-gu-ta	from Agu
Reverse	
kišib Bí-du$_{11}$-ga	seal of Biduga
mu-ús-sa Si-ma-núm^{ki} ba-ḫul	ŠS 4
Seal	
Bí-du$_{11}$-ga	Biduga
dub-sar	scribe
dumu La-a-ša$_6$	son of Laaša

no. 377 (ŠS 6) [copy]

Obverse	
2 gi kid	2 reed mats
šer$_{7}$-ru-um	
ki-lá-bi ⅓ sar	its weight ⅓ sar
má-zì-da-ka <ba-a->dul9	to cover a boat with flour
ki A-gu-ta	from Agu
Reverse	
kišib Ur-^{d}Nin-tu	seal of Ur-Nintu
šà bala-a	during the *bala*
mu-ús-sa bàd mar-tu mu-ús-sa-a-bi	ŠS 6
Seal	
Ur-^{d}Nin-tu	Ur-Nintu
dub-sar	scribe
dumu A-ab-ba-ni	son of Abbani
šabra ^{d}Nin-ur$_{4}$-ra	steward of Ninurra

no. 378 (IS 1 x) [copy]

Obverse	
1.20 sa gi zi	80 bundles of fresh reed
gu kilib-ba 5 sa-ta	in each bale there are 5 bundles
šà-gal udu niga	fodder for barley-fed sheep
ki Ur-é-maḫ-ta	from Ur-emaḫ
Reverse	
kišib A-lu$_{5}$-lu$_{5}$	seal of Alulu
iti ezem-^{d}Šul-gi	month 8
mu ^{d}I-bí-^{d}EN.ZU lugal	IS 1
Seal	
A-lu$_{5}$-lu$_{5}$	Alulu
dumu Inim-^{d}[Šara$_{2}$]	son of Inim-Šara
kurušda ^{d}[Šara$_{2}$-ka]	fattener of Šara

In the last years of the kingdom of Ur, barley was no longer easily available; more often animals were fed reeds, even supposed "barley-fed" sheep.

no. 379 (ŠS 6) [copy]

Obverse	
1 guruš u$_4$-1-šè	1 workmen for1 day
a-šà a-gestin-na-ta	from the field Ageštinna
é-udu a-šà lá-maḫ-šè	to the sheepfold in the field Lamaḫ
gi zi íl-gá	to carry fresh reeds
ugula Ab-ba-sig$_5$	overseer Abbasig
Reverse	
kišib I-šar-ru-um	responsible Išarrum
mu ^{d}Šu-^{d}EN.ZU lugal	ŠS 6
na-rú-a maḫ ^{d}En-líl ^{d}Nin-líl-ra mu-ne-rú	
Seal	
I-šar-ru-um	Išarrum
dub-sar	scribe
dumu Ur-^{d}En-líl-lá	son of Ur-Enlilla

no. 380 (ŠS 5) [copy]

Summary tablet of the activities of workmen to reinforce a dam or the banks of a canal.

Obverse	
23 guruš u$_4$-1-šè	23 workmen for 1 day
gi-gilim sur-ra	to braid reed tips
1.8 guruš u$_4$-1-šè	68 workmen for 1 day
ka-gìr-da ki-sur-ra saḫar si-ga ù	to fill with earth the road in Kisurra
gi uru$_4$ ku$_5$-ta gi íl	to carry reeds cut with the plow
Reverse	
ugula Šeš-kal-la	overseer Šeškalla
kišib Kù-ga-ni	seal of Kugani
mu-ús-sa bàd mar-tu ba-dù	ŠS 5
Seal	
Kù-ga-ni	Kugani
dub-sar	scribe
dumu Ur-ša$_6$-ga	son of Uršaga

no. 381 (ŠS 4 x) [copy]

Obverse	
6 gi-gur-dub	6 baskets
an-za-gàr-šè	for the fortification
ki A-gu-ta	from Agu
kišib Lú-du$_{10}$-ga	seal of Luduga

Reverse

iti ezem-^{d}Šul-gi	month 8
mu bàd mar-tu ba-dù	ŠS 4

Seal

Lú-du$_{10}$-ga	Luduga
dub-sar	scribe
dumu Lú-^{d}Šara$_{2}$	son of Lu-Šara
sa$_{12}$-du$_{5}$	field surveyor

no. 382 (ŠS 6) [copy]

Obverse

1.1 gi-gur 60 sila$_{3}$-ta	11 baskets containing 60 sila each
ki-su$_{7}$ gu-la a-šà lá-maḫ-šè	for the great threshing floor of the field Lamaḫ
ki A-gu-ta	from Agu

Reverse

kišib ^{d}Šara$_{2}$-ba-zi-ge	seal of Šara-bazige
mu ^{d}Šu-^{d}EN.ZU lugal-e	ŠS 6
na-<rú-a> maḫ in-rú	

Seal

Ur-^{d}Li$_{9}$-si$_{4}$	Ur-Lisi
ensi$_{2}$ Umma^{ki}	governor of Umma
^{d}Šara$_{2}$-ba-zi-ge	Šara-bazige
dub-sar ir$_{11}$-zu	scribe, is your servant

no. 383 (AS 6) [copy]

Obverse

4 gi-ḫal esír su-ba	1 basket covered with bitumen
ki-lá-bi ⅓ sar	its weight is ⅓ sar
1.0 kak-si-tag	60 nails
Ad-da-ti é-maš	Addati in the Emaš
ùr-ra-a	has deposited

Reverse

ki Lú-igi-ša$_{6}$-ša$_{6}$-ta	from Luigišaša
kišib A-du	seal of Adu
mu Šà-aš-ru-um^{ki} ba-ḫul	AS 6

Seal

A-du dub-sar	Adu scribe
dumu Lú-ga	son of Luga
aga$_{3}$-uš ensi$_{2}$	soldier of the governor

no. 384 (AS4) [copy]

Obverse	
6 á guruš u$_{4}$-1-šè	6 workmen for 1 day
^{giš}ù-suḫ$_{5}$ ù ^{giš}dusu íl-la	to carry pine-wood and baskets
gìr Ur-mes	responsible: Urmes
ki Ur-ša$_{6}$-ga-ta	disbursed
Reverse	
ba-zi	by Uršaga
mu en maḫ gal-an-na en ^{d}Nanna ba-ḫun	AS 4

no. 385 (Š 46/AS 3) [copy]

Obverse	
7 gi-kaskal	7 baskets in reed
é-gu$_{4}$-gaz-šè	for the slaughterhouse
ki Lú-igi-ša$_{6}$-ša$_{6}$-ta	from Lu-igišaša
kišib Lú-du$_{10}$-ga	seal of Luduga
šà bala-a	during the *bala*
Reverse	
mu-ús-sa Ur-bí-lum^{ki} ba-ḫul	Š46/AS 3
Seal	
Lú-du$_{10}$-ga	Luduga
dub-sar	scribe
dumu Lugal-nì-lagar-e	son of Lugalnilagare

no. 386 (ŠS 3 vii) [copy]

Obverse	
22 gi-kaskal [še 20 sila$_{3}$-ta]	22 baskets containing 20 sila each
5 gi-kaskal 30 sila$_{3}$-ta	5 baskets containing 30 sila each
15 gi-gur 60 sila$_{3}$-ta	15 baskets containing 60 sila each
šu-ba-an-si	were filled (with barley?)
ki A-gu-ta	from Agu
Reverse	
kišib Lú-du$_{10}$-ga	seal of Luduga
iti min-èš	month 7
mu-ús-sa Si-ma-[núm^{ki} ba-ḫul]	ŠS 3
Seal	
Lú-du$_{10}$-ga	Luduga
dub-sar	scribe
dumu Lú-^{d}Šara$_{2}$ sa$_{12}$-du$_{5}$	son of Lu-Šara the field surveyor

no. 387 (ŠS 3 v) [copy]

Obverse	
4 gi-kaskal ninda	4 baskets of bread
ki A-gu-ta	from Agu
ninda íl-íl-dè	to carry bread
In-ša$_{6}$-ša$_{6}$	Inšaša
šu-ba-ti	received
Reverse	
iti ri	month 5
mu-ús-sa Si-ma-núm^{ki} ba-ḫul	ŠS 3
Seal	
In-ša$_{6}$-ša$_{6}$	Inšaša
dumu Bí-du$_{11}$-mu	son of Bidumu

no. 388 (ŠS 8)

Obverse	
5 gi-su$_{7}$-su$_{7}$	5 sieves
3 gi-ma-an-sim zì-gu	3 baskets for pea-flour
1 gi-ma-an-sim nì-àr-ra	1 basket for groats
1 gi-ma-an-sim dabin	1 basket for barley flour
Reverse	
bala-šè	for the *bala*
ki A-gu-ta	from Agu
kišib Ur-^{giš}gigir	seal of Urgigir
mu má-gur$_{8}$-maḫ ba-dím	ŠS 8
Seal	
Ur-^{giš}gigir	Urgigir
dub-sar	scribe
dumu Ba-ša$_{6}$	son of Baša

no. 389 (Š 43)

Obverse	
4 gu kilib gi-zi	4 bundles of fresh reed
ki Ur-é-nun-na-ta	from Urenunna
kišib Uš-mu	seal of Ušmu
a-šà en-gaba-rá	in the field Engabara
Reverse	
[iti]	[month]
mu en ^{d}Nanna	Š 43
máš-e <ì>-pàd	

Seal

Uš-mu	Ušmu
dub-sar	scribe
dumu Lugal-ša$_6$-ga	son of Lugalšaga

no. 390 (ŠS 4) [copy]

Obverse

12 kid má šà-ga	12 reed mats for the center of the boat
ki-lá-bi (*written*: lá-ki-bi)	. . .
ki A-gu-ta	from Agu
kišib Ur-^{d}Ma-mi	seal of Ur-Mami

Reverse

má é-anše lugal	the boat for the house of the donkeys of the king
mu bàd mar-tu ba-dù	ŠS 4

Seal

Gìr-ni-ì-[ša$_6$]	Girnii[ša]
dub-sar	scribe
dumu Lugal-gù-dé-a	son of Lugal-Gudea

Commodities: Various (nos. 391–407)

no. 391 (Š 46) [copy]

Obverse

1 gír udu tag-ga	1 knife to slaughter sheep
ga-àm-bi [ ]	. . .
1 gír udu tag-ga	1 knife to slaughter sheep
ga-àm-bi	its handle
ki-lá-bi $2^{5}/_{6}$ ma-na	its weight is of $2^{5}/_{6}$ mana
mu-túm ^{d}[Šara$_2$]	delivery for [Šara]

Reverse

ki Na-ú-a-ta	from Naua
La-a-mu šu-ba-ti	Laamu received
mu Ki-maš^{ki} ba-ḫul	Š 46

Seal

Lú-^{d}Šara$_2$	Lu-Šara
agrig ^{d}Šara$_2$	agrig of Šara
dumu Ba-bí-za	son of Babiza

The term ga-àm is otherwise unattested. Perhaps it is a syllabic writing for gàm *gamlum* "handle."

no. 392 (Š 44 iii)

Obverse	
10 gìr-lam ^{giš}ḫašḫur 10-sila$_3$-ta	10 baskets of apples each containing 10 sila
1 gur ^{giš}ḫašḫur	1 gur of apples
é-^{d}Al-la-gu-la	the temple of Alla-gula
8 gìr-lam ^{giš}ḫašḫur 5 sila$_3$-ta	8 baskets of apples each containing 5 sila
0; 3.4. ^{giš}ḫašḫur	220 sila of apples
^{d}Nin-líl	Ninlil
Reverse	
2 gìr-lam 5 sila$_3$-ta	2 baskets of apples each containing 5 sila
0; 2.3. ^{giš}ḫašḫur	½ gur of apples
^{d}Nin-gá-gi$_4$-a	Ningagia
ezem gu$_4$-é-si	for the ...-festival
šà Nibru^{ki}	in Nippur
zi-ga šabra	disbursement of the steward
iti zaḫ$_x$-da-gu$_7$	month 3
mu Si-mu-rum	Š 44
Lu-lu-pu^{ki} ba-ḫul	

In the second month, the gu$_4$-si-su festival was celebrated in Nippur. But this elsewhere unattested festival name gu$_4$-é-si refers here to a festival in the third month. So it may not simply be a variant writing for gu$_4$-si-su.

no. 393 (Š 32 vii)

Obverse	
½ ma-na su-gán urudu	½ mana of lead and copper
ki Pàd-da-ta	from Padda
La-a-mu šu-ba-ti	Laamu received
Reverse	
iti min-èš	month 7
mu Si-mu-ru^{ki}	Š 32
a-rá 3-kam ba-ḫul	

no. 394 (Š 44 xi) [copy]

Obverse	
1 ma-na zabar	1 mana of bronze
ki Da-da-ga-ta	from Dadaga

Lugal-e-ba-an-ša$_6$	Lugalebanša
su-su-dam	will return
iti pa$_4$-kùš-e	month 11
Reverse	
mu Si-mu-ru-um	Š 44
Lu-lu-bun a-rá 10 lá 1-kam ba-ḫul	
Seal	
Lugal-e-ba-an-ša$_6$	Lugalebanša
dub-sar	scribe
dumu Ur-^{d}Ištaran	son of Ur-Ištaran

The scribe Lugalebanša almost exclusively seals tablets concerning reed. Our text is an exception.

no. 395 (ŠS 1 viii) [copy]

Obverse	
21 guruš ḫun-gá	21 hired workmen
u$_4$-22-kam	for 22 days
20 lá 1 guruš ḫun-gá	19 hired workmen
u$_4$-23-kam	for 23 days
20 guruš u$_4$-24-kam	20 workmen for 24 days
Reverse	
^{ú}kišig$_2$ ku$_5$-a 13 [sar]	to cut weeds, 13 sar per day
17½ guruš ḫun-gá	17½ hired workmen
al ak 4 sar	to dig 4 sar per day
u$_4$-25-kam	for 25 days
a-šà gíd-da	in the long field
ugula Ur-^{d}Šul-pa-è	overseer Ur-Šulpae
iti é iti 6 mu ^{d}Šu-^{d}EN.ZU lugal	month 8, ŠS 1
Seal	
Úr-ra-ni	Urrani
dub-sar	scribe
dumu Lugal-é-maḫ	son of Lugalemaḫ

no. 396 (AS 6) [copy]

Obverse	
30 gú ^{giš}ma-nu	30 talents of willow
gìr Ur-é-maš	responsible: Uremaš
30 gú ^{giš}ma-nu	30 talents of willow
gìr Ìr-ri-ib	responsible: Irrib

ki Lú-du$_{10}$-ga dumu Ni$_{9}$-gar-ki-du$_{10}$-ta	from Luduga son of Nigarkidu
ugú Lú-dingir-ra <ba-a-gar>	on the account of Ludingirra
Reverse	
kišib Ur-^{d}Nu-muš-da	seal of Ur-Numušda
mu a-rá 2-kam ša-aš-ru^{ki} ba-ḫul	AS 6
Seal	
Ur-^{d}Nu-muš-da	Ur-Numušda
dub-sar	scribe
dumu Lugal-gu$_{4}$-e	son of Lugalgue

no. 397 (AS 6)

Obverse	
10 gú ^{giš}ab-ba	10 talents of thornbush
ki Ur-é-maš-ta	from Uremaš
ugú Lú-dingir-ra ba-a-gar	on the account of Ludingirra
kišib Ur-^{d}Nu-muš-da	seal of Ur-Numušda
Reverse	
mu Ša-aš-šú-ru-um^{ki} ba-ḫul	AS 6
Seal	
Ur-^{d}Nu-muš-da	Ur-Numušda
dub-sar	scribe
dumu Lugal-gu$_{4}$-e	son of Lugalgue

no. 398 (Š 42) [copy]

Obverse	
4 ^{giš}dal é-da	4 planks for a cabin
ki Ur-é-maš-ta	from Uremaš
kišib Ḫé-ša$_{6}$	seal of Ḫeša
bala-[a u$_{4}$] 6-kam	during the *bala*, on the 6th day
Reverse	
mu Ša-aš-šú-ru-um^{ki}	Š 42
Seal	
Ḫé-ša$_{6}$	Ḫeša
dumu Ukken-né	son of Ukkenne

no. 399 (ŠS 4 vi 27) [copy]

Obverse	
5 gú ^{giš}ma-nu	5 talents of willow
siskur$_{2}$-šè	as an offering
ki Ur-é-maš-ta	from Uremaš

Reverse	
kišib Lú-^{d}Nin-šubur	seal of Lu-Ninšubur
u$_{4}$-27-kam	on the 27th day
iti šu-numun-na	month 6
mu-ús-sa Si-ma-núm^{ki} ba-ḫul	ŠS 4
Seal	
Lú-^{d}Nin-šubur	Lu-Ninšubur
dub-sar	scribe
dumu Du$_{10}$-ga	son of Dugga
šabra ^{d}Šara$_{2}$-ka	steward of Šara

no. 400 (ŠS) [copy]

Obverse	
1 in-nu gur	1 gur of straw
ki Ir$_{11}$-mu-ta	disbursed
ba-zi	by Irmu
Seal	
^{d}Šu-^{d}EN.ZU	Šu-Sîn
lugal kala-ga	strong king
lugal Uri$_{5}$^{ki}-ma	king of Ur
lugal an-ub-da limmu$_{2}$-ba	king of the four quarters of the universe
Lú-a-da-[kal]	Luada[kal]
dub-sar	scribe
dumu [ ]	son of [ ]
ir$_{11}$-zu	is your servant

Straw is not often mentioned in the tablets, although its use must not have been small. It could serve as fodder, used for making mats, or used in the production of mudbricks.

no. 401 (ŠS 5) [copy]

Obverse	
⅔ kuš gu$_{4}$ ú-ḫúb	⅔ of a tanned oxhide
3 kuš udu a ^{ú}ì-ri-<na>-ka	3 tanned sheepskins tanned with oak bark
^{giš}gigir-ra sag-uš	to be fixed in front of the chariot
gìr Nu-úr-Eš$_{4}$-tár sukkal	responsible: Nur-Eštar the vizier
Reverse	
mu-ús-sa bàd mar-tu ba-dù	ŠS 5

ú-ḫúb and ì-ri-na indicate two methods of tanning, as well as the colors obtained after the process. Leathers of various colors were strapped onto the chariot as decoration as well as affording protection.

no. 402 (Š 38) [copy]

Obverse

15 kuš-nì sumun	15 old leather sacks
ka-bi 1 [ ] ùr	…
ù ar-[ ]-ra	and [ ]
kaš-dé-a	for the banquet
ki A-du-ta	from Adu

Reverse

kišib Lugal-nì-lagar-e	seal of Lugalnilagare
mu-ús-sa bàd ba-dù	Š 38

Seal

Lugal-si-dè-e	Lugalsidee
dub-sar	scribe
dumu Lugal-ša$_6$-ga	son of Lugalšaga
lú ùr-ra-ka	the harrower(?)

no. 403 [copy]

Obverse

3.37 ^{kuš}e-sír é-ba-an	217 pairs of leather sandals
2.45 ^{kuš}ummud	165 leather bags
2.0 kuš-máš ì-dub	120 goat hides for containers
4.30 ^{kuš}a-gá-lá	270 leather pouches
2 túg uš-bar sag (*erasure*)	2 garments for weavers

no. 404 (Š 45 vii) [copy]

Obverse

1 kuš udu	1 sheepskin
ki Lú-Zabalam^{ki}-ta	from Lu-Zabalam
kišib Na-ba-sá	son of Nabasa
iti min-èš	month 7

Reverse

mu-ús-sa Si-mu-ru-um^{ki} Lu-lu-pu^{ki}	Š 45
a-rá 9-kam-aš ba-ḫul	

Seal

Na-ba-sá	Nabasa
dub-sar	scribe
dumu A-ka-dul	son of Akadul

If an animal was killed or even eaten by a wild beast, it was necessary to write a tablet removing the dead animal from the account. At the same time, the office of hides and leather would need to write another tablet to enter into the account the new skin in order to follow it through the administrative and tanning processing stream.

no. 405 (Š 35 iv) [copy]

Obverse	
40 lá 2 kuš ḫi-a	38 hides of various origin
ki Ur-ša$_6$-ga-ta	from Uršaga
^{giš}Dúr-gar-ni	Durgani
šu-ba-ti	received
Reverse	
iti nesag-<e>	month 4
mu dumu-lugal	Š 35
ensi$_2$ An-ša-<an>^{ki} ba-an-tuk	

no. 406 (AS 5 i) [copy]

Obverse	
3.0 kuš gu$_4$ síg mú	180 oxhides with the hairs still on them
2.30 kuš máš šu-<gíd> e-sír	150 hairless kidskins for sandals
1.30 kuš udu kurušda	90 sheepskins from the fattener
32.27 kuš udu	1947 sheepskins
12.41 kuš udu du$_{10}$-gan	761 sheepskins for bags
kuš síg mú-àm	hides with hair
12 ma-na sa udu	12 mana of sinews of sheep
Reverse	
ki ^{d}Šara$_2$-kam-ta	from Šarakam
Puzur$_4$-ì-lí	Puzur-ili
šu-ba-an-ti	received
iti še-kin-ku$_5$	month 1
mu en unu$_5$-gal ^{d}Inanna Unug^{ki} ba-ḫun	AS 5

The first two lines concern hides from sheep that were not barley-fed, whereas line 3 indicates hides of sheep coming from the fattener. Lines 4 and 5 give the amount of hides used for bags. All these hides were tanned, but the process did not remove the hairs.

no. 407 (AS 2)

Obverse	
3 ^{kuš}e-sír [ ] é-ba-an	3 pairs of sandals [ ]
7 ^{kuš}e-sír giš? é-ba-an	7 pairs of sandals [ ]?
10 ^{kuš}ummud	10 leather bags

dub-sar lugal a-šà gíd-da-a	the royal scribe measuring the field
Reverse	
šu-ba-ab-ti	received
gìr Lú-^{d}Nanna	responsible: Lu-Nanna
dumu Inim-^{d}Šara$_{2}$-ka	son of Inim-Šara
ki A-kal-la ašgab nin	from Akalla the leatherworker (of) the queen
kišib Lú-kal-la	seal of Lukalla
mu ^{d}Amar-^{d}EN.ZU lugal-e	AS 2
Ur-bí-lum^{ki} mu-ḫul	
Seal	
Lú-kal-la	Lukalla
dub-sar	scribe
dumu Ur-e$_{11}$-e kuš$_{7}$	son of Uree the equerry

LOANS (nos. 408–423)

no. 408 (ŠS 2 x)

Loan of silver at the interest rate of 20%.

Obverse	
1 gín kù-babbar ur$_{5}$-šè	1 shekel of silver for loan
máš 5 gín 1 gín-ta	the interest is 1 shekel for 5 shekels
ki Inim-kù-ga-ta	from Inimkuga
Sipa-ša$_{6}$-ga	Sipašaga
šu-ba-ti	received
Reverse	
ǀ Ur-^{d}En-líl-lá	Ur-Enlila
ǀ La-la-ma	Lalama
lú inim-ma-bi-me	are the witnesses
iti ab-è	month 10
mu má dara$_{4}$-abzu ba-ab-du$_{8}$	ŠS 2
Seal	
Sipa-ša$_{6}$-ga	Sipašaga
dumu Šu-[ ]	son of Šu[ ]

no. 409 (IS 3) [copy]

Obverse

0; 3.1.8 $sila_3$ še	198 sila
sá-du_{11} sag-bi gíd-da	verified regular deliveries
máš igi-3-gál si-gi_4-dé	its interest, ⅓ of the capital has to be returned
ki Gu-du-du-ta	from Gududu
Reverse	
Lugal-é-gal-e-si	Lugalegalesi
su-su-dam	will return it
mu-ús-sa en ^{d}Inanna Unug^{ki} máš-e ì-pàd	IS 3
Seal	
Lugal-é-gal-e-si	Lugalegalesi
dumu Inim-é-nun-na	son of Inimenunna
lú-lunga ^{d}Šara$_2$	the brewer of Šara

no. 410 (Š 32 ix)

Obverse

6 gín kù-babbar	6 shekels of silver
ki Lú-^{d}Bìl lú Má-gur_8-re-ta	from Lu-Bil servant of Magurre
Lú-ì-zu	Luizu
šu-ba-ti	received
Reverse	
iti ^{d}Li$_9$-si_4	month 9
mu a-rá 3-kam Si-mu-ru-um^{ki} ba-ḫul	Š 32

no. 411 (Š 44 iv 1)

Obverse

5 gín kù-babbar	5 shekels of silver
máš 5 gín 1 gín-ta	the interest is 1 shekel for 5 shekels
ki Ur-^{d}EN.ZU-ta	from Ur-Sîn
Ur-^{d}EN.ZU	Ur-Sîn
šu-ba-ti	received
Reverse	
iti šu-numun-a	month 4
u_4 1 ba-zal	the first day having elapsed
mu si-mu-ru-um^{ki} ba-ḫul	Š 44

no. 412 (IS 3 vii) [copy]

Obverse

1 gín kù-babbar	1 shekel of silver
máš 5 gín 1 gín-ta	the interest is 1 shekel for 5 shekels
ki Ur-^{d}EN.ZU-ta	from Ur-Sîn
Lú-bala-ša$_{6}$-ga	Lubalašaga

Reverse

šu-ba-ti	received
iti du$_{6}$-kù	month 7
mu en ^{d}Inanna Unug^{ki}-ga	IS 3
máš-e ì-pàd	

no. 413 (IS 3 vi) [copy]

Obverse

6 gín kù-babbar	6 shekel of silver
ki Ur-^{d}EN.ZU-ta	from Ur-Sîn
mu-túm	delivery

Reverse

iti kin-^{d}Inanna	month 6
mu en ^{d}Inanna Unug^{ki}-ga	IS 3
máš-e ì-pàd	

Seal

[ ]	
ir$_{11}$ lugal	servant of the king
dumu Šeš-a-ni	son of Šešani

no. 414 (IS 3 iv)

Obverse

2 še gur	1 shekel of silver
máš 1 gur 100 sila$_{3}$-ta-àm	interest 100 sila for each gur
ki Ur-^{d}EN.ZU-ta	from Ur-Sîn
Ur-^{d}Šul-pa-è	Ur-Šulpae
šu-ba-ti	received

Reverse

iti šu-numun-na	month 4
mu ^{d}I-bí-^{d}EN.ZU lugal-e	IS 3
Si-mu-ru-um^{ki} mu-ḫul	

no. 415 (AS 7 vi)

Obverse	
5 gín kù-babbar	5 shekel of silver
máš-bi 1 gín-ta	interest of 1 shekel
100 $sila_3$ še máš-bi 33 $sila_3$	100 sila barley its interest 33 sila
ki Ur-^{d}Iškur-ta	from Ur-Iškur
Ur-gu unù	Urgu the cowherd
Reverse	
šu-ba-ti	received
Nam-ḫa-ni dam-gàr	Namḫani the merchant
Ku_5-da	Kuda
lú inim-ma-bi-me	are the witnesses
iti kin-^{d}Inanna	month 6
u_4 6 ba-zal mu	the 6th day has elapsed
Hu-úḫ-nu-ri^{ki} ba-ḫul	AS 7

no. 416 (IS 2 xi)

Obverse	
1 gín kù-babbar	1 shekel of silver
máš 5 gín 1 gín-ta	interest 1 shekel for 5 shekel
ki Gemé-é-zi-da-ta	from Geme-ezida
Kal-la-kal-la-a	Kallakallaa
šu-ba-ti	received
iti úd-$duru_5$	month 11
Reverse	
mu en ^{d}Inanna Unug^{ki}	IS 2
máš-e ì-pàd	
Seal	
kal-la-kal-la(?)	

no. 417 (IS 2 vi)

Obverse	
⅓ gín kù-babbar ur_5-šè	⅓ shekel of silver for loan
máš gín 5 gín 1-ta	interest 1 shekel for 5 shekels
ki U-bar-um-ta	from Ubarum
Ú?-da-li šu-ba-ti	Udali received
igi Ur-^{d}En-ki sukkal	witness: Ur-Enki the vizier
igi Lugal-agrig-zi	witness: Lugalagrigzi
igi Lugal-kù-zu	witness: Lugalkuzu

Reverse

Ur-^{d}EN.ZU	witness: Ur-Sîn
lú inim-ma-bi-me	the witnesses
iti kin-^{d}Inanna	month 6
mu en Unug^{ki} máš-e ba-ḫun-gá	IS 2

Seal

^{d}I-bí-^{d}EN.ZU
lugal kalag-ga
lugal Uri$_{5}$^{ki}-ma
Ù-da-li
[ ]
dumu [ ]
[ ]

no. 418 (ŠS 8 ix)

Obverse

1 gín kù-babbar	1 shekel of silver
máš 5 gín 1 gín-ta	the interest is 1 shekel for 5 shekels
ki Ur-^{d}EN.ZU-ta	from Ur-Sîn
[ ]-^{d}Da-mu	[ ]-Damu
šu-ba-ti	received

Reverse

Á-da-da	Adada
Lugal-agrig-zi	Lugalagrigzi
lú inim-ma-bi-meš	are the witnesses
iti gan-gan-è	month 9
mu-ús-sa Za-ab-ša-li^{ki} ba-ḫul	ŠS 8

Seal

[ ]	[ ]
dumu Ur-^{d}[ ]	son of Ur-[ ]

no. 419 (ŠS 6 ix)

Obverse

1 kù ma-na kù-babbar	1 mana of silver
máš 5 gín 1-ta	interest 1 shekel for 5 shekels
ki Ur-^{d}EN.ZU-ta	from Ur-Sîn
Ur-^{d}EN.ZU nu-banda$_{3}$	Ur-Sîn the lieutenant
šu-ba-ti	received
| Lú-ša$_{6}$-ga	Lušaga

Reverse

| Á-da-da	Adada
| [Lú-dingir]-ra	Ludingirra
| Ur-dingir-si$_4$-an-na	Urdingirsianna
lú inim-ma-bi-me	are the witnesses
iti gan-gan-è	month 9
mu na-rú-a maḫ ba-dù	ŠS 6

Seal illegible

no. 420 (AS 9 diri)

Obverse

8½ gín kù-babbar	8½ shekels of silver
máš 5 gín 1 gín-ta	the interest is 1 shekel for 5 shekels
ki Inim-kù-ga-ta	from Inimkuga
Ur-^{d}En-líl-lá-ke$_4$	Ur-Enlilla
šu-ba-ti	received
iti diri!(SI) še-kin-ku$_5$	intercalary month
| Nam-ḫa-ni	Namḫani

Reverse

| Ur-ru-ma	Urruma
| Ga-ga	Gaga
| Na-na-a	Nanaa
lú inim-ma-bi-me	are the witnesses
mu en ^{d}Nanna kar-zi-da ba-ḫun	AS 9

Seal

Lugal-é-maḫ-e	Lugalemaḫe
dub-sar	scribe
dumu Lugal-kù-ga-ni	son of Lugalkugani

no. 421 (ŠS 6 iv)

Obverse

13 gín kù-babbar	13 shekels of silver
máš 5 gín 1 gín	the interest is 1 shekel for 5 shekels
ki Ur-^{d}EN.ZU-ta	from Ur-Sîn
Ur-du$_6$-kù-ke$_4$	Urduku
šu-ba-ti	received

Reverse

Lú-ša$_6$-ga	Lušaga
Inim-ša$_6$-ša$_6$	Inimšaša
^{d}Utu-ḫé-zu	Utu-ḫezu

lú inim-ma-bi-me	are the witnesses
mu lugal-e na maḫ mu-rú	ŠS 6

no. 422 (IS 2 vi)

Obverse

1 gín kù-babbar	1 shekel of silver
máš 5 gín 1 gín-ta	the interest is 1 shekel for 5 shekels
ki U-bar-ta	from Ubar
Ur-^{d}Lugal-bàn-da	Ur-Lugalbanda
ù Ur-^{d}EN.ZU-ke$_{4}$	and Ur-Sîn

Reverse

šu-ba-ti-eš	received
| Ur-^{d}Nám-maḫ	Ur-Nammaḫ
| Lugal-gú-gal	Lugalgugal
lú inim-ma-bi-me	are the witnesses
iti kin-^{d}Inanna	month 6
mu en ^{d}Inanna Unug^{ki}-ga máš-e ì-pàd	IS 2

no. 423 (IS 1)

Obverse

10 gín kù-babbar	10 shekels of silver
máš 5 gín 1 gín-ta	the interest is 1 shekel for 5 shekels
iti še-kin-ku$_{5}$ u$_{4}$ 15-ba-zal-ta	from month 12, the 15th day
iti sig$_{4}$-šè gi$_{4}$-dam	to month 2; he shall return it
ki Lugal-ezem-ta	from Lugalezem
Un-da-ga	Undaga

Reverse

šu-ba-ti	received
mu lugal-bi ì-pàd	they swore in the name of the king
mu ^{d}I-bí-^{d}EN.ZU lugal	IS 1

VARIOUS ADMINISTRATIVE TABLET TYPES (nos. 424–447)

Records were kept for verification needs. They were stored in reed baskets with a tag affixed to the handle. The tag was inscribed clay with a seal. Very often we can still see the two holes in the clay tag through which the reed fastener was placed. Tags are interesting for retrieving the administrative and accounting categories used by the scribes to classify the tablets kept in the baskets.

no. 424 (Š43) [copy]

pisan-dub-ba	tablet basket <containing>
im gi-na	the verified tablets (accounting for)
še giš è-a	the threshed barley
gìr Bù-bù	responsible: Bubu
mu en ^{d}Nanna maš-e ì-pàd	Š 43
ì-gál	

no. 425

This tag is sealed with three different seals, but there is no writing on the tag.

Seal 1

Lú-du$_{10}$-ga	Luduga
dub-sar	scribe
dumu Du$_{11}$-ga	son of Dugga

Seal 2

Ur-^{d}Nun-gal	Ur-Nungal
dub-sar	scribe
dumu Ur-^{d}Šara$_2$	son of Ur-Šara
ša$_{13}$-dub-ba	archivist

Seal 3

Ur-^{d}Šara$_2$	Ur-Šara
dub-sar	scribe
dumu [ ]	son of [ ]

no. 426 (Š 34) [copy]

Obverse

pisan-dub-ba	tablet-basket (containing the tablets about)
gurum$_2$-ak	the inspection
gìr-sì-ga gu$_4$-apin	of the team of plowoxen
mu-ús-sa a-rá [3]-kam Si-mu-ru-um	Š 34

gìr-sì-ga is a well-attested expression in Umma and Lagash. Sometimes the word is translated "household," in other words, all the persons and animals belonging to a given sector of the economy of a large estate. The term occurs also in the expressions gìr-sì-ga ensi$_2$ and gìr-sì-ga gu$_4$-apin, as in our text. Here, a translation "team" is more appropriate, referring to all that is needed for plowing to take place, i.e., workmen, cattle, and implements.

no. 427 (Š 46) [copy]

Obverse	
pisan-dub-ba	basket tablet
še-zì-da	about the flour of barley
kišib Ur-zu	seal of Urzu
ù kišib ugula kikken-na-ke$_4$-ne	and seal of the overseer of the grinder
ì-gál	
Reverse	
mu Ki-maš^{ki} ba-ḫul	Š 46

no. 428 (ŠS 6) [copy]

Obverse	
pisan-dub-ba	tablet basket (containing)
nì-ka$_9$-ak	the accounts
á erin$_2$-na	of the work of erin
nu-banda$_3$ gu$_4$ íd-pa-è	lieutenant of the oxen Idpae
Reverse	
mu na-rú-a maḫ ba-dù	ŠS 6
ì-gál	

no. 429 (ŠS 9 vi) [copy]

Obverse	
14 guruš ḫun-gá	14 hired workmen
al-[ak x-sar]-ta	to dig at the rate of x sar per day
ugula Ur-^{d}Šul-pa-è	overseer Ur-Šulpae
a-šà ì-sum	in the field Isum
gurum$_2$-ak u$_4$-15-kam	inspection on the 15th day
Reverse	
iti šu-numun	month 6
mu é-^{d}Šara$_2$ ba-dù	ŠS 9

no. 430 (ŠS 2)

Obverse	
12 guruš u$_4$-1-šè	12 workmen for 1 day
ki-su$_7$ ^{d}Amar-^{d}EN.ZU-^{d}Šara$_2$-ki-ág gub-ba	stationed on the threshing floor Amar-Sîn-beloved-of-Šara
ugula Lugal-é-maḫ-e	overseer Lugalemaḫe
Reverse	
kišib I-šar-ru-um	seal Išarrum

mu má ^{d}En-ki ba-ab-du$_8$	ŠS 2
Seal 1	
I-šar-ru-um	Išarrum
dub-sar	scribe
dumu Ur-^{d}En-líl-lá	son of Ur-Enlilla
Seal 2	
Šeš-kal-la	Šeškalla
dub-sar	scribe
dumu Tir-gu	son of Tirgu

no. 431 [copy]

This could be an exercise tablet.

Obverse	
159	159
159 udu	159 sheep

no. 432 (ŠS 5) [copy]

Obverse	
1.50 lá 1 guruš u$_4$-1-šè	109 workmen for 1 day
ugú Íd-pa-è ba-a-gar	on the account of Idpae
ugula A-a-kal-la	overseer Aakalla
kišib Lú-dingir-[ra]	seal of Ludingirra
Reverse	
mu-ús-sa bàd mar-tu ba-dù	ŠS 5
Seal	
Lú-dingir-ra	Ludingirra
dub-sar	scribe
dumu Ḫa-ba-lug-gé	son of Ḫabalugge

no. 433 (Š 32)

Obverse	
diri 1⅓ sila$_3$ 4 gín [ ]	debit 1⅓ sila 4 shekels of [silver]
gana$_2$ Ur-^{d}Nin-su	from the field of Ur-Ninsu
diri 15 gín	debit 15 gin
gana$_2$ A-ab-ba	field of Aabba
diri ½ gín	debit ½ gin
gana$_2$ me-en-kara$_2$	field Menkara
[ ]	[ ]
Reverse	
inim káb-[du$_{11}$-ga]-ta	according to the record of the tax office

Ur-^{d}Nin-su šabra	Ur-Ninsu is the steward
mu a-rá 3-kam Si-mu-ru-um^{ki} ba-ḫul	Š 32

no. 434

Obverse

[ ] še gur-lugal	[ ] gur of barley according to the royal measurement
[ ] kišib Ur-ni$_{9}$-[gar] ì-dab$_{5}$	[ ] tablet of Urni[gar] has taken into possession
[ ] gur kišib Lugal-inim-gi-na	[ ] gur tablet of Lugalinimgina
1; 2.0. še gur A.IGI.sar	$1\frac{2}{5}$ gur of barley A.IGI.sar
1 še gur Dingir-en-a-a	1 gur of barley for Dingirenaa
1.0 še gur Ur-tur muḫaldim unù ^{d}Nanna	60 gur of barley for Urtur the cook in the kitchen of Nanna

Reverse

nì-ka$_{9}$-ak	account of
Ur-^{d}A-šár dumu Ur-^{d}EN.ZU	Ur-Ašar son of Ur-Sîn
muḫaldim dumu lugal	cook of the son of the king

no. 435 (ŠS 9) [copy]

Obverse

Col. i

5.41 máš	341 goats
libir-àm	from the old account
20 máš	20 goats
máš ^{giš}gigir ^{d}Nin-gis-zi-da	goats for the chariot of Ningišida
udu gub-ba-àm	sheep on hand
1.2 máš 20 [udu]	62 goats 20 sheep

Col. ii

Ki-tuš-lú na-gada	Kitušlu the shepherd
3.0 lá 2 udu	178 sheep
bí-ri KU	Biri …
ki Ki-tuš-lú	from Kitušlu
1.1 udu	61 sheep
udu Ur-^{d}Iškur	sheep of Ur-Iškur
1.2 udu	62 sheep
udu Ì-tur-ra KU	sheep of Iturra …
[35 udu] ú	35 grass-fed sheep

Col. iii

udu Ur-^{d}Ba-ba$_{6}$ šabra	sheep of Ur-Baba the steward

2.31 udu	151 sheep
30 lá 1 máš	29 goats
udu Ur-^{d}Lama sa$_{12}$-du$_{5}$	sheep of Ur-Lama the recorder
1.2 udu 2 máš	62 sheep 2 goats
udu Ur-an-ki	sheep of Uranki
1.52 udu	112 sheep
1.29 máš	89 goats
[ ] lú-maḫ [ ]	[for] the *lumaḫ*-priest
Reverse	
Col. i	
38 [udu]	38 sheep
udu Lú-^{d}Šul-gi KU	sheep of Lu-Šulgi ...
48 udu 2 máš	48 sheep 2 goats
udu Amar-kù KU	sheep of Amarku ...
9 udu 1 máš	9 sheep 1 goat
udu Ur-^{d}Ba-ba$_{6}$ KU-ÀR	sheep of Ur-Baba ...
52 udu 1.2 máš	52 sheep 62 goats
udu Lú-ša$_{6}$-ša$_{6}$-ga KU	sheep of Lušašaga ...
19 udu 3 máš	19 sheep 3 goats
udu Nì-lagar-di-e KU	sheep of Nilagardie ...
Col. ii	
[udu]	[ ] sheep
[ ] máš	[ ] goats
udu Lú-^{d}En-ki [ ] kaskal	sheep of Lu-Enki [ ] ...
2.10 udu 10 máš	139 sheep 10 goats
Ur-zu sipa	Urzu the shepherd
1.41 udu 20 máš	101 sheep 20 goats
Lú-me-lám sipa	Lu-melam the shepherd
udu É-maḫ	sheep of the Emaḫ
1.51 udu	111 sheep
46 máš	46 goats
La-gú sipa	Lagu the shepherd
udu Lú-kiri$_{3}$-zal nu-banda$_{3}$ ki [ ]	sheep of Lu-kirizal the lieutenant of the place [ ]
Col. iii	
[ ]	[ ]
[ ]	[ ]
nì-[ka$_{9}$-ak]	account
a-šà é-^{d}Inanna	of the field of E-Inanna
mu é ^{d}Šara$_{2}$ ba-dù	ŠS 9

no. 436

This tablet seems to be a memo, recording four transactions that would be later transcribed onto separate dated tablets. That is why this memo is not dated.

Obverse	
1 gig gur	1 gur of wheat
1 zíz gur	1 gur of emmer
zi-ga ensi$_2$	disbursement of the governor
gìr Ukken-né	responsible: Ukkenne
0; 2.2.4 <sila$_3$> esír a-é sa$_{10}$	144 sila of bought bitumen
gìr Lugal-nì-lagar-e dumu Gìr-ni	responsible: Lugalnilagare son of Girni
Reverse	
3 zì gur kišib nu-ra-a	3 gur of flour; the tablet (for the transaction) was not sealed
A-tu	for Atu
7 gur A-ba-dingir-mu-gim	7 gur for Abadingirmugim and
ù Ḫa-ba-lug-gé	Ḫabalugge

Note that the scribe mentions that the tablet of Atu is not sealed. This note indicates that there is not an irregularity, when later this tablet of Atu will be presented.

Line 5 should probably be emended to esír-é-a.

no. 437 (Š 44 ix) [copy]

Obverse	
0; 1.0. še lugal	60 sila of barley according to the royal measurement
lá-ni-ta su-ga	from the arrears that were returned
ki Lú-kal-la-ta	from Lukalla
Ur-dingir-ra kuš$_7$	Urdingirra the equerry
Reverse	
šu-ba-ti	received
iti ^{d}Li$_9$-si$_4$	month 9
mu-ús-sa a-rá!	Š 44
Si-mu-ru-um^{ki} ba-ḫul	
Seal	
Ur-dingir-ra kuš$_7$	Urdingirra the equerry
dumu A-zi	son of Azi

no. 438 (AS 7) [copy]

Obverse	
29; 1.0. še gur	$29\frac{1}{5}$ gur of barley
gur sá-du$_{11}$-ta	gur according to the *sattukku*-measurement
lá-ni še zi-ga	surplus from the disbursed barley
šà-bi-ta	from it
26; 4.5.8 sila$_{3}$ gur	27 gur minus 2 sila
zi-ga-àm	disbursed
Reverse	
diri 2; 0.3.3 sila$_{3}$ še gur	deficit 2 gur 33 sila of barley
nì-ka$_{9}$-ak lá-ni še zi-ga	account of surplus from the disbursed barley
^{d}Šara$_{2}$-ba-zi-ge	by Šara-bazige
mu Ḫu-úḫ-nu-ri^{ki} ba-ḫul	AS 7

Balanced account, income and expenses are balanced and the balance can be positive lá-ni or negative diri. Here one should expect in the first line of the reverse lá-ni and not diri. There is also an error of 31 sila in the account.

no. 439 (AS 9 xi) [copy]

A tax adjustment.

Obverse	
lá-ni 4; 4.3.8. sila$_{3}$ še gur-lugal	difference 4 gur 278 sila of barley according to the royal measurement
kab-du$_{11}$-ga še-a-ak	tax of the barley
ki Ur-^{d}Li$_{9}$-si$_{4}$-ta	from Ur-Lisi
Reverse	
Lugal-nì-lagar-e	Lugalnilagare
su-su-dam	has to return
mu Lugal-nì-lagar-e-šè	instead of Lugalnilagare
kišib Šeš-a-ni dumu-na ì-gál	there is the seal of Šešani his son
iti pa$_{4}$-kùš-e mu-ús-sa en Eridu^{ki} ba-ḫun-gá	month 11, AS 9
Seal	
Šeš-a-ni	Šešanai
dub-sar	scribe
dumu Lugal-nì-lagar-e	son of Lugalnilagare

no. 440 (Š 31)

Obverse

lá-ni 2 še gur-lugal	surplus of 2 gur of barley according to the royal measurement
[ ] še zi-ga	disbursement of barley
gur zabar-ta	according to the bronze measurement
[ki] Lú-bàn-da-ta	from Lubanda

Reverse

a-šà gú-eden-na	in the field Guedenna
Šeš-ki-ág-mu su-su-dam	Šeškiagmu will return
mu a-rá 2-kam	Š 31
Kara$_2$-ḫar^{ki} ba-ḫul	

no. 441 (Š 30) [copy]

Obverse

lá-ni 14; 0.3. še gur-lugal	surplus of 14 gur and 30 sila of barley according to the royal measurement
lá-ni su-su engar-e-ne	surplus returned by the plowmen
ki Ur-^{d}Li$_9$-si$_4$-ta	from Ur-Lisi
Lugal-kù-ga-ni	Lugalkugani

Reverse

šu-ba-ti	received
mu dumu-munus lugal ensi$_2$	Š 30
An-<ša-an^{ki}>-na ba-an-tuk	

no. 442

Obverse

4 še gur-lugal	4 gur of barley according to the royal measurement
maš-bi 1; 1.4. gur	its interest is 400 sila
šu-nigín 5; 1.4. gur	total, 5⅓ gur
šà-bi-ta	from it
1; 3.0. Lugal-á-ga	1 3/5 for Lugalaga
0; 1.2.5 sila$_3$ Ba-ba-a	85 sila for Babaa
1 gín kù-babbar	1 gin of silver
še-bi 1 še gur	its barley 1 gur of barley
Al-la-mu	for Allamu

Reverse

šu-nigín 2; 4.2.5 sila$_3$ gur	total 2 gur 265 sila
mu-túm	delivery

si-ì-tum	rest of barley
2; 2.1.5 $sila_3$ gur	2 gur 135 sila
ki An-na-ḫi-gál gál-la-àm	in the place of Annaḫegal

The interest rate of 33% is standard for a loan of grain. Of the loaned barley with its interest, so far, 865 sila have been repaid. Grain outstanding or on debt is 735 sila, to be paid by Annaḫegal.

no. 443 (ŠS 9) [copy]

Dugagina, probably a ox-driver, has an excess of grain. Part of it has been returned and will be deducted from his overall debt.

Obverse	
14; 4.[ ] še [gur]	14⁴⁄₅ [ ] gur of barley
lá-ni Du_{11}-ga-gi-na	surplus of Duggagina
nì su-ga-bi íb-ta-zi	the amount of what has been returned is to be discounted
ki Gu-du-du-ta	from Gududu
Reverse	
Ur-^{d}Nun-gal	Ur-Nungal
su-su-dam	will return
mu é ^{d}Šara$_2$ Umma^{ki}-ka ba-dù	ŠS 9
Seal	
Ur-^{d}[Nun-gal]	Ur-[Nungal]
dub-sar	scribe
dumu Lugal-é-maḫ-e	son of Lugalemaḫe

no. 444 (IS 3)

Obverse	
5 še gur	5 gur of barley
lá-ni su-ga gu_4	from the arrears that were returned from the oxen of
Ur-é-maḫ dumu Lugal-kù-ga-ni	Ur-emaḫ son of Lugalkugani
ki Ur-^{d}Nun-gal-ta	from Ur-Nungal
Reverse	
gaba-ri kišib-ba	copy of the sealed tablet of
Gu-du-du	Gududu
mu Si-mu-ru-um^{ki} ba-ḫul	IS 3

The barley given to Lubanda was considered expended (zi-ga), had been subtracted from the account and had disappeared from the books. Now that some barley has been returned, its origin of the barley must again appear on the books (lá-ni-ta su-ga). But it is also necessary to indicate that it is a delivery (mu-túm), to make sure that the scribe records it in the correct column of his account. Mu-túm marks a delivery to the central administration, while zi-ga is an expenditure from the storerooms to the users.

no. 445 (Š 30 diri) [copy]

Obverse	
1.32;2.0. še gur lugal	$92^{2}/_{5}$ gur of barley according to the royal measurement
lá-ni-ta su-ga	returned from the surplus
ki Lú-bàn-da-ta	from Lubanda
mu-túm	delivery
Reverse	
Ur-^{d}Li$_{9}$-si$_{4}$ šu-ba-ti	Ur-Lisi received
iti diri	intercalary month
mu dumu-lugal	Š 30

no. 446 (Š 31 viii)

Obverse	
20 lá 1 še gur-lugal	19 gur of barley according to the royal measurement
lá-ni su-ga	surplus returned
ki Ur-^{d}A-šár-ta	from Ur-Ašar
gìr Lugal-inim-gi-na	responsible: Lugalinimgina
Ur-^{d}Li$_{9}$-si$_{4}$	Ur-Lisi
šu-ba-ti	received
iti é-iti-6	month 8
Reverse	
mu a-rá 2-[kam]	Š 31
Kara$_{2}$-ḫar^{ki} ba-[ḫul]	

The scribe does not write mu-túm because it is an internal transfer, not a return to the central granary. Nevertheless a gìr-official is present at this return of the barley, because such a procedure is unusual.

no. 447 (AS 7 vi)

Obverse	
1.11; 2.0. še zì-gu gur	$71^{2}/_{5}$ gur of barley for pea-flour
29; 1.0. gig gur	$29^{1}/_{5}$ gur of wheat

še nu-ub-ta-ri-ri	barley was not collected
ki-su$_7$ a-kun-ne-ta	from the threshing floor Akunne
20 še àr-ra gur	20 gur of barley for grinding
ki Ur-^{giš}gigir šabra-ta	from Urgigir the steward
Reverse	
má-a si-ga Nibru^{ki}	(all this barley, $120\frac{3}{5}$ gur) was filled in the boat (for) Nippur
gìr É-gal-e-si	responsible: Egalesi
kišib nu-ra-a	the tablet was not sealed
iti šu-numun	month 6
mu Ḫu-úḫ-nu-ri^{ki} ba-ḫul	AS 7

Navigation (nos. 448–457)

no. 448 (AS 7 vi) [copy]

Obverse	
15; 1.0. gig gur	$5\frac{1}{5}$ gur of wheat
še ri-ri-ga-bi 1; 4.3. <gur>	its lost barley is 1 gur 270 sila
nu-banda$_3$ Ur-^{giš}gigir dumu Bar-ra-an	the lieutenant is Urgigir the son of Barran
14 gig gur	14 gur of wheat
še ri-ri-ga-bi 1; 1.0. gur	its lost barley is 1 gur 360 sila
Reverse	
nu-banda$_3$ gu$_4$ Ur-^{giš}gigir dumu Lugal-lú-ni	the lieutenant of the oxen is Urgigir the son of Lugalluni
má-a si-ga Nibru^{ki}-šè	loaded on the boat for Nippur
gìr É-gal-e-si	responsible: Egalesi
ki-su$_7$ a-kun-ne	threshing floor Akunne
iti šu-numun	month 6
mu Ḫu-ḫu-nu-ri^{ki} ba-ḫul	AS 7

no. 449 (AS 2) [copy]

Obverse	
5.0 še gur-lugal	300 gur of barley according to the royal measurement
ì-dub ^{giš}tir-gaba-gíd-da	(from) the silo of the field Tirgabagidda
má-a si-ga Nibru^{ki}-šè	loaded on a boat for Nippur
ki Nam-maḫ-ta	from Nammaḫ
Ur-^{d}Šul-pa-è	Ur-Šulpae

Reverse

Lú-^{d}Nin-gír-su	(and) Lu-Ningirsu
šu-ba-ti	received
gìr Ur-^{d}Dumu-zi	responsible: Ur-Dumuzi
mu ^{d}Amar-^{d}EN.ZU lugal-e	AS 2
Ur-bí-lum^{ki} mu-ḫul	

no. 450 (AS 1) [copy]

Obverse

7 guruš u$_4$-2-šè	7 workmen for 2 days
Gir$_{13}$-giš^{ki}-ta še má-a si-ga	from Girgiš loading barley in the boat
7 guruš u$_4$-5-šè má diri-ga-<<ga>>	7 workmen for 5 days to move downstream
7 guruš u$_4$-2-šè kun-zi	7 workmen for 2 days at the dam of Patibira
-da Pa$_5$-tibira-ka	
sag-má gu-apin-ka	the front of the boat with plow strings
7 guruš u$_4$-5-šè	7 workmen for 5 days
má ba-al-la še bala	to unload the boat and to store the barley

Reverse

7 guruš u$_4$-5-šè	7 workmen for 5 days
má sud gíd-da	to tow the empty boat
ugula Ur-^{d}Da-mu	overseer Ur-Damu
kišib La-ni mu	seal of Lani the cook
šà Uri$_5^{ki}$	in Ur
še na-kab-tum-ma ku$_4$-ra	to bring the barley into the storehouse
mu ^{d}Amar-^{d}EN.ZU lugal	AS 1

Seal

La-ni muḫaldim	Lani the cook
dub-sar	scribe
dumu Ur-ni$_9$-gar	son of Urnigar

no. 451 (AS 6 v–x)

Obverse

10 má-laḫ$_4$? [ ] ná? sumun	10 boatmen [ ] old bed(?)
1 dumu Ú-ga	1 son of Uga
1 Ir$_{11}$-gi-na	1 Irgina
1 dumu An-né-ba-ab-du$_7$	1 the son of Annebabdu
1 dumu Lugal-má-gur$_8$-re	1 the son of Lugalmagurre
1 ^{d}Šara$_2$-in-zu	1 Šara-inzu

Reverse

1 dumu É-úr-bi	1 the son of Eurbi

1 dumu Ur-^{giš}gigir	1 the son of Urgigir
iti 6-šè	for 6 months
iti ri-ta iti ezem-^{d}Šul-gi-šè	from month 5 to month 8
á-bi Lugal-e-ba-an-ša$_6$	this work(ing time controlled by) Lugalebanša
ki-bi gi$_4$-gi$_4$-dam	shall be credited back
mu a-rá 2-kam Ša-aš-ru-um^{ki} ba-ḫul	AS 6
Seal	
Lugal-e-ba-an-ša$_6$	Lugalebanša
dub-sar	scribe
dumu Ur-^{d}Ištaran	son of Ur-Ištaran

no. 452 (ŠS 3) [copy]

Obverse	
15 guruš u$_4$-1-šè	15 workmen for 1 day
kar Umma^{ki}-ta	from the quay of Umma
ka íd-da-šè	to the mouth of the canal
má bala-a gíd-da	to turn around and tow a boat
ugula Ur-^{giš}gigir	overseer Urgigir
Reverse	
kišib Ukken-né	seal of Ukkenne
mu Si-ma-núm^{ki} ba-ḫul	ŠS 3
Seal	
Ukken-né	Ukkenne
dub-sar	scribe
dumu Ur-^{giš}gigir	son of Urgigir

no. 453 (ŠS 5) [copy]

Obverse	
5 guruš u$_4$-3-šè	5 workmen for 3 days
tir é lugal [ ]	in the forest of the palace of the king (...)
giš a-ta du$_8$-a má-a si-ga	to take out the wood from the water and to load it onto boats
kar-ra-šè má gíd-da	to tow the boat to the quay
ù má ba-al-la	and to unload the boat
5 guruš u$_4$-5-šè	5 workmen for 5 days
kar-ra é-dím-du gub-ba	to station at the quay of the Edimdu
Reverse	
ugula Íd-pa-è	overseer Idpae
kišib Lú-kal-la	seal of Lukalla
mu-ús-sa ^{d}Šu-^{d}EN.ZU lugal Uri$_5$^{ki}-ma-ke$_4$	ŠS 5

bàd mar-tu mu-dù

Seal

Lú-kal-la	Lukalla
dub-sar	scribe
dumu Ur-e_{11}-e $kuš_7$	son of Uree the equerry

no. 454 (ŠS 3)

Obverse

1 guruš u_4-15-šè	1 workman for 15 days
$Uri_5{}^{ki}$-šè	to Ur
má-še gíd-da	to tow a barley boat
ù má gur-ra	and to turn the boat around

Reverse

še-ba nar-ke_4-ne	(containing the) barley rations for the singers
ugula ^{d}Šara$_2$-a-mu	overseer Šara-amu
kišib Ur-àm-ma $kuš_7$?	seal of Uramma the equerry
mu Si-ma-núm^{ki} ba-ḫul	ŠS 3

Seal

Ur-àm-ma	Uramma
dub-sar	scribe
dumu Na-di	son of Nadi

no. 455 (ŠS 4 ix) [copy]

Obverse

1.50 še gur	110 gur of barley
kišib Ur-^{d}EN.ZU	tablet of Ur-Sîn
1.50 še gur	110 gur of barley
kišib Lú-nesag-e	tablet of Lunesage
[1.50] še gur	[110] gur of barley
kišib A-gu	tablet of Agu

Reverse

1.0 gur	60 gur of barley
kišib Ur-^{d}EN.ZU dub-sar	tablet of Ur-Sîn the scribe
má-a si-ga Umma^{ki}-šè	loaded onto a boat for Umma
gur_7 kam-sal_4-la-ta	from the granary of Kamsalla
ki É-gal-e-si-ta	from Egalesi
Lú-^{d}Nám-an-ka	Lu-Namanka
ba-an-díb	received
iti ^{d}Li$_9$-si_4	month 9
mu-ús-sa Si-ma-núm^{ki} ba-ḫul	ŠS 4

Seal

Lú-^{d}Nám-an-ka	Lu-Namanka
dub-sar	scribe
dumu Lú-^{d}Šara$_{2}$	son of Lu-Šara
sa$_{12}$-du$_{5}$-ka	field surveyor

no. 456 (ŠS 5) [copy]

Obverse

4 guruš u$_{4}$-1-šè	4 workmen for 1 day
má-lá-a gi šeg$_{6}$ kéš-rá	to knot a raft with dried reed
u$_{4}$ 7-šè má-gíd-da	to tow the boat for 7 days
u$_{4}$-1-šè [má bala-a]	to unload the boat during one day

Reverse

Umma^{ki}-ta	from Umma
Nibru^{ki}-šè	to Nippur
ugula Lugal-iti-da	overseer Lugalitida
kišib Uš-mu	seal of Ušmu
mu-ús-sa ^{d}Šu-^{d}EN.ZU lugal-e	ŠS 5
bàd mar-tu mu-dù	

Seal

Uš-mu	Ušmu
dub-sar	scribe
dumu Lugal-ša$_{6}$-ga	son of Lugalšaga

no. 457 (Š 36 i) [copy]

Obverse

1 guruš nagar	1 workman carpenter
iti 2 u$_{4}$-15-šè	for 2 months until the 15th day
mar-sa gub-ba	stationed at the navigation office
nu-banda$_{3}$ gu$_{4}$ Lugal-ukken-né	lieutenant of the oxen Lugalukkenne
ugula Lugal-^{giš}kiri$_{6}$	overseer Lugalkiri
iti še-kin-ku$_{5}$	month 1

Reverse

mu-ús-sa An-ša-an^{ki} mu-ús-sa-bi	Š 36
kišib Lú-kal-la	seal of Lukalla

Seal

Lú-kal-la	Lukalla
dub-sar	scribe
dumu Lugal-[en-nun]	son of Lugal[ennun]

MESSENGER TEXTS (nos. 458–467)

no. 458

Obverse

Col. i

1; 1.0.1 sila$_3$ kaš gin 20 sila$_3$	361 sila of average-quality beer at 20 sila of barley
6 gur dida gin	6 gur of beer, second category
1; 0.5. dabin	350 sila barley flour
4 it-gúr	4 containers
ì-bi 4 sila$_3$ 6 gín	its oil 4 sila and 6 gin
⅔ ì-giš	⅔ oil
kaš$_4$ didli-me	for the messengers
0;1.0 kaš 0; 1.2.5 sila$_3$ zì	60 sila beer 85 sila of flour
1 sila$_3$ ì-giš	1 sila oil
NE Ḫu-rìm^{ki}-me	for the Ḫurim-people
1 sila$_3$ zì	1 sila flour
[it]-gúr ì-bi 1 sila$_3$	[ ] containers its oil 1 sila
sukkal	vizier
[ ]	

Col. ii

šu-nigín 2; 1.3.1 sila$_3$ kaš gin gur	total 691 sila of average-quality beer
šu-nigín 6 gur dida gin	total 6 gur of second-class beer
še-bi 2; 4.3.1 sila$_3$ gur	its barley 871 sila
šu-nigín 4 sila$_3$ nì-àr-ra zíz-an	total 4 sila of fine emmer-flour
šu-nigín 2; 0.1. 6 sila$_3$ zì gur	total 616 sila of flour
še-bi 2; 0.2.4 sila$_3$ gur	its barley 624 sila
šu-nigín 9⅓ sila$_3$ 6 gín ì-giš	total 9⅓ sila and 6 gin of oil
iti ezem-^{d}Ba-ba$_6$	month 8
1; 2.4.1 sila$_3$ kaš gin gur	461 sila of average-quality beer
13 gur dida gin	13 gin of beer of second category
1; 4.3.8 sila$_3$ gur	578 sila

Col. iii

Uš-lu^{ki}-šè gin-né	going to Ušlu
0; 2.0. kaš 0; 2.0. zì	120 sila of beer 120 sila of flour
0; 0.0.1½ sila$_3$ ì-giš	1½ sila of oil
NIM Ši-ma-aš-ki-me	for the Elamites of Šimaški
gìr Ur-^{d}Da-mu sukkal	responsible: Ur-Damu the vizier
Ši-ma-aš-ki-šè gin-né	going to Šimaski

0; 2.0. kaš 0; 2.0. zì 2 sila$_3$ ì-giš	120 sila of beer 120 sila of flour 2 sila of oil
Še-li-bu-um ensi$_2$ Sa-bu-um	for Šelibum the governor of Sabum
gìr Za-na-ti sukkal	responsible: Zanati the vizier
Sa-bu-um[^{ki}]	Sabum
[ ]	[ ]
Col. iv	
šu-nigín 4; 1.0.6 sila$_3$	total 1266 sila of regular beer
šu-nigín 13 gur dida gin	total 13 gur of regular beer of second category
še-bi 5; 1.2.6 sila$_3$ gur	its barley 1586 gur
šu-nigín 4 sila$_3$ nì-àr-ra zíz-an	total 4 sila of fine emmer-flour
šu-nigín 6; 2.2.6 sila$_3$ zì gur	total 1946 sila of flour
šu-nigín 2; 2.0. še gur	total 720 sila
še-bi 8; 4.3.3 sila$_3$ gur	its barley 2673 sila
šu-nigín 17 sila$_3$ 16 gín	total 17 sila and 16 gin (oil)
[ ]	[ ]
[ ]	[ ]
Reverse	
Col. i	
[ ]	[ ]
1 gur kaš	1 gur of beer
6 sila$_3$ zì	6 sila of flour
4 sila$_3$ nì-àr-ra zíz-an	4 sila of fine emmer-flour
^{d}Šul-pa-è-[é-gal]	for Šulpae-egal
0; 2.0. kaš 0;1.0 zì 1 sila$_3$ ì	120 sila of beer 60 sila of flour 1 sila of oil
Ilum-á-lí-ik mar-tu	Ilum-malik the Amorite
0; 0.4. kaš sig$_5$ 0; 1.5 kaš	40 sila of top-quality beer 110 sila of regular beer
0; 1.0.4 sila$_3$ zì 10 sila$_3$ nì-àr-ra	64 sila of flour 10 sila of groats
⅓ sila$_3$ ì	⅓ sila of oil
Lú-^{d}En-ki-šè gin-né	going to Lu-Enki
0; 3.0. še anše	180 sila for donkeys
šà Ḫu-rím^{ki}	in Ḫurim
0; 3.0. še šà íd	180 sila barley in the river
Col. ii	
gìr šu-[ ]	responsible: Šu[ ]
Ši-ma-aš-ki-šè gin-né	going to Šimaški
40 sila$_3$ kaš 40 sila$_3$ zì ½ sila$_3$ ì	40 sila of beer 40 sila of flour ½ sila of oil
NIM Ḫu-ur$_5$-ti^{ki}-me	for the Elamites of Ḫurti
gìr Ú-ka-a nu-banda$_3$	responsible: Ukaa the lieutenant

Ḫu-ur$_5$-ti^{ki}-ta gin-né	coming from Ḫurti
0; 2.0. kaš 0; 1.0. zì 1 sila$_3$ ì	120 sila of beer 60 sila of flour 1 sila of oil
Ilum-á-lí-ik mar-tu	for Ilum-malik the Amorite
0; 1.0. kaš 0; 1.0. zì ½ sila$_3$ ì	60 sila of beer 60 sila of flour ½ sila of oil
Pu-ga mušen-dù	for Puga the fowler
2 gur dida-gin 10 sila$_3$ zì	2 gur of regular beer of second category and 10 sila of flour
5 sila$_3$ nì-àr-ra zíz-an	5 sila fine emmer-flour
siskur$_2$ A-ab-ba-ka	the offering of Abbaka
gìr Pu-ga mušen-dù	responsible: Puga the fowler
0; 1.2.5 sila$_3$ kaš 0; 1.2.5 sila$_3$ zì 1½ sila$_3$ ì	85 sila of beer 85 sila of flour 1½ sila of oil
Col. iii	
gìr Inim-gi-na sukkal	responsible: Inimgina the vizier
Si-ù<ki>-ta gin-né	coming from Siu
1 še gur šà Ḫu-rìm^{ki}	1 gur of barley in Ḫurim
1 gur šà Á-gul	1 gur in Agul
1 gur šà Gú-ab-ba^{ki}	1 gur in Guabba
šà-gal anše zi-kum-ma-a	fodder for the dispatch service donkeys
1; 1.0. kaš sig$_5$ 10 gín ì	360 sila of top-quality beer 10 gin of oil
èš-èš lugal	for the royal *ešeš*-(festival)
15 sila$_3$ kaš sig$_5$ 10 sila$_3$ kaš gin	15 sila of top-quality beer 10 sila of average-quality beer
12 sila$_3$ zì 2 sila$_3$ nì-àr-ra zíz-an	12 sila of flour 2 sila of fine emmer flour
^{d}Gù-dé-a	for Gudea
1 gur dida sig$_5$	1 gur of top-quality beer
6 sila$_3$ zì-dub-dub	6 sila of ...-flour
4 sila$_3$ nì-àr-ra zíz-an	4 sila of fine emmer-flour
^{d}Šul-pa-è é-gal	for Šulpae of the palace
Col. iv	
[ ]-ḫé GAR GAR a-sum-ni?	...
zi-ga gìr kaš$_4$-ke$_4$-ne	disbursement, responsible: the messengers
šà Gú-ab-ba^{ki}-ka	in Guabba
kišib Ur-^{d}Lama dumu Lú-^{d}Ba-ba$_6$	seal of Ur-Lama son of Lu-Baba
iti ezem-^{d}Ba-ba$_6$-ta	from month 8
iti še-íl-la-šè	to month 12
iti 5-kam	span of 5 months
mu ^{d}[	year [ ]

no. 459 (viii)

Obverse

kaš sig$_5$ sila$_3$	kaš sila$_3$	ninda sila$_3$	sum gín	ì gín	tè gín	
5	5	5	3	2		Šu-Ìr-ra
5	5	5	3	2		[ ]
5	5	5	3	2		Šar-ru-um-ì-lí
5	5	5	3	2		^{d}Šul-gi-ba-ni
5	5	5	3	2		Ì-lí-dan
5	5	5	3	2		Lugal-á-zi-da
5	5	5	3	2		[ ]-ar-tum
5	5	5	3	2		Ḫa-ra-na-i-ša$_6$
Reverse						
5	5	5	3	2		Ur-^{d}Nin-sún
5	5	5	3	2		Ir$_{11}$-dam
5	5	5	3	2		Ma-at-ì-lí
3	2	5	3	2		Ùr-re-ba-ab-du$_7$
3	2	5	3	2		La-al-la-a
3	2	5	3	2		[ ]-dan

15 49 61 1 sila$_3$ + 10 gín
⅔ sila$_3$ + 2 gín
⅓ sila$_3$ 8 gín

u$_4$ [ ] + 2-kam
iti é-iti-6

no. 460 (ŠS 4 ii)

Obverse

1 dug dida 5 sila$_3$ kaš sig$_5$	1 jug of beer 5 sila of top-quality beer
10 sila$_3$ ninda 2 gín ì 2 gín tè	10 sila of bread 2 gin of oil 2 gin of alkali
3 sa sum	3 bundles of onion
^{d}Nanna-ì-ša$_6$-e gaba-aš	for Nanna-iša going to the seashore
5 sila$_3$ kaš 2 sila$_3$ ninda	5 sila of beer 2 sila of bread
2 gín ì 2 gín tè	2 gin of oil 2 gin of alkali
1 sa sum	1 bundle of onion
Nì-^{d}Ba-ba$_6$ gaba-ta	for Ni-Baba coming from the seashore
3 sila$_3$ kaš 2 sila$_3$ ninda	3 sila of beer 2 sila of bread
Reverse	
2 gín ì 2 gín tè	2 gin of oil 2 gin of alkali
1 sa sum	1 bundle of onion

Ba-a-a ka-ús-sá	for Baaa …
šu-nigín 1 dug dida gin 10 sila$_3$	total: 1 jug of beer of ordinary quality 10 sila
šu-nigín 5 sila$_3$ kaš sig$_5$ šu-nigín 6 sila$_3$ kaš	total 5 sila of top-quality beer, total 6 sila of beer
šu-nigín 14 sila$_3$ ninda šu-nigín 6 gín ì	total 14 sila of bread total 6 gin of oil
šu-nigín 6 sila$_3$ tè	total: 6 gin of alkali
šu-nigín 5 sa sum	total: 5 bundles of onion
u$_4$-13-kam iti sig$_4$ giš-ì-šub-ba-gar	on the 13th day on month 2
mu-ús-sa Si-ma-núm^{ki} ba-ḫul	ŠS 4

no. 461 (A S8 iii)

Obverse

5 sila$_3$ kaš	3 sila$_3$ ninda	2 gín ì	Ur-^{d}Nin-ereš
3	2	2	Lugal-dingir

Reverse

5	3	2	Ḫu-ba-a sukkal

iti ezem-^{d}Li$_9$-si$_4$

mu en Eridu^{ki} ba-a-ḫun

Obverse

5 sila$_3$ beer	3 sila$_3$ bread	2 gín oil	Ur-^{d}Nin-ereš
3	2	2	Lugal-dingir

Reverse

5	3	2	Ḫu-ba-a sukkal

month 9

AS8

no. 462 (vii)

Obverse

2 sila$_3$ kaš 2 sila$_3$ ninda	Šu-^{d}Adad	2 sila beer 2 sila bread	Šu-Adad
1	Nì-ú-rum	1	Niurum
3	Li-iš-^{d}Šul-gi dub-sar	3	Liš-Šulgi the scribe
3	Ur-gi$_7$	3	Urgi
1	Puzur$_4$-Eš$_4$-tár	1	Puzur-Eštar

Reverse

1 àd udu ur-re íb-dab$_5$	1 sheep carcass taken by the dogs
½ udu é-kaš$_4$	½ sheep for the house of the messengers
1 udu NIM ù Aš-gi$_4$^{ki}-šè	1 sheep for the people going to Elam and Ašgi
2 sila$_3$ Lú-^{d}Utu maškim	2 sila Lu-Utu is the conveyer;
zi-ga u$_4$-29-kam	disbursement on the 29th day

šukur ensi$_2$	rations of the governor
iti ezem-^{d}Šu-li?	month 8(?)

no. 463 (ŠS 2 i 11)

Obverse

kaš	ninda	sum	ì	tè	
sila$_3$	sila$_3$	gín	gín	gín	
5	3	5	3	3	Ur-^{d}Šul-pa-è
5	3	5	3	3	Ma-áš
5	3	5	3	3	Šu-^{d}Nin-šubur
5	3	5	3	3	Lú-kiri$_3$-zal
5	3	5	3	3	Šu-Ma-ma
5	3	5	3	3	Kal-la-mu
5	3	5	3	3	Ar-ši-aḫ

Reverse

5	3	5	3	2	A-ḫu-ni
3	2	5	3	2	Ur-^{d}Ba-ba$_6$
3	2	5	3	2	Bù-ka
3	2	5	3	2	Ur-é-babbár
3	2	5	3	2	Im-ti-dam

20

1 dug dida 30 sila$_3$

10 sila$_3$ ninda 50 sila$_3$ dabin

½ sila$_3$ ì ½ sila$_3$ tè Ip-qú-ša

šu-nigín 72 sila$_3$ kaš

1 dug dida 30 sila$_3$

42 sila$_3$ ninda zì

50 sila$_3$ dabin

1 sila$_3$ sum

1 sila$_3$ 6 gín ì

1 sila$_4$ 4 gín tè

u$_4$-11-kam iti še-kin-ku$_5$

mu má ^{d}En-ki ba-ab-du$_8$

no. 464 (ŠS 4 xi)

Obverse

kaš	ninda	sum	ì	tè	
sila$_3$	sila$_3$	gín	gín	gín	
5	3	3	3	2	Nu-úr-Eš$_4$-tár

5 3 3 3 2 Puzur$_4$-Ma-ma

5 3 3 3 2 Ìl-šu-ba-ni

5 3 3 3 2 Šu-ga-tum

5 3 3 3 2 Lú-kiri$_3$-zal

5 3 3 3 2 Ar-ši-aḫ

Reverse

5 3 3 3 2 <A>-ḫu-zu

5 3 3 3 2 Ur-^{d}[Ba-ba$_6$]

3 2 3 3 2 A-kal-la

3 2 3 3 2 Ip-qú-ša

3 2 3 3 2 Nu-úr-^{d}EN.ZU

10 1 dug dida 20 sila$_3$ 30 sila$_3$ dabin

½ sila$_3$ ì Nu-úr-zu NIM

šu-nigín

59 sila$_3$ kaš

1 dug dida 20 sila$_3$

30 sila$_3$ ninda 30 sila$_3$ dabin

½ sila$_3$ sum

1 sila$_3$ 3 gín ì

⅓ sila$_3$ 3 gín tè

u$_4$-2-kam

iti pa$_5$-kùš-e

mu bàd mar-tu ba-dù

no. 465

This messenger tablet lists quantities of beer, bread, onions, and oil.

Obverse

kaš sig$_5$ sila$_3$	kaš sila$_3$	ninda sila$_3$	sum gín	ì gín	tè gín	
5	5	5	3	2		^{d}Šul-gi-dan
5	5	5	3	2		Lugal-maš-zu
5	5	5	3	2		Gu-da-núm
5	5	5	3	2		Dan-ì-lí
5	5	5	3	2		La-la-a
5	5	5	3	2		A-gu-za-núm
5	3	3	3	2		Šu-ì-lí

Reverse

3	2	5	3	2		Ur-^{d}[Ba-ba$_6$]

3	2	5	3	2	Bù-ú-a
3	2	5	3	2	Šu-na-a
3	2	5	3	2	Kal-zì-DAB
3	2	5	3	2	Ù-ma-ni

10 sila$_3$ kaš sig$_5$

40 sila$_3$ kaš gin

45 sila$_3$ ninda

1 sila$_3$ sum

½ + 7 gín ì

⅓ sila$_3$ 4 gín tè

u$_4$ 3-kam

iti ^{d}Dumu-zi

mu Si-ma-núm^{ki} ba-ḫul

no. 466 (xii 22)

Obverse

sila$_3$ kaš	sila$_3$ ninda	gín ì	
2	2	2	Šar-ru-um-ì-lí
2	2	2	En-um-ì-lí
2	2	4	A-da-làl lú ^{giš}tukul gu-la
1	1		lú zi-kum
2	2	2	Šà-ku-núm rá-gaba
2	2	2	lú nin-gá mar-tu
2	2	2	[ ]-da-da

Reverse

2	2	2	[ ]-núm-ma-nu-zi
5	5	10	^{d}Nanna-ma-an-sì
5	5	10	^{d}Amar-^{d}EN.ZU-ba-ni
2	2	2	I-ti-zu lú kaš$_4$
2	2	2	é-uš-bi ninda-šè gin-na
4	4	2	Lugal-nám-maḫ kú-šè gin
5	5	2	bar-du$_8$-ša-um nì-nesag-šè gin
10			I-ti-AN

u$_4$-22-kam

iti še-íl-la

no. 467

Obverse

1 giš-kešda$_2$-a šu-[ ]	1 tied wood
10 sila$_3$ té	10 sila alkali
40 [ ]	40 [ ]
3 sag [ ] ḫa-a	3 [ ]
Ur-ki sukkal	Urki vizier
1 [ ] ḫi-a	1 [ ]
4 sila$_3$ kaš sig$_5$	4 sila of top-quality beer
1 duk dabin gin	1 vessel of average-quality barley flour
Ur-gi$_6$-par$_4$	Urgipar
1 giš-kešda$_2$ du$_7$-a	1 perfect tied wood
5 sila$_3$ kaš sig$_5$	5 sila of top-quality beer
1 duk kaš gin	1 vessel of average-quality beer
Ur-^{d}[ ]	Ur-[ ]

Reverse

[ ] ^{giš}šakir zú-lum	[ ] container for dates
[dub]-sar Lú-^{d}Nin-šubur	[scribe?] Lu-Ninšubur
2 ^{giš}šakir Lugal-ti-da	2 containers for Lugaltida
2 Inim-^{d}Šara$_2$-ì-zu	2 for Inim-Šara-izu
2 Ì-zu-zu	2 Izuzu
2 Ad-da-mu	2 Addamu
2 Ki-tuš-lú	2 Kitušlu
2 A-ḫa-ma-ti	2 Aḫamati
1 ^{giš}šakir 5 sa Sila$_4$-ki-ág-mu	1 container 5 strings for Silakiagmu
1 Ur-^{d}Utu	1 Ur-Utu
1 Lugal-ezem	1 Lugalezem
2 [ ]	2 [ ]
1 gi-gan [ ]	1 basket
1 gi-gan zú-lum [ ]	1 basket for dates
Ur-lugal	Urlugal
1 ^{giš}dusu dug sal$_4$	1 basket for small containers
2 Lú-sukkal	2 Lusukkal
2 Ur-^{d}Nanše	2 Ur-Nanše

FOOD PREPARATION (nos. 468–477)

no. 468 (x) [copy]

Obverse

3; 2.2 ninda gur	3 ⅔ gur of bread
má u_4-zal-la	for the boat of the shining day
kišib Lugal-ki-gal-la	seal Lugalkigal
4.29; 3.3 gur	269 gur 210 sila
a-ka-a gar-ra šabra sanga-me	on the accounts of the steward (and) the chief temple official
2.20 gur	140 gur
kišib Šu-na ù Ur-gú-eden-na	seal of Šuna and Urguedenna
2.0 gur Ur-^{d}Nanše dumu Ur-é-an-na	120 gur Ur-Nanše son of Ur-Eanna
43; 2.0. gur šà še udu Lú-^{d}Kal-kal	43⅖ gur from the barley for the sheep of Lu-Kalkal
Lú-igi-$ša_6$-$ša_6$	(and) Luigišaša
7.20; 1.0.5 $sila_3$ gur	440 gur 65 sila
á ḫun-gá-a ^{íd}Idiglat	for work of hired men on the Tigris river

Reverse

1.0 gur nì šám esír-é-a	60 gur to buy bitumen
3-àm lú-mar-sa	3 times for the men at the navigation office
30 gur Lugal-gú-gal	30 gur Lugalgugal
kišib ka_9 gar-ra zi-ga	account tablet of the disbursements
nu gíd-da	was not …
Ma-ni	Mani
iti amar-a-a-si	month 10

no. 469 (ŠS 7 xi 4) [copy]

1 $sila_4$ é-uzug-ga	1 lamb for the sanctuary
šà Uri_5^{ki}-ki-du_{10} muḫaldim	(from the deliveries of) Urikidu the cook
Ri-ba-ga-da maškim	Ribagada is the conveyer;
šà-mu-er10-ra-ta	from the deliveries
u_4-4-kam	on the 4th day
ki In-ta-è-a-ta	disbursed
ba-zi	by Intaea

Reverse

gìr Nu-úr-^{d}EN.ZU dub-sar	responsible: Nur-Sîn the scribe
iti ezem-an-na	month 11
mu ^{d}Šu-^{d}EN.ZU lugal Uri_5^{ki}-ma-ke_4	ŠS 7
ma-da Za-ab-ša-li^{ki} mu-ḫul	

Edge

1 udu	1 sheep

no. 470 (Š 46 ii)

In this tablet dealing with fattening, oxen receive 10 sila barley per day while the cows only half.

Obverse

21 gu$_4$ niga 10 sila$_3$-ta	21 barley-fed oxen, each receiving 10 sila
15 áb mu-2 niga 5 sila$_3$	15 two-year-old barley-fed cows, each receiving 5 sila
še-bi 0; 4.4.5 sila$_3$ lugal	its barley (needed) 285 sila according to the royal measurement
sá-du$_{11}$ u$_4$-1-kam	the (amount of the) regular delivery per day

Reverse

iti sig$_4$-giš-ì-šub-ba-gá-ra	month 2
mu-ús-sa Ur-bí-lum^{ki} ba-ḫul	Š 46

no. 471 (AS 7 ix) [copy]

Obverse

1.0 udu niga 1⅓ sila$_3$ še-ta	60 barley-fed sheep 1⅓ sila of barley for each
45 udu niga 1 sila$_3$-ta	45 barley-fed sheep 1 sila of barley for each
10 u$_8$ ½ sila$_3$ še-ta	10 ewes ½ sila of barley for each
44 sila$_3$ duḫ sig$_5$ 6 sila$_3$ duḫ gin-ta	44 sila of top-quality bran 6 sila of average-quality bran
u$_4$-15-šè	for 15 days
1.0 udu niga 1⅓ sila$_3$-ta	60 barley-fed sheep 1⅓ sila of barley for each
38 udu niga 1 sila$_3$ še-ta	38 barley-fed sheep 1 sila of barley for each
10 u$_8$ ½ sila$_3$ še-ta	10 ewes ½ sila of barley for each

Reverse

44 sila$_3$ duḫ sig$_5$ 6 sila$_3$ duḫ gin-ta	44 sila of top-quality bran 6 sila of average-quality bran
u$_4$ 14-šè	for 14 days
šu-nigin3 12; 1.1.2 sila$_3$ še gur	total: 12 gur 72 sila of barley
šu-nigin3 4; 1.1.6 sila$_3$ duḫ sig$_5$ gur	total: 4 gur 76 sila of top-quality bran
šu-nigin3 0; 2.5.4 sila$_3$ duḫ gin	total: 174 sila of average-quality bran
An-na-ḫi-li-bi ì-dab$_5$	Annaḫilibi has taken into possession
iti ^{d}Li$_9$-si$_4$	month 9
mu Ḫu-ḫu-nu-ri^{ki} ba-ḫul	AS 7

no. 472 (1 i) [copy]

Obverse	
1; 4.0. še gur-lugal	$1\frac{4}{5}$ gur of barley according to the royal measurement
2; 2.0. zíz gur	$2\frac{2}{5}$ gur of emmer
iti še-kin-ku$_5$	month 1
Reverse	
0; 2.2.4 sila$_3$ še	144 sila of barley
0; 1.1.2 sila$_3$ zíz	72 sila of emmer
nì-dab$_5$ še-kin-ku$_5$	stuff for the harvest
Da-da-a šu-ba-ti	Dadaa received
iti še-kin-ku$_5$	month 1

no. 473 (Š 40) [copy]

Obverse	
4 še gur-lugal	4 gur of barley according to the royal measurement
nì-ezem Ur-^{d}Dumu-zi	item for the festival of Ur-Dumuzi
a-šà lá-maḫ-ta	from the field Lamaḫ
ki Ir$_{11}$-ta	from Ir
Reverse	
[Ḫa]-ma-ti	Ḫamati
[šu]-ba-ti	received
mu-ús-sa é Puzur$_4$-Da-gan ba-dù	Š 40
Seal	
Ḫé-na-ša$_6$	Ḫenaša
dub-sar	scribe
dumu Ur-^{d}Dumu-zi	son of Ur-Dumuzi

no. 474 (ŠS 4 xii)

Obverse	
1 máš	1 goat
ka-^{d}[ ]-šè	for the gate of [ ]
1 máš Ki-an^{ki}-šè	1 goat for Kian
1 máš ki ^{d}Utu	1 goat for cultic place of the sun-god
é ^{d}Dumu-zi-da-ka	in the temple of Dumuzi
Reverse	
gìr [ ]	responsible: [ ]
Uš-mu šu-ba-ti	Ušmu received
iti ^{d}Dumu-zi	month 12
mu bàd ba-dù	ŠS 4

This tablet concerning cattle for cultic purposes presents a number of difficulties. Line 2 could be ka for ká, gate of the temple of a god. Line 5 seems to be gur, but this reading is meaningless. Furthermore it is difficult to explain the use of šu-ba-ti for living animals when the verbal form ì-dab$_5$ is expected.

no. 475 (AS 8–9) [copy]

Obverse

0; 2.2. kaš 30 sila$_3$ lugal	140 sila of beer produced with 30 sila of barley according to the royal measurement
0; 2.4. kaš gin	160 sila of average-quality beer
0; 1.1.5 sila$_3$ zì-gu	75 sila of pea-flour
0; 1.3.6 sila$_3$ dabin	96 sila of barley flour
0; 0.1.7.sila$_3$ eša	17 sila of flour
0; 0.1. sila$_3$ gig sa-a	10 sila of roasted wheat
5 sila$_3$ še sa-a	5 sila of roasted barley
15 sila$_3$ zì-sig$_{15}$	15 sila of coarse flour
1⅓ sila$_3$ ì-nun	1⅓ sila of ghee
2 sila$_3$ ga gazi	2 sila of spiced milk
3 sila$_3$ ga-àr-gal	3 sila of large cheese
⅔ sila$_3$ geštin ḫád	⅔ sila of dried grapes
10 sila$_3$ zú-lum	10 sila of dates
8 gìr-lam zú-lum ^{giš}pèš 2 sila$_3$-ta	3 baskets of dates (and) figs, capacity of 2 sila
[ ] ^{giš}pèš še-ir-gu	[ ] strings of figs
[ ] sila$_3$ ^{giš}pèš	[ ] figs
nì-dab$_5$ u$_4$-sakar nì diri ezem-ta	foodstuffs for the festival of the new moon, additional coming from the festival
<<ma>> iti ^{d}Li$_9$-si$_4$	month 9
ù ^{d}Dumu-zi	and month 12
mu en Eridu^{ki} ba-ḫun	AS 8

Reverse

0;4.0.5 sila$_3$ kaš 30 sila$_3$	245 sila of beer 30 sila of barley
0;3.2. sila$_3$ kaš gin	200 sila of average-quality beer
21 sila$_3$ zì-sig$_{15}$	21 sila of coarse flour
0;4.3.1 sila$_3$ zì-gu	271 sila of pea-flour
26 sila$_3$ eša	26 sila of flour
13 sila$_3$ gig sa-a	13 sila of roasted wheat
5 sila$_3$ še sa-a	5 sila of roasted barley
2 ⅔ sila$_3$ ì-nun	2 ⅔ sila of ghee
3 sila$_3$ ga-gazi	3 sila of spiced milk
5 sila$_3$ ga-àr-gal	5 sila of large cheese

1 sila$_3$ geštin-ḫád	⅔ sila of dried grapes
2 sila$_3$ ^{giš}ḫašḫur-ḫád	2 sila of dried apple
18 ^{giš}pèš še-ir-gu	18 sila of a string of figs
13 sila$_3$ zú-lum	13 sila of dates
27 gìr-lam zú-<lum> ^{giš}ḫašḫur 2 sila$_3$-ta	27 baskets of dates and apples, capacity of 2 sila
2 gìr-lam zú-lum 2 sila$_3$-ta	2 baskets of dates, capacity of 2 sila
nì-dab$_5$ iti-da ù nì-ezem-ma zag-mu-ka	foodstuffs for the month and the festival of the new year
mu-ús-sa en Eridu^{ki} ba-ḫun	AS 9
Edge	
nì-dab$_5$ ki-a-nag šabra-ke$_4$-ne	goods for the *kianag* of the steward

no. 476 (Š or AS)

Obverse	
0;1.0. zú-lum	60 sila of dates
10 sila$_3$ geštin-ḫád	10 sila of dried grapes
10 sila$_3$ ^{giš}gi$_6$-par$_4$	10 sila of *gipar*-fruit
5 sila$_3$ ^{giš}pèš še-ir-gu	5 sila of a string of figs
[ ]-ra-zu-ta	from! [ ]
ki ensi$_2$-ta	from the governor
Reverse	
unug^{ki}-šè siskur-šè	for the offering in Uruk
kišib Ur-^{d}Šul-pa-è	seal of Ur-Šulpae
Seal	
Ur-^{d}Šul-pa-è	Ur-Šulpae
dub-sar	scribe
dumu Lugal-kù-ga-ni	son of Lugalkugani

no 477

Obverse	
8.10 še gur-lugal	490 gur of barley according to the royal measurement
gìr Ur-ša$_6$-[ga]	responsible: Uršaga
kišib [ ]	seal of [ ]

WOOL AND CLOTHING (nos. 478–491)

no. 478

Obverse

3 ma-na síg	3 mana of wool
Ši-šar-ra-at	for Ši-šarrat
2 Ba-a-a	2 <mana of wool for> Baaa
2 A-a-ar	2 <mana of wool for> Aaar
2 Nin-gá-bí-du$_{11}$	2 <mana of wool for> Ningabidu
1 U4-ma-ni-gar	1 <mana of wool for> Umanigar
2 Ì-za-tum	2 <mana of wool for> Izatum
2 Zì-bí-ni-ib	2 <mana of wool for> Zibinib
2 Gal-la-a	2 <mana of wool for> Gallaa
2 Az-za-at	2 <mana of wool for> Azzat
2 Ša-at-ì-lí	2 <mana of wool for> Šat-ili
2 ^{d}Ba-ba$_{6}$-nin-àm	2 <mana of wool for> Baba-ninam

Reverse

2 Nin-^{d}Lama muḫaldim	2 <mana of wool for> Nin-Lama the cook
2 [	2 <mana of wool for> [ ]
3 [	3 <mana of wool for> [ ]
1 [	1 <mana of wool for> [ ]
šu-nigín 30 ma-na	total 30 mana
síg geme$_{2}$ é-duru$_{5}$	wool for workwomen in the encampment
mu [ba-]ḫul	year [ ]

no. 479 (AS 5 ii) [copy]

Obverse

4 ma-na síg nì-lám 3 kam uš	4 mana of third-grade *nilam*-wool
7 ma-na síg túg guz-za 3 kam uš	7 mana of wool for third-grade *guzza*-garments
3 gú 32 ma-na síg túg guz-za 4 kam uš	3 talents 32 mana of wool for fourth-grade *guzza*-garments
2 gú 14 ma-na síg túg guz-za gin	2 talents 14 mana of wool for average-quality *guzza*-garments
1 gú síg uš-bar	1 talent of wool for the weaver

Reverse

síg sumun síg kur-ra	old wool and wool from mountain sheep
ki ensi$_{2}$-ta	from the governor
Ur-^{d}Nin-tu šu-ba-ti	Ur-Nintu received
iti sig$_{4}$-giš-ì-šub-ba-gar	month 2
mu en unu$_{6}$-gal ^{d}Inanna ba-ḫun	AS 5

no. 480 (Š 43 xii) [copy]

Obverse	
7½ ma-na	7½ mana
nì-u-nu-a síg-ùz	to make goat-hair strings
á-bi u_4 13-kam-	the work is 13 days
ma gi-kid má $ensi_2$-ka-šè	for reed mats for the governor's boat
ki Lú-^{d}Nagar-pa-è-ta	from Lu-Nagarpae
Reverse	
kišib Lú-igi-$ša_6$-$ša_6$	seal of Luigišaša
iti ^{d}Dumu-zi	month 12
mu en-^{d}Nanna maš-e ì-pàd	Š 43
Seal	
Ur-$^{d}Li_9$-si_4	Ur-Lisi
$ensi_2$ $Umma^{ki}$	governor of Umma
Lú-igi-$ša_6$-$ša_6$	Luigišaša
dub-sar	scribe
ir_{11}-zu	(is) your servant

This nì-u-nu preparation of the wool is a very long procedure, taking 13 days to prepare a reed mat for the governor's boat.

no. 481 (AS 9) [copy]

Wool, silver and three kinds of fat partially used in the weaving of the weaver women.

Obverse	
1 gú lá 5 ma-na síg gír-gul	1 talent minus 5 mana of *girgul*-wool
11 gín igi-3-gál kù-babbar	11 gin ⅓ of silver
1 $sila_3$ ì-nun ku_6	1 sila of fish oil
8⅓ $sila_3$ ì-giš	8⅓ sila of oil
35 $sila_3$ ì-šáḫ	35 sila of lard
Reverse	
ki Ki-dúr-re-ta	from Kidurre
^{giš}Dúr-gar-ni	Durgarni
šu-ba-ti	received
mu-ús-sa en $Eridu^{ki}$ ba-ḫun-gá	AS 9

no. 482

Obverse

[ ]-gi ù-um-gi-[in]	[ ] has certified
nì-ka$_9$ na-ki-a-ga? la-ta tùm-[dam]	… he will bring
nì-ka$_9$-ak sipa Umma^{ki}	account of the shepherd of Umma
A-tu ru-na-ne	Atu …
ki Da-da-ga-ta tùm-dam	from Dadaga he will bring
ù-um-túm nì-ka$_9$-šè zi-ga tùm-dam	if he brings for the account disbursement he will bring
sipa ki [Da]-da-ta tùm-dam	the shepherd from Dada he will bring

Reverse

lá-ni sipad-de-ne	deficit of the shepherds
Ì-lí-mu in-[ ]-sar	Ilimu inscribed
kišib-ta sar du$_8$ [ ]	from the tablet …
Da-da-ga ù Na-du	Dadaga and Nadu
di-di-dam	…
èn-bi tar-re-dam	the matter shall be investigated

no. 483 [copy]

Obverse

8 túg 5⅓ sila$_3$ ì	8 garments ⅓ sila of oil for
^{d}Šara$_2$-a-mu	Šara-amu
7 túg 4 ⅔ sila$_3$ ì	7 garment ⅔ sila of oil
Ur-si-gar	for Ursigar
1 túg 1 sila$_3$ ì Ì-kal-la	1 garment 1 sila of oil for Ikalla
1 túg ⅔ sila$_3$ ì In-ša$_6$-ša$_6$	1 garment ⅔ sila of oil for Inšaša
1 túg 1 sila$_3$ ì ^{d}Šara$_2$-ì-zu	1 garment 1 sila of oil for Šara-izu
1 túg 1 sila$_3$ ì É-úr-bi	1 garment 1 sila of oil for Eurbi
1 túg ⅔ sila$_3$ ì Ur-^{d}En-[ ]	1 garment ⅔ sila of oil for Ur-En[ ]
1 túg 1 sila$_3$ ì Uš-mu	1 garment 1 sila of oil for Ušmu
1 túg ⅔ sila$_3$ ì Ur-^{d}A-šár dam-gàr	1 garment ⅔ sila of oil for Ur-Ašar the merchant
1 túg ⅔ sila$_3$ ì Im-a-ni	1 garment ⅔ sila of oil for Imani
1 túg ⅔ sila$_3$ ì Lugal-nì-lagar-e	1 garment ⅔ sila of oil for Lugalnilagare
1 túg 1 sila$_3$ ì Kaš$_4$	1 garment 1 sila of oil for Kaš
1 túg 1 sila$_3$ ì Inim-^{d}Šara$_2$	1 garment 1 sila of oil for Inim-Šara
1 túg [ ] sila$_3$ ì Kù-dingir-ra	1 garment [ ] sila of oil for Kudingirra
1 túg ⅔ sila$_3$ ì Ur-^{d}[ ]	1 garment ⅔ sila of oil for Ur-[ ]
1 túg ⅔ sila$_3$ ì Lú-[ ]	1 garment ⅔ sila of oil for Lu-[ ]

no. 484 (AS 9) [copy]

Obverse

1 túg gú-na	1 garment from the tax
Lugal-úr-ra-ni lú-azlág	for Lugalurrani the fuller
1 túg A-tu	1 garment for Atu
1 túg Ur-e_{11}-e	1 garment for Uree
1 túg Nì-bi	1 garment for Nibi
1 túg Šeš-kal-la dumu Uš-mu	1 garment for Šeškalla son of Ušmu
1 túg Na-mu	1 garment for Namu
1 túg Ba-ta-ab-è	1 garment for Batabe
lú azlág-me	fullers
ugula Ì-kal-la	overseer Ikalla

Reverse

1 túg nar-munus	1 garment for a female singer
ugula A-da-làl	overseer Adalal
1 túg Lú-dingir-ra muḫaldim	1 garment for Ludingirra the cook
1 túg Ad-da ašgab	1 garment for Adda the leatherworker
1 túg Lugal-uru-ni-šè	1 garment for Lugaluruniše
ugula Ba-sig_5	overseer Basig
túg mu-túm mu en Ga-$eš^{ki}$ ba-ḫun	delivery of garments; AS 9

no. 485 (AS 8 iii) [copy]

Obverse

5 túg ú gi_6 KAL	5 black ...-garments
8 túg ú gi_6 $muru_{13}$-a	8 black ...-garments
ki-lá-bi 40 ma-na	weighing 40 mana
13 túg ú $muru_{13}$	13 ...-garments
ki-lá-bi 43 ⅔ ma-na	weighing 43 ⅔ mana

Reverse

túg ki-lá-tag-ga	garments according to their weight
ki Lú-bala-sig_5-ta	from Lubalasig
Ì-kal-la šu-ba-ti	Ikalla received
$ensi_2$-ke_4 in-lá	the governor weighted
iti še-kar-ra-gál-la	month 3
mu en $Eridu^{ki}$ ba-ḫun	AS 8

no. 486 (ŠS 8 xii) [copy]

Obverse

3 túg nì-lám 3 kam uš	3 third-grade *nilam*-garments
5 túg nì-lám 4 kam uš	5 fourth-grade *nilam*-garments

4 túg nì-lám gin	4 average-quality *nilam*-garments
33 túg guz-za gin	33 average-quality *guzza*-garments
40 túg sag uš-bar	40 first-grade garments for the weavers
1.30 lá 1 túg uš-bar	89 garments for the weavers
8 gada gin	8 of average-quality linen
ki Ur-àm-ma-ta	from Uramma
3 túg nì-lám 3 kam uš	3 third-grade *nilam*-garments
4 túg nì-lám 4 kam uš	4 fourth-grade *nilam*-garments
6 túg nì-lám gin	6 average-quality *nilam*-garments
20 túg guz-za gin	20 average-quality *guzza*-garments
40 túg sag uš-bar	40 first-grade garments for the weavers
1.48 túg uš-bar	108 garments for the weavers
8 gada gin	8 of average-quality linen
ki Lú-du$_{10}$-ga-ta	from Luduga
9 túg nì-lám 3 kam uš	9 third-grade *nilam*-garments
20 túg guz-za gin	20 average-quality *guzza*-garments
40 túg sag uš-bar	40 first-grade garments for the weavers
1.34 túg uš-bar	94 garments for the weavers
Reverse	
4 gada gin	4 of average-quality linen
ki Ur-^{d}A-šár-ta	from Ur-Ašar
2 túg nì-lám 4 kam us	2 fourth-grade *nilam*-garments
7 túg guz-za gin	7 average-quality *guzza*-garments
ki A-kal-la-ta	from Akalla
šu-nigín 15 túg nì-lám 3 kam uš	a total of 15 third-grade *nilam*-garments
šu-nigín 10 túg nì-lám 4 kam uš	a total of 10 fourth-grade *nilam*-garments
šu-nigín 10 túg nì-lám gin	a total of 10 average-quality *nilam*-garments
šu-nigín 1.20 túg guz-za gin	a total of 80 average-quality *guzza*-garments
šu-nigín 2.0 túg sag uš-bar	a total of 120 first-grade garments for the weavers
šu-nigín 4.51 túg uš-bar	a total of 291 garments for the weavers
šu-nigín 20 gada gin	a total of 20 of average-quality linen
9.6 túg-ḫi-a	546 garments
túg é-gal-la ku$_{4}$-ra šà Nibru^{ki}	garments brought into the palace in Nippur
^{d}Šul-gi-uru-mu šu-ba-ti	Šulgi-urumu received
iti ^{d}Dumu-zi	month 12
mu ^{d}Šu-^{d}EN.ZU lugal Uri$_{5}$^{ki}-ma-ke$_{4}$ má-gur$_{8}$-maḫ ^{d}En-líl ^{d}Nin-líl-ra mu-ne-dù	ŠS 8

no. 487 (ŠS 9 ix)

Obverse

40 túg ú-gi$_6$-kal	40 ...-garments
ki-lá-bi 2 gú 24 ma-na	weighing 2 talents and 24 mana
ki Ì-kal-la-ta	from Ikalla
túg-ba-a bala-a-šè	its garments amount for the *bala*

Reverse

Kù-^{d}Nin-ur$_4$-ra	Ku-Ninurra
in-lá	weighed
iti ^{d}Li$_9$-si$_4$	month 9
mu é-^{d}Šara$_2$ ba-dù	ŠS 9

no. 488 (IS 3) [copy]

Obverse

1 túg nì-lam gin ki-lá-bi 2 ma-na	1 average-quality *nilam*-garment weighing 2 mana
síg-mug-bi ⅔ ma-na 2 gín	...-wool needed weighs ⅔ mana and 2 gin
bí-kú-bi 17 gín	the loss is 17 gin
U-bar-tum	<brought> by Ubartum
1 Nin-é-gal-e-<si>	1 <brought> by Ninegale<si>
1 Nin-mu-ma-an-ne-šè	1 <brought> by Ninmumanše
1 Ama-nesag-<e>	1 <brought> by Amanesage
1 Gemé-^{d}Dumu-zi-da	1 <brought> by Geme-Dumuzida
1 Nin-ama-mu	1 <brought> by Ninamamu
1 Ba-a-sig$_5$	1 <brought> by Baasig
1 Sag-nin$_{10}$-zu-zu	1 <brought> by Sagninzuzu
1 Gemé-^{d}Šara$_2$-bi	1 <brought> by Geme-Šarabi
1 Ša-at-^{d}Ìr-ra	1 <brought> by Šat-Irra
1 Su-ḫi	1 <brought> by Suḫi
1 Nin-má-gur$_8$-re muš	1 <brought> by Nin-magurre ...
12	12
lú túg nì-lám gin-me-šè	for the fullers ...
túg guz-za gin ki-lá-bi 4 ma-[na]	*guzza*-garments weighing 4 mana
broken	

Reverse

1 túg ú-gi$_6$ kal ki-lá-bi 3 [ma-na] 9 gín	1 ...-garment weighing 3 mana and 9 gin
bí-kú-bi ⅓ ma-na 4 gín	the loss ⅓ mana 4 gin
A-ḫa-ti	1 <brought> by Aḫati
1 Nin-a-zu	1 <brought> by Ninazu

1 Šir-šir	1 <brought> by Širšir
túg mu-túm	delivery of garments
mu Si-mu-ru-um^{ki} ba-ḫul	IS 3

Two types of wool are employed. The loss of wool during the weaving is called bí-kú-bi "the part that is eaten."

no. 489 (Š 24, 31, 33 vi)

Obverse	
1 túg guz-za	1 *guzza*-garment
síg-bi 5½ ma-na	its wool 5½ mana
ki Lugal-nì-lagar-e	from Lugalnilagare
Kù-ga-ni	Kugani
šu-ba-ti	received
Reverse	
iti šu-numun	month 6
mu-ús-sa Kara$_2$-ḫar^{ki}	Š 24
a-rá [ ] ba-ḫul	

LETTERS (nos. 490–491)

no. 490

Obverse	
Ur-e$_{11}$-e-[ra]	to Uree
ù-na-a-du$_{11}$	say
3;3.0. še gur	$3^{3}/_{5}$ gur of barley
buru$_x$(GANA$_2$)-maḫ-ta	from (the field) Burumaḫ
lú Lú-^{d}[ ] šaggina-ra	to the man of Lu-[ ], for the military governor
Reverse	
ḫé-[ ]	may [ ]
ḫé-na-[ab-sum-mu]	give.
kišib-ba ba-[ ]	on the tablet [ ]
ki ensi$_2$	from the governor
še sag ba- [ ]	the barley [ ]
na-kab-[tum-ma]	into the storehouse
ba-an-ku$_4$	was brought

no. 491 (Š 48)

Obverse	
5 gú 0 ma-na síg gi	5 talents 0 mana of ...-wool
á uš-bar-šè	for the wages of the weavers
ki Ur-e_{11}-e-ta	from Uree
Šeš-sig_5 šu-ba-ti	Šešsig received
Reverse	
mu Ḫa-ar-$ši^{ki}$	Š 48
Ḫu-ur_5-ti^{ki}	
ù Ki-$maš^{ki}$ ba-ḫul	

Letter Orders (nos. 492–495)

no. 492 [copy]

Obverse	
^{d}Šara$_2$-in-[zu-ra]	to Šara-inzu
ù-na-a-du_{11}	say
0; 3.0. še šukur-ra	180 sila of barley as ration
Ur-^{d}Dumu-zi	to Ur-Dumuzi
Reverse	
ḫé-na-ab-sum-mu	give!

no. 493 [copy]

Obverse	
Ur-mes	to Urmes
ù-na-a-du_{11}	say
2 udu ú sig_5	2 top-quality grass-fed sheep
ki $ensi_2$ bala-a-ta	from the *bala*-delivery of the governor
Gír-la-bi	to Girlabi
Reverse	
lú Du_{11}-ga muḫaldim-ra	the assistant of Dugga, the cook
ḫé-na-ab-sum-mu	give
a-ma-ru-kam	it is urgent
na-mi-gur-re	do not delay!
Seal	
Du_{11}-ga dub-sar	Dugga the scribe
dumu Lú-^{d}Nin-gír-su	son of Lu-Ningirsu
sipa na-kab-tum	shepherd of the storehouse

no. 494 [copy]

Obverse

^{d}Šul-gi-na-da	to Šulgi-nada
ù-na-a-du$_{11}$	say
| Dan-ì-lí	Dan-ili
| Šu-Eš$_{4}$-tár lú kin-gi$_{4}$-a lugal	Šu-Eštar, messenger of the king
| A-la-bi	Alabi
| Šu-ku-pu-um	Šukupum
| I-pí-iq-Na-ni	Ipiq-Nani
| Šu-Iš-ḫa-ra	Šu-Išhara

Reverse

| Šu-ti-ru-um	Šu-Tirum
| I-la-ak-šu-qir	Ilak-šuqir
| Im-ti-dam	Imtidam
| Za-ri-qum	Zariqum
| A-ḫu-ṭab	Ahu-ṭab
| A-la-ḫu-um	Alaḫum
| Ip-qú-ša	Ipquša
| I-na-zu	Inazu
| Šu-^{d}Šamaš	Šu-Šamaš
| Pu-zu-núm	Puzunum

Edge

šu ḫé-bar-ri	set <them> free!

no. 495 (Š) [copy]

Obverse

4.0 sa gi šid	240 bundles of ...-reed
gi-kid DU/gin	for regular reed mats
Da-da-ga	Dadaga
ḫé-na-ab-sum-mu	shall give.

Seal

[^{d}Šul-gi	(o) ^{d}Šulgi
nita-kalag-ga	the strong man
lugal Urí^{ki}-ma	king of Ur
lugal an-ub-da limmu$_{2}$-ba	the king of the 4 corners of the universe
Ur-^{d}Li$_{9}$-si$_{4}$	Ur-Lisi
ensi$_{2}$	the governor
Umma^{ki}	of Umma
ir$_{11}$-zu	is your servant

School Exercise Tablets (nos. 496–506)

no. 496 [copy]

Obverse

nì áb-ba
nì DU è-a
nì šu-sikil

no. 497 [copy]

Obverse

Lú-me-lám
Lú-me-$ša_4$
Lú-šu-me-$ša_4$

no. 498 [copy]

Ur-si-gar-ra
Ur-^{d}Nin-sún-ka
Ur-^{d}Nin-pa

no. 499 [copy]

ki-lugal-gub	pedestal
ki-lugal-gub-en-na	pedestal of the *en*
ki-lugal-gub-[ ] lugal	pedestal of the king
lugal	king

no. 500 [copy]

^{d}Nanna-e-ba-an-[$ša_6$]
^{d}Nanna-e-dím
^{d}Nanna-dingir-mu

no. 501 [copy]

^{giš}tukul-wa-tar-?

no. 502 [copy]

gi gu-gu-
gi gu-gu-un-
gi gu-un

no. 503 [copy]

I-pí-iq-la-aš
I-pí-iq-^{d}Da-gan
I-pí-iq-^{d}Da-mu

no. 504 [copy]

dub-sar ugnim-ma	scribe of the army
dub-sar zag-ga	scribe of the tithe

no. 505 [copy]

gi-ba-an-du	drinking vessel
gi-ba-an-du$_8$	
gi-ba-an-du$_8$-du$_8$	

no. 506 [copy]

nì-šu-gál-la-ni
i-bí-gim
dingir nigin-ba-è-dè

Old Akkadian (nos. 507–510)

no. 507 (Old Akkadian) [copy]

no. 508 (Old Akkadian) [copy]

no. 509 (Old Akkadian) [copy]

no. 510 (Old Akkadian) [copy]

Personal Names

Divine Names

Toponyms

Glossary

Seals

^{d}Šul-gi nita kalag-ga lugal Uri$_5$^{ki}-ma Lú-d[ ] dub-sar ir$_{11}$-zu, seal 280
^{d}Šul-gi nita kalag-ga lugal Urí^{ki}-ma lugal an-ub-da limmu$_2$-ba Ur-^{d}Li$_9$-si$_4$ ensi$_2$ Umma^{ki} ir$_{11}$-zu, seal 495
[^{d}Šul-gi] nita kalag-ga lugal Uri$_5$^{ki}-ma lugal an-ub-da limmu$_2$-ba [ ] [ ] [ir$_{11}$-zu], seal 83
Da-da nu-banda$_3$ gu$_4$, seal 123
Da-da-ga dub-sar dumu Ur-ni$_9$-gar kuš$_7$, seal 140, seal 149, seal 362
Du$_{11}$-ga dub-sar dumu Lú-^{d}Nin-gír-su sipa na-kab-tum, seal 493

E-lu-lu dub-sar dumu Dingir-a-zu, seal 325
É-gal-e-si dub-sar dumu Lú-^{d}Šara$_2$ sa$_{12}$-du$_5$-ka, seal 145
É-gal-e-si dub-sar dumu Ur-[kù], seal 7
En-kaš$_4$ dub-sar dumu Ur-^{d}Ištaran, seal 185
En-mí-ús-sa dumu Lu$_5$-ú-lu$_5$ gudu$_4$ e$_{11}$-e-[ka?], seal 110
En-ú-šim-e dumu Ir$_{11}$-dam sanga ^{d}Nin-e$_{11}$-e, seal 11

Gìr-ni-ì-ša$_6$ dub-sar dumu Lugal-gù-dé-a, seal 390
^{giš}Dúr-gar-ni dub-sar dumu Lugal-gaba šabra, seal 301
Gu-ú-gu-a dub-sar dumu Ma-an-sum, seal 143, seal 151, seal 370
Gur$_8$-za-an dumu Al-la, seal 12
Gur$_4$-za-an dumu Al-la, seal 13
Gur$_4$-za-an dumu Du-la-a-bi muḫaldim ensi$_2$, seal 286

Ḫé-na-ša$_6$ dub-sar dumu Ur-^{d}Dumu-zi, seal 473
Ḫé-ša$_6$ dumu Ukken-né, seal 398

I-la-ak-šu-qir dumu Ur-^{giš}kiri$_6$ dub-sar, seal 141
I-šar-ru-um dub-sar dumu Ur-^{d}En-líl-lá, seal 193, seal 194, seal 379, seal 430
Ì-kal-la dub-sar dumu Lú-[ša$_6$-ga], seal 348
Ì-kal-la dub-sar dumu Lú-ša$_6$-ga, seal 179
Igi-^{d}Šara$_2$-šè ir$_{11}$ ^{d}Šara$_2$, seal 15, seal 16, seal 17
In-ša$_6$-ša$_6$ dumu Bí-du$_{11}$-mu, seal 387
Inim-^{d}Šara$_2$ dub-sar dumu Ur-ni$_9$-gar kuš$_7$, seal 171, seal 258
Inim-^{d}Šara$_2$ dumu Ur-dingir-ra kurušda ^{d}Šara$_2$, seal 18, 19
Inim-ma-ni-zi dumu Ba-a-mu lú bappir nì-lagar, seal 251
Ir$_{11}$-mu dub-sar dumu Ur-ni$_9$-gar kuš$_7$, seal 246, seal 338

kal-la-kal-la?, seal 416
Ku-li dub-sar dumu Ur-ki-ág-mu, seal 21
Kù-ga-ni dub-sar dumu Ur-ša$_6$-ga, seal 380

La-ni muḫaldim dub-sar dumu Ur-ni$_{9}$-gar, seal 239, seal 450
Lú-bàn-da mu$_{6}$-šùb-^{d}Šara$_{2}$ dumu ^{giš}gigir-re, seal 22, seal 23, 24-33
Lú-^{d}Ḫa-ià dub-sar dumu Ur-e$_{11}$-e kuš$_{7}$, seal 154
Lú-^{d}Nám-an-ka dub-sar dumu Lú-^{d}Šara$_{2}$ sa$_{12}$-du$_{5}$-ka, seal 304, seal 455
Lú-d Nin-šubur dub-sar dumu Du$_{10}$-ga šabra ^{d}Šara$_{2}$-ka, seal 399
Lú-^{d}Nin-šubur ir$_{11}$ ^{d}Šara$_{2}$, seal 35, seal 36, seal 40, seal 41, seal 42, seal 43, seal 44, seal 46
Lú-^{d}Nin-šubur kuš$_{7}$ ir$_{11}$ ^{d}Šara$_{2}$, seal 37, seal 38, seal 39, seal 45, seal 47, seal 48
Lú-^{d}Šara$_{2}$ agrig ^{d}Šara$_{2}$ dumu Ba-bí-za, seal 391
Lú-d Šara$_{2}$ dub-sar dumu [ ], seal 321
Lú-^{d}Šara$_{2}$ dub-sar dumu Lugal-inim-gi-na, seal 373
Lú-^{d}Šara$_{2}$ dub-sar dumu Ur-^{giš}gigir, seal 172
Lú-^{d}Šara$_{2}$ dumu Ur-^{giš}gigir išib ^{d}Šara$_{2}$, seal 104
Lú-d Šul-gi-ra dub-sar dumu Da-da-ga, seal 186
Lú-dingir-ra dub-sar dumu Á-an-du-ru, seal 281
Lú-dingir-ra dub-sar dumu Da-da-a, seal 34
Lú-dingir-ra dub-sar dumu Ḫa-ba-lug-gé, seal 169, seal 432
Lú-dingir-ra dub-sar dumu Ḫé-ma-túm, seal 176
Lú-dingir-ra dumu Ù-ma-ni, seal 114
Lú-^{d}Nám-an-ka dub-sar dumu Lú-^{d}Sara$_{2}$ sa$_{12}$-du$_{5}$-ka, seal 91
Lú-du$_{10}$-ga dub-sar dumu Du$_{11}$-ga, seal 425
Lú-du$_{10}$-ga dub-sar dumu Ḫé-ma-túm, seal 208
Lú-du$_{10}$-ga dub-sar dumu Lú-^{d}Šara$_{2}$ sa$_{12}$-du$_{5}$, seal 381, seal 386
Lú-du$_{10}$-ga dub-sar dumu Lugal-nì-lagar-e, seal 385
Lú-du$_{10}$-ga dub-sar dumu Ur-^{d}Nin-tu gudu$_{4}$-E$_{11}$-e-ka, seal 111
Lú-du$_{10}$-ga dub-sar dumu Ur-ni$_{9}$-gar, seal 207, seal 219
Lú-é-maḫ-e dub-sar dumu Ur-^{d}Li$_{9}$-si$_{4}$ ensi$_{2}$ Umma^{ki}-ka, seal 330
Lú-é-maḫ-e dub-sar dumu Ur-^{d}Li$_{9}$-si$_{4}$-na ensi$_{2}$ Umma^{ki}-ka, seal 297
Lú-eb-gal dub-sar dumu Ur-gi$_{6}$-par$_{4}$, seal 341
Lú-Eridu^{ki} dumu Lugal-ga, seal 104, seal 106
Lú-ezem dub-sar dumu al-ùr-dingir, seal 347
Lú-gi-na dub-sar dumu Da-da, seal 134, seal 224
Lú-gi-na dumu É-gal-e-si, seal 188
Lú-gišgal dumu Bí-du$_{11}$-mu, seal 365
Lú-ib-gal dub-sar dumu Ur-gi$_{6}$-par$_{4}$, seal 324
Lú-ib-gal dub-sar dumu Ur-gi$_{6}$-par$_{4}$ gudu$_{4}$ ^{d}Inanna, seal 355
Lú-ib-gal dub-sar dumu Ur-gi$_{6}$-par$_{4}$ gudu$_{4}$ ^{d}Inanna, seal 184
Lú-kal-la dub-sar dumu Lugal-[en-nun], seal 457
Lú-kal-la dub-sar dumu Ur-e$_{11}$-e kuš$_{7}$, seal 407, seal 453
Lú-ša$_{6}$-ša$_{6}$ dub-sar dumu Bí-du$_{11}$-ga, seal 295
Lugal-á-zi-da dub-sar dumu Ur-du$_{6}$-kù-ga?, seal 210
Lugal-á-zi-da dumu Lugal-kù-ga-ni, seal 49

Lugal-Anzu^{mušen} dub-sar dumu Ba-[ ], seal 197
Lugal-e-2-maḫ-e dub-sar dumu Lugal-kù-ga-ni, seal 139
Lugal-e-ba-an-ša$_6$ dub-sar dumu Ur-^{d}Ištaran, seal 394, seal 451
Lugal-é-gal-e-si dumu Inim-é-nun-na lú-lunga ^{d}Šara$_2$, s, seal 51, seal 150, seal 191, seal 420
Lugal-é-maḫ-e dumu Lú-^{d}Nin-šubur kuš$_7$, seal 52, seal 53, seal 54
Lugal-é-maḫ-e dumu Ur-^{d}Dumu-zi, seal 375
Lugal-ezem dub-sar dumu Lugal-é-maḫ-e šabra, seal 196
Lugal-ḫé-gál dub-sar dumu Ur-^{d}Utu, seal 276
Lugal-ḫé-gál dub-sar dumu Ur-ni$_9$-gar, seal 144
Lugal-ḫé-gál mu$_6$-šùb-^{d}Šara$_2$ dumu Ur-ni$_9$-gar, seal 55, seal 56
Lugal-kù-ga-ni dumu Lú-^{d}Nin-[ur$_4$-ra], seal 178
Lugal-kù-ga-ni dumu Ur-mes, seal 146, seal 164
Lugal-kù-zu dub-sar dumu Lugal-é-maḫ-e, seal 367
Lugal-kù-zu dub-sar dumu Ur-ni$_9$-gar kuš$_7$, seal 157, seal 303
Lugal-nì-lagar-e dub-sar dumu Da-da, seal 148
Lugal-nir dub-sar dumu Ur-^{d}Šara$_2$ ša$_{13}$-dub-ba-ka, seal 363
Lugal-si-dè-e dub-sar dumu Lugal-ša$_6$-ga Lugal-šaga lú ùr-ra-ka, seal 402
Lugal-ukken-né dumu Lugal-nì-lagar-e nu-banda$_3$ gu$_4$, seal 287
Lugal-zag-ge-[si] dumu Ur-^{d}Dumu-zi-da dub-sar, seal 331
Lugal-zag-ge-si lú-šim-^{d}Šara$_2$ dumu [Lugal]-lú-ni, seal 130

Mes-é dub-sar dumu Da-da, seal 173

Na-ba-sá dub-sar dumu A-ka-dul, seal 404
Nam-ḫa-ni dumu Ur-ni$_9$-gar, seal 126
Nam-lugal-ni-du$_{10}$ ir$_{11}$ ^{d}Šara$_2$, seal 136
nu-banda$_3$ Ur-[^{d}Nám-maḫ-ka] Ka$_5$-<a>-mu dumu-ni, seal 252

Sipa-ša$_6$-ga dumu Šu-[ ], seal 408

Šeš-a-ni dub-sar dumu Lugal-nì-lagar-e, seal 289, seal 439
Šeš-a-ni gudu$_4$-^{d}Šul-gi dumu Inim-kù, seal 105
Šeš-kal-la dub-sar dumu A-ka-DUL, seál69
Šeš-kal-la dub-sar dumu Na-di, seal 174
Šeš-kal-la dub-sar dumu Tir-gu, seal 430
Šeš-kal-la dub-sar dumu Ur-ni$_9$-gar kuš$_7$, seal 211
Šu-ú dumu Ga-ni, seal 58, seal 59

Ú-da-li dub-sar nu-banda$_3$-ne-ne ir$_{11}$ ^{d}Šu-^{d}EN.ZU, seal 233
Ú-li kir$_4$-díb ir$_{11}$ ^{d}Nin-líl-lá, seal 60
Ù-dag-ga dumu Ú-[da-li] ir$_{11}$ ^{d}Šara$_2$, seal 187

Ukken-né dub-sar dumu Ur-^{giš}gigir, seal 142, seal 152, seal 371, seal 452
Ur-àm-ma dub-sar dumu Na-di, seal 454
Ur-àm-ma dumu Lugal-ezem sukkal lugal, seal 175
Ur-àm-ma išib ^{d}Nin-da-lagaš^{ki} dumu [ ], seal 108
Ur-^{d}Ba-ba$_{6}$ dub-sar dumu Lugal-sig$_{5}$, seal 310
Ur-^{d}Ba-ba$_{6}$ dumu Ab-ba-dul, seal 319
Ur-^{d}EN.ZU dub-sar dumu Ur-^{giš}gigir, seal 163
Ur-^{d}EN.ZU dub-sar dumu Ur-^{giš}gigir šà-tam, seal 153, seal 155, seal 250
Ur-^{d}EN.ZU dumu ^{d}Šara$_{2}$-ka, seal 129
Ur-^{d}EN.ZU dumu Lú-^{d}Šara$_{2}$ nu-banda$_{3}$, seal 116, seal 117
Ur-^{d}En-líl-lá dumu Ḫa-la muḫaldim, seal 77
Ur-^{d}Lama dub-sar dumu [ ], seal 307
Ur-^{d}Li$_{9}$-si$_{4}$ ensi$_{2}$ Umma^{ki} Ba-ša$_{6}$ sagi ir$_{11}$-zu, seal 162
Ur-^{d}Li$_{9}$-si$_{4}$ ensi$_{2}$ Umma^{ki} ^{d}Šara$_{2}$-ba-zi-ge dub-sar ir$_{11}$-zu, seal 382, seal 179
Ur-^{d}Li$_{9}$-si$_{4}$ ensi$_{2}$ Umma^{ki} Lú-igi-ša$_{6}$-ša$_{6}$ dub-sar ir$_{11}$-zu, seal 480
Ur-^{d}Li$_{9}$-si$_{4}$ ensi$_{2}$ Umma^{ki} Puzur$_{4}$-ì-lí kir$_{4}$-díb ir$_{11}$-zu, seal 57
Ur-^{d}Li$_{9}$-si$_{4}$ ensi$_{2}$ Umma^{ki} Šeš-kal-la dub-sar dumu Na-di ir$_{11}$-zu, seal 372
Ur-^{d}Li$_{9}$-si$_{4}$ ensi$_{2}$ Umma^{ki} Lil-la ^{d}[ ] ir$_{11}$-zu, seal 287
Ur-^{d}Nanše dub-sar dumu A-[ ], seal 197
Ur-^{d}Nin-^{giš}zi-da gu-za-lá dumu Igi-[ ], seal 197
Ur-^{d}Nin-tu dub-sar dumu A-ab-ba-ni šabra ^{d}Nin-ur$_{4}$-ra, seal 377
Ur-^{d}Nu-muš-da dub-sar dumu Lugal-gu$_{4}$-e, seal 198, seal 396, seal 397
Ur-^{d}Nun-gal dub-sar dumu Lugal-é-maḫ-e, seal 443
Ur-^{d}Nun-gal dub-sar dumu Ur-^{d}Šara$_{2}$ ša$_{13}$-dub-ba, seal 425
Ur-^{d}Šara$_{2}$ dub-sar dumu [ ], seal 425
Ur-^{d}Šara$_{2}$ dub-sar dumu Lugal-nanga nu-banda$_{3}$-gu$_{4}$-^{d}Šara$_{2}$, seal 202
Ur-^{d}Šul-pa-è dub sar dumu Lugal-kù-ga-ni, seal 181
Ur-^{d}Šul-pa-è dub-sar dumu Lugal-kù-ga-ni, seal 177, seal 359, seal 476
Ur-^{d}Ùr-bar-tab dumu Lugal-á-zi-da gudu$_{4}$ é-maḫ, seal 167
Ur-Da-da išib ^{d}Šara$_{2}$-bàn-da, seal 235
Ur-dingir-ra kuš$_{7}$ dumu A-zi, seal 61, seal 437
Ur-dingir-ra kuš$_{7}$ dumu A-zi-da, seal 61, seal 62, seal 68, seal 69, seal 70, seal 84, seal 85
Ur-dingir-ra kuš$_{7}$ ensi$_{2}$-ka dumu A-zi-<da>, seal 65, seal 66, seal 67
Ur-dingir-ra kuš$_{7}$ ensi$_{2}$-ka dumu A-zi-da, seal 61, seal 63, seal 64, seal 71, seal 72, seal 73, seal 74, seal 75, seal 76
Ur-e$_{11}$-e dub-sar dumu Ur-ni$_{9}$-gar, seal 189, seal 256
Ur-é-gu-la ir$_{11}$-^{d}[ ] aga$_{3}$-uš A-a-kal-la, seal 279
Ur-gi$_{6}$-par$_{4}$ dub-sar dumu A-a-kal-la, seal 344
Ur-gi$_{6}$-par$_{4}$ dumu Ur-^{d}Ištaran, seal 131
Ur-^{giš}gigir dub-sar dumu Ba-ša$_{6}$, seal 170, seal 292, seal 296, seal 388
Ur-^{giš}gigir dub-sar dumu Bar-ra-an, seal 78, seal 351

Ur-^{giš}gigir dub-sar dumu Lugal-é-maḫ-e, seal 168, seal 368
Ur-^{giš}gigir dumu Lugal-má-gur$_8$-re, seal 358
Ur-gú-dè-na dub-sar dumu Lú-[kiri$_3$-zal, seal 293
Ur-ni$_9$-gar dumu Lugal-^{giš}gigir en-dub-lá, seal 106
Ur-^{ú}numun$_2$ ir$_{11}$ ^{d}Nin-ur$_4$-ra, seal 79, seal 80, seal 81, seal 82
Úr-ra-ni dub-sar dumu Lugal-é-maḫ, seal 395
Uš-mu dub-sar dumu Lugal-ša$_6$-ga, seal 389, seal 456

[ ] dub-sar ir$_{11}$ lugal, seal 314
[ ] dumu Ur-^{d}[ ], seal 418

Text 1

o.

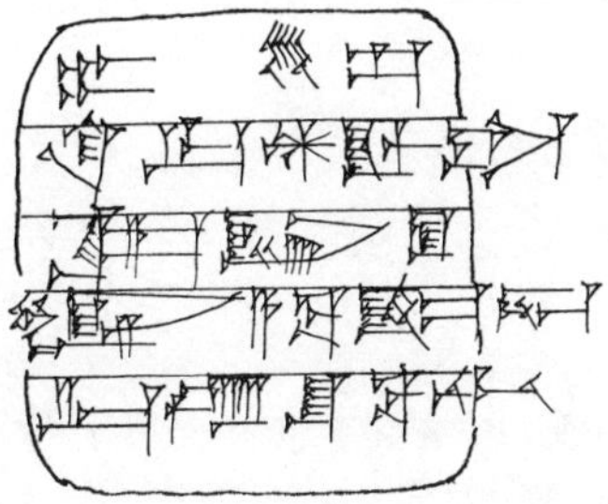

r.

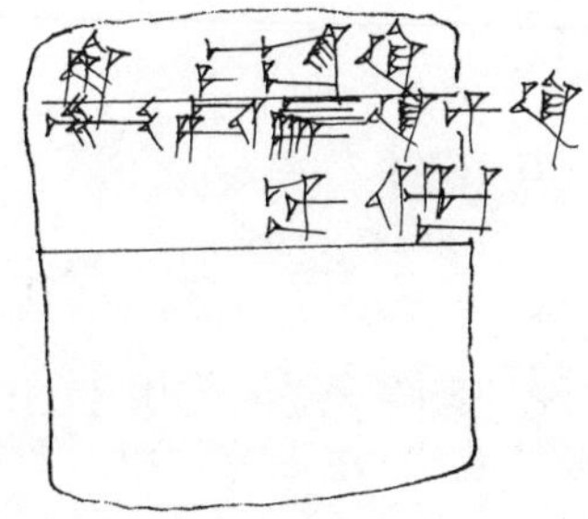

Text 2

o.

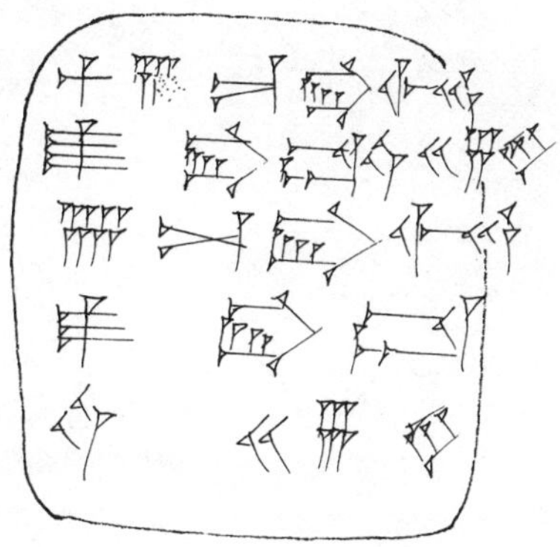

r.

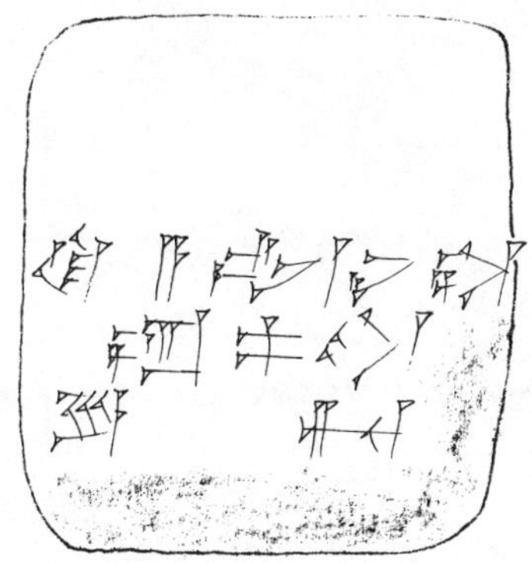

Text 3

o.

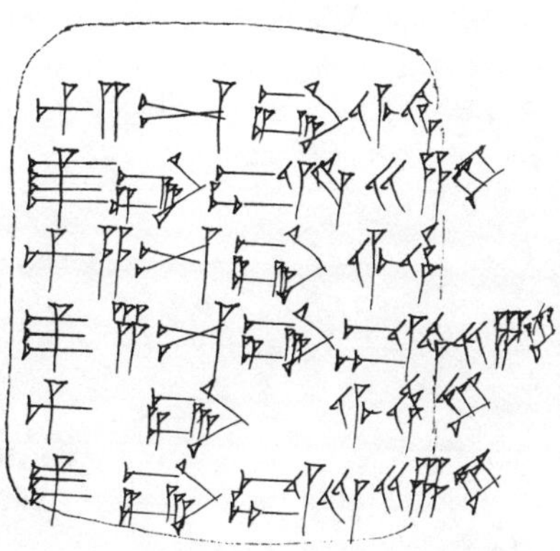

r.

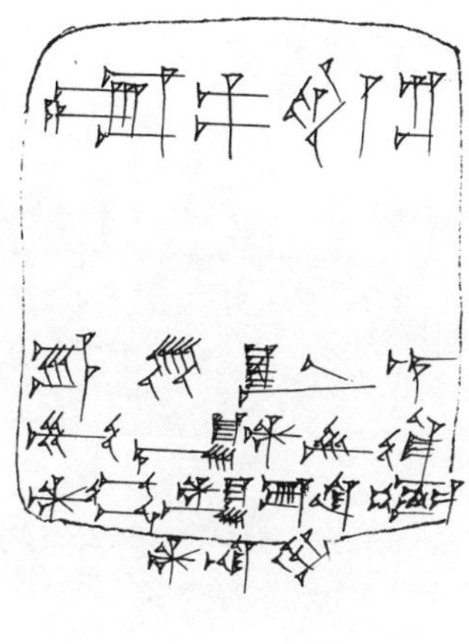

Text 4

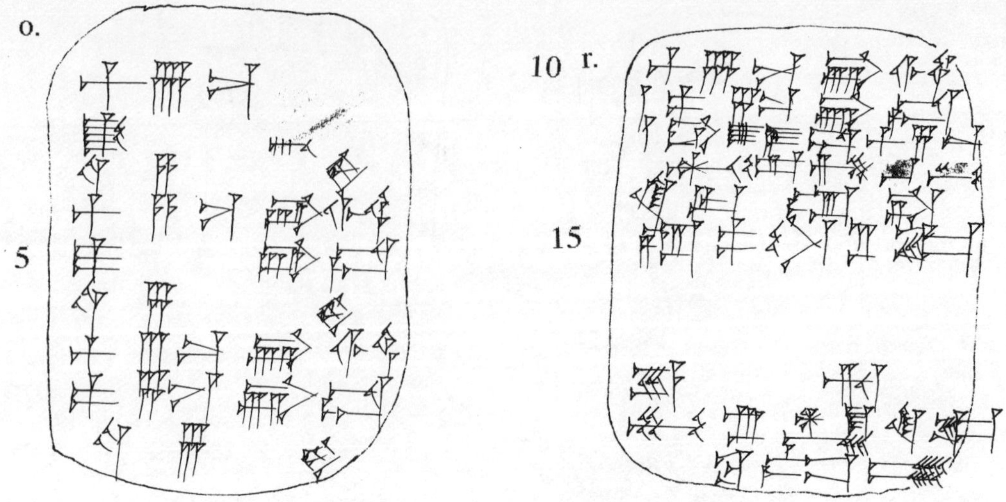

Text 5

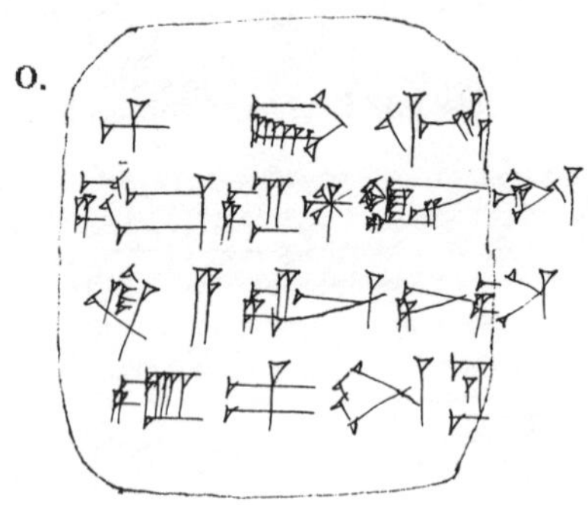

Text 7

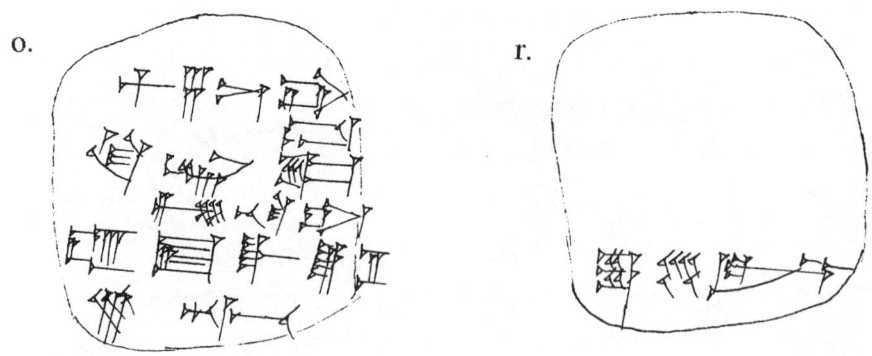

Text 10

o.

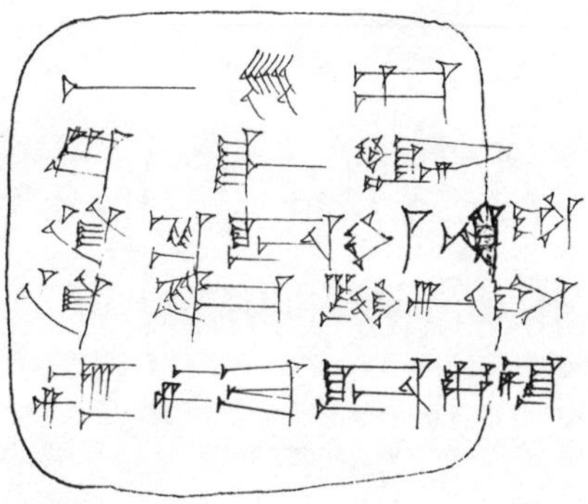

r.

Text 11

o.

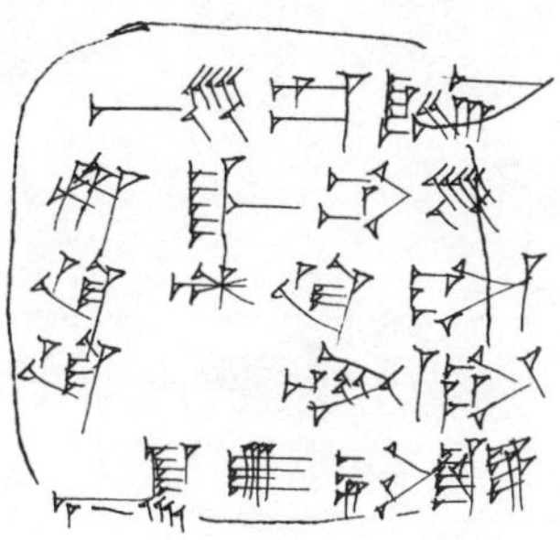

r.

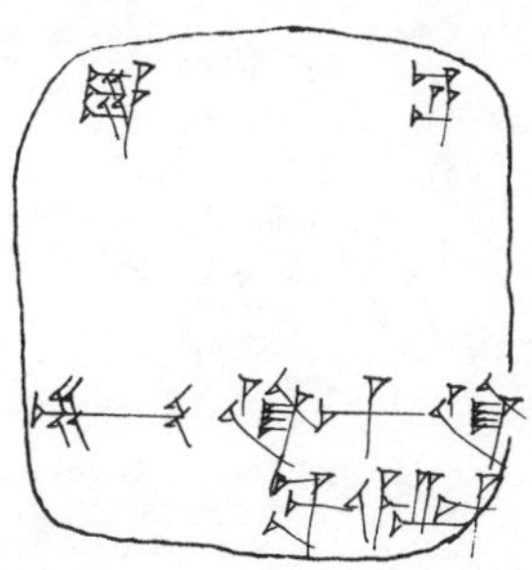

Text 14

o.

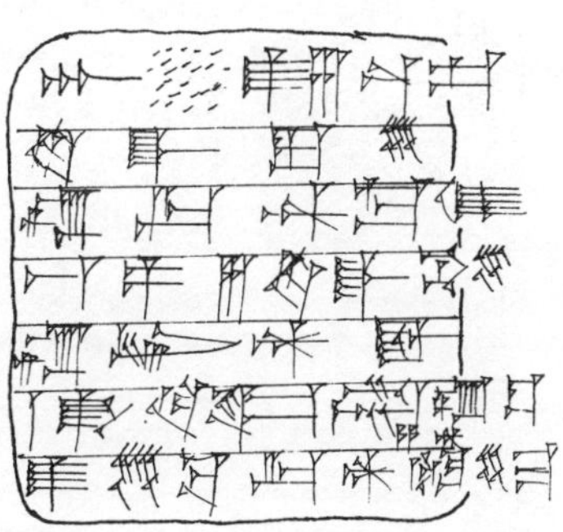

r.

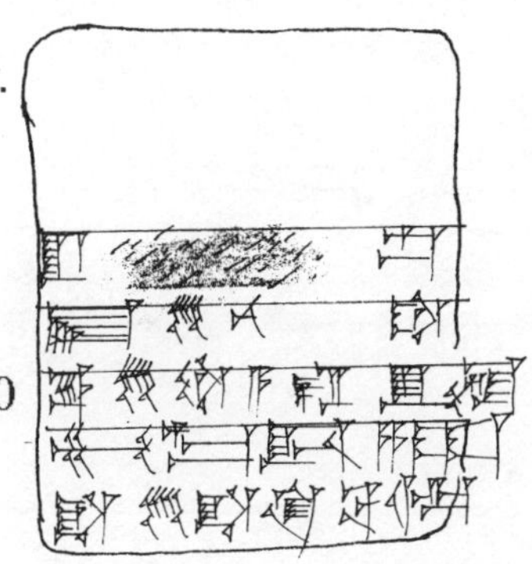

Text 15

o.

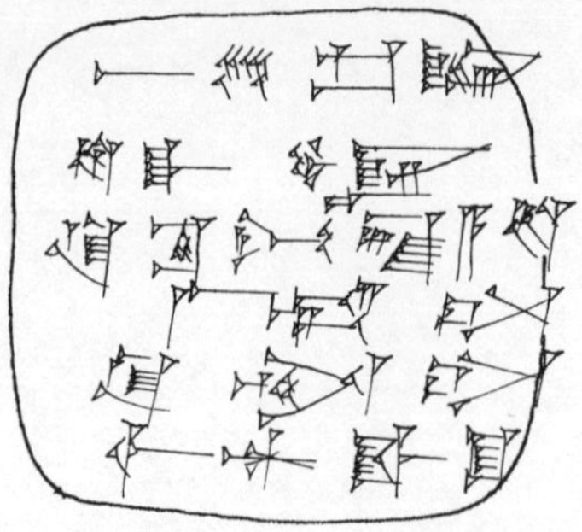

r.

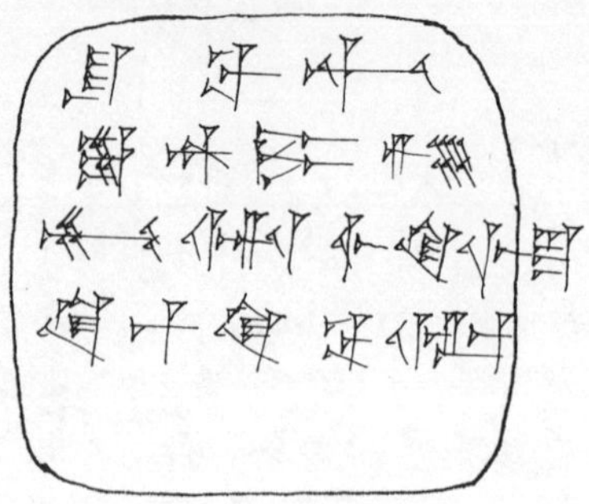

Text 18

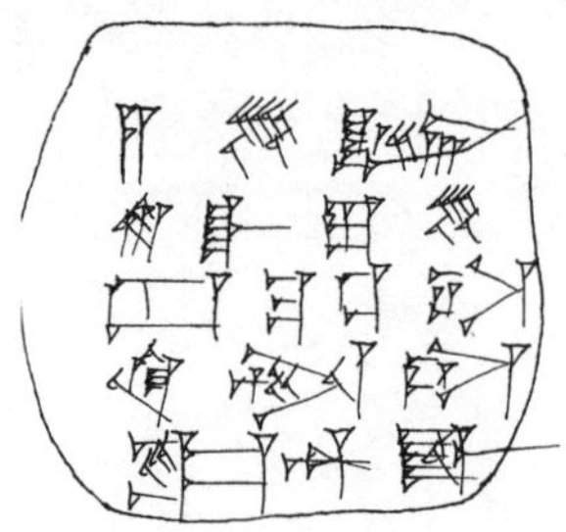

r.

Text 22

o.

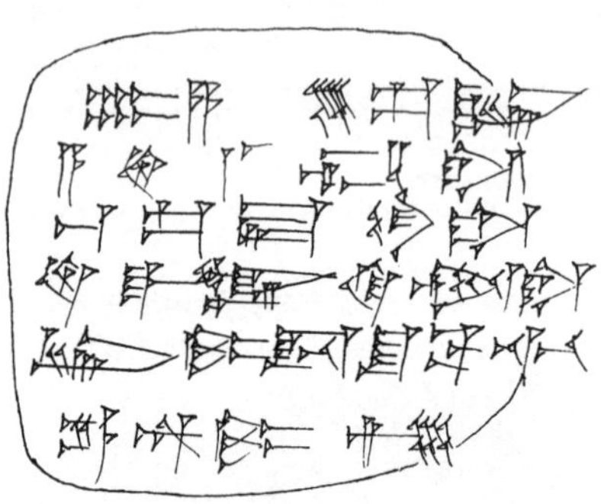

r.

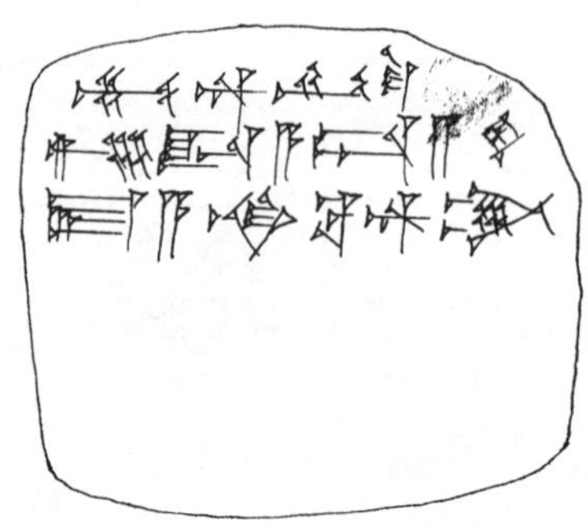

Text 26

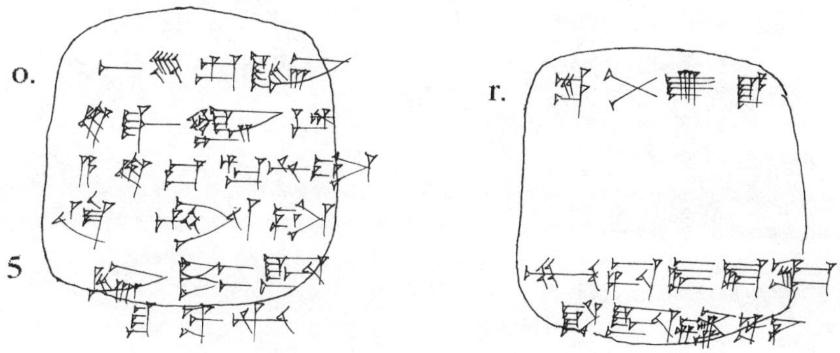

Text 27

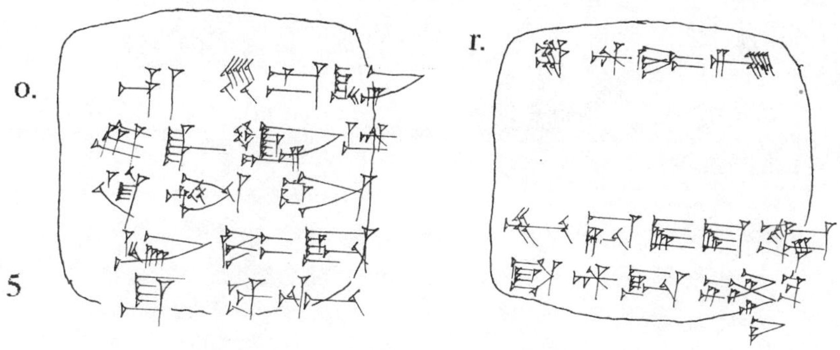

Text 30

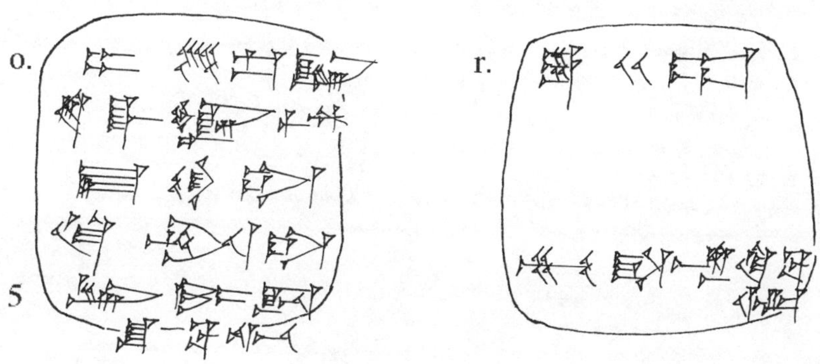

Text 33

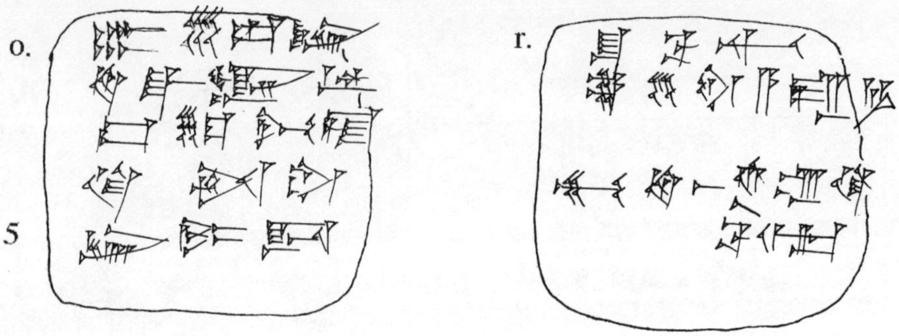

Text 36

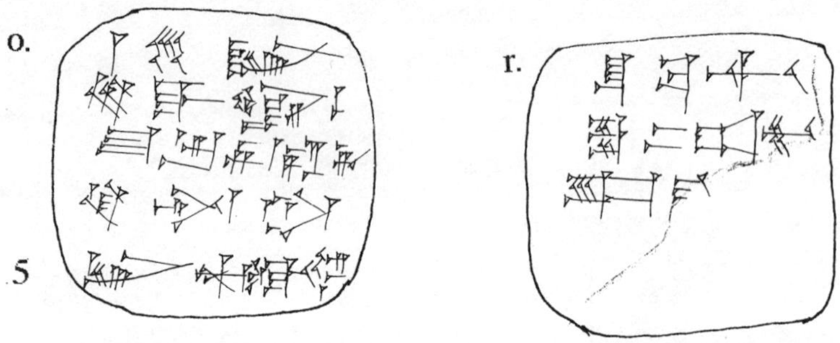

Text 37

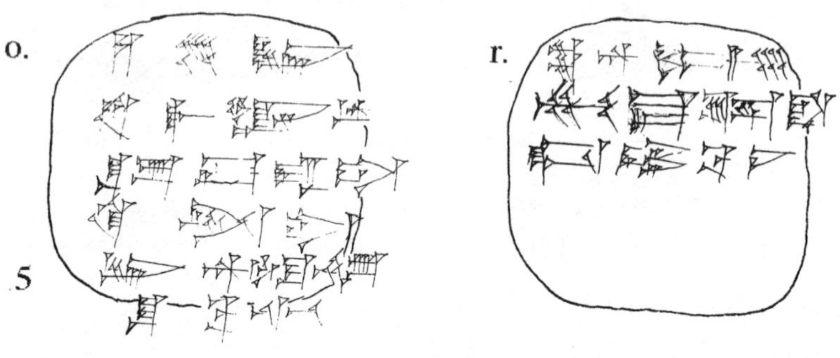

Text 41

o.

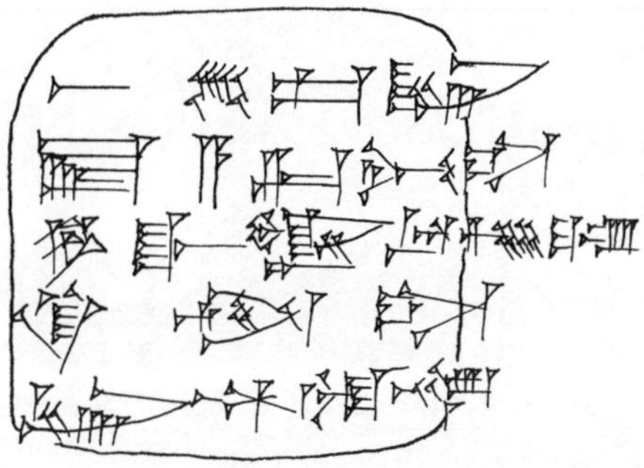

r.

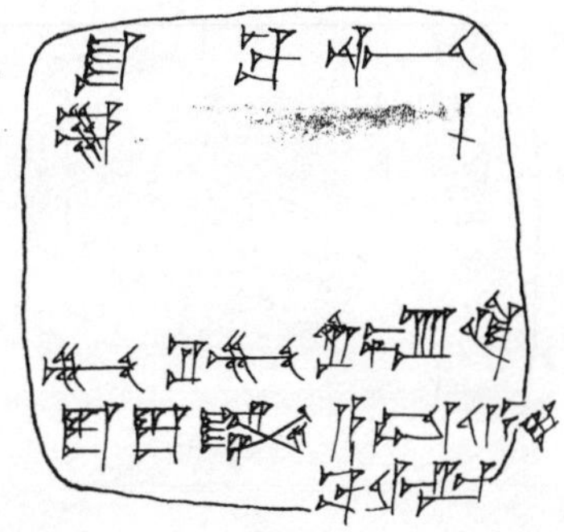

Text 42

o.

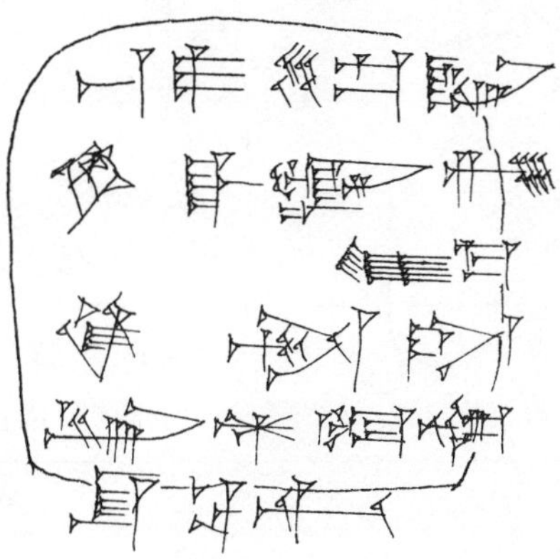

r.

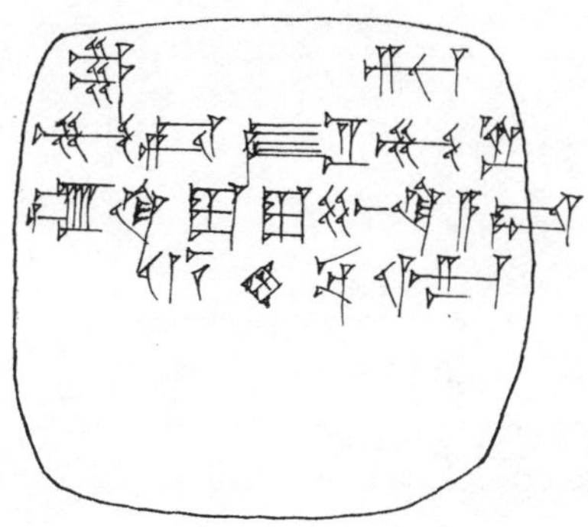

Text 45

o.

r.

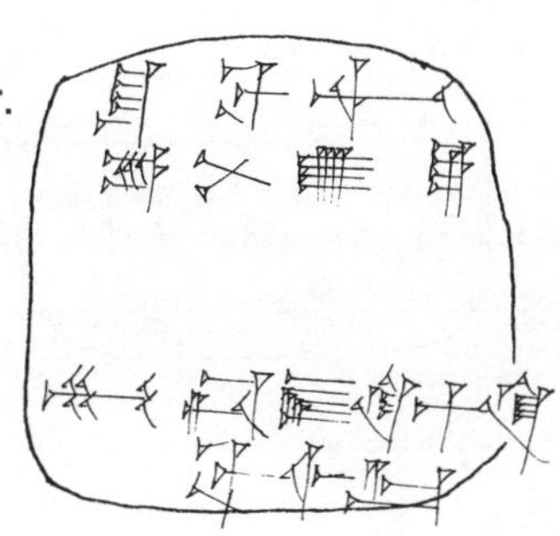

Text 51

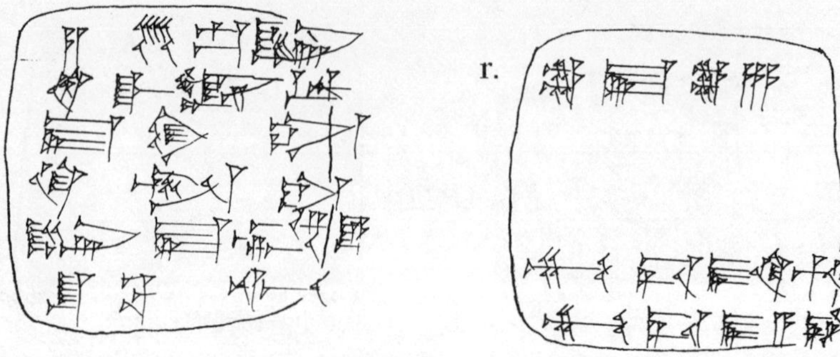

Text 54

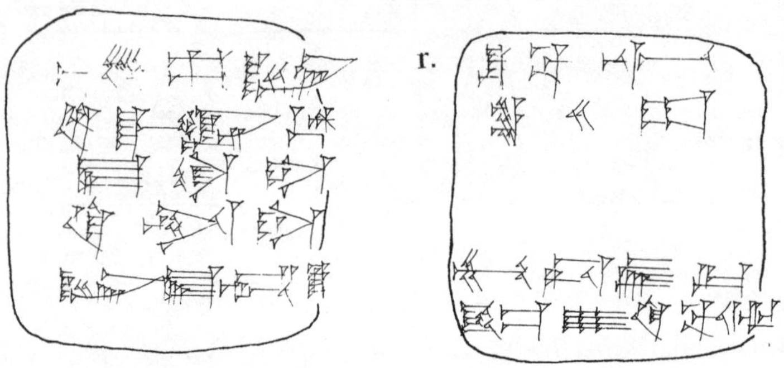

Text 56

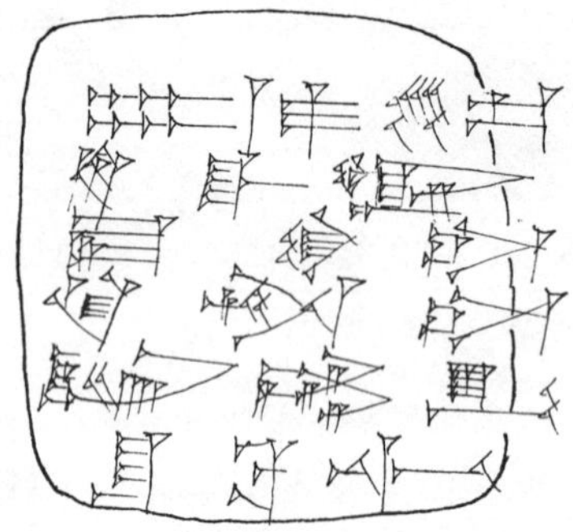

Text 59

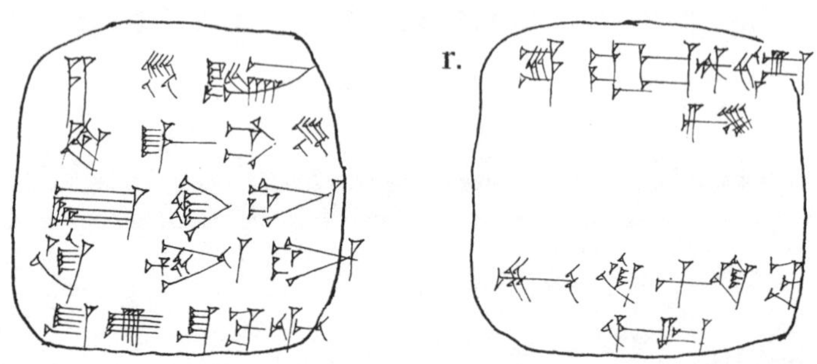

Text 63

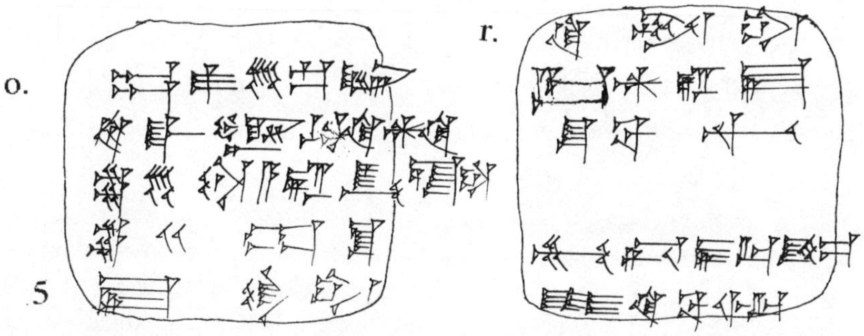

Text 64

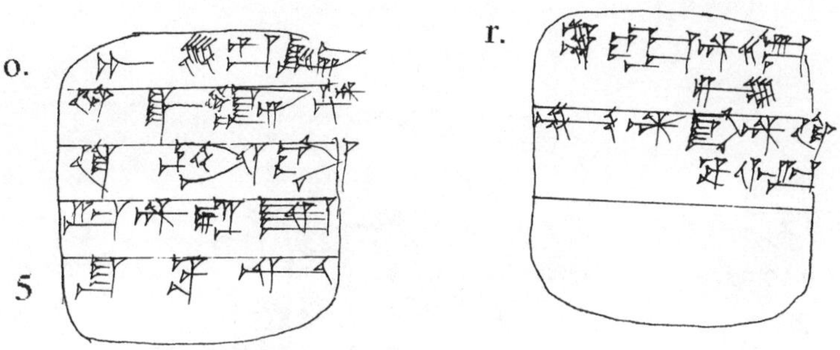

Text 71

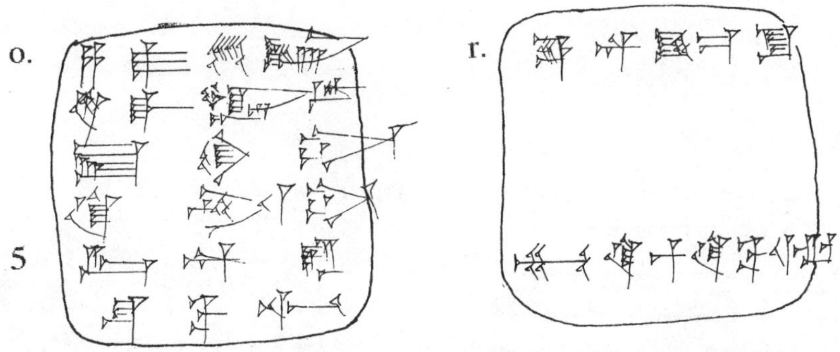

Text 75

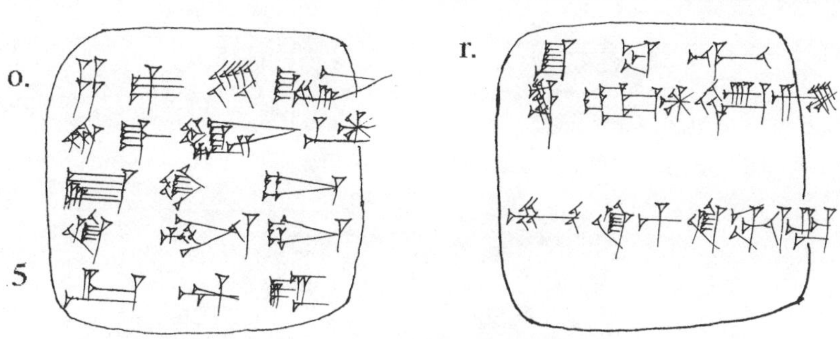

Text 82

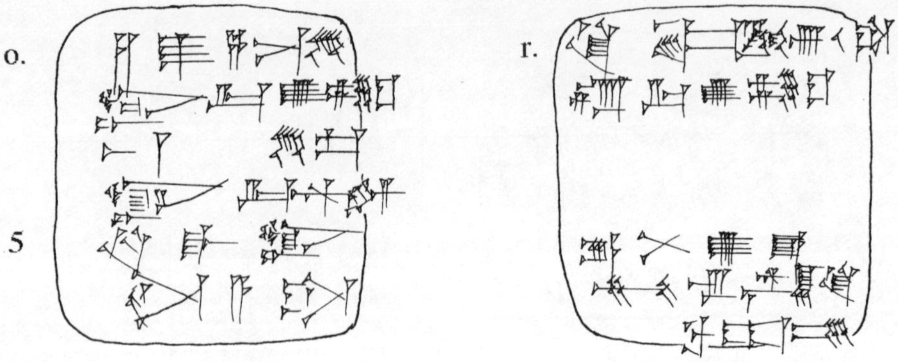

Text 87

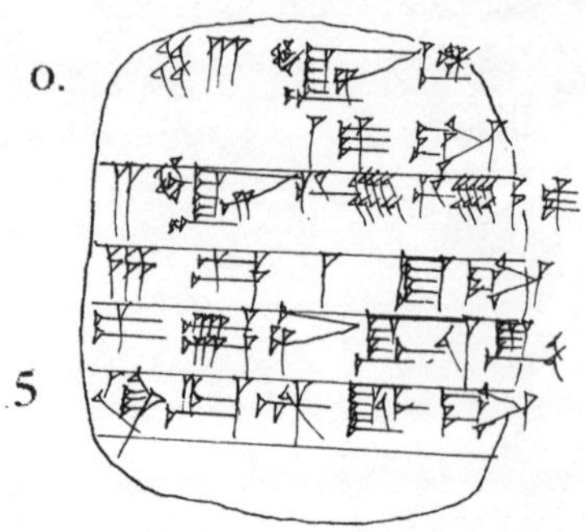

Text 88

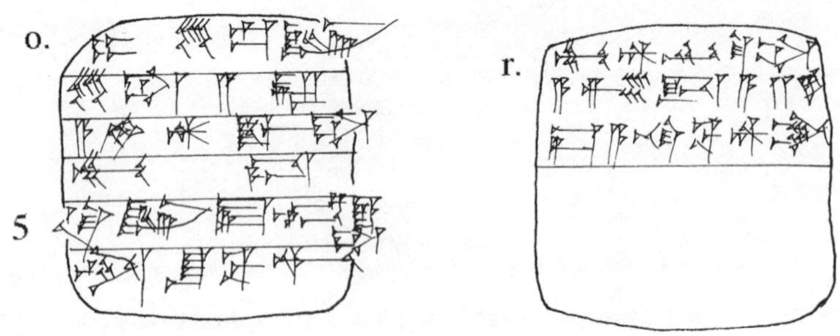

Text 89

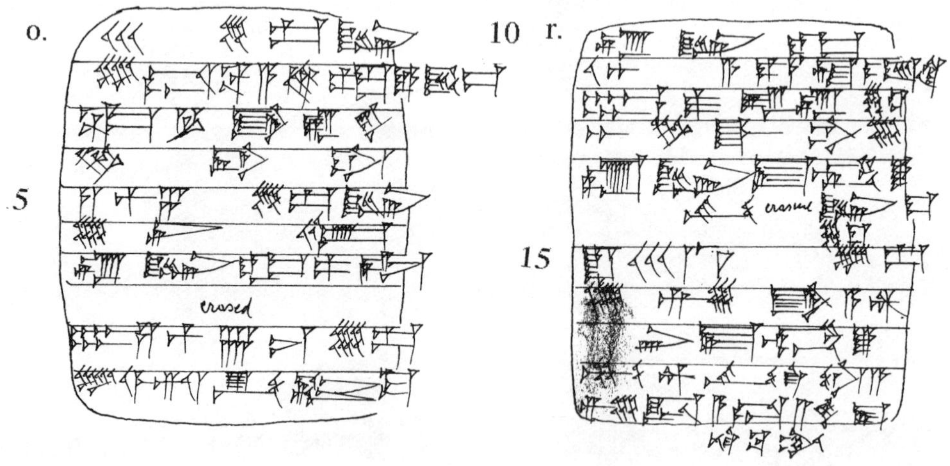

Text 91

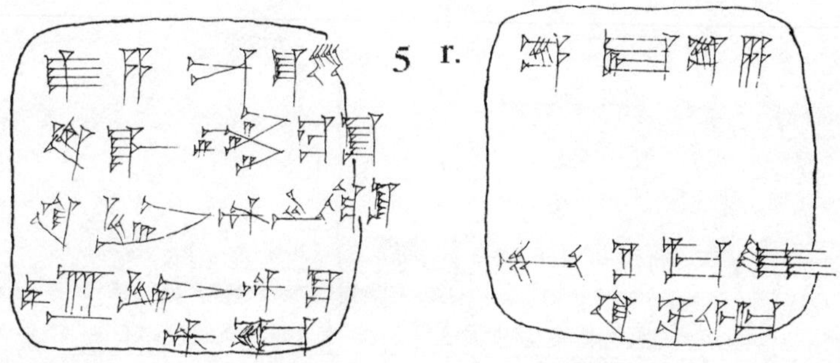

Text 92

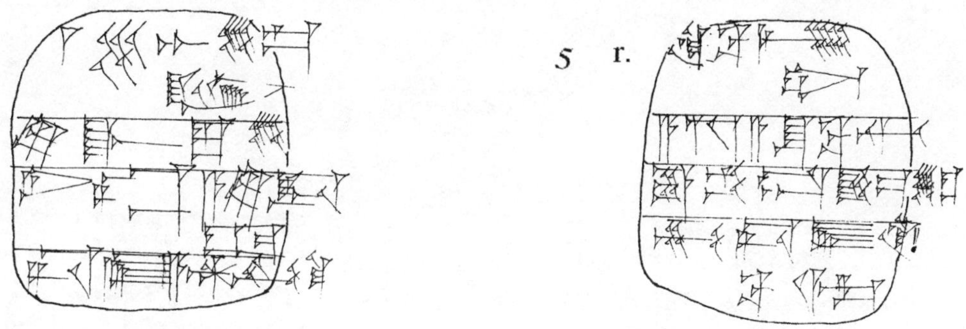

Text 95

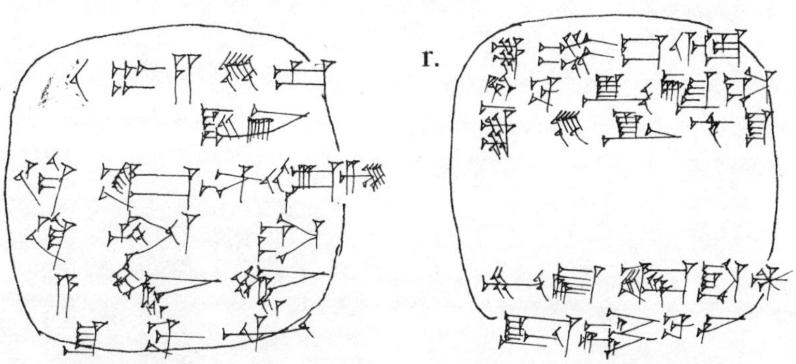

Text 98

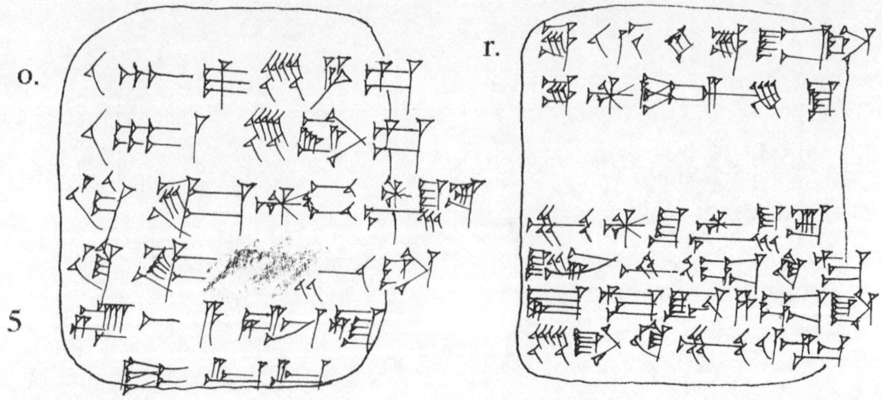

Text 99

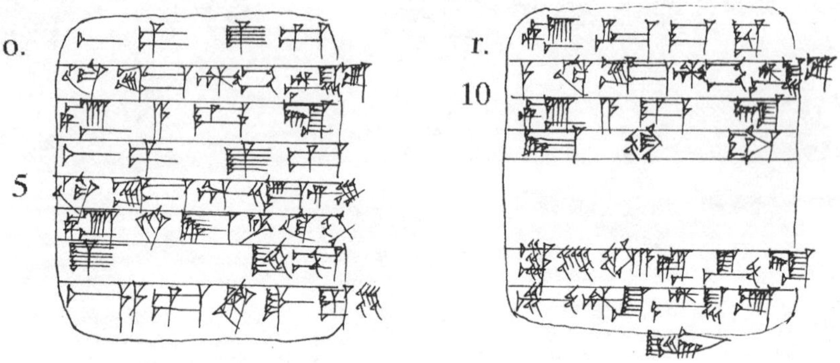

Text 100

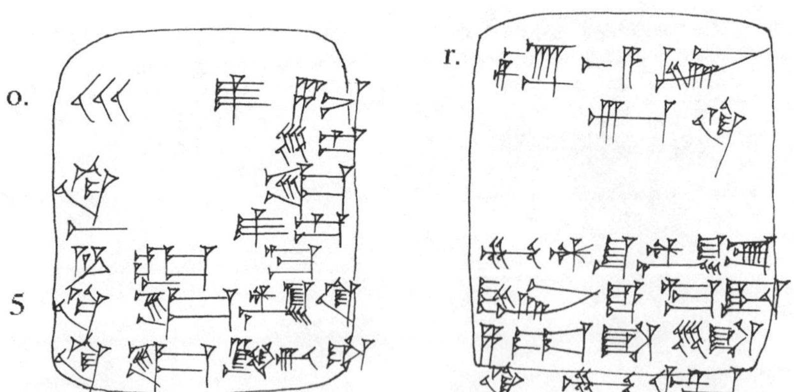

Text 101

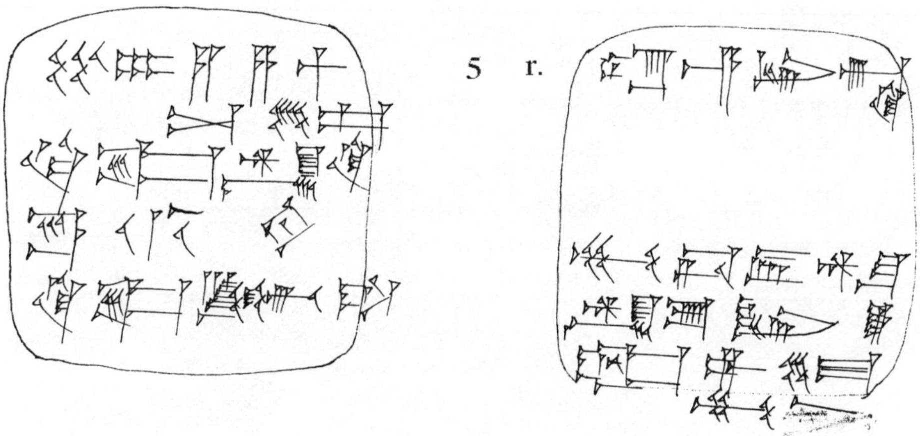

Text 103

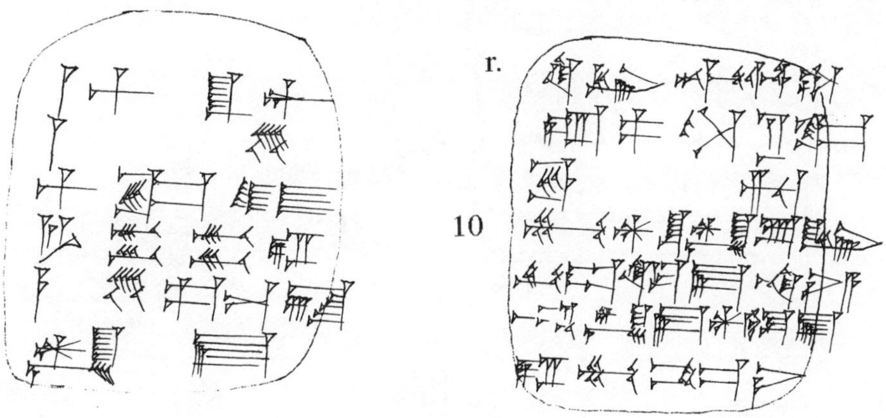

Text 104

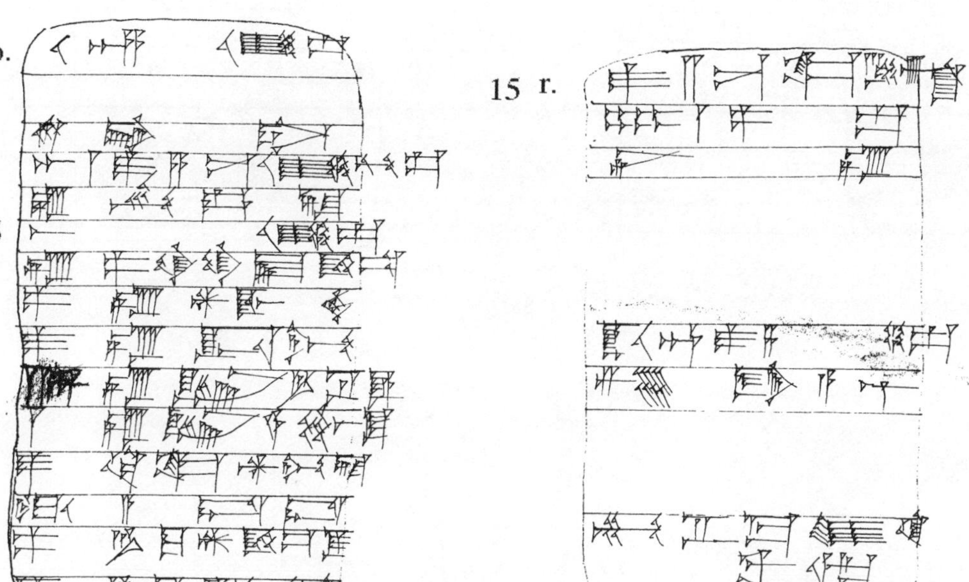

Text 105

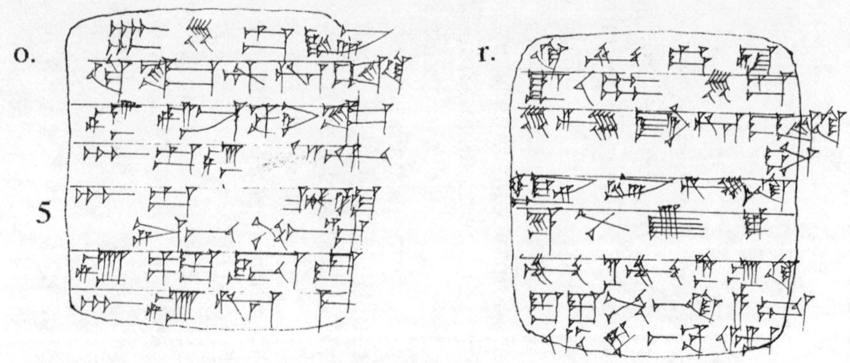

Text 106

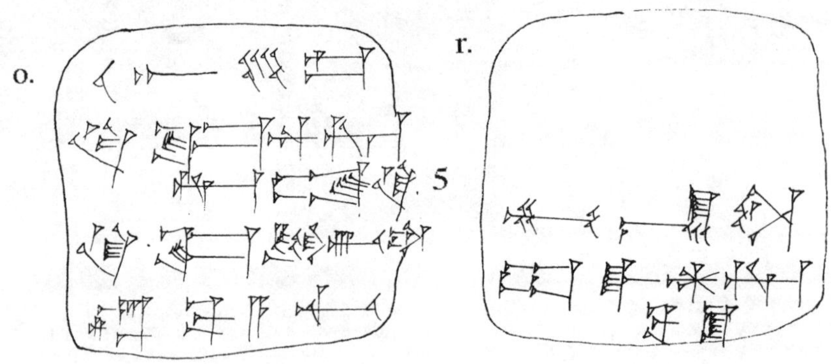

Text 108

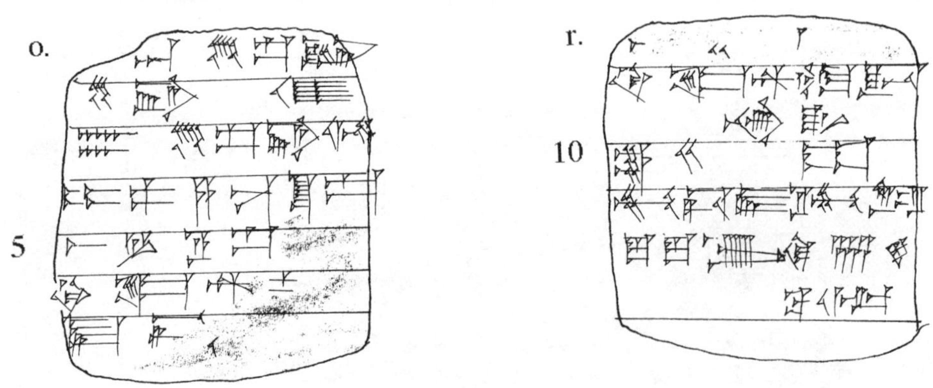

Text 111

o.

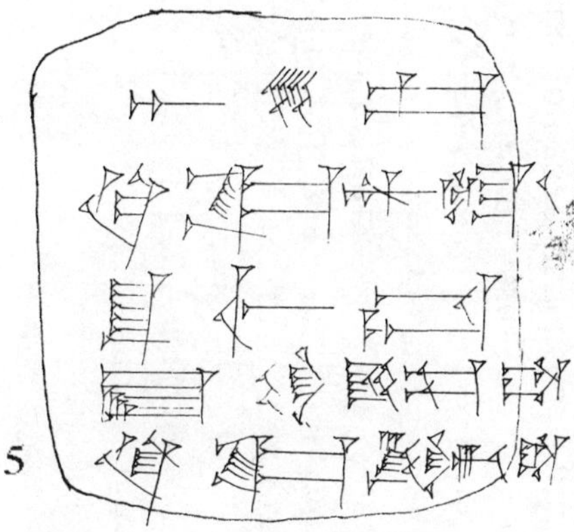

r.

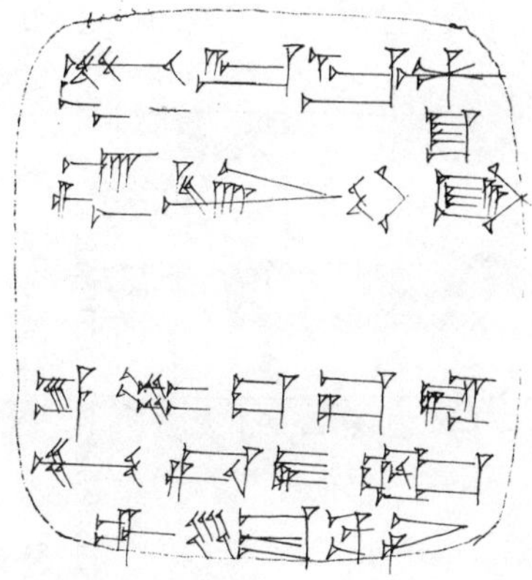

Text 112

o.

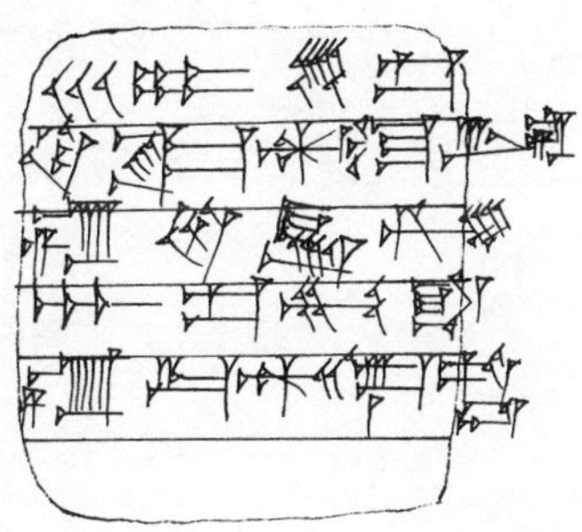

r.

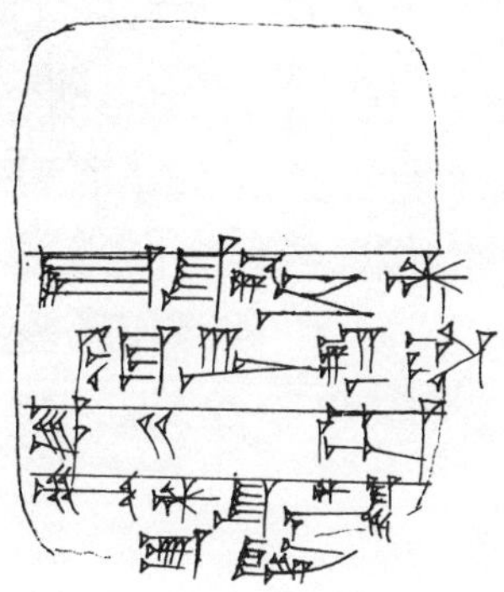

Text 114

o.

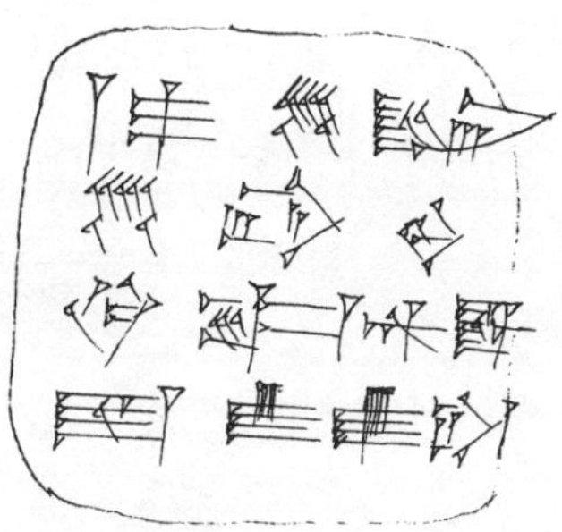

r.

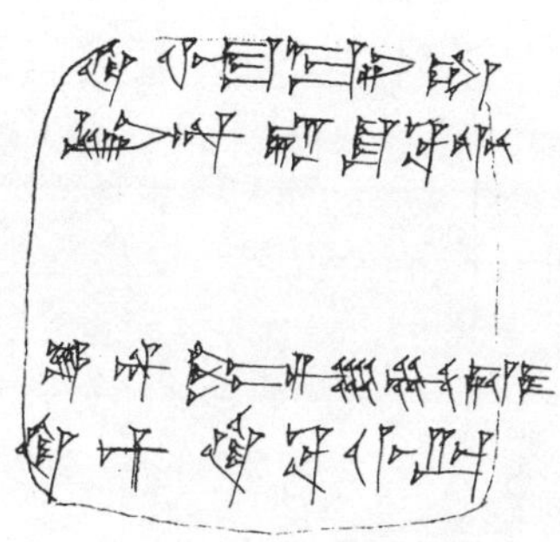

Text 115

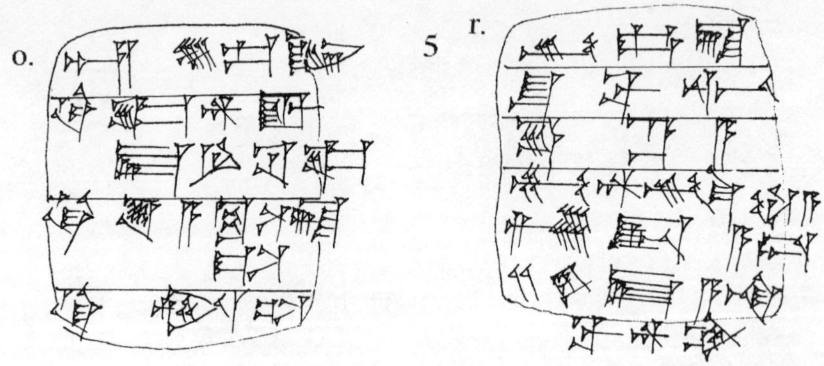

Text 116

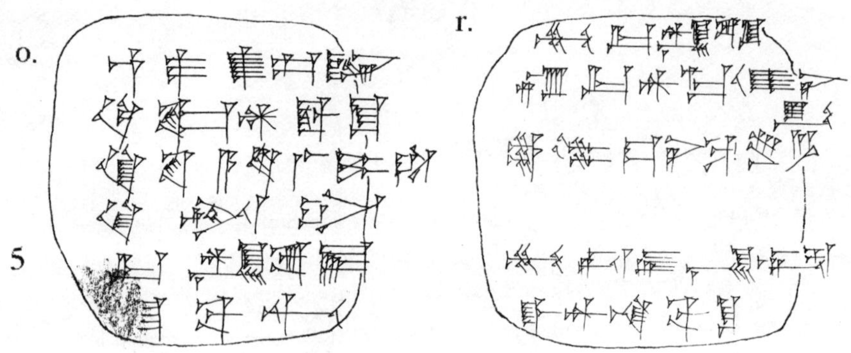

Text 117

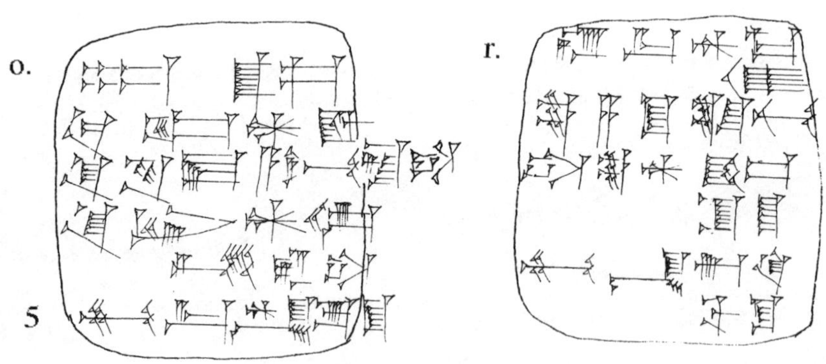

Text 118

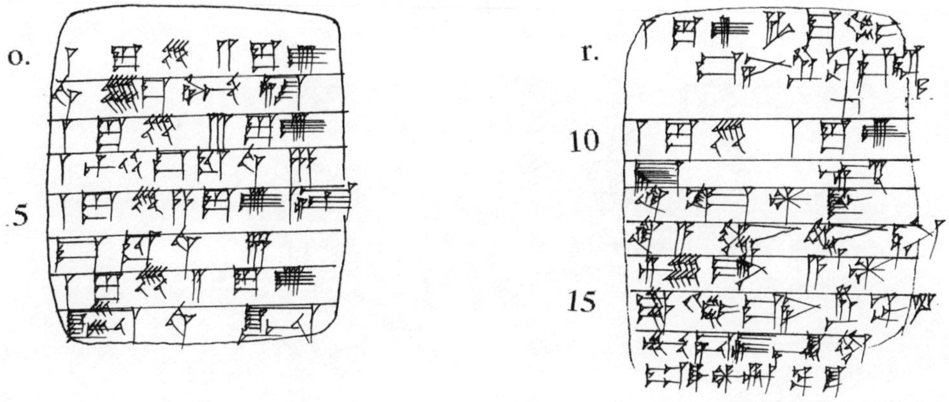

Text 119

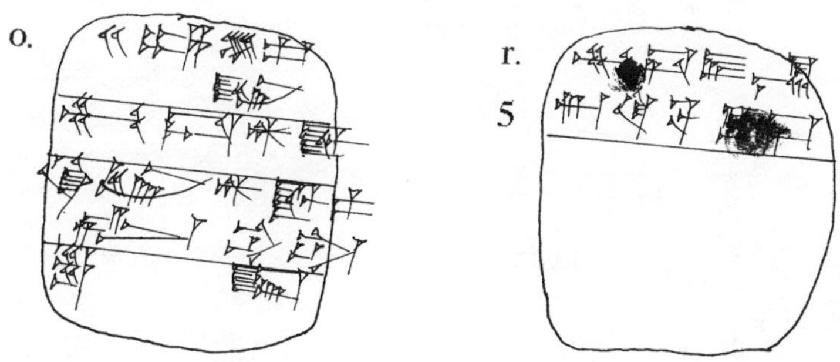

Text 120

o.

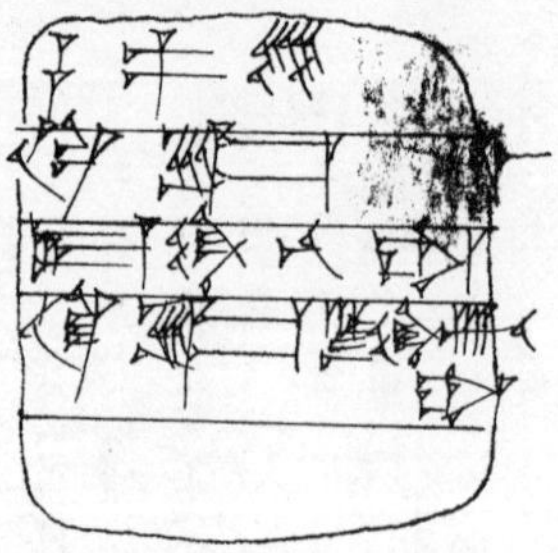

r.

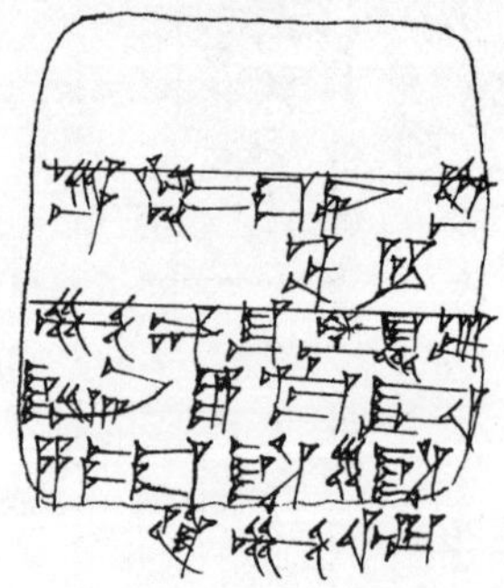

Text 122

o.

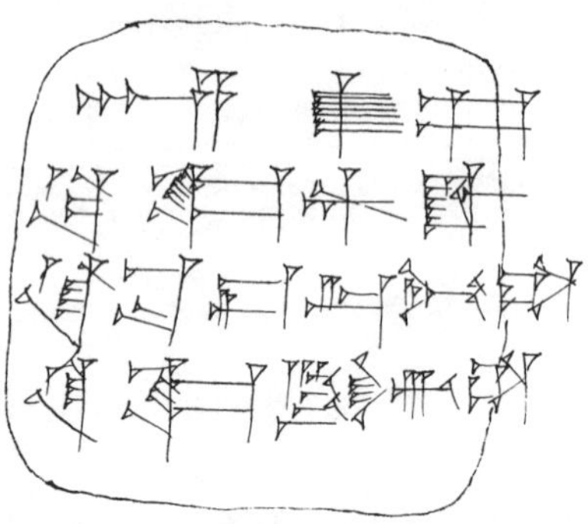

r.

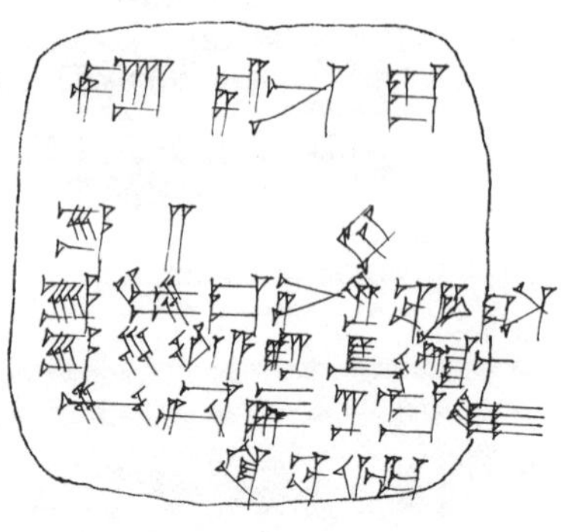

Text 123

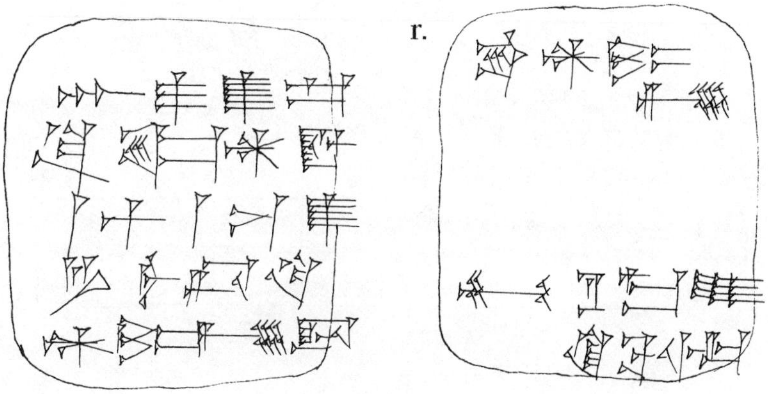

Text 125

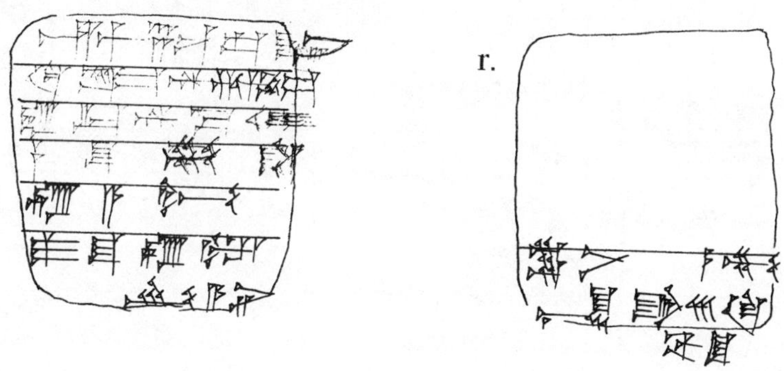

Text 126

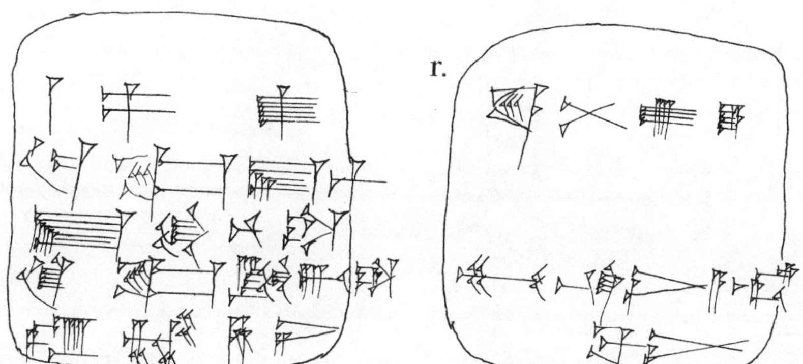

Text 127

o.

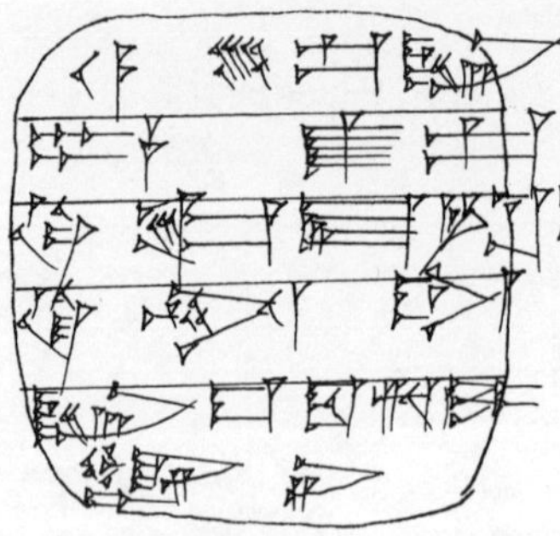

r.

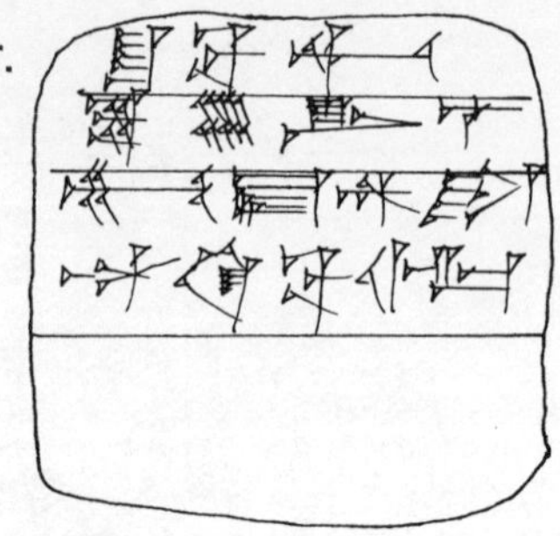

Text 128

o.

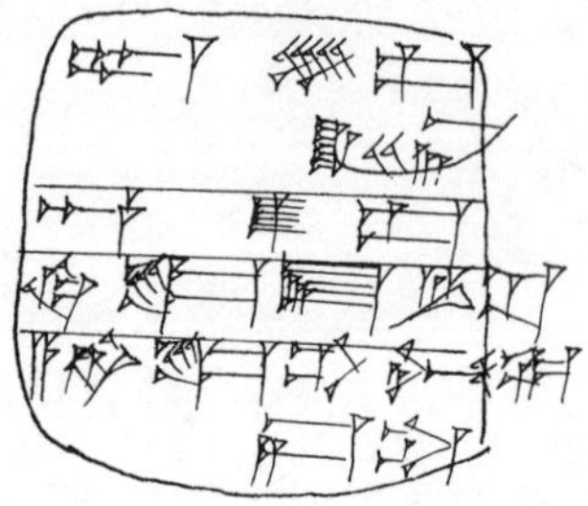

r.

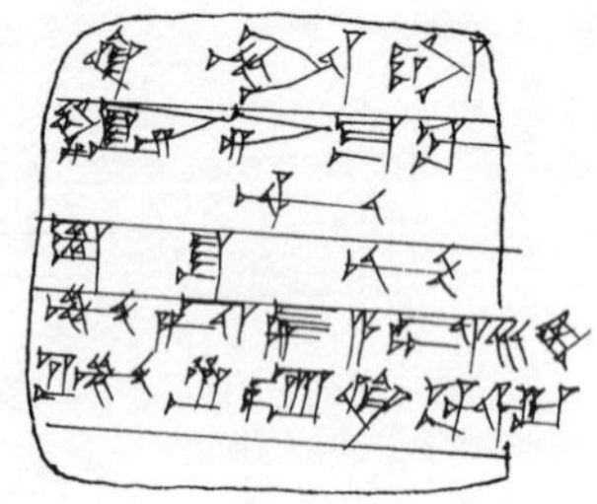

Text 129

o.

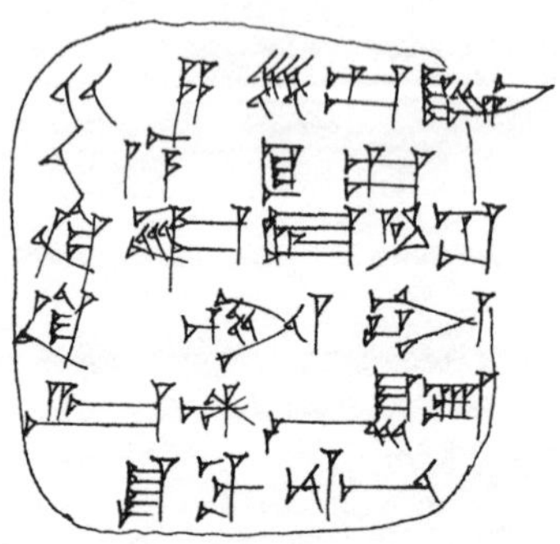

r.

Text 130

o.

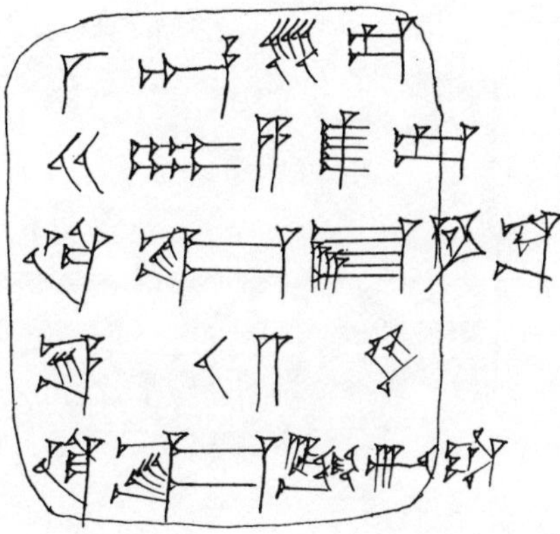

r.

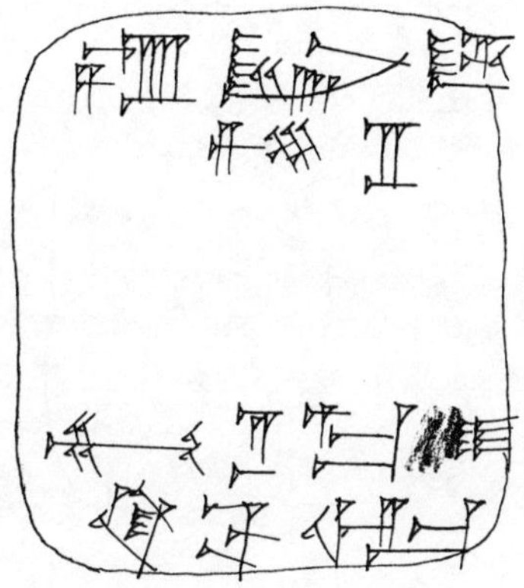

Text 131

o.

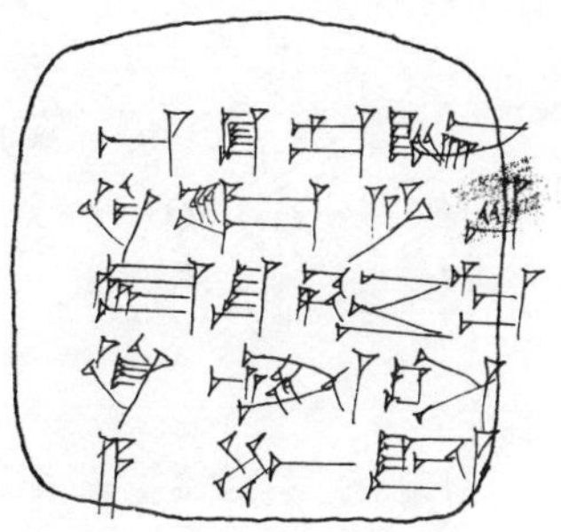

r.

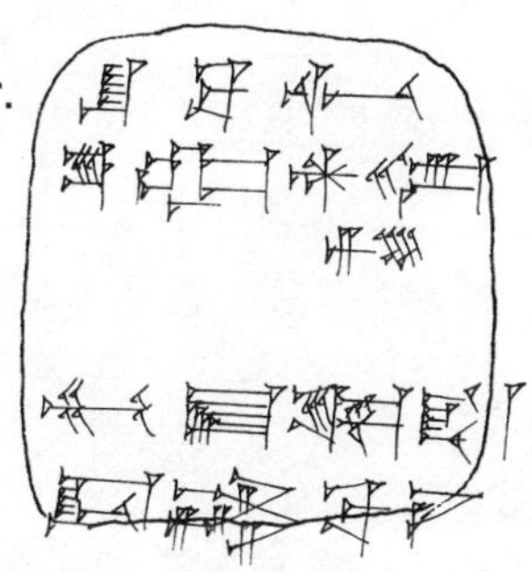

Text 133

o.

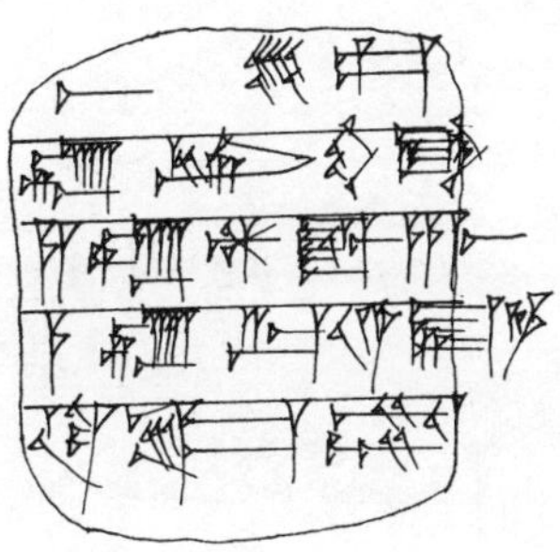

r.

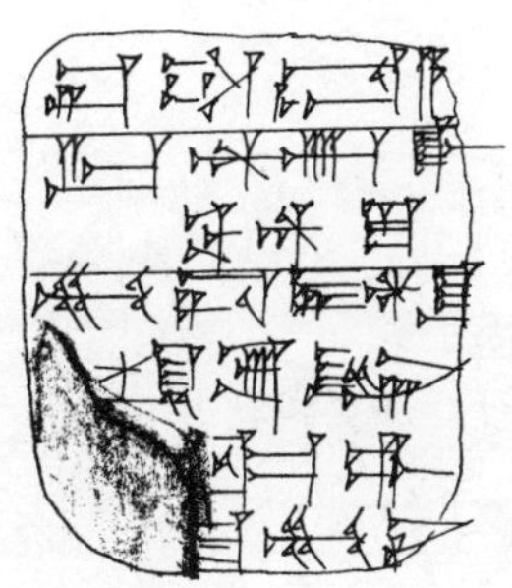

Text 135

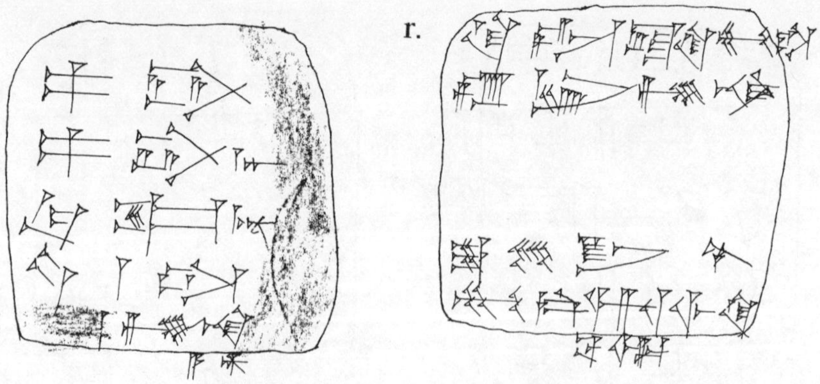

Text 139

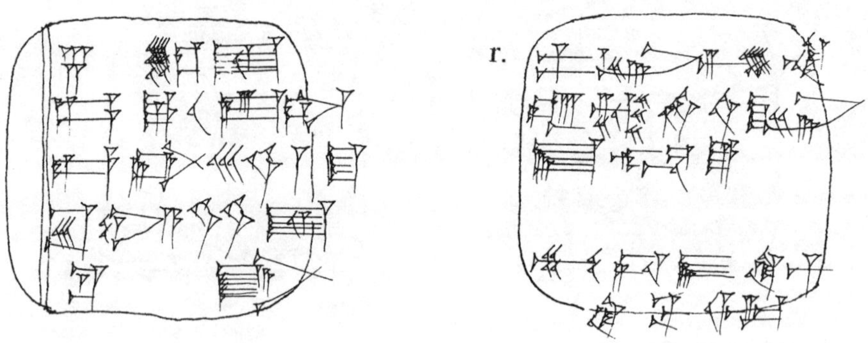

Text 140

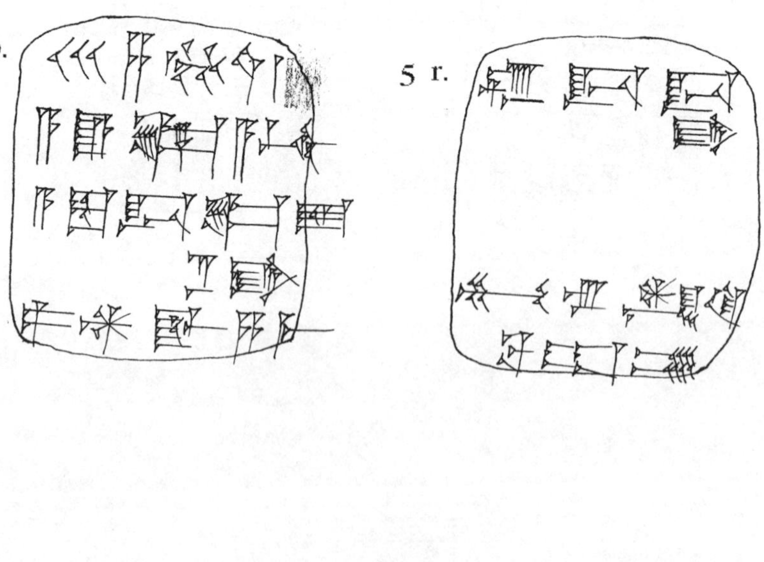

Text 141

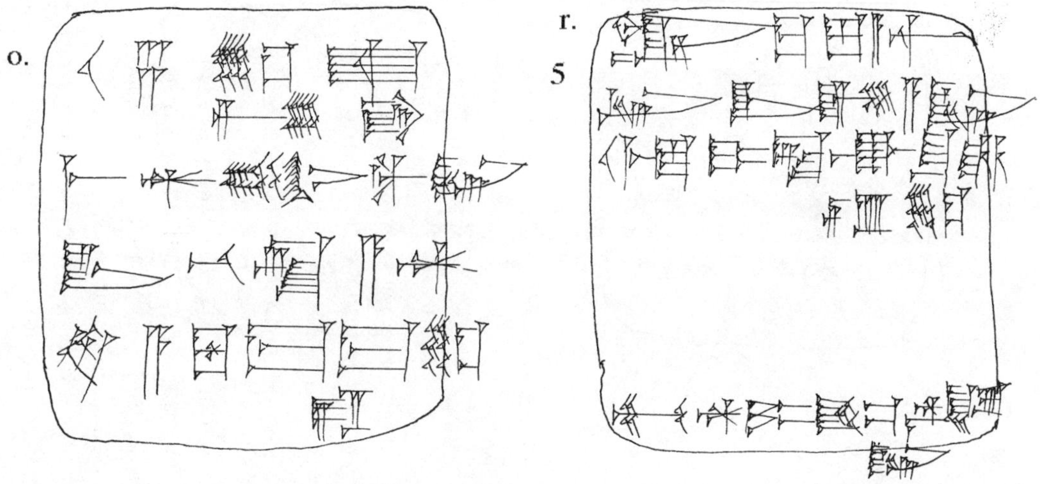

Text 143

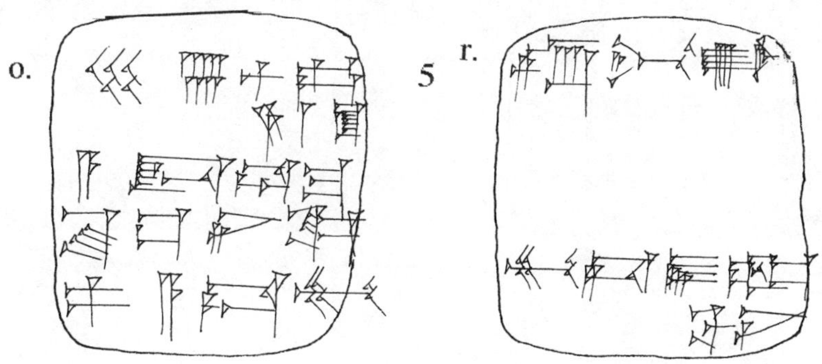

Text 145

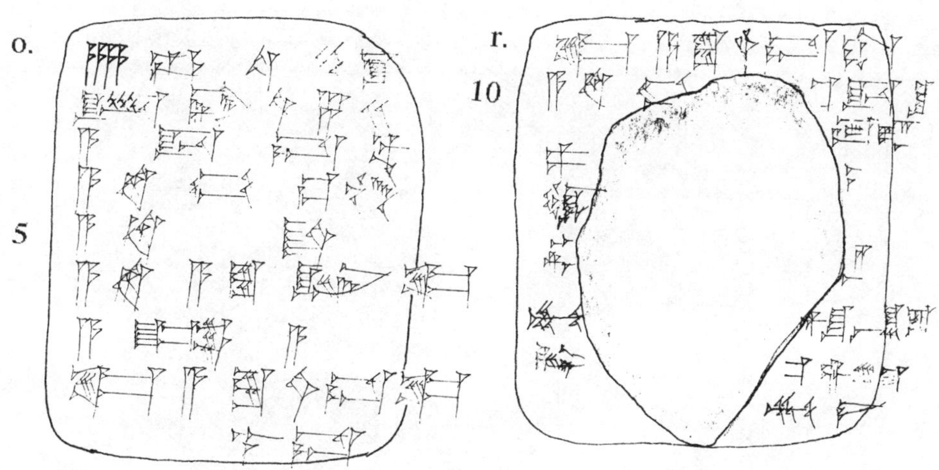

Text 146

o.

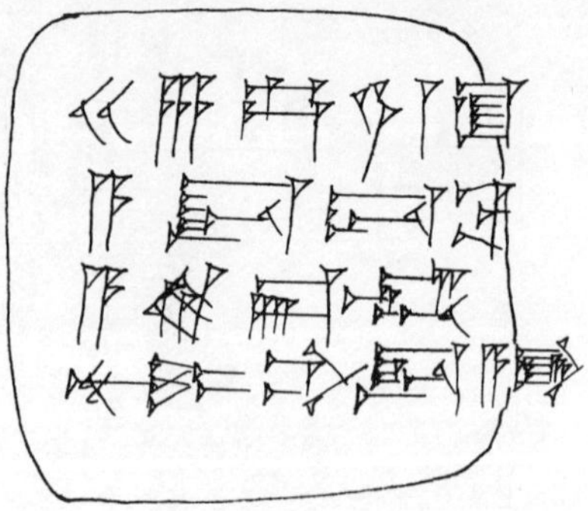

r.

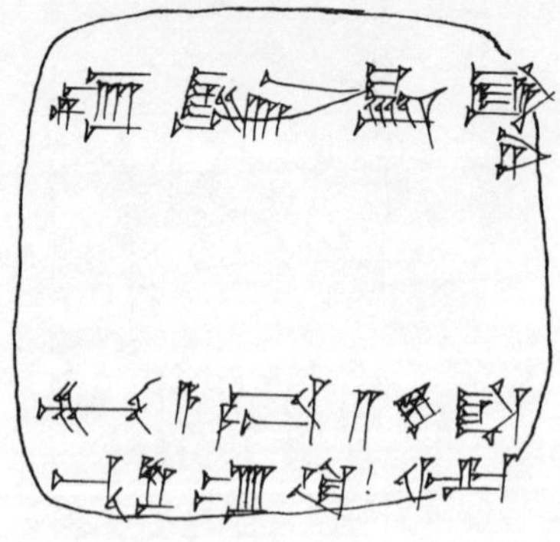

Text 147

o.

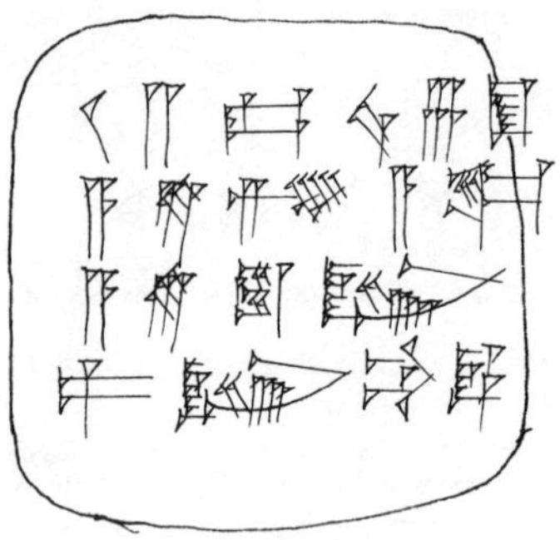

r.

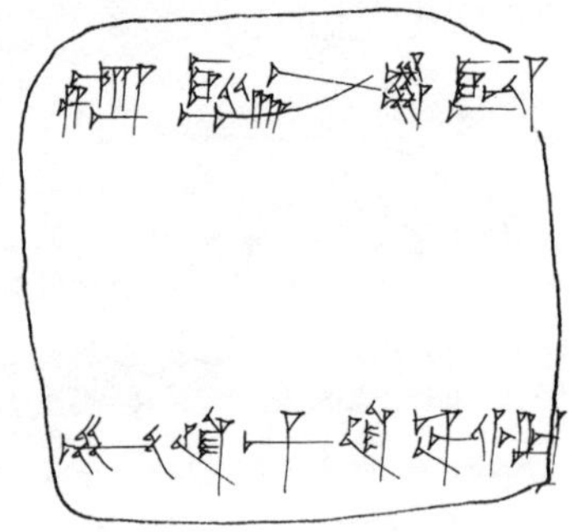

Text 149

o.

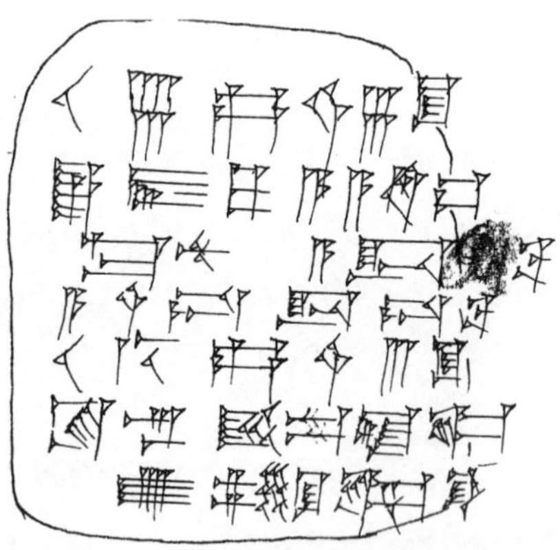

r.

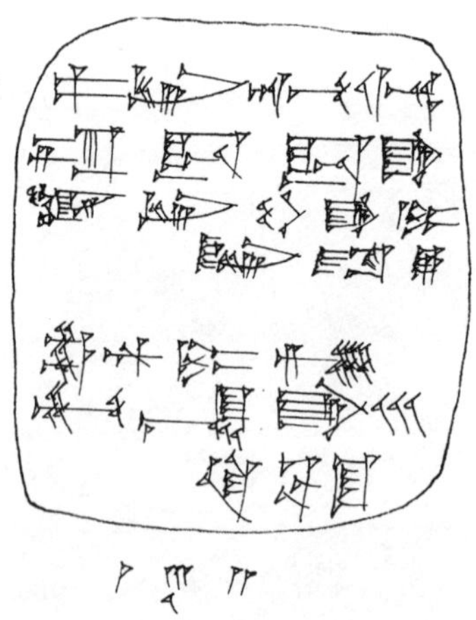

Text 152

o.

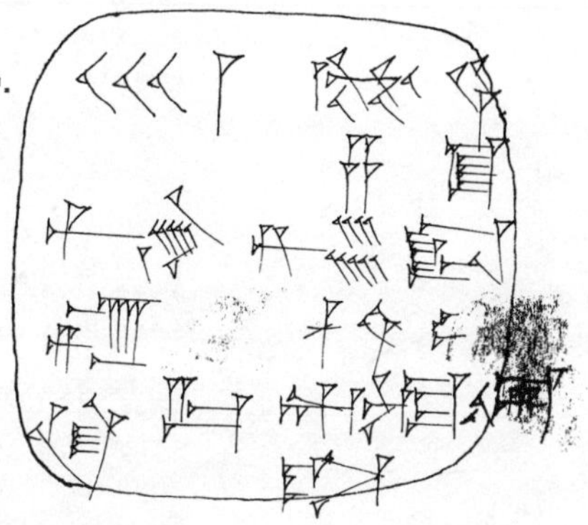

r.

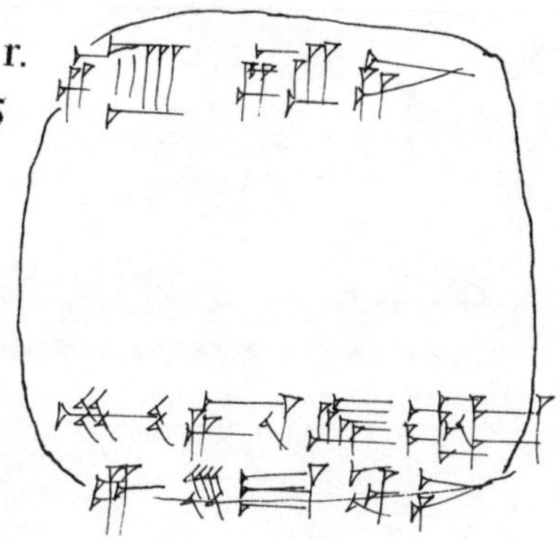

Text 153

o.

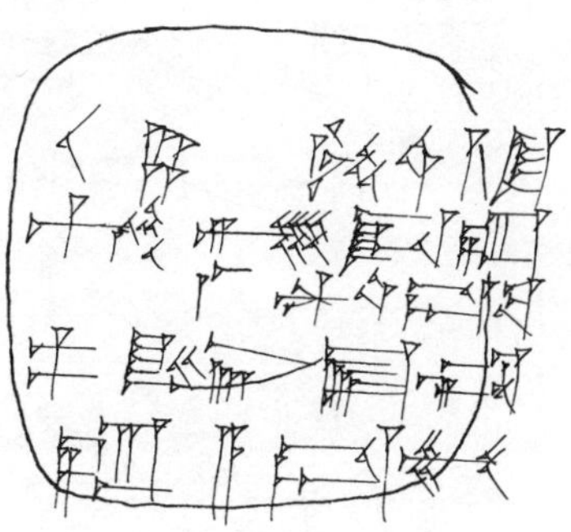

r.

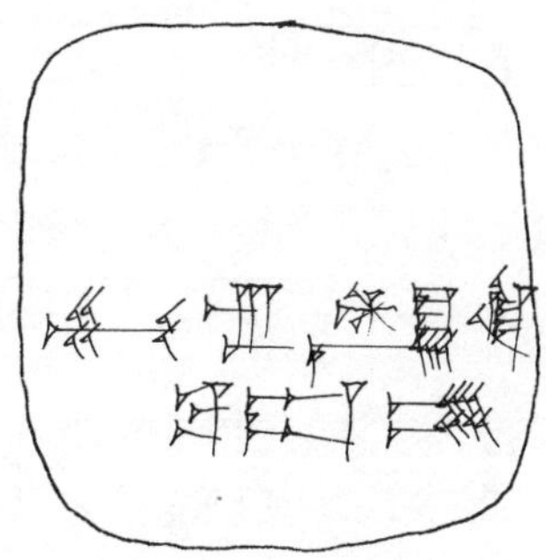

Text 154

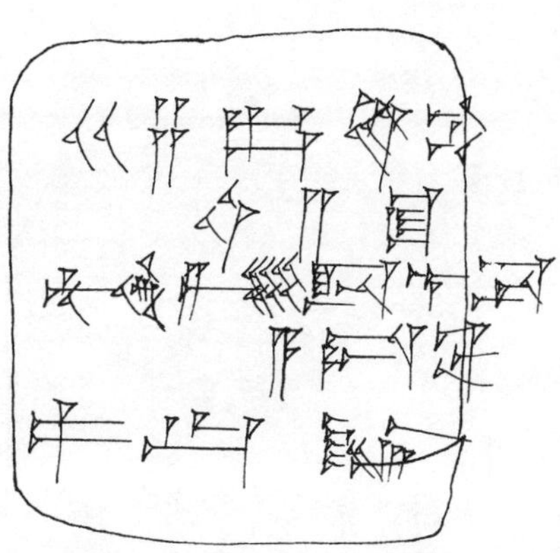

r.

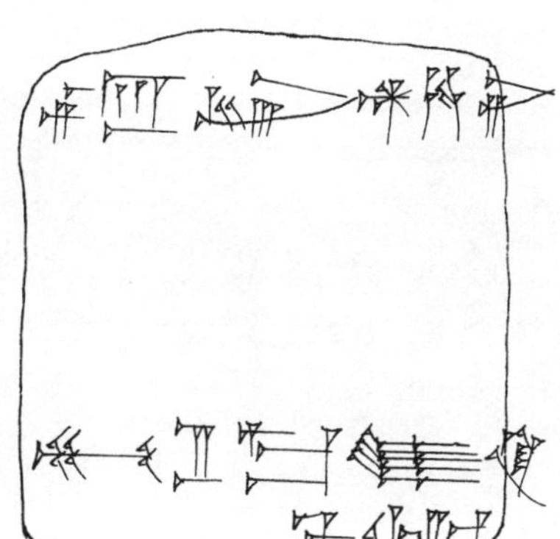

Text 155

o.

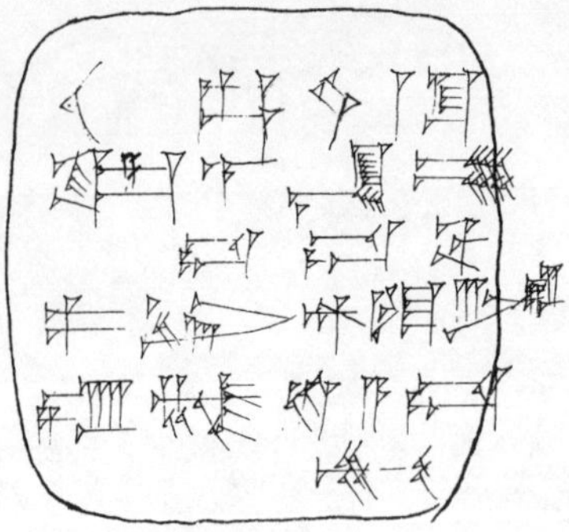

r.

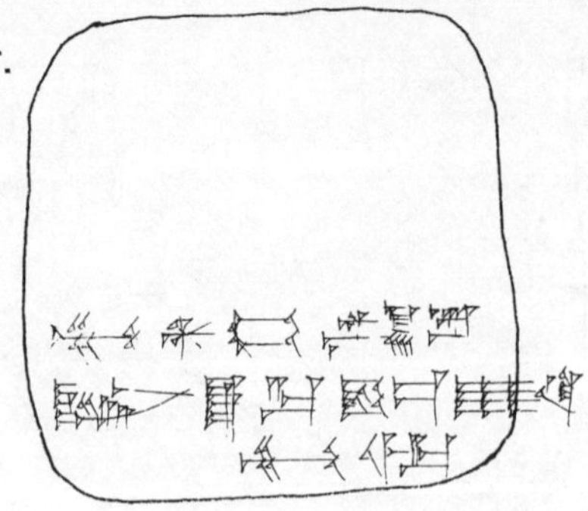

Text 156

o.

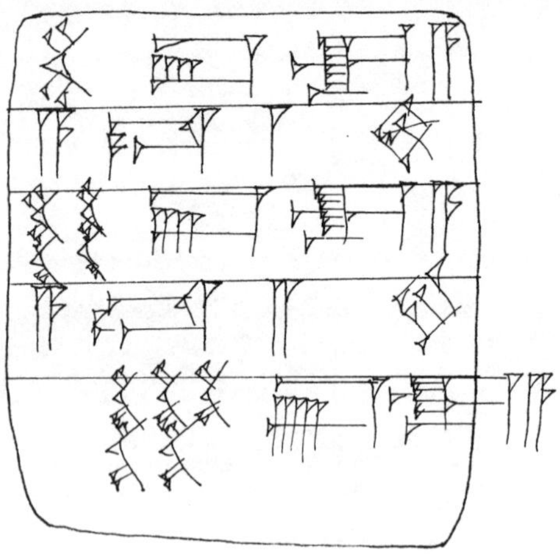

r.

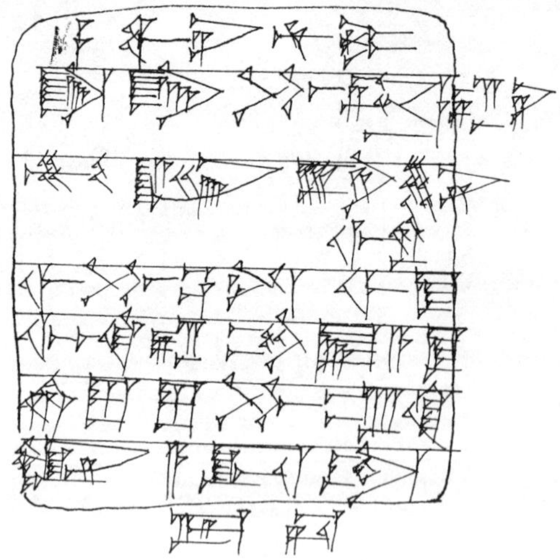

Text 157

o.

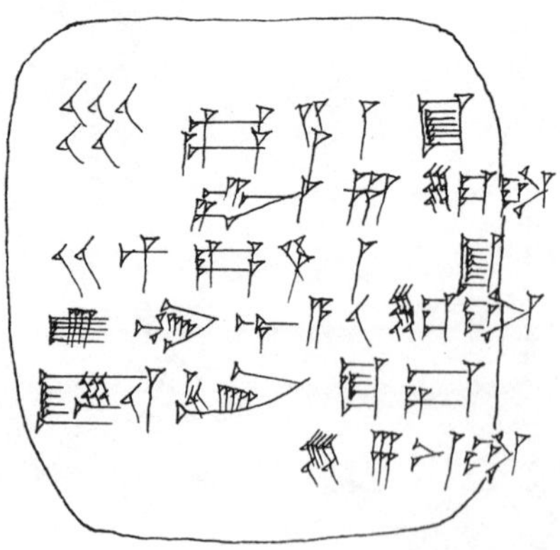

r.

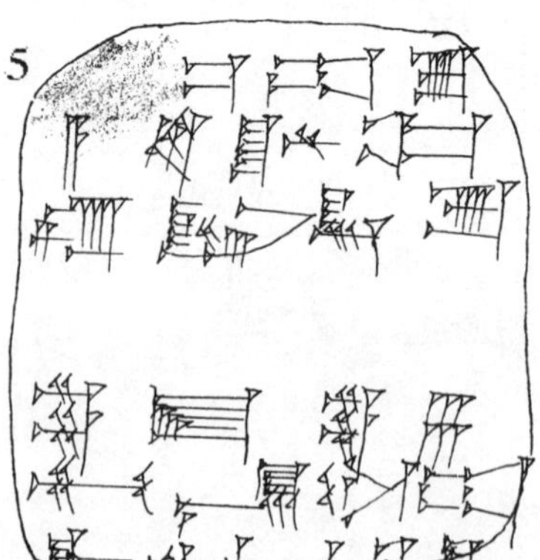

Text 158

o.

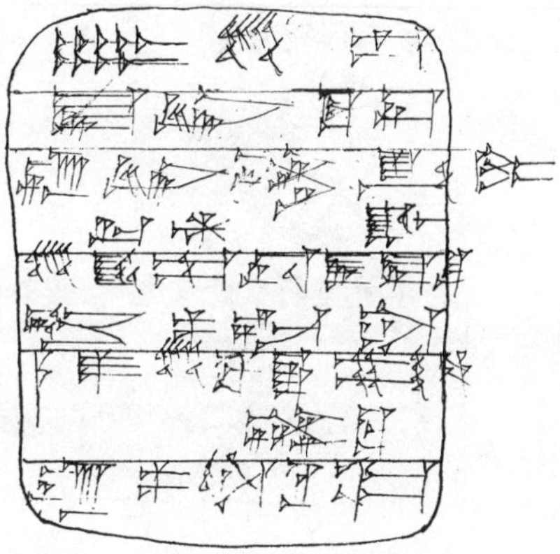

r.

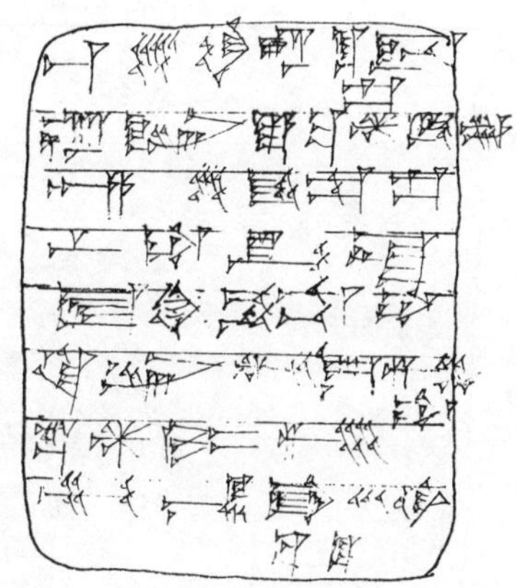

Text 159

o.

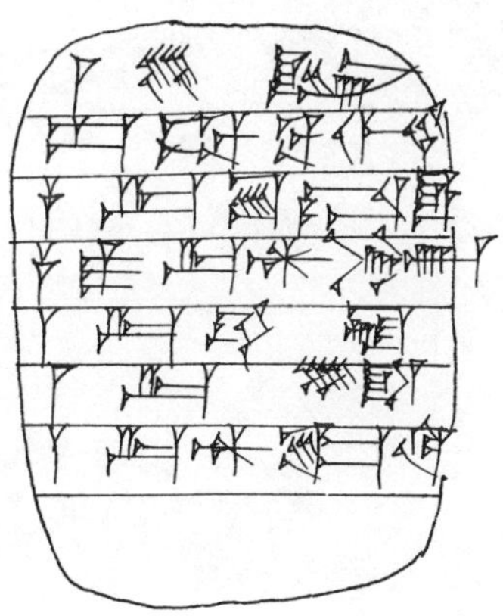

Text 163

o.

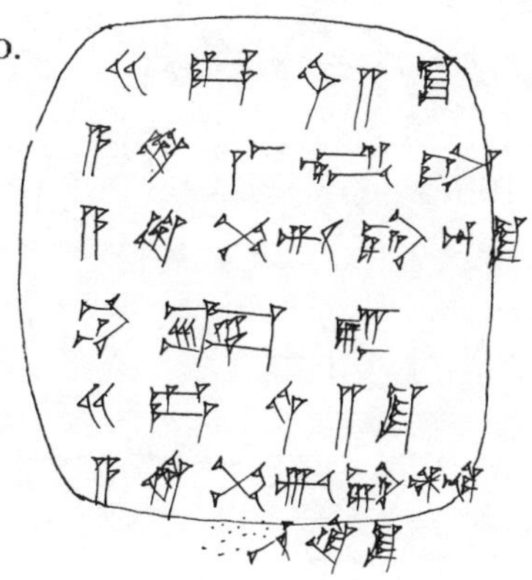

r.

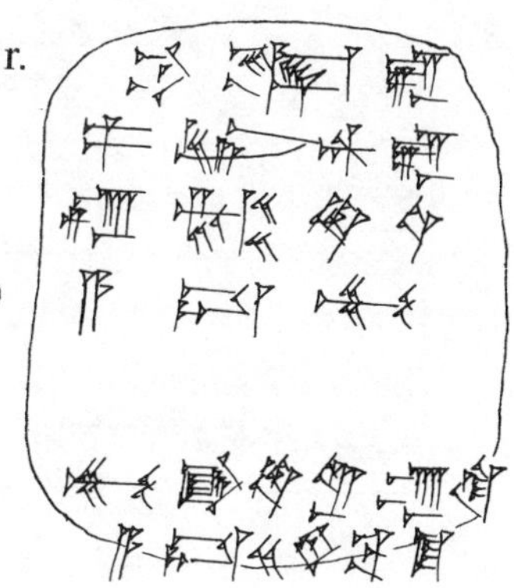

Text 164

o.

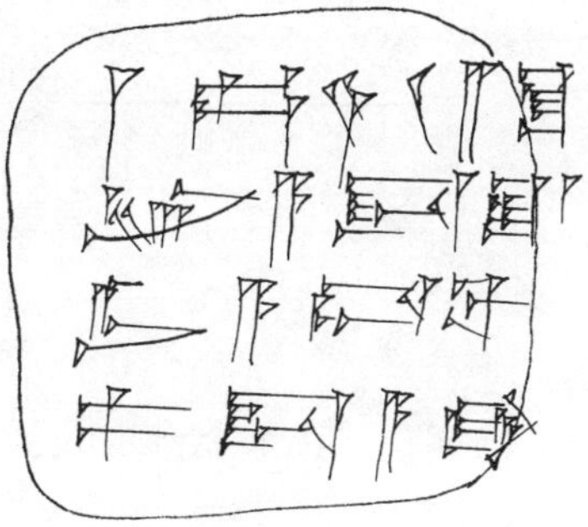

r.

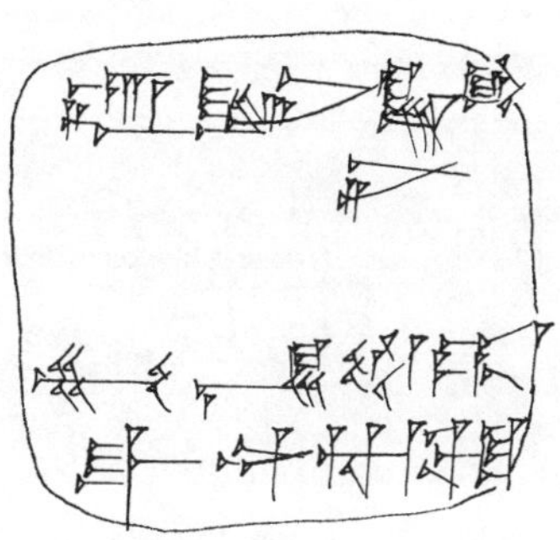

Text 165

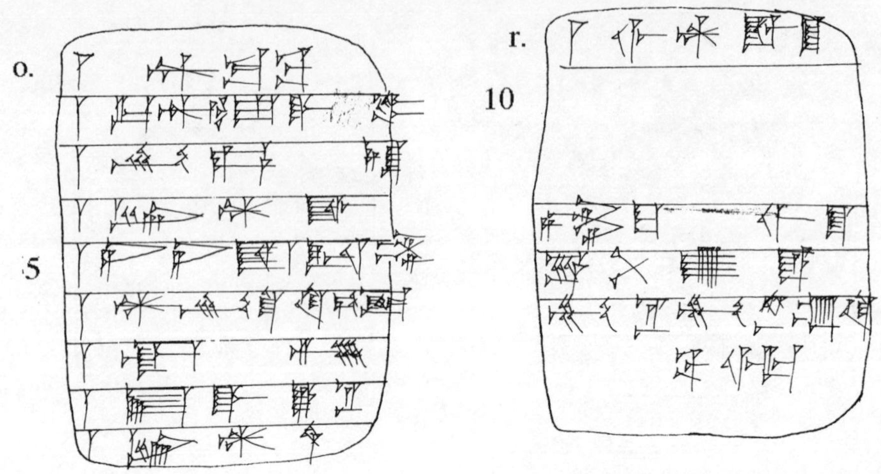

Text 166

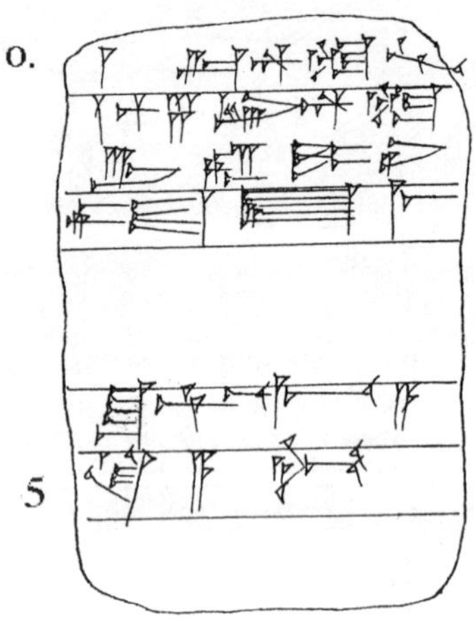

Text 167

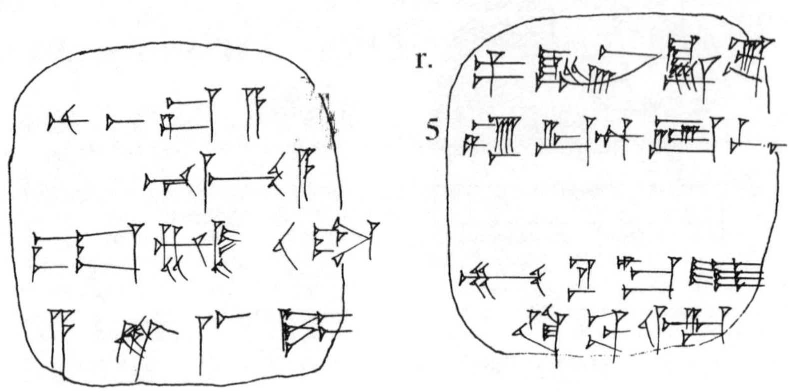

Text 168

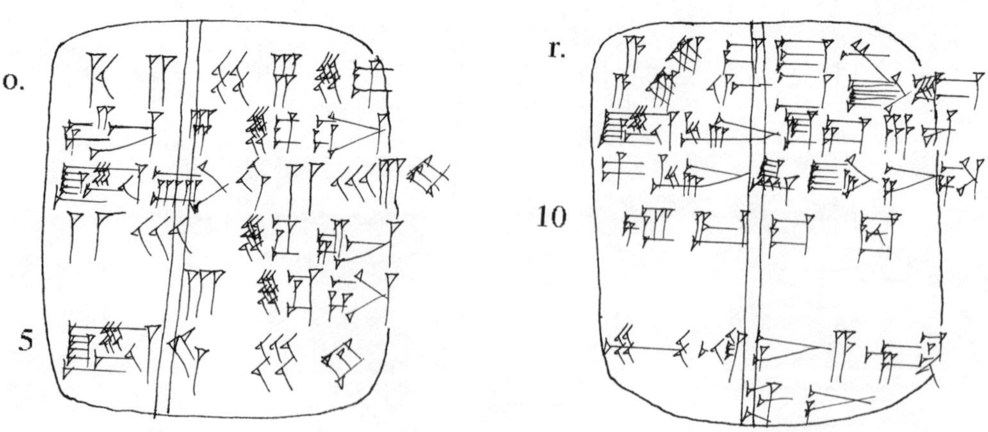

Text 169

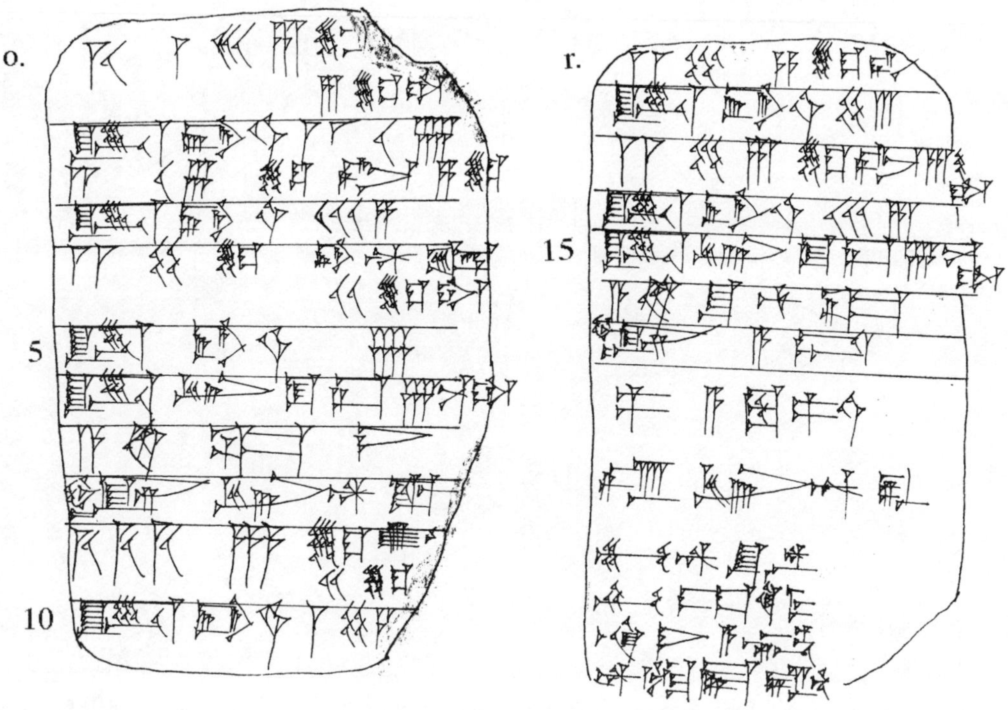

Text 170

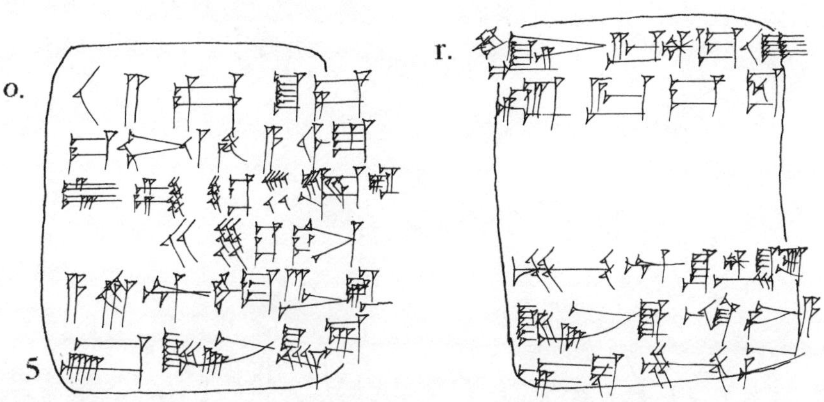

Text 171

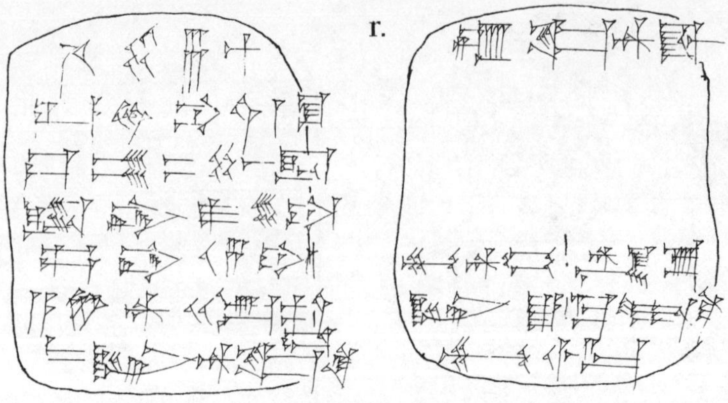

Text 172

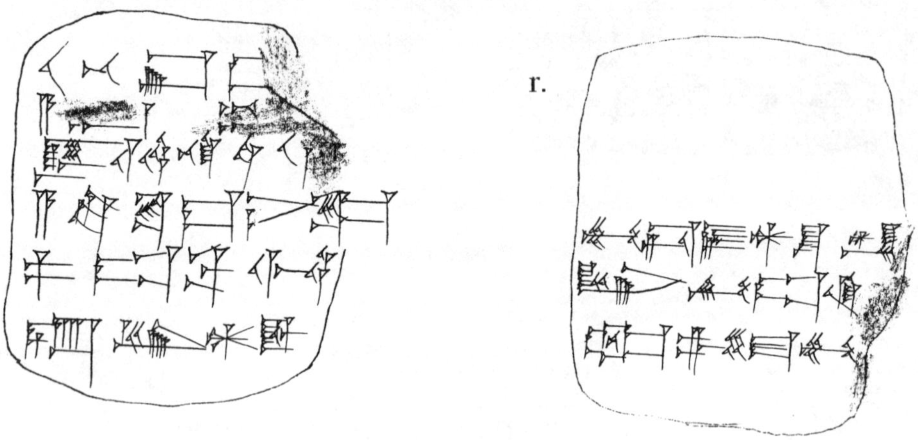

Text 173

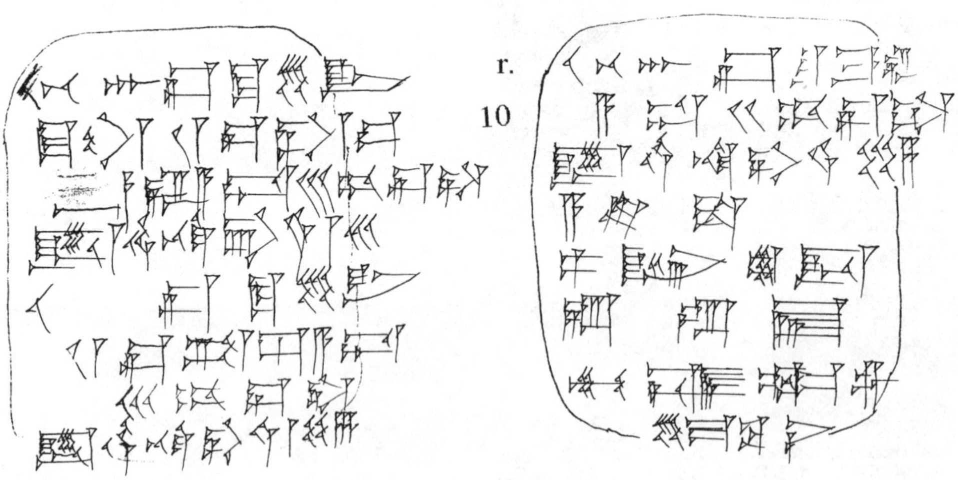

Text 174

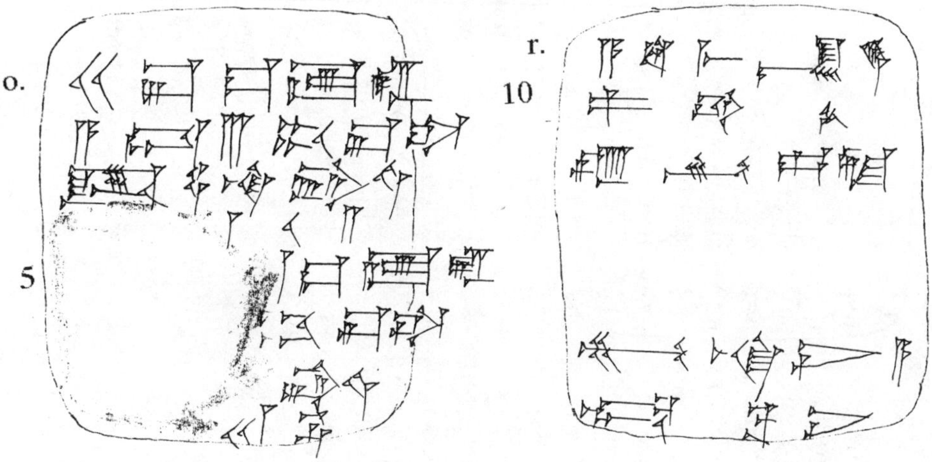

Text 175

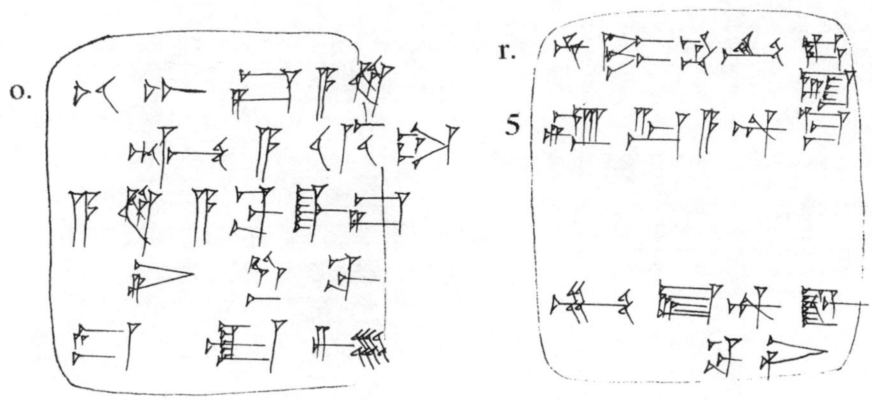

Text 176

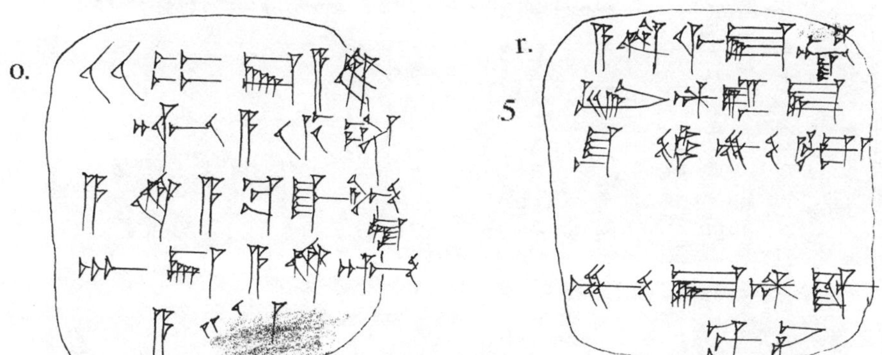

Text 179

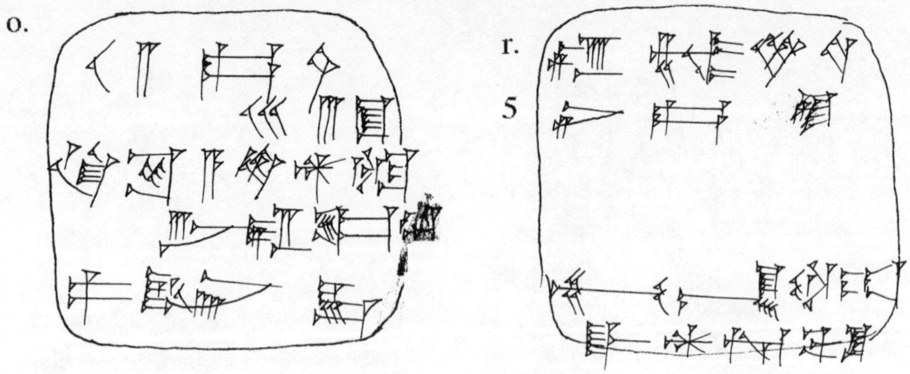

Text 180

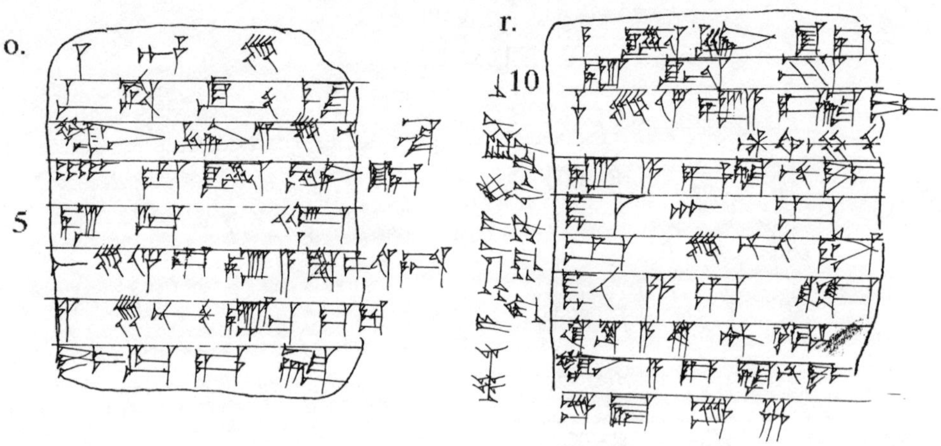

Text 181

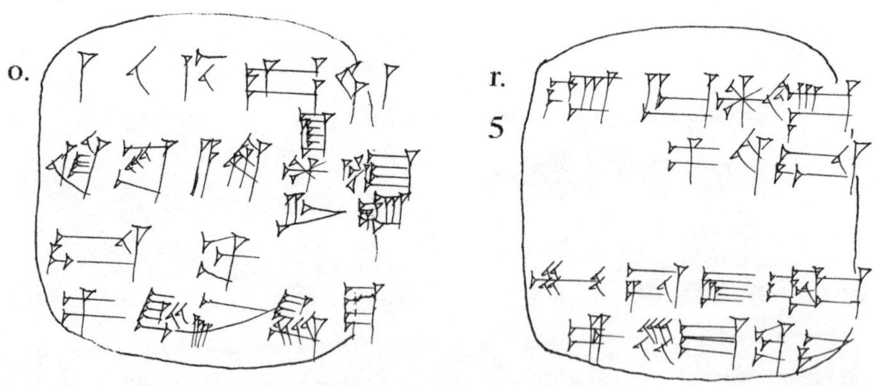

Text 182

o.

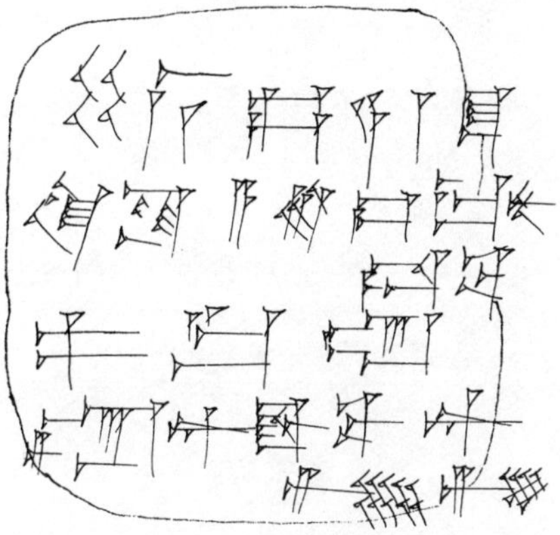

r.

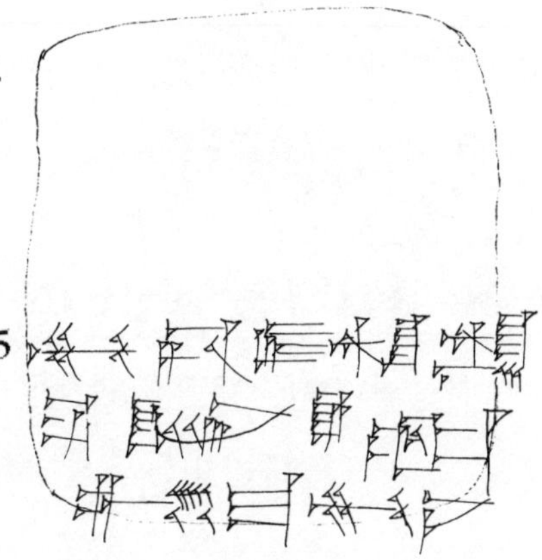

Text 184

o.

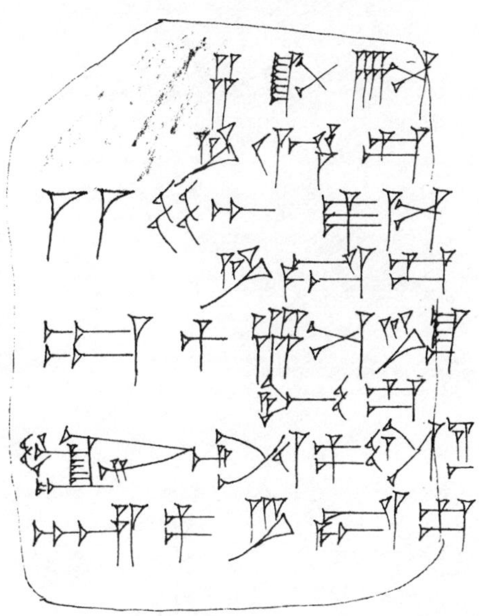

r.

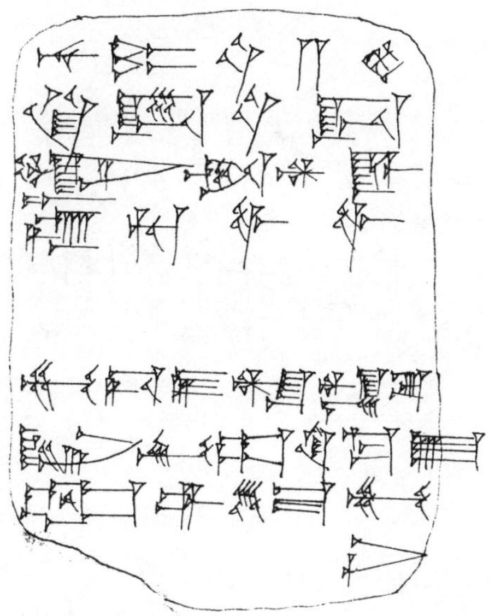

Text 186

o.

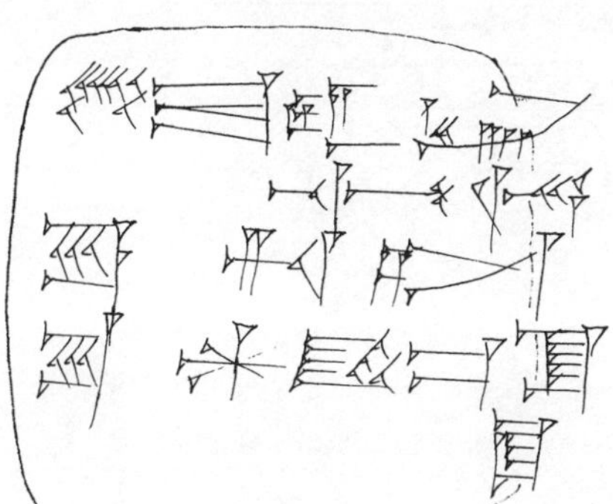

r.

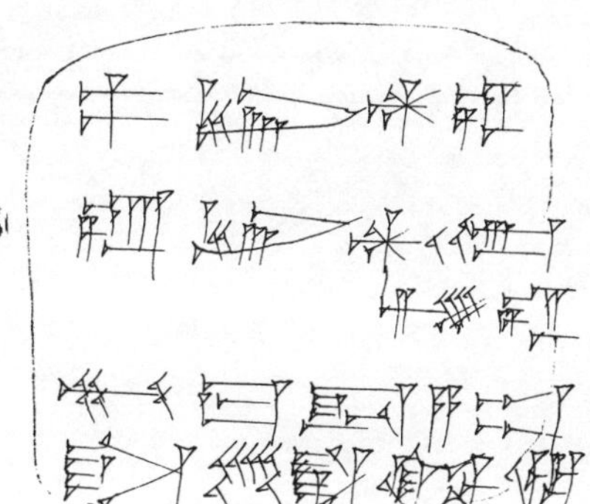

Text 189

o.

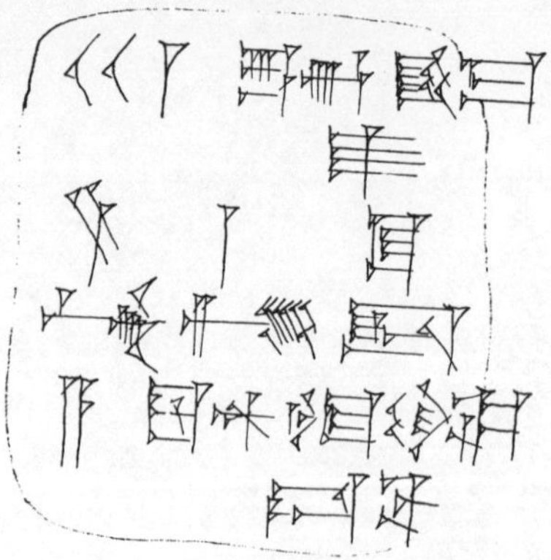

r.

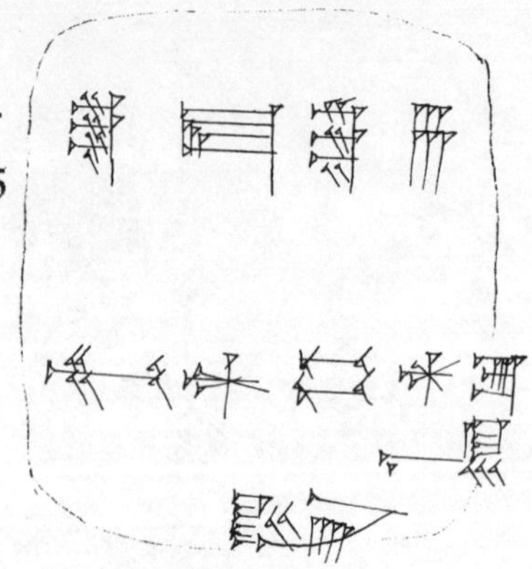

Text 191

o.

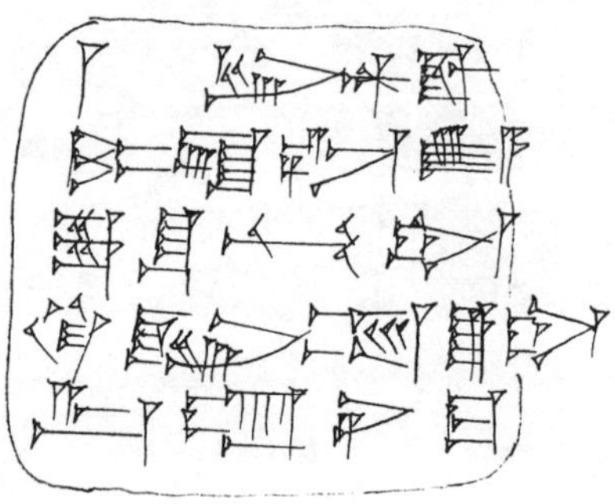

r.

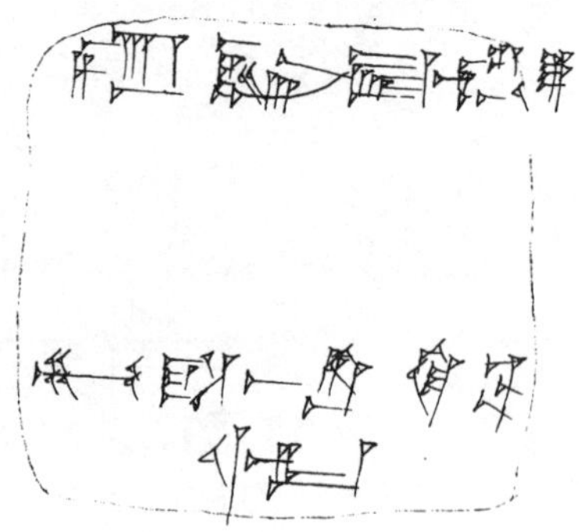

Text 192

o.

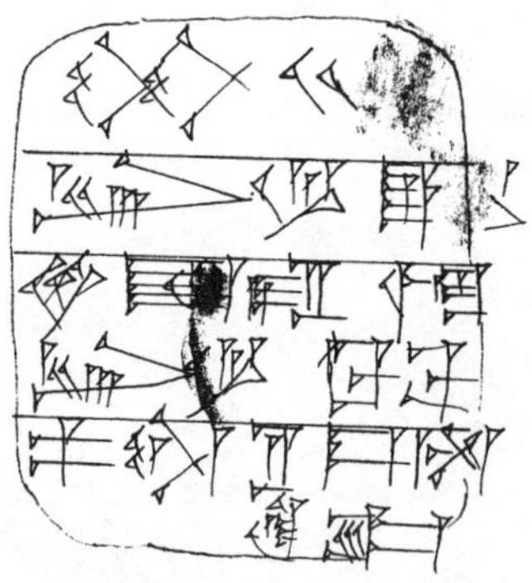

r.

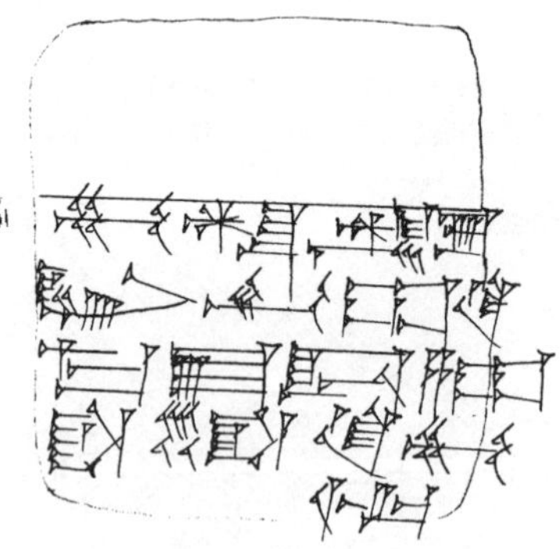

Text 193

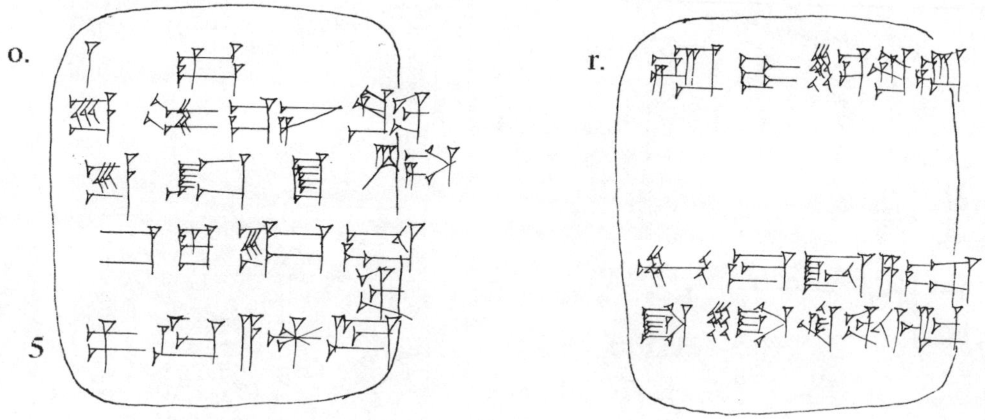

Text 194

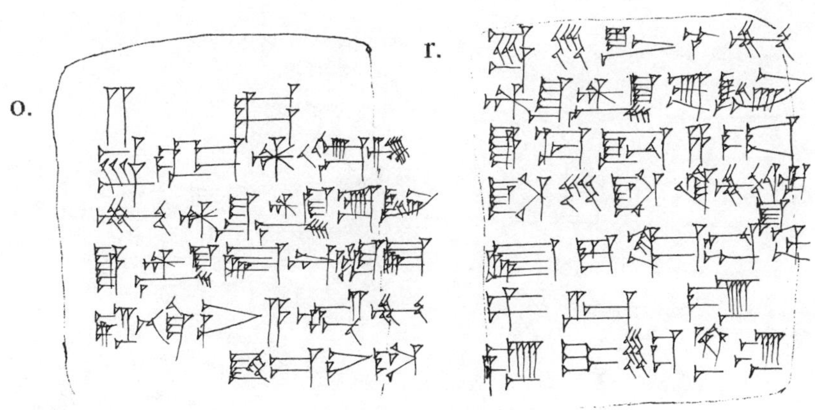

Text 196

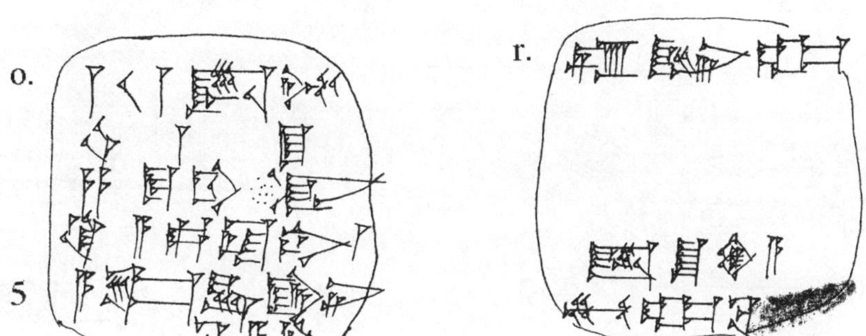

Text 197

o.

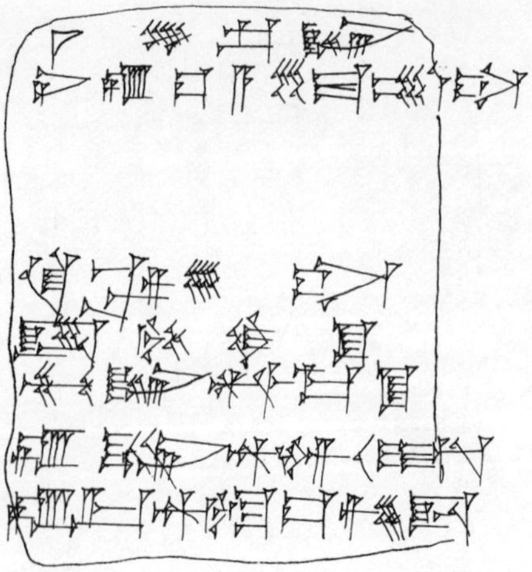

r.

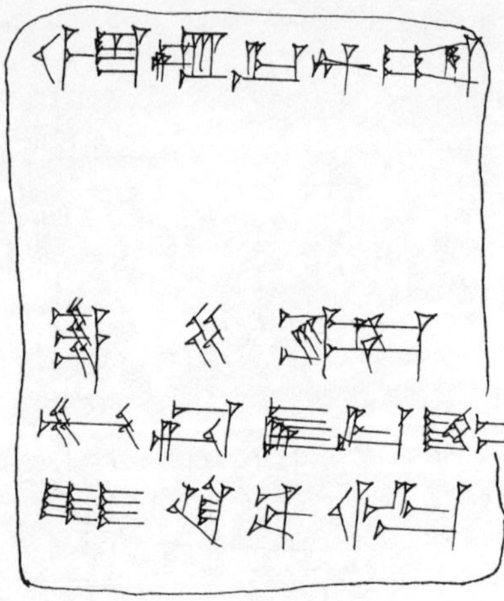

Text 198

o.

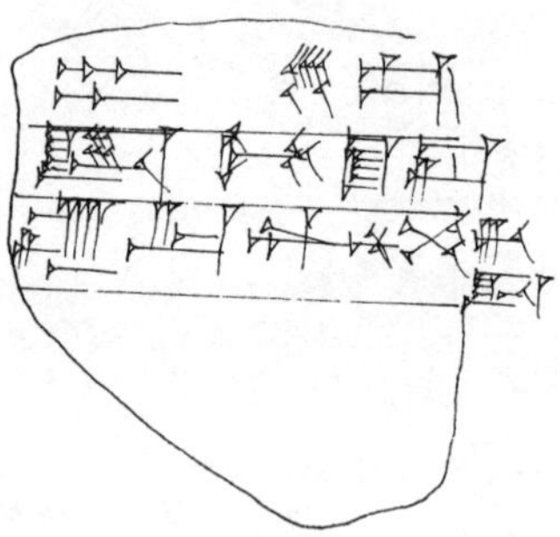

r.

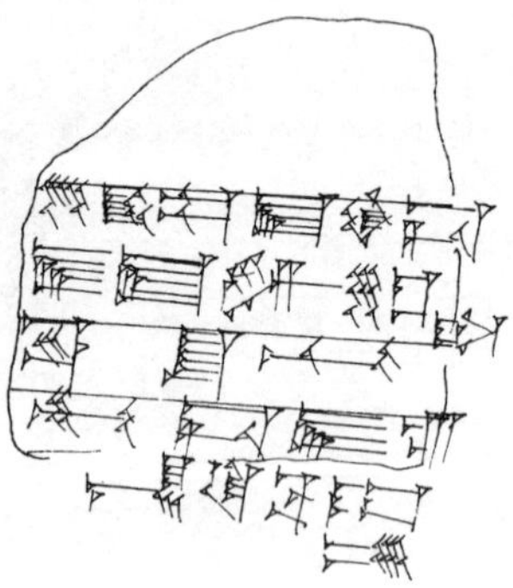

Text 199

o.

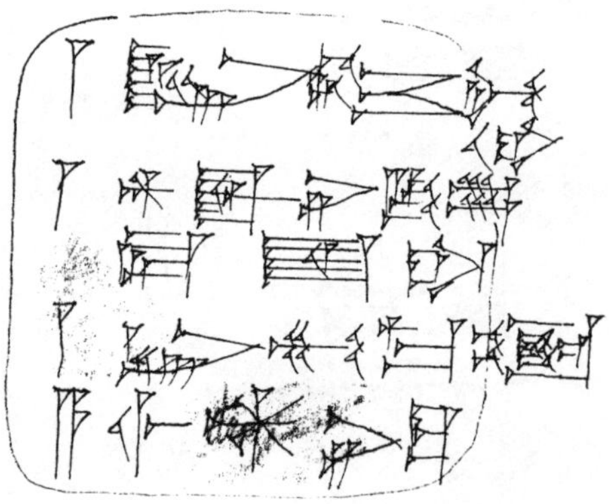

r.

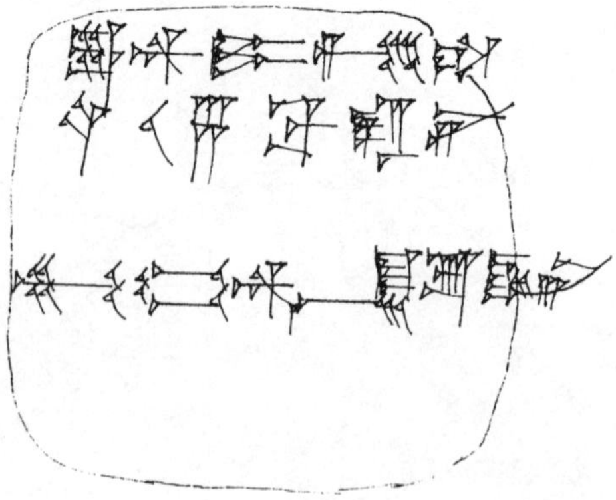

Text 201

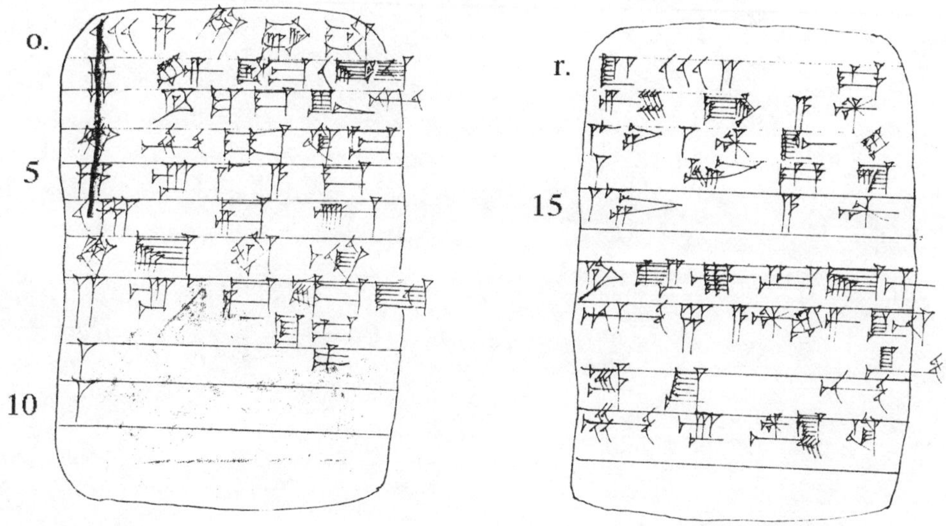

Text 206

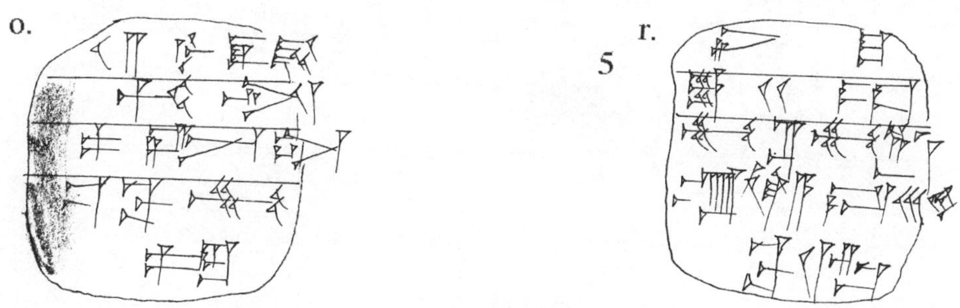

Text 208

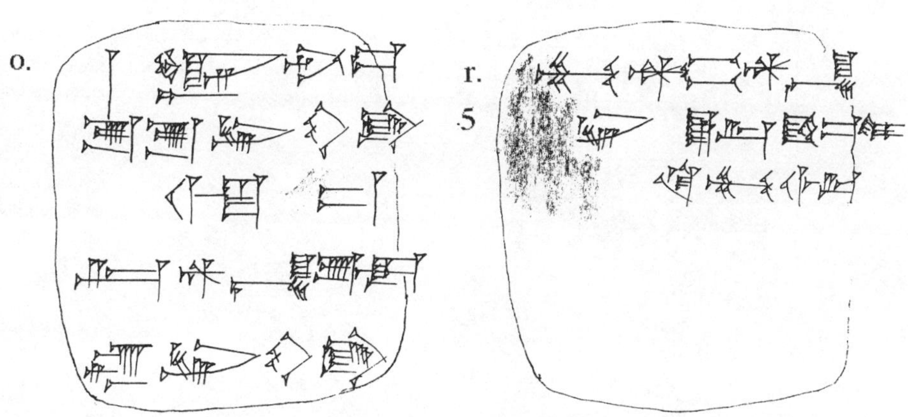

Text 209

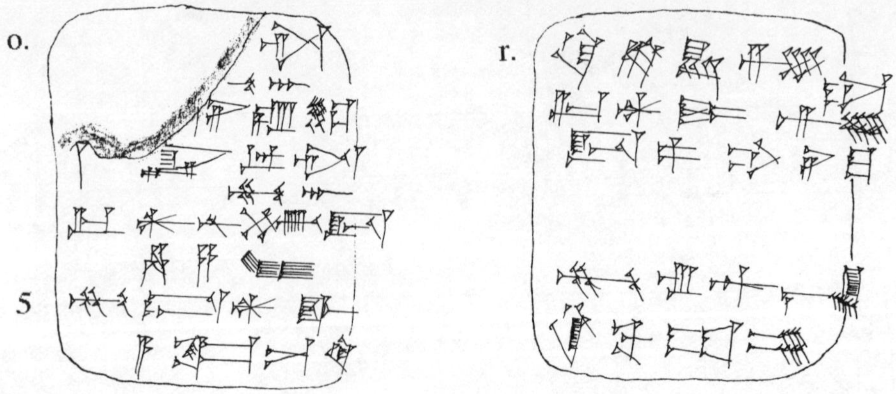

Text 210

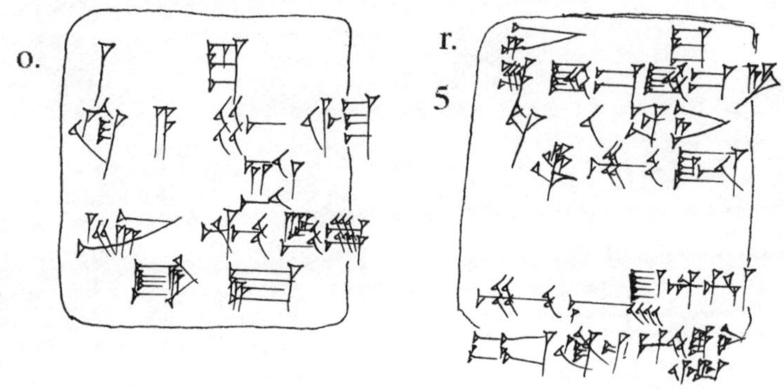

Text 211

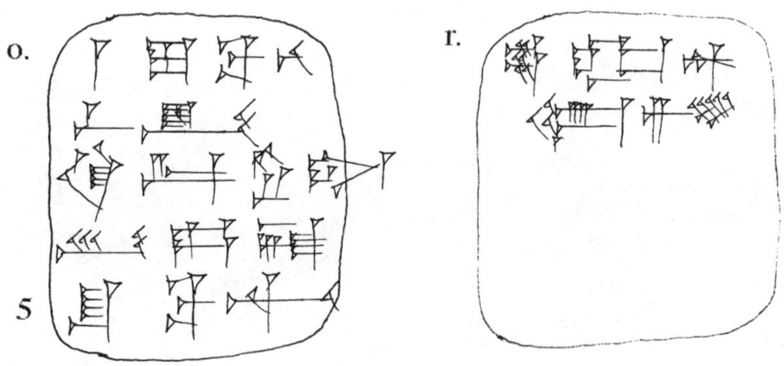

Text 215

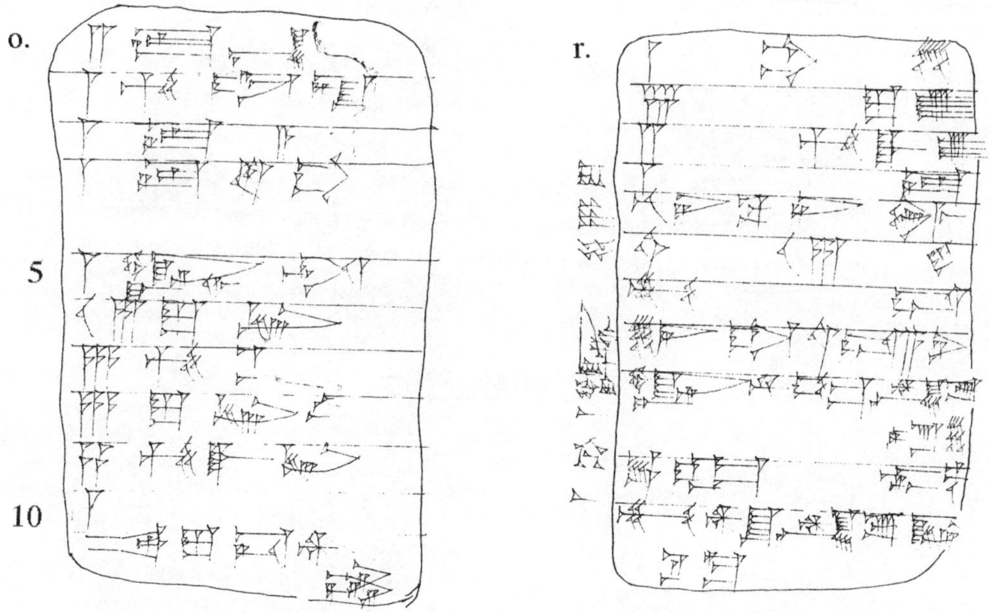

Text 219

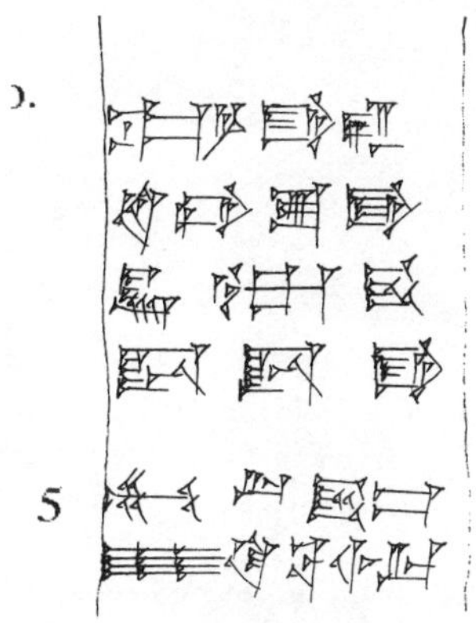

Text 222

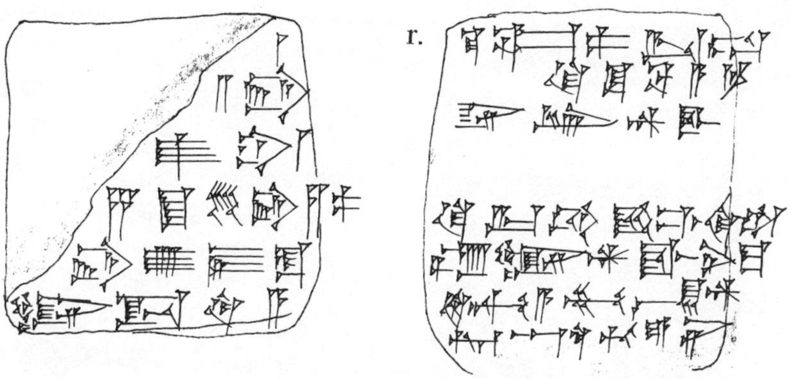

Text 223

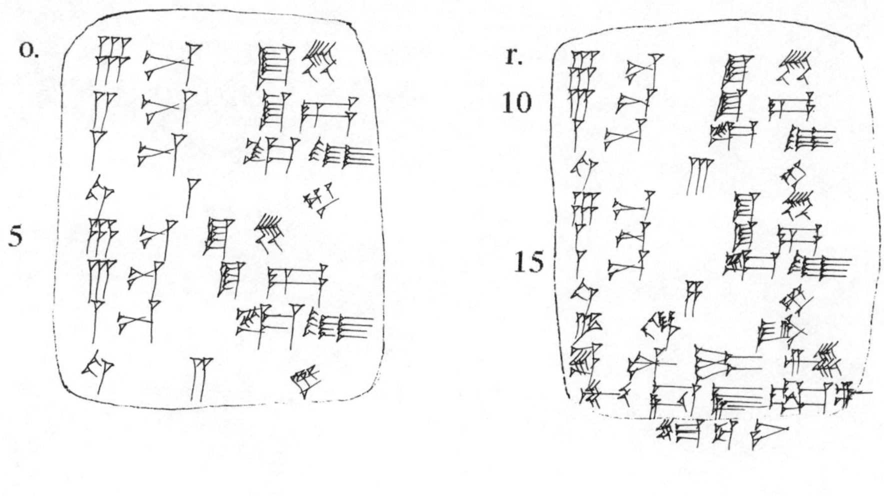

Text 224

o.

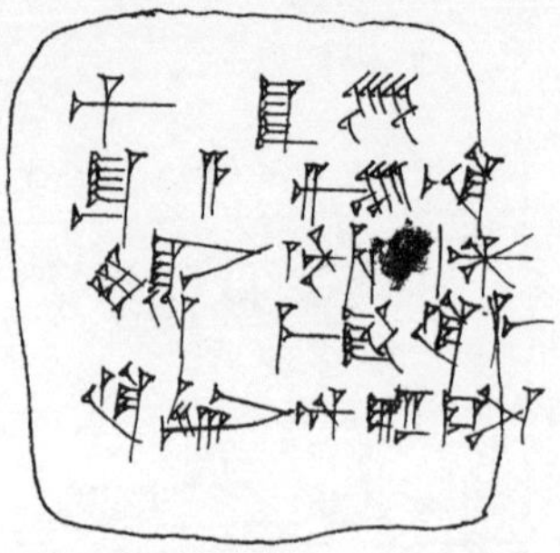

r.

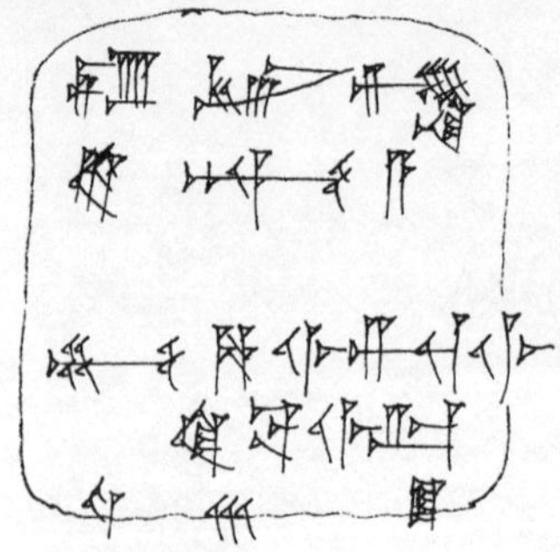

Text 225

o.

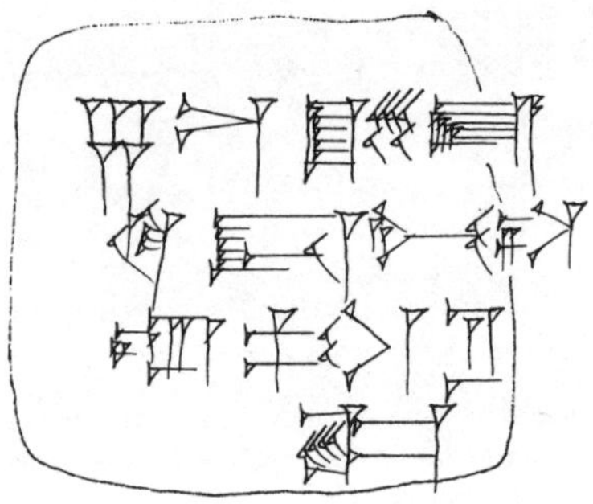

r.

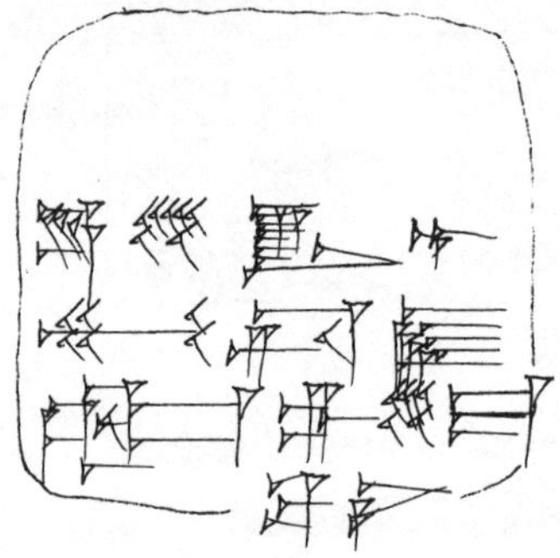

Text 226

o.

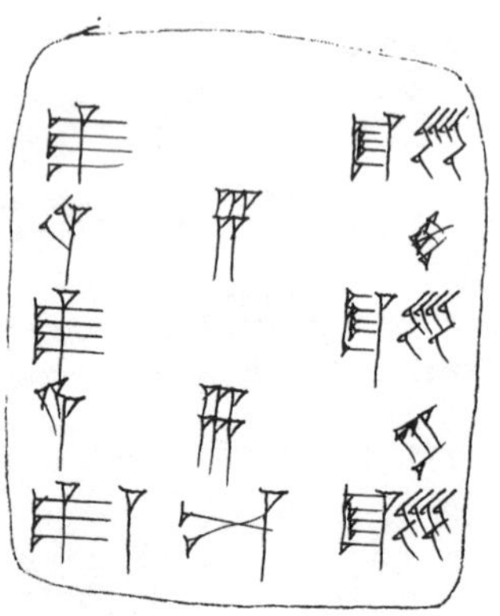

r.

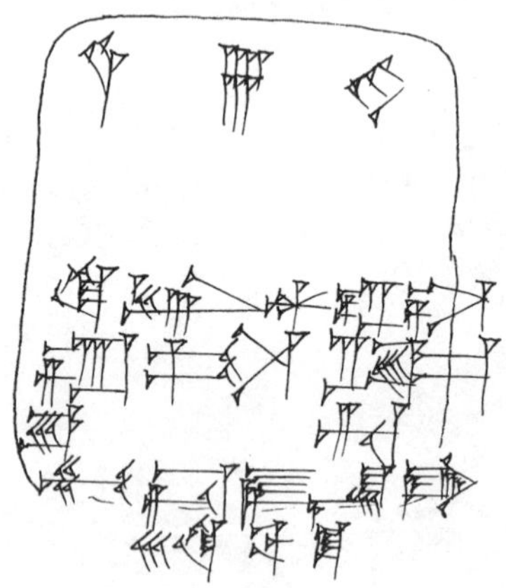

Text 227

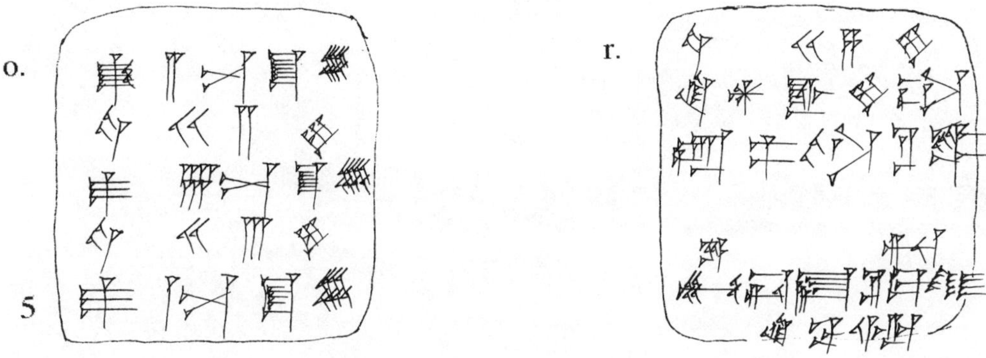

Text 228

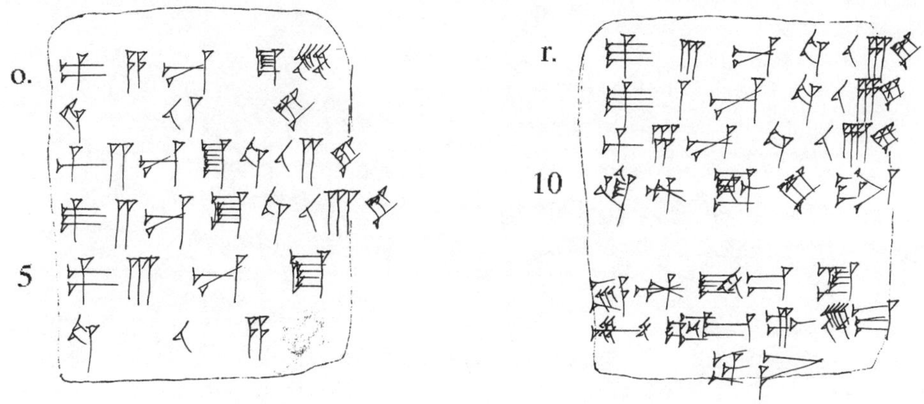

Text 229

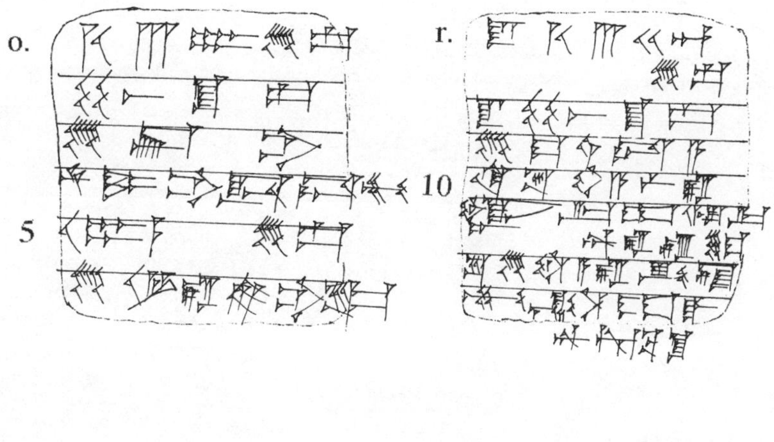

Text 233

o.

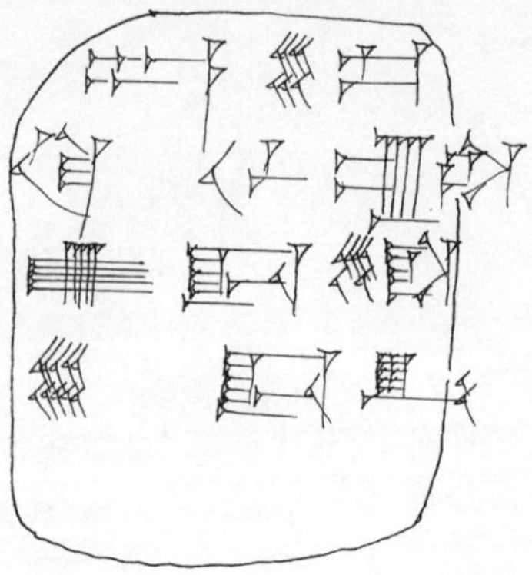

Text 235

o.

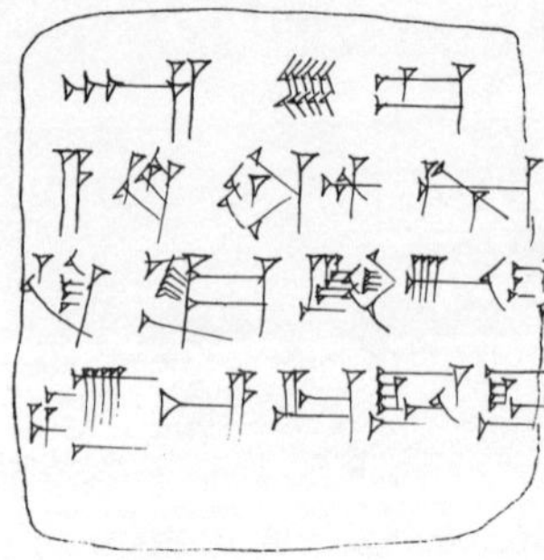

r.

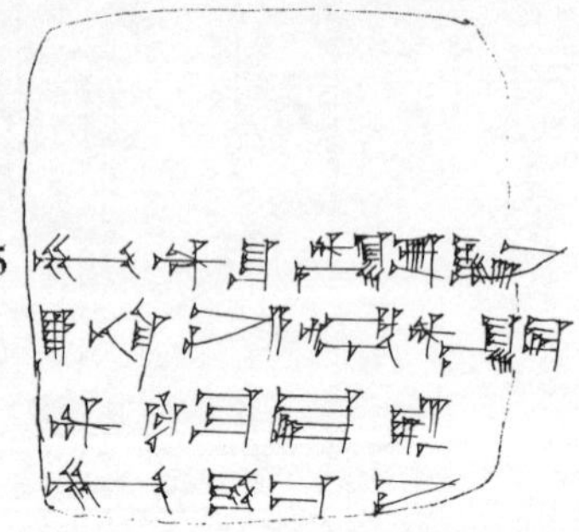

Text 236

o.

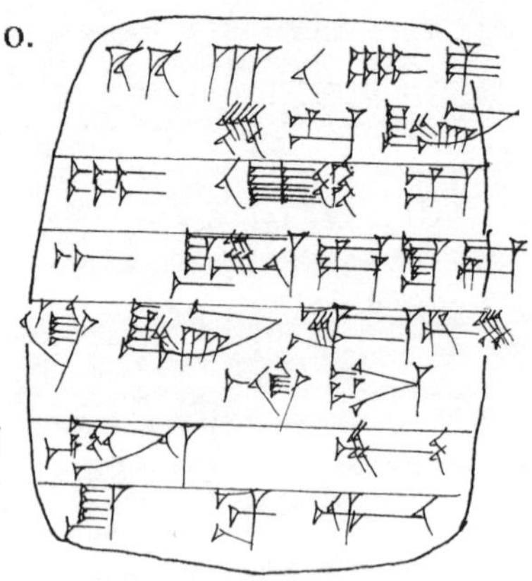

r.

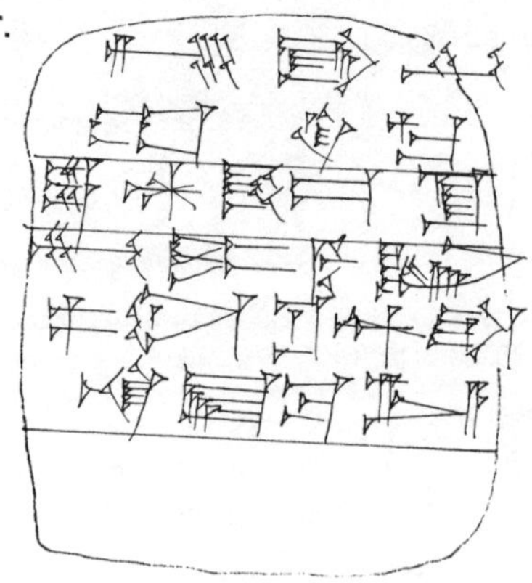

Text 237

o.

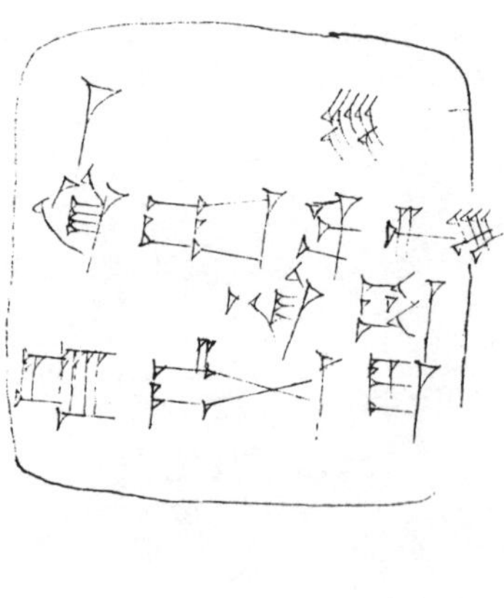

r.

Text 238

o. r.

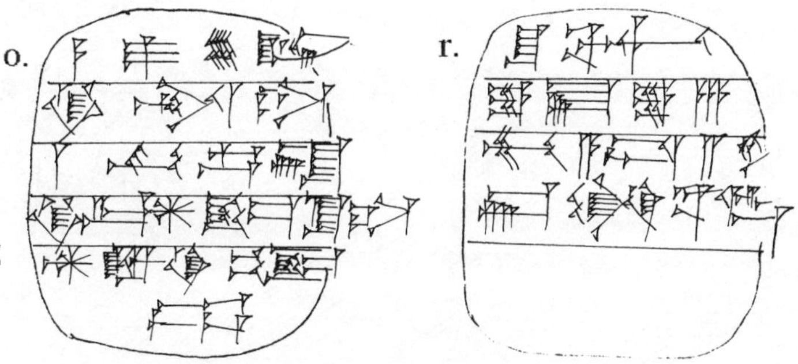

Text 239

o. r.

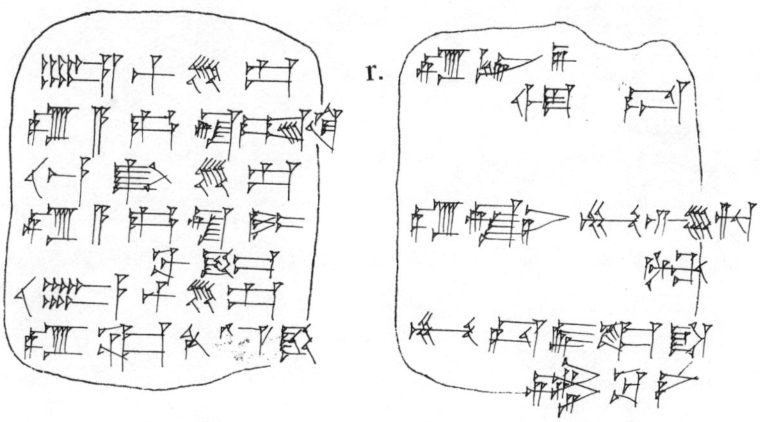

Text 240

o. r.

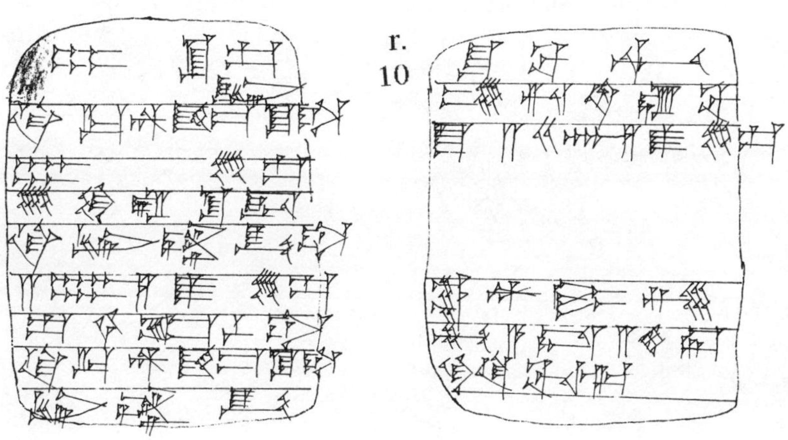

Text 241

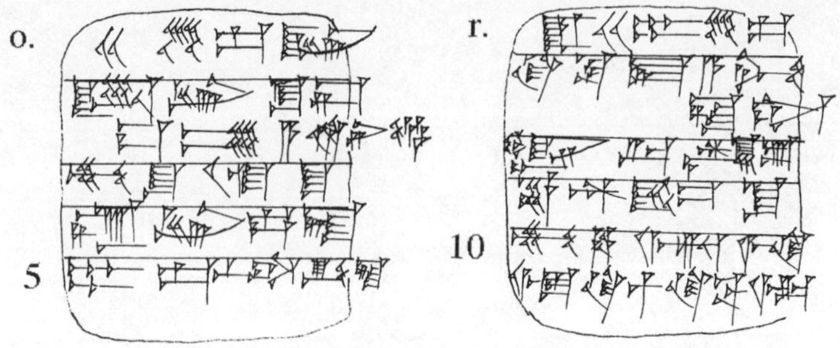

Text 245

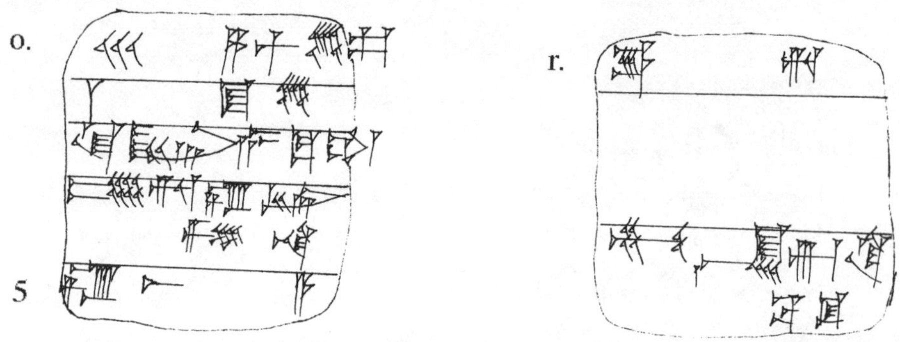

Text 246

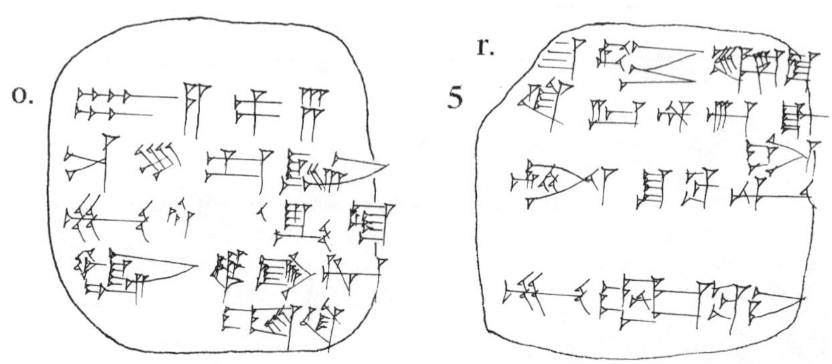

Text 247

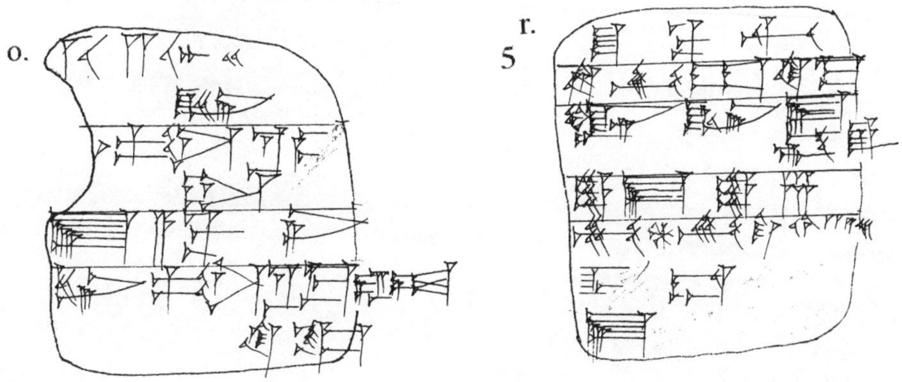

Text 249

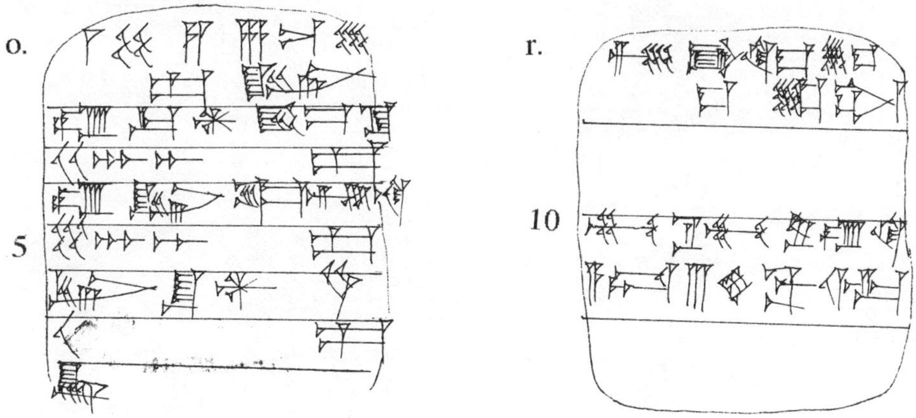

Text 250

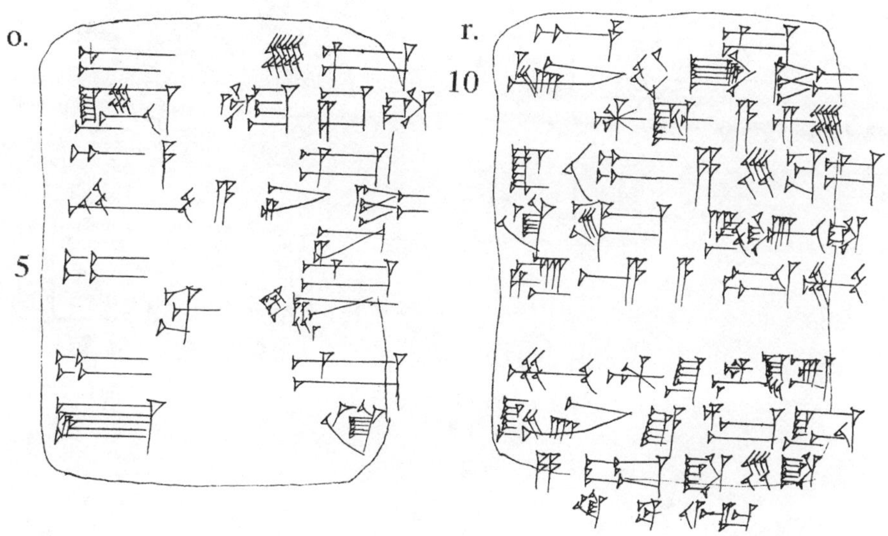

Text 254

o.

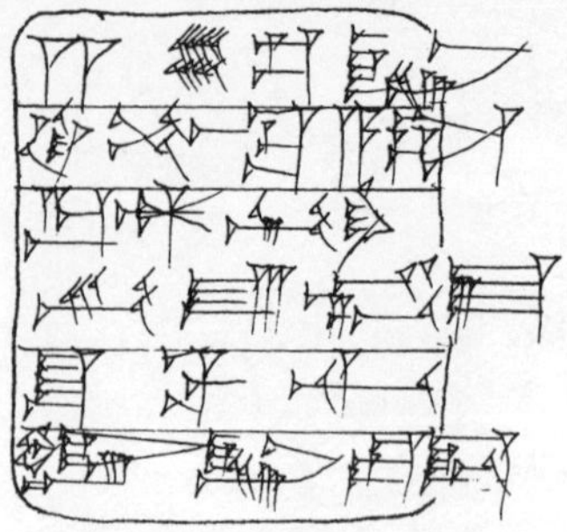

r.

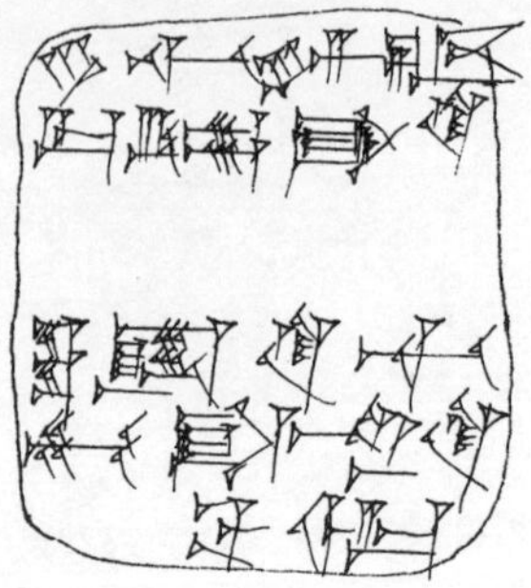

Text 255

o.

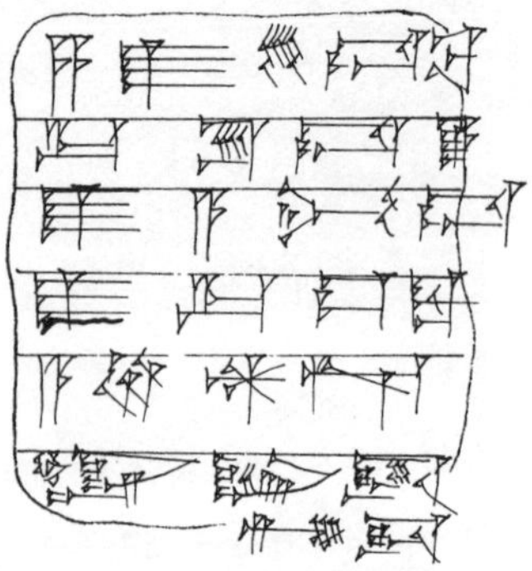

r.

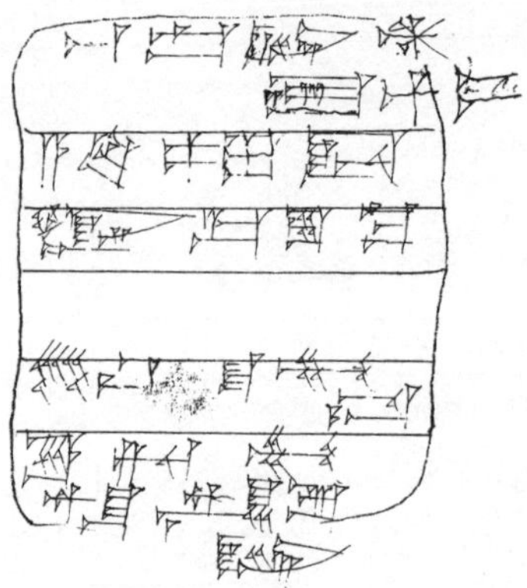

Text 256

o.

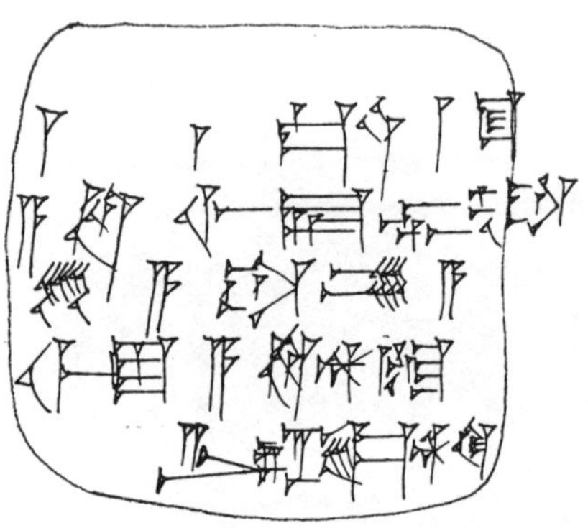

r.

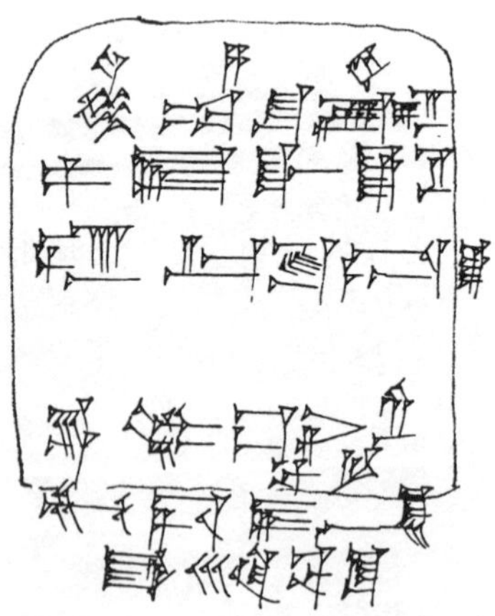

Text 258

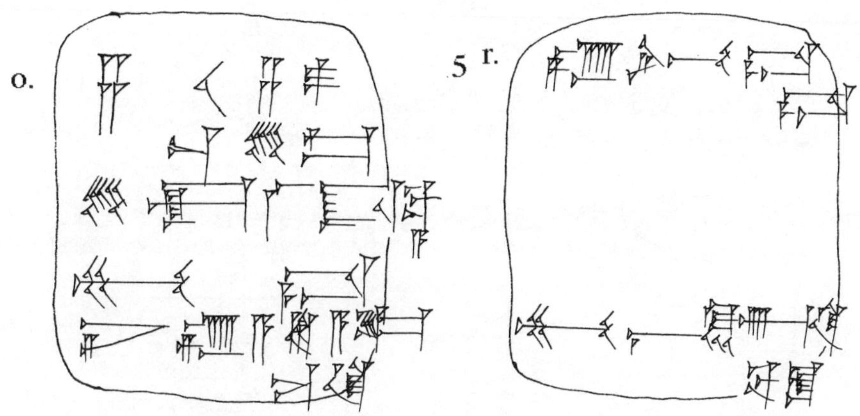

Text 263

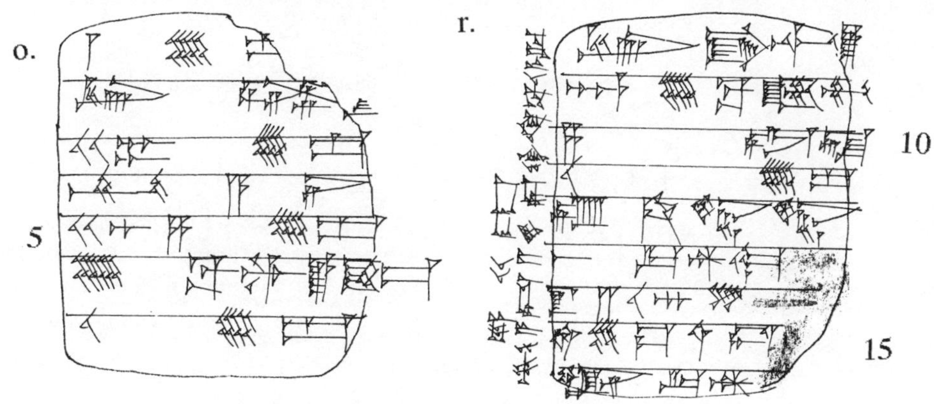

Text 267

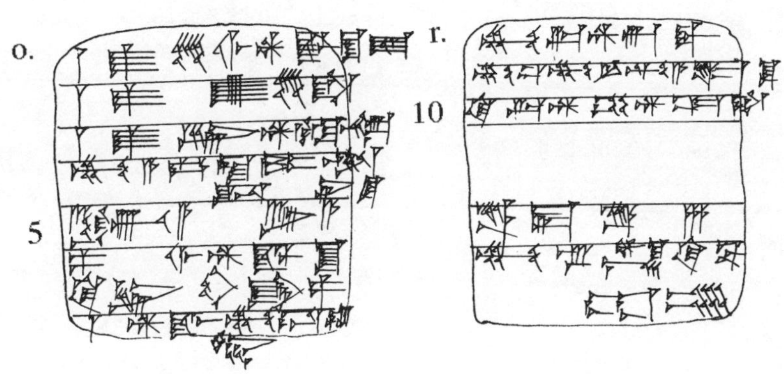

Text 268

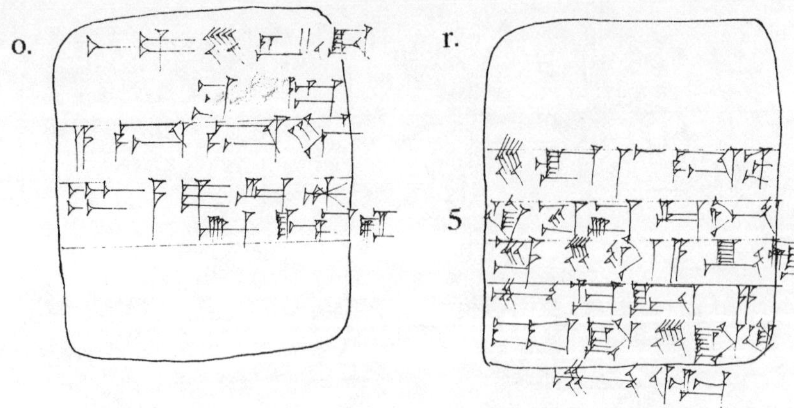

Text 269

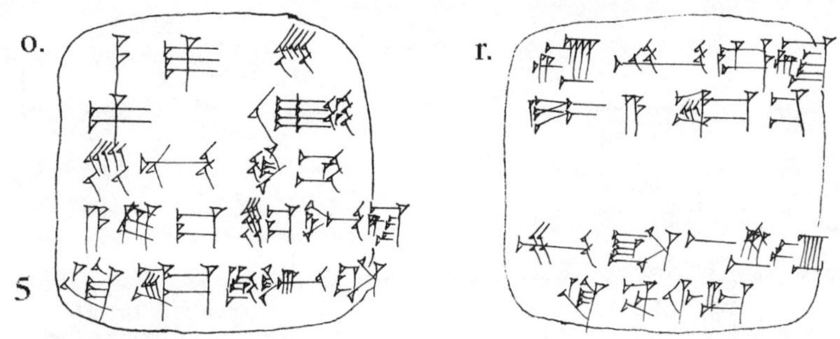

Text 271

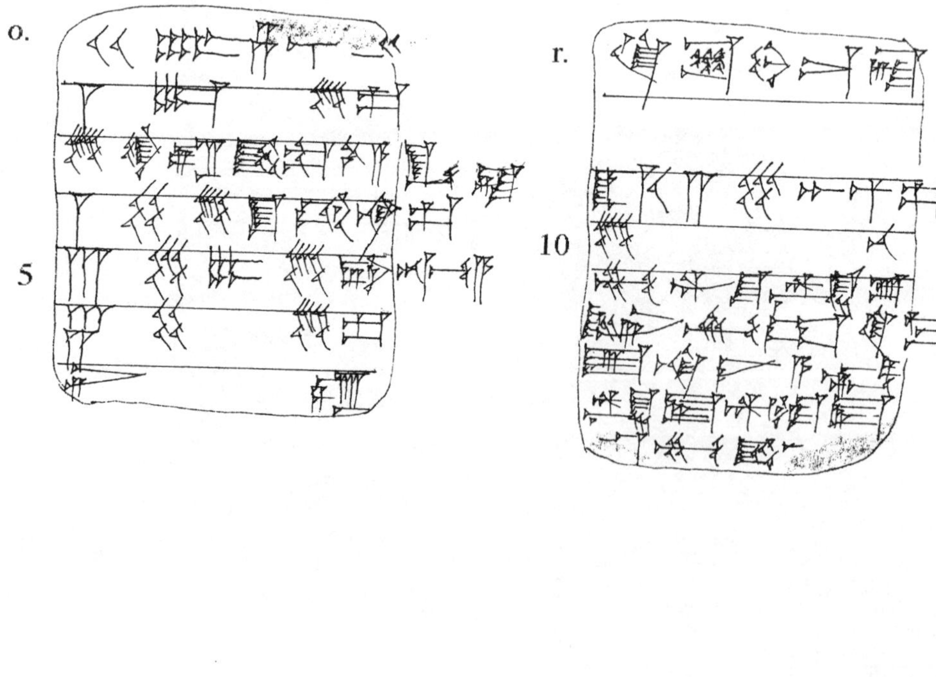

Text 272

o.

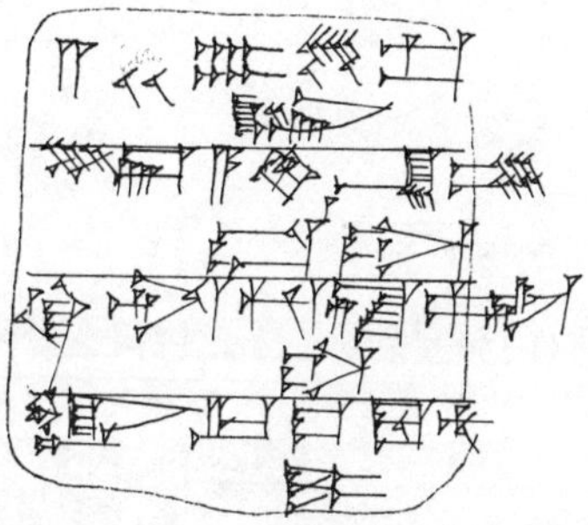

r.

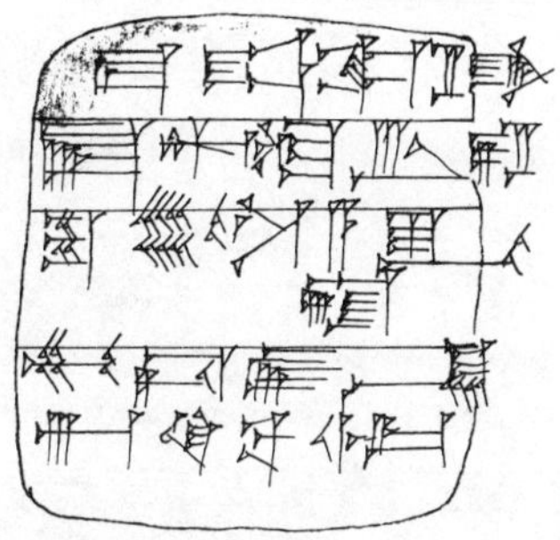

Text 274

o.

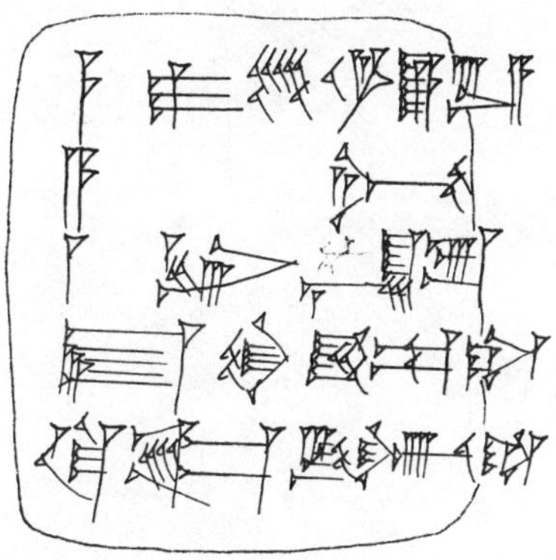

r.

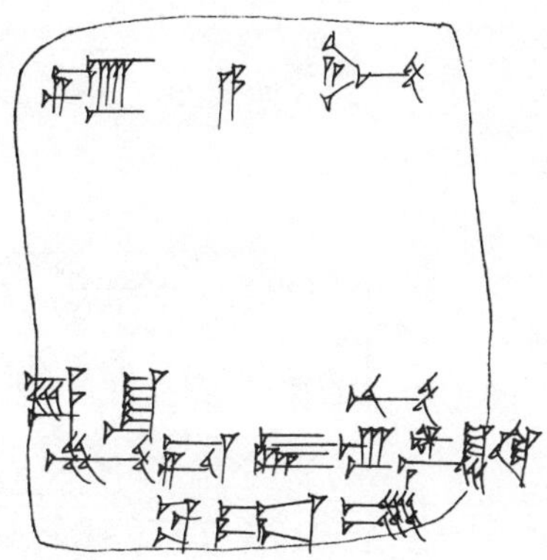

Text 275

o.

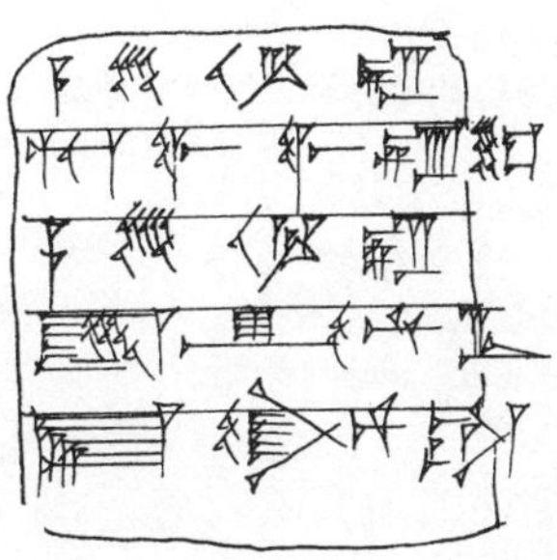

r.

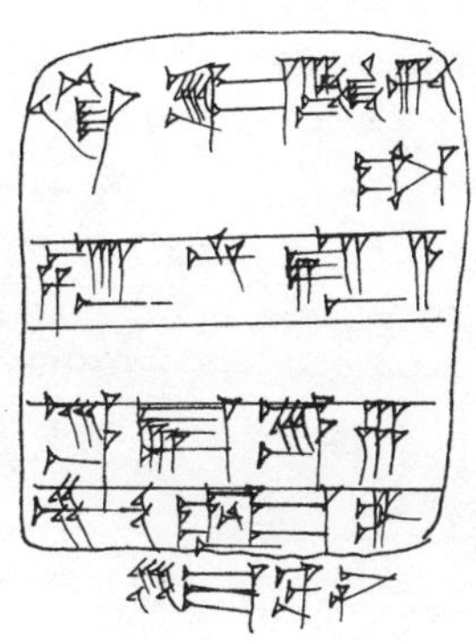

Text 277

o.

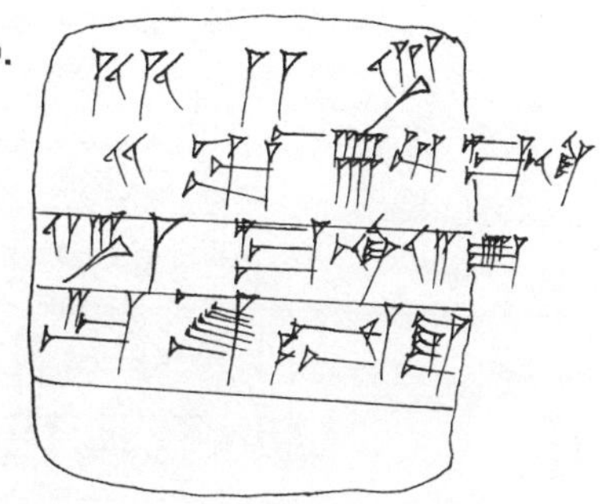

Text 278

o.

r.

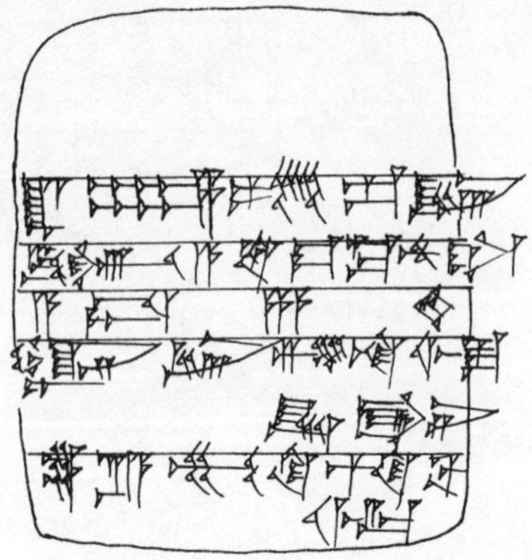

Text 279

o.

r.

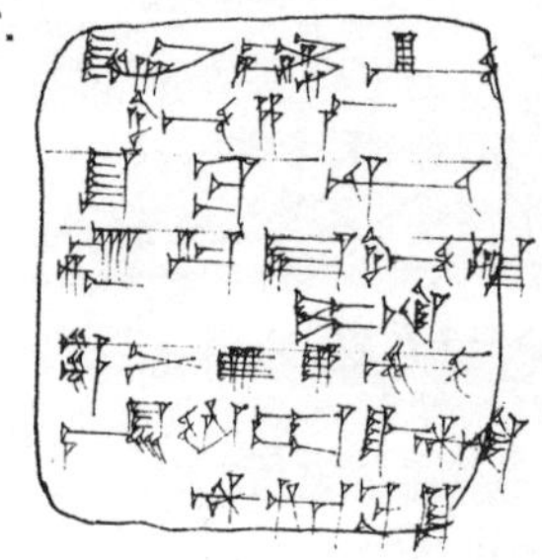

Text 282

o.

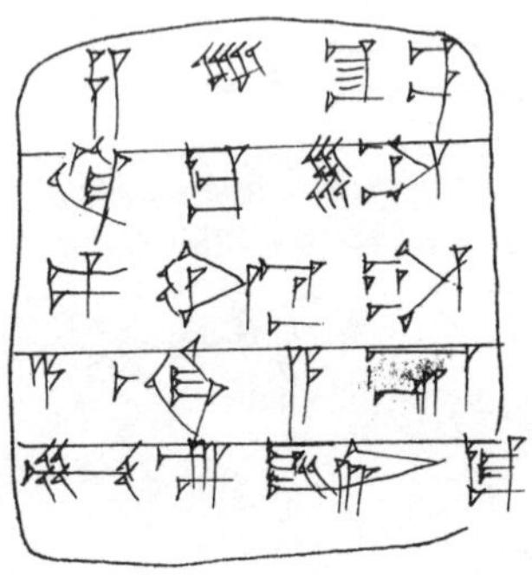

r.

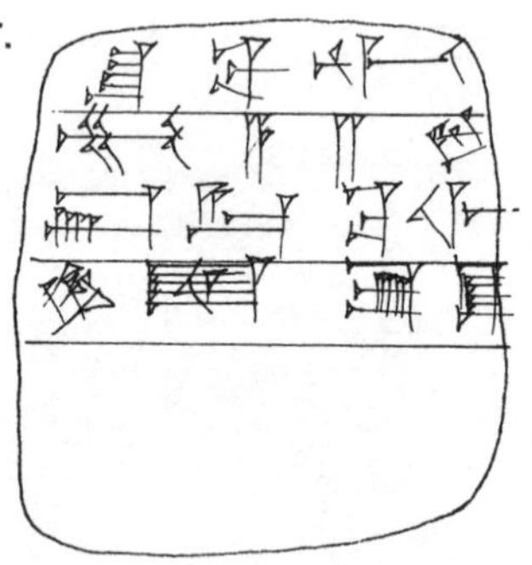

Text 283

o.

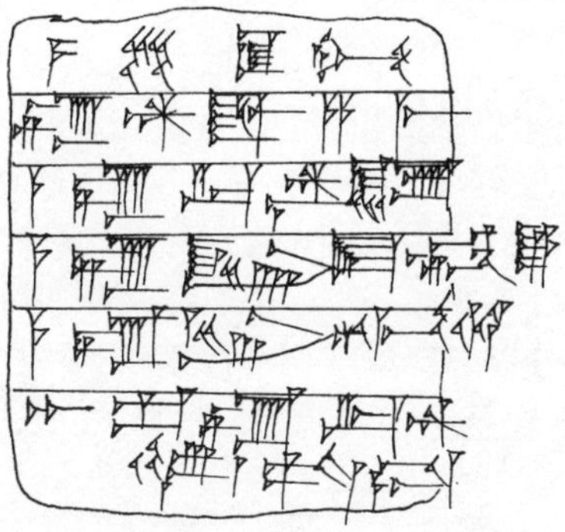

r.

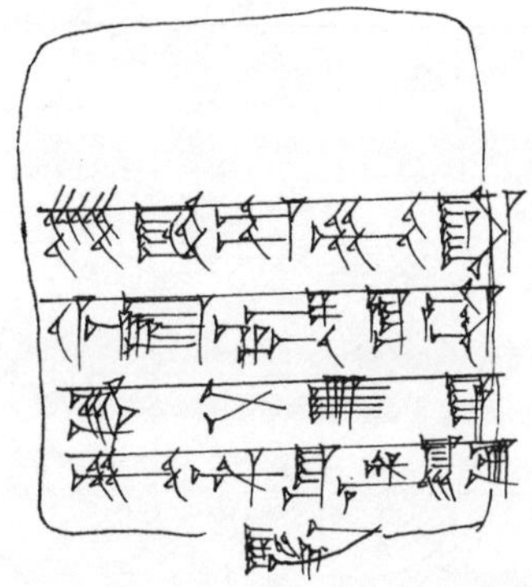

Text 288

o.

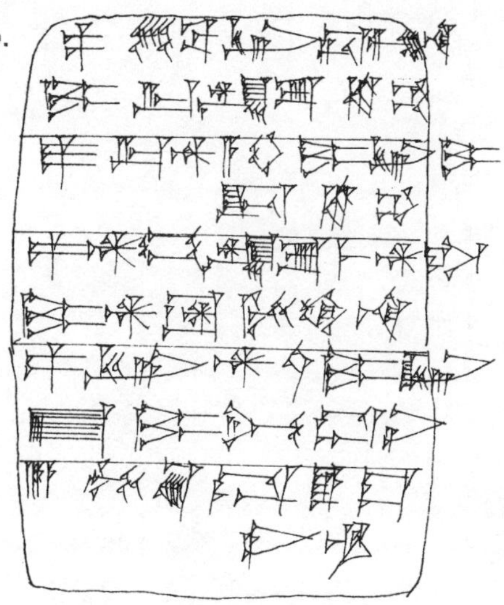

r.

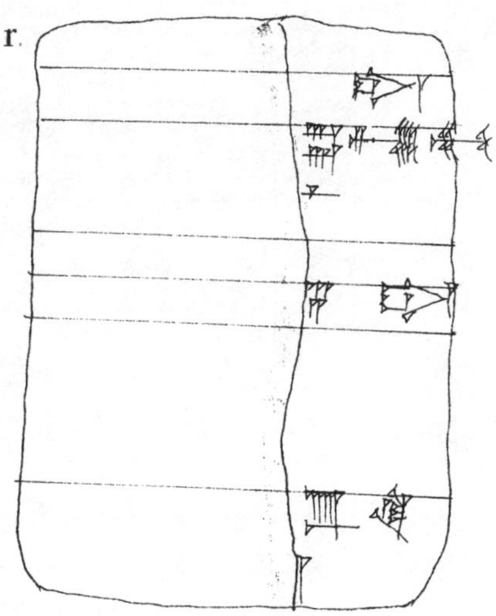

Text 289

o.

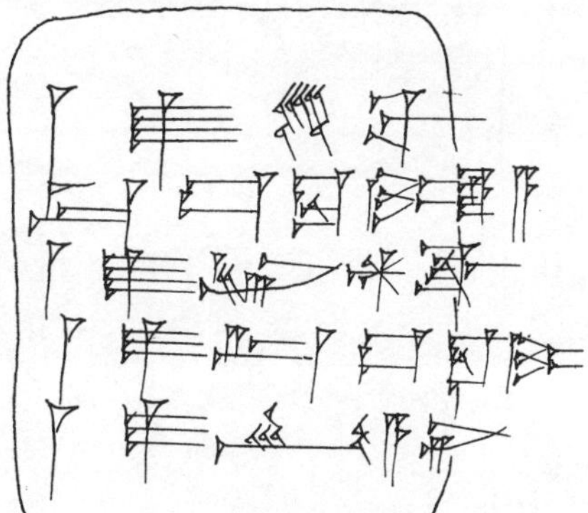

r.

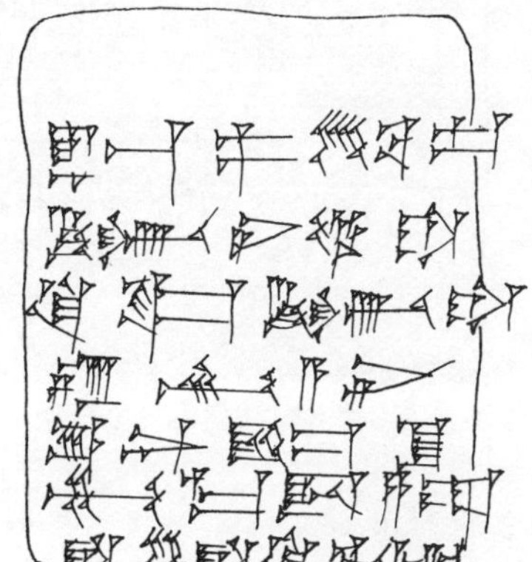

Text 290

o.

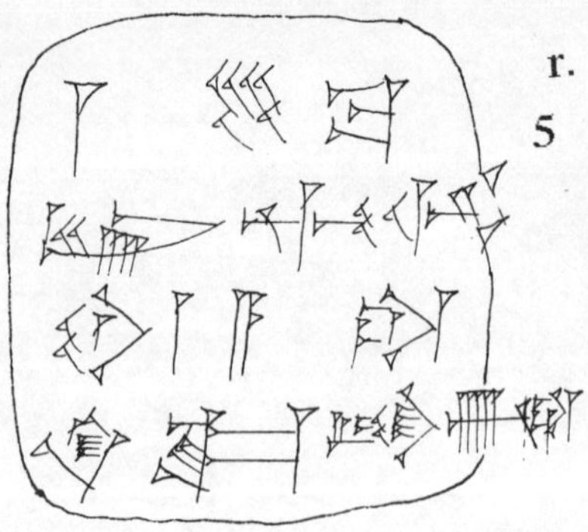

r.

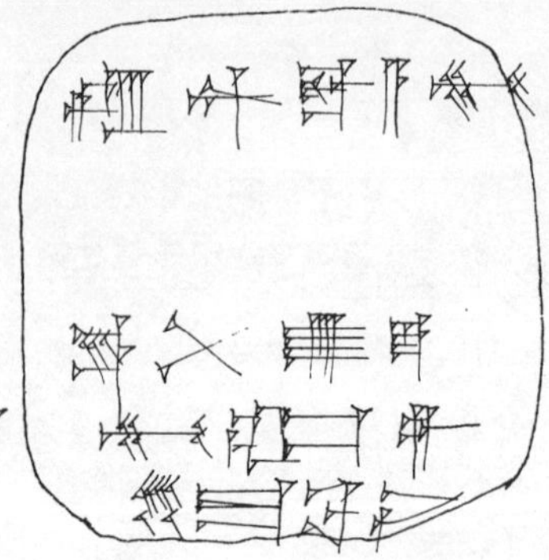

Text 291

o.

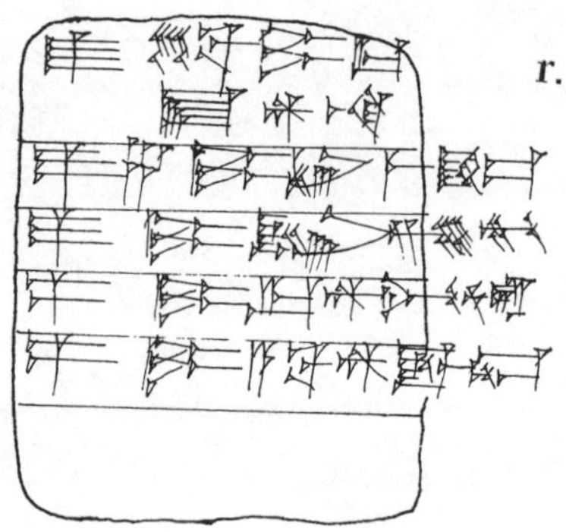

r.

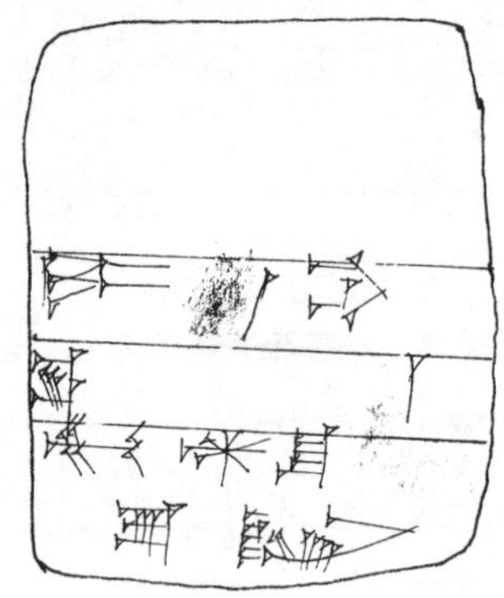

Text 292

o.

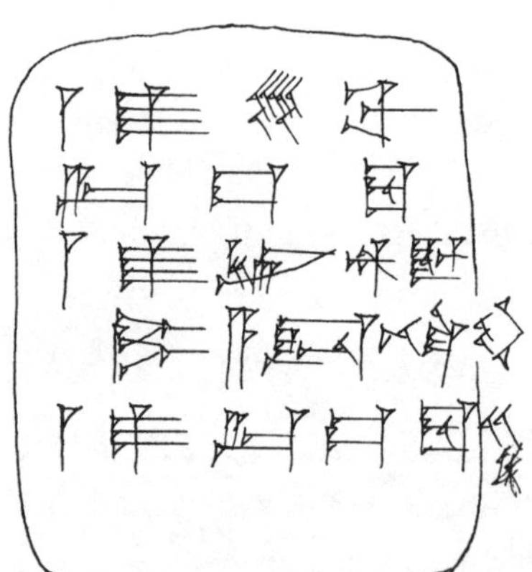

r.

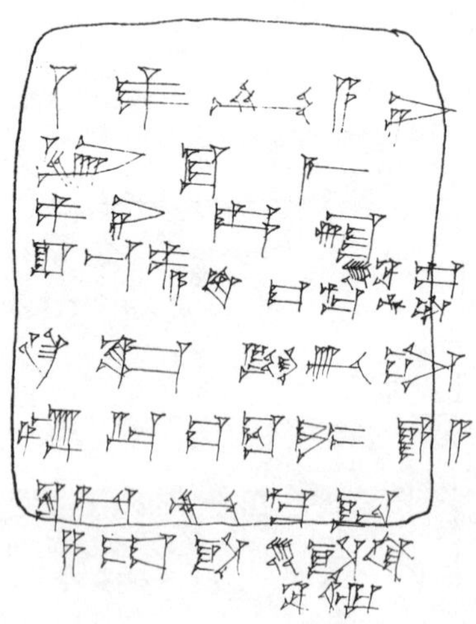

Text 293

o.

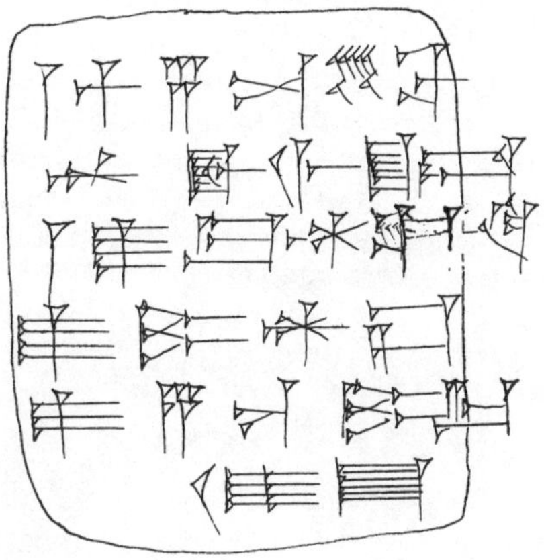

r.

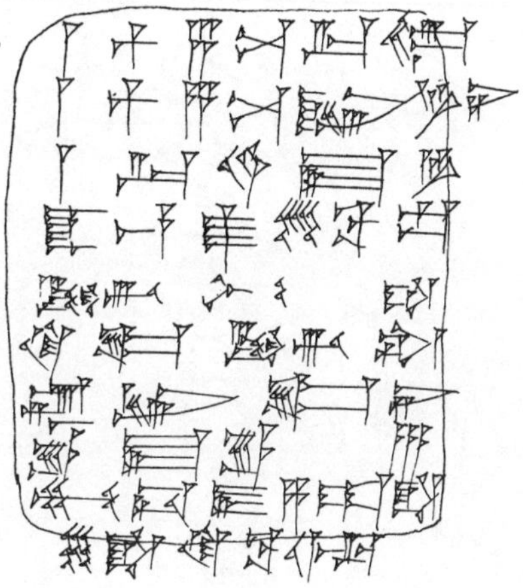

Text 296

o.

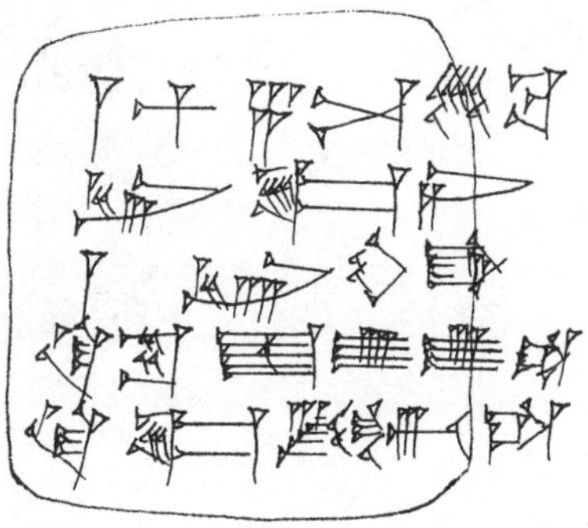

r.

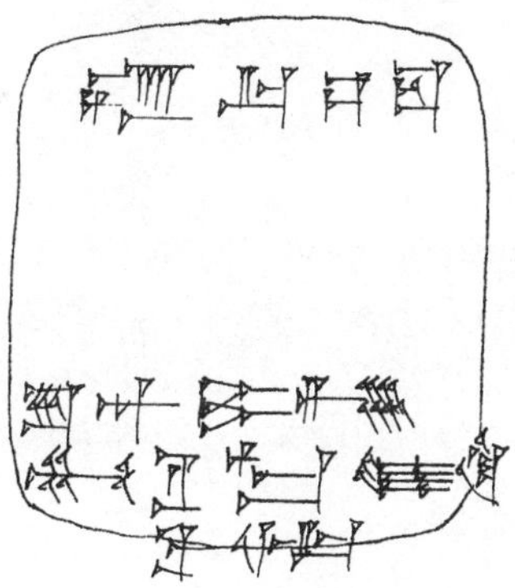

Text 297

o.

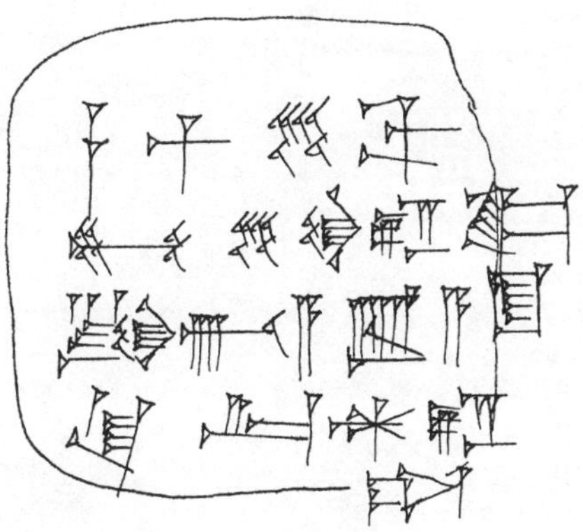

r.

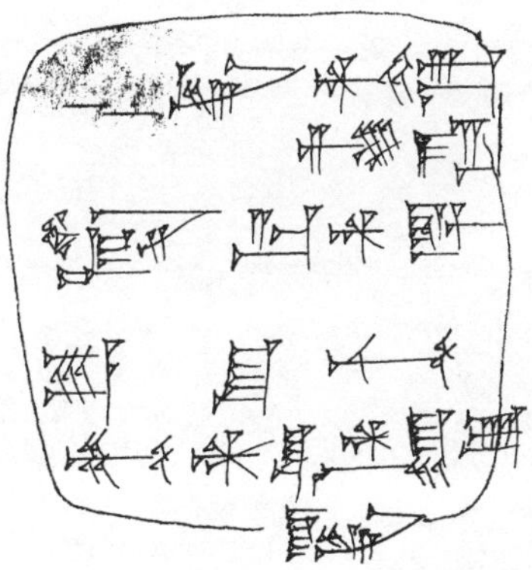

Text 299

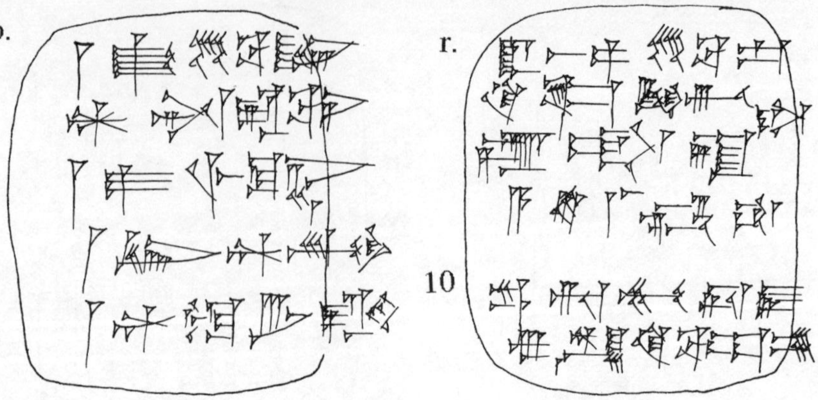

Text 300

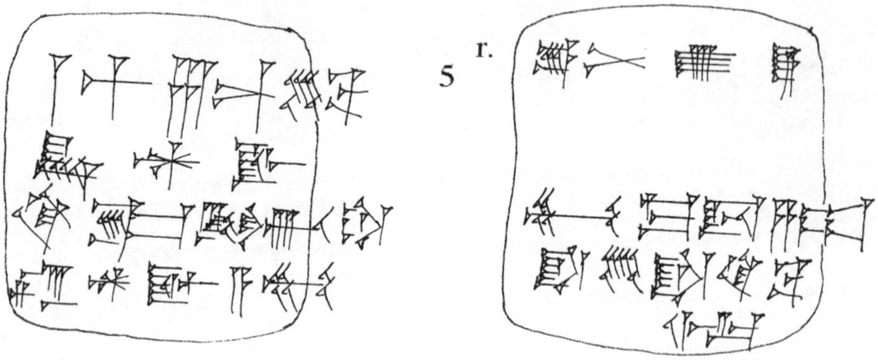

Text 301

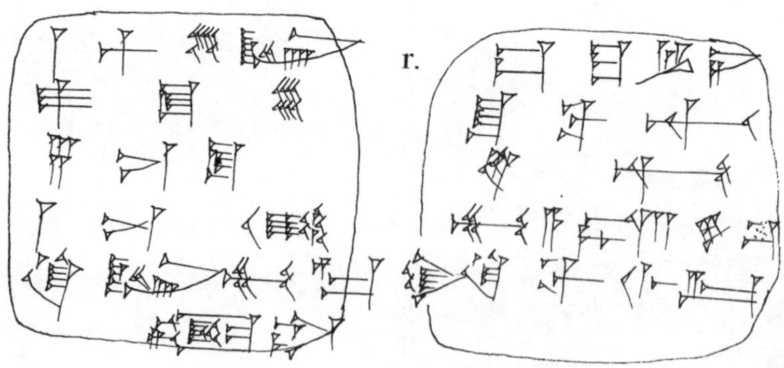

Text 303

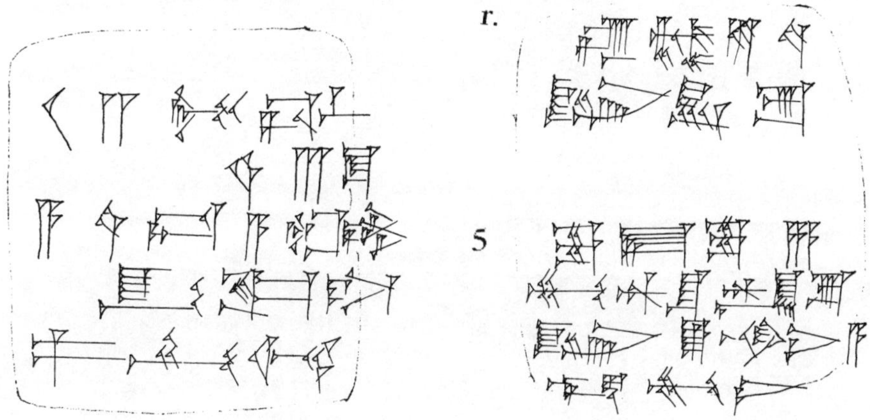

Text 307

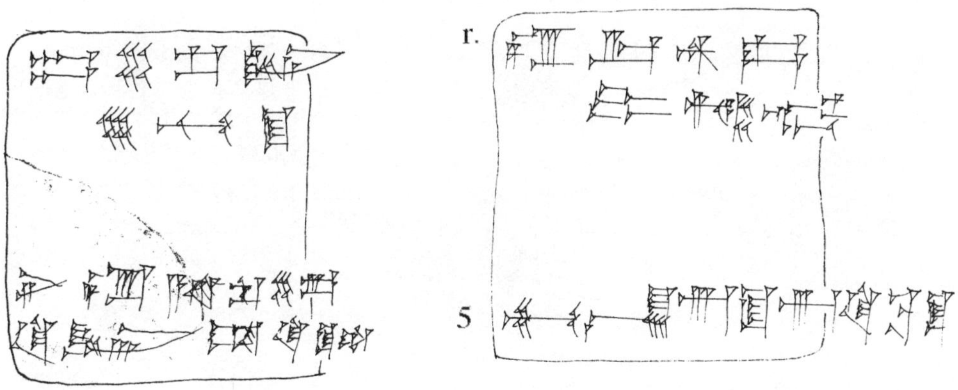

Text 309

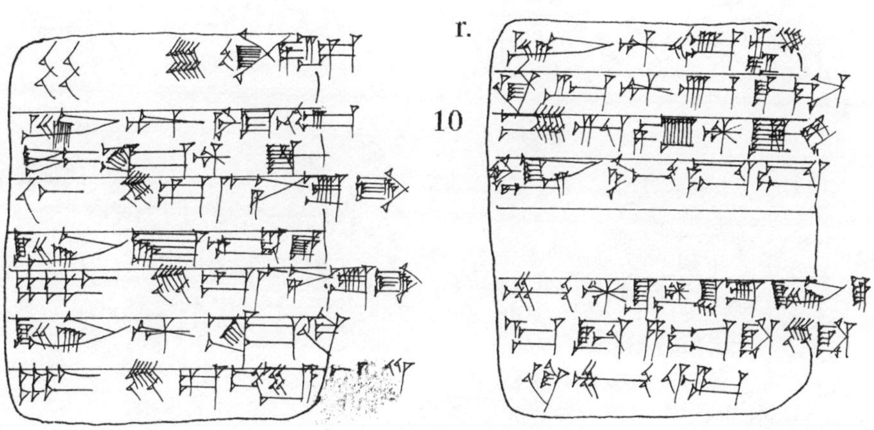

Text 310

o.

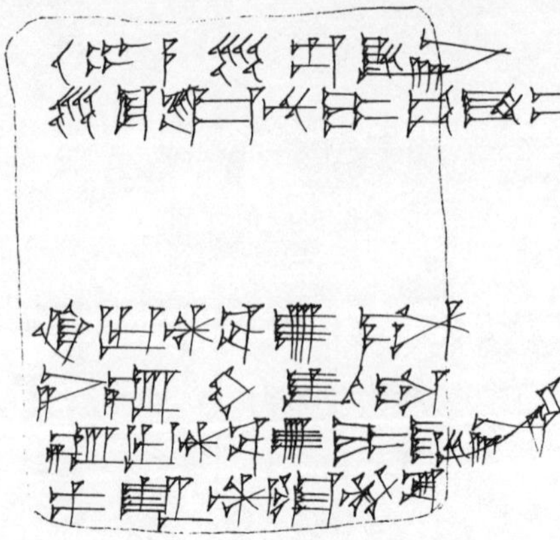

r.

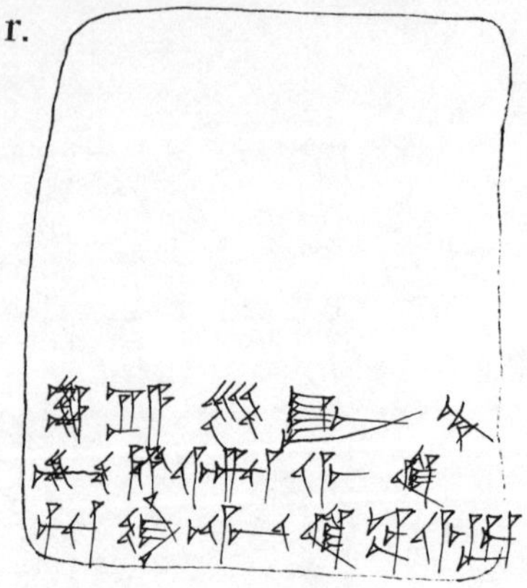

Text 313

o.

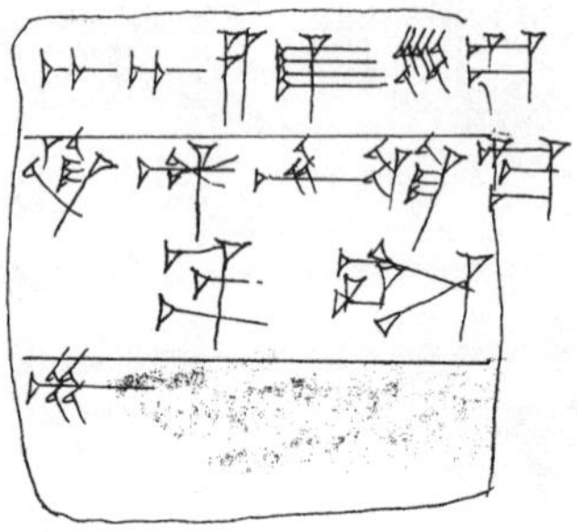

r.

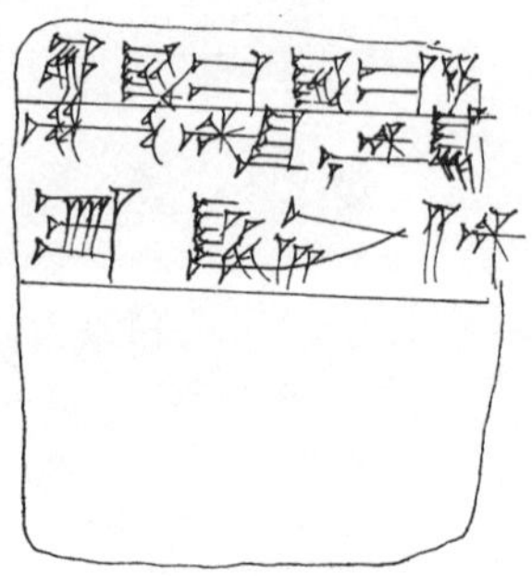

Text 314

o.

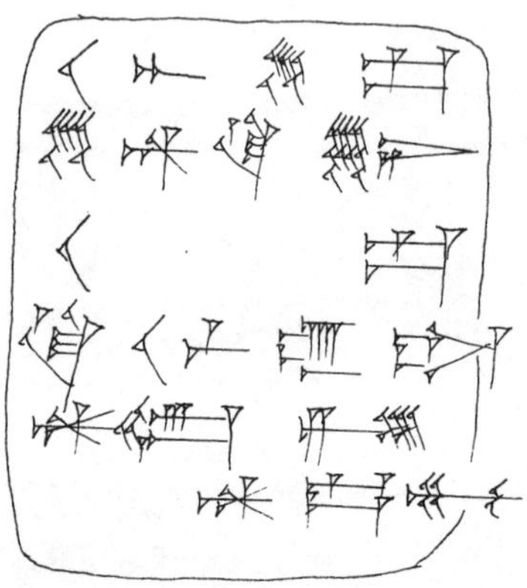

r.

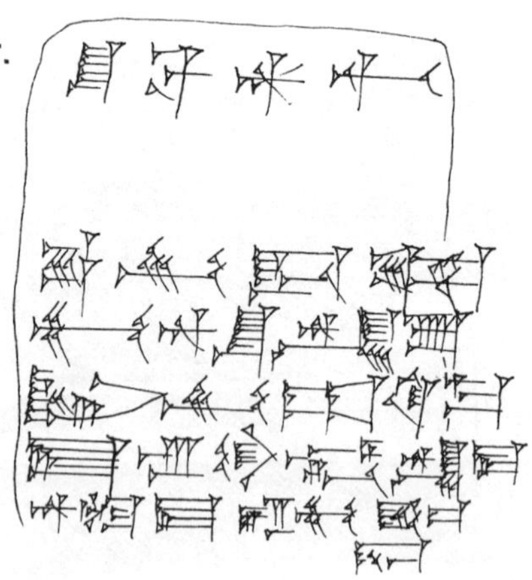

Text 321

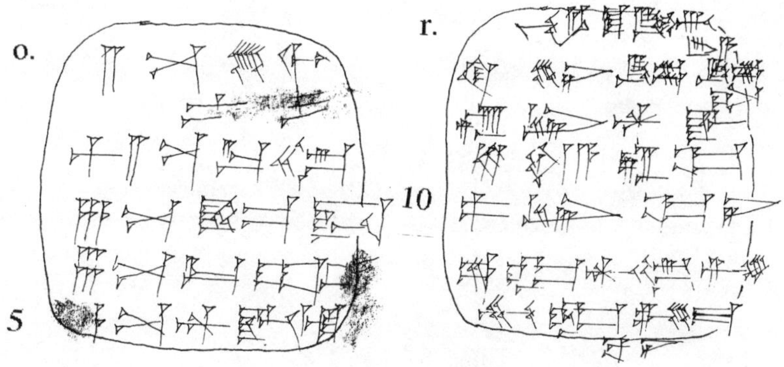

Text 322

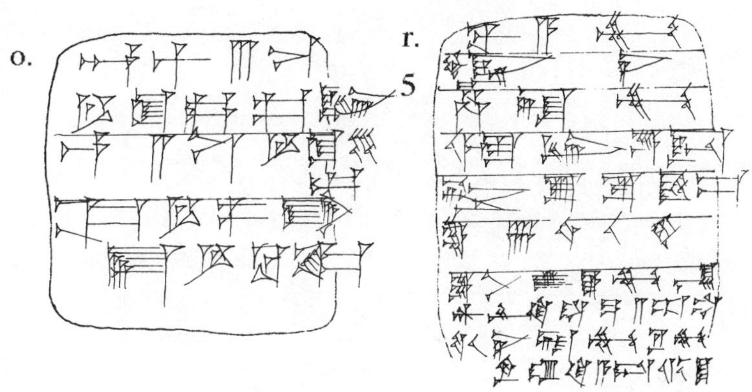

Text 323

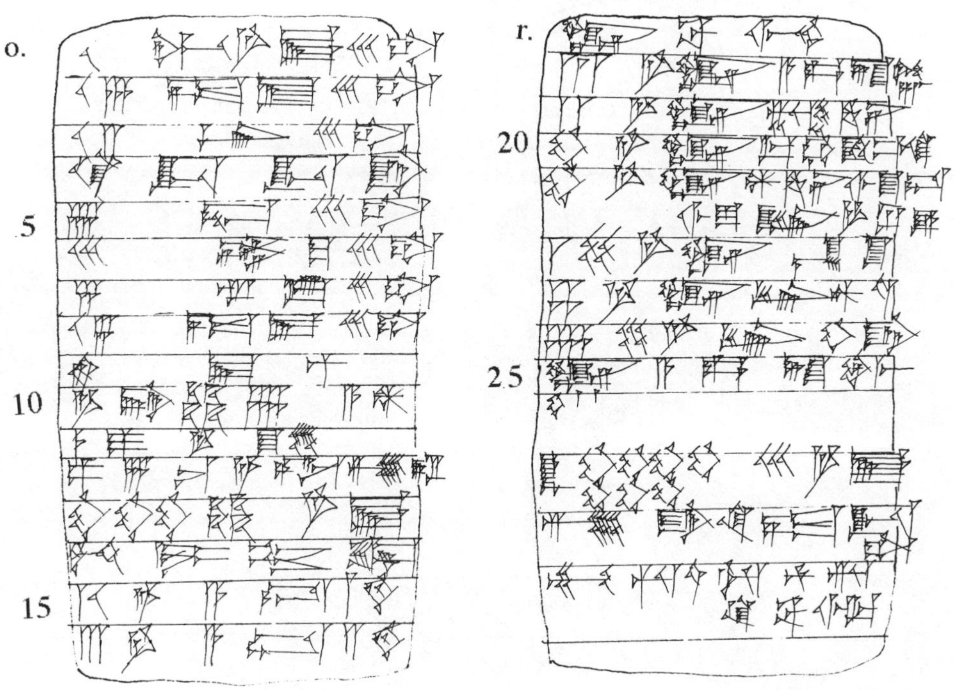

Text 325

o.

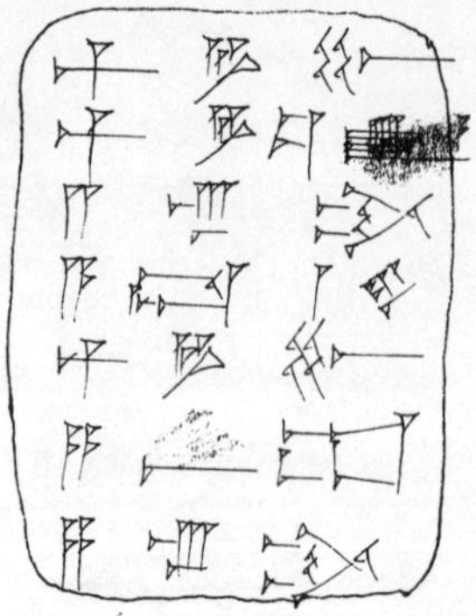

r.

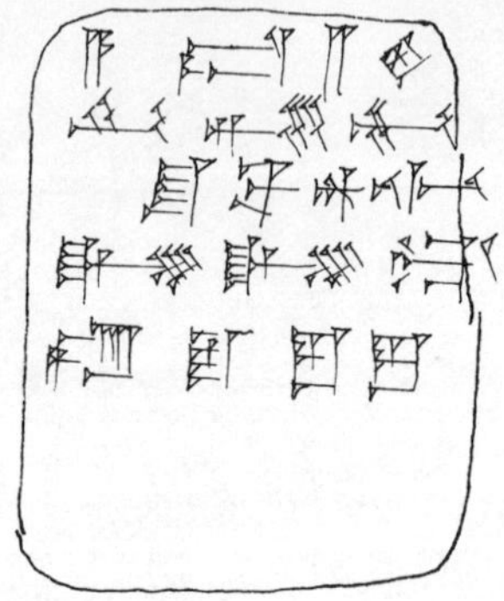

Text 327

o.

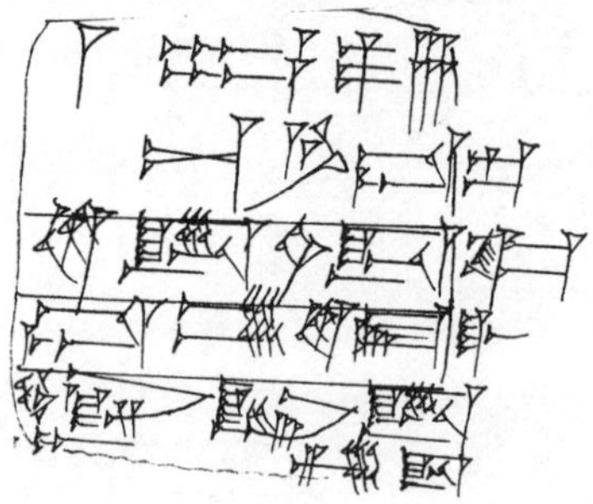

r.

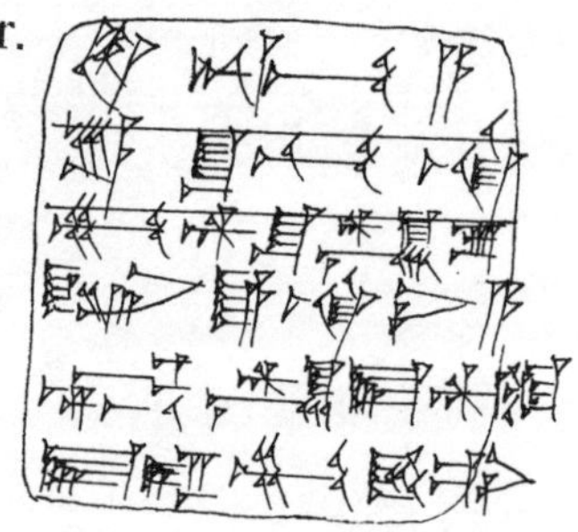

Text 330

o.

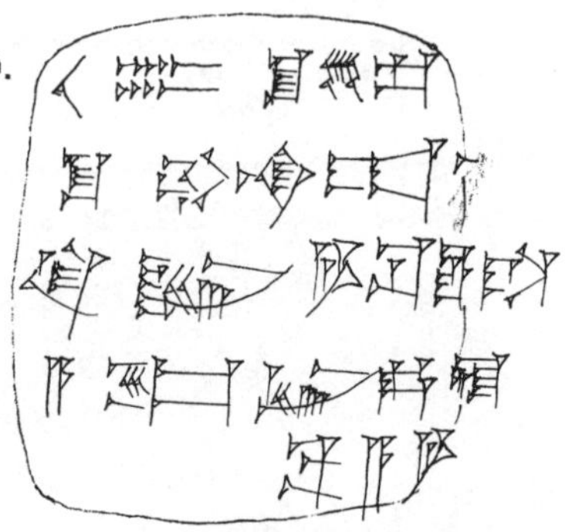

r.

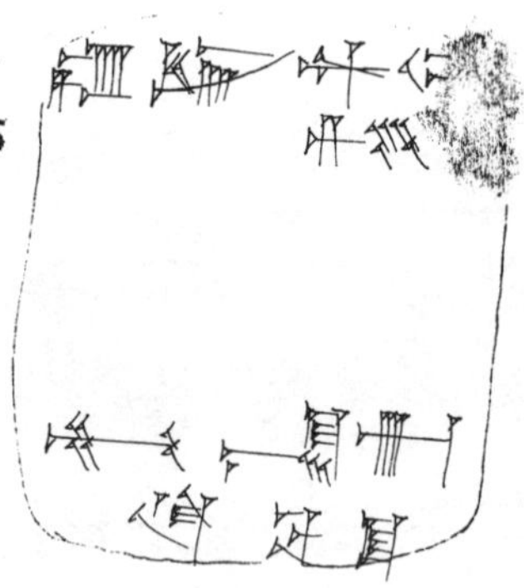

Text 333

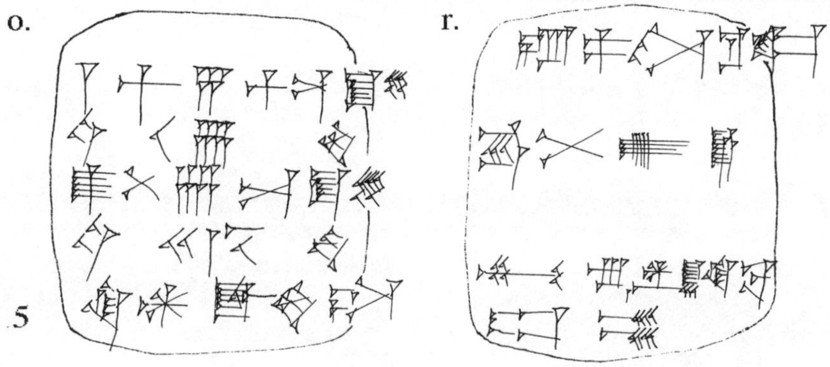

Text 334

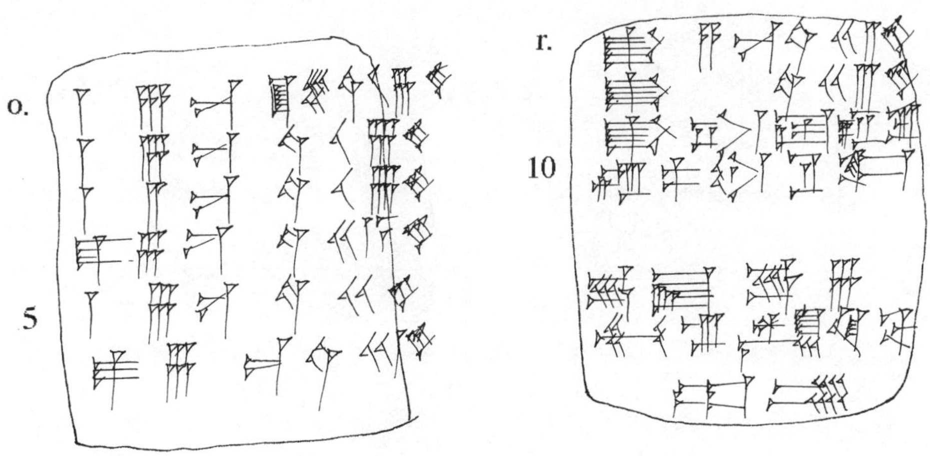

Text 336

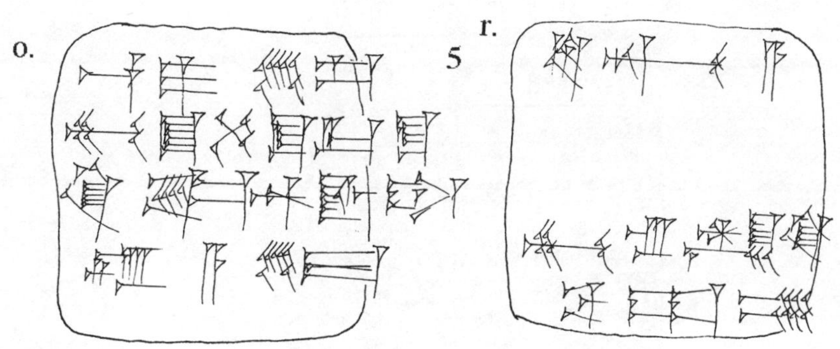

Text 338

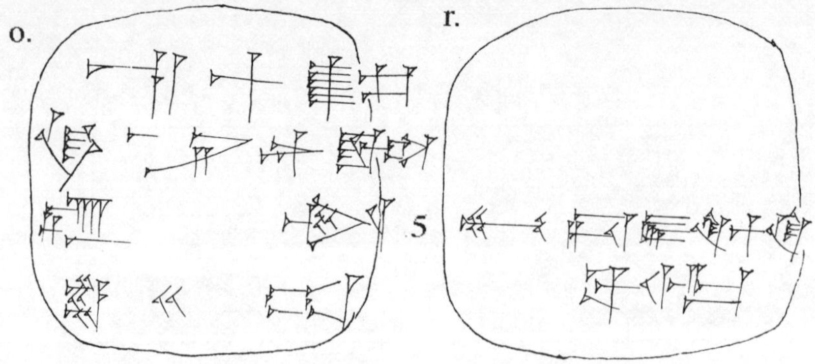

Text 341

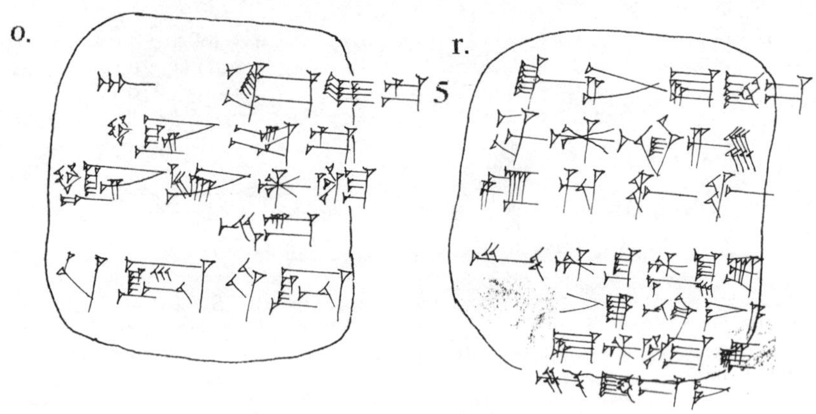

Text 343

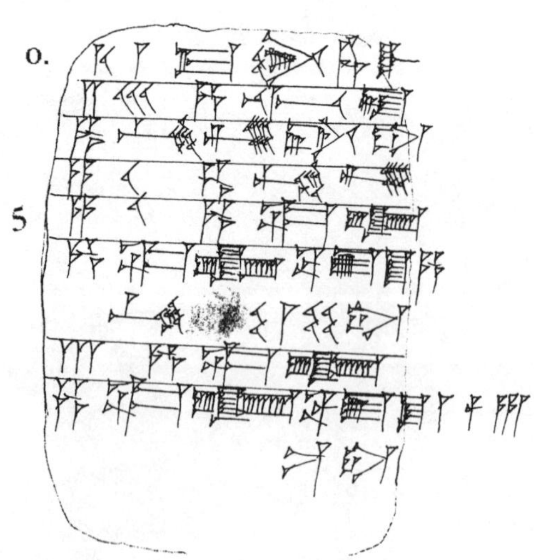

Text 345

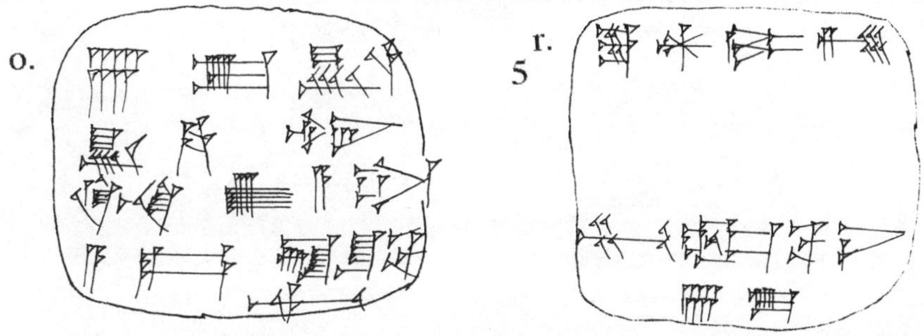

Text 346

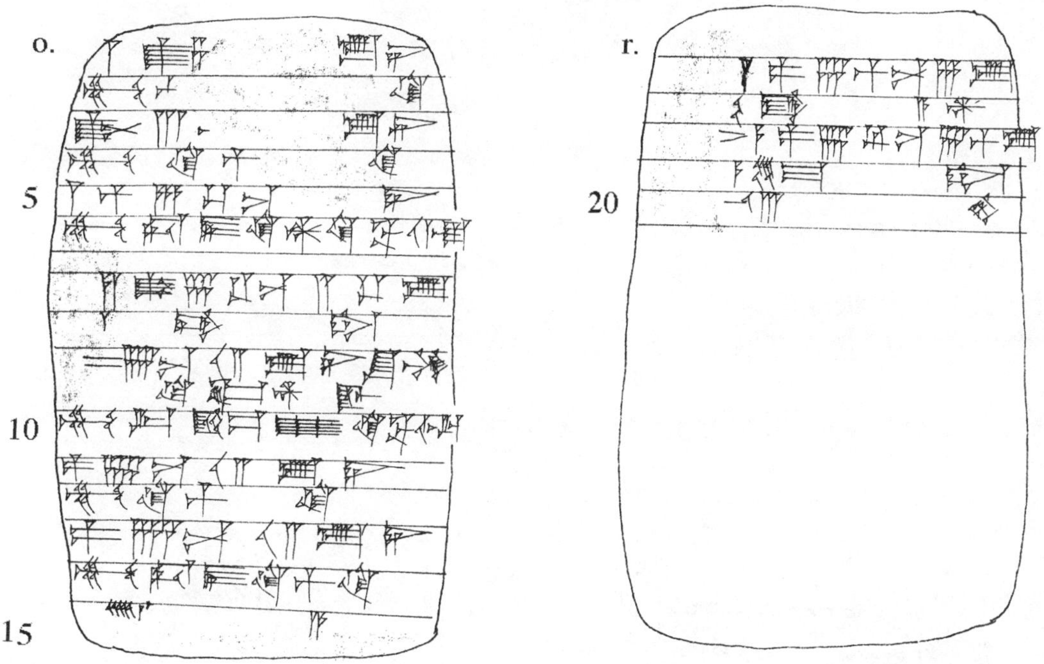

Text 349

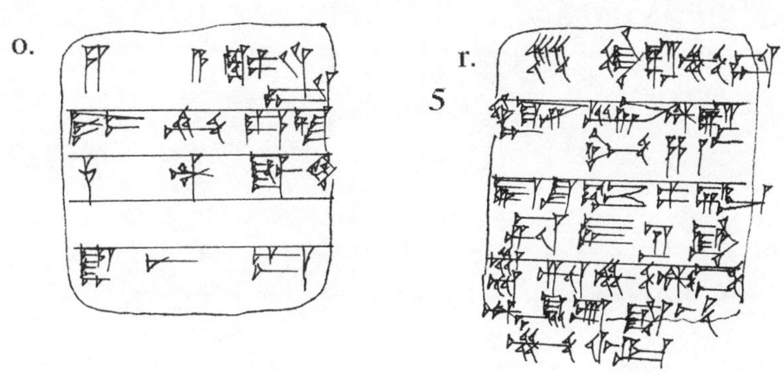

Text 350

o.

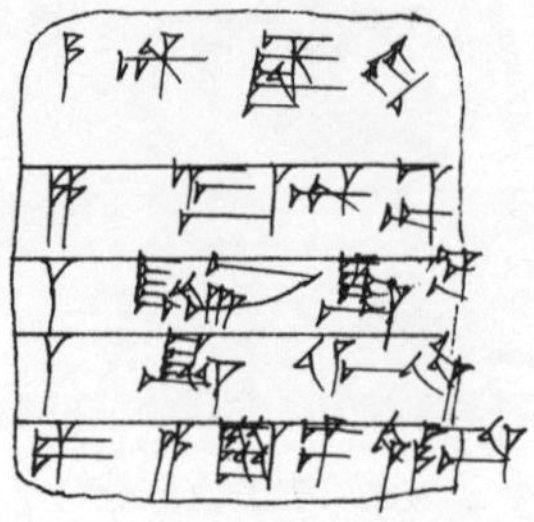

r.

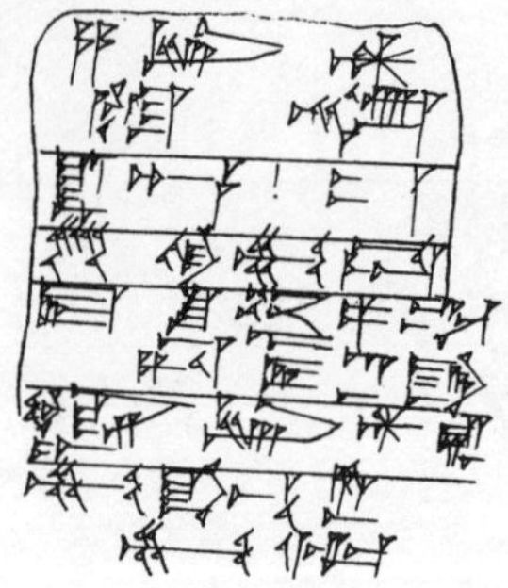

Text 352

o.

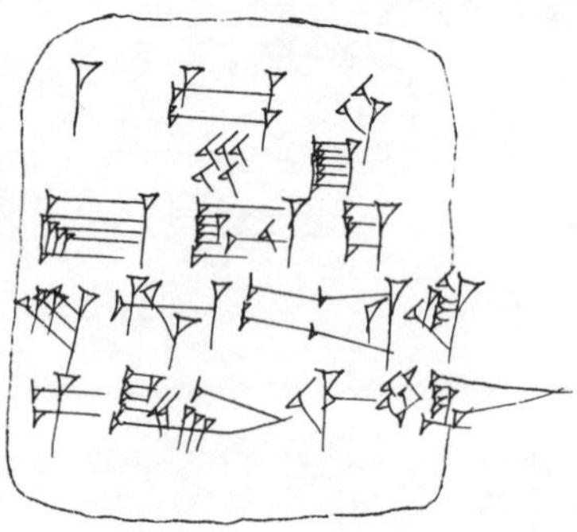

r.

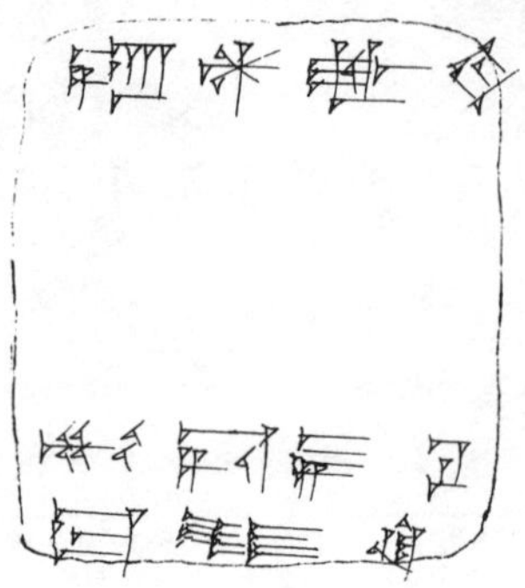

Text 354

o.

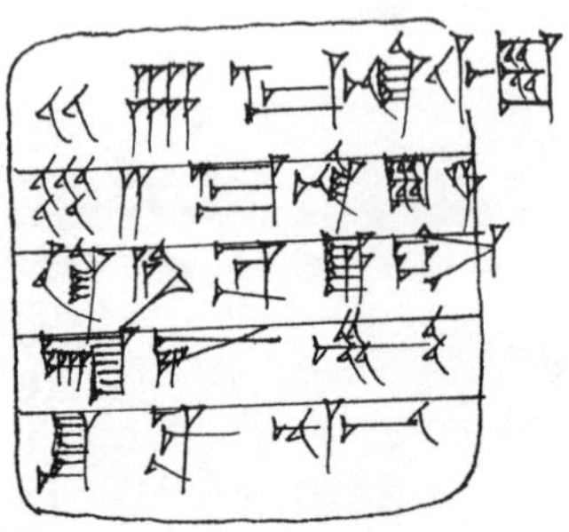

r.

Text 355

o.

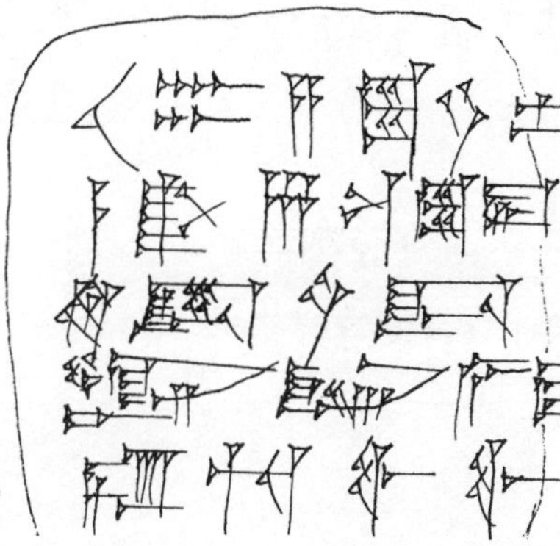

r.

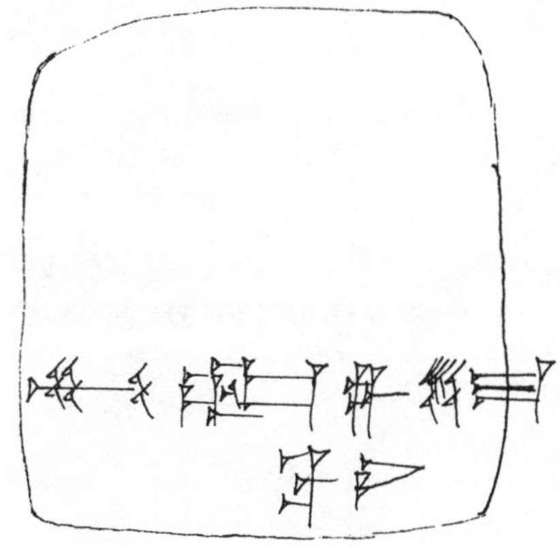

Text 356

o.

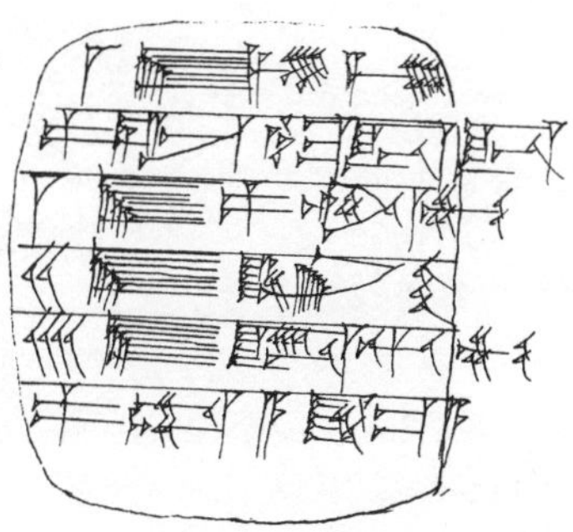

r.

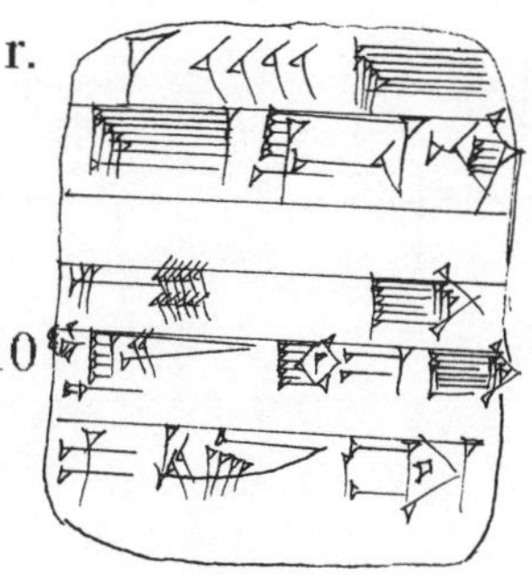

Text 357

o.

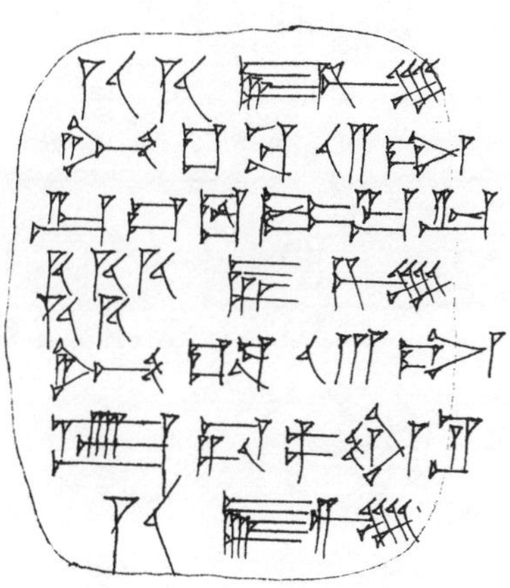

r.

Text 360

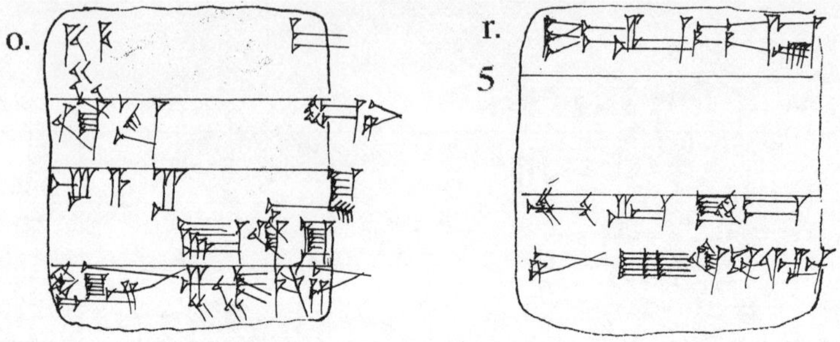

Text 361

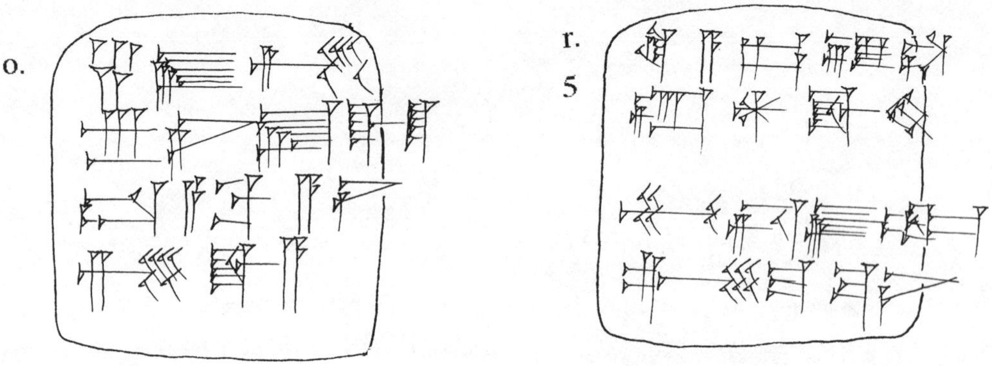

Text 362

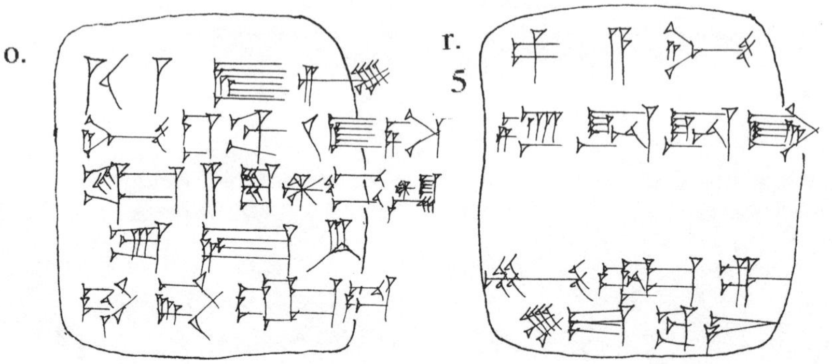

Text 363

o.

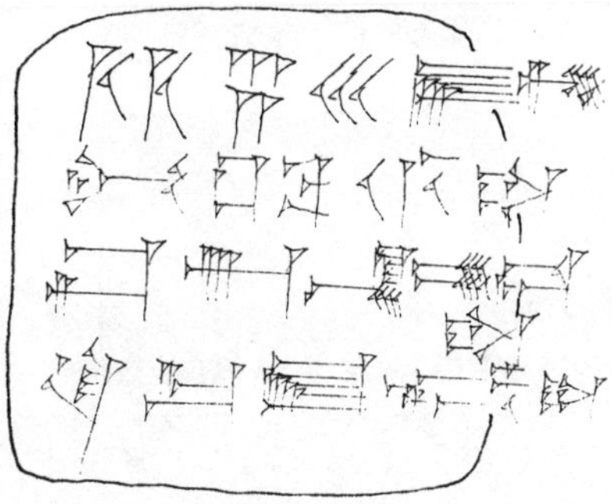

r.

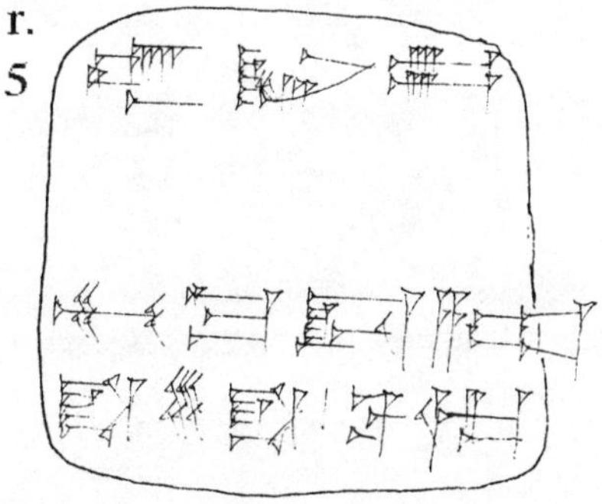

Text 364

o.

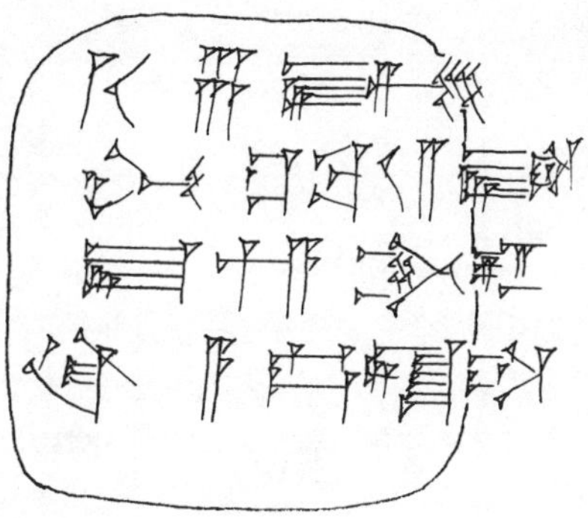

r.

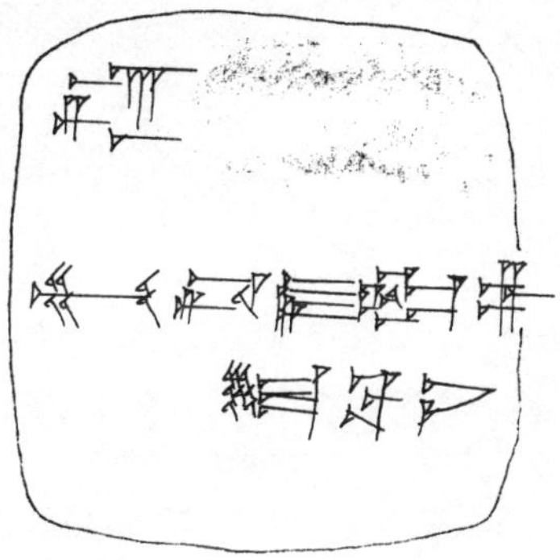

Text 365

o.

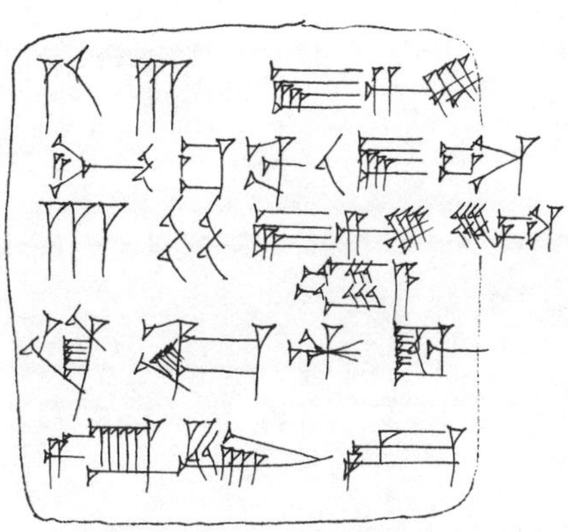

r.

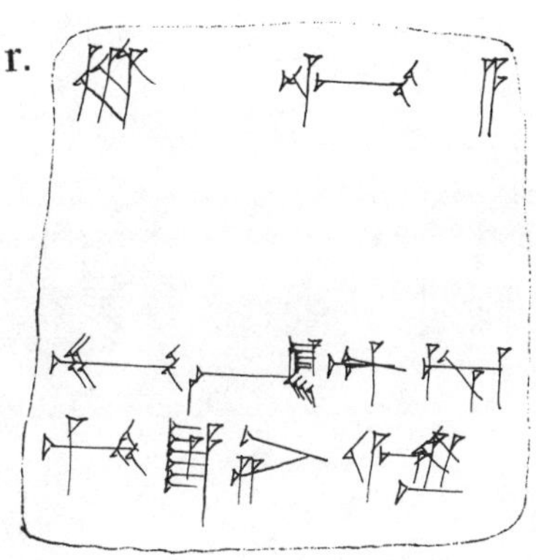

Text 367

o.

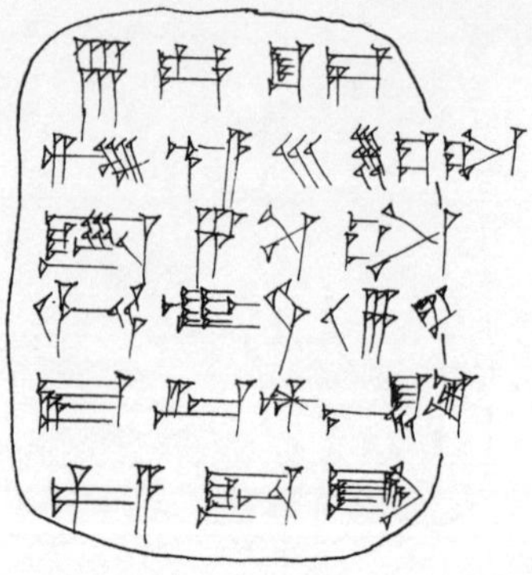

r.

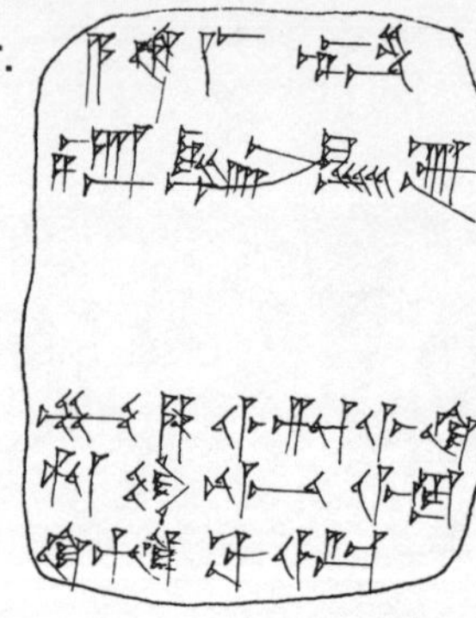

Text 368

o.

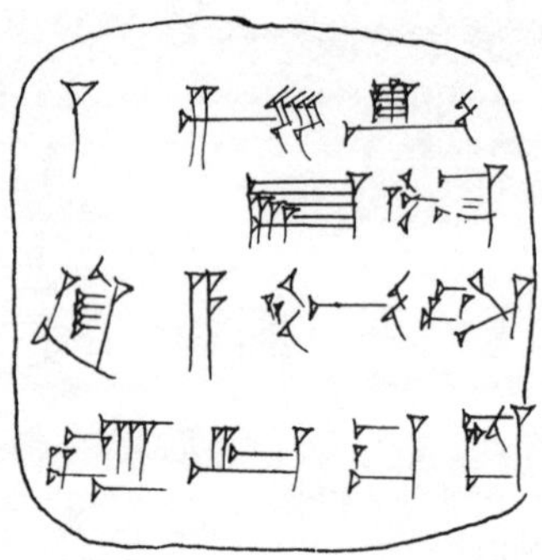

r.

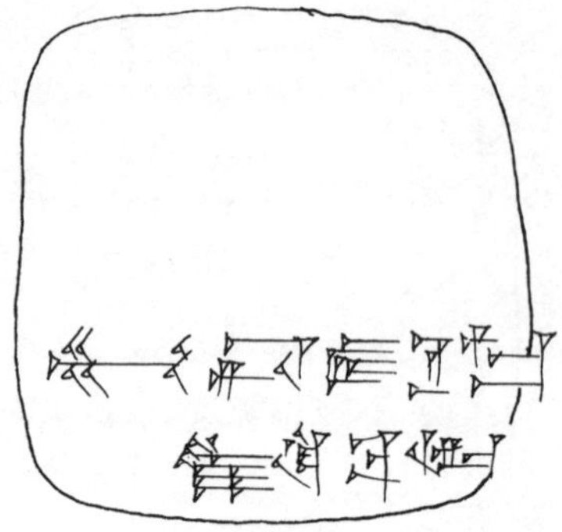

Text 369

o.

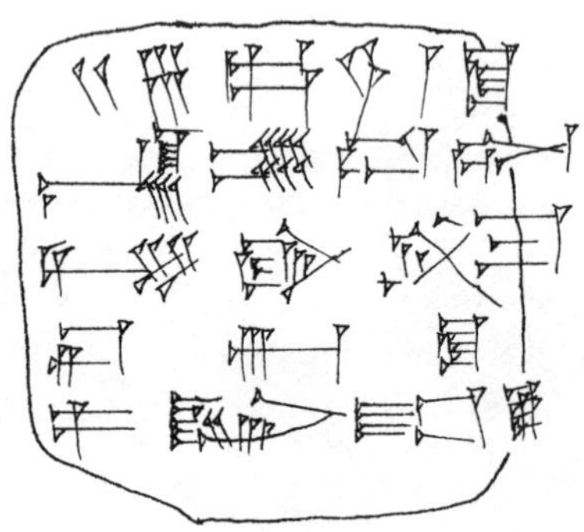

r.

Text 370

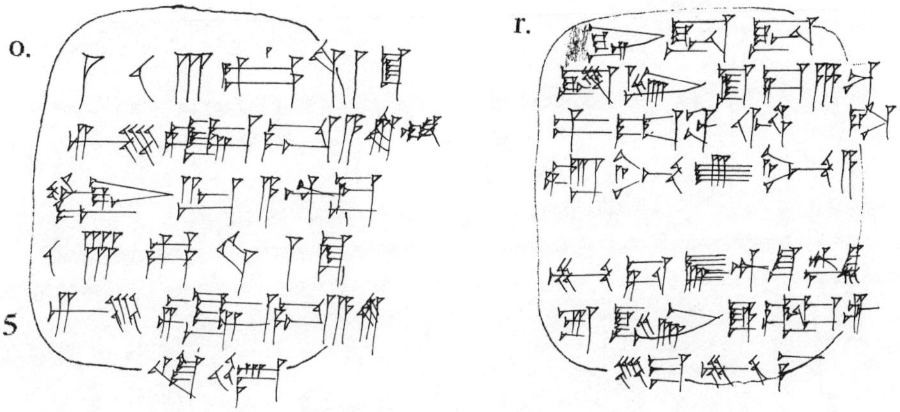

Text 371

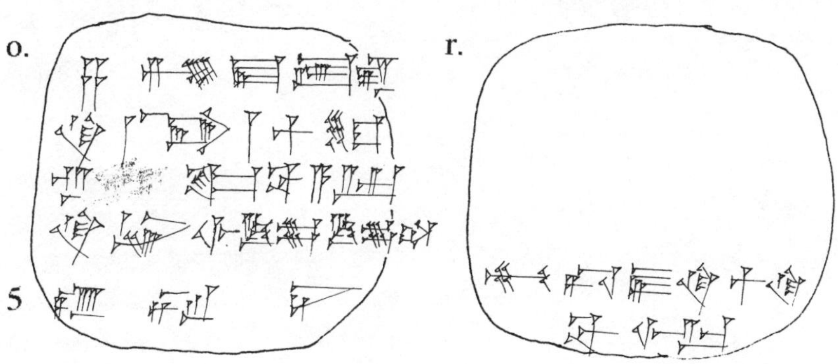

Text 372

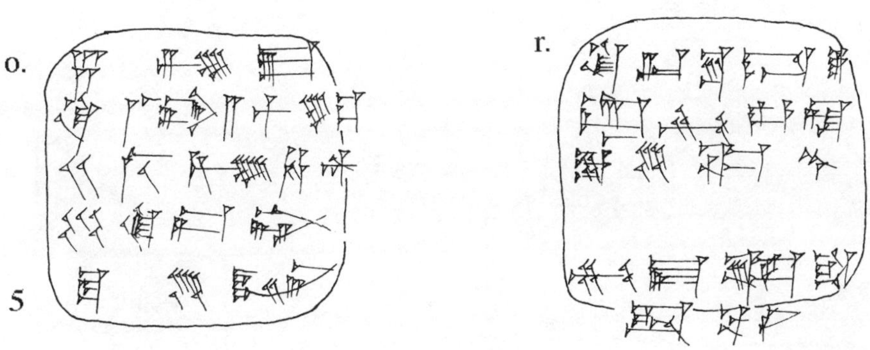

Text 374

o.

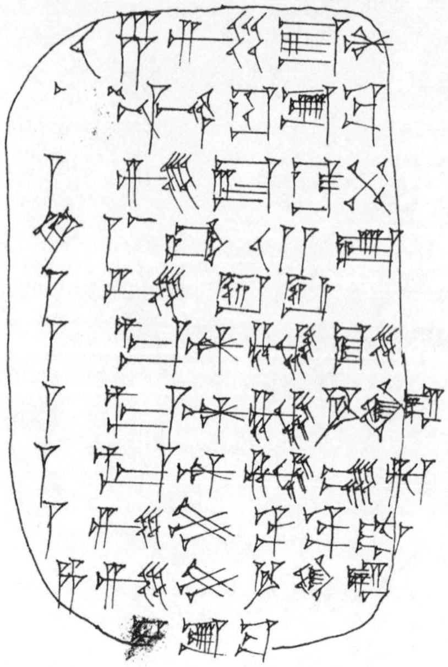

r.

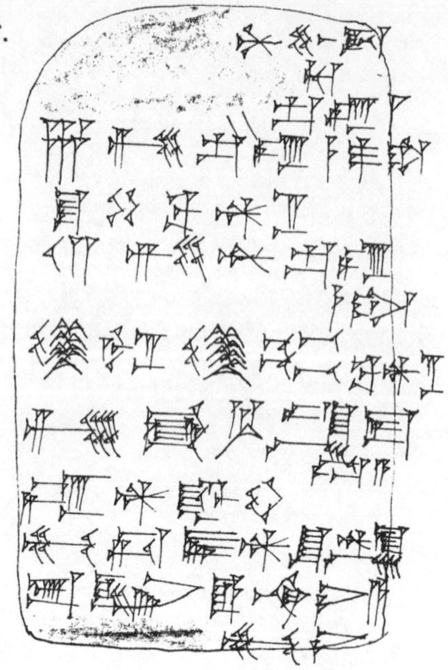

Text 375

o.

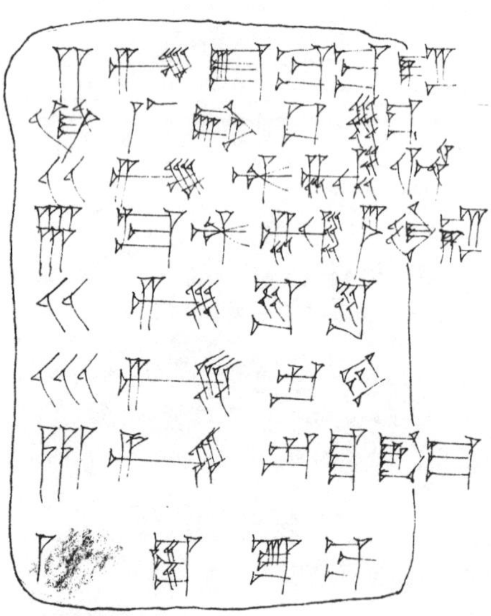

r.

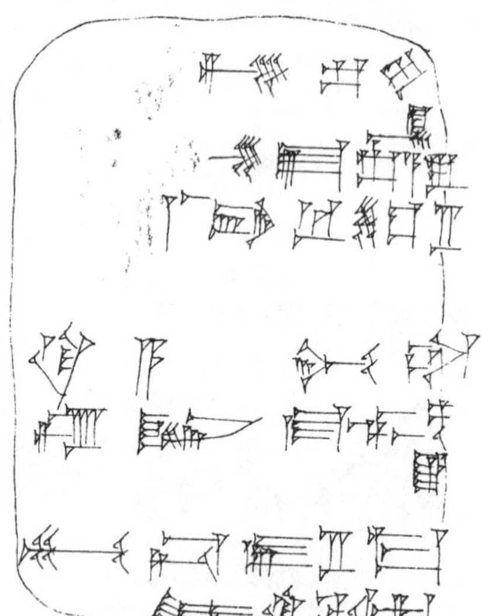

Text 376

o.

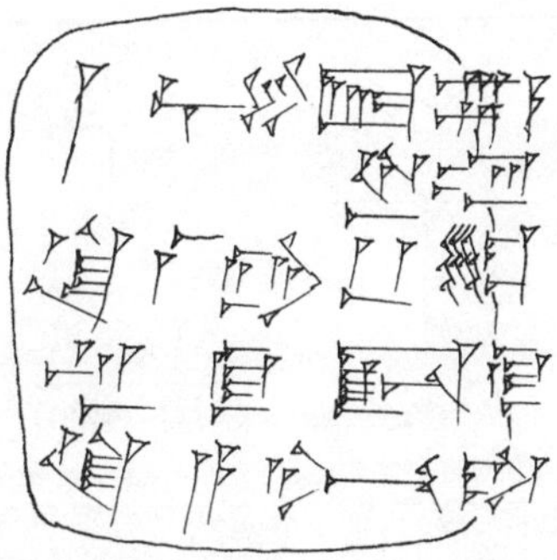

r.

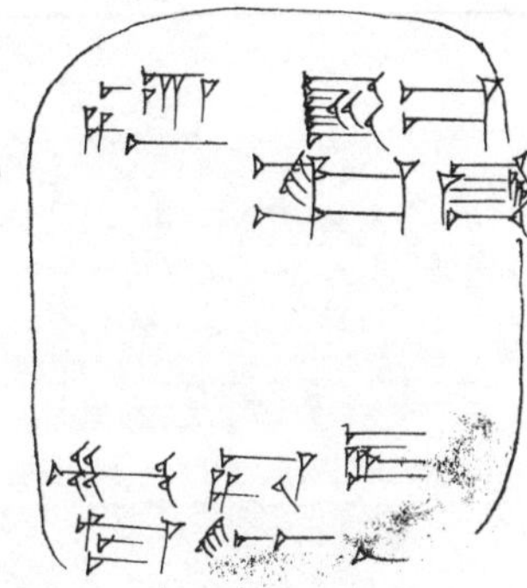

Text 377

o.

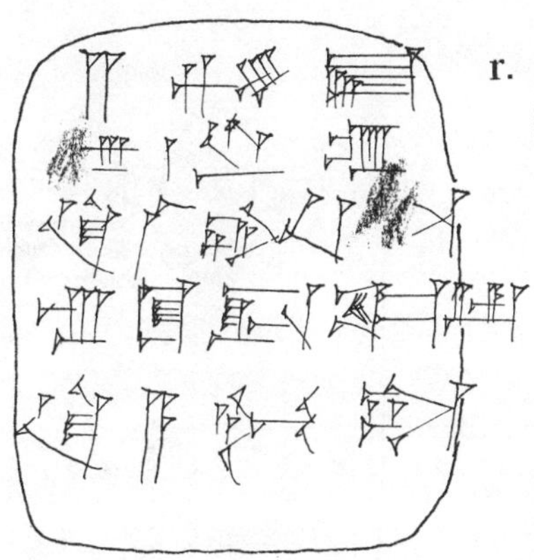

r.

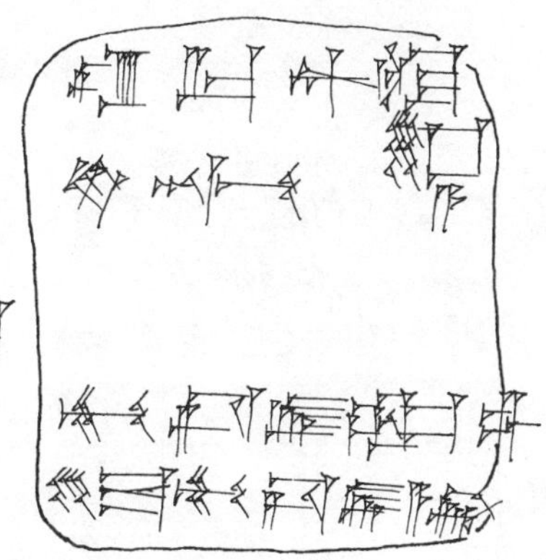

Text 378

o.

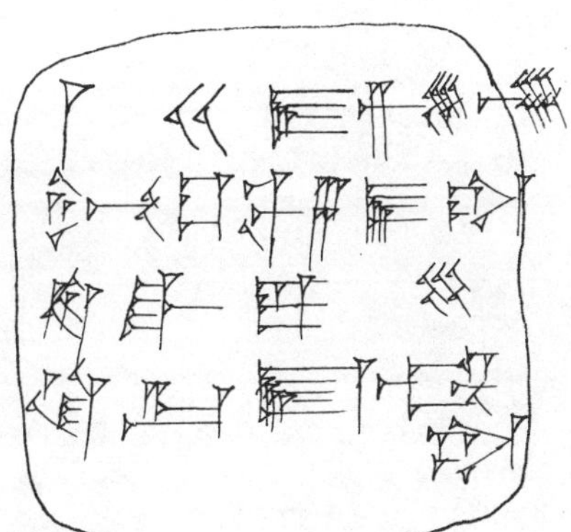

r.

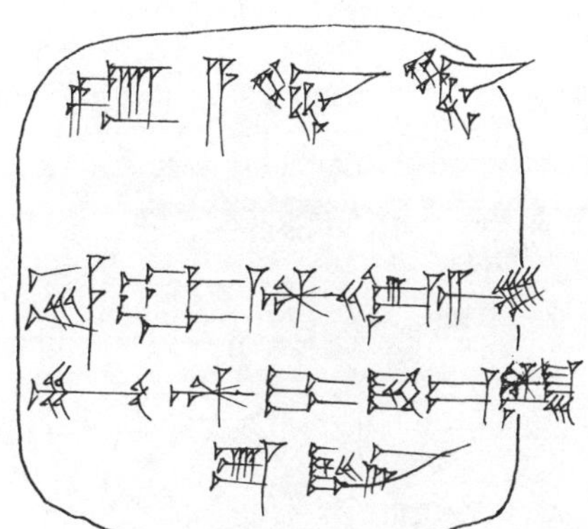

Text 379

o.

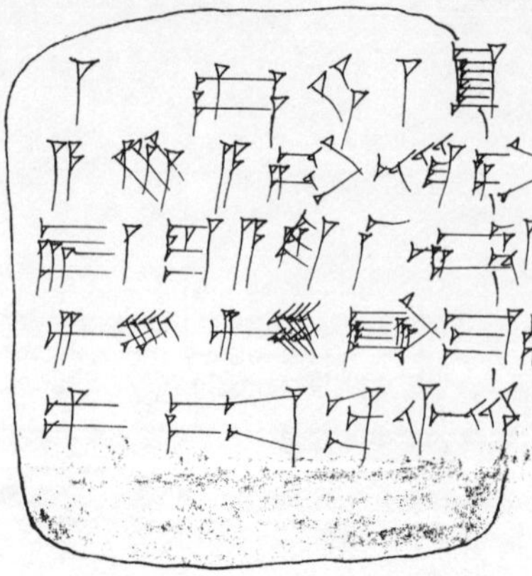

r.

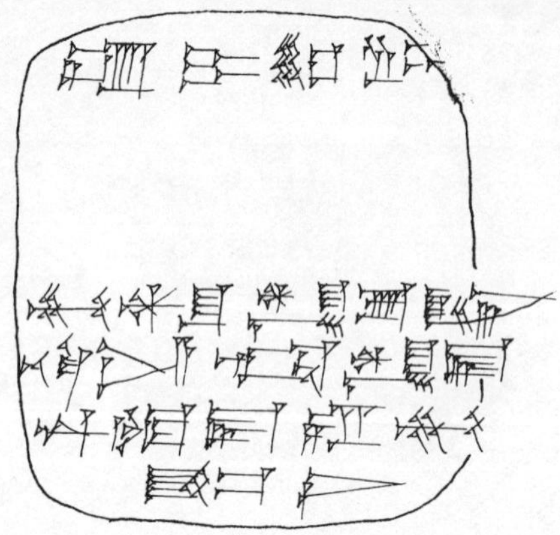

Text 380

o.

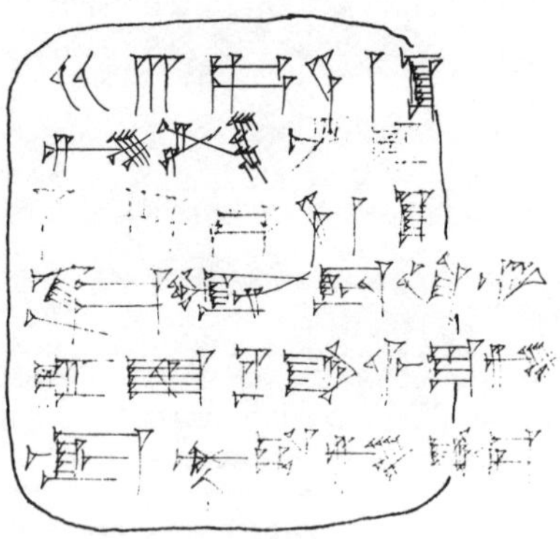

r.

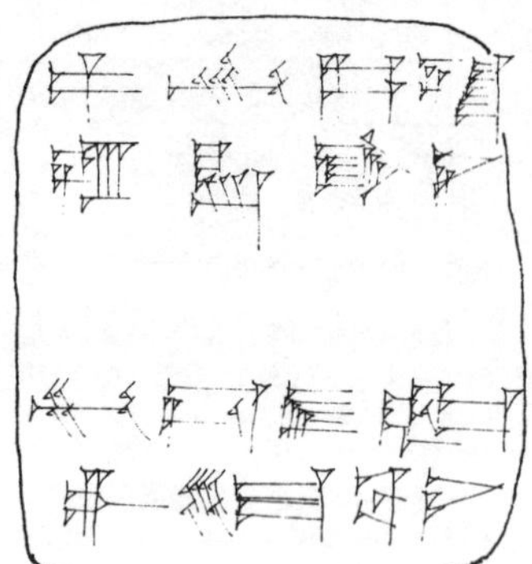

Text 381

o.

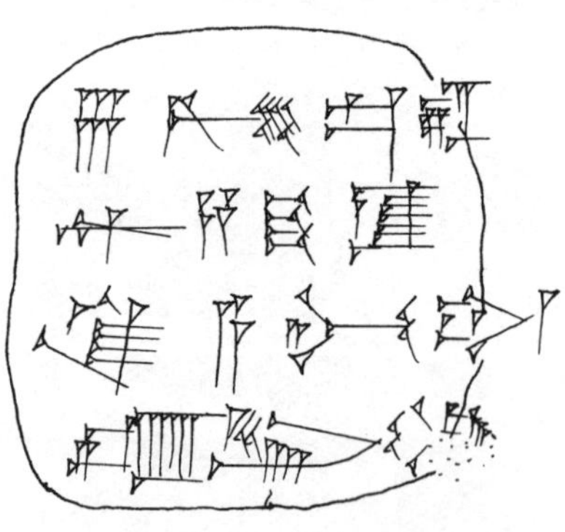

r.

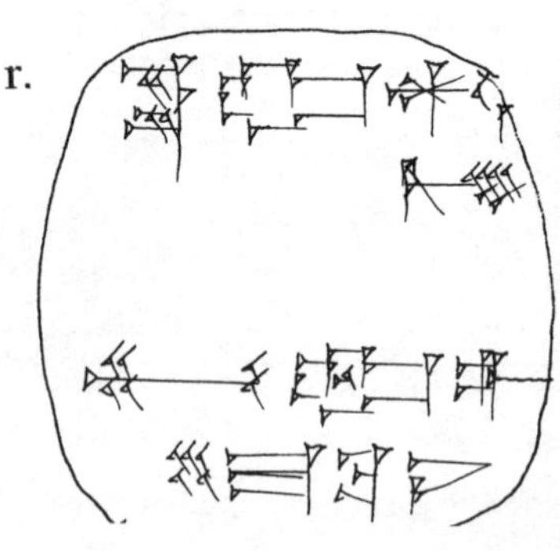

Text 382

o.

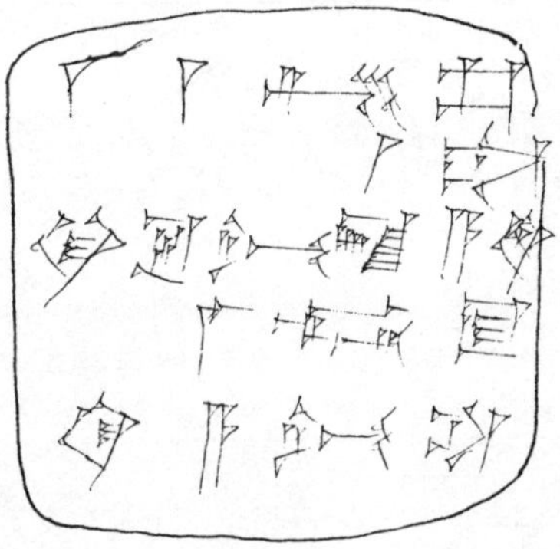

r.

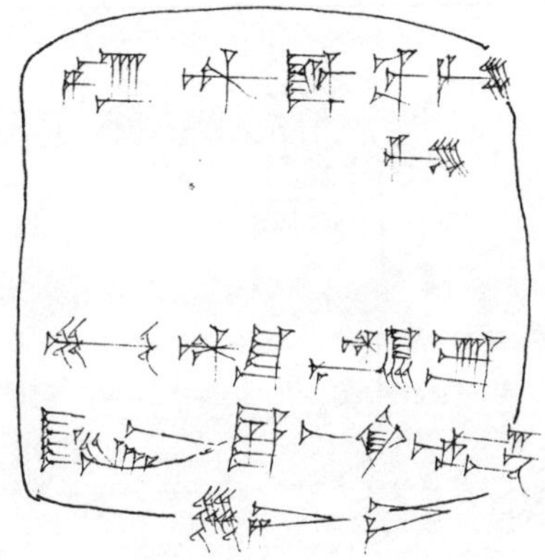

Text 383

o.

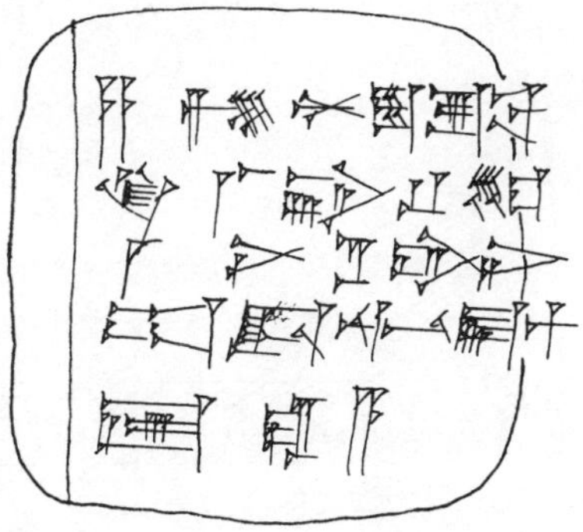

r.

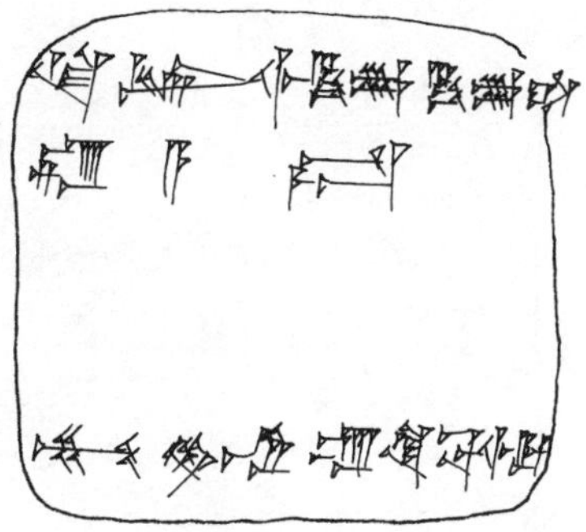

Text 384

o.

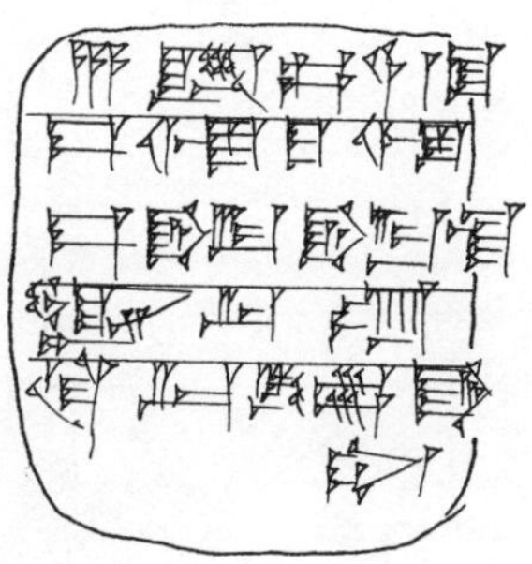

r.

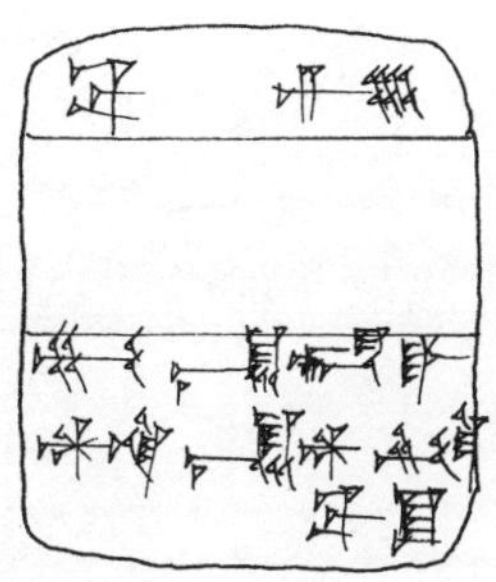

Text 385

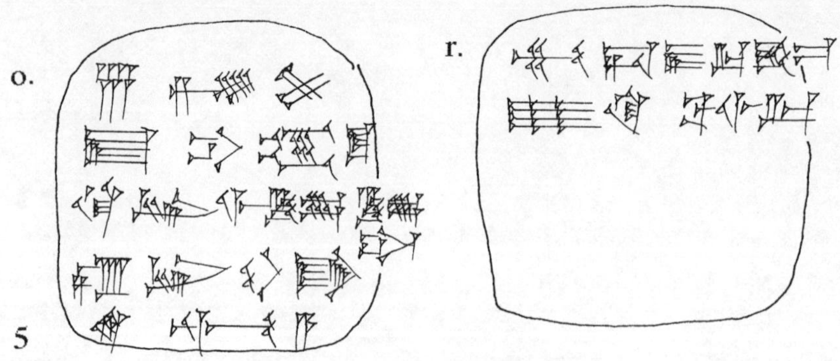

Text 386

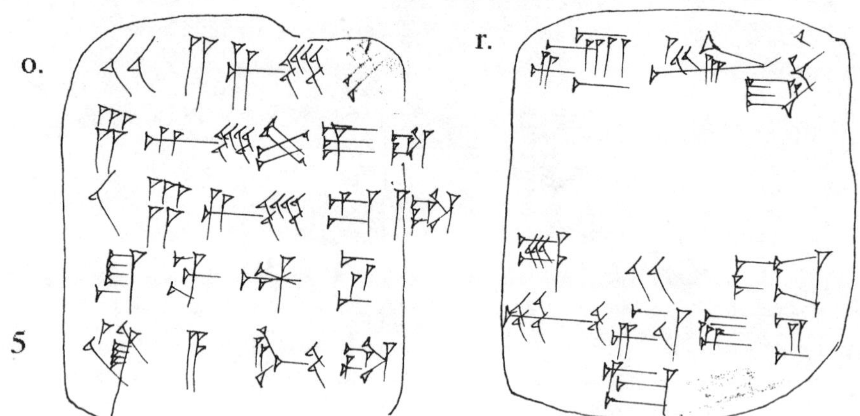

Text 387

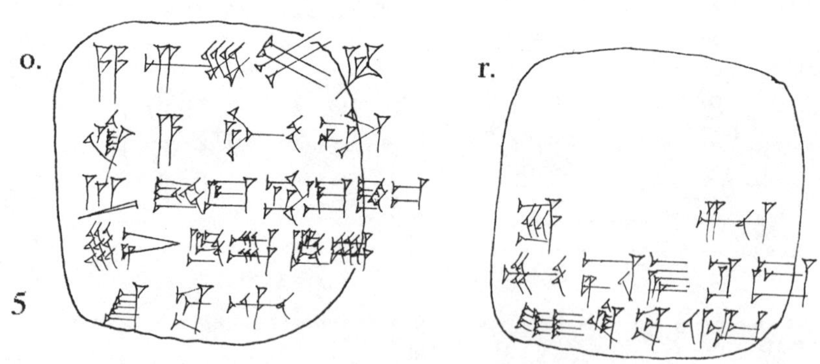

Text 390

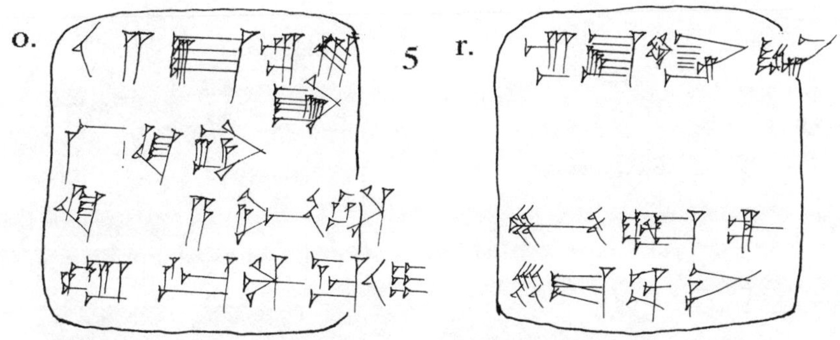

Text 391

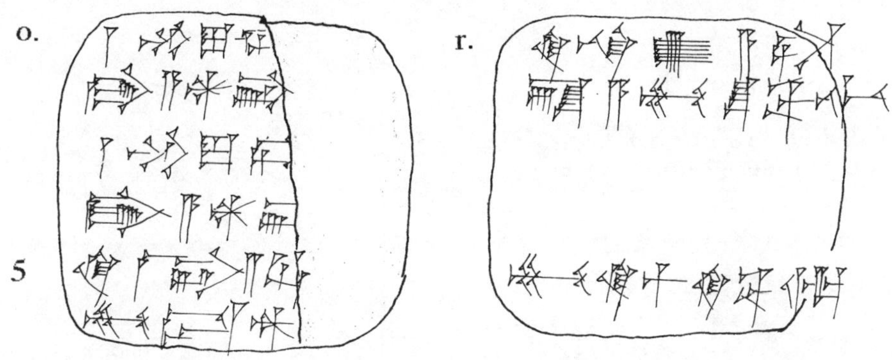

Text 394

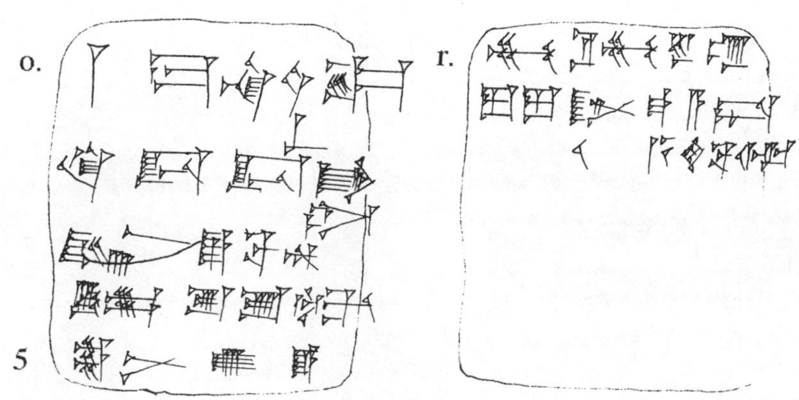

Text 395

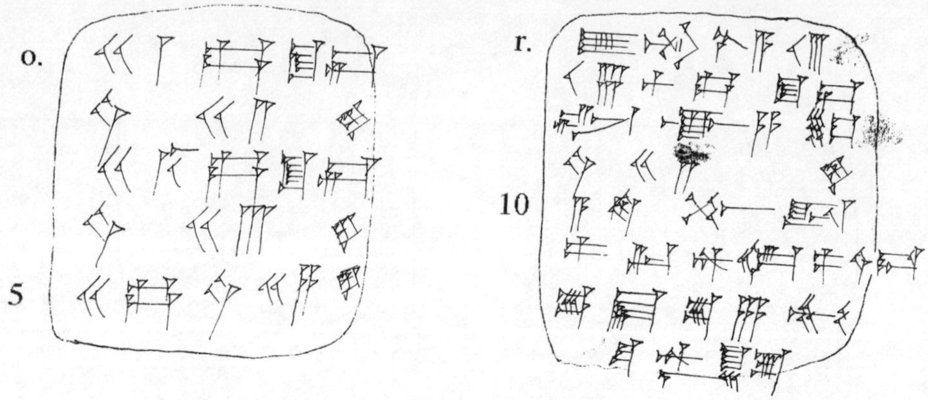

Text 396

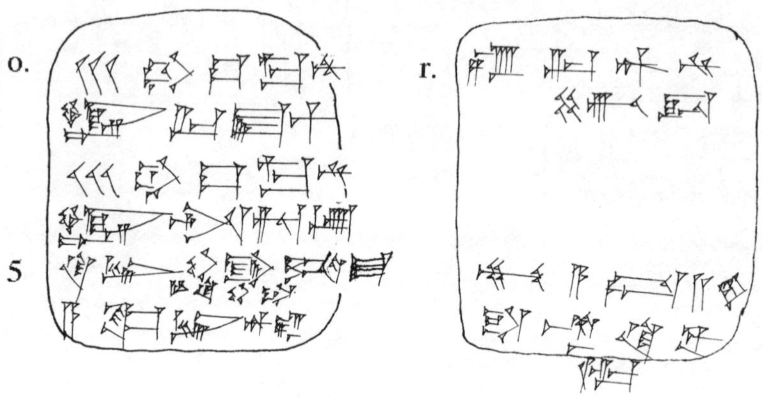

Text 398

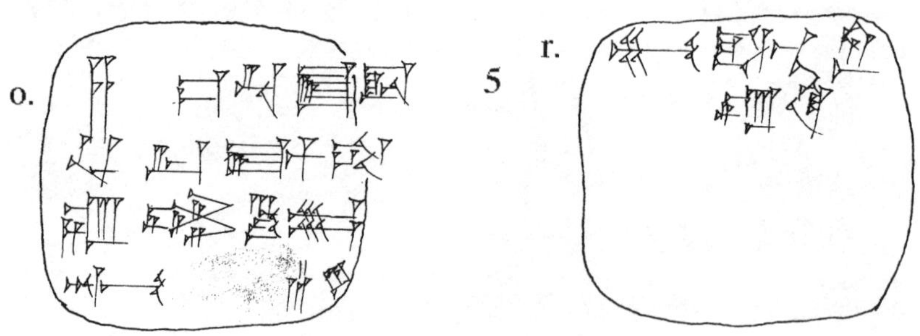

Text 399

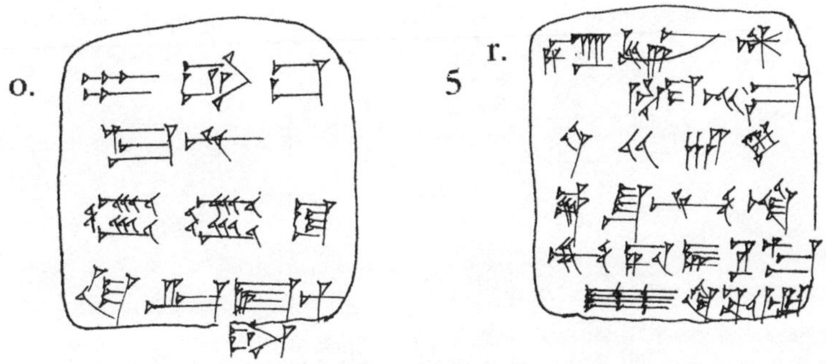

Text 400

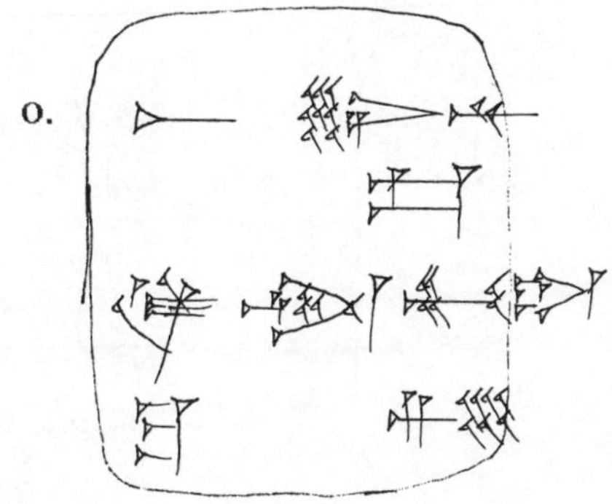

Text 401

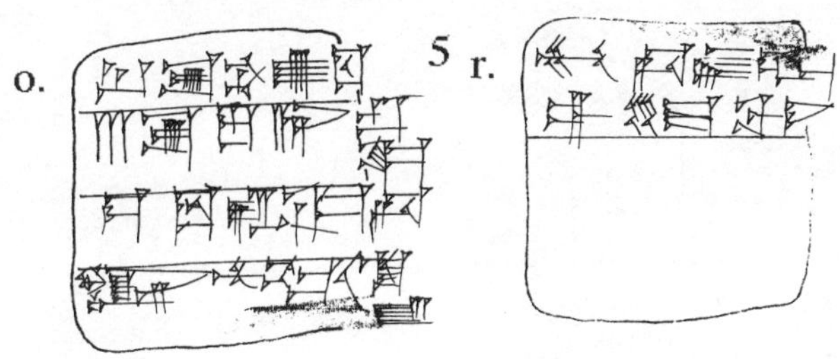

Text 403

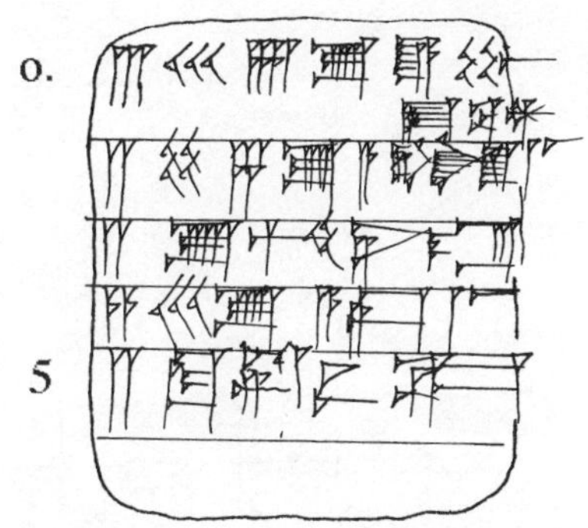

Text 404

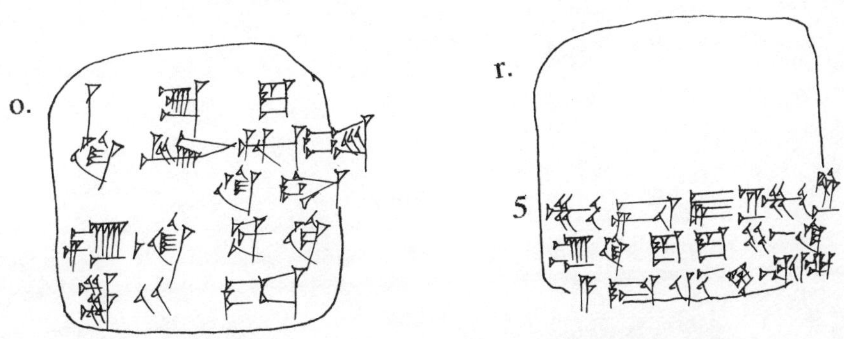

Text 405

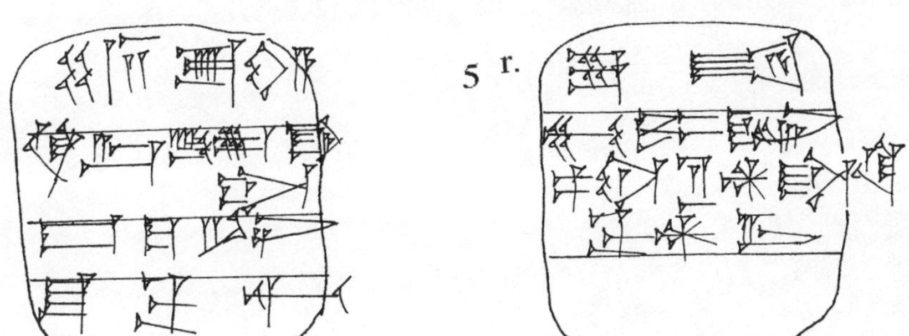

Text 406

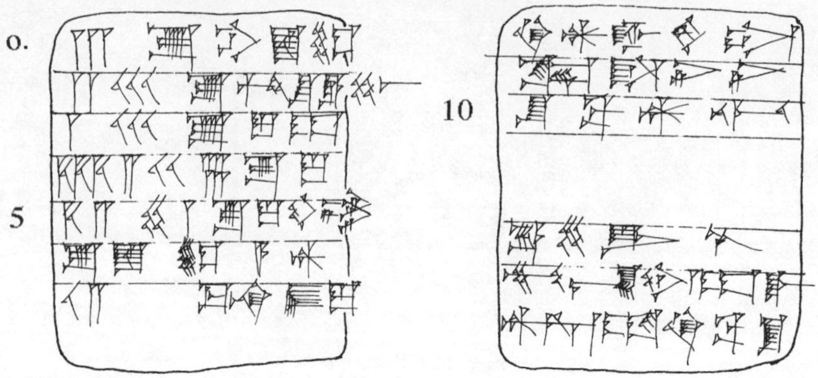

Text 409

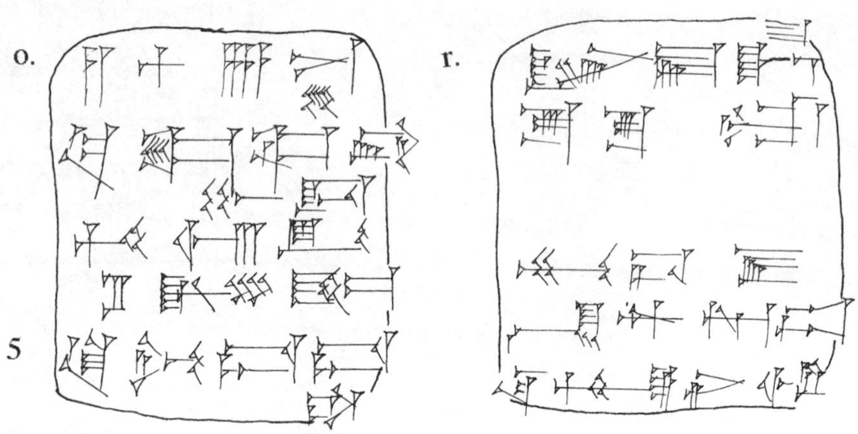

Text 412

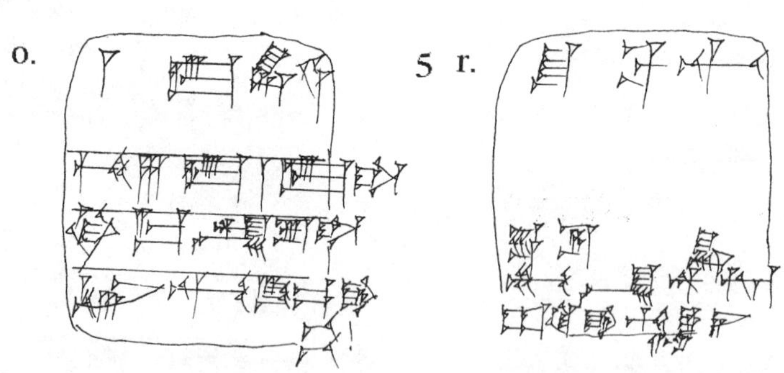

Text 413

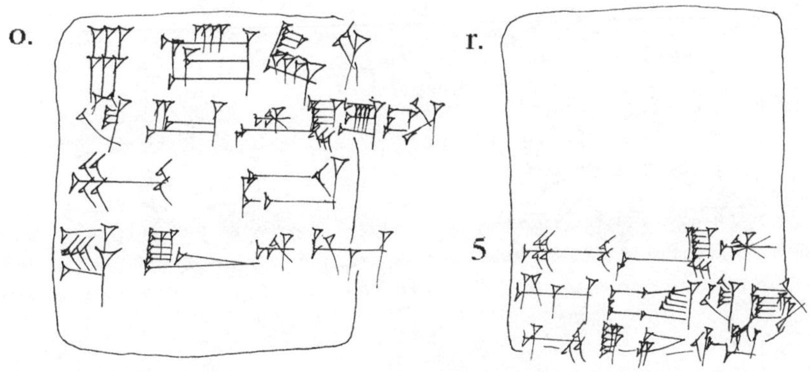

Text 424

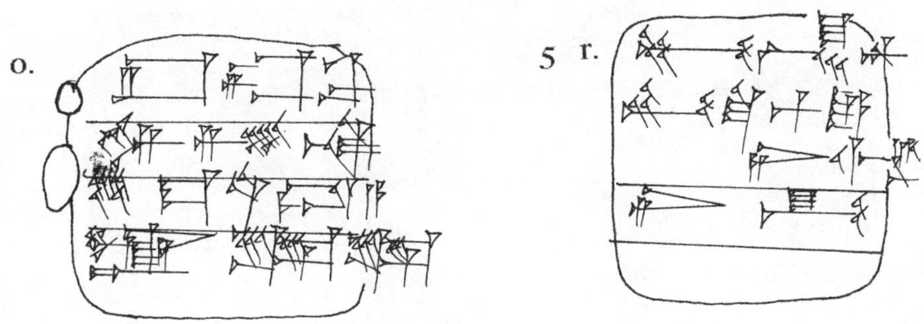

Text 426

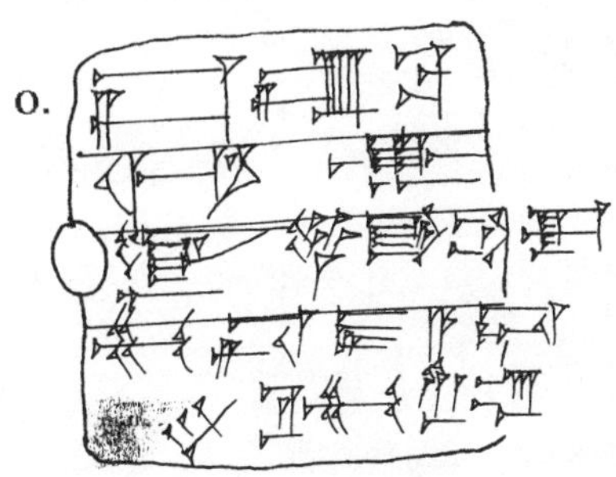

Text 427

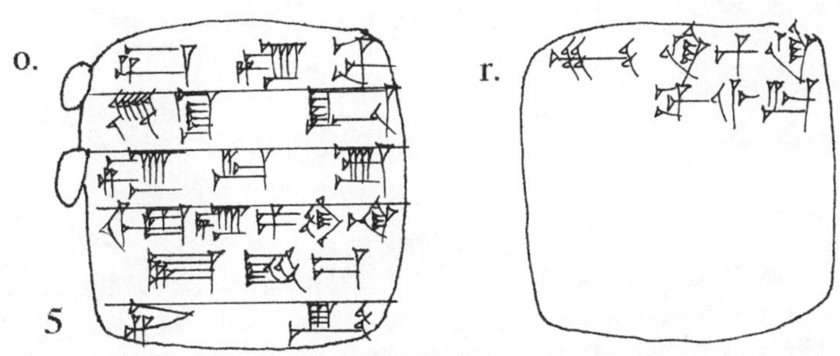

Text 428

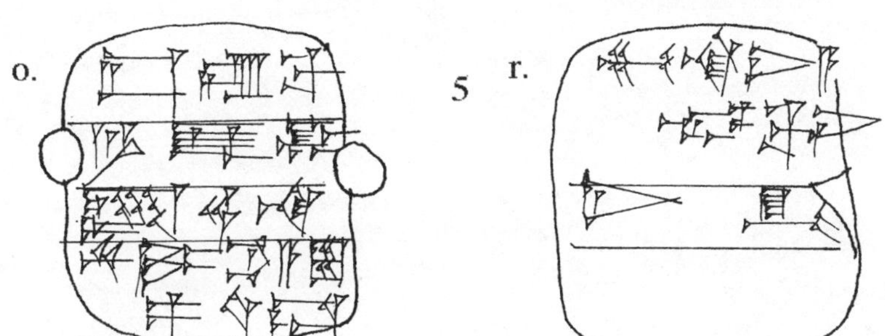

Text 429

o.

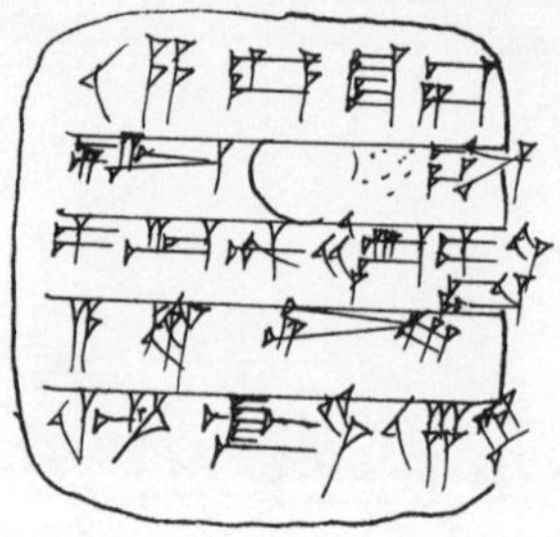

r.

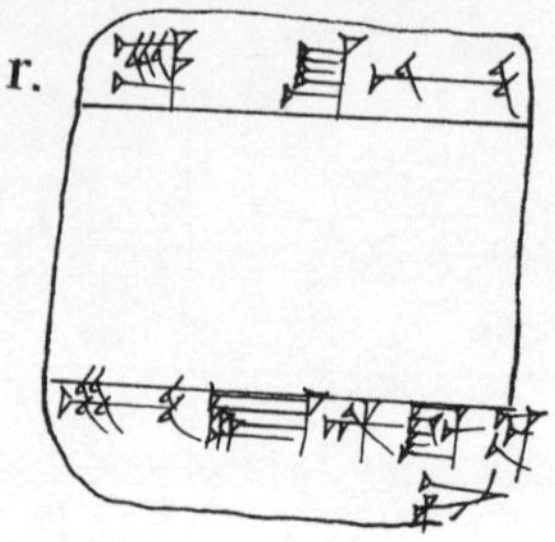

Text 430

o.

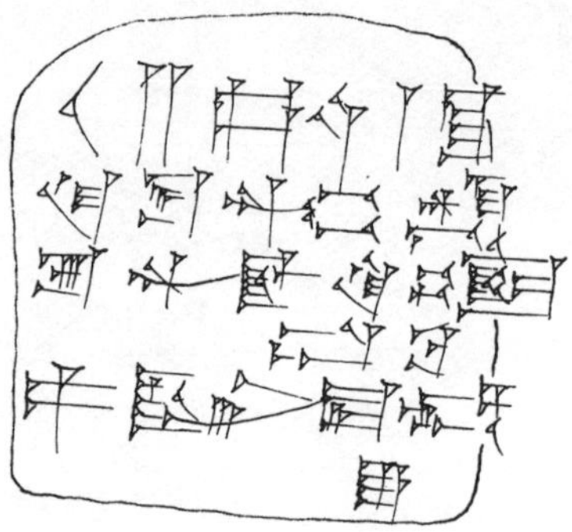

r.

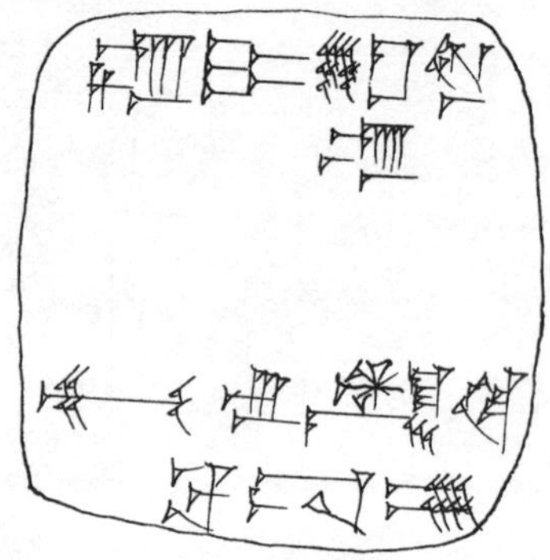

Text 431

o.

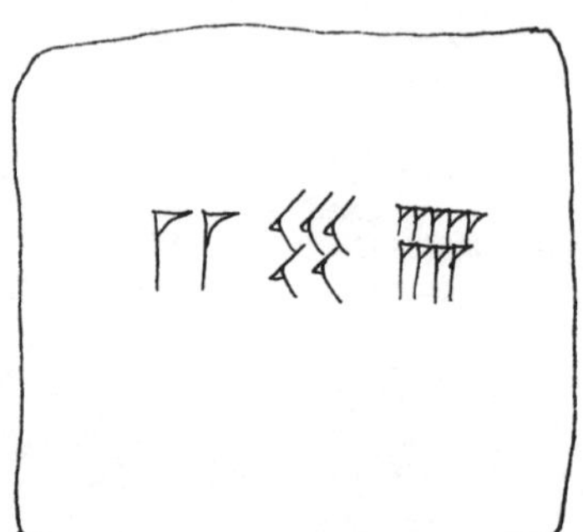

r.

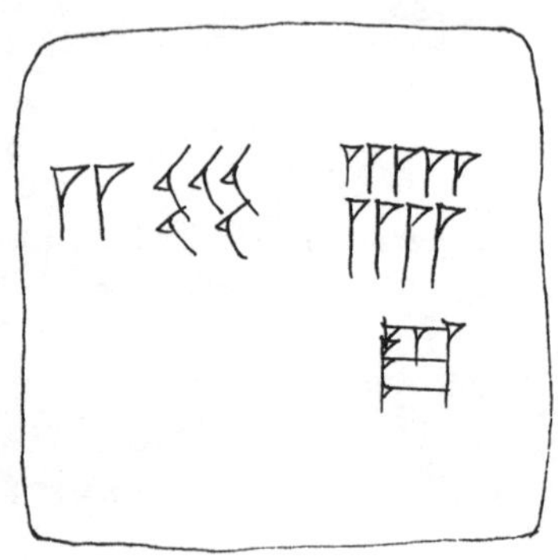

Text 432

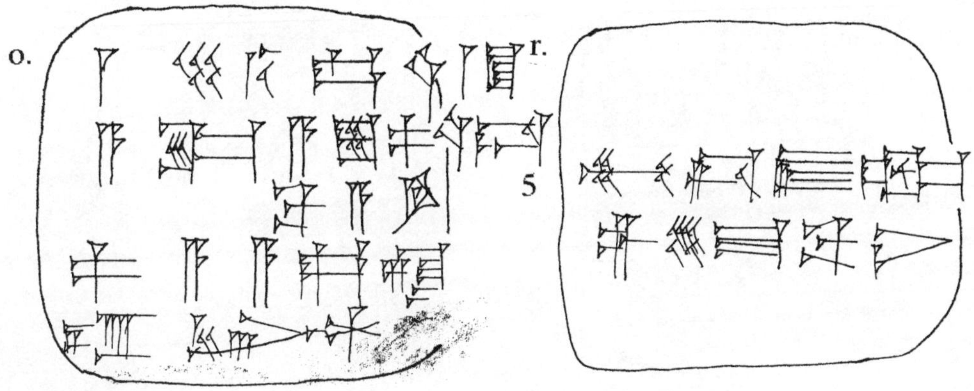

Text 435

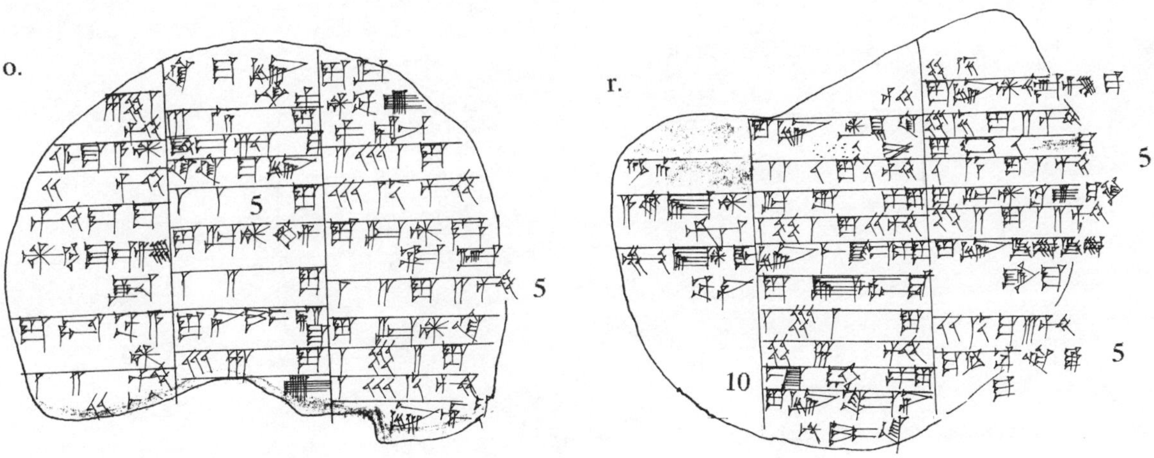

Text 437

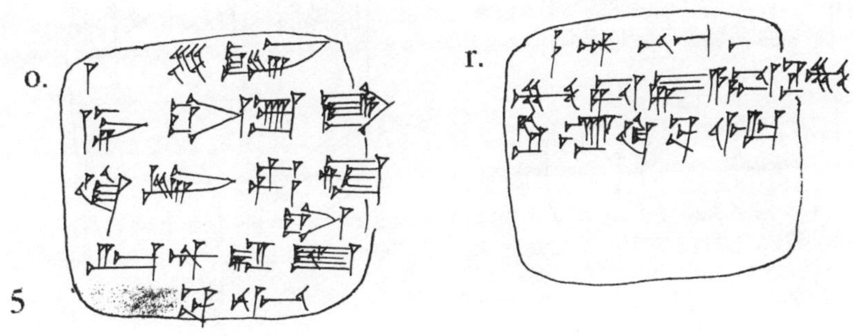

Text 438

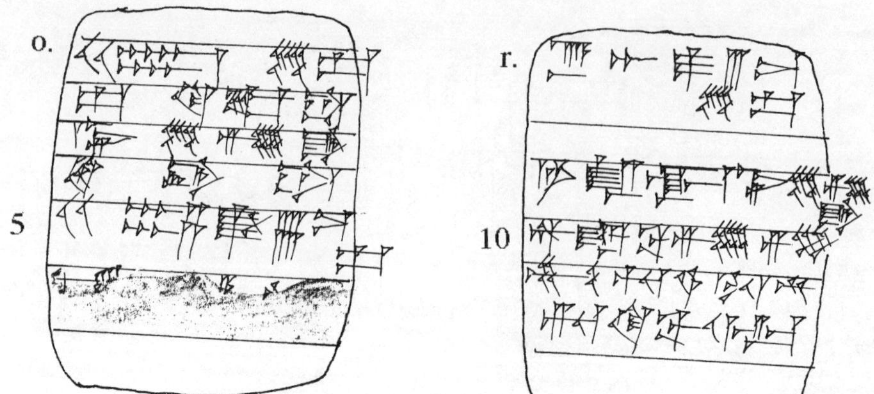

Text 439

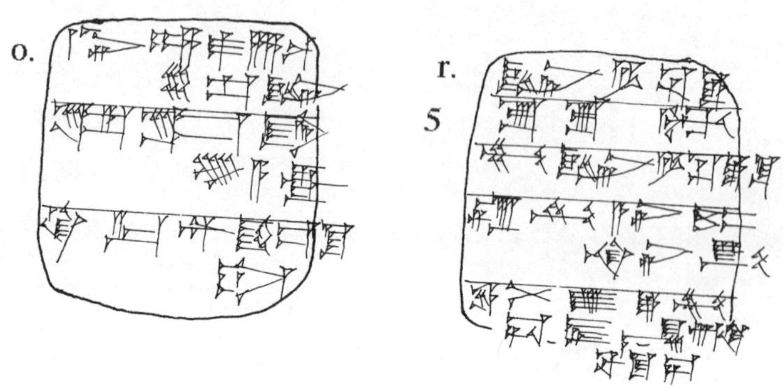

Text 441

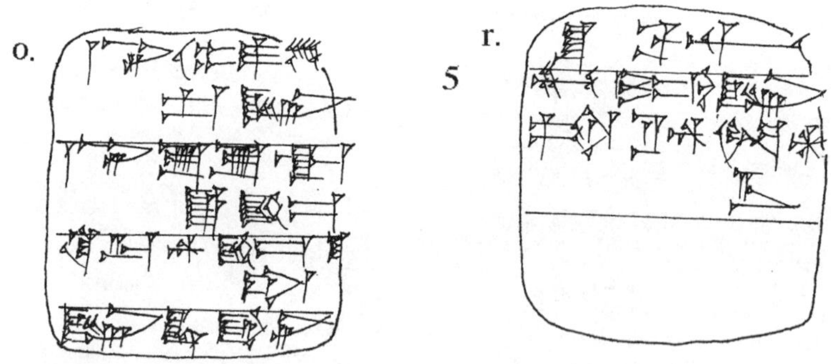

Text 443

o.

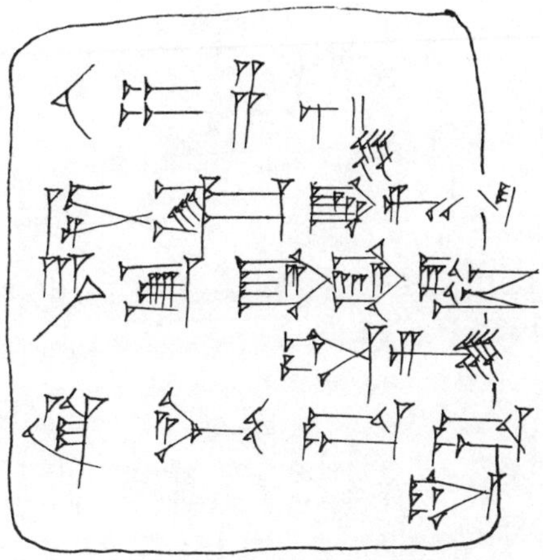

r.

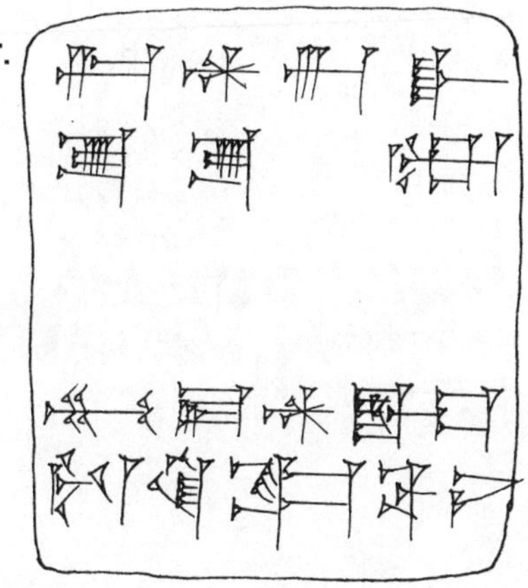

Text 445

o.

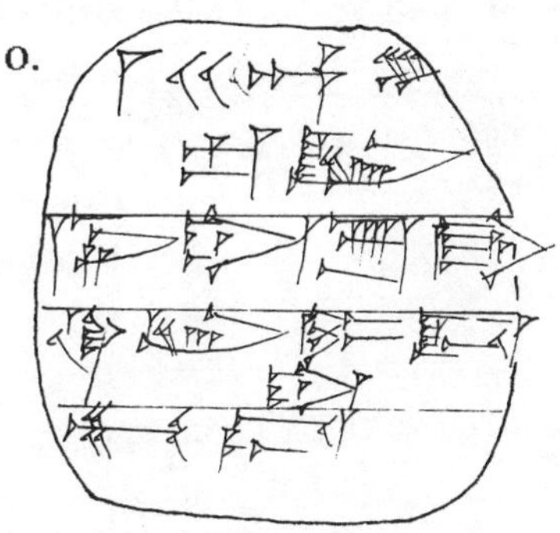

r.

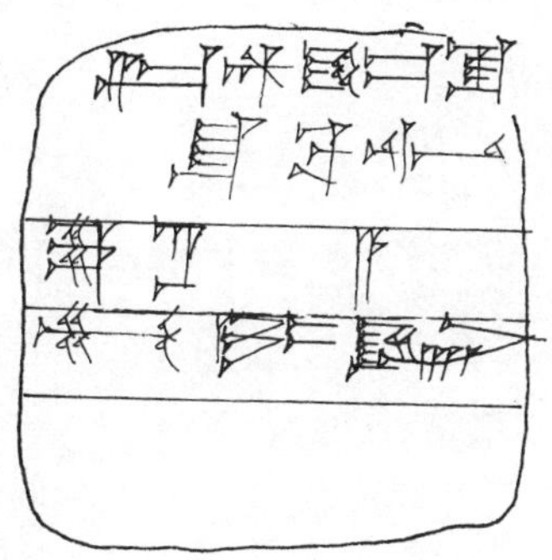

Text 448

o.

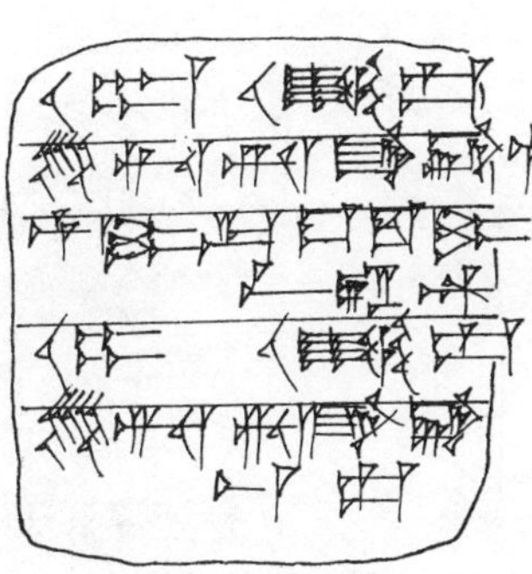

r.

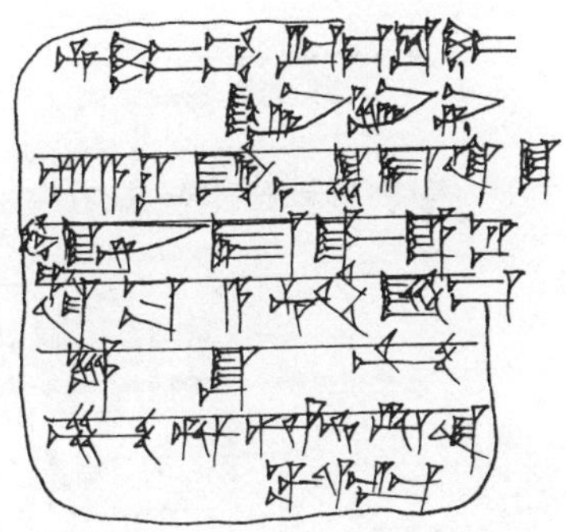

Text 449

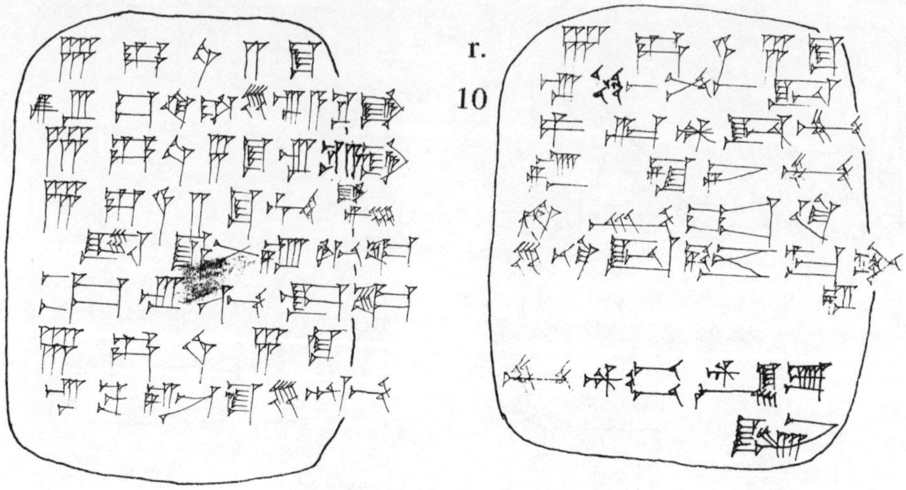

Text 450

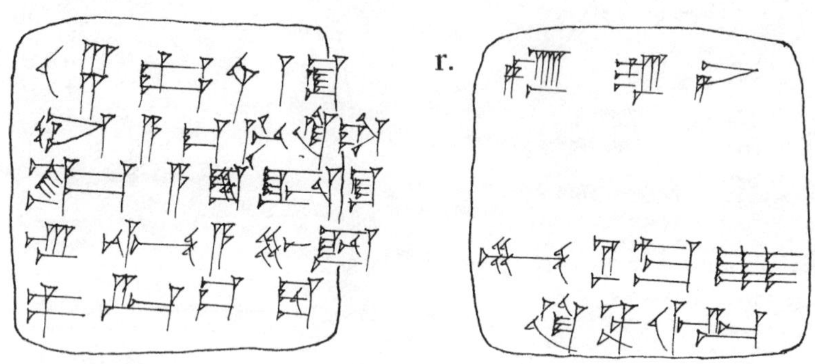

Text 452

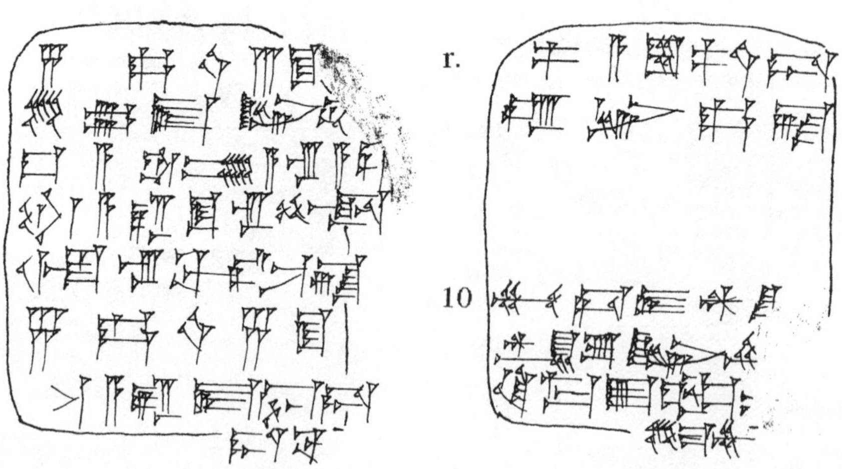

Text 453

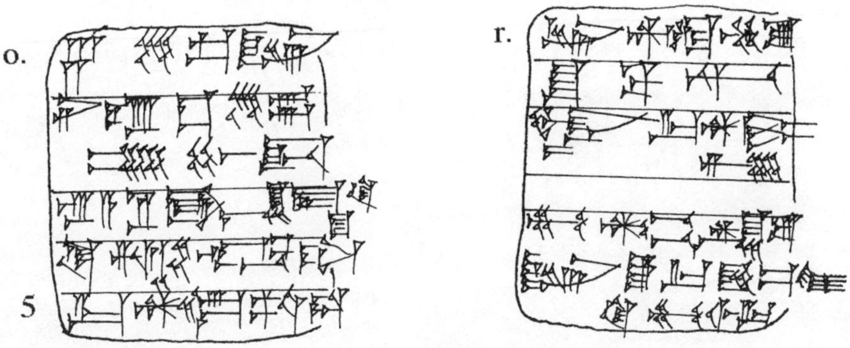

Text 455

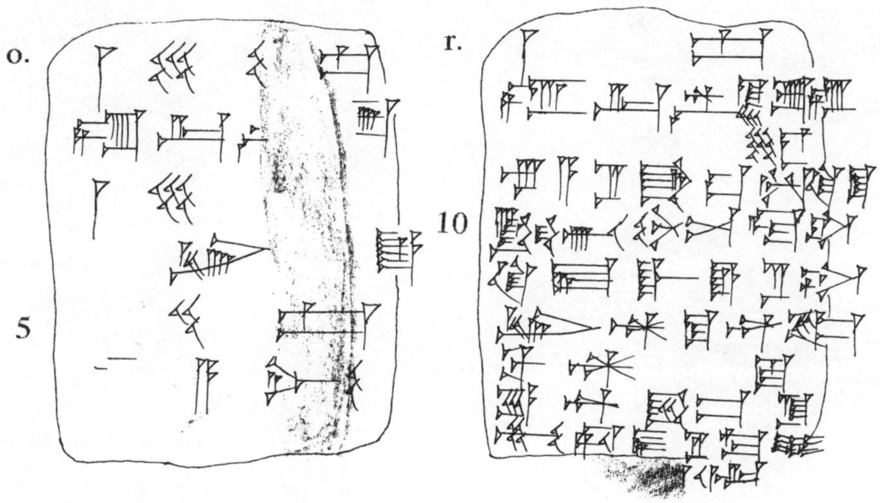

Text 456

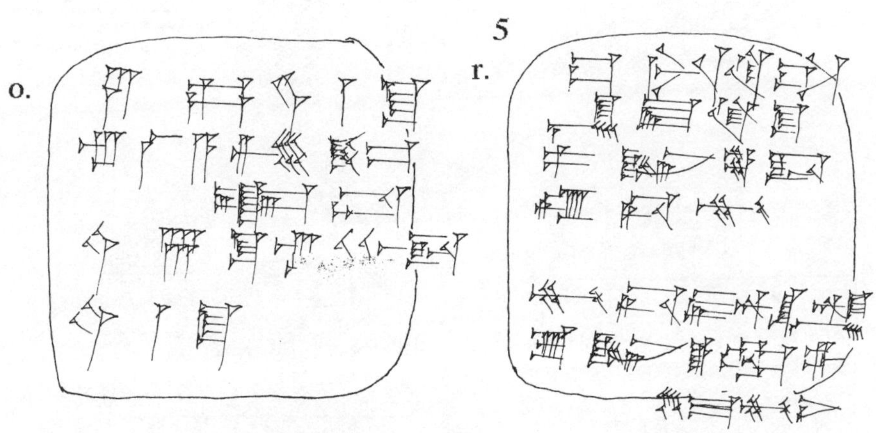

Text 457

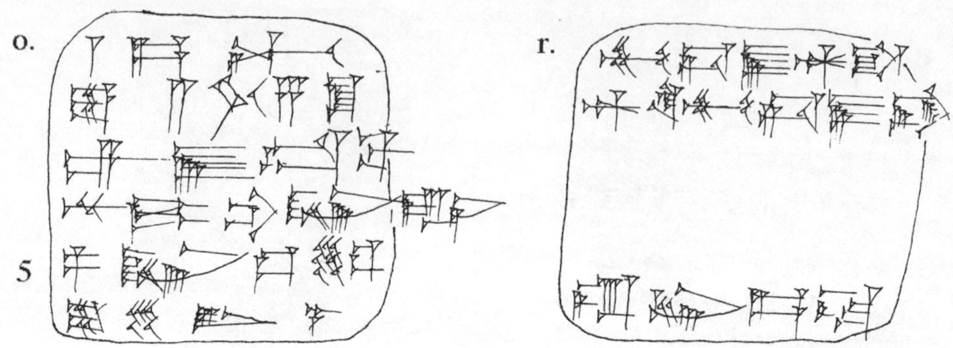

Text 468

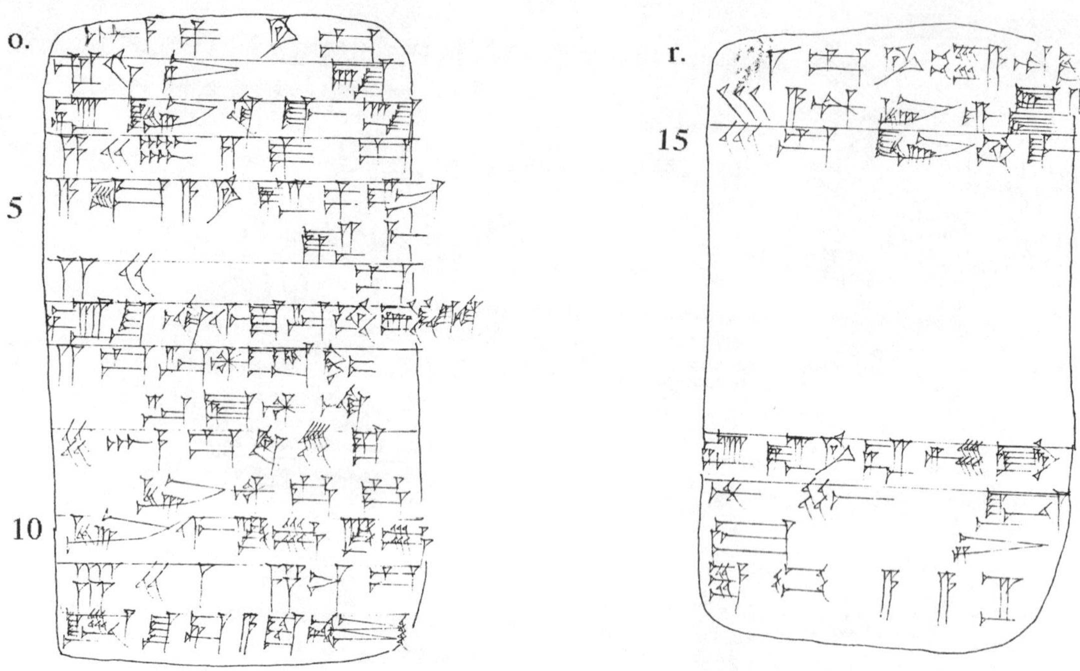

Text 469

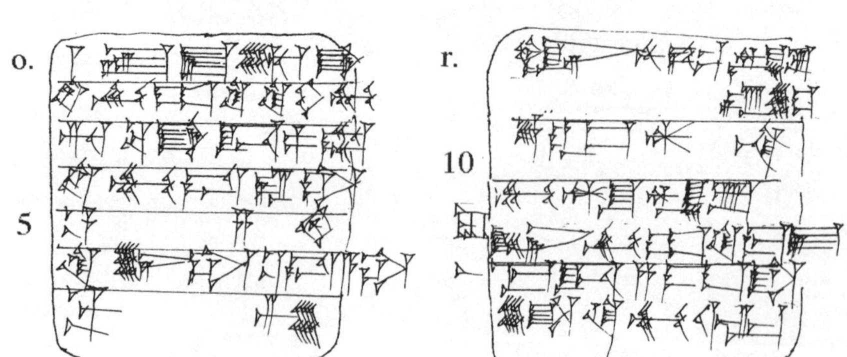

Text 471

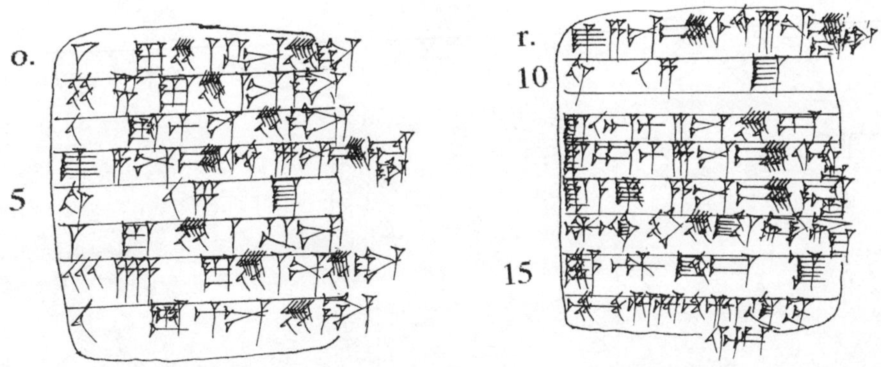

Text 472

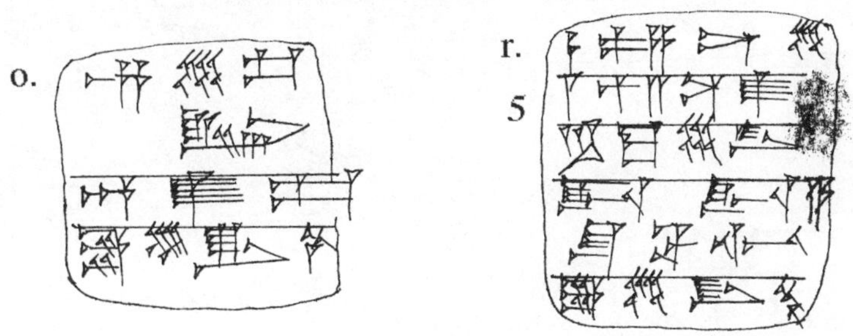

Text 473

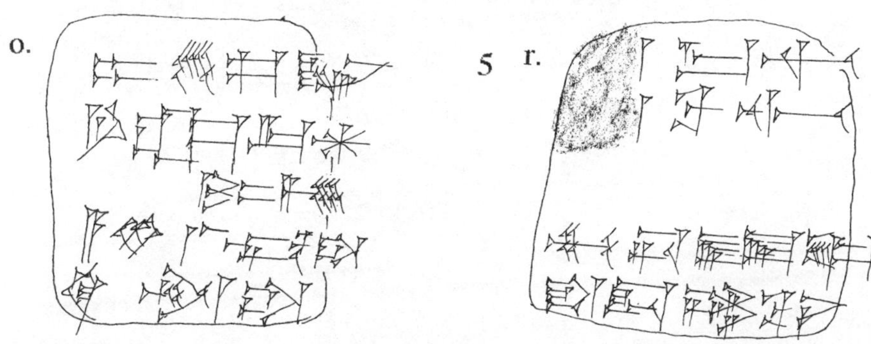

Text 475

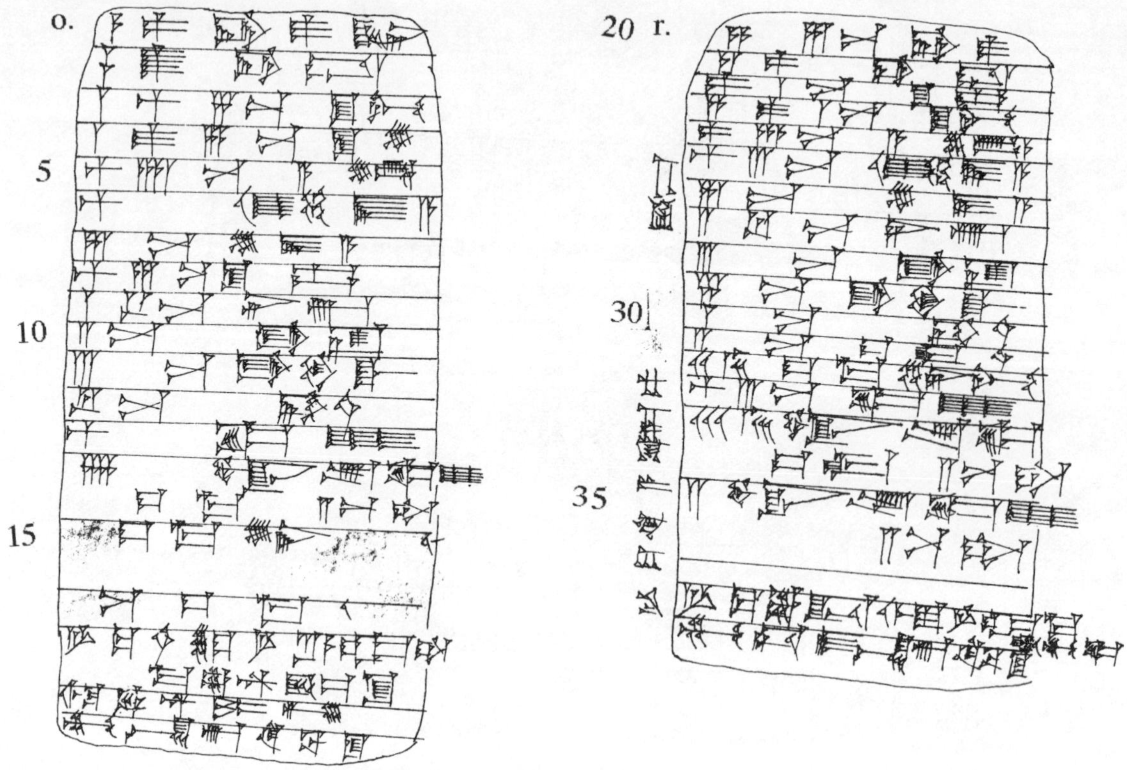

Text 479

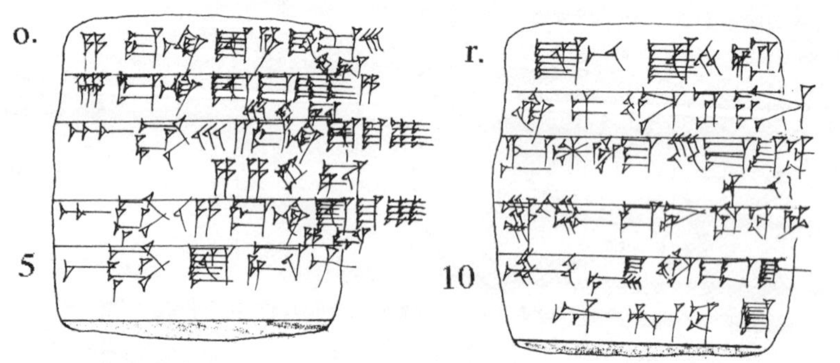

Text 480

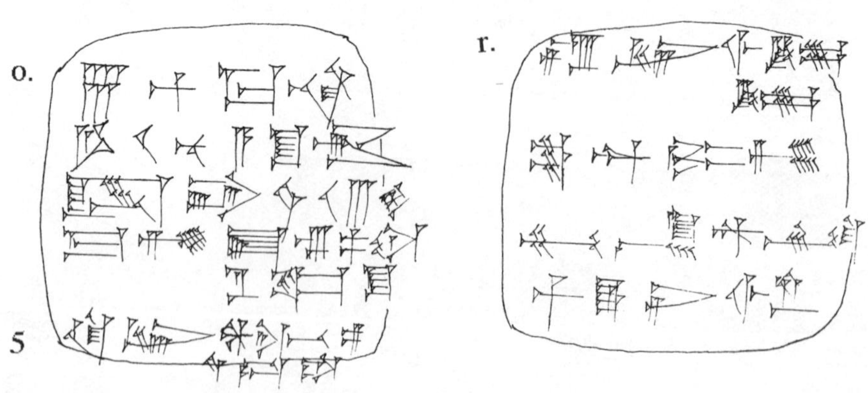

Text 481

o.

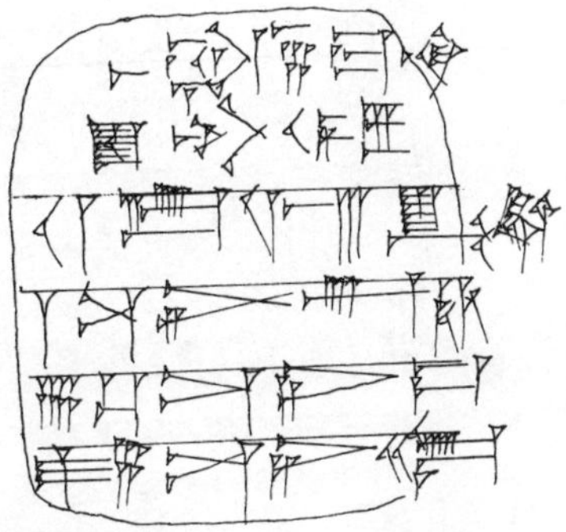

r.

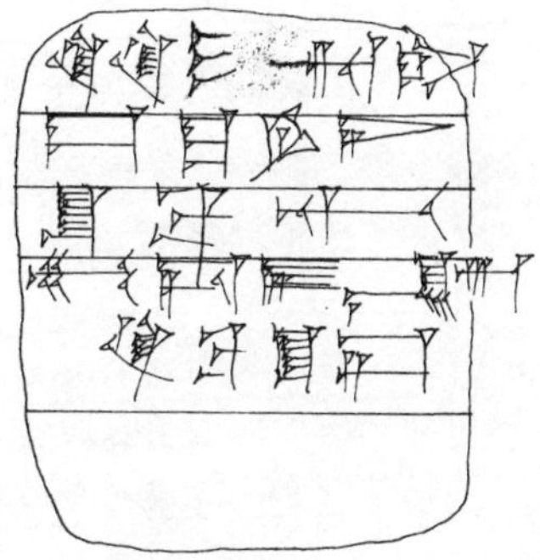

Text 483

o.

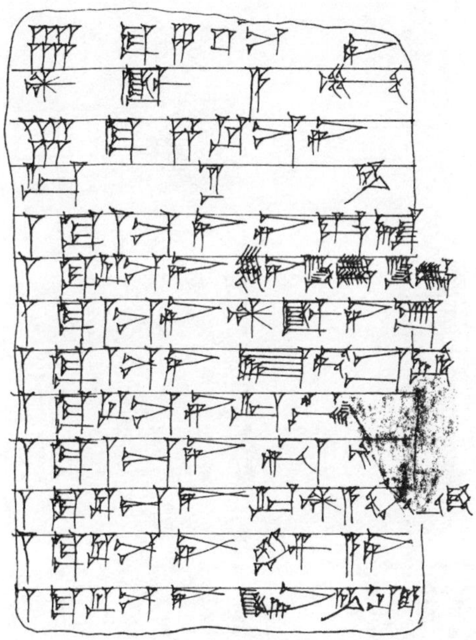

r.

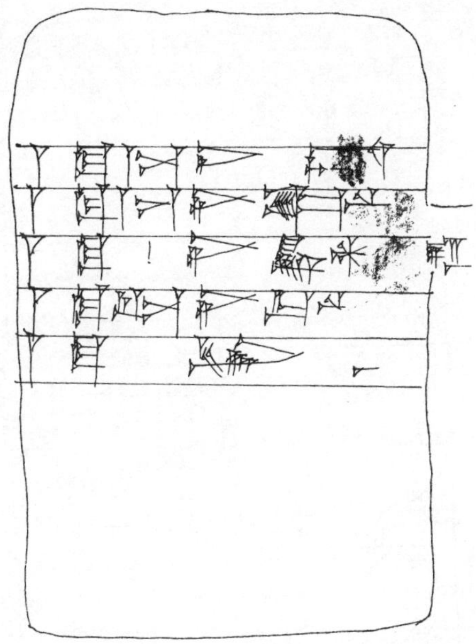

Text 484

o.

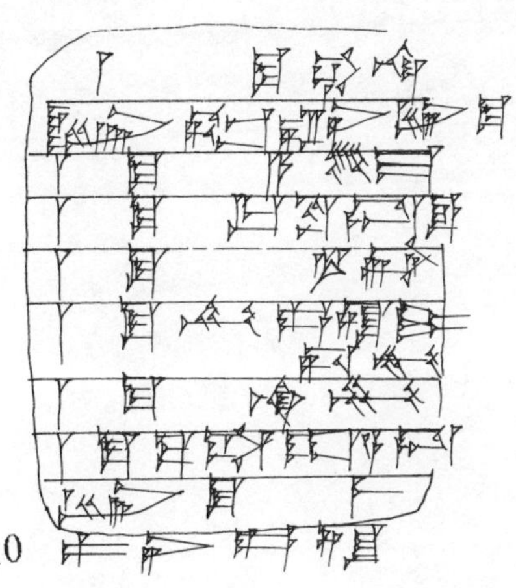

r.

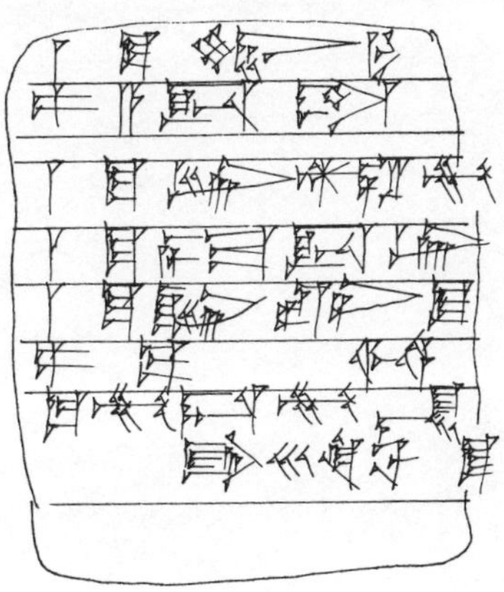

Text 485

o.

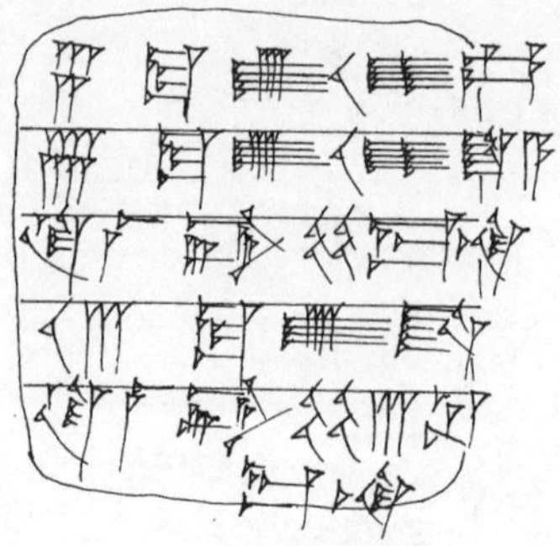

r.

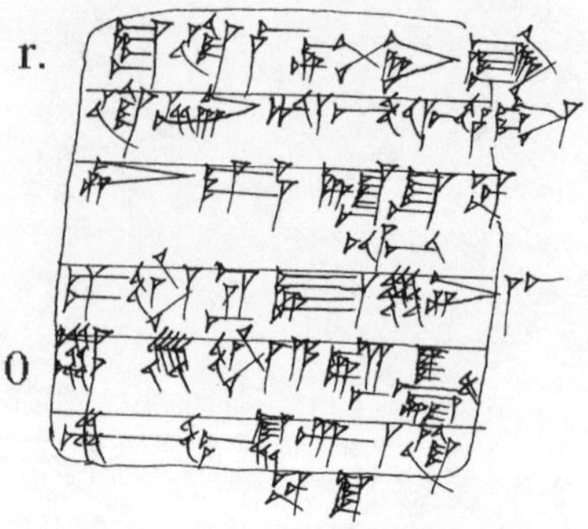

Text 486

o.

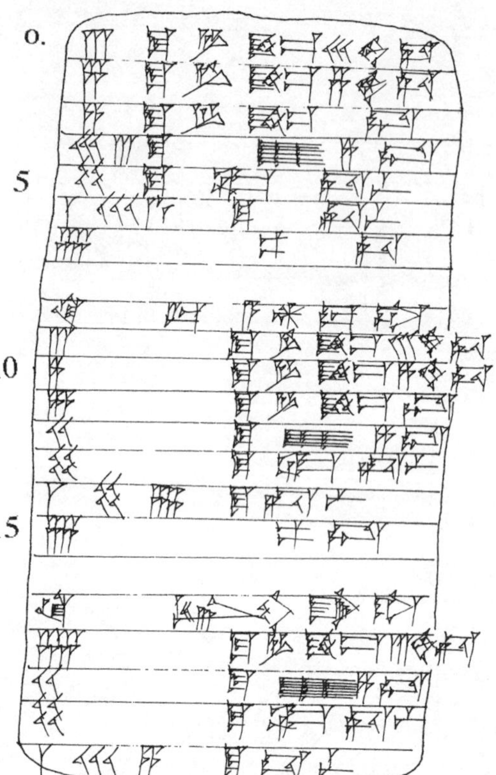

r.

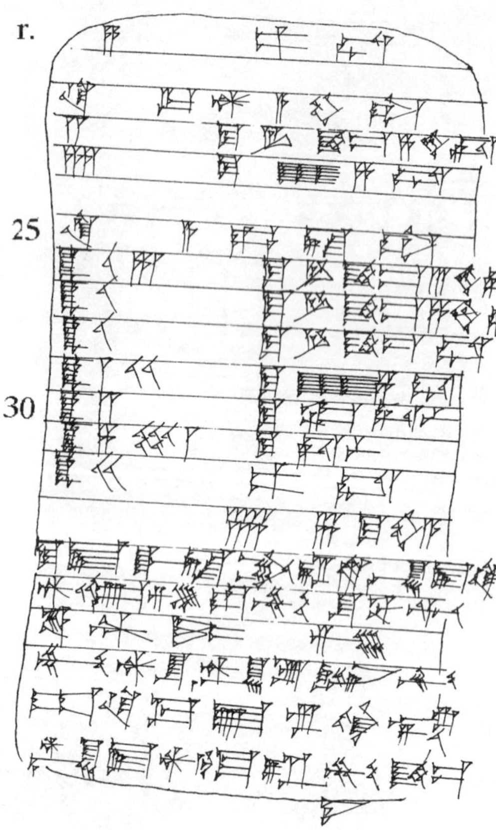

Text 488

o.

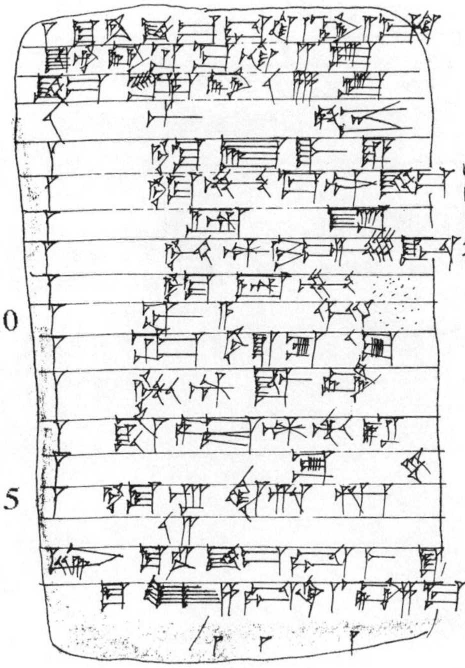

r.

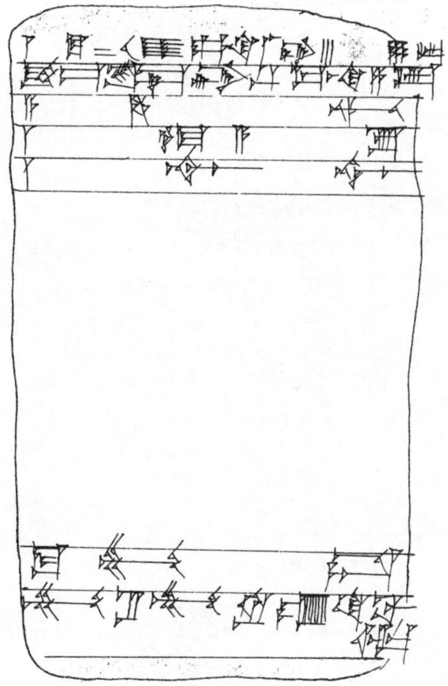

Text 492

o.

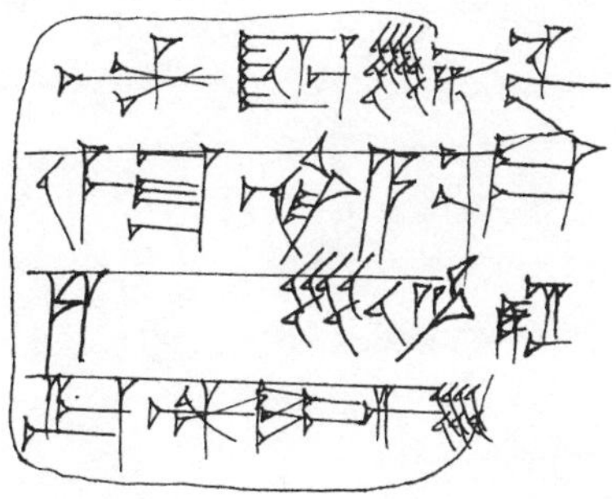

r.

Text 493

o.

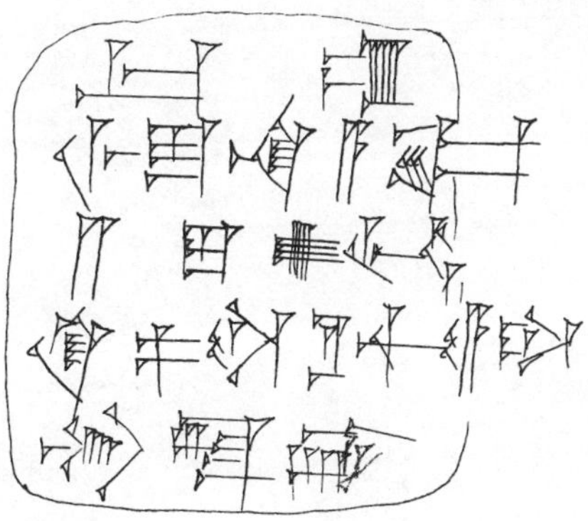

r.

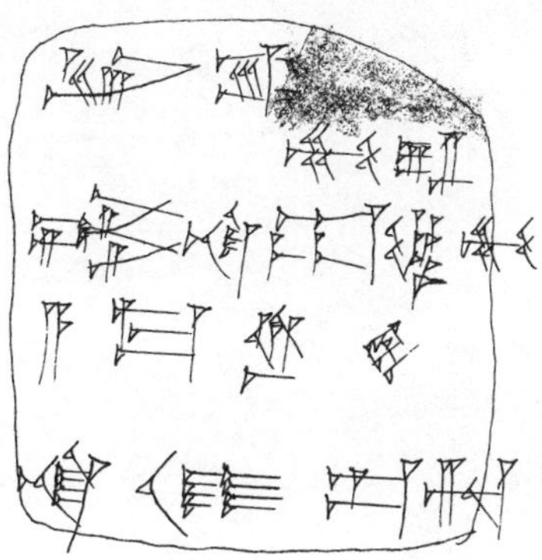

Text 494

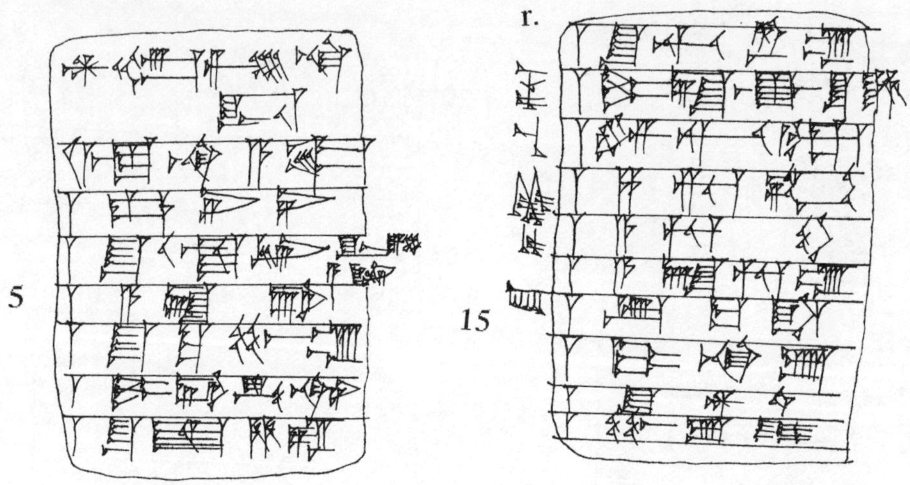

Text 495

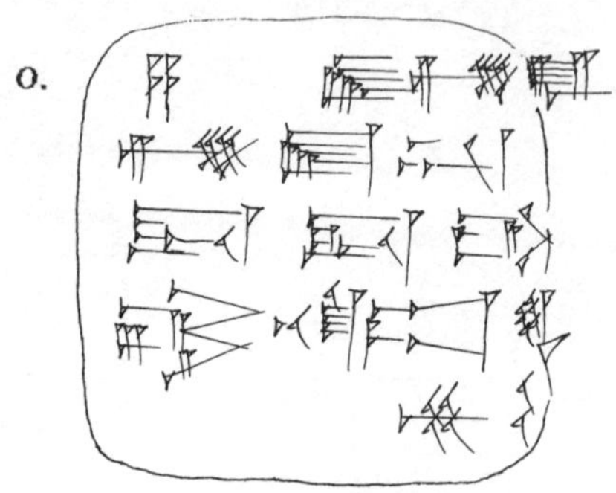

Text 496

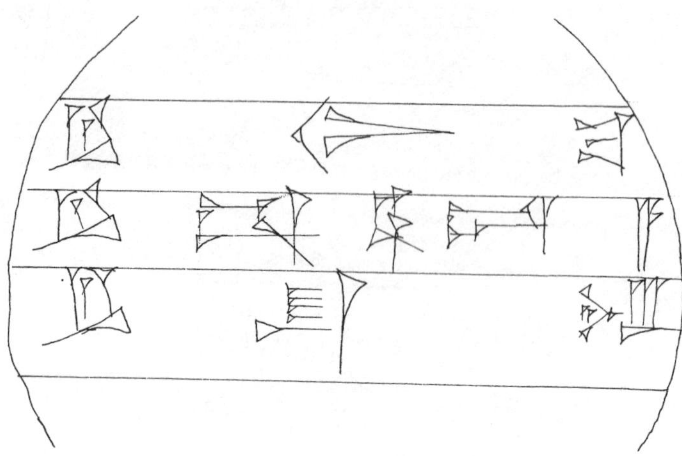

Text 497

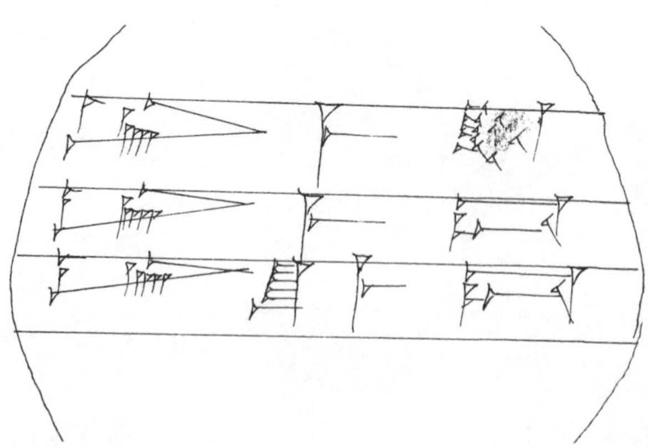

Text 498

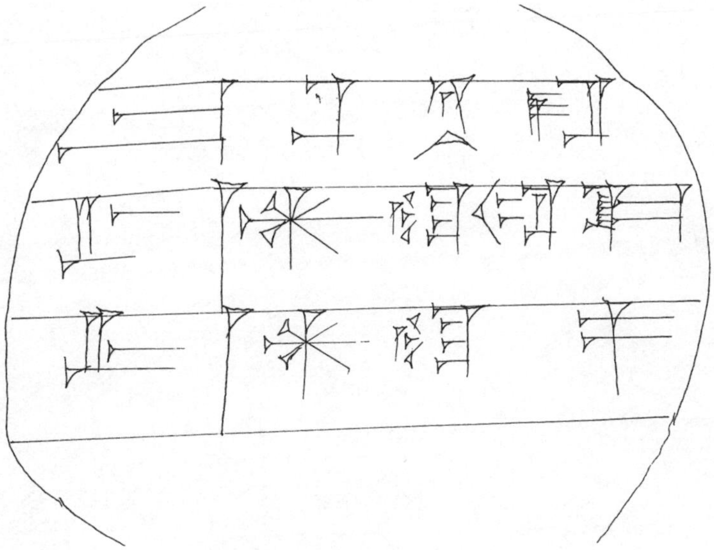

Text 499

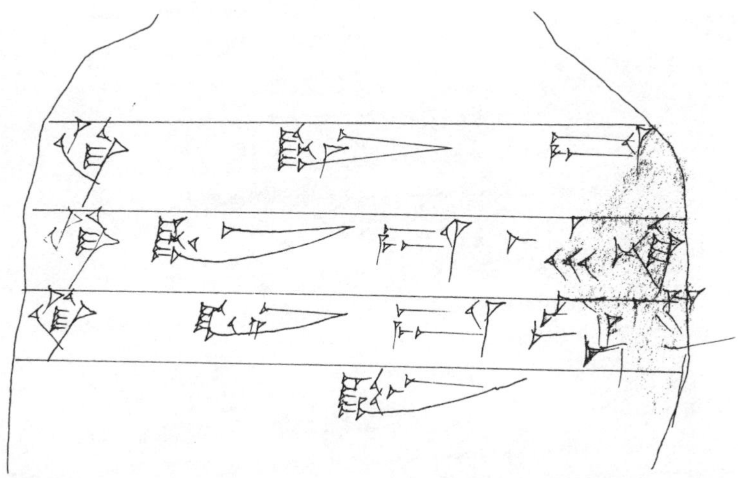

Text 500

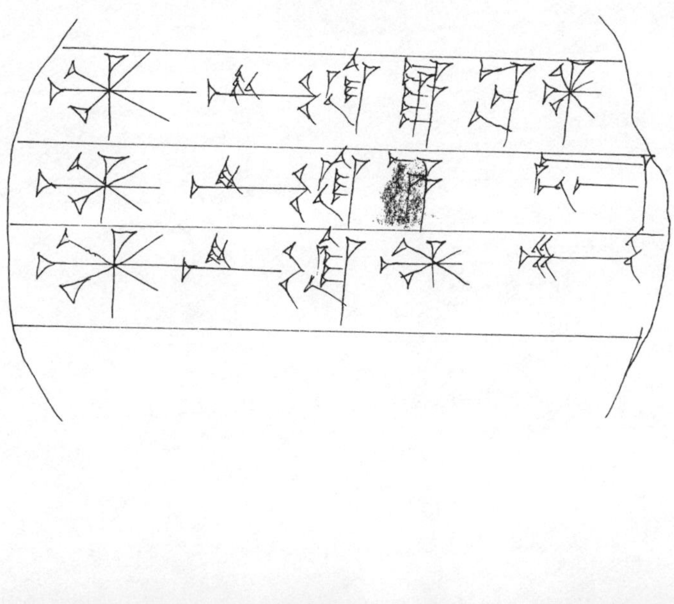

Text 501

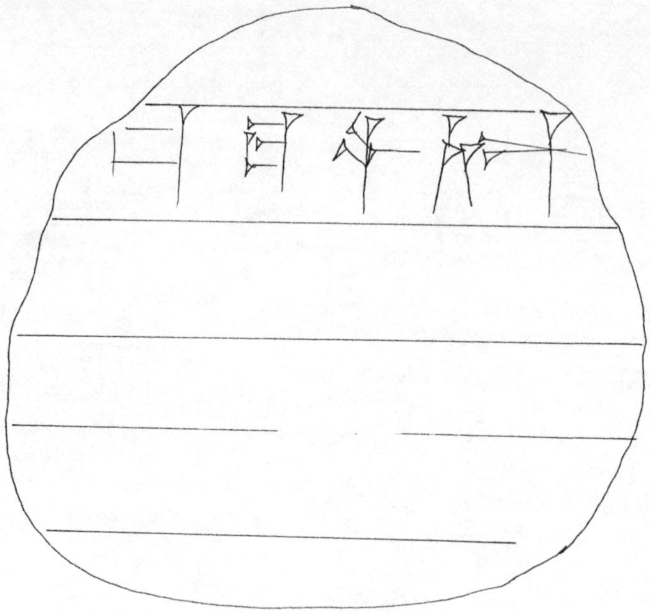

Text 502

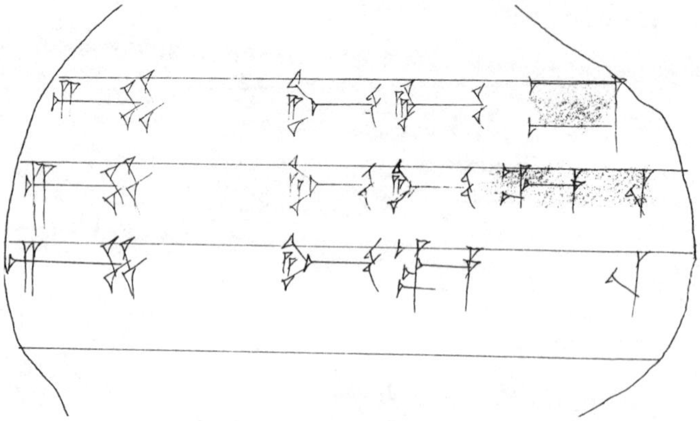

Text 503

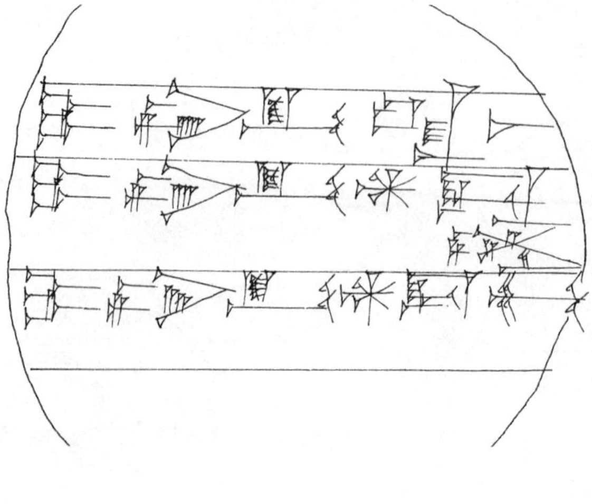

Text 504

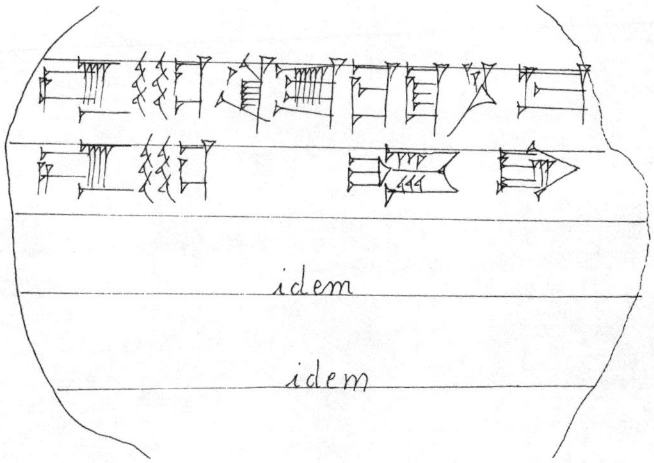

Text 505

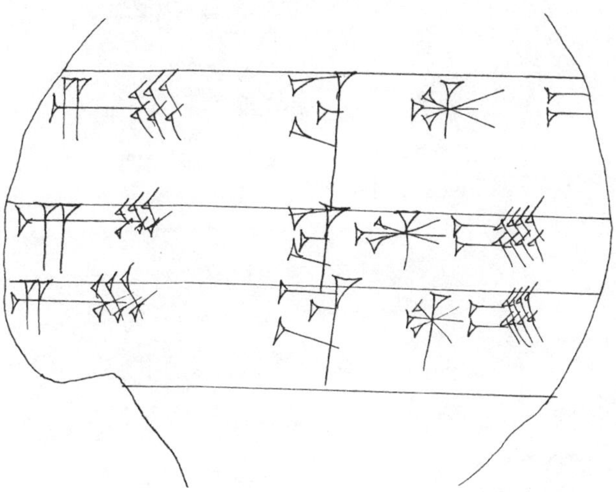

Text 506

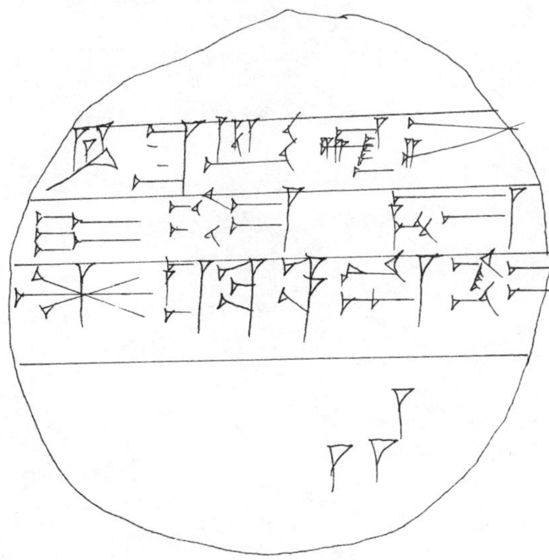

Text 507

o.

5

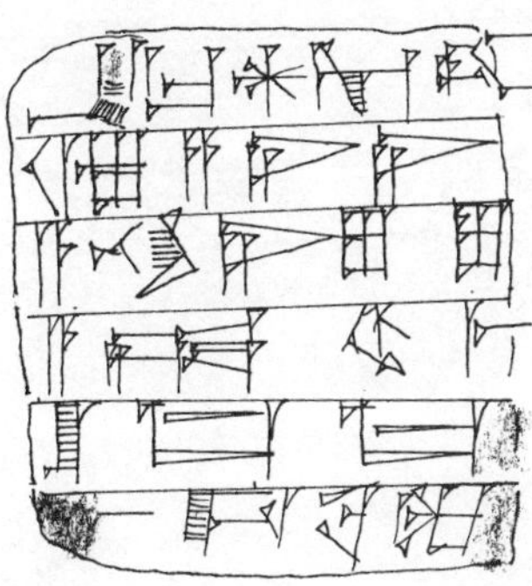

r.

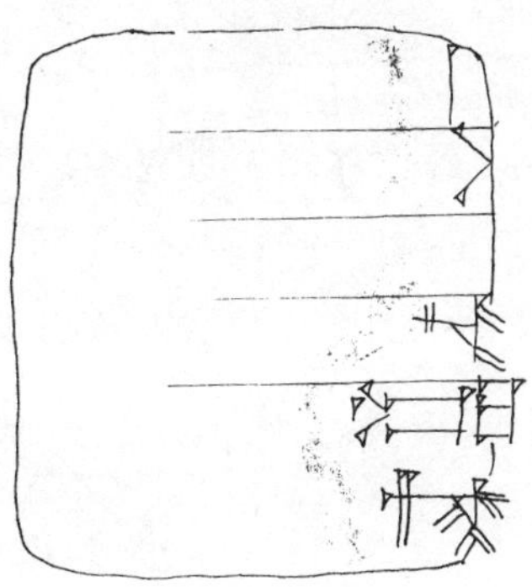

Text 508

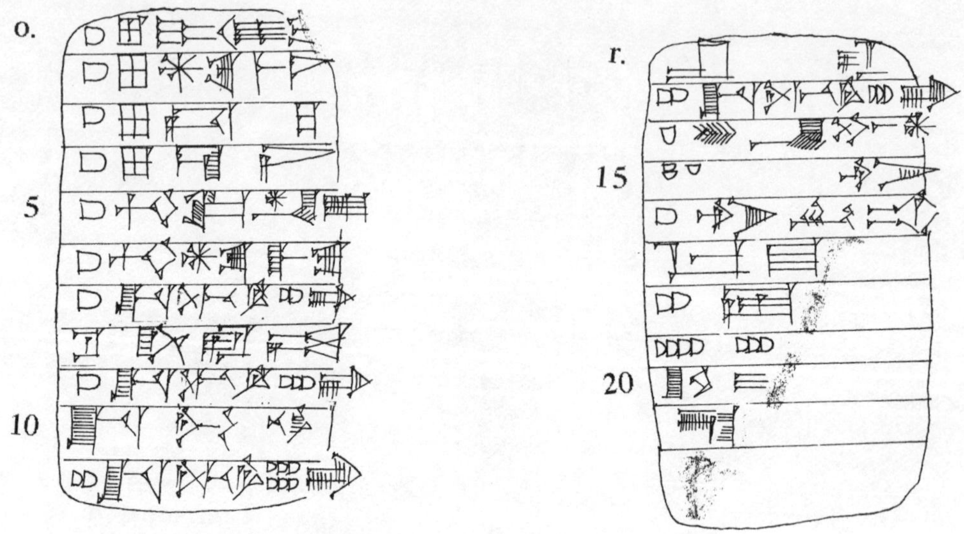

Text 509

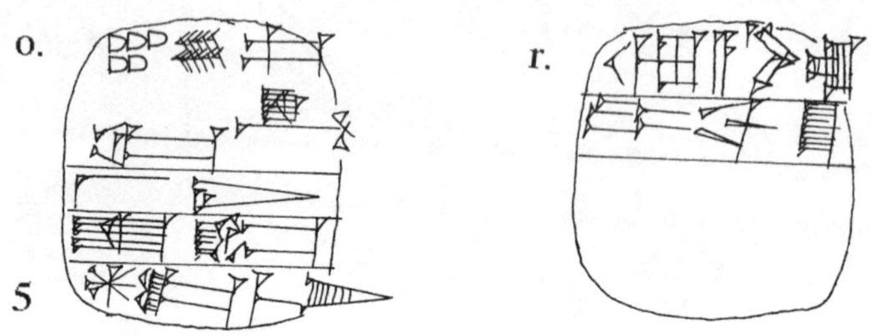

Text 510

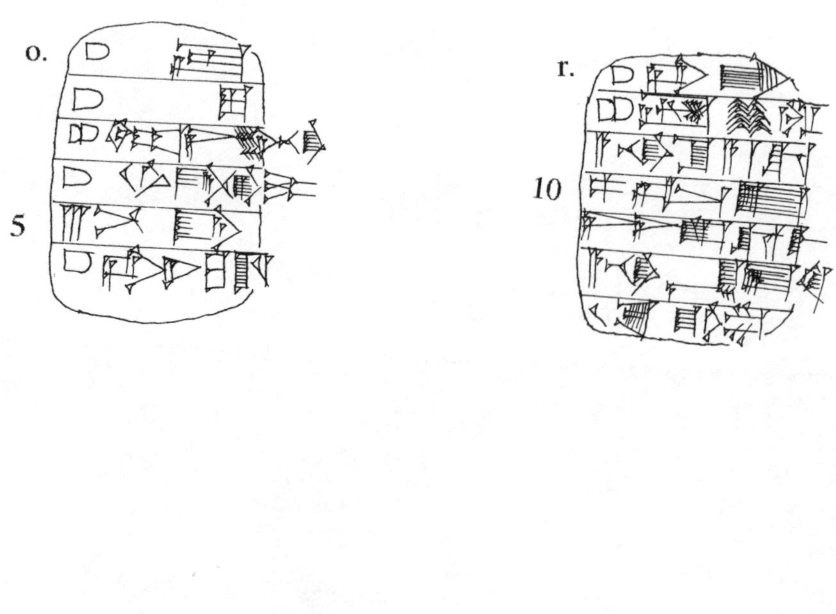